Learn Peachtree Accounting

Covers versions 4 through 2002

Deborah Bean

Wordware Publishing, Inc.

Contents

Month 2: The Balancing Month

Acknowledgments

A book such as this cannot be written without the support and assistance of numerous people — especially when the author has suffered a back injury and cannot drive a car. I'd like to thank Chris Blackhurst and Dawn Yarbro; as friends and former employees they have helped me get around to clients and doctor appointments. They also suffered through the inadequacies of their boss and the Peachtree program. I'd like to acknowledge Don Smith of Baldwin Metals, Sue Willard of Rockwall Dust Systems, and Budd and Marty Perlman of Texscape for their loyalty and friendship as clients. They've allowed me to straighten out their Peachtree books through power failures, company buyouts, and numerous program upgrades. Thanks to Jim Hill and Wes Beckwith of Wordware Publishing, who have exhibited much patience and long-suffering in waiting for the final production of this book. To editor Beth Kohler who makes sure that the thoughts in my head match the words on the page, I express my appreciation and apologies.

Last of all, I'd like to dedicate this book to my husband, Neal Berkowitz, who has supported and tolerated me for far longer than anyone else would. He once said, "I don't care what you do — just find one thing and stick to it for a little while!" Through all my careers, projects, and cloud-high dreams, he has been there for me as I have tried to be there for him. Our unique relationship is a point of gossip among my clients and is summarized in the words of my mother, "You're perfect for each other. You're both weird." I am proud and happy to have celebrated over 17 years of weirdness.

Introduction

In This Section

- Who should use this book
- About the author
- Determining if Peachtree is right for you and your business
- How to use this book
- Your accounting department

Welcome to my book on Peachtree Accounting. This book covers the following products: Peachtree® Complete Accounting, Peachtree® Accounting, and Peachtree First Accounting®. These products are all outgrowths of the original Peachtree Accounting for Windows.

We will be using the screens and features from Peachtree® Complete Accounting 2002 (Release 9.0). This book may also be used with older versions of Peachtree, going back as far as Release 3.5, although the earlier versions of the program are not really compliant with some of the latest versions of Microsoft Windows or with issues associated with Year 2000, and the icons will definitely have a different look. Some features shown in this book are not available in older versions. If you don't see the icon or menu item in your version, it is not available and you should skip that part. The basic features are still the same.

This book does not cover Peachtree Complete Accounting for DOS or Peachtree Office Accounting.

Who Should Use This Book

My book is designed for the non-accountant business owner, accounting manager, or office manager who is trying to find a lower-cost, easy-to-use method of getting a handle on their business processes. In my opinion, the Peachtree line of Windows-based accounting products is perfect for these business owners.

If you have any understanding of what an invoice or a bill is, you will be able to understand the steps involved in transferring your business to an accurate, easy-to-access method of keeping track of financial matters.

A word of caution, though. This book is <u>not</u> designed to replace your accountant. On the other hand, if you are using your accountant for basic write-up work, such as the month-end processing of the checking accounts, accounts receivable, and determining whether you actually made a profit last month, this book will teach you how to do those things yourself. That way your accountant can concentrate less on the day-to-day work and focus on how to make your business more competitive and profitable.

If your accountant is not supportive of your decision to move to Peachtree, consider carefully what he or she is doing for you. Getting an accurate listing of who owes you money is easily accomplished by the average $10- to $12-an-hour clerk. Don't pay big bucks for the little stuff.

As an example, a year after one of my clients converted to Peachtree he was audited by the state controller's office regarding sales taxes. The auditor was amazed that everything was documented and accounted for accurately. The state did not find a single item that was incorrect. More important, the company did not have to pay anything to their accountant to get ready for the audit; all the information was already in the computer and files.

Normally, an audit would send most companies screaming to their CPA for the pre-audit work to get their records in shape to be audited. This is a very expensive procedure for your average small company and an expense that can be avoided if a computerized accounting program is used correctly and consistently. Let me repeat — if a computerized accounting program is used correctly and consistently. If you are haphazard about what goes into the program, you won't get good information out.

In addition to showing you how to use Peachtree, I have included standardized procedure lists for common tasks in the downloadable companion files (www.wordware.com/peachtree). Some of these may seem simplistic to you, but I have found that they are invaluable to the data entry clerks who use them. They also provide you with a checklist to verify that everything is getting done correctly.

About the Author

My name is Deborah Bean. I have been the owner of a computer support company supplying a wide variety of services to small and mid-sized companies. My expertise is in advising companies of their actual computer and software needs. When I started, I became knowledgeable in the major accounting packages used at the time including an early version of Peachtree Accounting for Windows. I would spend large amounts of time getting to know the needs of my clients and then install the accounting program best suited to their needs. As Peachtree added new features and as I became more of an expert, I narrowed the list of programs that I recommended until I was eventually only recommending Peachtree.

I feel that I am uniquely qualified to offer some of the advice that I do because, unlike most people who try to teach you accounting software, I learned to do the work before I went to school for my degree in accounting and computer science.

Being young and stupid (as most teenagers are), I didn't go to college. When I discovered that I needed to support two children with no skills and no education, I had hard choices to make. Rather than becoming a "welfare mom," I worked a few years and eventually became an accounting clerk. I learned all the basics of day-to-day accounting in this way. I later moved upward from clerk to office manager, staff accountant, accountant, project business manager, and finally accounting software consultant. Most of these positions included responsibilities for not only the accounting functions but also some of the computer management functions.

Another fortunate and unique part of my career has been the fact that at each company I worked for, the company was somewhat at the forefront of converting to more modern, computerized accounting methods. I assisted with most of these conversions and learned a remarkable amount about what goes into creating and using an accounting package.

During all this time, I also went to school part time to finish my education. There I learned the theory behind all the tasks that I was performing. Because of my hands-on experience, I quickly understood the principles the teachers were trying to pass on.

So you see, I've not only sat in the manager's and consultant's chair, but also in the chair of the person who must deal with the day-to-day realities of getting the numbers and figures into and out of the computer. Because of this experience, I do feel uniquely qualified to guide you through the steps to get your business up and running with accurate information. I'm not talking to you from just the theoretical side, I'm also considering the practical experience side.

Is Peachtree Right for Me and My Business?

Peachtree is great for small to mid-sized offices. Of course, the definition of a small to mid-sized office varies with whom you talk to. Office size has nothing to do with company revenue or the total number of employees. I've seen companies that bring in millions of dollars in income and have hundreds of employees succeed with Peachtree. In evaluating Peachtree and office size, suitability has to do with other things such as the number of transactions and the number of people working in Peachtree. To discover if Peachtree is right for your business, answer the following questions:

- Do you send out fewer than 2,000 invoices per month?
- Are there ten or fewer people handling the day-to-day accounting functions of invoicing, paying bills, payroll, and cash receipts?

- Do you have a fairly standardized payroll? Peachtree can handle lots of types of salaried and hourly payment plans and almost any type of deduction. On the other hand, it doesn't do automatic calculation of all commissions.
- Can your business fit into a standardized business model? There are dozens to choose from, everything from flower shop to auto repair to construction company.
- Are you willing to make the commitment in time and energy to set up the program properly? A commitment to verify the accuracy of all the data could last from one to three months. This would be on top of your normal accounting procedures. This commitment would actually be required for any accounting software conversion that you participate in, not just Peachtree.
- Are you willing to standardize accounting procedures so that almost all transactions are handled in the same manner without a lot of exceptions?
- Do you have the computers to handle the software and transaction load? If more than one person is doing the accounting, are you willing to spend money to have your computers networked properly?

If you can answer these questions with a "Yes," then Peachtree could easily be the answer to your operations.

Some good reasons to move to Peachtree include that it does not have the massive initial setup time found in larger, more customizable packages. In many cases, you can start entering data as soon as your company is created in Peachtree. Information can be entered "on the fly," as you need it. You don't have to have beginning balances before you start, but can reenter them later.

Peachtree has a smaller learning curve for basic tasks that make it simple to use for the average, small-office, data entry person. A few simple tutorials will familiarize your employees with the steps necessary to perform their jobs.

You, and your employees, don't have to understand debits and credits to use Peachtree. The program's forms handle all that stuff behind the screens. You just do the data entry and the analysis.

How to Use This Book

This book can basically be divided into two parts. The first part covers the installation of the program, familiarization of the Peachtree window, and the setup of a new company. The second part is a Three-Month Plan to get you up and running with Peachtree. It covers all the basic data entry and reconciliation of your company's data. Unfortunately, due to space constraints, I could not cover everything that I wanted to in this book. But for now, this book will get you going.

You will want to go through most of the book straight though. Some chapters may be skipped for a short while, but the whole book is written in a semi-chronological order. See Chapter 4, "The Three-Month Plan," for more information.

Your Accounting Department

According to generally accepted accounting principles (GAAP), related accounting functions should be performed by different individuals to reduce the chances for fraud and embezzlement. You would be amazed at the number of offices where an accounting clerk has managed to pull some scheme and taken the company for thousands, and sometimes hundreds of thousands, of dollars. Two of the most common schemes are:

The A/R scheme — The employee who enters and prints the invoices also receives the checks. This person can set up a dummy bank account with a name very similar to yours, receive a check for your company, and destroy the evidence of the original invoice. This leaves you with all the costs of the work and none of the revenue.

The A/P scheme — The person who enters the A/P invoices also prints the checks. Again, a dummy bank account is set up, a dummy bill is received by your company, and a check is cut.

Although these scenarios are rare, they do exist and they are perpetrated by some of the most innocent-seeming and trustworthy-looking people around. The best way to avoid such corruption is to remove the opportunity. Don't let the person who does the data entry also handle the checks for both accounts receivable and accounts payable.

In the smallest companies you might not be able to avoid this but, as the business owner, there are some simple auditing techniques you can employ to better protect yourself. Talk to your CPA to help you practice these methods.

In the typical offices that I set up, there are usually three people and an office manager to do the administrative work, in addition to one or two salespeople. We usually set up the tasks as follows:

Salespeople — They enter the initial invoice information using the quotes or sales order functions. These functions can also be used to create work orders for some shops.

Office Person 1 — This person enters additional invoices and converts quotes and sales orders to customers. This person is responsible for getting the invoices to the customer. This person does not enter cash receipts.

Office Person 2 — This person is responsible for entering cash receipts and creating the bank deposit. This person may also print the checks to pay bills and verify and enter payroll information.

Office Person 3 — This person is responsible for verifying and entering bills into the accounts payable system. Sometimes this person may be used to assist with invoice data entry. This person does not print checks to pay bills.

Office Manager — This person is responsible for printing checks to pay bills and reconciling the cash receipts and the bank statement at the end of the month. This person always verifies payroll before it is printed and usually handles the payroll tax deposits.

In some offices, these tasks are combined or expanded. Some offices have the salespeople enter sales information, while other offices have only the admin people do this work, though it only makes sense to have the people doing the initial write-up of sales to do the actual data entry to reduce errors and increase efficiency.

Some offices allow the shop manager to view and make changes to sales or work orders. In offices that are very small, the salesperson does the invoice data entry and the admin assistant does all other work except for signing checks. Then, of course, there is the one-person office where the owner does it all.

In all of these cases, we have made Peachtree fulfill the company's needs. It will work for you, too.

Chapter 1

Installation

In This Chapter

- Installing Peachtree — stand-alone and custom configurations
- Upgrading from a previous version of Peachtree
- Network installation and concerns
- Registering Peachtree
- Converting your data files from earlier versions of Peachtree

Protecting Your Network and Your Computers

Before you begin installing Peachtree on any computer or network, you should first take two precautions to protect your systems.

The first investment that should not be ignored is power protection. Every computer, monitor, hub, and server should be attached to a good UPS (uninterruptible power supply). Some people believe that a surge protector provides all the needed protection. This might have been true in the days of DOS, but Windows is far more temperamental. When a surge hit a DOS computer protected with a surge protector, the protector would kick in to stop the surge and all power to the computer and the computer itself would shut down. The probability of having a critical file open that could not be recovered was minimal. But now we have Windows. Windows constantly creates and moves temporary files to disk. Other files are opened and left in an indeterminate state until a specific operation completes. The net effect is that when power goes off, the system may not be in a stable state and a graceful recovery might not be possible. If we had the aforementioned surge protector, it would successfully perform the operation of preventing the surge from hitting the computer — and possibly kill the patient in the process. A UPS will not only prevent the surges from getting to your computer, it will also keep brownouts from destroying your system (brownouts are actually more harmful than surges), keep the computer from stopping when a power outage occurs, and let you gracefully bring down the system during a long-term power outage. With a UPS on every machine, if the power goes out you still have several minutes to save your work and close down your computer. And if it is only a momentary outage, you have lost nothing because the computer kept on going.

The second investment you need to make to protect your computer equipment and data is to purchase good anti-virus software. This is particularly important if anyone on your network has outside e-mail or Internet access. Since that includes just about everyone today, you don't have an excuse. I like some of the new subscription anti-virus services because they keep me updated with the latest protection. I am an average user and I get hit two or three times a week with various viruses, many of them brand new. My virus protection software has worked in every case because I keep it updated. Also, explain to your employees the importance of not opening any file sent in an e-mail unless they are absolutely sure of who it came from and what the file actually contains.

Installation

There are several different types of installations for Peachtree. You will need to select from one of the following types:

Standard — The Standard installation is used for the average user on a stand-alone computer.

Custom — If you have limited space on your hard drive, you may choose not to install some components of Peachtree. This choice will allow you to choose what parts of the program to install.

Upgrade — This installation is used to upgrade from an earlier version of Peachtree to a newer version.

Network — Select this installation if you have a network and more than one computer is to run Peachtree or if the data files are to reside on a computer and the program run from another machine.

Later versions of Peachtree come on a CD and are easily installed by following the steps shown below.

Note: Peachtree 2002 requires that Microsoft Internet Explorer 5 (or higher) be installed on your system in order to run. You may still use another Internet browser, but Internet Explorer must be installed. This should not be much of a problem since if you are running Windows 98, ME, or 2000, you have Internet Explorer installed whether you want it or not. If you are running Windows 95 and do not have IE5, you may be prompted to install Internet Explorer. Just follow the instructions to install.

Standard Installation on a Stand-alone Computer

To install Peachtree on a stand-alone computer, perform the following steps:

1. Close all programs that are running on your computer. This includes virus protection software, e-mail systems, and fax programs that may be running in the background. Peachtree is one of the more finicky programs to install so the advice to close all applications should not be brushed aside. I have seen a few installations seem to

install correctly only to have problems down the road which could only be attributed to a bad install. Place the Peachtree CD in the computer's CD-ROM drive.

2. The Welcome to Peachtree Accounting screen appears.

   If it does not appear, click **Start**, **Run** on the Windows taskbar. The Run dialog box will appear.

   Click the **Browse** button to open the Windows Browse dialog box.

   In the Look in field, choose your CD-ROM drive. Generally, it will be the D drive, although a different drive letter may be used. Select the **Setup.exe** file in the window or select the **Setup** file if your computer is not set up to display file extensions. Click **Open**.

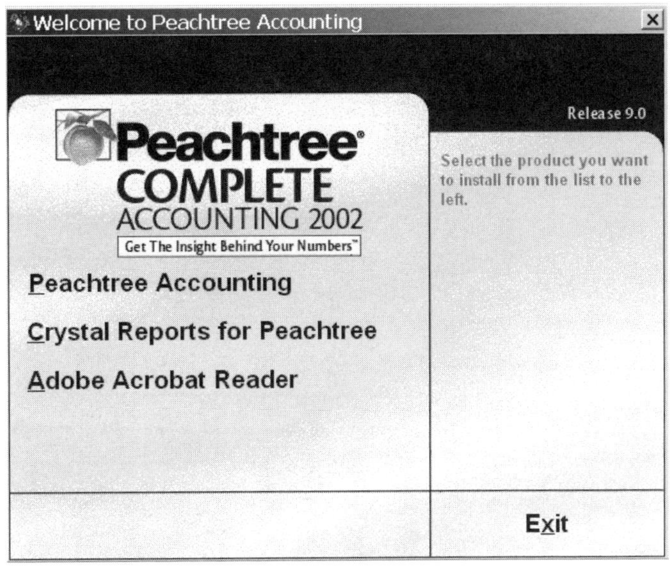

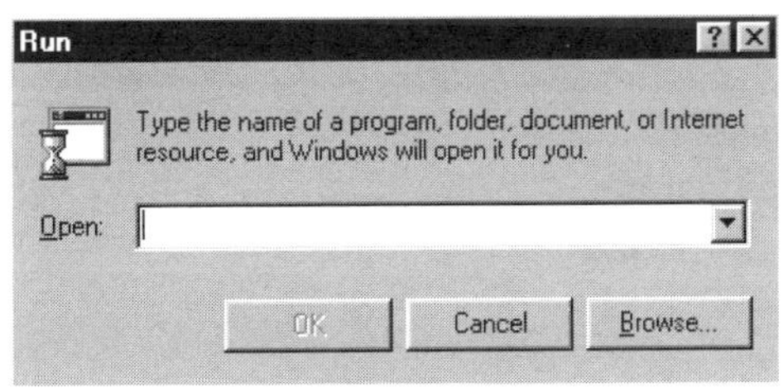

   The path appears in the Open field. Click **OK.** The Welcome to Peachtree Accounting screen will appear.

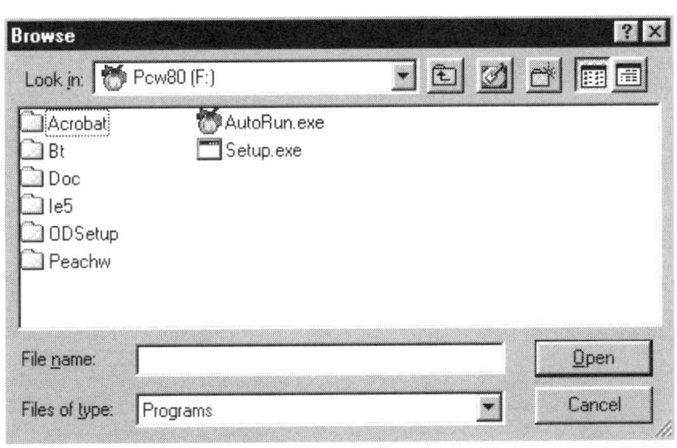

3. Click on the line that says **Peachtree Accounting**. The Peachtree splash screen and the Setup display meter appear for several seconds.

   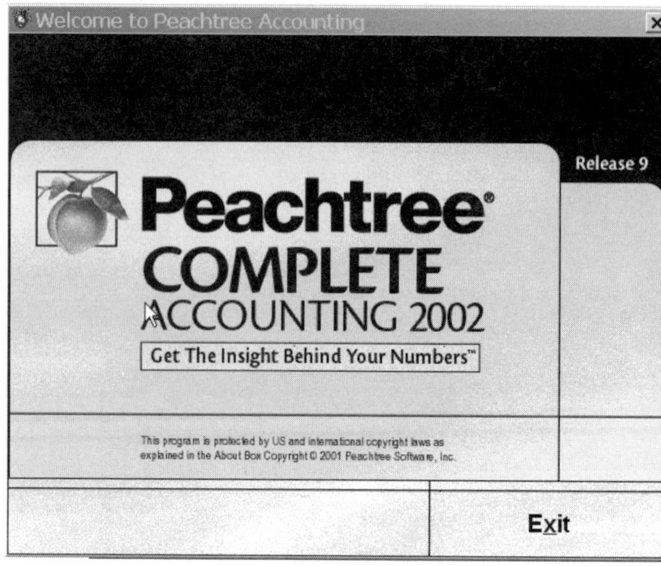

   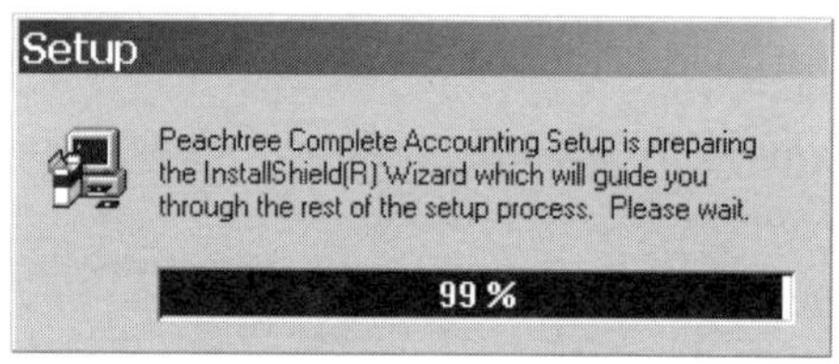

   For some reason, Peachtree may crash or disappear at this point and you may need to start the process over. Usually this happens if you have other programs running in the background. Remember the earlier admonition to close all programs? Be sure that you have closed or disabled all programs. Wait several minutes first, though, to verify that the installation has actually crashed and is not just working in the background.

4. Finally, InstallShield will appear in the background and the Peachtree Complete Accounting Setup Welcome screen will appear with several warnings and instructions.

   Click **Next** to continue.

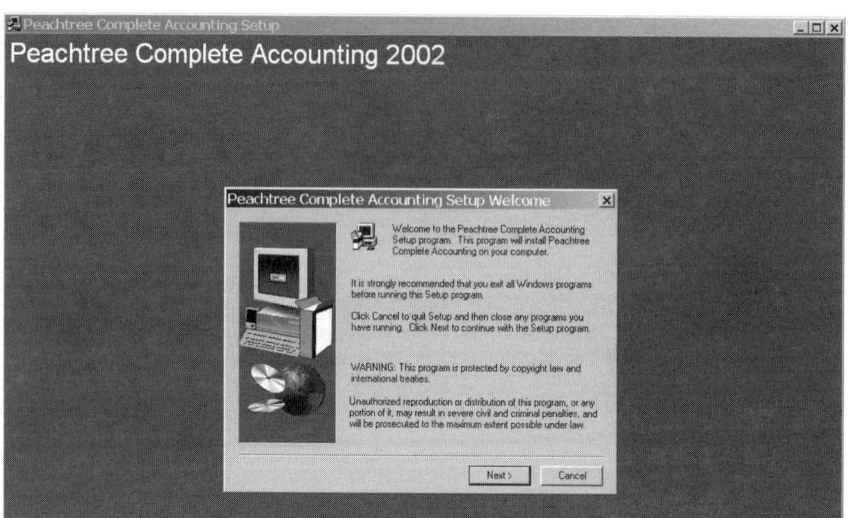

5. The License Agreement screen appears.

   In order to install Peachtree, you must accept the agreement and click **Yes** to continue.

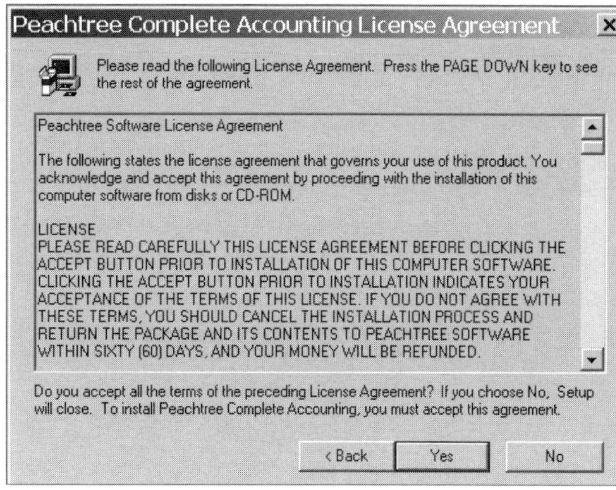

6. The Select Setup Type screen appears.

   Depending on whether you have previously installed Peachtree on your system or your network, this screen may look slightly different and could possibly have up to four buttons showing. In Peachtree 2002 I only saw three buttons, regardless of the type of installation I performed.

   For a new, stand-alone installation, click the **Standard** or the **Custom** button. Selecting Custom will present you with additional options later in the installation. Generally, if you don't care about file locations or having more control over the actual features installed, just select Standard.

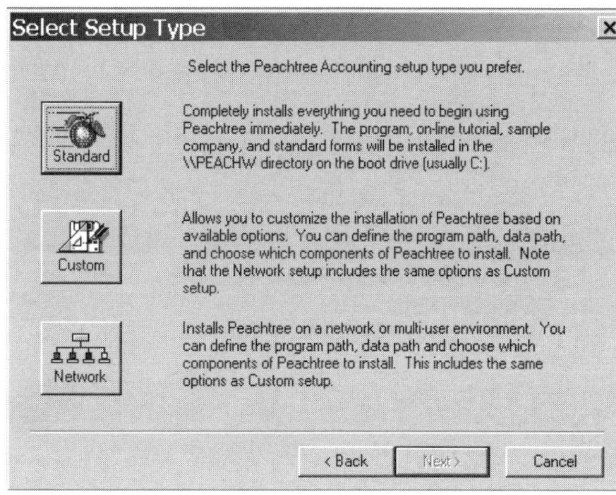

7. The Select Location screen appears.

   For a stand-alone installation you may leave the settings as they are (and click **Next** to proceed to Step 11) or change the location of either the program or the data files by clicking one of the **Browse** buttons. The Choose Folder dialog box will appear.

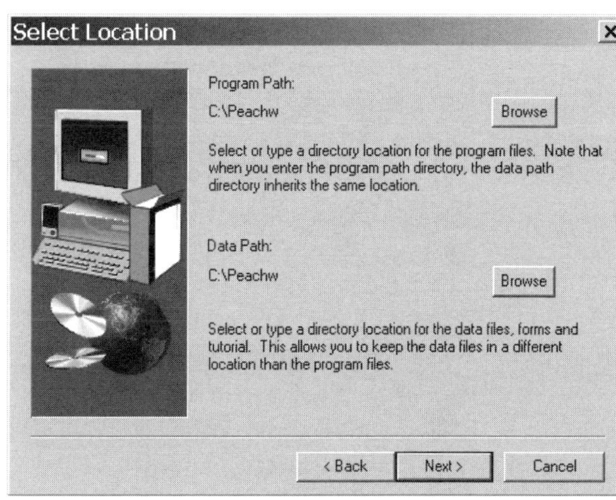

8. You may enter the path directly or select it from the Directories window. Click **OK** once the path is entered correctly.

9. If a folder does not exist — and it should not unless you have previously started a Peachtree installation — you may get a confirmation message. (Peachtree 2002 may have changed this so that the folder is added first.)

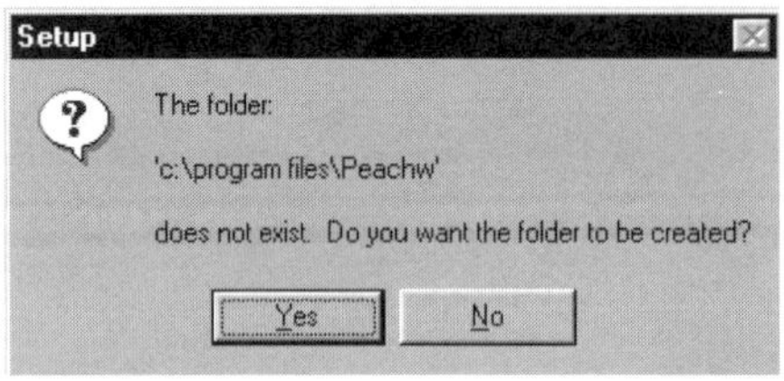

Click **Yes** to create the new folder.

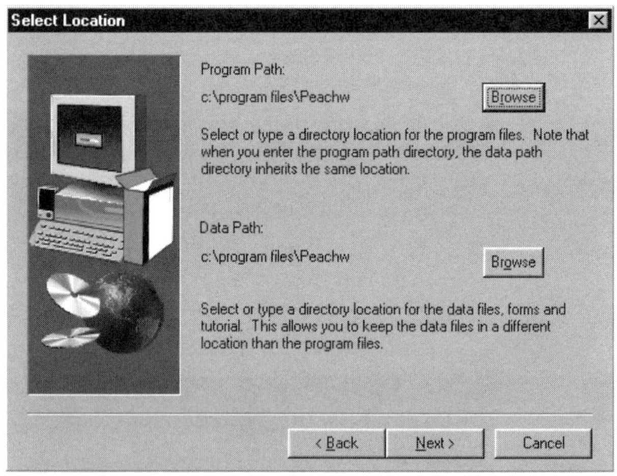

10. The new filenames will now appear on the Select Location screen.

    Click **Next** to continue.

11. The Select Peachtree Accounting Folder screen appears.

    The program defaults to the Peachtree Complete Accounting folder. This is where the program will show up when you select Start, Program Files from your Windows taskbar. Accept the default unless you have a compelling reason not to. If you select an existing folder, Peachtree will install all of its shortcuts into the indicated folder, combining the folder contents with the shortcuts Peachtree creates. I prefer to install to the default folder and then move the folder using the taskbar function in Windows after installation completes. Click **Next** to continue.

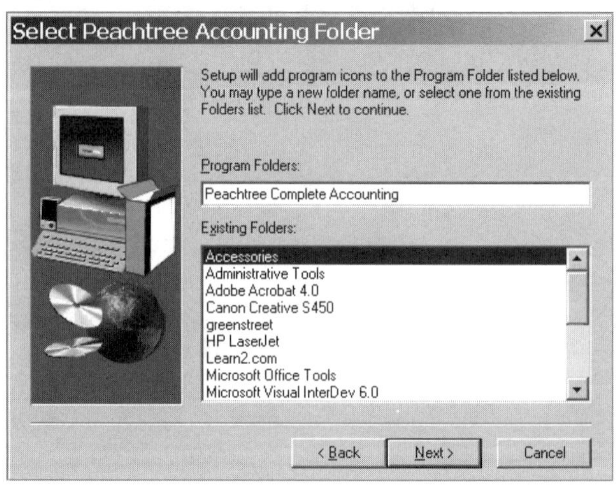

12. The program copies the needed files to the locations that you specified. A meter appears showing that the copying is taking place and indicating the percentage complete.

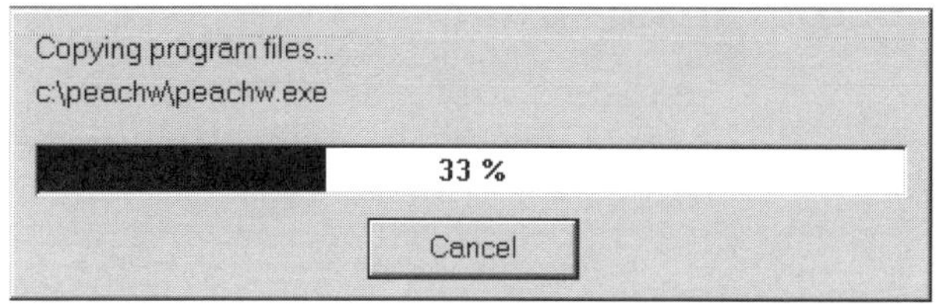

After all the files are copied to the hard drive, the installation process will register the program and set up additional components to the operating system.

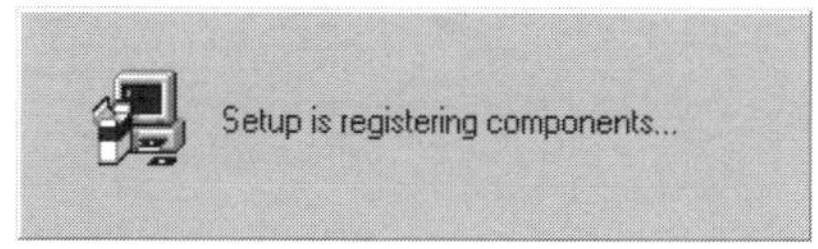

13. The Setup Complete window will then appear and ask you to restart your computer.

    Selecting **Yes** will reboot the computer automatically when you click **Finish**. If you select **No**, you will need to reboot your computer manually.

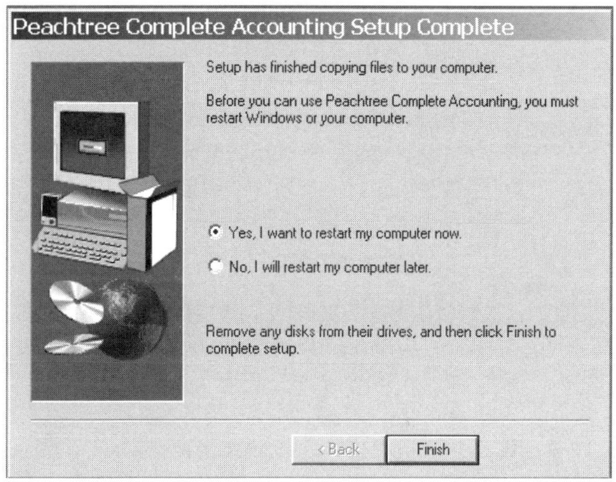

14. When Windows restarts, a system configuration message will appear as the final components of Peachtree are installed on the computer.

    If you selected to install the program or the data files on a drive on another computer in your network, you may receive the following message.

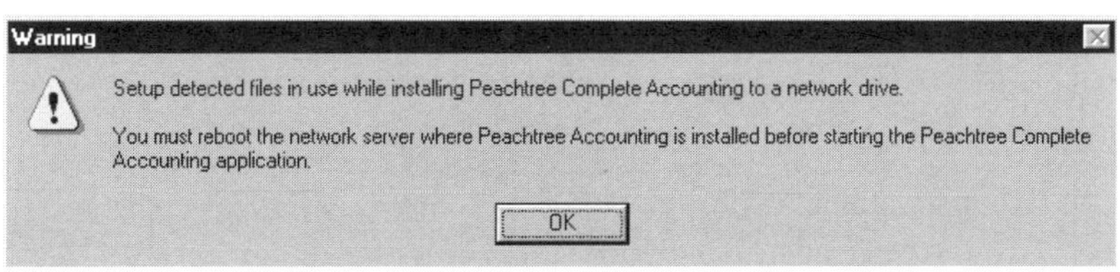

Simply reboot the other computer to finish the installation.

Peachtree is now installed on the computer. The next step is to create a new company, which is discussed in Chapter 3.

Custom Installation

A custom installation of Peachtree can be used to change the components that are installed on the computer. When doing a standard installation, the following files are installed:

Peachtree Accounting program files	59 MB (approx.)
Sample Company Data	10 MB
Standard Forms	7 MB
Tutorial and Manual Files	62 MB
Fixed Assets program files	3 MB

The files add up to approximately 140 MB of hard drive space. Actual company files that you create will range in size from 2 MB to 40 MB. You also need lots of room for backups — at least three times the size of your company files to be safe. So altogether you are looking at 200 to 300 MB needed in the near future. If your hard drive space is limited, you may not want to install the sample data, tutorial files, or fixed assets. On the other hand, with hard drive space as cheap as it is, if room on your hard drive is a critical issue, you might want to just add a larger hard drive on your computer.

When doing a custom installation, you will follow the same steps as in the previous section. After you have chosen the location and folders for the program, the Select Components screen will appear.

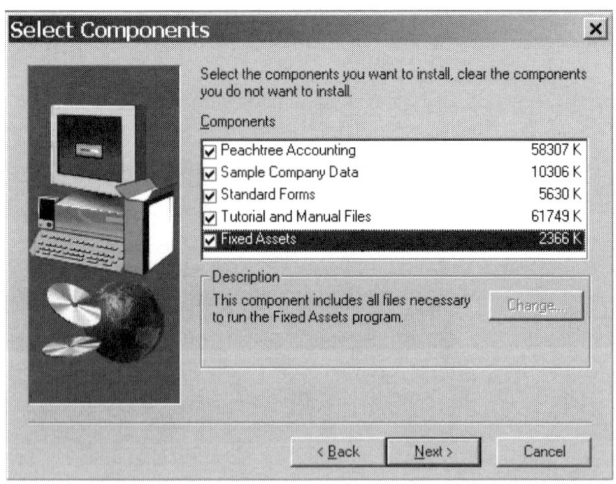

Unselect the components that you do not want to add and click the **Next** button to continue with the rest of the installation.

The Select Components screen will also appear when you choose the Upgrade or Network installations.

Upgrading Peachtree from a Previous Version

If you have a previous version of Peachtree on your computer, you can upgrade it to the newest version. I have tried to determine the oldest version of Peachtree that can be upgraded without intermediate steps, but I have not yet gotten a definitive answer. I do know that versions 5, 6, and 7 can be upgraded directly to 2002 without intermediate steps.

Running the upgrade is very similar to the Standard installation.

1. Before you do anything, I strongly suggest that you make an extra backup of your company files before beginning the upgrade procedure. This backup should be in a location that is not on the same hard drive as your files.
2. Close all programs that are running on your computer. Place the Peachtree CD in the computer's CD-ROM drive.
3. The Welcome to Peachtree Accounting screen appears.

4. Click **Peachtree Accounting.**
5. A Peachtree splash screen appears, along with a Setup window that prepares to install Peachtree.

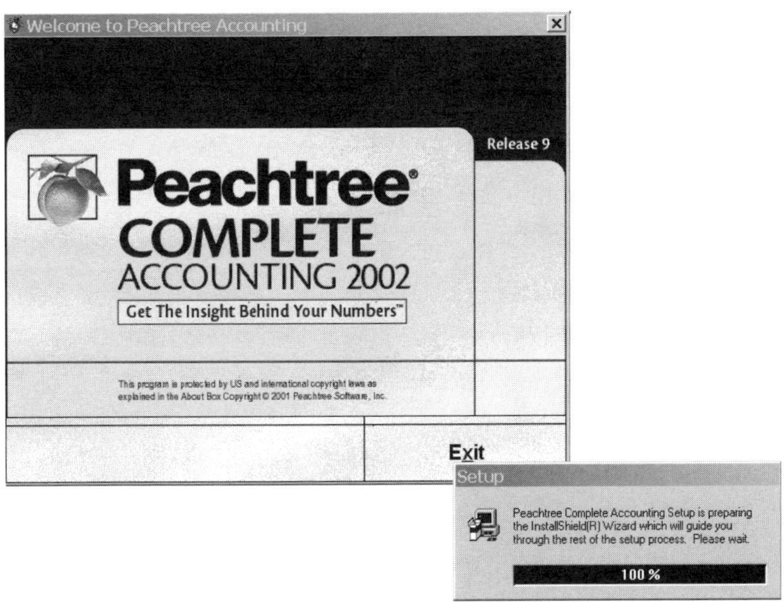

6. After several seconds, Peachtree InstallShield appears, covering up the screen. Inside InstallShield is the Peachtree Welcome screen.

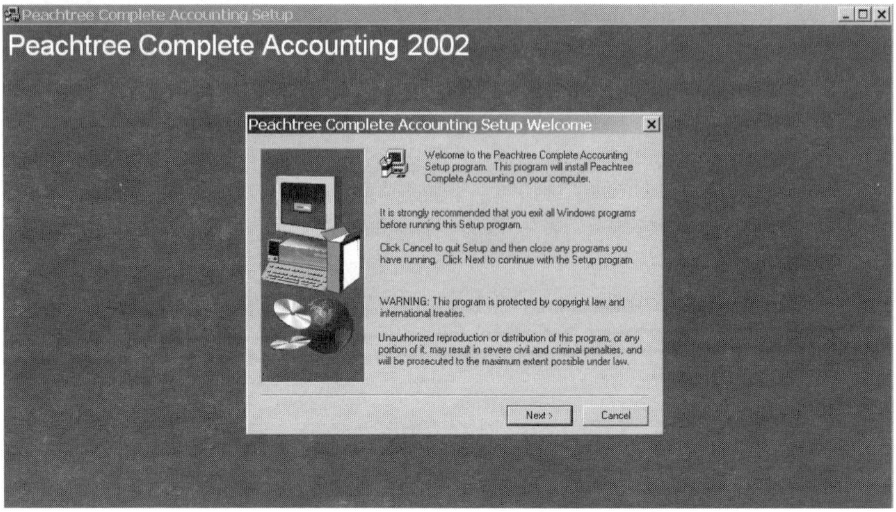

Click the **Next** button to continue the installation.

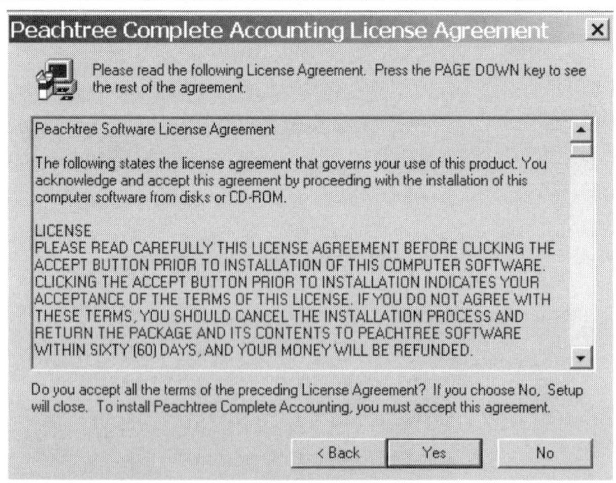

7. The Peachtree License Agreement screen appears.

   You must click **Yes** to continue the installation. Clicking **No** will abort the installation.

8. The Select Setup Type screen appears.

   Because this is an upgrade installation, Peachtree does not show the Standard setup option. Click the **Upgrade** button. Upgrade will work for both single installations and network installations.

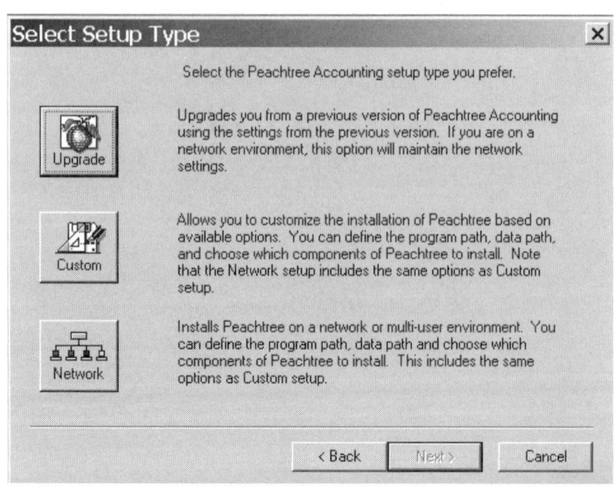

9. The Select Location screen appears.

   Peachtree will always try to find the location of the current Peachtree program files and the company files. In this case, the program is located on the user's C drive and the company files are located on a mapped network drive named n.

   To change the location of either the program path or the data path, click the **Browse** button.

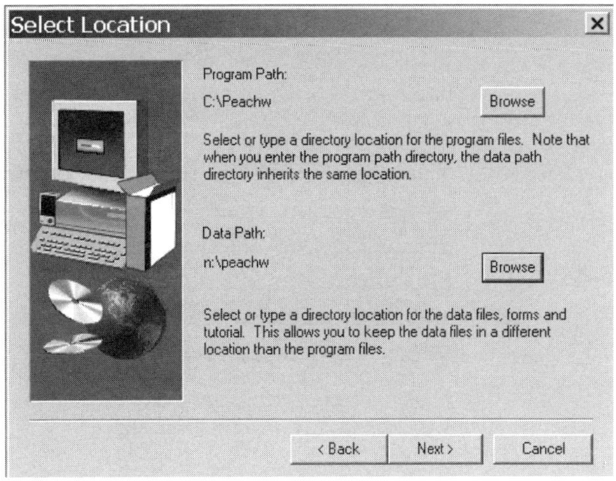

Note: If you change the folder that the program is to be installed to, the older version of the program will remain in its old location. This situation can sometimes cause havoc in both versions of the program because some shared files in the Windows directory may be converted incorrectly. It is best to leave the program path in the default location.

10. The Choose Folder dialog box appears.

    Select the correct location of the files and click **OK**.

11. You are returned to the Select Location screen with the new location showing. Click the **Next** button to continue.

12. The Select Peachtree Accounting Folder screen appears.

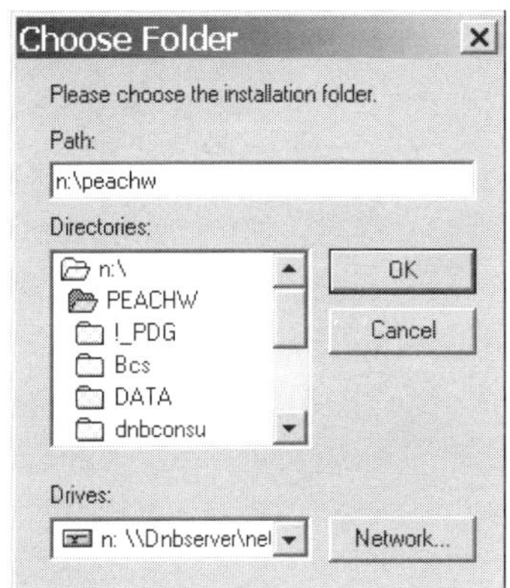

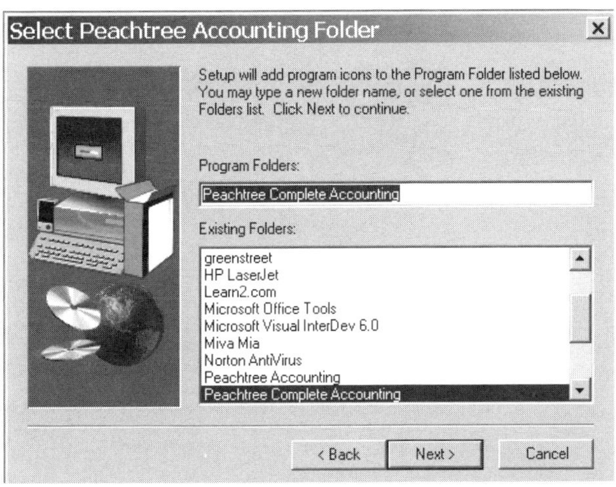

The program defaults to the Peachtree Complete Accounting folder. This is where the program will show up when you select Start, Program Files from your Windows taskbar. As with the standard installation, accept the default unless you have a compelling reason not to. Click **Next** to continue.

13. The Select Components screen appears. See the "Custom Installation" section for the options available. Generally you will leave the selected options as they are.

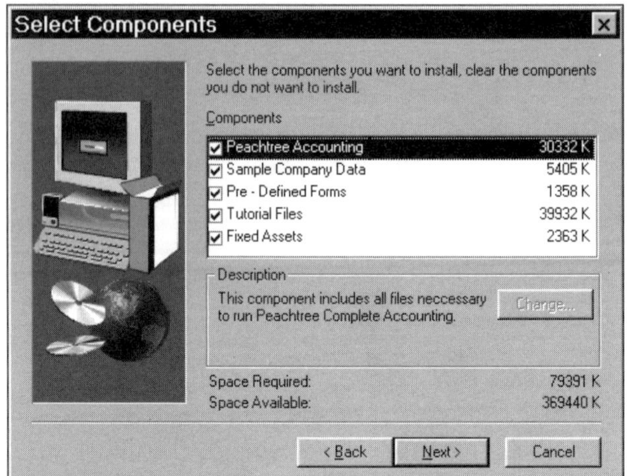

14. Press **Next**. The program copies the needed files to the locations that you specified. A meter appears showing that the copying is taking place and the percentage complete.

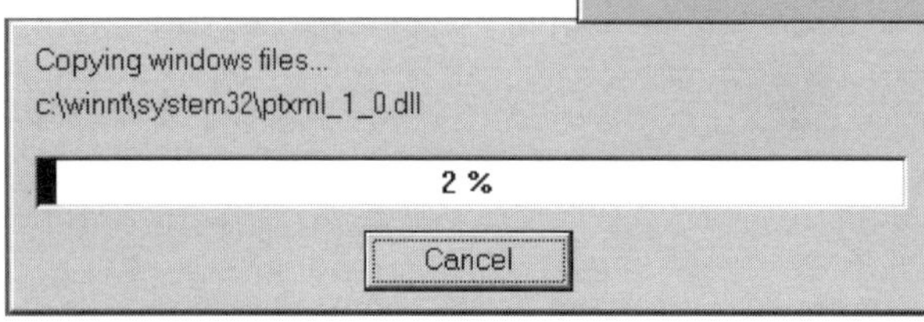

After all the files are copied to the hard drive, the installation process will register the program with your computer system and install additional components.

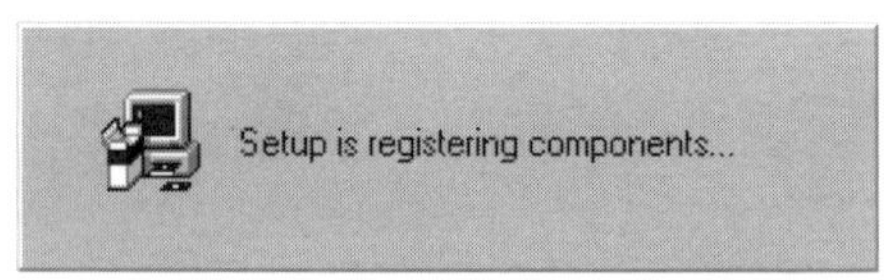

15. The Setup Complete window will then appear and ask you to restart your computer.

    Selecting **Yes** will reboot the computer automatically when you click **Finish**. If you select **No**, you will need to reboot your computer manually.

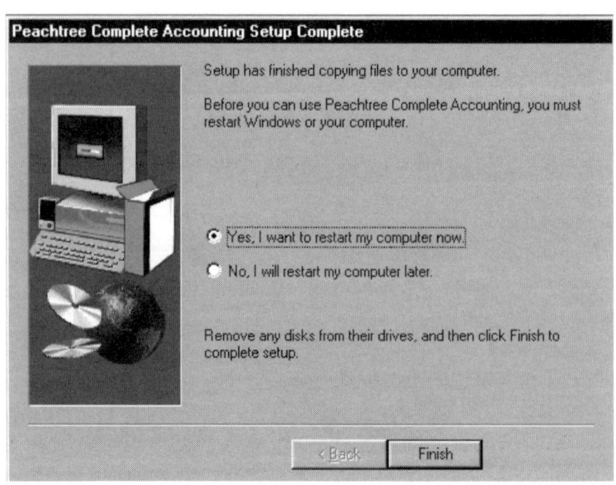

16. When Windows restarts, a system configuration message may appear while the remaining portions of the installation complete.

If you are doing a network installation and the network is being used, you may receive a message telling you to reboot your server before opening Peachtree.

Notify others on the network to log off the server, including yourself, and then simply reboot the server computer to finish the installation. All users may then log on to the server again.

If you wish to close the Peachtree setup before the installation is complete, you will get the message shown to the right.

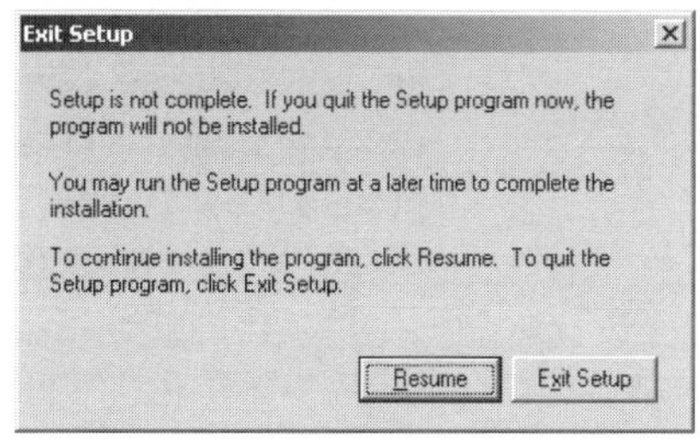

Network Installations and Concerns

In a network environment, the Peachtree data files reside on a computer called a *server*. Other computers that have the Peachtree program installed on them and which run the program are called *workstations* and connect to the server to use the data files. In very small offices with only two or three computers, the server may also function as a workstation. With computers as cheap as they are now, I do not recommend the dual function server/workstation for several reasons. First, since the machine is doing double duty, it runs slower for the person using the machine. It also means slower access for those who are accessing the machine since the machine is having to split its processing between the user who is on it and sending files to the other users. More important, the stability of a dedicated server is far greater than that of a dual-purpose machine. With fewer programs installed on it and fewer programs running on it, a dedicated server has a tendency to not crash as often or have as many intermittent problems.

Peachtree can be used on both peer-to-peer and client/server networks. A *client/server network* is defined as a network that has one or more machines that function as dedicated servers and have server-based software running on them. All machines access the servers to log into the network, to share files, and to access common applications. *Peer-to-peer networks* are those networks that have a more distributed functionality where any machine can function as a source for files or applications. Login occurs at an individual machine and each machine then controls who has access to that machine. In the case of peer-to-peer networks, the machines can be any flavor of workstation Windows including Windows 95, 98, ME, NT Workstation, or 2000 Professional. For client/server systems, the server can be NT

Server, NT 2000 Advanced Server, or Novell Netware 4 or higher. The workstations can be any of the Windows configurations listed for peer-to-peer.

It is strongly suggested that regardless of the operating systems chosen for the client and server machines all service packs be applied to the machines before Peachtree is installed. This will generally prevent accidentally wiping out Peachtree files when the operating system is upgraded.

Network Requirements

Because computers are changing so rapidly, I will not give actual specs for computers here beyond a few basics. No matter what I suggest for a machine configuration, the suggestion will be out of date in six months, and a year in the future you will probably not be able to even buy the suggested configurations! In general, the server machine should be configured with emphasis on hard drive access and amount of memory. Since hard drive speeds do not seem to be increasing very rapidly, you can assume that any contemporary drive will be fast enough. The server should have a minimum of 256 MB of RAM.

The same general rules apply to the workstations. They should have adequate hard drive space, at least 10 GB, plenty of processing power, and at least 64 MB of RAM (Peachtree says 32; I really suggest 128 MB). With the average new machine being at least 1.7 gigahertz, it is suggested that any machine less than one-third that speed be replaced and serious consideration made to replacing any machine at less than half that speed. If you are upgrading from a previous version of Peachtree, and you are unhappy with your current computer speed, you will be very unhappy after the upgrade. Think about new machines.

Often overlooked by most companies is the type and quality of their network wiring. While BNC coax wire was the standard several years ago, it has been superseded by twisted-pair wires and hubs. The real consideration is reliability. Twisted-pair wiring goes from a central hub to each of the machines on the network. If a wire goes bad, only the connection between the hub and the one computer goes down. With coax wire, a problem anywhere along the daisy chain of wires will result in the whole network going down. When I move clients from coax to twisted pair the speed, reliability, and stability of the network always seem to improve.

To compound this issue is the matter of Peachtree not being tolerant about dropped network connections. A dropped connection at the wrong time can result in a corrupted database. With the drop in the cost of wiring and the inexpensive prices of hubs, if you have old coax wire just go ahead and replace it.

It is also a good idea to upgrade your wiring and components to 100 megabit Ethernet. With the sizes of files drastically increasing you will appreciate the speed differential over the slower 10 Mb Ethernet. The upgrade in speed will be well worth it. If you cannot do this job yourself, call on a reliable computer person to install the network. And do not go with the cheapest parts. Your network is an area in which you want to have a name-brand hub and network cards. I also recommend that you stick to the same brand for all parts whenever possible.

The following figure shows a sample network with four workstations connected by 10 or 100 Mb wiring to a central hub, which is connected to the server.

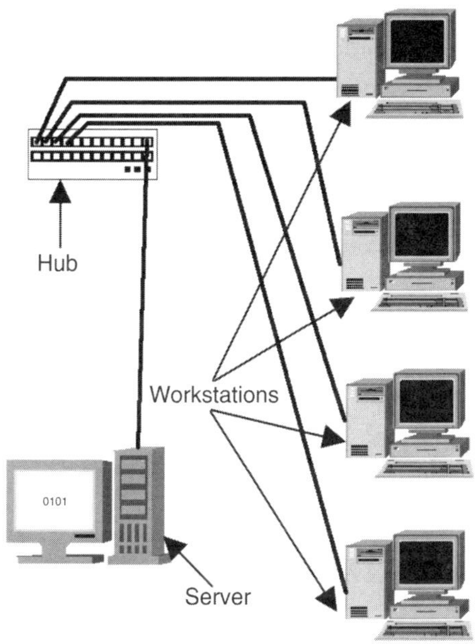

Installing Peachtree on the Server

Before you install Peachtree on the server, you need to decide if the server is actually going to be used as a workstation or not. Because of the requirements of Peachtree, I recommend against server/workstations, but am sometimes overruled. If the server will not be used as a workstation, you may not want to install one of your Peachtree licenses on the server. Instead, create a folder on the server called PEACHW. This folder should be able to be backed up regularly, so you might want to put it in a common data folder along with all your other data files in an orderly hierarchical arrangement.

If you decide to install Peachtree on the server, follow these steps:

1. Start the installation process the same as you do for a stand-alone or custom installation. When you get to the Select Setup Type screen, click the **Network** button.
2. The Select Location screen appears. Change the location of either the program or the data files, if needed, by clicking the **Browse** button.
3. The Choose Folder dialog box will appear. You may enter the path directly or select it from the Directories window. Click **OK** once the path is entered correctly.
4. If you are asked if you want to create a new folder, click **Yes**. The new filenames will now appear on the Select Location screen. Click **Next** to continue.

5. The Select Peachtree Accounting Folder screen appears. Accept the default folder, select an existing folder, or create a new folder for Peachtree. Click **Next** to continue.
6. Just as in the stand-alone installation, Peachtree will install the files and ask you to reboot the computer. After rebooting, the server needs no more work.
7. After the PEACHW folder is installed, you need to share the folder in which it resides. To do this, open Windows Explorer and find the PEACHW folder. Highlight the folder by clicking on it with the left mouse button.
8. Right-click on the folder to bring up the shortcut menu and select **Sharing**.

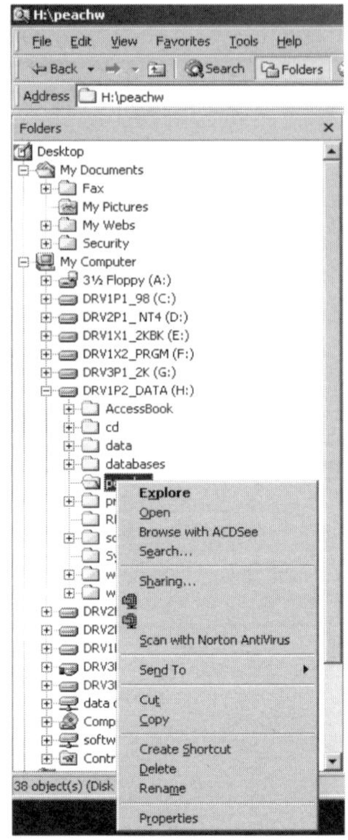

9. The properties screen appears with the Sharing tab selected. Select **Share this folder** and keep the default value PEACHW for the share name. Click **OK**. The following screen is for Windows 2000; depending upon the version of Windows that you have on your server, this screen may look a bit different.

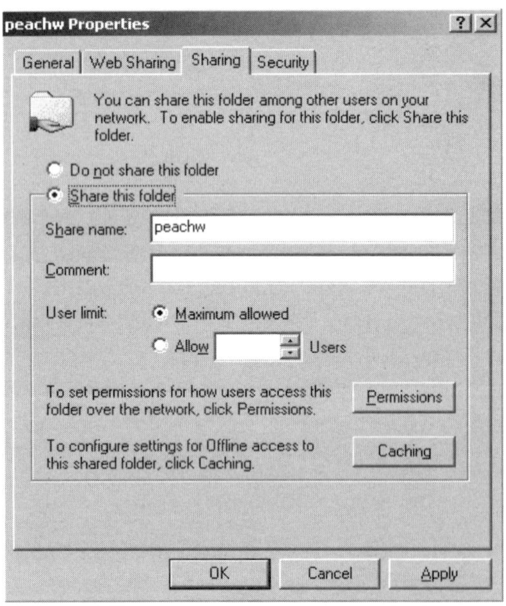

For Windows 95, 98, and ME, the screen will look more like the following. Select the **Shared As** option and select **Full** for Access Type. Click **OK** to continue.

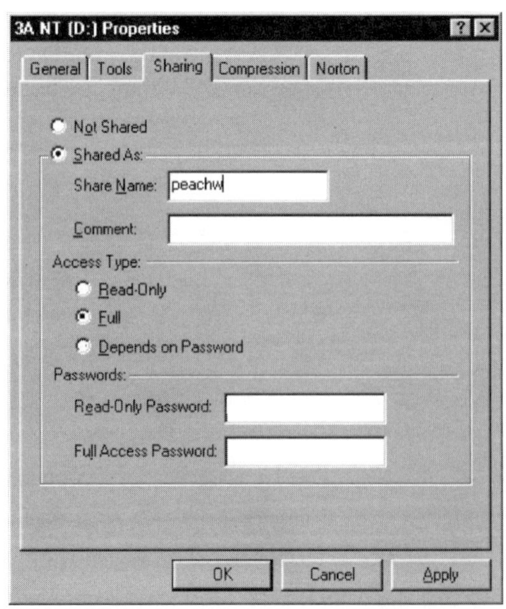

At this point the Peachtree directory is shared and is available for all users. This is represented by a little open hand under the directory icon.

Installing Peachtree on the Network Workstations

Once the system is installed on the network server, you may install it on the workstations.

1. Before you begin, you must map each workstation to the PEACHW folder on the network. Open Windows Explorer on the workstation. Go to **My Network Places** and open the folder **Entire Network**, under which is the folder **Microsoft Windows Network**, under which is the name of your workgroup or domain. Open your workgroup or domain and find the computer on which you have placed the Peachtree data files. Open it and you should see a folder labeled PEACHW. Right-click on this folder to bring up the shortcut menu. Depending upon how many drives and computers you have, and the general network setup, this window can vary significantly.

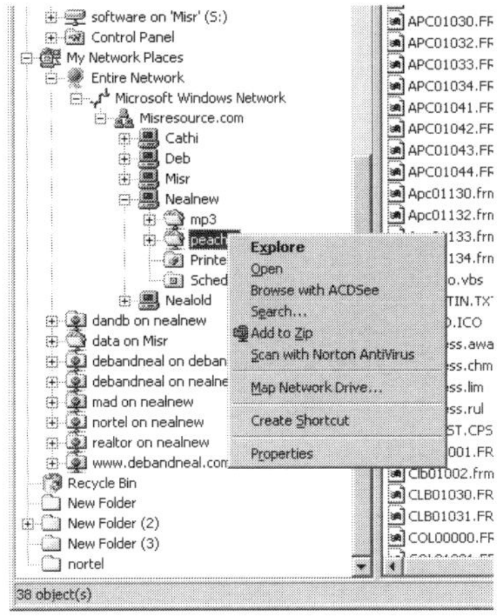

2. Select **Map Network Drive** to bring up the Map Network Drive window. Once again, the appearance of this window will vary based on your version of Windows. This is the Windows 2000 screen:

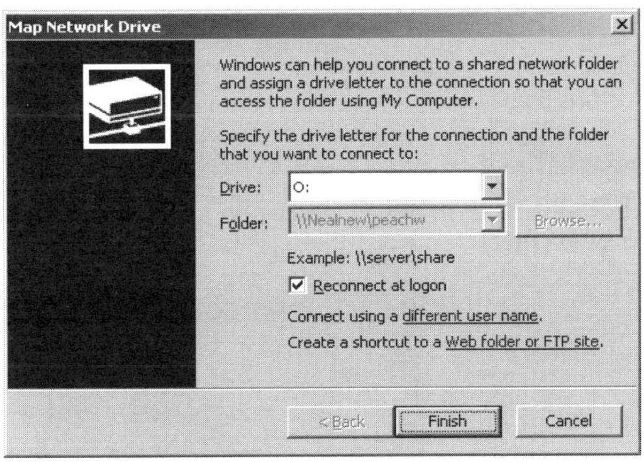

and this is from Windows 98:

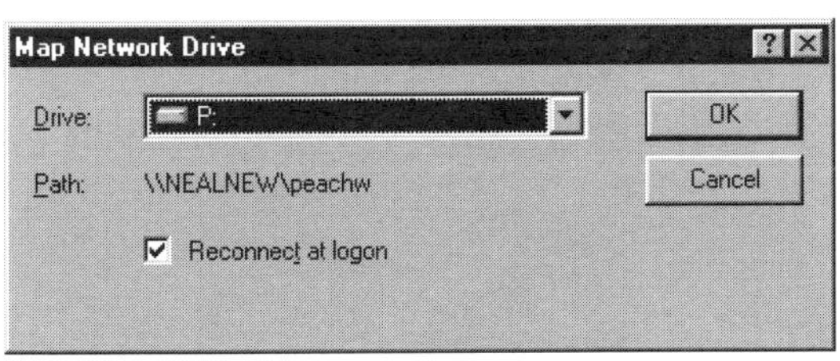

3. Select the desired drive letter from the drop-down box. I suggest P for Peachtree, if it is not already in use. Check the **Reconnect at logon** check box and click **Finish** or **OK**.

   The drive is now mapped and will appear in your list of drives in Windows Explorer as drive P.

4. Once the PEACHW folder is mapped, you may start installing Peachtree. When you get to the Select Setup Type screen, click the **Network** button.
5. Follow the instructions for installation. When you get to the Select Location screen, the data path should point to the mapped network drive. Click the **Browse** button to locate the mapped drive.
6. When you get to the Select Components screen, select the components that you want to install. If the server has a complete Peachtree installation, you can choose not to install the Tutorial files or Fixed Assets. If hard drive space is critical, you can choose only to install Peachtree Accounting. If hard drive space is no problem, I generally install everything.
7. Finish the installation as we discussed earlier in the chapter. You will need to reboot the server before you open Peachtree on any of the machines.

Opening Peachtree for the First Time

Now that Peachtree is installed and the system has been rebooted, it is time to start working in Peachtree.

Open Peachtree by selecting **Start**, **Programs**, **Peachtree Complete Accounting**, and **Peachtree Complete Accounting** from the Windows taskbar.

You can also click the **Peachtree** icon on the Windows desktop.

Peachtree will open.
Here you may see one of several different screens or messages. These include looking for online program updates, registering the program, and converting an existing company to the new version. Depending upon which message appears, you will need to go to the appropriate section below.

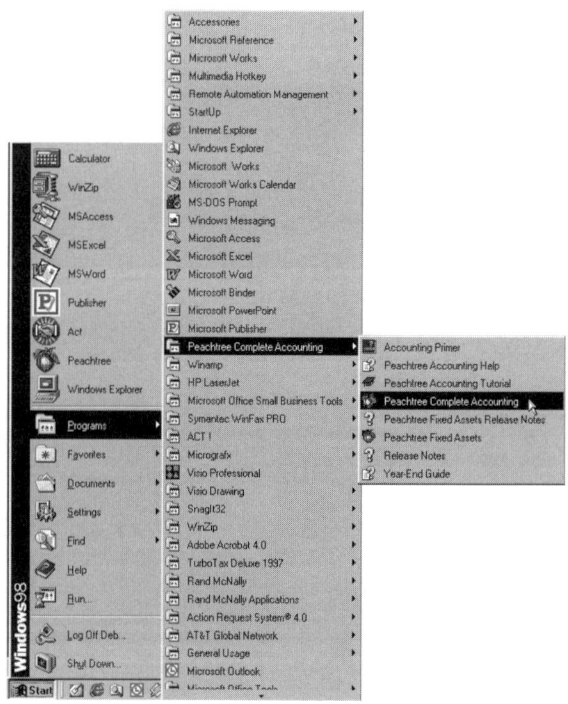

Peachtree Updates

As with any program, Peachtree updates can be vital to the running of the program. Sometimes when you open Peachtree, the Peachtree Online Update screen comes up automatically. The available updates can also be found at the bottom of the Welcome tab in Peachtree Today (see Chapter 2).

The update screen informs you of available updates to the Peachtree program and can include bug fixes, new features, and other changes. The online update feature allows you to check for program updates over the Internet. If you do not have an Internet connection, it is strongly recommended that you get one. With so much computer support now taking place over the Internet, a connection is vital. If you do not have a connection (yet), select **Close** to stop the online update process, and skip to the next section.

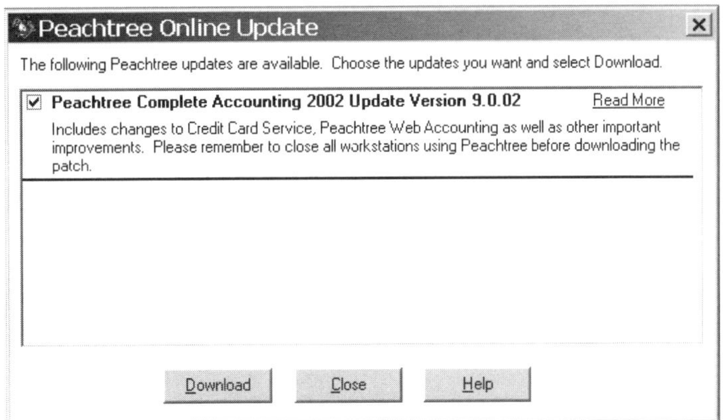

1. Click **Download** or **Check Now**, depending on your version of Peachtree, to get any existing program updates.
2. A Peachtree Online Update reminder appears.

   You can have the program prompt you to look for updates regularly by selecting the Remind me check box and setting the Day(s) field. Click the **Check Now** button.

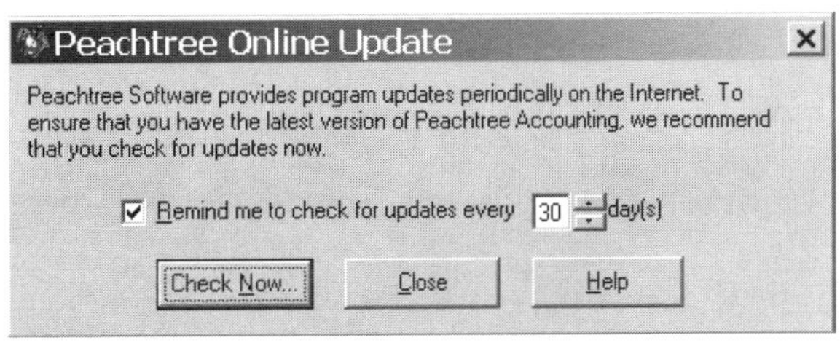

3. The Internet Connection Setup dialog box appears if you have not yet set up an Internet connection method (see Chapter 2). This dialog box can also be reached by selecting **Options**, **Define Internet Connection** from the menu bar.

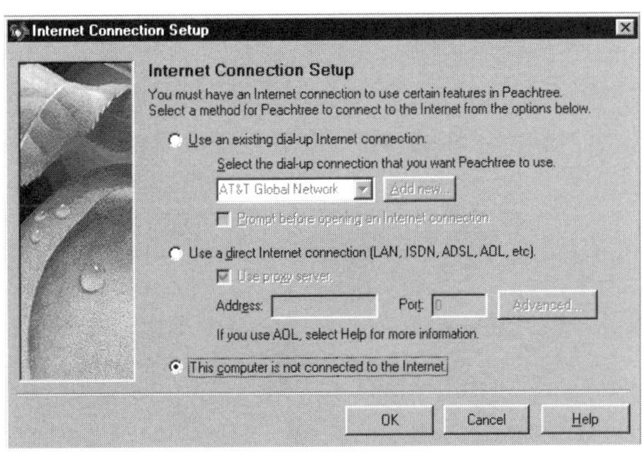

Select the appropriate Internet connection type from the options. Click **OK**.

4. Peachtree will begin the download and a download progress window appears.

   Once the download is complete, a message box will confirm the process and tell you that the update will be installed when Peachtree is closed.

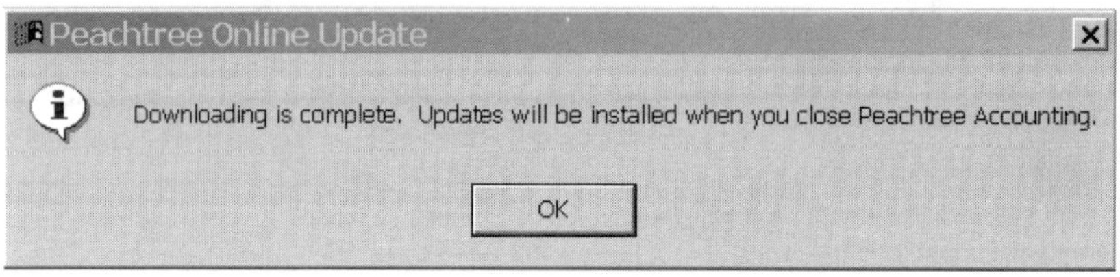

5. Click **OK**. When you reopen Peachtree, you will be taken through an installation process to finish updating the program. You may be asked to reboot your machine at the end of the update. This process may take several minutes and it may appear that your computer has locked up. Be patient and try not to interrupt the process at any time. When the update is completed, you may view the update log.
6. Open Peachtree Today and go to the Welcome tab. Select **Product Update Center**.

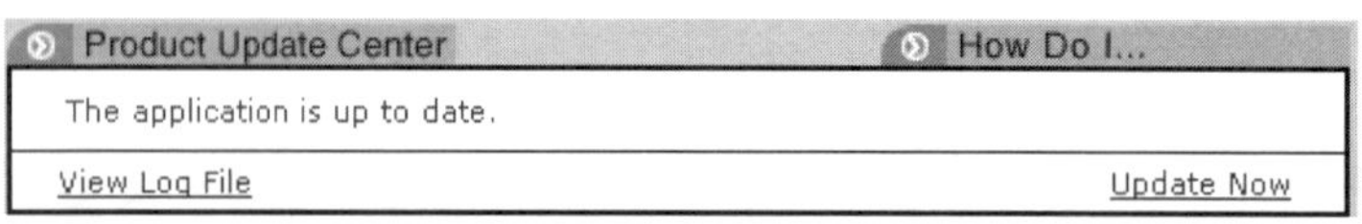

7. Click the **View Log File** link. The log file will appear.

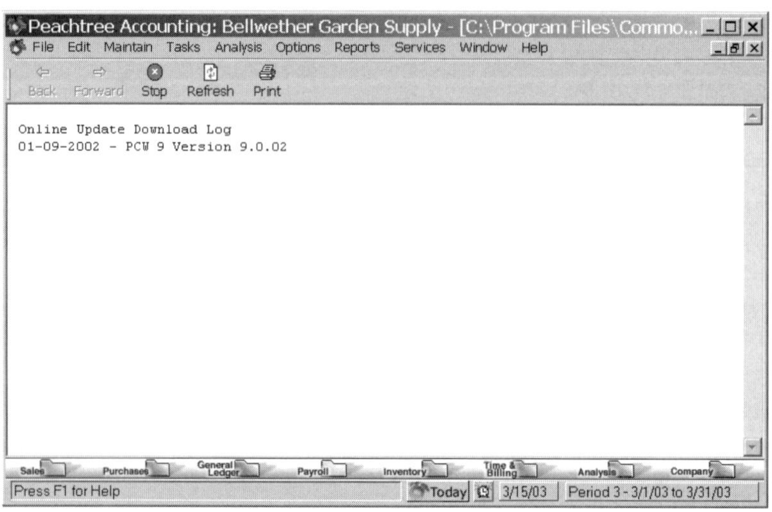

This list may be printed by clicking the **Print** button.

Registering Peachtree

When Peachtree opens, you will get a dialog box asking you to register either now or later.

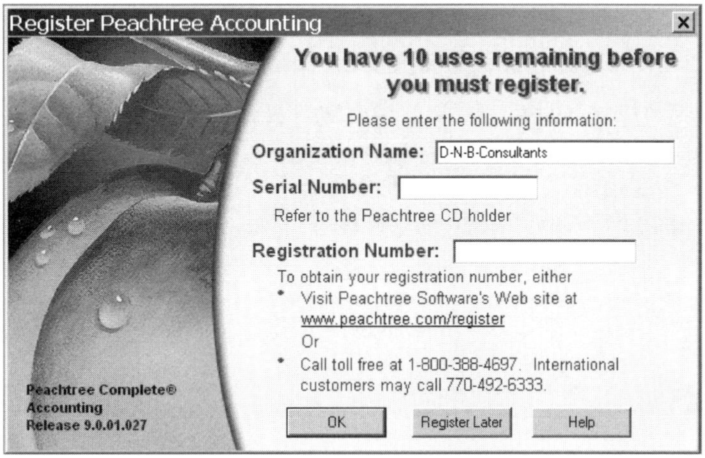

You must register your Peachtree software. The program will only allow you to open Peachtree a limited number of times. You may want to hold off registering a little while for only one reason: Peachtree offers 30 days of free support from the day you register. Since it takes a few days before you even know you have a problem, waiting until the last minute to register can increase the amount of time you have to call for support. And if you don't register until you have the first big problem, you can guarantee that you will not have to pay for this first support question.

1. Click the **Register Later** button if you want to postpone registering, and skip to the next section.
2. To register, enter your company name in the Organization Name field.
3. Enter the serial number in the appropriate field. The serial number is located on the Peachtree CD-ROM sleeve.

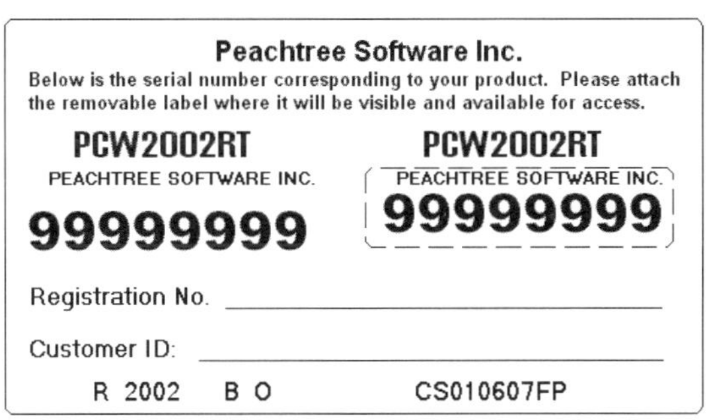

In earlier versions, it is on the inside front page of the "Getting Started" guide. Locate the sticker that looks like one of those shown here or on the previous page.

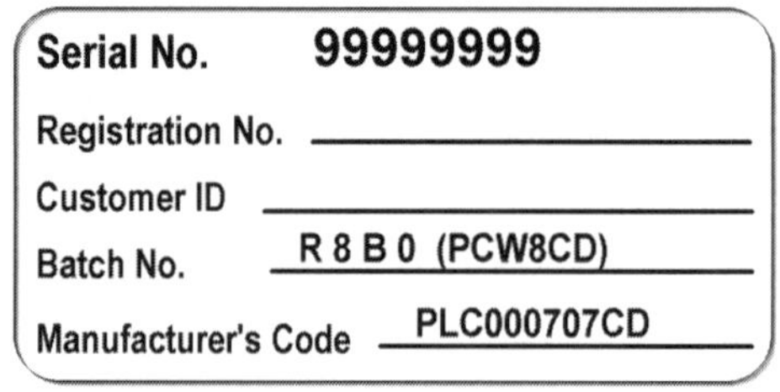

4. If you do not have Internet access, you will need to call the toll-free number shown. Otherwise, click the **www.peachtree.com/register** link.
5. The Peachtree Product Registration web page appears.

Select the **Peachtree Desktop Product** option for the product type and whether you are a new or existing Peachtree customer. Then click **Continue**.

6. The Online Registration web page appears.

Although the page states that you must log into Peachtree Passport before you register, it is more for marketing reasons than security reasons. Peachtree, like many other software companies, is trying to force its customers into the subscription model for software rather than the licensing model.

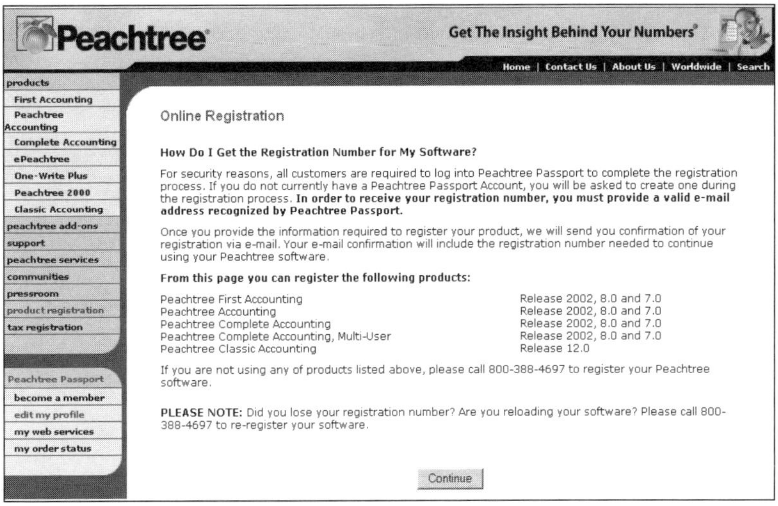

If your version of Peachtree is one of those listed, click **Continue**; otherwise, call the number given on the web page. Notice that you must have an e-mail address to register online.

7. The Passport Login Page appears.

   If you have previously become a member, enter the appropriate information in the E-mail Address and Password fields. Click **Log In** and continue with Step 14. Otherwise, click the **Become a Member** button.

8. The Create Account page appears.

Enter your e-mail address in the field provided.

9. Enter a password to be used when accessing Peachtree's web site. Make sure it is something you will remember. Write it down! (A good place to write it down may be on the serial number sticker.) Type the password again in the Confirm field.
10. Click **Continue**.
11. The Member Profile page appears.

    Enter the requested information. There are fields in the lower section of the page requesting information about your company and whether you want to receive regular information from Peachtree.

    Click **Continue** when you have filled in the information.

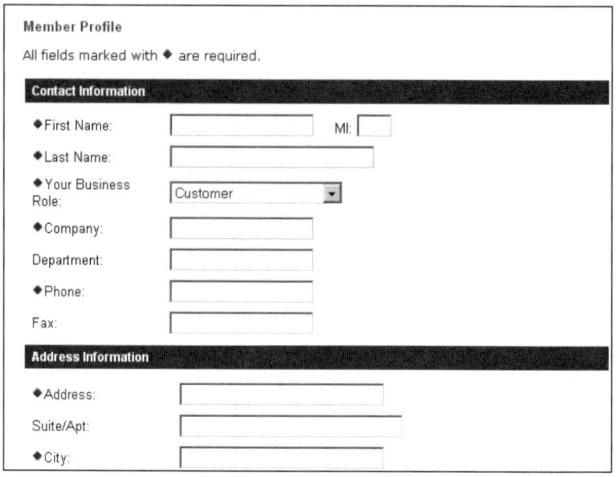

12. The Your Passport Account Has Been Created confirmation will appear.

    Click **Continue**.

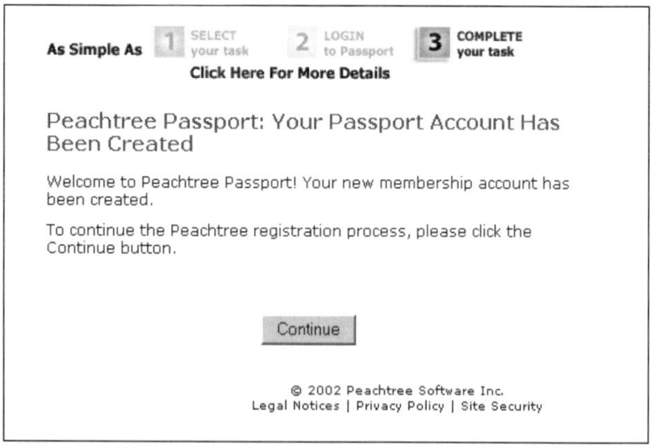

13. The Welcome Peachtree Customer page appears.

    Click **Continue**.

14. The Online Registration page appears.

    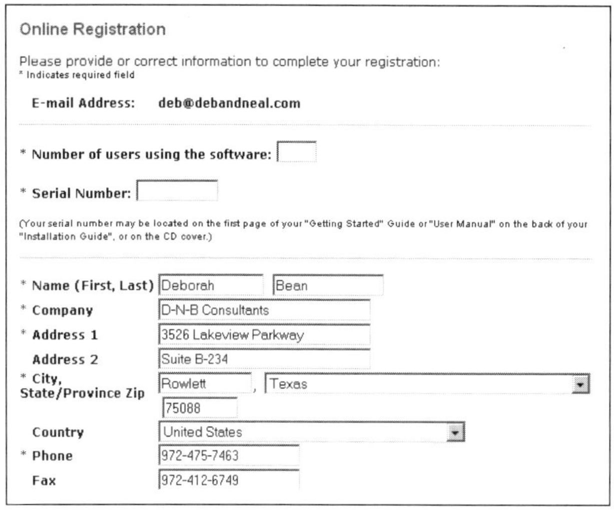

    In the Number of users using the software field, enter the number of machines that Peachtree will reside on. This is the program, not the data. If the data files are on a server computer but the program is only run on a connected workstation, you should count the users as just one, not two. Likewise, two employees who share a computer should only be counted as one user.

Note: If you are using Peachtree on more than one computer, as of Release 8.0 Peachtree requires a separate license for each computer running Peachtree. You can purchase additional copies of the software from the web site. Note that for a little more than the cost of two copies, you can get the Value Pack Single-Site version. This version allows you to add as many users to the system as you need as long as they are at the same location. If you have other locations, you must purchase a separate license for the other sites.

15. Enter the serial number in the appropriate field. Click **Continue** at the bottom of the page.
16. A Review Registration Information page appears.

    Click **Continue** if all the information is correct. Use the **Back** button if you need to correct any information. Notice the warning that says to not click the button a second time.

    If you do click a second time, Peachtree's files could become confused and would consider that the same serial number was being registered illegally. This would require you to call Peachtree and spend time convincing them that you are the legal owner of the software in order to obtain your registration number.

17. A questionnaire screen appears.

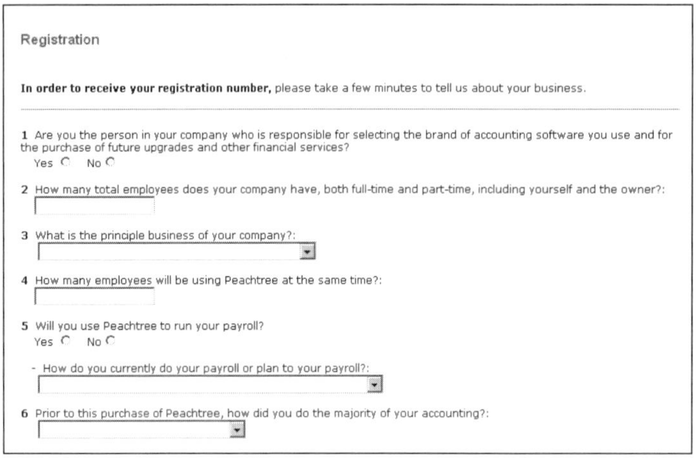

Fill in the information and click **Next.**

18. The Registration Complete page appears.

The new registration number will show on this page. (It is blacked out here for obvious reasons.) Write down the registration number! This will save many headaches if you have to reinstall your software. The "Getting Started" guide sticker has a line for this number, but I also suggest that you make a copy of these numbers and file them where they won't get lost.

19. Close your web browser and return to the Peachtree Registration dialog box.
20. In the Registration Number field, enter the number you received and then click **OK.**
21. A Thank You message appears.

Click **Continue.**

22. The Peachtree Open menu appears.

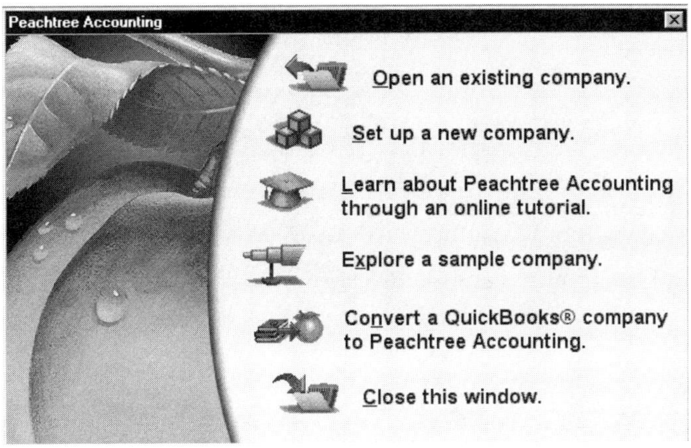

From this menu, you can now do a number of things that will all be discussed later in this book.

Converting an Existing Company File to the Latest Version

If you have upgraded your program from an earlier version of Peachtree, your company files will need to be upgraded to the latest version before you can use the program. Although this is a simple process, I strongly suggest that you make an extra backup before you start this process. This backup can be made from the System Explorer window by copying the folder to another location. Many of my clients have had trouble when the upgrade process failed and they didn't have an adequate backup.

1. Open the Peachtree program. The Peachtree Accounting menu should appear in most cases. If this is the first time you have opened Peachtree, the software may first go to the Peachtree Registration screen, in which case you will need to either register the program first or close the registration screen and open your existing company. In Peachtree 2002 the program may detect your old company files and go directly to the conversion wizard, skipping the opening menu.
2. Select **Open an existing company.**
3. The Open an Existing Company dialog box appears.

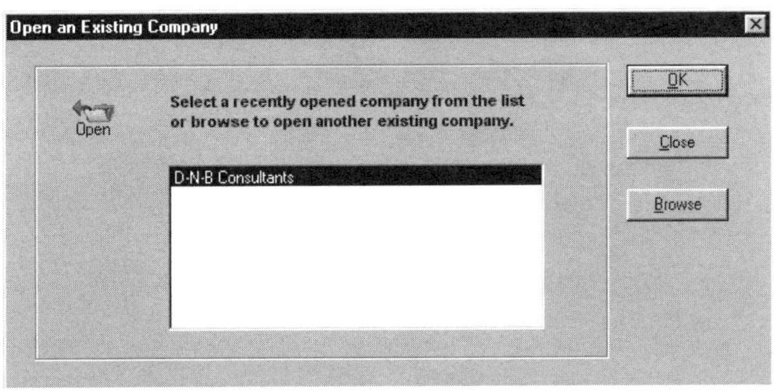

The list may or may not show company files. If the company you want is not listed, or you are not sure it is the right file, click the **Browse** button to locate the desired file. Select the company from the Company Name list and click **OK.**

4. The Open Company dialog box appears.

   Select the correct location and the company from the list and click **OK**.

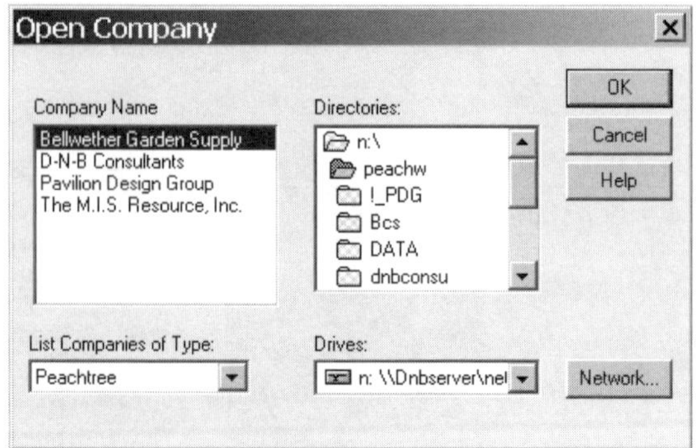

5. Peachtree will determine that the company you selected is from an older version of the program and will bring up the Data Conversion Wizard.

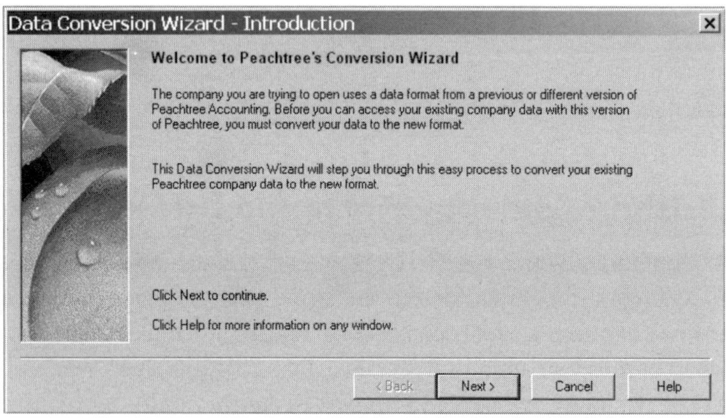

   Click **Next.**

6. The Confirm Company to Convert screen appears.

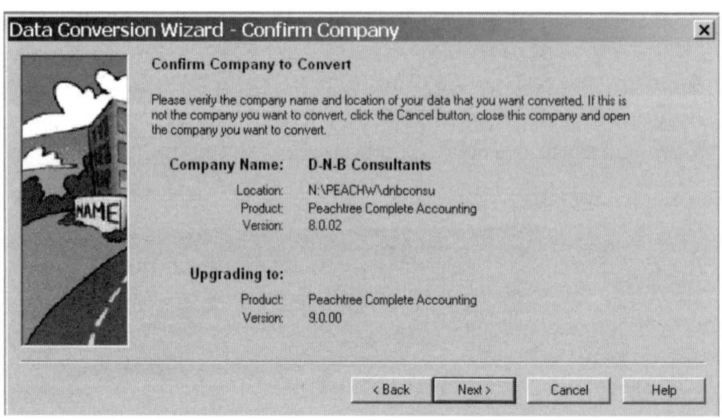

   Verify that this is the correct company to convert and click **Next.**

7. The Back Up screen appears.

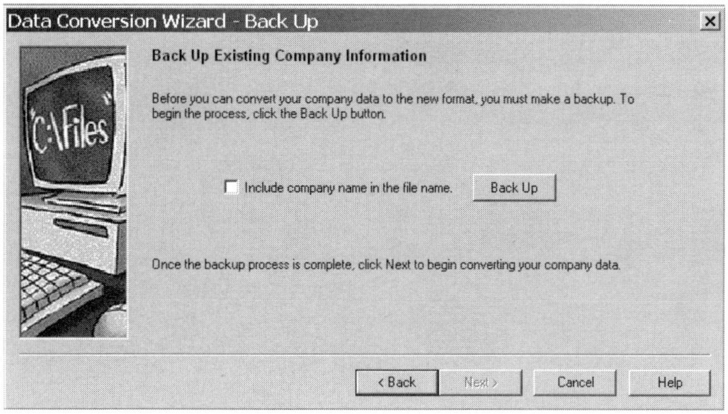

The program automatically names the backup backupv9.ptb or, if you check the Include company name in the file name check box, Co Name-backupv9.ptb. Do not use a filename that could be later confused as your standard backup name. Click **Back Up** or **Save**.

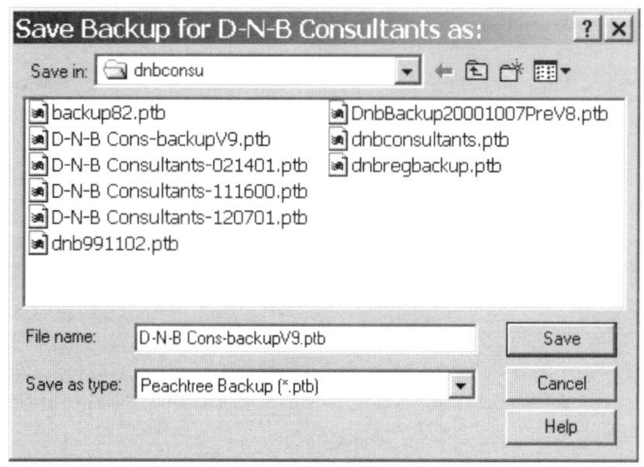

8. The program copies the files into a buffer to calculate the size of the program. It shows the different files' names as it is copying.

9. After the file size is calculated, the hard drive space needed to back up the file displays.

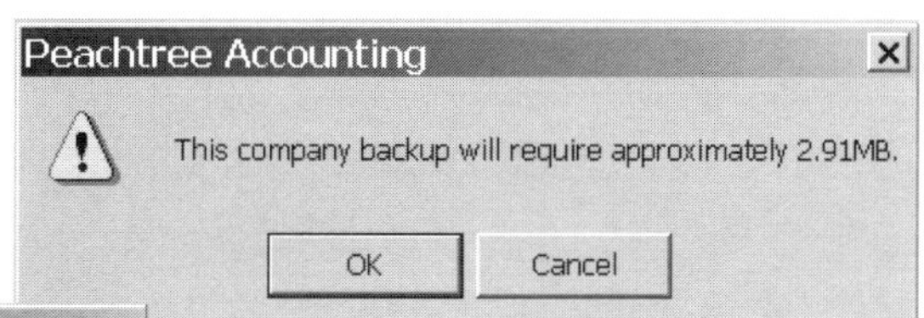

Press **OK** to back up the files.

10. When the backup is complete, click **Next** to start upgrading all the files. Each file will be displayed along with a percent completed bar.

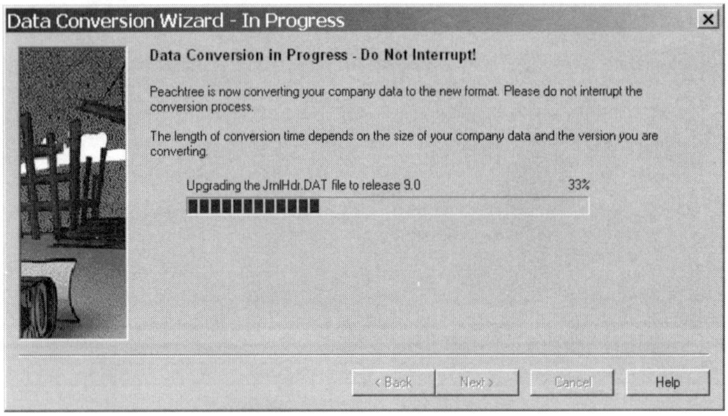

11. Be very careful not to interrupt the process. Restoring an older version can be very messy. When the conversion is complete, a confirmation appears.

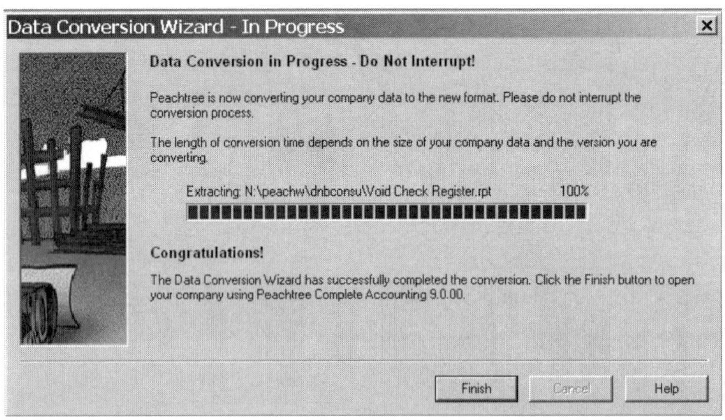

12. After all the files have been upgraded, click **Finish**. Peachtree opens the company.

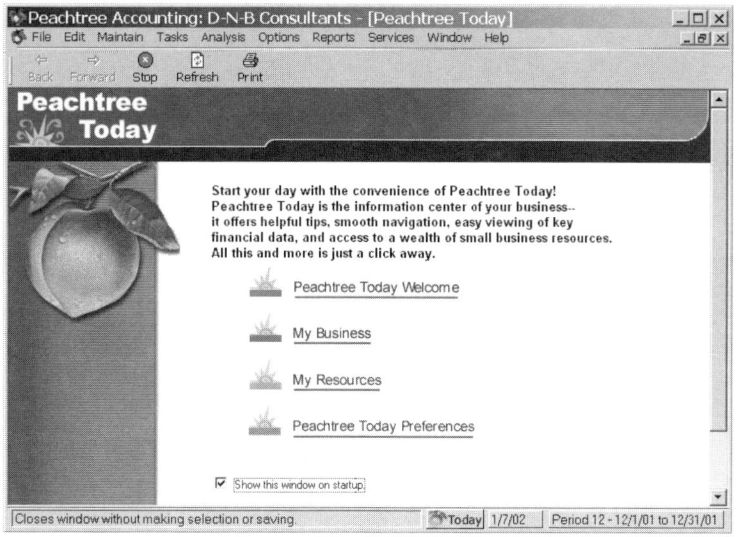

Summary

Now that Peachtree is correctly installed, we need to look at the layout of the Peachtree window and set up your new company files. These topics will be discussed in Chapters 2 and 3. If you are new to Peachtree, you will want to pay special attention to Chapter 4. There I outline how the rest of the book will work with converting your company to Peachtree so that all information comes over accurately.

Chapter 2

The Peachtree Window

In This Chapter

- A description of and look at the Peachtree window
- The navigation aid, menu bar, toolbars, and status bar
- A few specific terms used in this book and Peachtree
- The accounting period
- Toolbar buttons — Post/Save, Edit/New, Delete
- Using multiple printers and how to change your default printer
- Peachtree options

Before we dive into setting up Peachtree, let us examine the Peachtree window and all it contains. There is lots of information to understand before you start working in the program. A clear understanding of this chapter can make learning the rest of the program much easier. Some of the things we mention here may seem out of place or just plain obvious, but in my many years of teaching the program these are the items that continuously cause problems and misunderstandings. That's why I always stress them up front before teaching any other Peachtree tasks.

Opening the Sample Companies

To explore Peachtree, we will use one of the two sample companies included with Peachtree throughout this book. Each company has different requirements showing different types of functions.

1. Open Peachtree Accounting by clicking on the **Peachtree** icon on your desktop.

Alternately, click on the Windows **Start** button, select **Programs**, select the **Peachtree Accounting** menu, and select the **Peachtree Accounting** program.

Depending upon your version of Peachtree, it may be titled **Peachtree Complete Accounting** or **Peachtree First Accounting.**

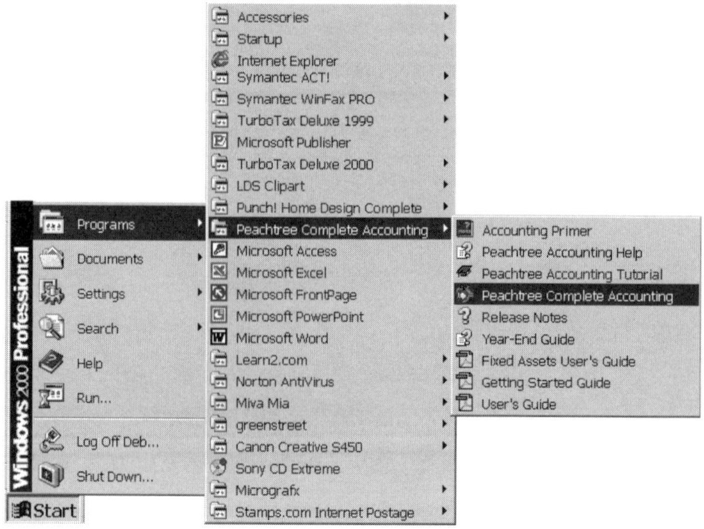

2. The Startup screen appears.

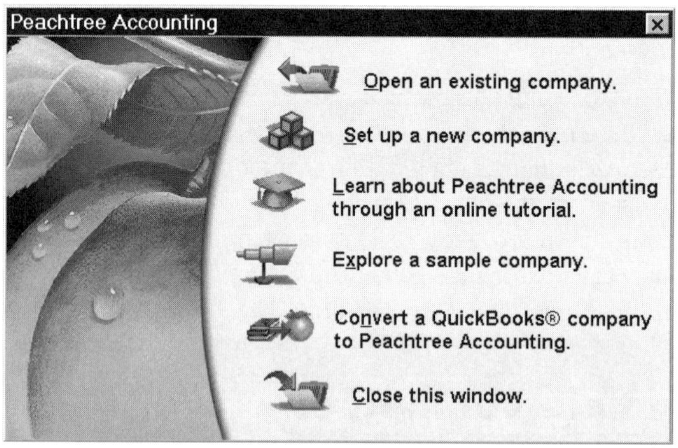

Click **Explore a sample company.**

3. The Explore dialog box appears.

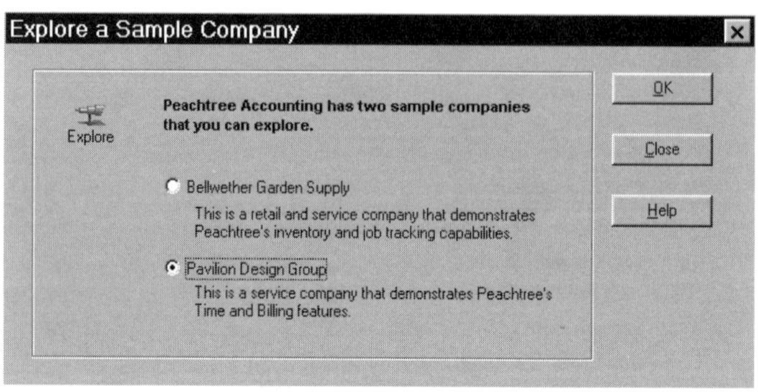

Select one of the two companies and click **OK.**

4. The company opens to the Peachtree window.

   If the Startup menu does not appear, follow these steps to open a sample company:

1. Open Peachtree.

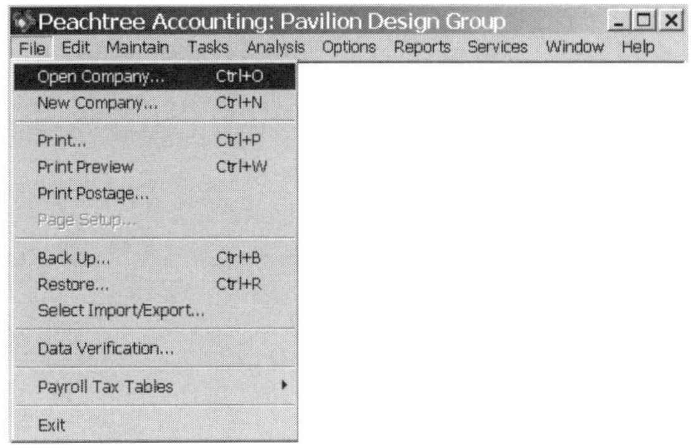

2. Select **File** from the menu bar and then **Open Company.**
3. If the following warning message appears, don't panic; just click **OK.**

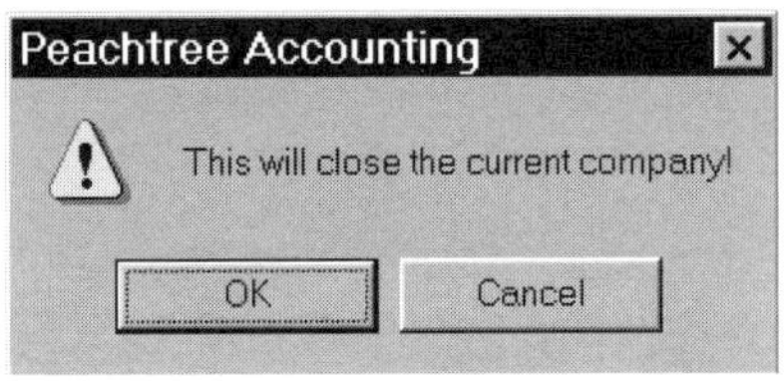

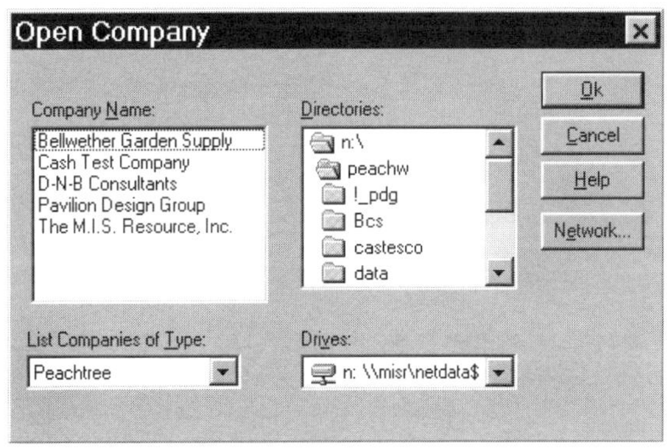

4. The Open Company dialog box appears. It is a little different from the standard Windows Open dialog box in that the drives are selected from a drop-down field in the lower right portion of the window and the directory (folder) is selected from the Directories list.

   Peachtree will try to locate the companies associated with the program. If you installed Peachtree directly to your computer's C hard drive and chose to add the sample company data, the companies should automatically show up in the Company Name list. If you installed Peachtree to your network, you may need to change to the correct network location by selecting a mapped drive from the drop-down list in the Drives field.
5. Select one of the sample companies in the Company Name list (Bellwether or Pavilion), and click **OK.**

6. The company opens to the Peachtree Today window.

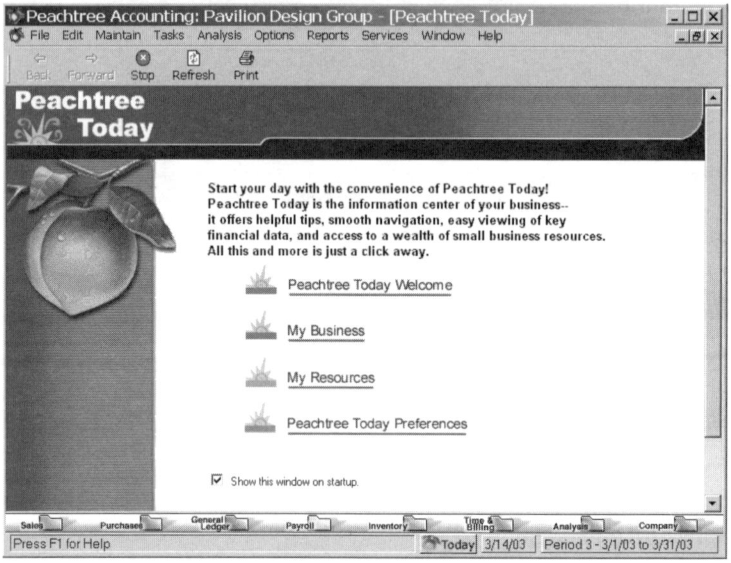

Click the **Close** button for the window — not the program. You will have a blank window as shown in the example in the next section.

The Peachtree Window

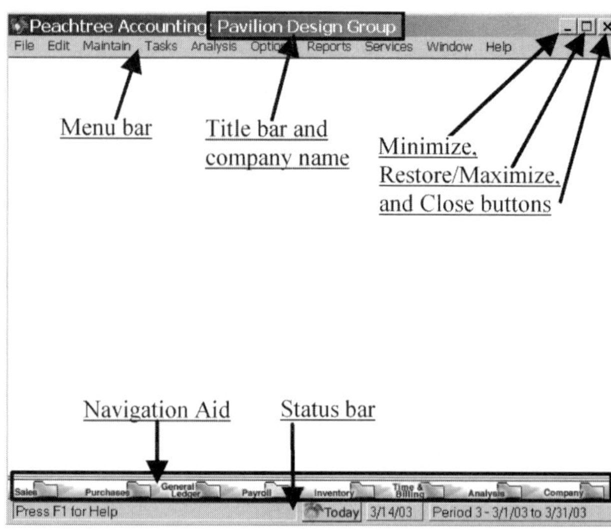

All work performed in Peachtree is done is this window.

At the very top is the standard Windows title bar with the Minimize, Restore/Maximize, and Close buttons in the right-hand corner. Minimize moves the program to a button on the Windows taskbar. Clicking on the taskbar button puts the program back on the desktop. When minimized, Peachtree is not closed, just hidden.

The Restore/Maximize button is a dual-purpose button. When it looks like a box and is clicked, the program enlarges to fill the entire Windows desktop. When maximized, the button changes to two boxes and clicking it restores the program to a customizable size. You can change the size of the window by moving your mouse pointer to any border, where the pointer will change to a double arrow ↔↕⤢. Click the left mouse button and drag it in the direction of the arrow to make the screen smaller or larger.

Also located on the title bar is the name of the current open company.

The Menu Bar

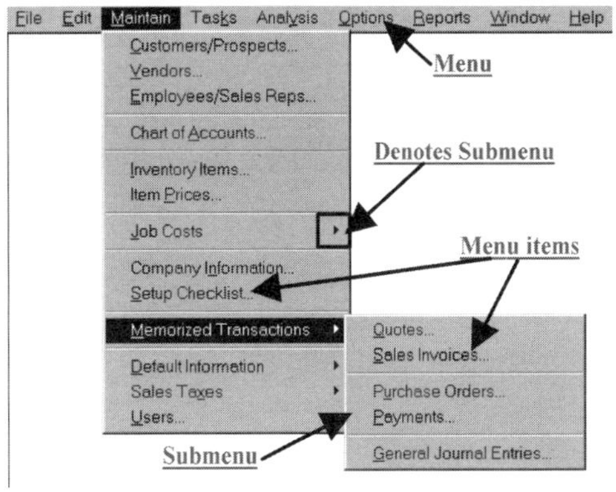

Immediately below the title bar is the menu bar. It separates all the Peachtree functions into logical groupings.

Selecting any menu item causes the menu to expand via a drop-down. Selecting any menu item in the drop-down list brings up the associated screen or dialog box to perform the desired function. Any menu item with an arrow to the right has a submenu and selecting it causes the associated submenu to appear.

You will find that some of the menus are similar to other Windows programs such as File, Edit, Window, and Help. The other menus are uniquely Peachtree's. As we need them, we will identify their individual functions in depth. In this chapter, we'll describe their collective functions.

Maintain — This menu deals with different kinds of files or lists in Peachtree like the customer list or the inventory items. It also allows you to maintain the data used in running each company file in Peachtree with information such as the sales tax rates, the company name, and users on the system.

Tasks — This menu has the items to let you add, modify, and delete transactions in the system. These are the day-to-day jobs that the accounting clerks perform every day. Also included in this menu is the System submenu, used to perform period end tasks.

Analysis — Management tools are found in this menu, which will give you quick access to the state of your company right now. It helps answer such questions as "when can I expect cash in?" and "what payments do I need to make next week?"

Options — These personalized options control the user's view of Peachtree and the individual control preferences.

Reports — Obviously, this is where you access the reports that you will view or print to get accurate information about all areas of Peachtree. This is also where you customize forms.

Help — In addition to standard help features, this menu includes online assistance that takes you to the Peachtree web site to get program updates and other information. The online features are functional only if you have Internet access.

The Navigation Aid

At the bottom of the Peachtree window is a row of what looks like file folders. (In earlier versions it looked like a row of file tabs.) Each folder represents a module or functional accounting area of Peachtree. Whereas the menu bar breaks down the program into lists and tasks, the navigation aid divides the program into accounts receivable, payroll, and other types of common accounting functions.

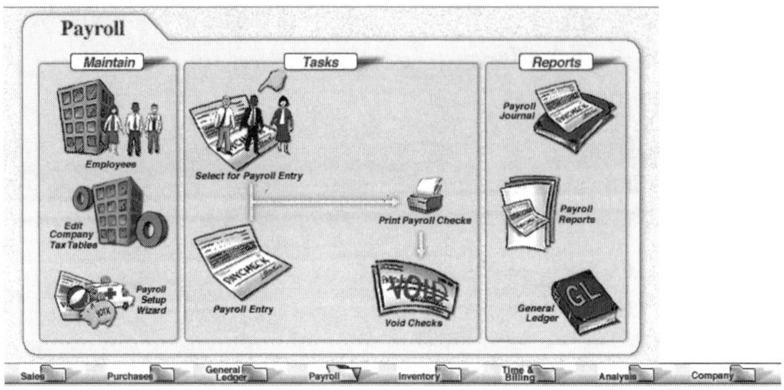

Each folder, when clicked and opened, displays the navigation menu. The menu has a graphical interface to help you identify where you need to go quickly and easily. The first six navigation menus (five for some versions) are also subdivided into the Maintain, Tasks, and Reports functions to match the menu bar. The Analysis menu has its own folder to match the menu bar. The last folder, Company, includes many of the less-used items from the menus.

You will notice that many of the navigation menus have arrows pointing from one task to another. These describe the workflow of the system and show how transactions should progress through the accounting process. Not every business will use all the functions. Some companies may also have additional tasks that are performed outside the program.

There are three ways to do almost everything in Peachtree. For those with the need for a graphical interface, the navigation aid will probably become their function access tool of choice. Others will use the menu bar. Those raised in the old DOS days will be happy to discover the keyboard shortcuts. Throughout the book I will always try to show you all three ways of getting to the functions.

The Status Bar

The status bar contains five items, two of which are vital.

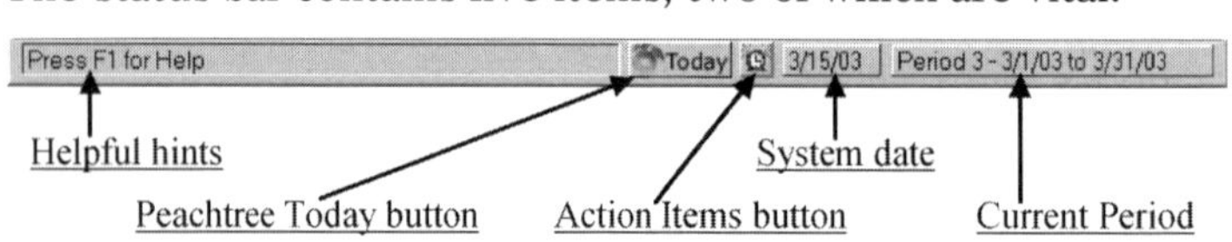

Helpful Hints

The left-hand section of the status bar contains helpful hints regarding whatever area of the program you currently are in. If the mouse pointer were in the Sales navigation aid and pointing to the Sales/Invoicing icon, you would see the hint "Click to enter an invoice."

Peachtree Today

Next is the Peachtree Today button. Click the button to bring up the Peachtree Today screen.

This screen is customizable and can help you track many important details about your company.

The Peachtree Today screen opens to a menu of Peachtree resources. Clicking on any menu will bring up the associated screen. At the bottom of the screen is the Show this window on startup check box. For those who want to skip this information when Peachtree is opened, you can unselect the check box.

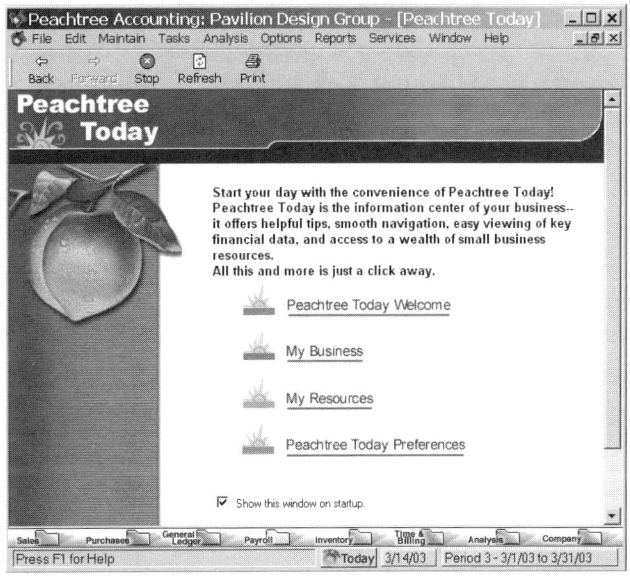

Clicking the first menu item, Peachtree Today Welcome, will take you to the Welcome screen. This window has information such as product tips, help, and how-tos. It also includes links to the Peachtree web site. Once you have left the Peachtree Today screen, the other menu items are available by clicking the associated tab in the upper section of the window.

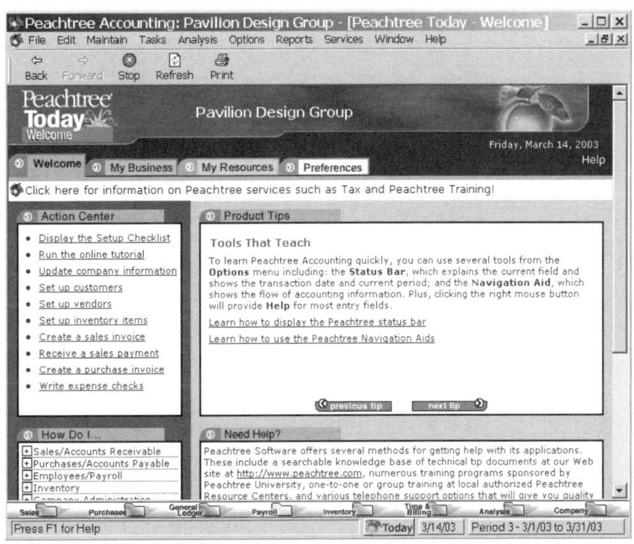

The second menu item on the Peachtree Today screen, or the second tab on the Welcome screen, is My Business. This area contains important information about your company's current financial position, including overdue sales invoices, current bills due, and revenue.

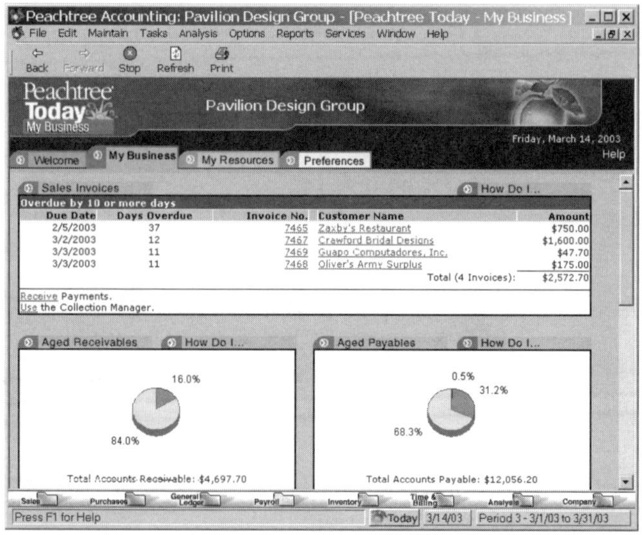

Depending upon your screen resolution and how much of the display you are using for Peachtree, you may have to scroll down to see the full display on all of the screens.

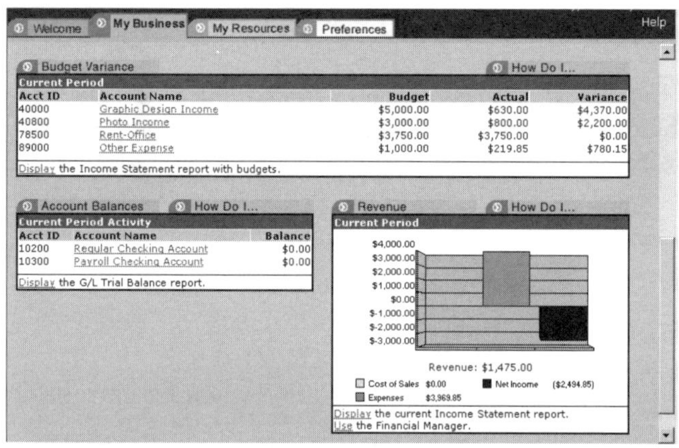

The next tab is My Resources. This area contains ads for Peachtree products, links to Peachtree registration sites, and sites and ads for small businesses. Check them out: Some may be very beneficial to your company such as Stamps.com and UPS tracking; others may be considered the electronic version of junk mail.

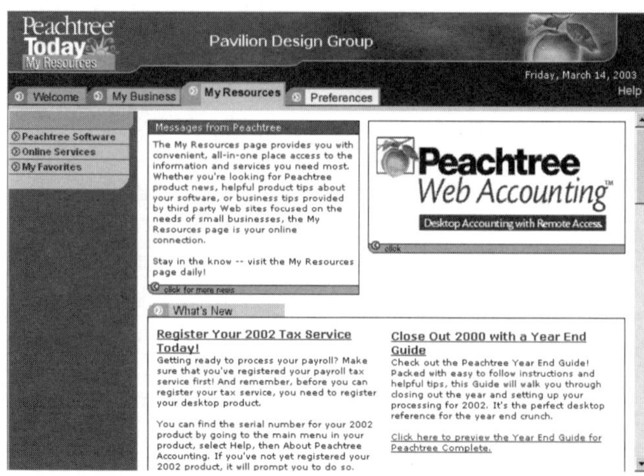

Next in the list of tabs is Preferences. This screen has two pages, each of which may be selected by clicking on the menu on the left. The first, the General page, allows you to modify the default page, connect to the Internet, and select whether you want to show the Today window each time Peachtree is opened.

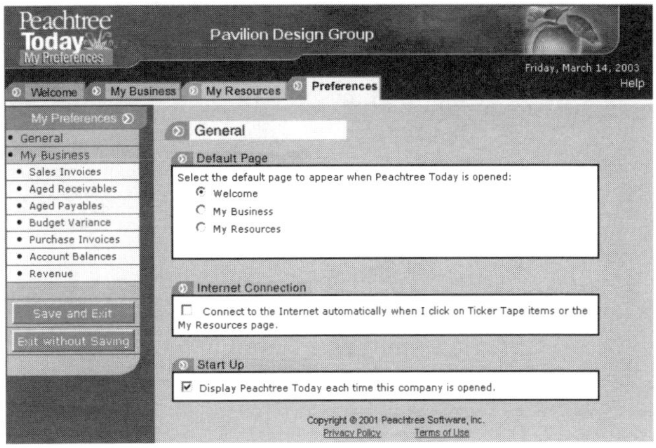

The second page, My Business, allows you to change the parameters for viewing the My Business screen. You can view the parameters by scrolling down the page or access a specific parameter by clicking on the submenu under the My Business menu item. Click the **Save** button to save any changes you make.

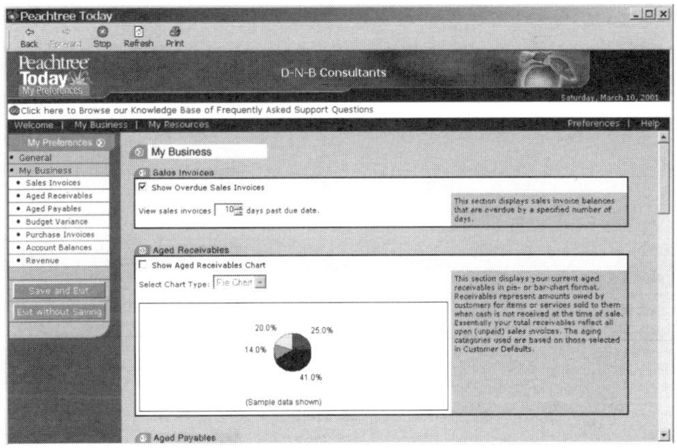

Action Items

The second button on the status bar is Action Items. The action items can be used as a sort of to-do list for contact management and cash management. Click the **Action Items** button to bring up the window.

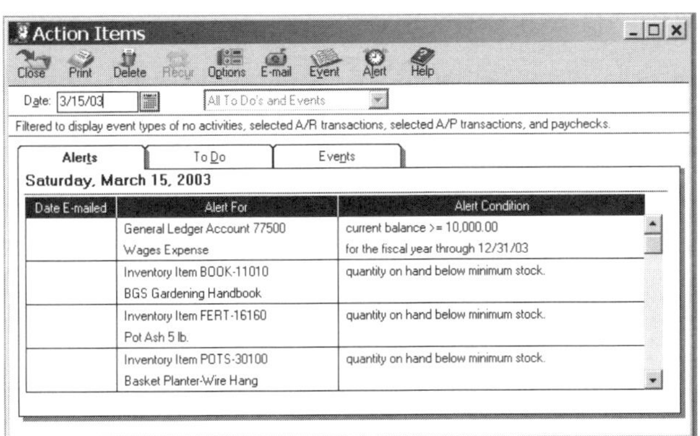

Click the **Options** button in the toolbar to open the Action Items and Event Log Options dialog box. This window allows you to choose what types of activities and transactions you want to appear in the Action Items screen. Select the items that you want to appear and enter the number of days before the event that you want to be reminded on both the Activities and the Transactions tabs.

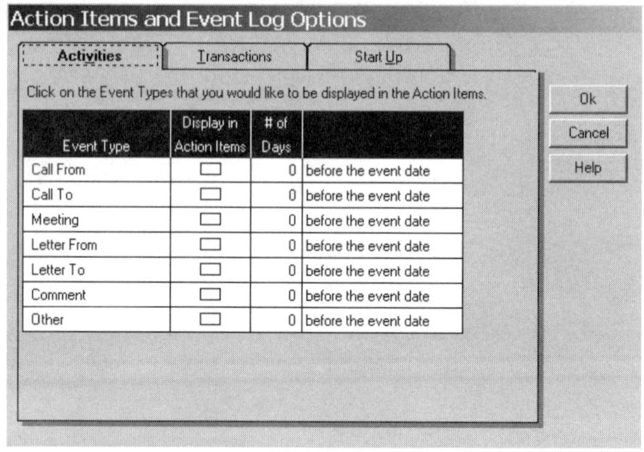

On the Start Up tab is a check box where you can indicate whether you want the action items to be displayed each time you open the company.

System Date

The system date is displayed next on the status bar. It is controlled by Windows and is changed through the Date/Time properties in the Control Panel. The system date is vital to the operation of your Peachtree program. If it is not set to today's date, or appears as if it is not keeping correct time, you should contact your computer maintenance person as this can seriously damage your Peachtree files and result in erroneous recording of data.

Note: One thing I have noticed is that if you leave Peachtree open all night, the system date does not change. This can sometimes play tricks with your data. Therefore, all employees should be instructed to close Peachtree at the end of the day or any time they leave their desk for an extended period.

Current Accounting Period

Last in the status bar is the current accounting period. An *accounting period* is a unit of time, usually a calendar month or a four-week period, that a fiscal year is divided into. The period that appears in this area of the status bar is the current period. Transactions can only be entered into the current or future accounting periods. Accounting periods are very important to Peachtree and will be discussed later in this chapter.

Terms and Meanings

Warning!! This is the boring part of the book, but I want to let you know what I mean when I use specific words to describe Peachtree and the accounting process.

Program — The Peachtree Accounting program as a whole with functions and tools that are used for any company.

Company — When you create a new company, Peachtree creates a group of data files found within a folder (or directory) that is named by the program. You do not work with the data files individually. The program manipulates them when you have the company open. Most of these data files have a .dat extension and include all the data related to the company. Errors and warnings may identify a specific data file by name within the company.

File — A group of Windows files that are used for a single purpose, such as the accounts receivables file or the vendor file.

Record — A semi-permanent item to which things are done and that is used to create transactions. An example would be a customer record that includes the address and the tax rate, or an employee record with the social security number and pay rates. The content of a record does not change very often.

Transaction — Transactions are things that occur in relation to a record. For a customer, this would be an invoice or a cash receipt against an invoice. These often are the result of a document that has been sent to you, such as a customer receipt or vendor bill, or a document you send out, such as an invoice or a check.

Account — These are the general ledger accounts. Each represents a line on the balance sheet or income statement. Every line in a transaction is applied to two different accounts, even though the accounts themselves may be hidden.

Two specific areas of accounting can be confusing because of the similarity in terms. Many people become puzzled as to whether a bill refers to something you send to a client or something you receive from a client. To make these distinctions clear I will use the following terms consistently throughout this book.

For accounts receivable:

Invoice — A document you send a customer for goods or services.

Invoicing — Also referred to by the program as sales. The act of sending invoices to customers. Some programs refer to this as billing, but since that could be confused with an accounts payable function I will always use the term invoicing.

Receipt — A check from a customer to be applied to an invoice or as a down payment.

Customer Credit Memo — A credit memo sent to a customer to be applied to an invoice.

For accounts payable:

Bill — A document you receive from a vendor that you must pay. These are invoices sent to you, but since every transaction will be expressed in relation to you, in this book I will always use bill.

Purchases — Also known as accounts payable. The act of entering bills received from vendors.

Payment — A check you send to a vendor. It may be applied to a bill or entered separately.

Vendor Credit Memo — A credit memo received by you that will be applied against a bill you owe a vendor.

Accounting Periods

If you've ever used computerized accounting software, you've probably run into posting to accounting periods. Many programs go to great lengths to keep transactions in specific periods, and moving from one period to another takes time and effort to balance and write transactions to the program. For small companies, this process would be a nightmare in overtime.

Peachtree Accounting has simplified the process tremendously. Peachtree does not assign a transaction to an accounting period, but bases the period upon the transaction date.

The good news is that it is now very easy to edit, move, or delete a transaction in a previous period.

The bad news is that it is now very easy to edit, move, or delete a transaction in a previous period.

Fortunately, Peachtree can be set up to warn you if such a change is being made.

The reason for having accounting periods and the ability to show and change them is so transactions cannot be added to a previous period. The transaction date must be in the current or a future accounting period. This reduces the chance of posting a transaction to a previous period and thereby changing all the financial statements.

To change the current accounting period, follow these steps:

1. Click on **General Ledger** in the navigation aid and click **Change Accounting Period.**

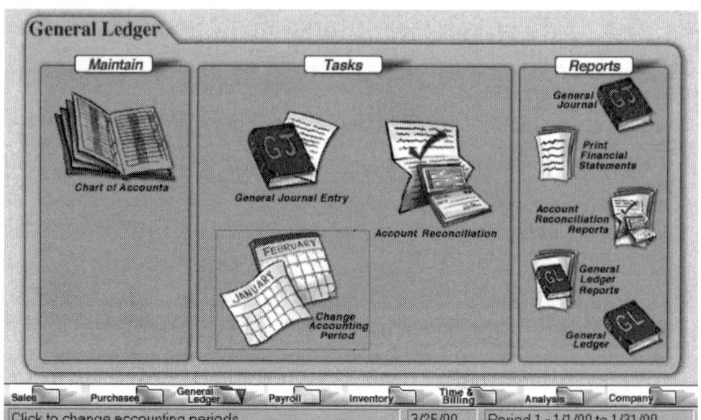

Or from the menu bar, select **Tasks**, **System**, **Change Accounting Period.**

Or using the keyboard, press **Alt+K**, then **T**, then **A**.

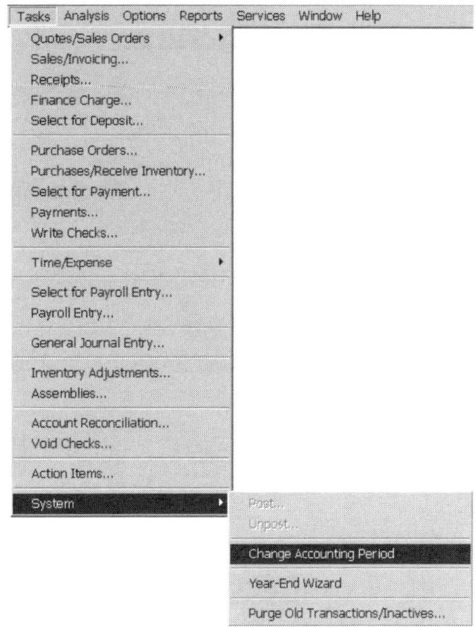

2. The Change Accounting Period dialog box appears.

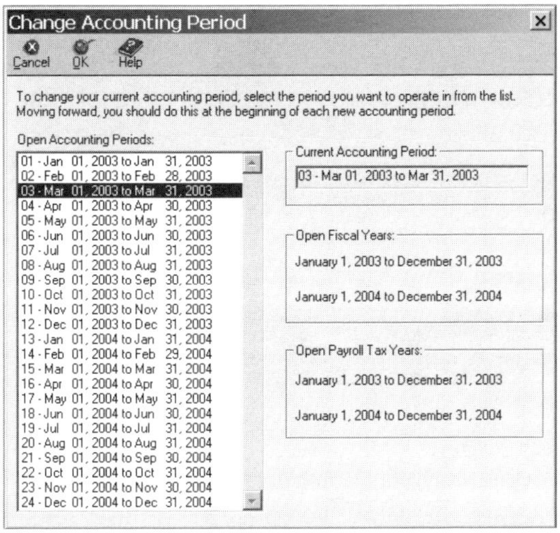

In older versions, the dialog box will appear like this.

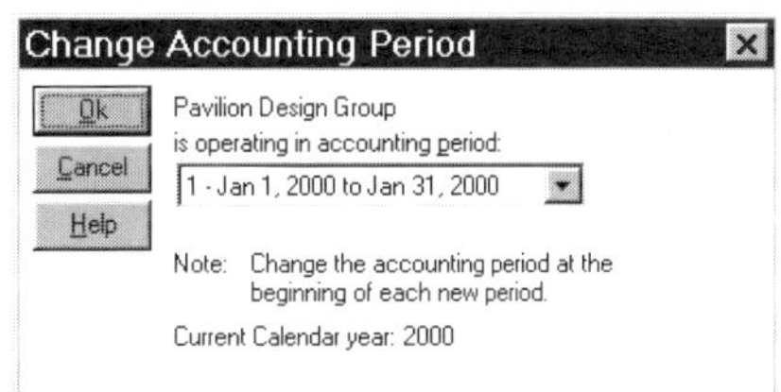

The dialog box shows the current accounting period, the current open fiscal year, and the current open payroll year.

3. Select the new accounting period in the Open Accounting Periods list or by clicking the drop-down button in the Is operating in accounting period field.

   Click the **OK** button.

   The new current accounting period shows on the status bar.

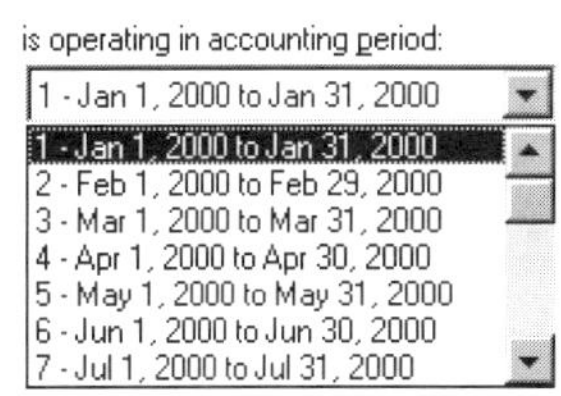

Special Peachtree Buttons

Customers, vendors, stock items, services, and employees all have their own records. You create transactions or documents (invoices, checks, quotes, etc.) for these records. After a transaction is created, you can save, edit, or delete the transaction using one of several buttons located on the toolbar of the different tasks. We look at some of the buttons here because they can be a bit confusing to the new user.

Saving Transactions

In Peachtree 2002, when you want to save a transaction you click the Save button on the form toolbar.

Save button for 2002 Batch or Real-time Posting

In older versions of Peachtree, depending upon whether you selected the batch or real-time mode of posting transactions, the Save buttons will appear as either Post or Save.

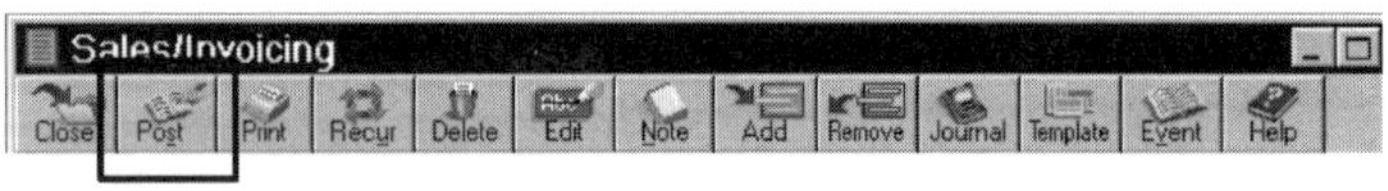

Real-time posting method

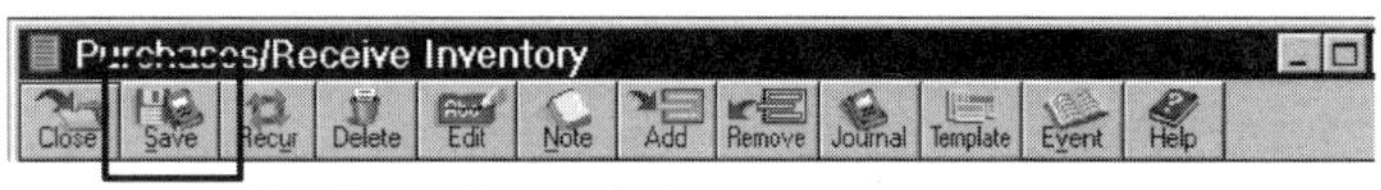

Batch posting method

When you use the batch posting method, transactions are saved to a temporary file and are not saved to the general ledger until you post the transactions, so this button says Save. If you use real-time posting, the transactions are posted at the same time that they are saved, so the button says Post in older versions. That was very confusing for many users, so the button was changed to be the same regardless of which method is used. Selecting which posting method is best for you will be discussed in Chapter 3.

When you need to print a transaction, the Print button on the toolbar not only prints but also saves or posts the transaction.

Editing Transactions

On occasion you will need to make a change to a transaction because of data entry errors, changes in quantities or prices, or additions to existing orders. To change a transaction, you must first locate it. The method of locating existing transactions has changed dramatically in the latest version.

In Peachtree 2002, there is both a New button, used to bring up a blank form on the screen, and an Open button, used to locate an existing transaction. The Open button replaces the old Edit button.

2 buttons - New and Open (edit existing)

In earlier versions, one button was used to both create a new transaction and locate existing transactions. The button changed depending upon whether a transaction was currently in the task window.

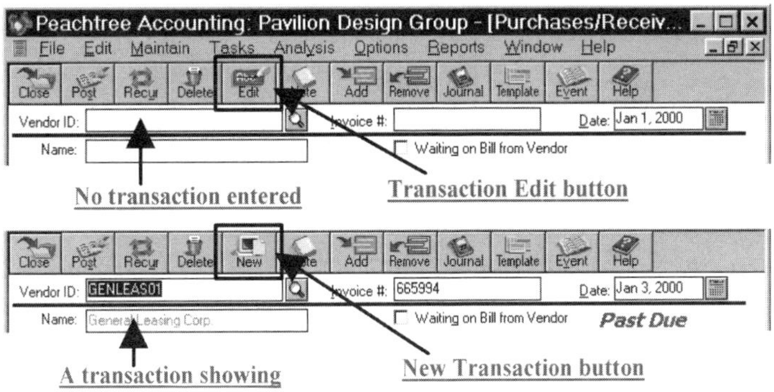

1. When you click the **Open** or **Edit** button, a list of transactions appears.

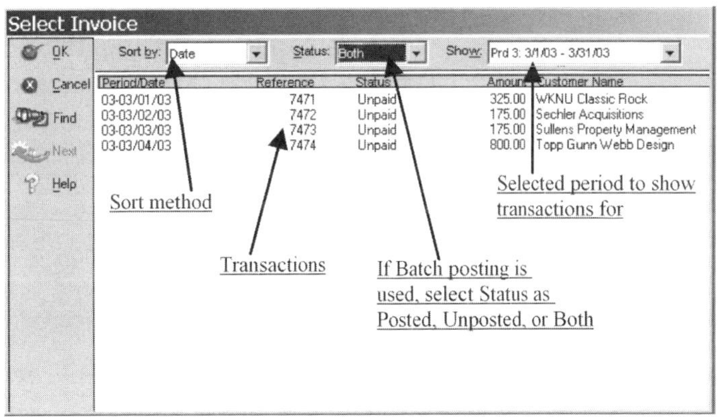

These are the transactions for the accounting period listed in the Show field. To get other transactions, you can change the period to the one needed.

If you are using the batch posting method, the Status field will allow you to choose from posted transactions, unposted transactions, or both. If you are using real-time posting, the Status field will not be visible.

Note: One of the most common, and panicked, calls I get from new users is "I opened up the transactions and they are all gone!" In every case this has occurred because the client has already posted all of their transactions. This window opens showing only unposted transactions. Changing to Posted or Both brings up their transactions — much to their relief and embarrassment.

You can sort the transactions — by date, reference, or ID — to make them easier to find.

2. Choose the transaction that you need to edit by clicking on the line so that it is highlighted.
3. Click **OK** to bring up the transaction for editing.

When edited, you use the Post or Save button again to save the changes.

Deleting Transactions

Many accounting programs never allow you to delete a transaction To eliminate a transaction you had to void it or apply a counter-balancing transaction. Peachtree lets you handle deleting transactions in two different ways. You may void the transaction by clicking the Delete button and then selecting Void, or you may totally remove the transaction from the system by selecting Delete after clicking the Delete button.

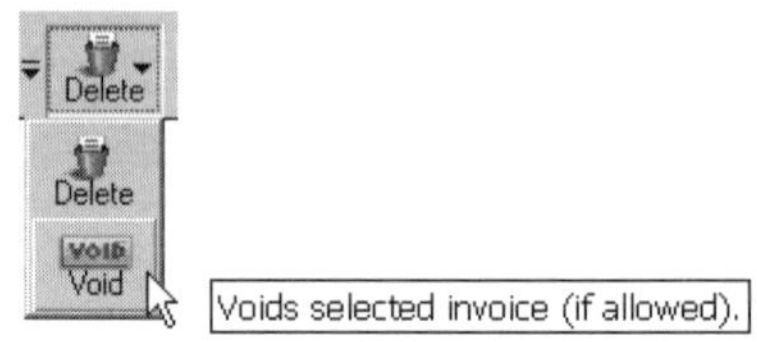

When you use the Delete option (in earlier versions this was called the Erase button), the only way to know that the transaction ever existed after that point is to use the audit trail log — if it is enabled — to see what happened.

When you select the Void option, a reversing transaction is created and will appear as a separate transaction in the file.

If a transaction has another linked transaction, such as an invoice that has a receipt applied or a bill that has been paid, the Delete or Void buttons will be grayed out and inactive. To delete that type of transaction, you will first need to edit or delete the linked transaction. Only then can the current transaction be deleted.

In the beginning you will probably delete a number of transactions as you make errors and adjustments, but after the program is set up and data entry people are trained, deleting should be minimized to the greatest extent possible to maintain the best possible audit trail. Data entry people can be denied the delete function when you set up their security and user rights. We discuss user setup in Chapter 3.

Printers

In older versions of Peachtree, if you had more than one printer on your network and you needed to print Peachtree forms to multiple printers, you could change the Printer Setup before you printed. By selecting File and Printer Setup from the menu bar, you could then choose the printer you wanted to send the form to. That printer was then the default printer for all forms and reports until you changed it again.

Newer versions of Peachtree have taken a more "network-centric" approach of assuming that specific printers are used for specific functions. Because of this change in thinking, Peachtree has removed the Printer Setup option from the File menu.

I personally feel it was a bad idea, but there are workarounds.

Changing the Printer for a Specific Form

Most companies modify existing forms to their own specifications. In Chapter 18 we will discuss more about customizing forms, but here is where you can designate the specific printer for each form. Many companies print to a multipart dot-matrix printer for invoices and use a laser or inkjet printer for checks or reports. Other companies want to ensure that payroll checks and reports only print in the manager's office. If you want a form to go to a specific printer, follow these steps:

1. Open the form in Form Design mode. It is a button that will appear when you have selected the form to print.

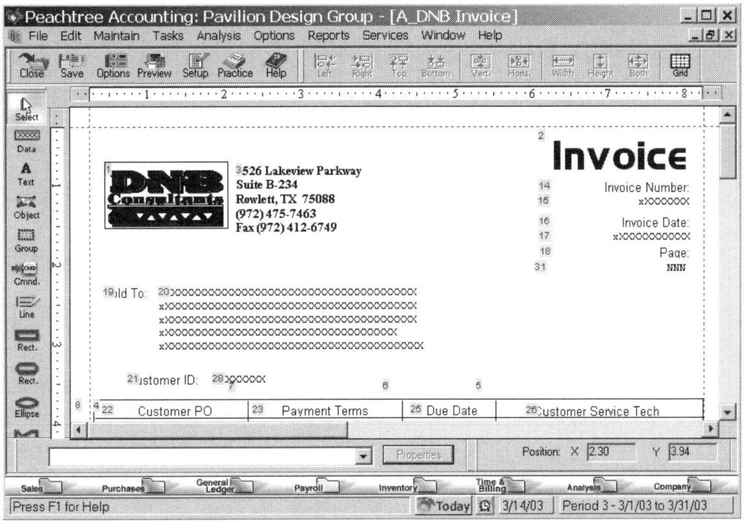

2. Select the **File** menu on the menu bar and then select **Page Setup**.

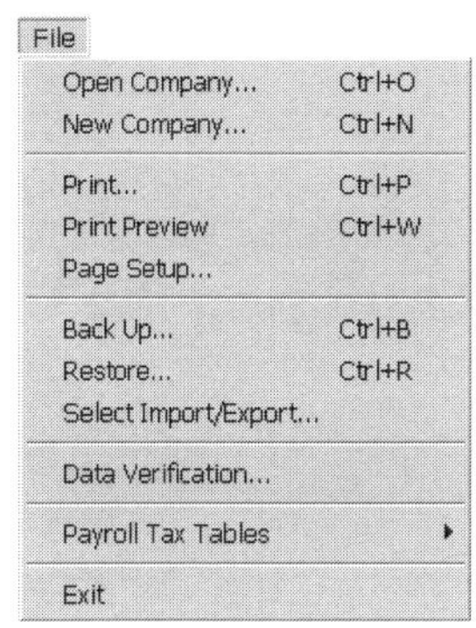

3. The Page Setup dialog box appears.

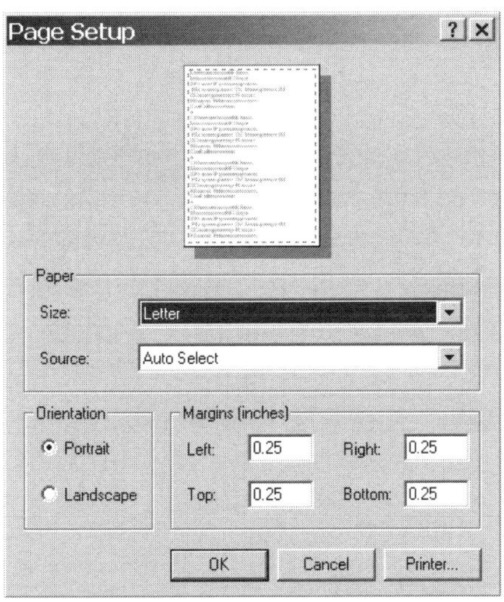

Click the **Printer** button.

4. Another Page Setup dialog box appears.

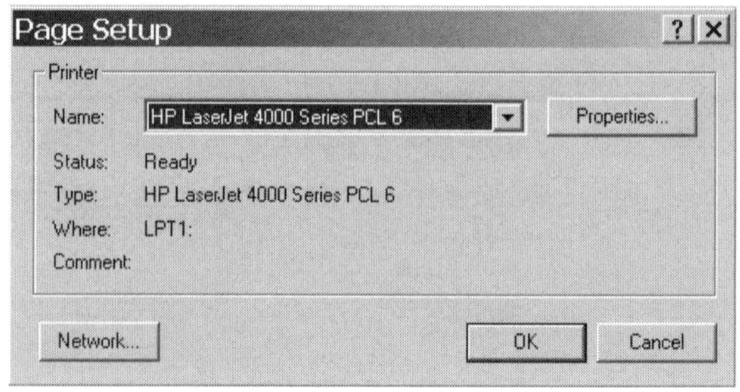

   Select the correct printer from the drop-down in the Name field. Click **OK** until you get back to the Form Design window.

5. Click the **Save** button to keep the changes to the form and then click **Close** to shut the Form Design window.

6. When you return to the transaction screen, print the form or record again to verify that it prints to the correct printer.

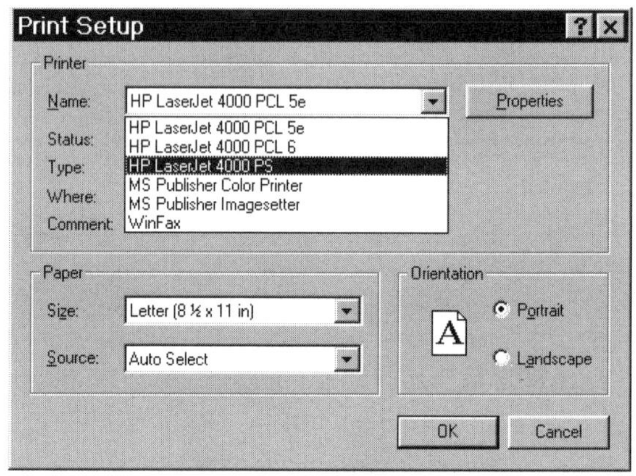

   In older versions of Peachtree, instead of going to the File menu you should click the **Options** button on the toolbar and go to the **Format** tab to change the printer.

   The form will now be associated with the specific printer that you have chosen and will always go to the specified destination even if the default printer changes.

Changing the Printer "On the Fly"

Some companies need the flexibility to be able to print any form to any printer they want. Changing the printer in this manner uses the Windows tools rather than the Peachtree tools. Unless you change it, each form prints to the default printer. Changing the default printer in Windows changes the destination of the print job.

To change the printer on the fly, meaning whenever you are in the middle of one task and want to jump over to a different function without leaving the current task, follow these steps:

1. From the Windows **Start** button, select **Settings**, then **Printers** and then right-click on the printer that you want to print to.

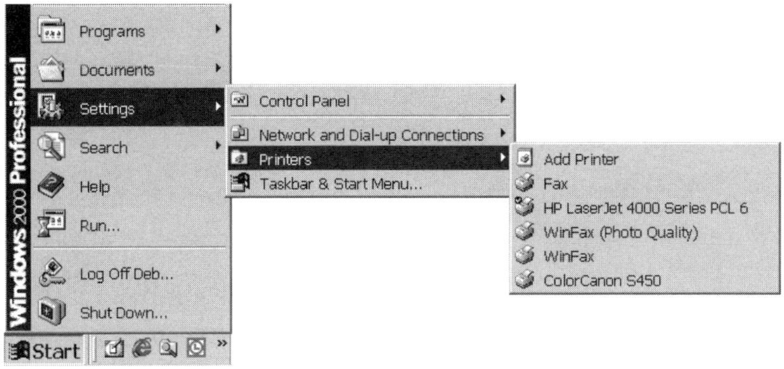

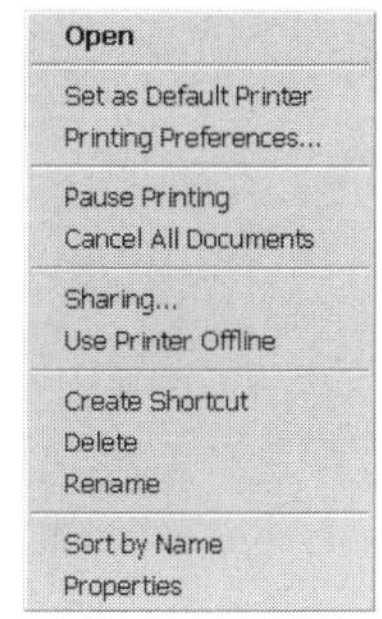

2. The shortcut menu appears.

   Select **Set as Default Printer** from the list.

   All new print jobs that are not preassigned to a specific printer will print to the default printer until a new printer is selected.

Tip: If you are going to be printing to different printers a lot, I suggest that you leave the Printers window minimized on the Windows taskbar so that you can access it at any time. You can access the Printers window by double-clicking the menu item.

Looking Up Records

In almost all the Peachtree windows you need to select a record before attaching information to it. This record could be a customer, an inventory item, or a G/L account. Records are selected through their IDs. To assist you in locating the needed record, Peachtree has two tools.

The Lookup Button and the Lookup List

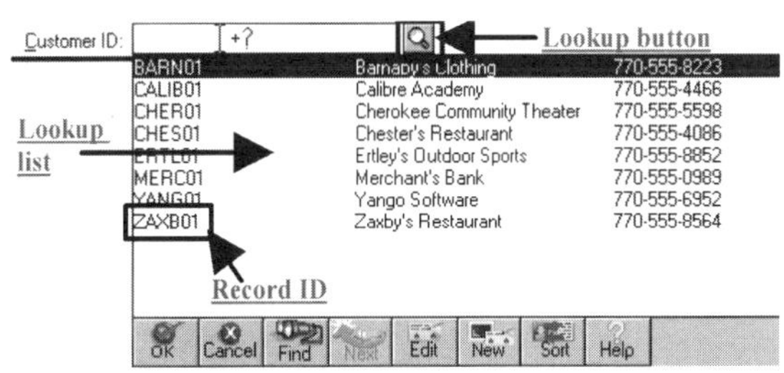

The first locator tool is the Lookup button. It looks like a tiny magnifying glass.

When you click on the Lookup button, the lookup list drops down. Scroll through the lookup list until you find the record that you want to use. Select the record by clicking on it with the mouse and then click **OK**. Alternately, you can double-click on the record ID. The selected record ID then appears in the ID field.

When the lookup list is open, the lookup toolbar has several features, accessed by clicking the buttons on the bottom of the lookup list.

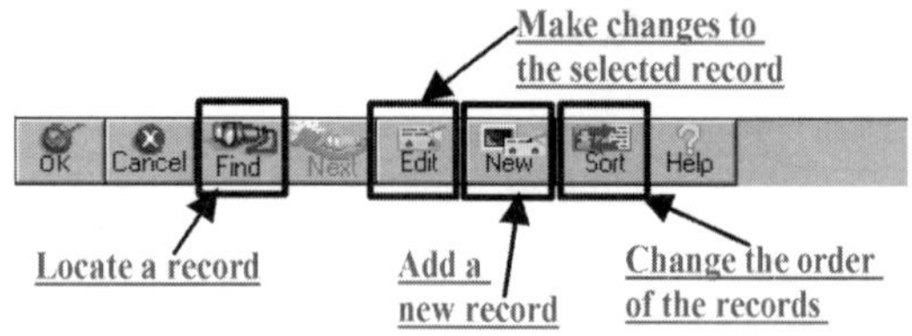

Find — Clicking this button pops up the Find dialog box. Enter the information that you wish to locate in the lookup list and click OK. Peachtree will go through the list until it finds the first matching record. If more than one record matches, the Next button on the toolbar will become active and clicking it will take you to the next matching record. You do not have to type an entire word. Typing "ch" would first find Cherokee, then find Chester's. The Find tool is not case sensitive, so typing upper- or lowercase letters will not affect the find operation.

Edit — While entering an invoice for a company, you might have a need to change the company's address or some other parameter. You can enter the new information "on the fly" by selecting the record in the lookup list and clicking the Edit button. The Maintain dialog box appears so that you can make the changes. Click Save and then select the record so that it appears in the transaction window. The new changes also appear.

New — In addition to changing existing records, you may also add new records when entering transactions. The New button takes you to a blank Maintain screen to add the new record. After saving the record, it appears in the lookup list.

Sort — Records in the lookup list are automatically sorted in ascending order by the record ID. You can change the sort order to sort alphabetically by the record name by clicking the Sort button. Clicking it a second time returns the sort order to the record ID.

Smart Data Entry

Smart data entry is a way to enter part of the information in the ID field and have Peachtree try to find the correct record. For example, if I wanted to create an invoice for Chester's Restaurant, I would go to the record ID and start by typing the letter "C" in that field.

Peachtree would go through the records and locate the first record ID that starts with that letter, in this case Calibre Academy. Typing the second letter, "H," would take me to the first record that began with "CH," Cherokee Community Theater. Typing the third letter, "E," would not change the selection because Cherokee is still the first matching record. Typing the fourth letter, "S," would locate Chester's. At that point, press Tab or Enter to accept the selection.

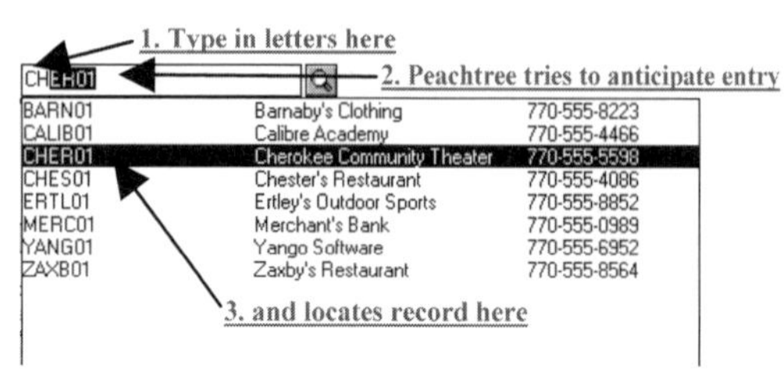

Be aware that record IDs are case sensitive. Capital letters must be entered as capitals and lowercase letters must be entered as lowercase. Typing "chcs" or "Ches" will not locate the record ID that begins with "CHES."

Keyboard Lookups

When entering data into the record ID field you will notice that the mouse cursor changes from an arrow to one of three other forms: an I-bar, a plus sign, and a question mark. These show the keyboard strokes to use in this field.

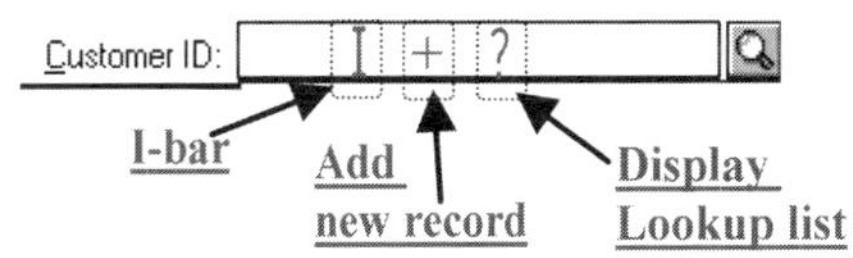

I-bar — This means the field is active and you can enter information by clicking once in the field and then starting to type.

Plus sign (+) — Typing a plus sign brings up a blank Maintain record window so that a new record may be added.

Question mark (?) — Typing this character causes the lookup list to be displayed. You may scroll through the list using the up and down arrow keys. Use the Enter key to select a highlighted record and put it in the record ID field.

Tip: You can also right-click the mouse to bring up the lookup list.

All Caps or Lowercase

One last item before we delve into the program. I am often asked whether it is better to enter data and record IDs in all capital letters or lowercase. The answer is — it depends! Many older accounting programs automatically required everything to be in caps. Data entry people coped with this requirement by leaving the Caps Lock key engaged all the time. You can do that in Peachtree and have `EVERYTHING PRINT LIKE THIS.`

On the other hand, reports, checks, and invoices are easier to read when they are written in upper- and lowercase. It does take an additional small fraction of time to use the Shift key to capitalize `Some Of the Words`, but the miniscule time more than makes up for itself in the professional look of your documents.

So it doesn't really matter which you use, as long as you do it consistently. Make it clear to all data entry people what the standard is for your company. If you don't, you will end up with customer addresses that look like this:

```
ABC COMPANY
123 Main Street, Suite 101
ROWLETT, Tx 75089
```

The second reason to have a standard is that record IDs are sensitive to upper- and lowercase letters. The sort order is such that all capital letters are sorted before all small letters. Capital "Z" comes before small "a."

ID Numbers

Let's take the example of the record IDs used earlier for the Smart Data Entry. The three IDs, CALIB01, CHER01, and CHES01, all sort in true alphabetical order. But if you add a new record for a company called Chernook Gallery, you would want to type it as "CHERN01." That way it will show up in the list in the correct order. If the record ID were entered as "chern01," the record would not show in the correct order but, because of the way Peachtree sorts, it would actually be placed in the list after ZAXB01.

Decide which way you want information entered into Peachtree and have all your data entry people use that standard for entering data. It can save you hours locating records and changing and editing records to bring them to a consistent look.

Note: Record IDs are very important. I know it looks very organized to have IDs such as those cited above, but with the expanded length of the ID field I prefer to make my IDs as close to the actual name as possible. I just cut out all spaces, dashes, and other characters. I also use only lowercase letters in my IDs because I don't like all caps and I'm too lazy to use the Shift key. So my IDs look as follows:

Name	Type	ID
D-N-B Consultants	company	dnbconsultants
RDS Metals	client	rds
Southwestern Bell	vendor	swbell
Contract Hours Used	inventory item	usecontract
Dawn Yarbro	employee	yarbrod

Peachtree Options

The Peachtree options can customize your program for you and your users. These options control how the screens look and what certain actions will accomplish. Options can be changed at any time. After you start working in Peachtree and start to understand all the features and abilities of the program, you may discover the need to review these options again.

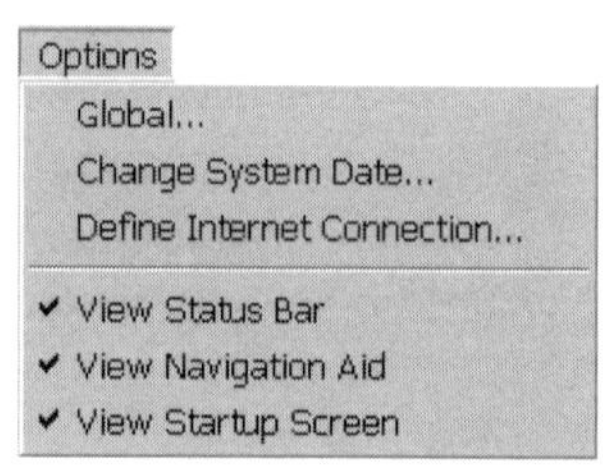

Options are accessed through the Options menu on the menu bar.

For those companies with network installations, these options are set for each individual computer, not for the entire network. Different computers may have different settings according to the company's and the individual's needs.

Global Options

You can change the global options by selecting **Global** from the Options menu. Or, press **Alt+O**, then **G** using the keyboard shortcuts. The Maintain Global Options screen appears. It has two tabs, the first of which is the Accounting tab.

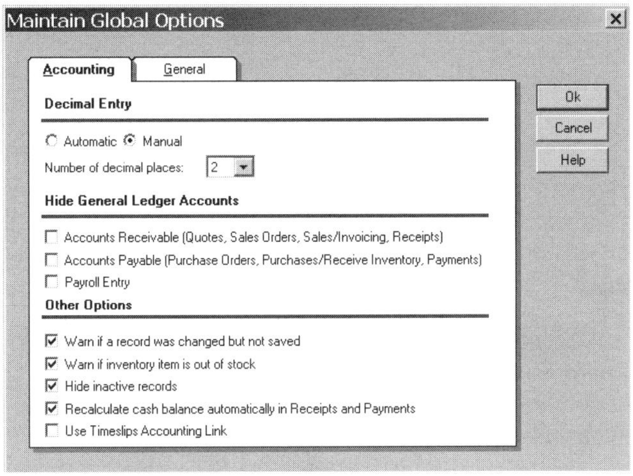

Decimal Entry

The options on the Accounting tab control how decimals are entered. There is a drop-down list for the Number of decimal places field. You may choose between 0 and 5 decimal places. The default is 2.

You can also choose whether you want automatic or manual decimal entry. Anyone who has some experience with a ten-key calculator will quickly see the difference between the two options. We will assume that the decimal places are set at 2. If you type 100 into a quantity or price field, the Automatic option will enter the decimal in the appropriate place and will show 1.00. If you choose Manual decimal entry, the program will not enter a decimal and will show 100.00.

Hide General Ledger Accounts

The next section of options allows you to hide the general ledger accounts on certain forms. These options are appropriate for companies that use inventory items to enter all line items on the associated forms. Inventory items are discussed in Chapter 10.

When the options are unselected, the GL Account field will appear on the forms.

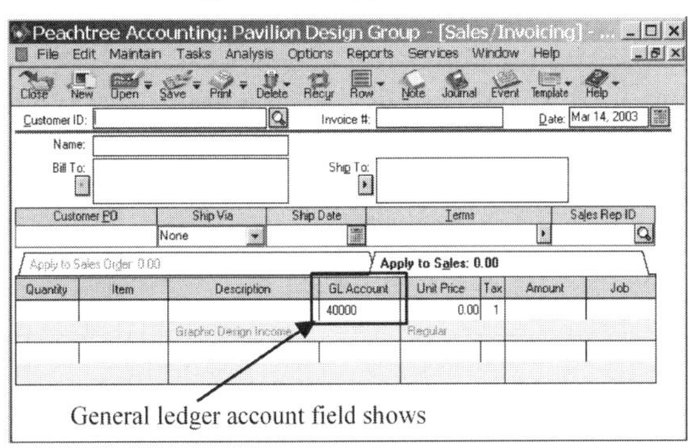

When these options are selected by clicking to place a checkmark in the check box, the GL Account field is hidden. You may select to hide the general ledger account fields for Accounts Receivable, Accounts Payable, or Payroll Entry forms.

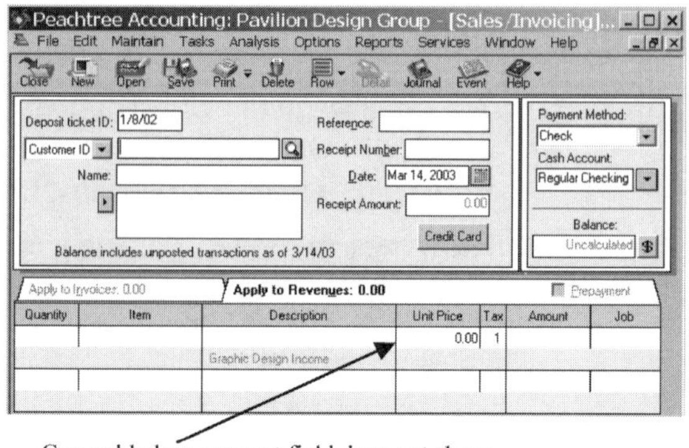

General ledger account field does not show

Other Options

The next set of options on the Accounting tab has several unrelated choices for the Peachtree program.

Warn if a record was changed but not saved — The first check box is to control whether a message box is displayed when records have been changed but not yet saved. To display the warning message, mark the check box.

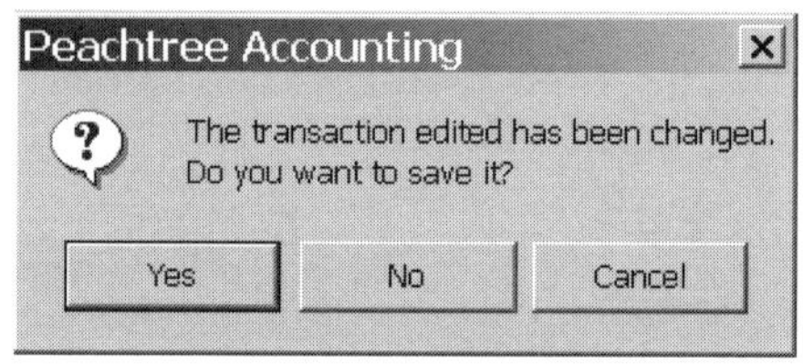

A quick word about the Yes, No, and Cancel buttons — if you were closing a record, such as an invoice, and received this message box, each button would have a separate result. **Yes** would close the window and save the changes. **No** would close the window without saving the changes. **Cancel** would cancel the close action and take you back to the record to view or make additional changes. The actions can sometimes be confusing because in some programs "No" and "Cancel" are the same thing.

Warn if inventory item is out of stock — The next option is for those companies with stock inventory items. Stock inventory is discussed in Chapter 10. When tracking inventory, you may decide to have Peachtree tell the invoice data entry people when the inventory is out of stock when the items are sold. Other companies may decide that the data entry people have no need for this information. Marking the check box will cause the warning message to appear when too many items are sold.

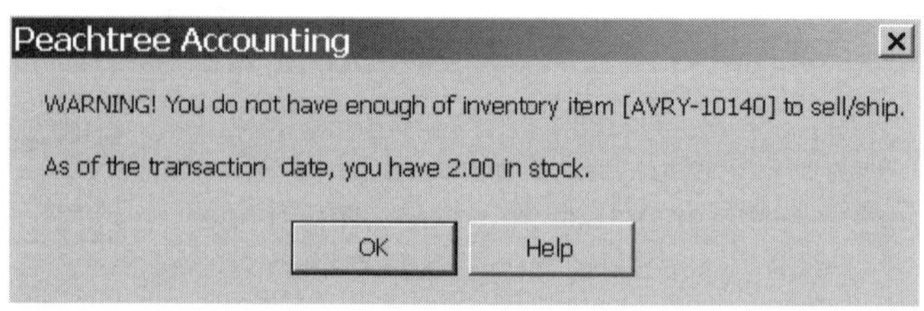

Hide inactive records — When records, such as a customer, are made inactive they will appear in drop-down lists with "Inactive" in the last field. After a while, these records can become cumbersome in the listing.

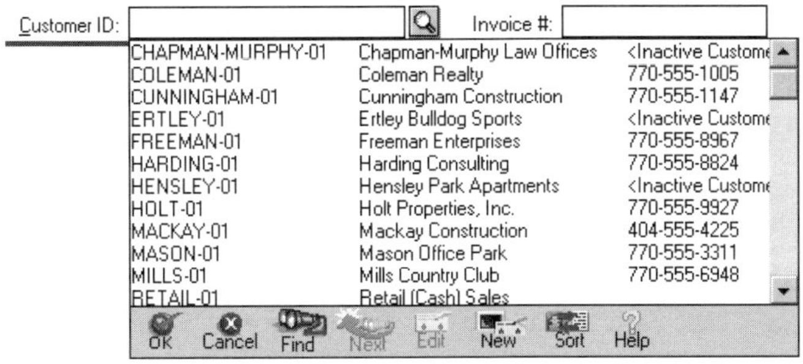

Marking this option will remove the inactive records from drop-down lists. If you choose this option, be sure that all transactions for the customer, vendor, or employee have been processed because you will not be able to pull up the ID to enter any more transactions. In order to view an inactive record, you will need to clear this check box first.

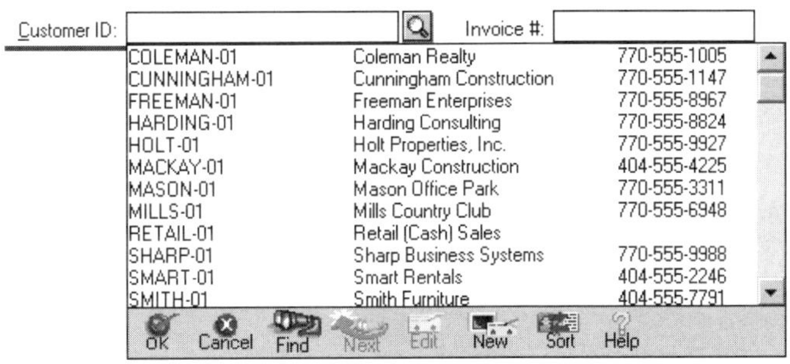

Recalculate cash balance automatically in Receipts and Payments — Both the Receipts form (see Chapter 6) and the Payments form (see Chapter 8) show the balance of the selected account in the Balance field. If this option is unselected, the balance will show as Uncalculated (or as ??????? in older versions).

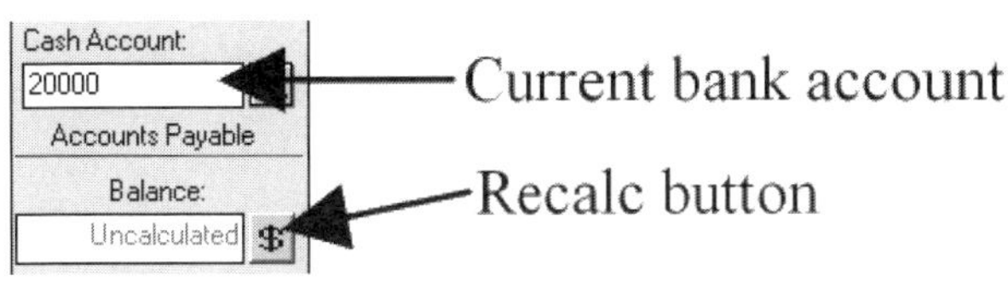

When you select this option, the balance will automatically appear when the form is opened. Unfortunately, this is not a way to permanently hide the account balance from the data entry people because clicking the **Recalc** button will cause the Balance field to be populated, regardless of the selection here.

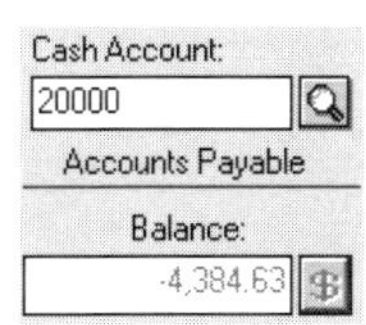

Use Timeslips Accounting Link — Timeslips is a time and billing program whose data may be imported into Peachtree if this option is selected. Timeslips is not covered in this text.

The remaining global options are found on the General tab.

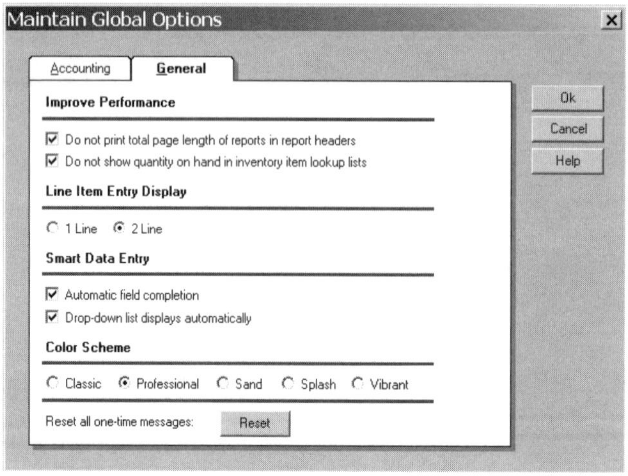

Improve Performance

The options in this section will help those companies that find that some tasks, such as invoicing, purchasing, and printing reports, are cumbersome. These options may help to improve performance a little. If your computers are still slow after selecting these, it may be time to consider replacing some machines.

Do not print total page length of reports in report headers — If you print a lot of multipage reports, this option may increase the printing speed. This option only works with printed reports, not previewed reports. Selecting the option removes the "Page n of n" header line in your reports.

Do not show quantity on hand in inventory item lookup lists — When invoices, receipts, purchases, or payments are entered using inventory items, a drop-down list will appear. Peachtree shows the quantity of items in stock in the list. Calculating the quantity takes a small amount of time and could slow down data entry on some systems.

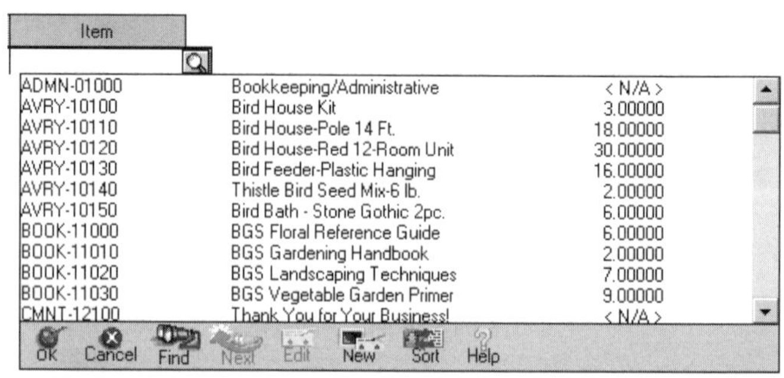

By marking the check box, the calculation can be eliminated so that processing time can be saved. When selected, the drop-down lists appear without the quantity showing.

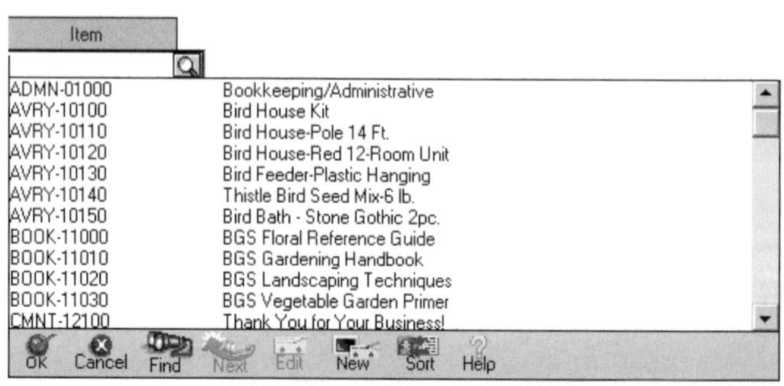

Line Item Entry Display

For those companies that have a lot of line items on their invoices and bills, selecting 1 Line as the number of lines to be displayed on forms can make data entry a little easier when viewing the lines. The lines on the form will appear as shown here.

Apply to Sales Order: 0.00 | **Apply to Sales: 179.90**

Quantity	Item	Description	GL Account	Unit Price	Tax	Amount	Job
2.00	EQWT-15160	Bell-Gro Impulse Sprinkler	40000-EQ	29.99	1	59.98	
6.00	FERT-16140	Bell-Gro Lawn Fertilizer 5 lb	40000-FF	9.99	1	59.94	
1.00	TOOL-35420	Bell-Gro Long-Handled Tin	40000-HT	19.99	1	19.99	
1.00	EQFF-13110	Bell-Gro Fertilizer Compres	40000-EQ	39.99	1	39.99	

Selecting the 2 Line option allows the data entry people to see some of the descriptions associated with the line items. This can be especially beneficial to new employees, as you can see in the following figure.

Apply to Sales Order: 0.00 | **Apply to Sales: 179.90**

Quantity	Item	Description	GL Account	Unit Price	Tax	Amount	Job
2.00	EQWT-15160	Bell-Gro Impulse Sprinkler	40000-EQ	29.99	1	59.98	
Sprinkler-Impulse		Sales - Equipment		Regular			
6.00	FERT-16140	Bell-Gro Lawn Fertilizer 5 lb	40000-FF	9.99	1	59.94	
Lawn Fertilizer 5 lb.		Sales - Food/Fert		Regular			
1.00	TOOL-35420	Bell-Gro Long-Handled Tin	40000-HT	19.99	1	19.99	
Long Handled Cultivator 4pr		Sales - Hand Tools		Regular			
1.00	EQFF-13110	Bell-Gro Fertilizer Compres	40000-EQ	39.99	1	39.99	
Fertilizer Compression Spraye		Sales - Equipment		Regular			

Smart Data Entry

Smart data entry is the automatic search for records that the computer performs when IDs are typed.

Automatic field completion — This feature was discussed earlier in this chapter. This check box must be marked to enable this feature.

Drop-down list displays automatically — When entering an ID field, you can determine whether you want the list to display automatically or remain hidden. To show the list automatically, mark the check box.

Color Scheme

Peachtree allows users to select their own color scheme for the program. Some of the colors are really interesting. Once a color scheme is selected, it does not become active until Peachtree is closed and reopened. Hopefully, you do not have two employees with wildly different tastes sharing a computer because the Vibrant scheme is really vibrant.

Reset All One-time Messages

As you begin using Peachtree, you will receive messages that include a check box saying "Do not display this message again." As employees become proficient in the program, they will probably want to select the check boxes to hide these messages. Occasionally, such as when you train a new employee, you will want these messages to appear to help teach the employee. If you click the Reset button, all messages will again appear at the appropriate times.

A number of other items are available directly from the Options menu.

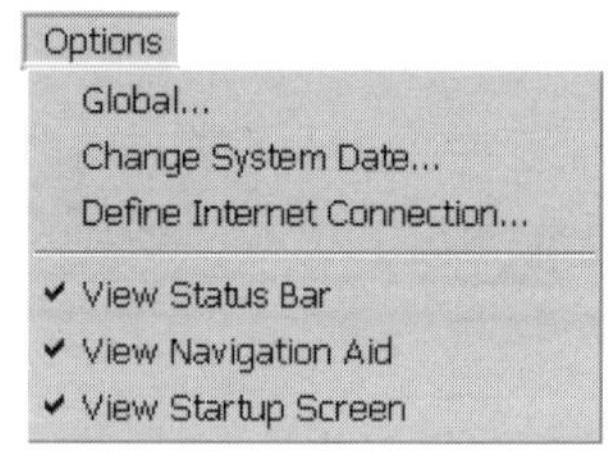

Change System Date

When you are working in the current accounting period, the current date appears automatically in the Date fields. The date that appears is the same date that shows on the status bar. You may change the system date for Peachtree by choosing Change System Date and selecting a new date. Changing the date here does not affect your Windows system date or the system date for any other programs.

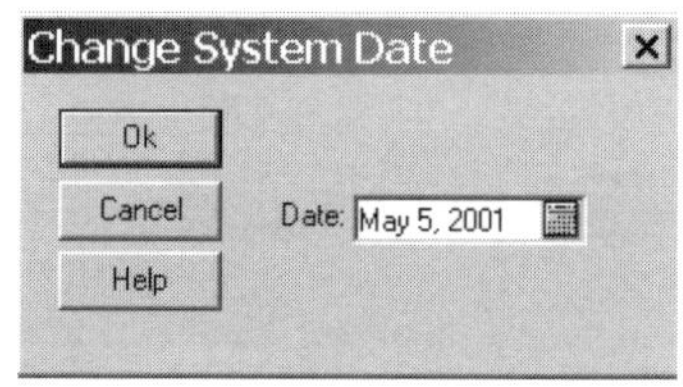

Define Internet Connection

When you select this menu item, the Internet Connection Setup dialog box appears.

Configure Peachtree to use your Internet connection using your modem dial-up or LAN specifications. If you have Internet access and this dialog box does not make any sense, you should contact your computer professional.

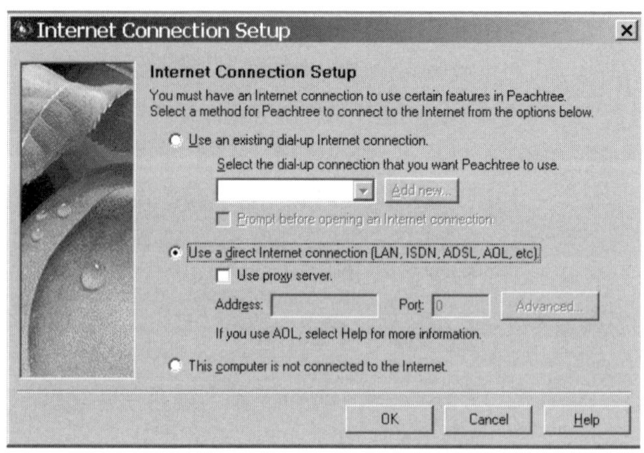

View Status Bar

This option and the next two act as toggles. This means that when you select the menu item, it enables or disables the option — sort of like turning a light switch on and off. If this option has a check mark in front of it, the option is enabled.

When the View Status Bar option is enabled, the status bar appears at the bottom of the Peachtree window. To keep from viewing the status bar, disable this option.

View Navigation Aid

The navigation aid is the graphical interface that appears just above the status bar. For people who prefer to use the mouse and icons to navigate through the program, this feature is very helpful. For those who prefer to use keyboard shortcuts or menus to navigate through Peachtree, this feature can be hidden by disabling the option.

View Startup Screen

When Peachtree is opened, the Startup screen appears. From it, you can choose to open a company, create a company, view tutorials, and perform other actions. Once you are familiar with the program, you may decide to skip those choices and open your company files immediately. If this option is disabled, the Startup screen will quit bothering you.

Summary

So now you know some basics, common tools, and special features to get you started in Peachtree. This chapter is filled with information that you will want to refer to often when you first begin working with Peachtree. In the next chapter you will learn to set up a company in Peachtree.

Chapter 3

Starting a New Company

In This Chapter

- What you need to begin a new company
- Using the Setup Wizard
- The chart of accounts
- Setting up users and security

Before we enter anything into Peachtree we need to set up the company. Most people will have one, and only one, company. It is very important that the company be set up correctly from the beginning because it is impossible to change some of the settings once you begin entering data into the files.

We will start this chapter by going through the wizard and explaining, in detail, every decision that must be made. Some of these may be obvious to you, but I guarantee that somewhere in here is a question that has been puzzling some of you for a long time.

If you have already set up a new company, you may still want to use this chapter to verify that you have set up Peachtree correctly. If you discover that you need to change something, it may point you to the right spot. If you are having problems with your current setup, some of you will discover that it might be best to chuck the old and start anew.

Before You Start a New Company

There are a few pieces of information and answers to specific questions that you need when starting a new company. Assemble these ahead of time to speed up the process of creating a new company. The company owner, office manager, or CPA can provide this information.

- Company name and address
- Federal and state employer IDs and unemployment numbers
- Unemployment tax rate
- Type of company — corporation, sole proprietorship, etc.
- The chart of accounts — you may employ the one used by your CPA or you may select one from Peachtree's charts of accounts.

- Whether your company uses the accrual or cash accounting method
- Your company's fiscal year and the number of accounting periods per year
- Standard terms and defaults for customers, vendors, and employees

In addition, you need to designate an individual as the Peachtree administrator. This is the person who is ultimately responsible for the Peachtree file and must be someone in the organization with the authority to make decisions regarding the day-to-day operations of the company. This person must also be available to data entry people on a regular basis to assist them in making changes and adjustments when problems occur. Generally, in small offices this is the office manager. For larger offices this is the accounting manager or controller. Unless you are in a very small, one- or two-person company, the owner is often not the ideal person for this job because he or she just isn't available and should be concentrating on the long-term goals and decisions of the company instead.

Five other pieces of information are needed to run Peachtree, but they are not actually necessary to start using the program. These are listed below.

- A beginning date for starting the company in Peachtree, especially if the company has existed for any length of time. Whenever possible, it is best to use the first day of the new fiscal year and to use the three months just previous to that date to get up and running and verify that all your balances are correct. Otherwise, you need to select the first date of any accounting period. This is the "Go Live" date for your Peachtree data; it is not usually the date you start entering transactions into the program. If you want to "go live" on June 1, you will usually begin adding transactions about March 1, which is called the "Begin Transactions" date. These dates are discussed more in the next chapter.
- For existing companies a general ledger trial balance report is needed. It shows the balance of every single account in your general ledger chart of accounts as of the specific date that the company will "go live" in Peachtree. This information must be accurate in order for Peachtree to give you a good record of your business! Your CPA can supply you with this report; it is often part of the reports she gives to you after closing a month or a year.
- An accurate Accounts Receivable ledger of all invoices owed to the company as of the "Go Live" date and as of the "Begin Transactions" date. This should be in an accessible, easy-to-read format and the total must match the A/R general ledger account balance for both dates. If the balance is off, you must get with your CPA to reconcile this ledger.
- An accurate Accounts Payable ledger of all bills owed by the company as of both dates. This should be in an accessible, easy-to-read format and the total must match the A/P general ledger account balance for both dates. If the balance is off, you must get with your CPA to reconcile this ledger.

- If you track inventory, you need the physical inventory count as of both dates also.

Creating a New Company Using the Wizard

To create a new company, follow these steps:

1. When Peachtree starts, select **Set up a new company** from the Startup screen.

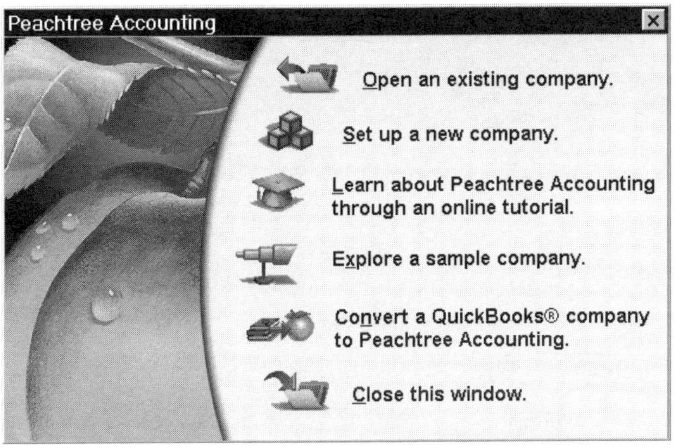

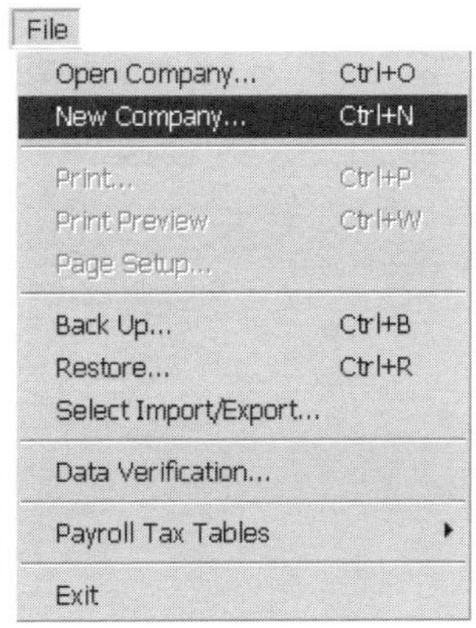

Or from the menu bar, select **File**, **New Company**.

Or from the navigation aid, click **Company**, **New Company Setup**.

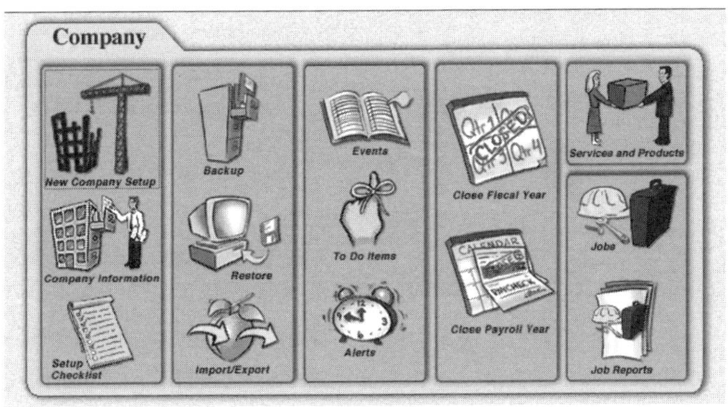

Or using the keyboard, press **Alt+F**, **N** or just **Ctrl+N**.

2. If another company is open, the following warning message will appear. Click **OK** to close.

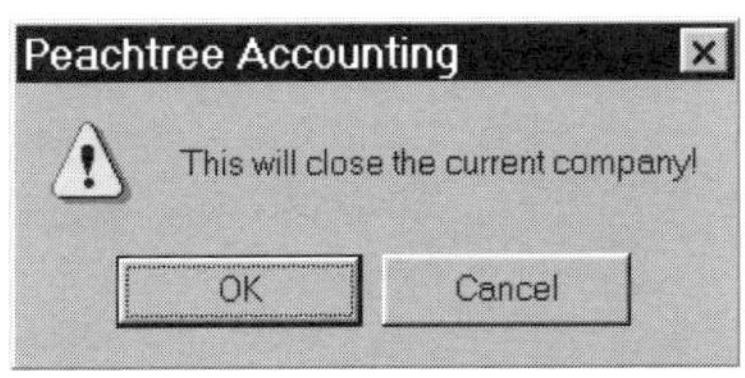

3. The New Company Setup wizard starts with the Introduction screen showing.

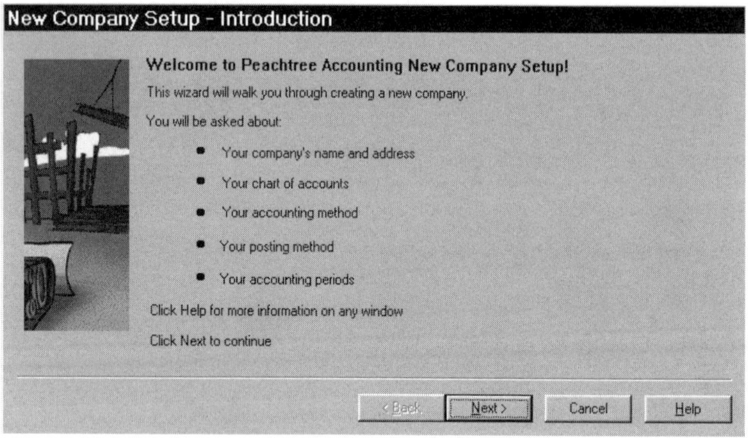

Click **Next** to continue.

4. The Company Information screen appears.

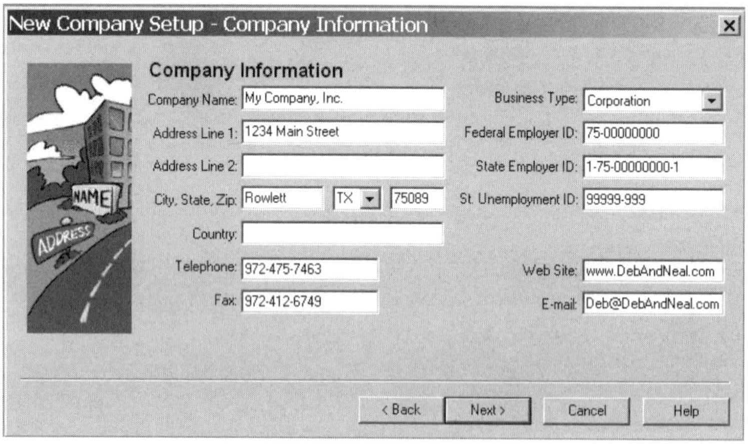

Fill in the Company Name and Address fields as you want it to appear on invoices and other correspondence. If you do not buy or sell outside the U.S., there is no need to fill in the Country box.

5. Enter your telephone and fax numbers. You may use any format you desire with parentheses, dots, or dashes. Peachtree does not format these fields for you.

6. Select the Business Type. This is the first big question in Peachtree. The choices are Corporation, S corporation, Partnership, Sole proprietorship, or Limited liability company. The owner or CPA should have the answer to this question. The type of business affects the equity accounts of the general ledger and each type has specific accounts that get closed, don't get closed, or are used for retained earnings.

7. Enter the ID numbers requested. Again, the owner or CPA should have the answers to these questions.
8. Fill in the Web Site and E-mail fields if you are on the Internet.
9. Click **Next** to continue.

Note: At any time, if you want to go back and review or change a previous screen, use the Back button. If you go back, answers placed in subsequent questions are not forgotten. The values previously entered into these fields will be remembered.

10. The Chart of Accounts screen appears.

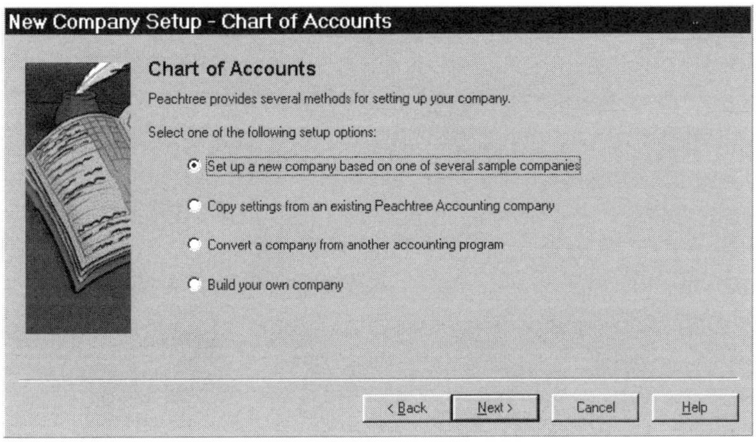

The chart of accounts (referred to hereafter as COA) is the listing of all accounts used to create the transactions in your accounting system. Each account is a way to track a specific type of information. Examples of accounts include an accounts receivable account to track amounts customers owe you, a telephone expenses account to track the amount you paid the phone company, and a checking account to keep the cash in the bank account.

You will need to decide where you get your COA. The easiest way is to let Peachtree create the COA based on a sample company or to get it from an existing company if one has already been established in Peachtree.

Select **Set up a new company based on one of several sample companies** and click **Next.**

11. This opens the sample Chart of Accounts screen.

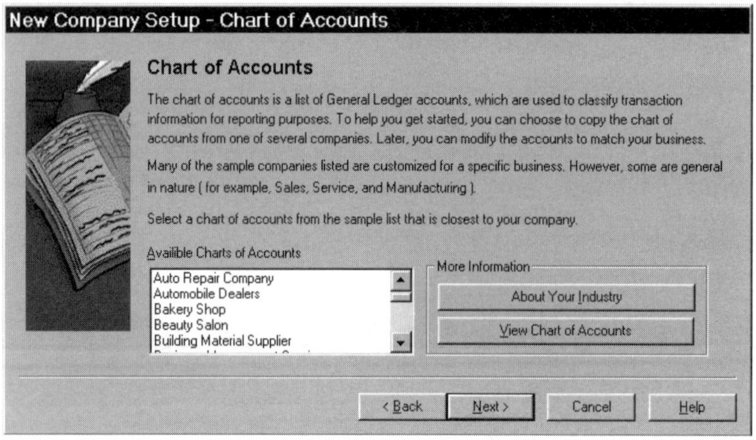

In the Available Charts of Accounts list box, you may select the type of company closest to yours. If you need additional help, click the **About Your Industry** button in the More Information section. A help window appears with some generalized information about this type of company. For example, the following window shows the information displayed for a caterer.

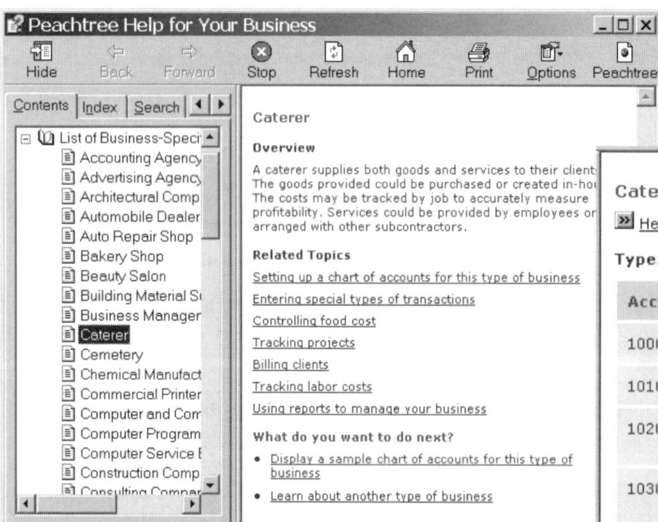

To see the COA that are set up for this type of company, click the **Display a sample chart of accounts** link to bring up the sample listing.

There is considerable hand-holding to help you select the best model for your company, and usually the end result is better than if you built the COA manually.

12. Click **Next** to move to the Accounting Method screen.

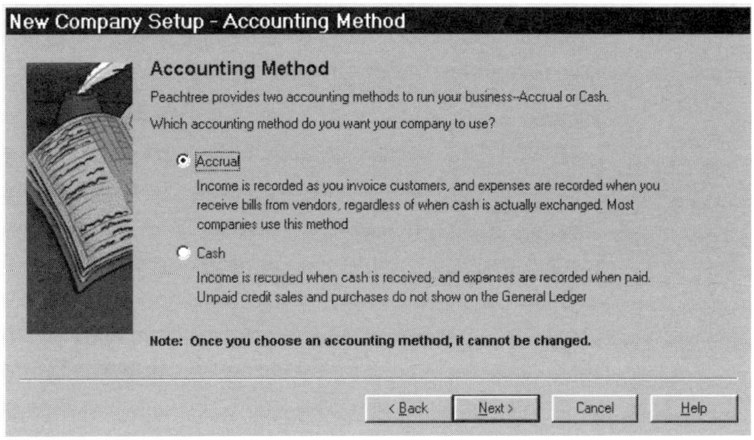

Another big question is how income and expenses are treated. Do invoices become income when you send the invoice or when you receive the payment? Are expenses counted when the check is sent or when the actual expense occurred? The answers to these questions are important and determine your accounting method. Both have tax consequences and affect your financial statements. The cash method can be advantageous in reducing taxes, but the accrual method will let you match the expenses related to the sales that you make to the month that they actually occur. Your CPA will tell you which method to use.

Note: If your company is growing and you want to track income and expenses in the month that they actually occur, this may be a great time to make the change from the cash to the accrual method.

Warning!! Once your accounting method is set, it cannot be changed. You can only copy the company to a new company and change it at that point.

13. Select an option and click **Next** to continue.
14. The Posting Method screen appears.

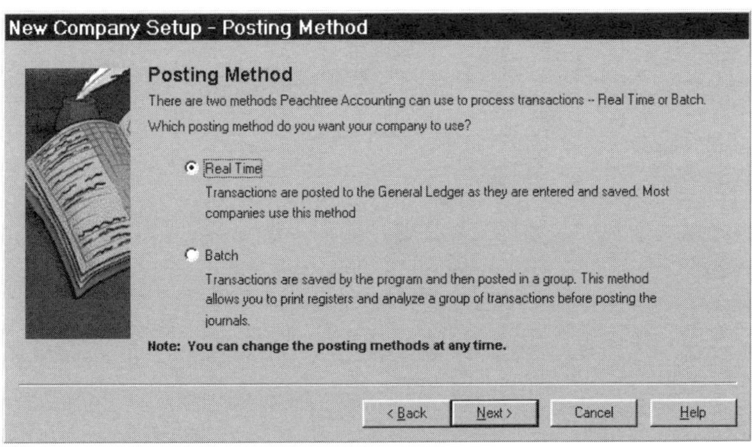

There are two types of posting methods. We briefly discussed these in the previous chapter. The posting method affects the saving of transactions.

Real Time — All transactions are immediately posted to the general ledger when saved. These transactions show up immediately in all linked functions and reports. This method is best used with smaller companies where there is no need for a lot of cross-checking of the data entry.

Batch — Transactions are saved to a temporary file. These transactions can be reviewed for accuracy before they are posted to the general ledger and therefore reduce errors made at data entry. Larger companies tend to use batch posting.

Another reason to use batch posting is that it helps optimize the use of your network if multiple people are simultaneously working in Peachtree. When Peachtree writes a transaction to the general ledger it must "lock" the General.dat file. As each transaction is performed the ledger is opened and closed, using a significant number of system resources. Also, during that time everyone else is locked out of the system until the first user completes the operation. When batch processing is used, temporary files are used to hold transactions, the ledger does not need to be exclusively locked, with the ensuing overhead, and overall processing goes smoother. If you get too many "file in use" messages that slow down data entry, changing to batch posting may help.

15. Select an option and click **Next** to continue.
16. The Accounting Periods screen appears.

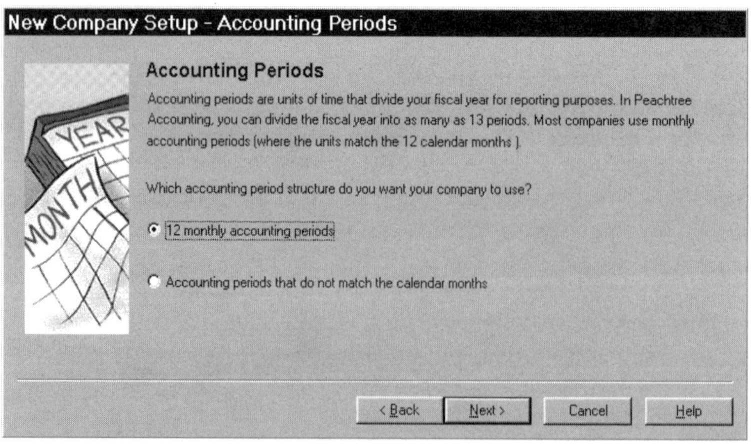

Accounting periods are the unit of time for which your company reports its transactions. Usually this is a month. Peachtree keeps two years open at the same time to allow you to view or make changes to the previous year or to apply transactions to next year. Nearly all smaller companies use the standard 12 monthly accounting periods.

In this case, select **12 monthly accounting periods** and click **Next** to go to the Monthly Accounting Periods screen in Step 21.

If your CPA wants you to use a different set of accounting periods, select **Accounting periods that do not match the calendar months** and click **Next**.

17. This brings up the Custom Accounting screen.

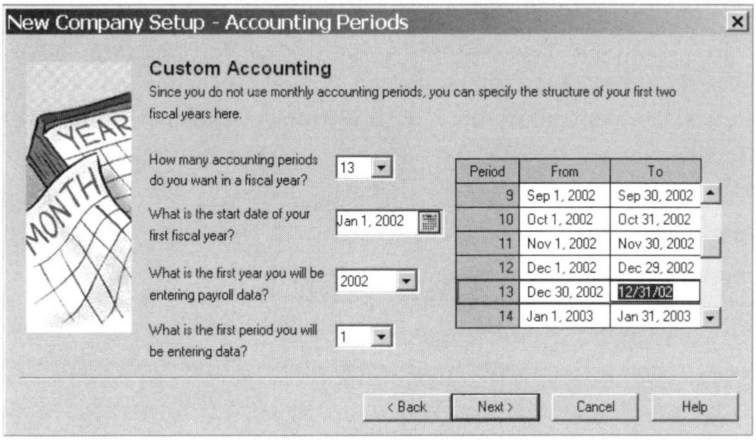

Select the number of accounting periods in a year from the How many accounting periods drop-down. Most companies use 12. Some companies break the year into 13 equal four-week periods. Other companies may use less. The smallest number of periods is one; it uses the entire year as a single accounting period. If you are a one-person office and don't want to be bothered with changing accounting periods during the year, you could make that choice here.

Some larger companies break their year into a different sort of 13 accounting periods. The periods still follow the monthly breaks but there is an additional period at the end of the year (sort of like midnight between December 31 and January 1) that they use for year-end adjustments. Peachtree does not support a 13th period in this manner.

Note: I tried a new 13-period method with a 13th period used for year-end adjustments by adjusting periods 1-11 and 14-24 so that they followed the calendar months January-November. I then made the 12th and 25th periods from December 1 to December 29 and the 13th and 26th periods from December 30 to December 31. This method appeared to work so if you wanted to use 13 periods and make December shorter, you could try this. Just remember that you would have no regular transactions, just adjustments, on the last two days of each year.

18. Select the What is the start date of your first fiscal year drop-down. Most companies follow the calendar year, but there are definite advantages to using a different start date. If your business specializes in catering parties, New Year's Eve would often be one of the busiest days of the year. By setting the fiscal year to another month, all your year-end tasks could be done during a slow period and would make the accounting tasks easier. As another example, an accounting firm generally does not

select April 16 to be the start of its financial year. Check with your CPA about the tax repercussions of changing your fiscal year.

19. The payroll year always follows the calendar year because it is used to create W-2s, 1099s, and payroll reports. Select the current payroll year for your company.

20. Select the What is the first period you will be entering data drop-down. If you are entering information from the beginning of your fiscal year, you would select 1. If your year started in January, but it is now June you may wish to start entering data in period 6 or 7.

    If you enter any of the custom periods incorrectly, you will receive the following error message. Click **OK** and go to Step 22.

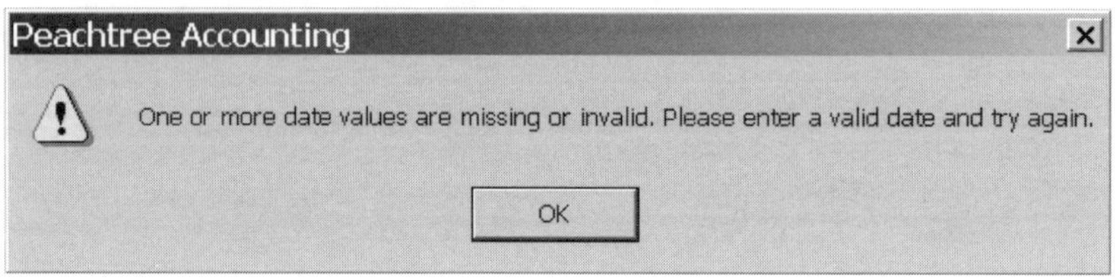

21. If you chose 12 monthly accounting periods, you still need to select the fiscal year, starting month for data entry, and first payroll year.

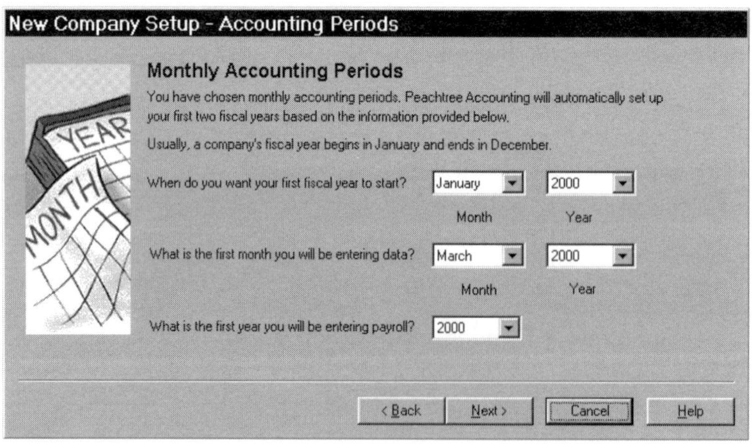

Warning!! You cannot change your accounting periods once they are set.

22. Click **Next** to go to the Defaults screen.

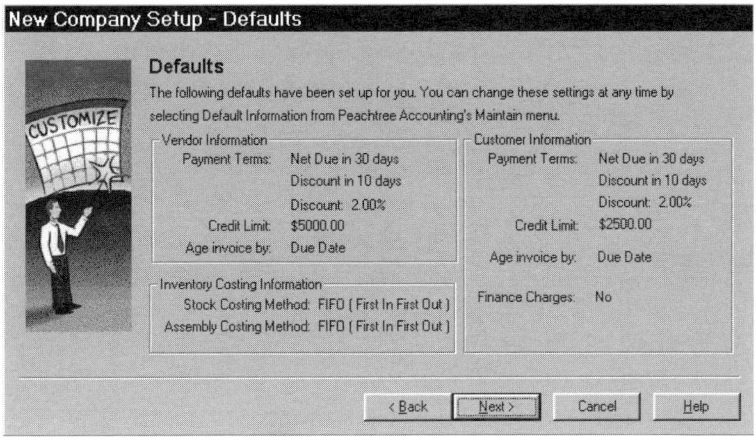

Peachtree shows you the current defaults here. In earlier versions, the program let you select your own defaults, but that function has been moved. We will discuss changing these defaults later in the book.

23. Click **Next** to go to the Finish screen.

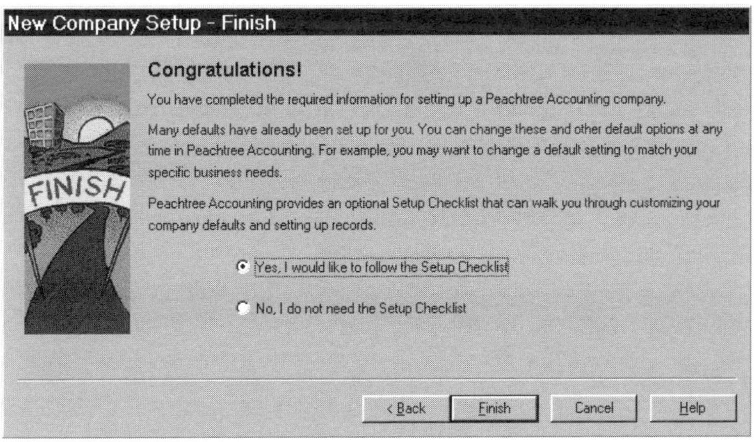

24. All information for creating your new company has now been entered. To check your settings, click the **Back** button to return to any screen and make any changes needed. Before clicking **Finish**, select **Yes, I would like to follow the Setup Checklist** to use the Setup Checklist. We will ignore it later, but for now we want to view the checklist. (This is discussed later in the chapter.)

25. After you click **Finish**, Peachtree will create your new company. First, the Creating Data Files processing window appears.

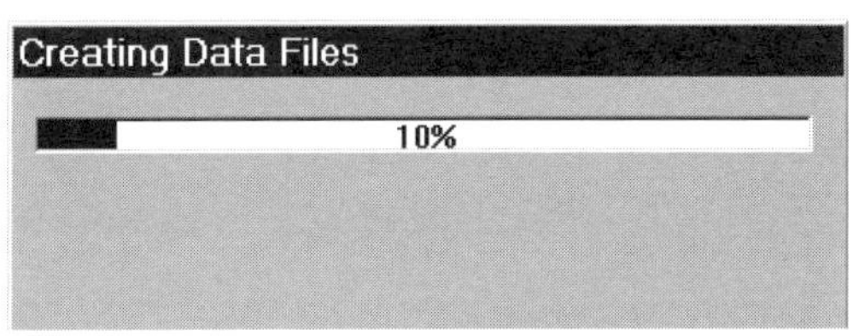

Then the Copying Company processing window appears. It may look different depending upon your version of Peachtree.

Both windows show the status of the company creation. Depending upon the speed and processing power of your computer, these could take a few minutes.

When completed, the newly created company will be opened in Peachtree with the Setup Checklist showing.

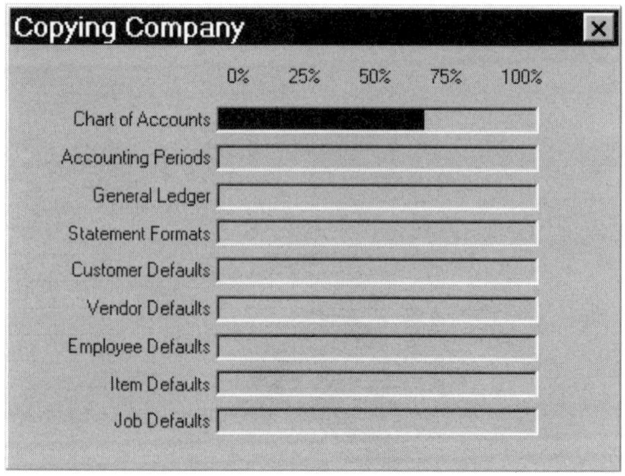

Creating a New Company by Copying an Existing Peachtree Company

If you have a company in Peachtree with a COA that you want to use for your new company, you can copy that information into your new company. Copying can be especially helpful when you work with more than one company and you have spent a large amount of time getting all the accounts and default information just the way you need it.

1. On the Chart of Accounts screen, select **Copy settings from an existing Peachtree Accounting company** and click **Next**.
2. The Chart of Accounts screen appears. Select a company from the Available Peachtree Companies listing. You may see an alphabetical listing of the associated COA by clicking **View Chart of Accounts**.

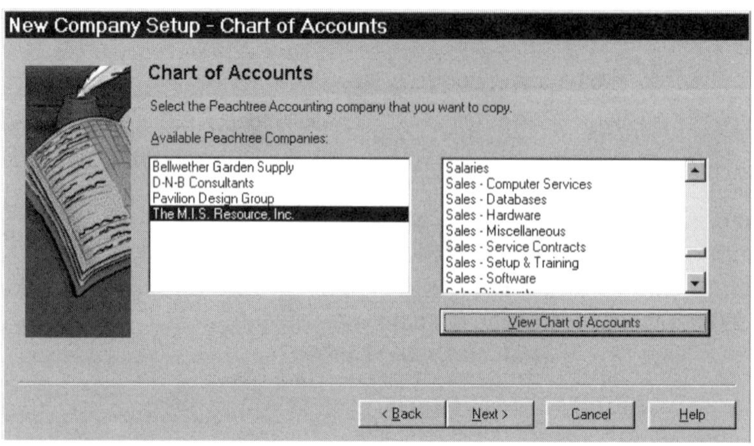

Press **Next** when you have selected which company to copy.

3. The Copy Company Information screen appears.

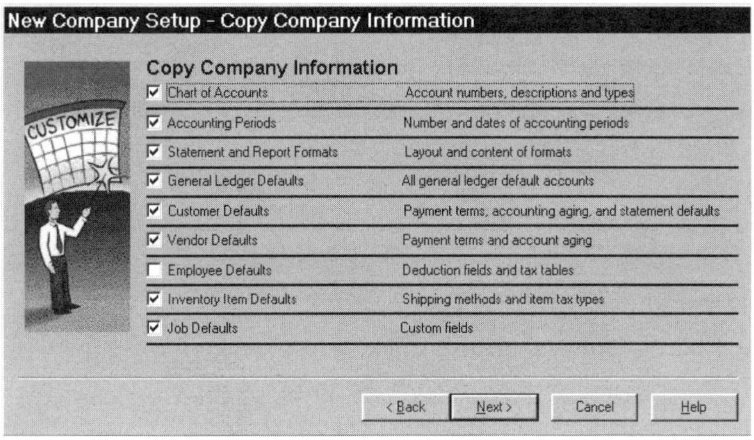

Select which elements of the existing company you want in the new company, and click **Next** to continue.

4. Select the accounting method — cash or accrual — and click **Next**. (For more information on these steps, see the descriptions of these screens in the previous section.)
5. Select the posting method — batch or real time — and click **Next**.
6. Click **Finish** to complete the copy process. The Creating Data Files and the Copying Company processing windows appear.

   When completed, the newly created company will be opened in Peachtree with the Setup Checklist showing.

Creating a New Company by Converting from Another Accounting Program

If you have a company already set up in another accounting program, such as Peachtree for DOS, Quicken, QuickBooks, or Veritask Write-Up (formerly Client Write-Up), you can import the company information into Peachtree for Windows. Which types of files you can import depends upon which version of Peachtree you are running. Peachtree 2002 can only convert Quicken and QuickBooks.

1. On the Chart of Accounts screen, select **Convert a company from another accounting program** and click **Next**.
2. Select the accounting method — cash or accrual — and click **Next**.
3. Select the posting method — batch or real time — and click **Next**.
4. Select the accounting periods and click **Next**.
5. Enter the fiscal and payroll years and the first month to enter data. Click **Next**.

6. Click **Finish** to complete the company creation process. The Creating Data Files and the Copying Company processing windows appear.

   When completed, the newly created company will be opened in Peachtree. At this point you will only have the basic skeleton of your company without any data. You must go to the Import function to bring in the data from the other accounting program. (Due to space constraints, the Import function is not covered here.)

Creating a New Company from Scratch

In some cases, you may decide to build your own company in Peachtree from the ground up.

1. On the Chart of Accounts screen, select **Build your own company.** Click **Next** to continue.
2. Select the accounting method — cash or accrual — and click **Next.**
3. Select the posting method — batch or real time — and click **Next.**
4. Select the accounting periods and click **Next.**
5. Enter the fiscal and payroll years and the first month to enter data. Click **Next.**
6. Click **Finish** to complete the copy process. The Creating Data Files and the Copying Company processing windows appear.

   When completed, the newly created company will be opened in Peachtree with the Setup Checklist showing.

   You will need to go through all the steps in the checklist to make sure that the company has been set up correctly.

The Setup Checklist

After your new company is created, the Setup Checklist appears on the screen. You can use the checklist to change or set up defaults for the company. These include such things as the terms you offer customers, deductions for employees, and beginning inventory balances. We will briefly go through the checklist here.

1. If the checklist is not available, it needs to be opened. Click the **Company** file in the navigation aid, then click the **Setup Checklist** icon.

   Or select **Maintain, Setup Checklist** from the menu bar.

   Or press **Alt+M, S** from the keyboard.

2. The Setup Checklist appears.

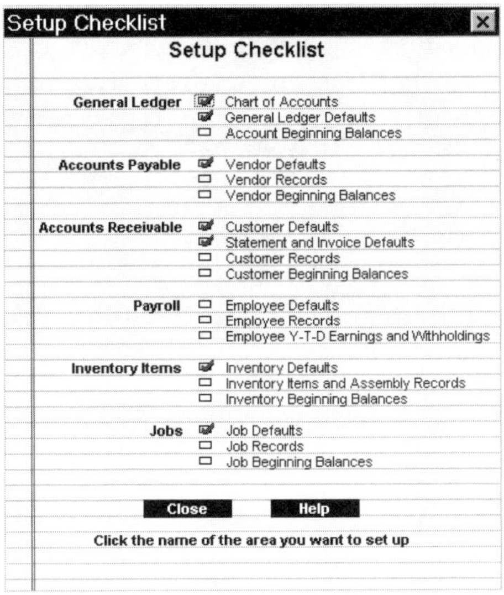

The checklist looks like a yellow legal pad with a list of tasks. Completed tasks are indicated by being checked off; uncompleted tasks are unmarked.

The checklist does not have a print option, an overlooked nuisance, so you can't get a printout. For those who desire a hard copy, one is provided (in both Word and Excel 97 formats) with the companion files.

3. When you leave each task, a message box appears asking if the task is completed.

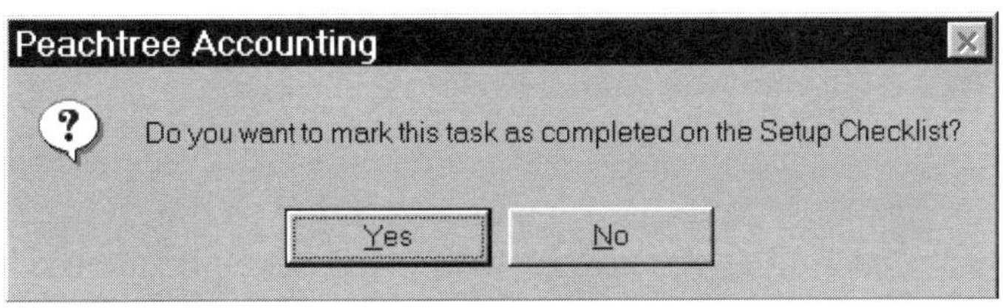

Clicking **Yes** puts a check mark in the appropriate box.

Items that have been checked off can still be accessed.

You may go through the checklist and add all necessary information in a linear fashion. I recommend that you don't do that, but instead work on your chart of accounts first, if it needs work, and then go to the next chapter and follow my Three-Month Plan setup procedure.

By following the setup I recommend, you can be using Peachtree immediately for the day-to-day tasks while waiting on the more complicated and final tasks until they are actually needed.

The Chart of Accounts

The first item on the Setup Checklist is the General Ledger Chart of Accounts. When you click on the item, the Maintain Chart of Accounts screen appears.

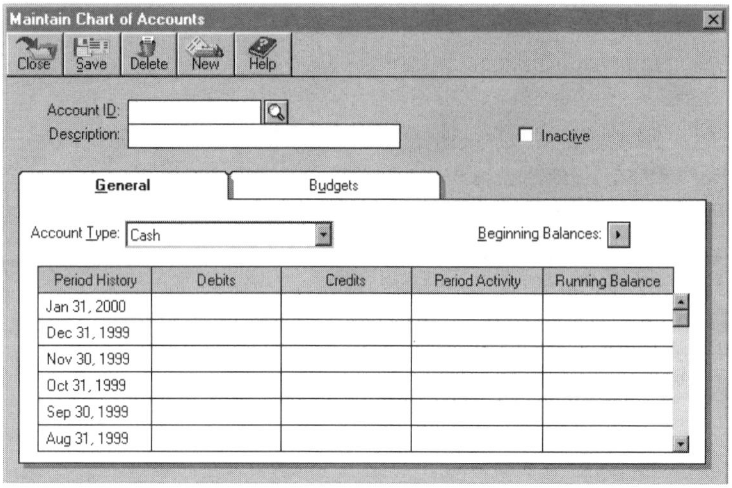

If you created your company using a Peachtree-supplied COA, a list of accounts is already installed in the company file. While the list of accounts is probably satisfactory the way Peachtree created it, you may want to make some minor changes. For example, you will probably want to change the names of some accounts to better suit your company's needs, delete some accounts that are unnecessary, and add new accounts.

The Parts of a General Ledger Account

An account has several parts that are very important to the setup of your company. You will need to pay very close attention to the section on the account ID and not add any new accounts until you understand the requirements for account IDs.

Account ID

The account ID is an identifying code that is used to sort and categorize your COA. Almost everyone uses a numerical code because this makes the sorting easiest. Although I recommend alphabetical codes for other Peachtree files, for the COA I strongly suggest a numerical code.

Generally, your accountant should give you a list of accounts. This list may or may not include account numbers, but even if it does have account numbers, you may still decide to modify them. Account IDs should all be the same length for simplicity and to facilitate sorting. Peachtree sorts the account IDs using an alphabetic rather than a numeric sort so that if you have the following account IDs:

```
1, 2, 3, 12, 14, 23, 168...
```

Peachtree will sort them as follows:

```
1, 12, 14, 168, 2, 23, 3
```

This is due to the alphabetic sort where the first letter in the IDs are compared, then the second letter, and so forth. The user may consider 12 to be greater than 4, but the computer doesn't since by the time it makes it to the second character the "1" has already been declared less than the "4"!

One way to overcome this problem is to make all the IDs the same length, preceding the smaller numbers with leading zeros. This way they sort in the order that you need them:

```
001, 002, 003, 012, 014, 023, 168...
```

I also recommend that codes be at least four digits long, with at least 10 or 100 between each code, to allow for future growth. Our list now starts to look like this:

```
0010, 0020, 0030, 0120, 0140, 0230, 1680...
```

It is even better to categorize accounts according to the type of balance sheet or income statement account. This categorization breaks the accounts into six types of accounts, with each type starting with 1 through 6. For a set of accounts with five digits, the breakdown is as follows:

10000 – 19999	Asset Accounts (Cash, Accounts Receivable, Fixed Assets)
20000 – 29999	Liability Accounts (Accounts Payable, P/R Taxes Due)
30000 – 39999	Equity Accounts (Retained Earnings, Owners Draw)
40000 – 49999	Revenue Accounts (Sales, Service Income, Interest Income)
50000 – 59999	Cost of Sales Accounts (Cost of Goods Sold, Direct Labor)
60000 – 69999	Expense Accounts (Salaries, Entertainment, Office Expenses)

Using this method, our list may now look like this:

```
10010, 10020, 20030, 30120, 40140, 50230, 61680...
```

If you need to, you can have expense accounts also use the 7 and 8 series. Peachtree uses these and also uses the 9 series for the Gain on Sale account. If in doubt, discuss this with your accountant.

Description

This is the account name. Try to be as specific as needed. If you have several checking accounts, describe them by their type, such as Payroll Checking, or by the bank, such as Great State Checking Account.

Account Type

In addition to the account breakdowns listed earlier, Peachtree breaks down accounts even further. There are 16 account types. These account types should be discussed in more detail with your CPA. Their purpose is to simplify reporting.

Inactive

An account cannot be deleted if there is any activity in it or in any part of the open accounting periods. Accounts that are not yet deleted are made inactive to keep transactions from posting to the account.

Viewing an Account

1. You may view an account by clicking on the **Lookup** button.

   The list of accounts will then drop down.

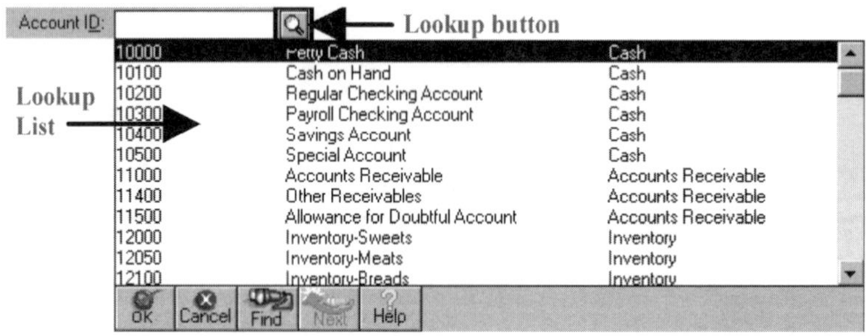

2. Select the account that you want to view, and click **OK**. Alternately, double-click on the account name.

   The selected account appears in the screen.

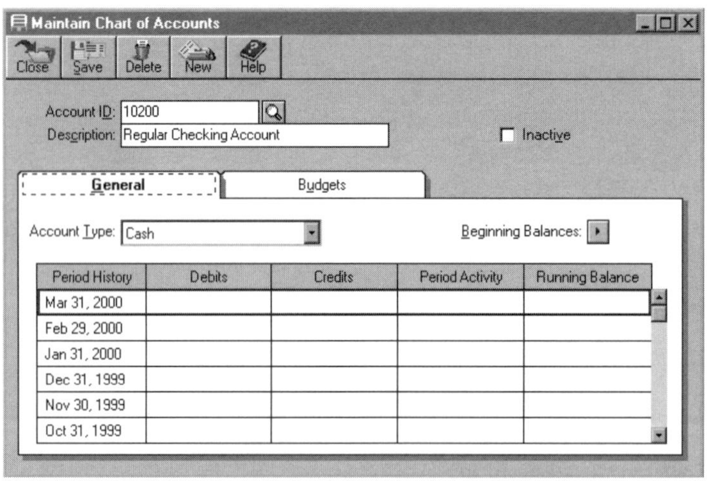

Changing an Account Name or Description

To change the description of an account, follow these steps:

1. Select the correct account from the drop-down list in the Account ID field.
2. Highlight the current name in the Description field, or click at the end of the name and use the Backspace key to delete the name.
3. Enter the new name or description.
4. Click the **Save** button.

If you try to leave the screen without saving the changes, you get the following warning message.

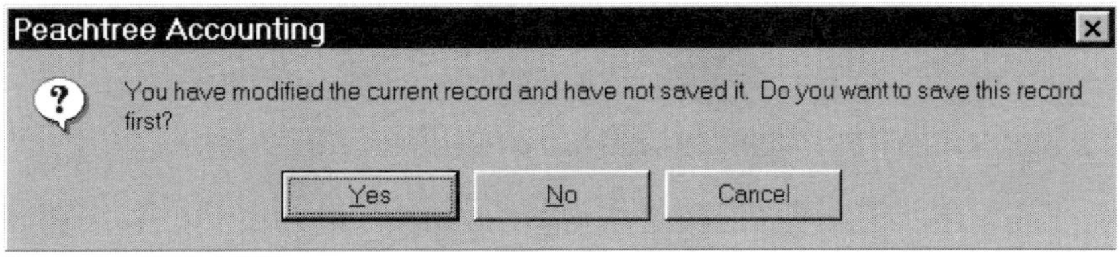

Click **Yes** to save the record, **No** to close the record without saving the changes, and **Cancel** to take you back to the screen without saving the record and without losing the changes.

Deleting an Account

To delete an account, follow these steps:

1. Bring up the correct account in the screen.
2. Verify that it is the correct account that you want to delete. There is no undo when you delete a record.
3. If this is the correct account to delete, click the **Delete** button.
4. A confirmation message appears.

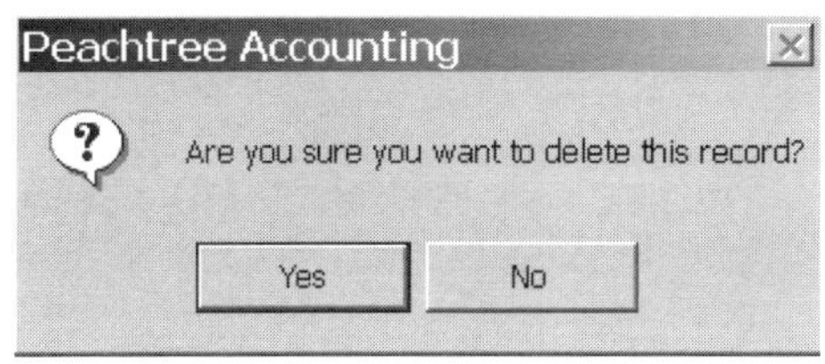

If you are still sure that this is the account that you want to delete, click **Yes**.

The account is removed from Peachtree.

If there has been any activity in the account in the last two open years, you cannot delete the account. Peachtree will notify you if you are attempting to delete such an account by displaying a message. The account will not be deleted. You will need to make the account inactive for now, and wait until the end of the year to delete it.

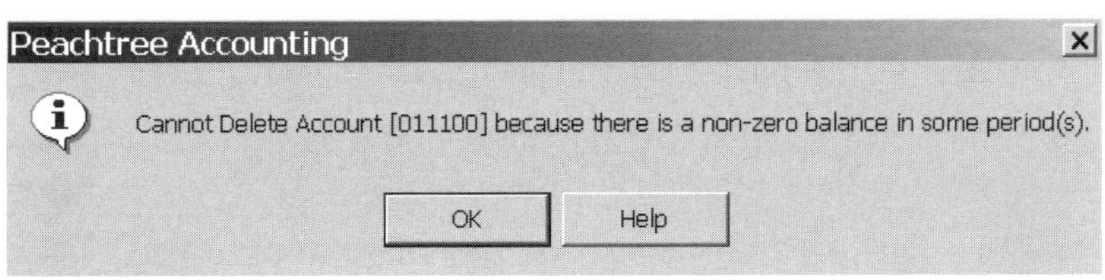

Adding an Account

To finish setting up your COA, you will probably need to add some accounts:

1. If an account is currently showing in the screen, click the **New** button.
2. A blank screen appears.

3. Determine the account ID by looking at existing accounts and inserting the ID in the correct position. Try to leave a count of at least 10 between each account ID.
4. Enter the new ID into the Account ID field.
5. Tab to the next field or click on the next field with the mouse.
6. Type the account name in the Description field.
7. In the Account Type field, select the correct category.
8. Click the **Save** button.
9. The new account now appears in the COA list.

Printing the COA

Unfortunately, you cannot print the COA from the Setup Checklist. You must close the checklist and do the following:

1. Click the **General Ledger** folder from the navigation aid, then click the **General Ledger Reports** icon.

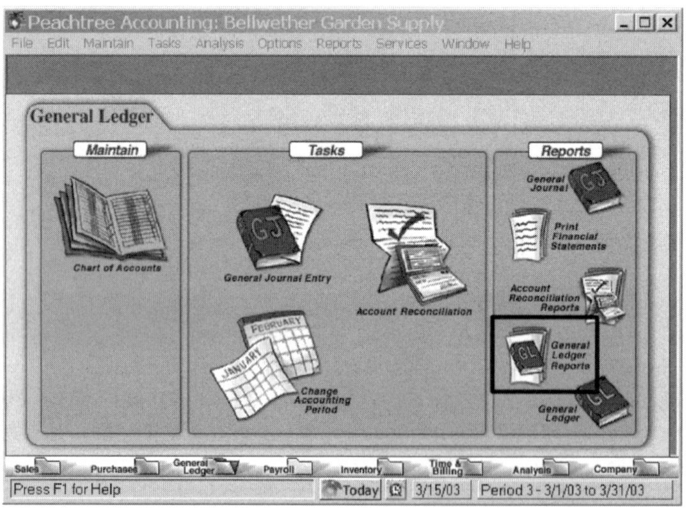

Or you can select **Reports** from the menu bar and then select **General Ledger**.

You can also use the keyboard shortcut and press **Alt+R**, then **G**.

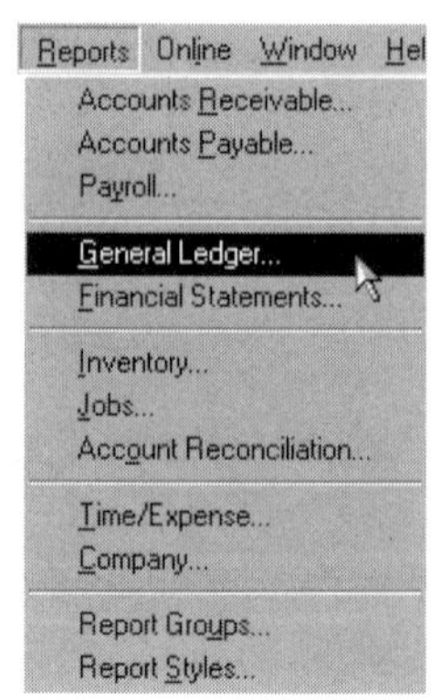

2. The Select a Report dialog box appears with the General Ledger reports showing.

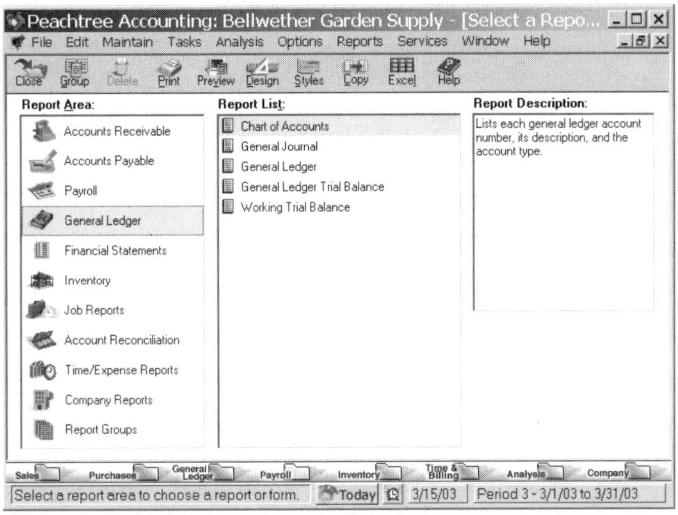

Highlight the **Chart of Accounts** report from the Report List.

3. Click the **Print** button in the toolbar to print to the default printer. To print to another printer, see the "Printers" section in Chapter 2.
4. The Chart of Accounts dialog box appears.

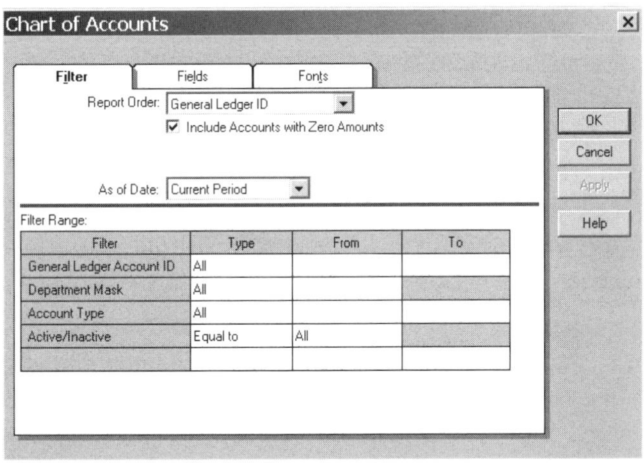

We don't need to change any options, so click **OK**. These options will be covered later in this book.

5. To view the COA on the computer, click the **Preview** button instead of **Print**. After you click **OK** on the options dialog box, the report will appear.

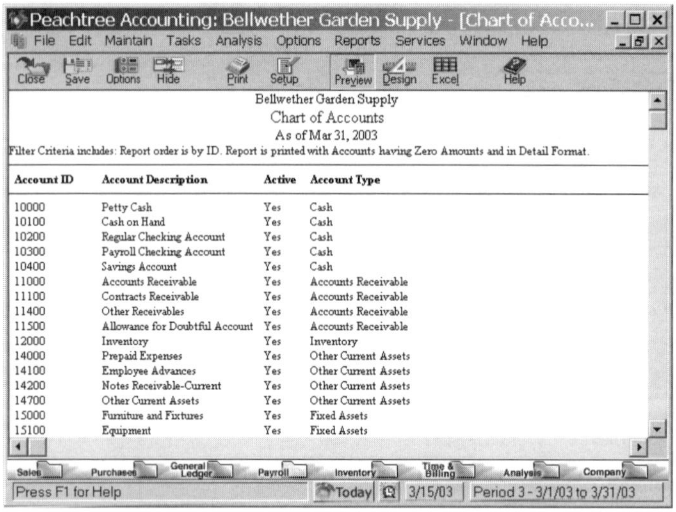

As you can see, you can also print the report while viewing it on the screen.

Setting Up Users and Security

Security is one area that is often ignored in a computer environment. People who lock up their file cabinets every time they leave the area and who have extensive security systems in their building often become complacent about the security of their computer. The questions to ask are "How important is your information to your company?" and "How much trouble or embarrassment or loss of business would occur if the private information about your company is suddenly made available to everyone?" While the PC does not have good security inherent in it, Peachtree has a built-in level of security that is fairly good.

If you have a one-person office and do not have to worry about anyone breaking into your computer, you may not need to worry about security or setting up as a user in Peachtree.

If there is any chance that someone could get into your computer and therefore your company accounting information, you will want to set up security and a user account. If you have a network installation, you must set up security and users.

Entering the Peachtree Administrator User Account

To implement security in Peachtree, you must first create at least one user account. To enter a new user account, follow these steps:

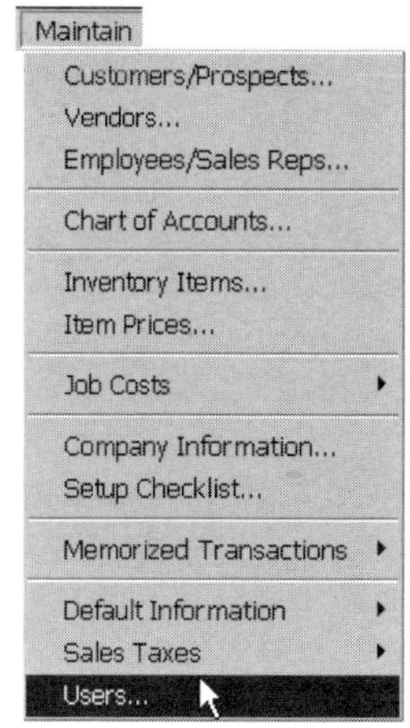

1. Select **Maintain**, **Users** from the menu bar.
2. If no users have yet been set up, a security message appears. Click **OK**.

3. The Maintain Users window appears.

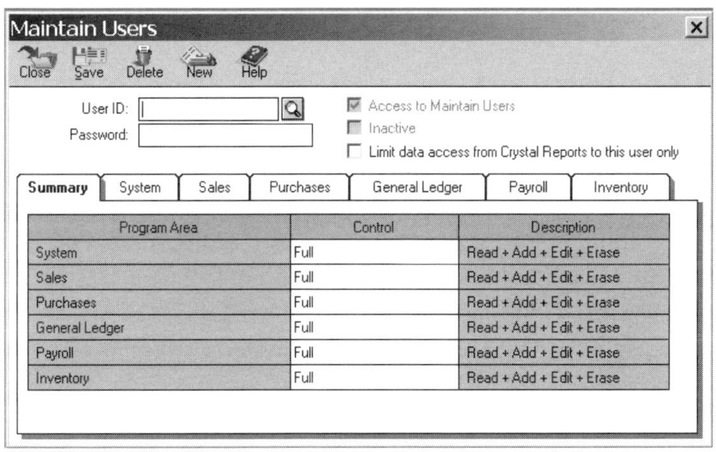

Enter an ID in the User ID field. This should be the account for the main user of Peachtree, probably yourself. Keep the user ID simple, such as Deb or Dbean instead of Deborah Bean. You may be typing this a lot and you want to make it easy to remember. If you are on a network, you may want to make it the same as your logon name.

4. Enter the password. Passwords are case sensitive and may be up to 13 characters in length.

   Notice that the Access to Maintain Users and the Inactive check boxes are disabled. Because this is the first, and main, user account, Peachtree assumes that this is the account of the main Peachtree administrator. When entering other accounts you will want to uncheck the Access to Maintain Users check box so that other users do not have access to the user account and passwords function.

Note: Unlike many programs, Peachtree does not print your password as ***. This is another reason to limit access to this function. It is still a deficiency on Peachtree's part that passwords are not changeable by the user of the password. This "miss" on Peachtree's part allows a Peachtree administrator to make changes to Peachtree in another user's name without anyone realizing that the wrong user is using that account.

The next check box, Limit data access..., will not be covered here.

5. In the lower half of the window are seven tabs. The Peachtree administrator only needs to be concerned with the Summary tab. Verify that all Program Areas have their Control set to **Full.**
6. Click **Save** to save the user account. The window will close.

   The next time you open Peachtree you will be required to fill in the User ID and Password fields.

   There is more detailed information on users and security in Chapter 19.

Entering Other User Accounts

You may enter other user accounts by repeating the steps in the previous section. Determine who should have access to the maintain users function. Limit their program access by changing the Control fields on the appropriate tabs. Be careful how your users are limited. Sometimes you can limit them so much that they can't enter the data that they need to. In this case, go back into the user account and change the access to the needed level.

Summary

Getting your company set up in Peachtree is very easy using the wizard. Getting your COA entered correctly is a bit more difficult and requires close attention to details. Once you have created a company and have your chart of accounts completed, you are ready to dive into actually doing business with Peachtree.

Chapter 4

The Three-Month Plan

In This Chapter

- How the Three-Month Plan has worked in the past
- What is covered in your Three-Month Plan
- The Go Live and the Begin Transactions dates
- Using systems in parallel
- Important lists

After many years of setting up Peachtree for many different types of companies, I have developed my own special way of getting a company up and running in Peachtree. My Three-Month Setup Plan is designed to make the transfer to Peachtree as painless as possible for your company. It is also designed to ensure that your data is as accurate as possible. Many of my clients have attended Peachtree classes and then come to me for help when they couldn't remember what was taught four days or six months ago. Rarely did these classes teach them how to reconcile their books when converting to Peachtree. My way takes a slower but much easier and more accurate path so that at the end of three months my clients are not only fully trained in Peachtree, they also have a completely balanced set of books.

How I Work the Three-Month Plan

Before I wrote this book, I would conduct the Three-Month Plan by going to companies and working with their employees and data to get the company through the details of installing and setting up Peachtree. My services would also include customization of forms and procedures. I charge between $2,500 and $5,000 for this service. By buying this book, you get the setup information. Unfortunately, I can't include all the customization features in this book, but then the book costs a lot less than what I would charge for a personal setup!

How my plan has worked in the past is described in this section. Your Three-Month Plan will follow similar steps and timeline.

1. After meeting with the client and making a commitment to convert to Peachtree, a time frame is established. The time frame is generally three months and a schedule is established for training sessions and reconciliation work. During that time the client makes the commitment to continue all old accounting methods until the end of the setup period so that we have numbers to balance the new Peachtree to.

2. During the first week, I create the new company and discuss with the owner or office manager what functions are required, what functions are not important, and what functions need special thought and development for procedures.

   I also enter the basics for sales taxes, default accounts, and users myself to get everything started. The beginning balances for accounts are not entered at this time. We want to start with getting the day-to-day procedures in place before we start worrying about reconciling.

3. After the initial company setup, we have one or two training sessions a week. The appropriate people, plus the office manager or owner, attend each session. I hold these sessions at the desks of the people doing the work. We work at their desks because that is where all the information will be such as customer files, inventory counts, and outstanding bills. If we did it at any other place, we would be jumping up and down searching for needed data.

4. I almost always start with invoicing, unless the company has a large inventory that needs tracking. The employees gather together current invoices or sales orders or work orders; these are entered into the computer, and real invoices are generated. The invoices are then filed with the old system invoices or are sent to the customers and the old system invoices are filed with the new copies. After discussing the correct procedures to follow, I give the invoicing data entry person some homework. All new invoices and any invoices going back to the first of the current month must be entered into Peachtree, in addition to being entered into the old system. I also tell them to write down any questions that they have for our next session.

5. If there are enough people in the office to distribute the A/R and A/P tasks among them, I go to A/P bill data entry and do the same thing. If not, I leave the company with its homework.

6. A few days later when I come back, I answer questions and fine-tune the procedures to match the way the customer does business. I then go to the next subject, cash receipts. I show them how to apply customer payments to invoices and how to enter beginning balances for customers whose invoices are not in the system. For A/P, I teach how to pay bills. During this time, I also begin to customize the invoices and checks for the company.

7. I cover payroll and inventory in the same manner, each time making sure that the appropriate people understand the tasks and have a procedure list to follow. I answer questions that are specific to how that business wants to do its work. I have found that often these questions are company specific and do not come up unless I am actually working with the people in their environment. Many of these questions are such that they would never come up in a regular classroom setting.

8. After about a month of data entry practice, I am able to teach the balancing functions. These include bank reconciliation, balancing accounts payable and receivable, and determining the sales taxes. We start customizing some of the reports needed by the company at this time also.

9. In the third month, we move to the final company reconciliations and payroll taxes. We make sure that the trial balance is correct and matches the CPA's records. Once the reconciliation is complete, the Peachtree system "goes live" and there is no more need to keep two sets of books.

   My plan may seem a little unorthodox, but it generally produces a smoother transition, with fewer "gotchas" than other methods. It also promotes a trusting relationship between my clients and myself which encourages questions and reduces uneasiness about the process. It also builds confidence in the operations, which means that the system will be used and the client will expand on their knowledge to use other capabilities of the system.

Your Three-Month Plan

Your Three-Month Plan will work in a similar manner. The remaining chapters in this book relate to the Three-Month Plan as follows:

Month 1 — The Practice Month

- Chapter 5 — Invoicing
- Chapter 6 — Cash Receipts
- Chapter 7 — Purchases
- Chapter 8 — Payments
- Chapter 9 — Payroll
- Chapter 10 — Inventory

Month 2 — The Balancing Month

- Chapter 11 — Balancing Checking and Credit Card Accounts
- Chapter 12 — Balancing Accounts Receivable
- Chapter 13 — Balancing Accounts Payable
- Chapter 14 — Sales Taxes
- Chapter 15 — Balancing Payroll

Month 3 — The Reconciliation Month (Note we did <u>not</u> call this the "final" month!)

- Chapter 16 — Reconciling the General Ledger
- Chapter 17 — Reconciling Inventory
- Chapter 18 — Reporting
- Chapter 19 — Finalization and Follow-Up

In each month you may vary the order of the chapters, but the months themselves must be completed sequentially.

Note: If your accounting periods are not based upon calendar months, the plan will cover three accounting periods — unless you use less than 12 accounting periods in a year. In this case you will have to tailor the plan somewhat.

Most chapters in the first month have a "Getting Started" and a "Homework" section. The Getting Started section includes some tasks that I usually complete when teaching. You should follow the steps exactly as shown. The homework tasks are those I assign when leaving appointments to be completed to help the data entry people learn about the program. It is vital that these are followed and completed the first month. If you get to the second and third months without completing the data entry of all transactions, you won't be able to balance your accounts.

Scheduling the Three-Month Plan

Try to schedule your Three-Month Plan during a downtime if your business is seasonal. If you have a strong Christmas rush, hold off until February or June. If tax season is crunch time, wait until September or January.

You do not have to start the very first day of the first month, but your Three-Month Plan will cover three calendar months. If you start midway through the month, you just need to enter all the transactions from the first of the month. If it is towards the end of the month, you should wait until the beginning of the next month.

For some reason, every year in December, often late December, I get calls from people who want me to come out a time or two so that they can start using Peachtree on January 1. They are amazed when it can't be done, that it will take three months to make the conversion, and that they need to continue using their old system during the entire conversion. So plan plenty of time to convert to Peachtree.

Why You Must Continue Using Your Old Accounting System

Warning!! You must continue to use your old accounting system, manual or automated, for the entire Three-Month Plan.

Using systems in parallel, meaning using two systems at the same time that do the same job, is an important practice of both accounting and computing conversions. Because the old system has been thoroughly tested, we know that the information in it is correct. Conversely, the new system has not been tested and we need to know that the entries we are making will balance the same way that the entries in the old system do. By running the systems in parallel, we can check the balances of Peachtree at the end of each month and know that our new system is working the way it is supposed to.

Many people try to avoid running systems in parallel. Don't be tempted. If your accounts receivable gets messed up, it is very easy to print out the general ledger of the accounts receivable account in Peachtree and compare it, line by line, to the listing of the same accounts receivable in the old system, even if the old system is manual. If you haven't run both systems, you could spend a very long time trying to figure out where the error is in the new system, possibly more than you saved by not using both systems. If you have any doubts, talk to your CPA; she will give you many more reasons to run both Peachtree and your old accounting system in parallel.

Important Dates for Your Three-Month Plan

In sketching out your Three-Month Plan, you need to determine two dates:

The "Go Live" date — This is the date that you will officially start using Peachtree. It is not the first date that you start entering transactions. It is always the first day of an accounting period.

The "Begin Transactions" date — This date is three months prior to your Go Live date. This is the date that you start entering transactions. The time between the Go Live date and the Begin Transactions date is the Three-Month Plan.

Important Lists for Your Three-Month Plan

In addition to the plan schedule, there are several lists that you need. You need these lists for the Begin Transactions date and the Go Live date. These lists must be verified by your CPA and must match the CPA's version of your financial statements. If any discrepancies are found, you and your CPA should discuss what should be done about the differences. Generally, your CPA will give you journal entries to be made in the old accounting system for the month preceding your Begin Transactions date. I suggest that these entries are made in that month so that the Begin Transactions amounts are correct. The lists that you need are as follows:

Company General Ledger Trial Balance — You need one each for the Go Live date and the Begin Transactions date. This information must be accurate in order for Peachtree to give you a good record of your business! If your company does not have a trial balance, one must be created by the Go Live date.

Accounts Receivable Ledger — An accurate listing of all invoices owed to the company for both dates. This should be in an accessible, easy-to-read format and the total must match the A/R general ledger account balance for both dates.

Accounts Payable Ledger — An accurate listing of all bills owed by the company for both dates. This should be in an accessible, easy-to-read format and the total must match the A/P general ledger account balance for both dates.

Physical Inventory Count — If you track inventory you need to have an accurate accounting of the items in inventory for the Go Live date. If you can also get a listing for the Begin Transactions date, that would be an additional benefit. If tracking a physical inventory is important to your company or you have a large physical inventory, I suggest that you start with Chapter 10, "Inventory," before any other chapter.

You do not have to have these lists before you start entering information into Peachtree, but you will need them during the second and third months of the plan.

A Three-Month Setup Plan list is included with the companion files.

Month 1

The Practice Month

- Invoicing
- Cash Receipts
- Purchases
- Payments
- Payroll
- Inventory

Chapter 5

Invoicing

In This Chapter

- All the basics on the day-to-day processes of sending out invoices in Peachtree
- Creating a sales tax account
- Entering, editing, and printing invoices
- Adding customers "on the fly" and maintaining customers
- Using inventory items to speed data entry
- Other invoicing forms and functions: sales orders, quotes, work orders, etc.
- Creating invoices from quotes and sales orders
- Quick invoicing reports

Invoicing — sending invoices to customers — is where most companies start in Peachtree. Before we actually begin, let me warn you of an important feature of making a successful transition into Peachtree.

Warning!! You must continue to enter all sales transactions into your existing system for the entire duration of the Three-Month Plan. Until the end of the third month, when all general ledger accounts are verified, you will be running both accounting programs in parallel.

Invoices are the pieces of paper that you send to a customer and what you use to get payment from the customer. It follows that the faster you can get the invoice into the hands of the customer, the faster you can get paid.

This section discusses the most basic instructions for entering invoices. If you need to track inventory, you should at least look over Chapter 10 before you start this chapter.

Getting Started

If you charge sales tax to your customers, you must set up sales taxes in Peachtree before you can enter invoices. Normally when I am doing an onsite setup for a customer, I just enter this information before beginning the actual training without explaining everything to the client. Then later when the client starts to have questions about sales taxes, we cover the subject in depth and set up the sales tax codes and authorities to meet the customer's requirements.

The only other thing that you need to start entering invoices is your customer information, such as address, sales tax status, and payment terms.

Setting Up for First-Time Sales Taxes

We have to take care of one important detail — the sales tax account — before we can continue. We will do the bare minimum here just to get you going and then cover sales taxes in greater detail later in Chapter 14.

If you do not need to charge sales tax to your customers, you can skip this section. If you need to track multiple sets of sales taxes, I suggest you enter one set first to get started and later make changes or add additional sales tax codes.

Although this looks like a lot of steps, you need to follow them exactly. If you make a mistake, click Cancel until you get back to the beginning and start over.

1. Click the **Receivables** folder in the navigation aid to open it and then click the **Sales Tax Codes** icon. In older versions, the Receivables folder is called the Sales folder or Sales tab.

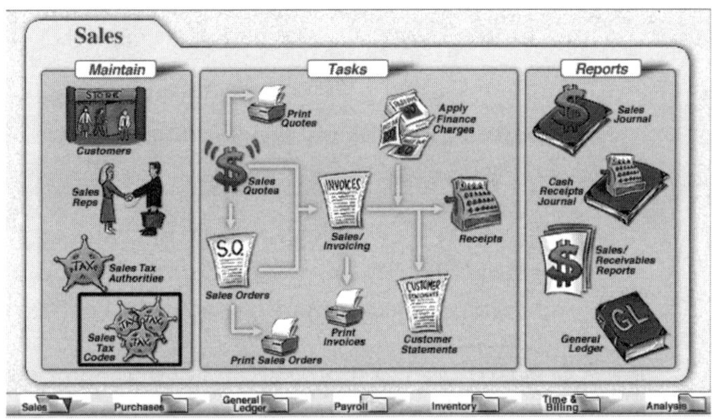

2. The Maintain Sales Tax Codes screen appears.

   In the Sales Tax Code field, enter the ID for this code such as **SalesTax**, **TexasST**, or **Main**. You are limited to eight characters.

3. Enter a description, such as **Sales Tax**, **Texas Sales Tax**, or **8.25% Taxes** in the Description field.

4. If freight is taxed, check the **Tax Freight** check box.

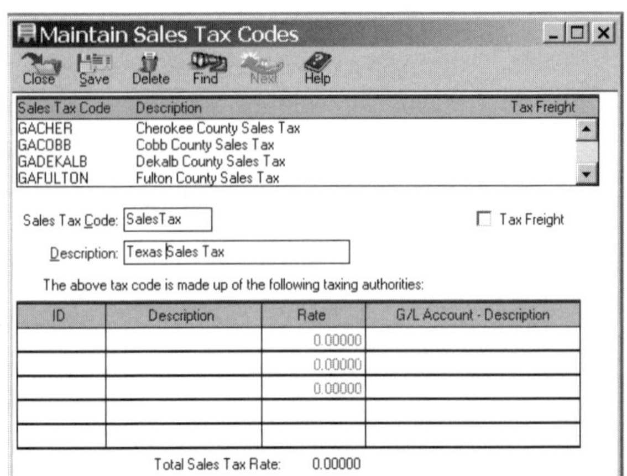

5. Right-click the mouse when the lookup keys are showing in the first ID field for the section that begins The above tax code.
6. Click the **New** button to add a taxing authority.
7. The Maintain Sales Tax Authorities screen appears.

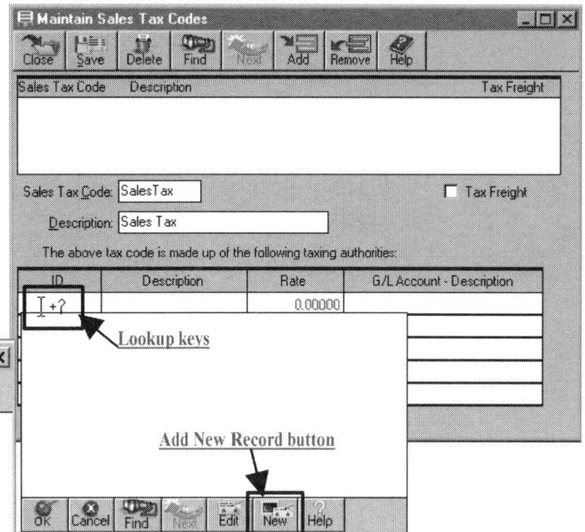

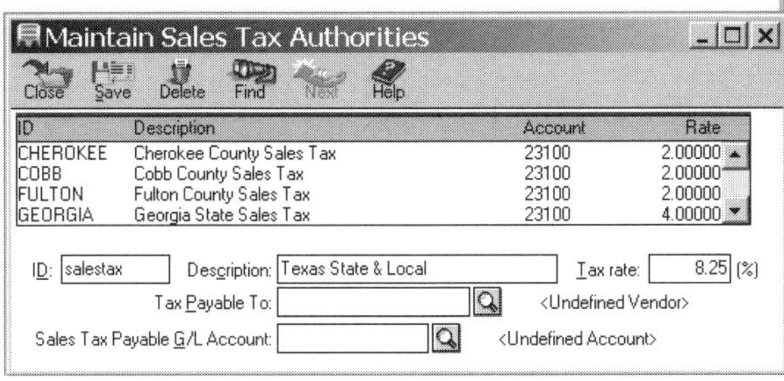

Enter a sales tax authority in the ID field, again using something simple, like **salestax.**

8. Fill in the Description box for this authority, such as **State, Local, and County Tax.**
9. Enter the tax rate as a percentage. If your sales tax rate is 8¼ % or, alternately, if you multiply your taxable sales by .0825 to determine your sales tax, enter **8.25.**
10. Right-click in the Tax Payable To field and then click the **New** button.
11. The Maintain Vendors screen appears. We are only going to enter the barest minimum of information here. Vendors are covered in Chapter 7.

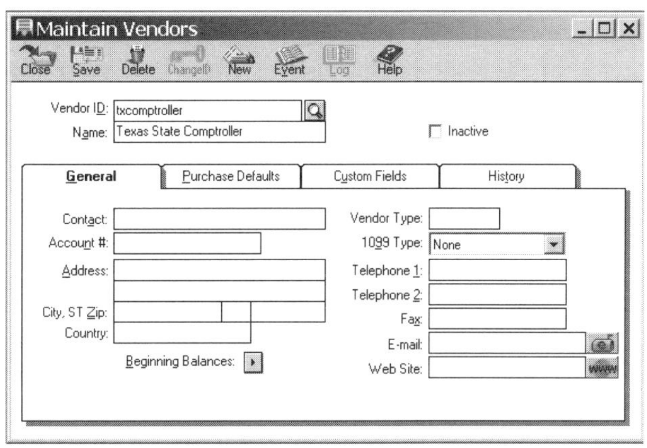

In the Vendor ID field, type a vendor code for the agency that you pay sales taxes to, such as **salestaxes**. I will go into the ramifications and thoughts behind vendor codes later. Unlike previous versions of Peachtree, the vendor ID need not be a permanent choice here, so don't worry about it too much.

12. Enter the agency name that you pay sales taxes to in the Name field. This is usually something like **Comptroller of Public Accounts**.

13. We will skip the General tab for now. Click on the **Purchase Defaults** tab.

    Use the Lookup button (the magnifying glass) to locate the general ledger account Sales Tax Payable. Peachtree's standard account is usually 23100.

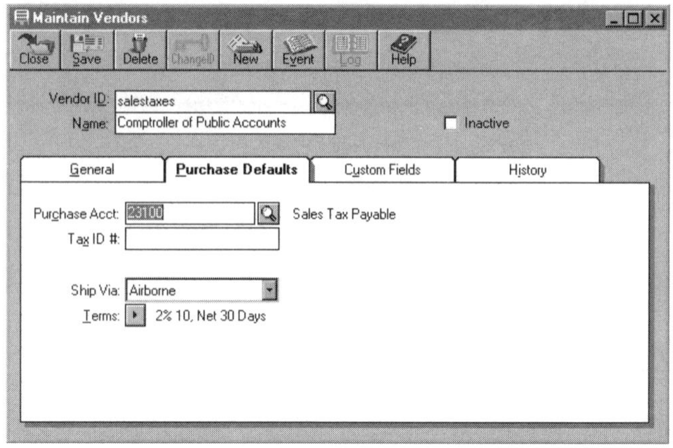

14. Click the **Save** button in the toolbar and then click the **Close** button.
15. You are now back at the Maintain Sales Tax Authorities screen. If you click on the Lookup button for the Tax Payable To field, you will now notice one vendor in the list. Select the vendor and then click **OK.**

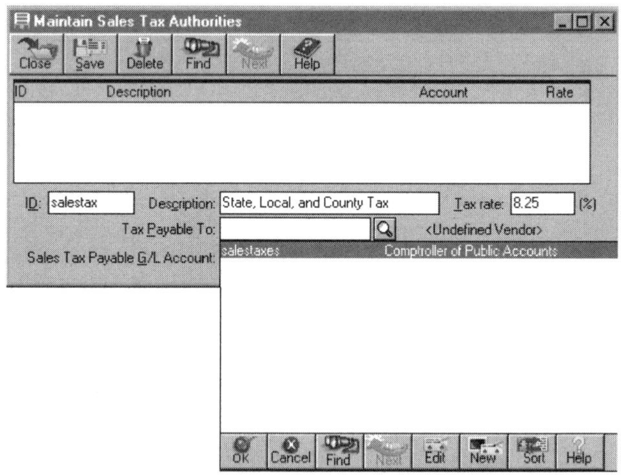

16. In the Sales Tax Payable G/L Account field, enter the same general ledger account that we used on the Maintain Vendors screen.
17. Click the **Save** button and then click **Close** to return to the Maintain Sales Tax Codes screen.
18. Back in the ID field, right-click the mouse to bring up the list of authorities and select the one we just created.
19. Click **Save** to finish creating the sales tax code.

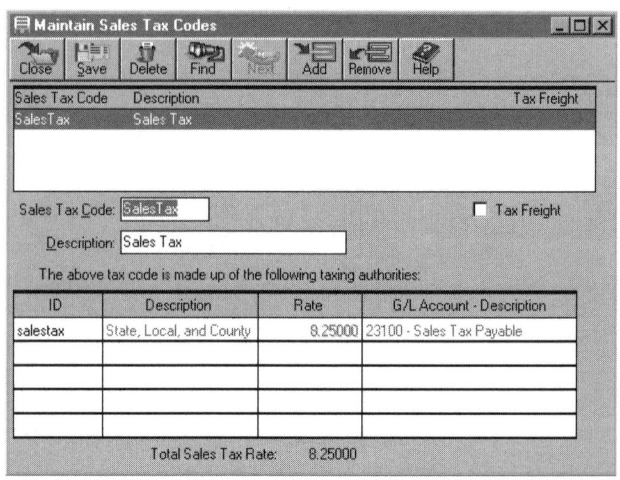

    I know this seems a great number of steps for such a little chore, but it's very important to get this first sales tax code in so we can correctly account for our sales taxes. It is interesting to note that many companies overpay their sales taxes. Correctly entering the sales taxes will result in money that is rightfully yours staying with you.

Entering Invoices

Once the sales tax account information is entered, we can enter our first invoice.

Note: If you need to keep strict track of inventory, you will want to go to Chapter 10 before you start entering invoices.

First, get all the information together to enter an invoice that was recently created in your current (pre-Peachtree) accounting system or an invoice that you are getting ready to enter.

1. On the navigation aid, click the **Receivables** or **Sales** folder, then click the **Sales/Invoicing** icon.

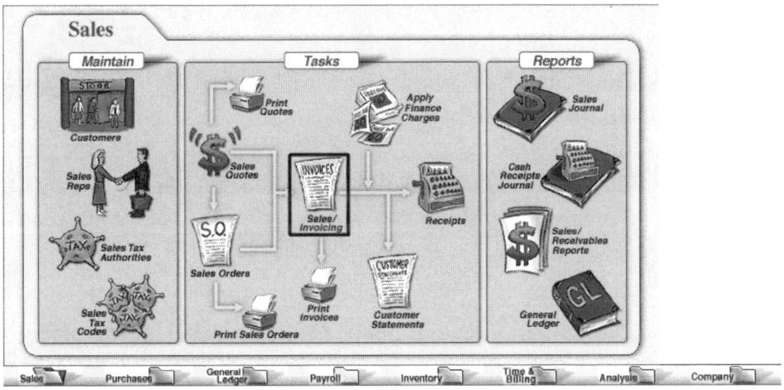

Or select **Tasks** from the menu bar and then select **Sales/Invoicing.**

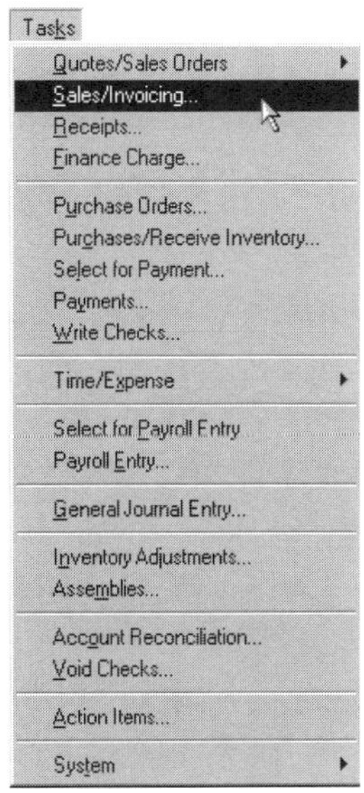

Or using the keyboard, press **Alt+K**, then **S**.

2. The Sales/Invoicing form appears.

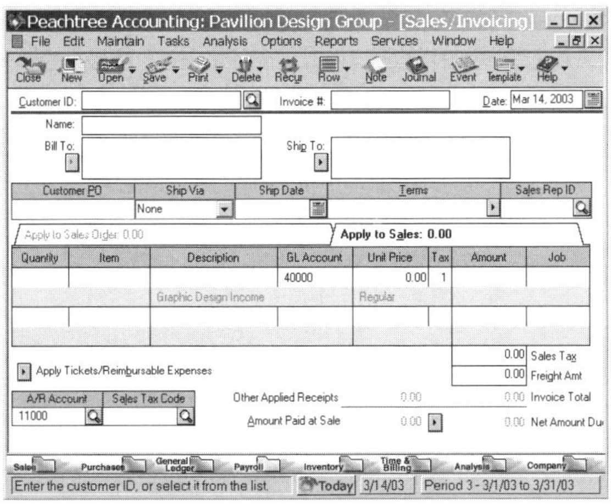

Take a quick look at the form and note a few things. We have maximized the Sales/Invoicing form so that it completely fills the Peachtree window. If you cannot see the A/R Account field in the lower left, click on the **Maximize** button in the upper right corner of the Sales/Invoicing form. The title bar of the program shows the name of the program — Peachtree Accounting, the company name — Bellwether Garden Supply, and the name of the form that we are using — Sales/Invoicing. You can always tell where you are by looking at the title bar.

In the lower right-hand corner is the system date and the current period. If the accounting period showing is not the current period, you need to change it. Changing the accounting period is covered in Chapter 2.

3. Click the **Lookup** button in the Customer ID field and select a customer from the list, or using the keyboard shortcut, type **?** in the field to display the list.

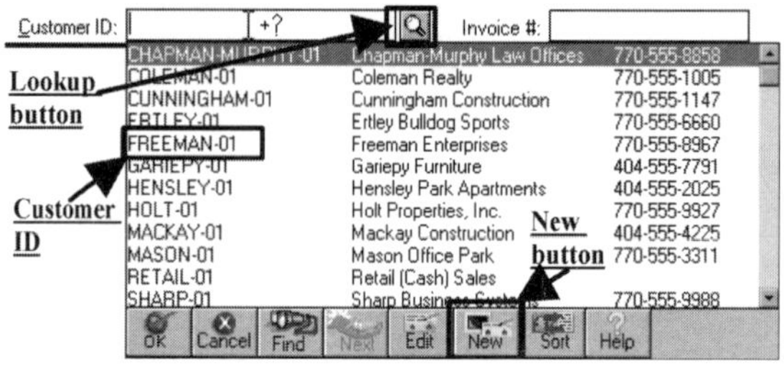

There is a good chance that you haven't entered any customers yet, in which case the list will be blank. We can add customers directly from the Peachtree Sales/Invoicing form. The program does not require us to back out of this screen and go to another part of the program. To add customers on the fly, skip ahead to the following section. If you already have customers, continue with Step 4.

4. After entering the customer in the Customer ID field, use the Tab key to move to the Invoice # field. Leave this field blank. Peachtree will add the invoice number when you print the invoice. Use the Tab key to move to the next field.

Note: The invoice number is how Peachtree determines if the invoice has been printed or not. If the Invoice # field has a number, it is assumed to have been printed. An empty field means that the invoice is waiting to print.

5. Enter the invoice date in the Date field. You can type it as **1/1/03** or **010103**; both will work the same way. You can also click on the Calendar button to view the mini-calendar. After clicking the button, click the date to select it or click the arrow buttons to move to a different month (single arrow) or year (double arrow).

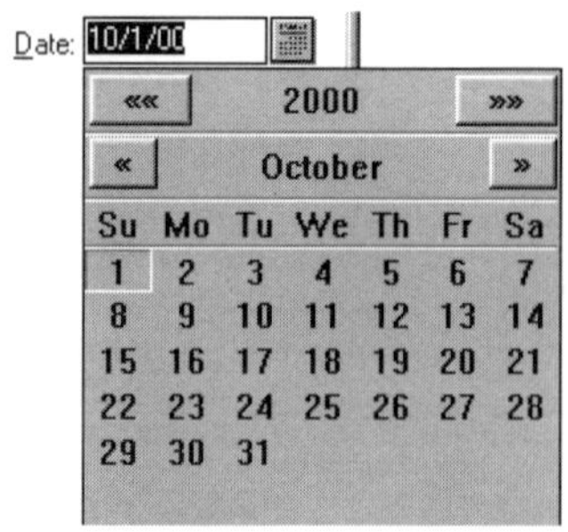

6. The Ship To field is where your product will be sent if it is not going to the billing address. Click on the **Ship To** button (the arrow below Ship To) and the Ship To Address dialog box appears.

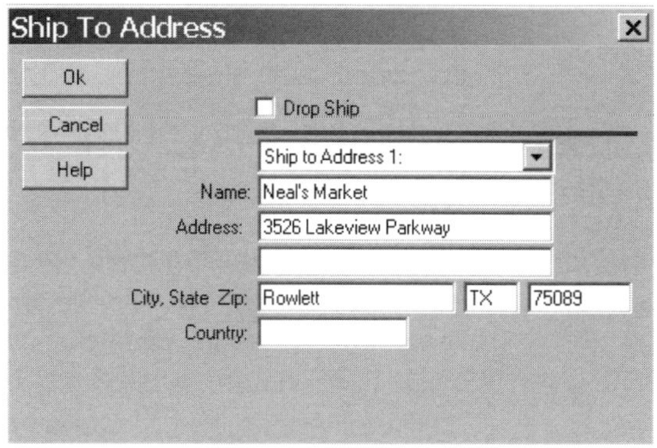

7. Enter the address where the order is to be sent or select one of the shipping addresses or the billing address for the customer. If the order is going to a site directly from the vendor, click the **Drop Ship** check box. Click **OK**.

Warning!! Ship to addresses added here will not be saved in the customer file for permanent use. The address is only saved with this invoice. To add a frequently used shipping address, go to the Maintain Customers form and add the address there.

8. The Customer PO (Customer Purchase Order) field is automatically filled in if the customer has a PO number in the Open P.O. # field on the customer form. If there is no PO showing or the wrong PO is showing, you may type a new number.
9. The customer's preferred shipping method appears in the Ship Via field. Change the shipping method by clicking the drop-down button and selecting a new method from the list.
10. The Ship Date field contains the date that the product left your company. It is often earlier than the invoice date. Change the date by clicking the Calendar button and selecting a date from the mini-calendar.
11. The customer's preferred payment terms appears in the Terms field. Click on the Terms drop-down button to view the Terms Information dialog box. Make the changes and click **OK**. Making a change here does not change the information on the customer form, only on this invoice.

12. The Sales Rep ID comes from the list of employees. Employees are covered in Chapter 9. If an employee is a sales rep, the person's employee ID will show in this list and can be assigned to this invoice.
13. The Apply to Sales tab will be showing and should be the only active tab. The Apply to Sales Order tab should be grayed out because there are no existing sales orders at this time.
14. Enter the line items as follows:

    Quantity — If this is a job, enter 1; if hours, sets, pieces, etc., enter the number of items. Depending upon how your options are set, numbers in this field are entered in different ways. Typing 3475 may give you 34.75 or it may give you 3475.00. We discussed changing decimal entry options in Chapter 2.

Item — If you sell a lot of the same services or items or you are tracking inventory, you will want to enter the item ID here. The item ID will automatically complete the Description, GL Account, Unit Price, and Tax fields. Items can be used for inventoried product or parts so that when you sell an item, it is deducted from the inventory. You can also use items to speed up your data entry. If you go on service calls and your employees bring back service call reports that are filled out, you might have an item called Service Call. The description could be See service call report for details. After entering the number of hours and the item ID, everything else on the line would be completed and would reduce the time to prepare an invoice. See Chapter 10 for more information on inventory.

Description — Type the full description. The maximum size of the description is about 160 characters or 5½ normal lines. To place a line break in the field, press **Ctrl+Enter**.

GL Account — This should be a G/L Income account unless this is an unusual item. A default account will populate this field from the default GL Sales Account field on the customer's record if an item was not entered. Change this to another account by clicking on the Lookup button and finding the account number in the list or by typing the number into the field directly.

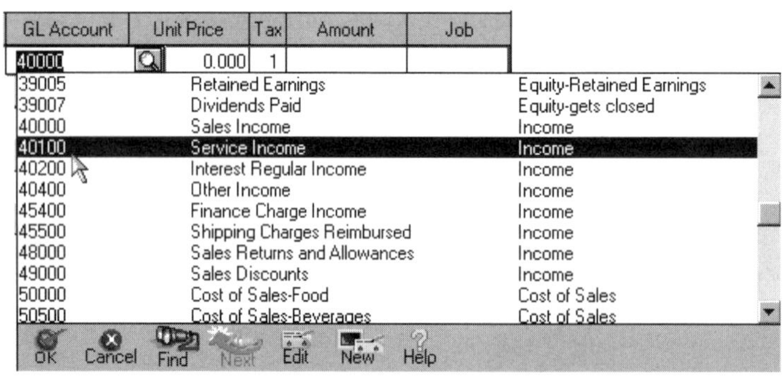

Unit Price — If you know the price per unit (and there is a number in Quantity), type it here. When you tab from the field, the value for Amount is calculated.

Tax — If the line item (service or item) is taxable, this should show a taxable number, such as 1. If the line item is non-taxable, this should show a 2 (or some other applicable number if more than one sales tax code is used) for exempt.

Amount — The amount is calculated from the Quantity and Unit Price fields. You can also work the calculations backward by leaving either the Quantity or the Unit Price fields blank. If you enter the Unit Price and Amount, the Quantity is calculated. If you enter the Quantity and Amount, the Unit Price is calculated.

Job — Jobs are not covered in this book.

15. Enter other line items on this invoice as needed.
16. Verify that the A/R Account field has the correct G/L account showing.
17. For taxable customers, verify that the sales tax code is showing. In order for sales tax to be charged, the customer needs to be a taxable customer and the items or services sold need to also be taxable. In the case where a non-taxable customer needs to be taxed, the Sales Tax Code field at the bottom of the Sales/Invoicing form must show a tax code. If the tax rate isn't the standard percent, figure the tax manually and enter the amount in the Sales Tax field on the lower right.
18. Verify that the values in the Sales Tax and Invoice Total fields are correct.
19. Fill in the Freight Amt field, if needed.

    A completed sample invoice is shown in the following figure.

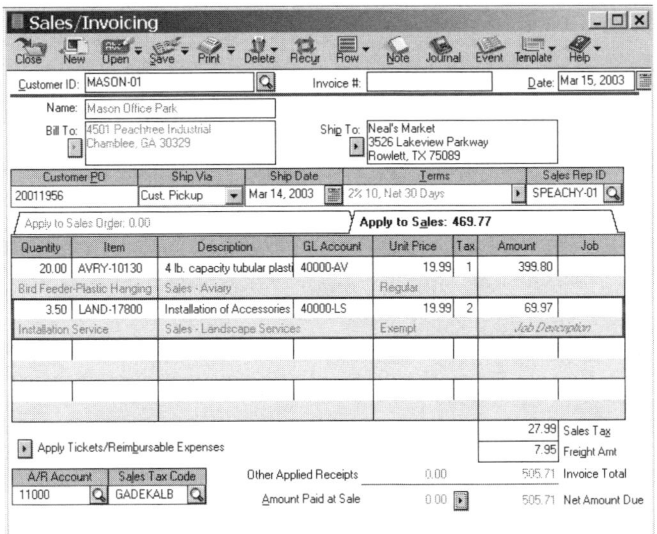

Adding a Customer "On the Fly"

1. If adding invoices, click the **Lookup** button in the Customer ID field and click the **New** button in the toolbar.

   Or enter + in the Customer ID field.

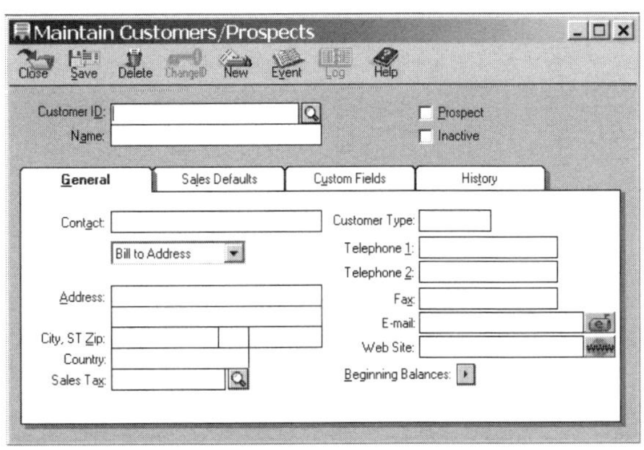

2. An empty Maintain Customers/Prospects form appears.

   Enter a unique identifier in the Customer ID field to describe this customer.

Note: What makes a good ID? A good ID is one that is consistent with other IDs so that all IDs are organized and sorted easily. We discussed ID sorting in Chapter 2. If you use Peachtree with the Caps Lock key on, your IDs should be in all capital letters. If you don't use all capitals, IDs should be in lowercase. Make sure that the data entry people use a consistent standard for entering IDs. I personally prefer IDs to be in all lowercase with no spaces or other punctuation (i.e., wolfcompany or dnbconsultants).

Warning!! Also, have a way for all the people entering customers to track the customers entered so as to not double-enter records. That way a client does not have two sets of records (i.e., THEWOLFCO and WOLFCOMPANY).

3. Fill in the Name and Contact fields.
4. Peachtree handles customer addresses with the Address Type field (located under Contact) since customers have an address that you send the invoices to and may also have different addresses that the product is sent to. Select **Bill to Address** in the Address Type field.

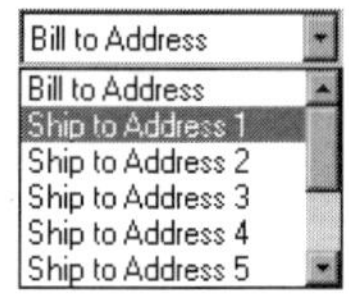

5. Enter the customer's mailing address in the fields provided. Peachtree only allows you two fields for the street address. The Country field can be ignored for U.S. addresses.
6. The next field is the Sales Tax field. This field should only have an entry if the customer is assessed sales tax. Leave this field blank for exempt customers. Select the correct sales tax code for customers that pay sales tax.

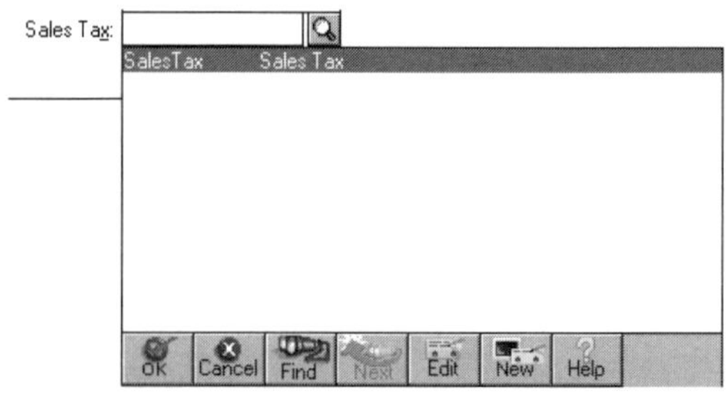

7. Ignore the Customer Type field for now.
8. Enter the phone numbers and other contact information. Be sure to use the correct fields.
9. Select the **Sales Defaults** tab. Ignore the Sales Rep field for now and go to the GL Sales Acct field. Enter the most used sales account for this customer in this field or use the Miscellaneous Sales account.

   Ignore the rest of this tab for now.

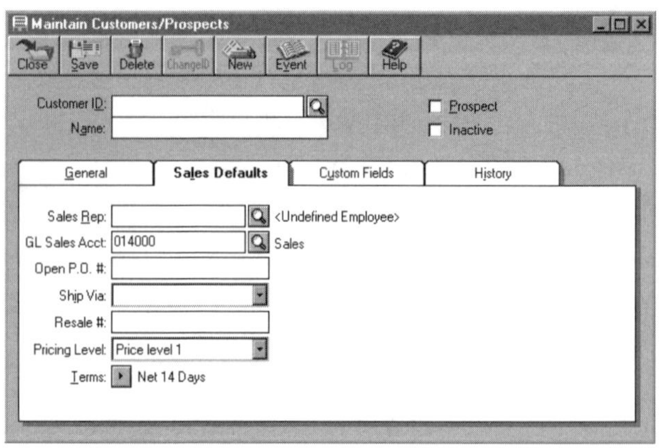

10. Click the **Save** button in the toolbar to save the new record.

11. Click the **Close** button to return to the Sales/Invoicing form.

    If you added customers on the fly while entering invoices, return to Step 4 in the previous section.

Printing and Saving an Invoice

Now that the invoice information has been entered, we need to save it and print it. Both tasks are accomplished by clicking the Print button.

1. Click the **Print** button on the toolbar or, if you want to see what the invoice looks like on the screen, click the drop-down button next to the Print button and click **Preview**. The Print and Preview dialogs are the same. Print sends the form to the printer, and Preview sends the form to the screen.
2. The Print Forms or Preview Forms dialog box appears.

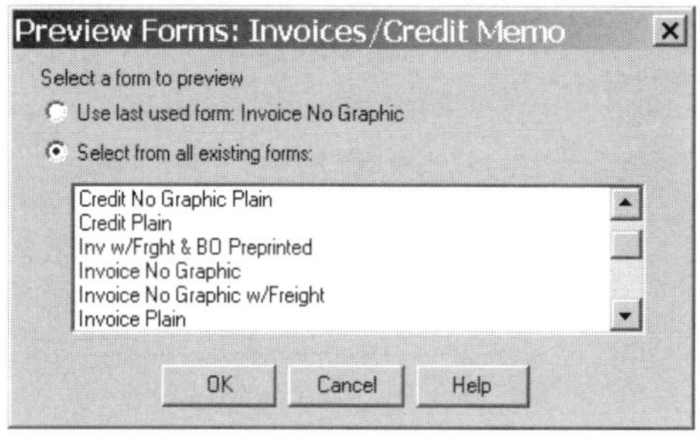

3. There are two options in this dialog box. The first allows you to print or preview the last form that you used. The first time you open this dialog box this option will be disabled. The second option lists all available forms.

   Select the appropriate form to use, such as Invoice Plain. You may want to preview some of the different forms by clicking the **Preview** button in the invoicing form before choosing a form to use.

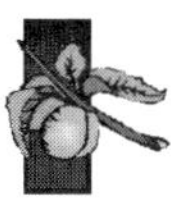

Note: I am often asked whether to use laser (or inkjet) forms or continuous dot-matrix forms and whether to use preprinted forms or plain paper. Whether you use preprinted forms or not is a matter of choice and how professional you want your invoices to look. I prefer plain paper for the cost savings. For companies that do a lot of invoices, I suggest using multipart dot-matrix plain paper or printed forms. You can easily print simple graphics and logos on a dot-matrix printer and you get multiple copies at the same time. On the other hand, it is becoming more common to print multiple times rather than go through the hassles of tractor-fed, multipart forms. With the growing scarcity of dot-matrix printers, the more professional look of laser printing, the drop in price of laser printers and supplies, and the speed of laser compared to dot matrix, laser printing is becoming the standard.

4. Click **OK**. Another, smaller, Print Forms dialog box appears.

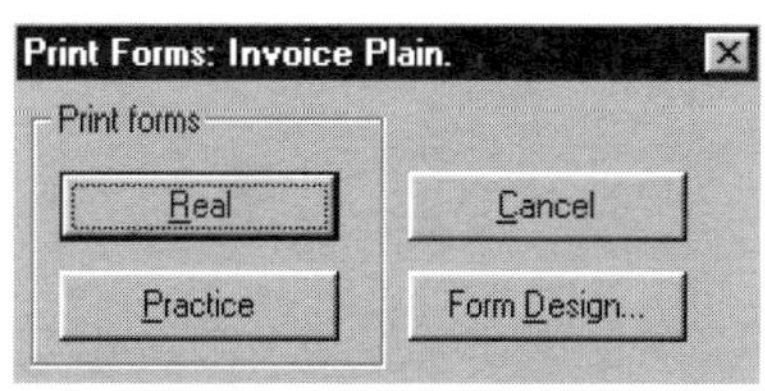

   I've never figured out why these choices are here. The Practice button prints a dummy invoice and the Form Design button takes you to the form designer. Both those functions are better handled in the Reports section. Click the **Real** button. With the exception of printing a dummy invoice to verify the alignment of tractor-fed forms and the unusual times when you will need to go to form design to temporarily select a different destination printer, the Real button will be the only one you use.

5. The About to Print Invoices dialog box appears.

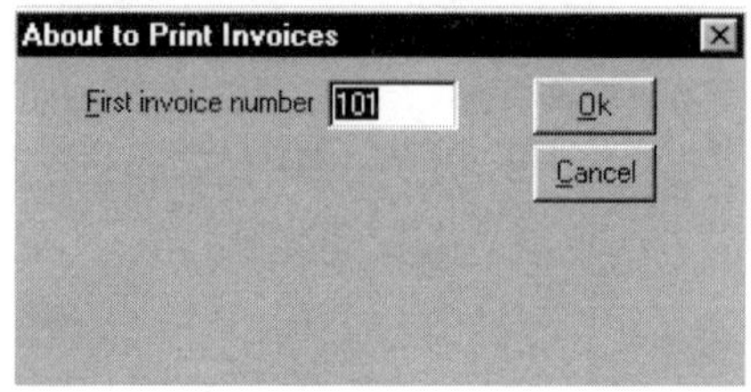

   Here is where you enter the invoice number for this invoice. If you use preprinted, prenumbered invoices, this should match the current form. If you use plain paper and generate invoice numbers, this can be any number either following your current sequence of invoices or not.

   Luckily, once the first invoice number is created, the program remembers the last number used and simply adds one to the current number. Peachtree also handles invoice numbers with letters in them, but not quite as successfully as numerical sequences.

6. Click **OK**.

   The invoice prints to the computer's current default printer. If you selected Invoice Plain and printed on a laser printer, the invoice will look something like this:

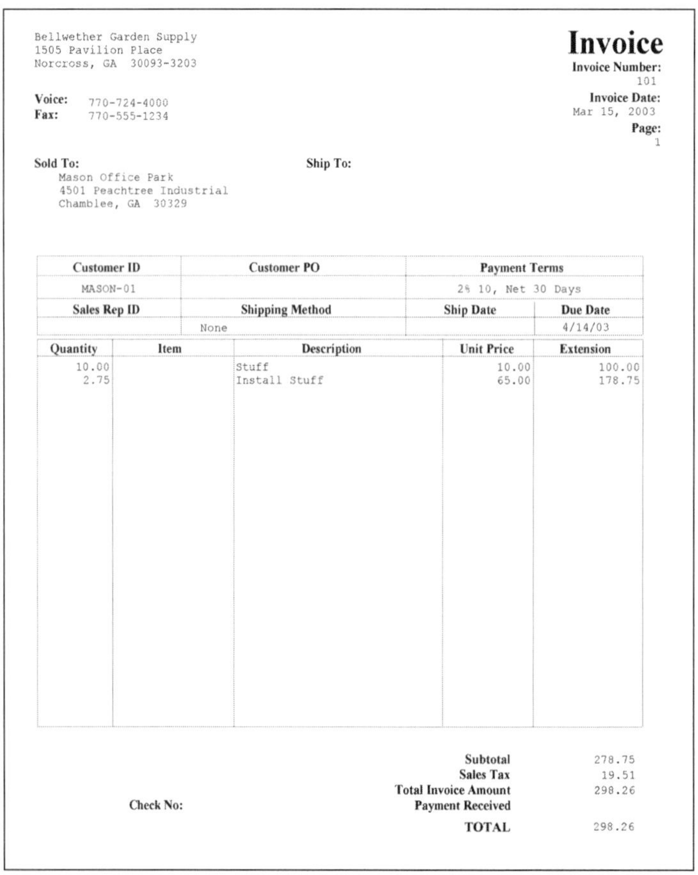

Bellwether Garden Supply
1505 Pavilion Place
Norcross, GA 30093-3203

Voice: 770-724-4000
Fax: 770-555-1234

Invoice

Invoice Number: 101
Invoice Date: Mar 15, 2003
Page: 1

Sold To:
Mason Office Park
4501 Peachtree Industrial
Chamblee, GA 30329

Ship To:

Customer ID	Customer PO	Payment Terms	
MASON-01		2% 10, Net 30 Days	
Sales Rep ID	**Shipping Method**	**Ship Date**	**Due Date**
	None		4/14/03

Quantity	Item	Description	Unit Price	Extension
10.00		Stuff	10.00	100.00
2.75		Install Stuff	65.00	178.75

Subtotal	278.75
Sales Tax	19.51
Total Invoice Amount	298.26
Payment Received	
TOTAL	298.26

Check No:

Click **Save** or **Post** to save the invoice without printing.

Note: A time-saver that I have discovered while printing invoices is to use the keyboard. It works as long as you print the same form and you don't change the invoice number. Press **Ctrl+P** to access the print function. Then press the **Enter** key four times (the About to Print dialog box takes two keystrokes). This eliminates the use of the mouse and speeds up your keyboard-driven data entry people.

Invoices and Accounting Behind the Scenes

One of the nice things about a computerized accounting program is that you rarely have to worry about the debits and credits of the transactions you are processing. On the rare occasion that you do want to view the actual entries, you can do so in the newer versions of the program.

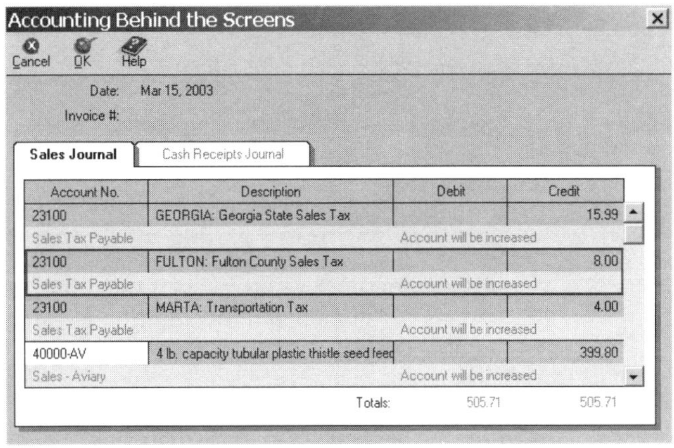

On the Sales/Invoicing form, click the **Journal** button on the toolbar. The Accounting Behind the Screens form appears.

The Sales Journal will be selected and the journal entry for this transaction will be showing. It is possible to change the sales account and the accounts receivable account on this form, but no other changes are permitted. Tax accounts, freight accounts, and COGS accounts are not changeable. The debits and credits will balance. Some lines, such as COGS, may show amounts that are to be calculated.

Entering Invoices Homework

After your first invoice is entered, you need to locate all invoices from earlier in this month and enter them here. The goal this month is to enter all invoices for this month in Peachtree, in addition to adding them to your old accounting system.

Once you have the knack of entering invoices, you may go on to another task.

Editing Invoices

Sometimes, you will need to make a change to an existing invoice. Peachtree makes it very easy to change existing transactions. This is both a good and a bad thing. It's good because it means you do not have to void incorrect transactions or create credit memos to fix incorrect invoices. You can just make the change on the original document and reprint it. It's bad because making the changes becomes very easy and you may make even more mistakes.

To edit an existing invoice, follow these steps:

1. From the Sales/Invoicing form, click the **Open** button.

   In earlier versions of the program this was the **Edit** button.

2. The Select Invoice window appears.

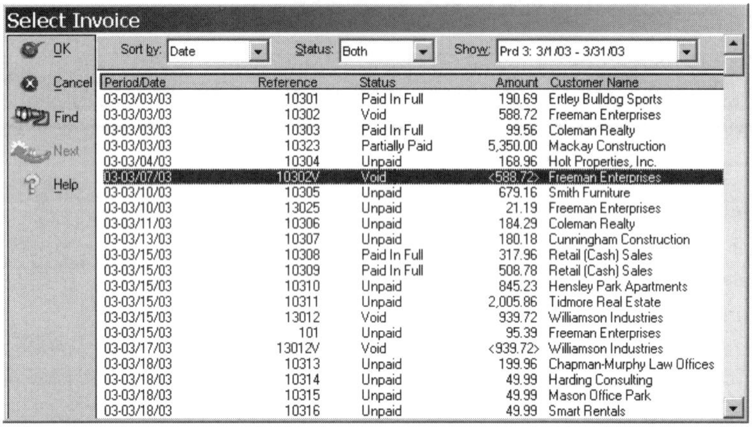

   Invoices may be sorted by date, by reference (the invoice number), or by ID (customer ID). The current accounting period transactions show in the window. You may select another period from the Show drop-down list. Remember, if you use batch posting, you can select to view invoices that are posted, unposted, or both.

3. Locate the desired invoice and click **OK** to return to the Sales/Invoicing form.

4. Edit the invoice as needed. If an invoice cannot be edited, information will be grayed out. In that case you will need to void the transaction or create a credit memo. Click **Save** or **Post** when you are done or click **Print** to reprint the invoice.

Voiding or Deleting an Invoice

There are two ways to get rid of an invoice. The first method, voiding an invoice, actually just reverses the invoice by creating a customer credit memo for the entire invoice. Both the original invoice and the credit memo show in reports and lists. The second method, deleting an invoice, totally removes the invoice from the system. No record is kept of the deletion. Generally, you will want to void invoices, not delete them, so that you will have a tracking of what has happened and can account for all changes. Deleting the invoice may appear to be easier, but the lack of accountability of the action falls into the category of "bad thing." Caution your employees about deleting invoices.

Voiding an Invoice — Customer Credit Memos

1. Select the invoice to be voided and bring it up on the Sales/Invoicing form.
2. Click the drop-down arrow next to the Delete button and then click the **Void** button. On earlier versions the Void button is separate on the toolbar.

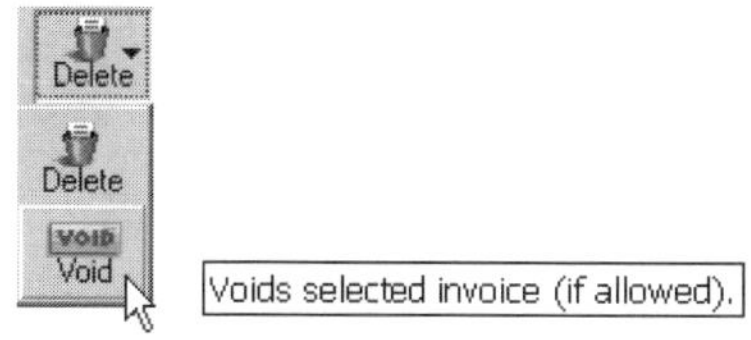

3. The Void Existing Invoice dialog box appears.

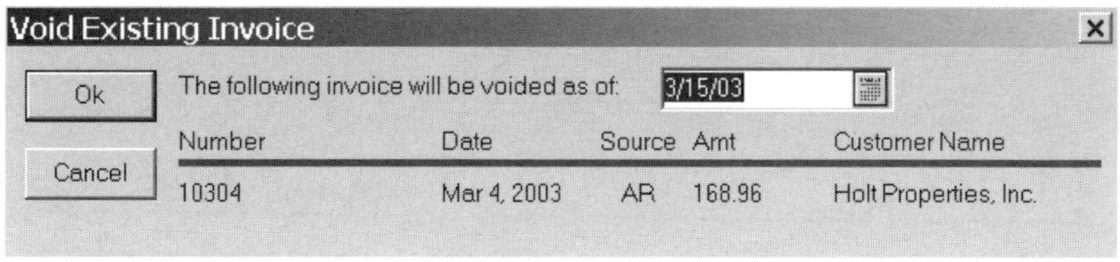

Verify that this is the correct invoice to void.

4. Select the date that the invoice is to be voided. Sometimes you will want this to be the same day as the original invoice and sometimes you will want it to be the actual date that it is voided.
5. Click **OK.**
6. In the Select Invoice window, notice that both the original and the new voided invoice appear with Void in the Status column. The voided invoice also has the same invoice number, but with a V at the end.

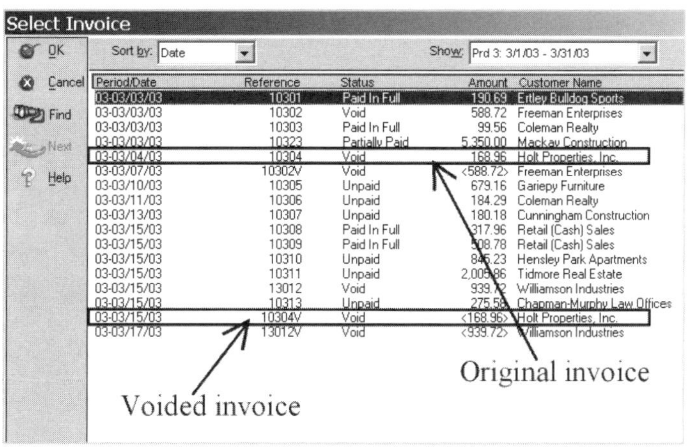

Some invoices, such as those that have already been paid, cannot be voided. In those cases, the Void button will be grayed out.

If you need to send out a customer credit memo, you can do so by printing the voided invoice and using one of the credit memos as the form to print.

Deleting an Invoice

1. Select the invoice to be deleted and bring it up on the Sales/Invoicing form.
2. Click the Delete drop-down arrow and then click the lower **Delete** button.

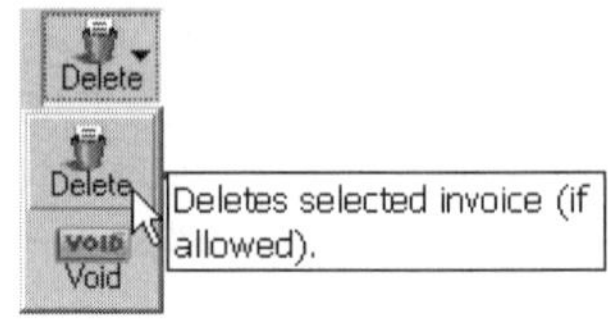

3. A confirmation message box appears.

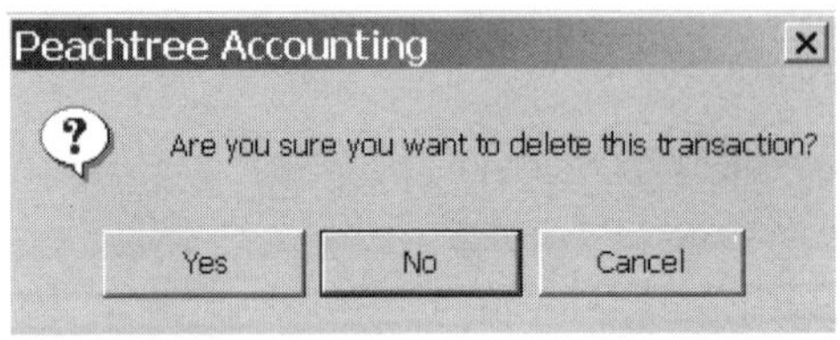

   Click **Yes** to delete.
4. In the Select Invoice window notice that the original invoice is no longer in the system.

   Some invoices, such as those that have already been paid, cannot be deleted. In those cases, the Delete button will be grayed out.

Other Invoicing Forms and Functions

After you have some of your invoices entered, you may decide that you should be entering information before you actually start work on a project or order. You may also discover the need to send out packing slips. Another situation is when you cannot void an invoice and you need to create a credit memo. Peachtree can meet all of these needs.

Quotes

Quotes are entered just like invoices with one important difference — quotes do not make changes to your general ledger or your inventory. They are held in a kind of limbo until converted or purged.

1. To enter quotes, click on **Receivables** or **Sales**, **Sales Quotes** on the navigation aid.

   Or select **Tasks**, **Quotes/Sales Orders**, **Quotes** from the menu bar or press **Alt+K**, then **Q**, and **Q** using the keyboard shortcuts.

2. The Quotes form appears.

   Fill in the Customer ID, Ship To, Date, Customer PO, Ship Via, Displayed Terms, and Sales Rep ID fields as you would on an invoice.

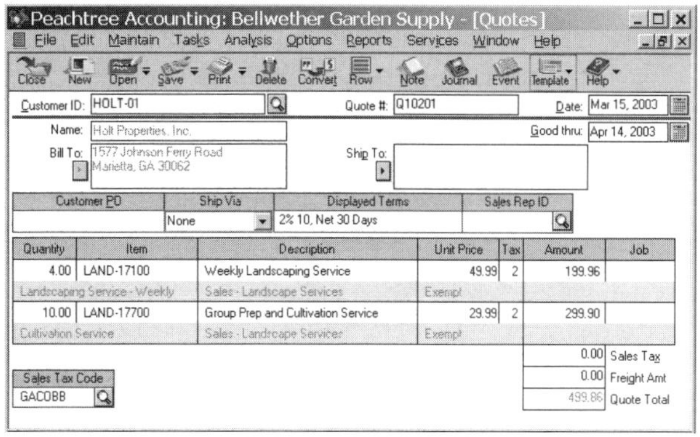

3. The Good thru field is the last date that this quote is usable by the customer. Peachtree defaults to 30 days, but you can change the date to whatever you desire.
4. The Quote # field is generally left empty and filled when the quote is printed. Remember that this field tells Peachtree whether the quote has been printed earlier.
5. Enter the line items for the quote. This information can be easily changed later.
6. The sales tax is automatically calculated. Verify the Sales Tax Code field. In earlier versions, the A/R Account also appears as a field on the form. Verify the account.
7. Fill in the Freight Amt field if freight is involved.
8. You can check the future journal entry for this quote, once it becomes an invoice, by clicking the **Journal** button. Notice the message on the Accounting Behind the Screens form.

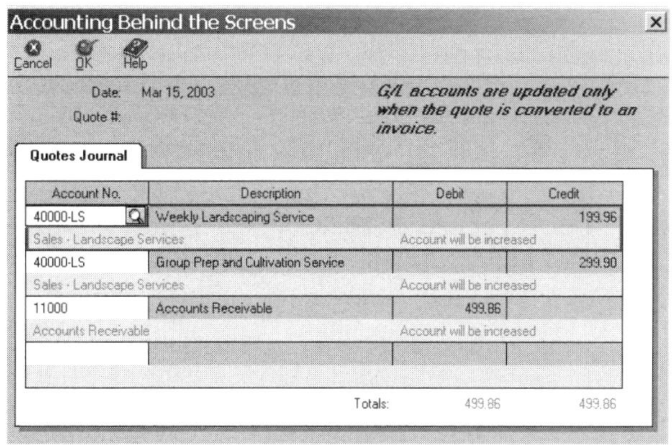

9. Print the quote by clicking the **Print** button and following the same steps for printing an invoice. The only difference is the forms.

Quotes are edited, voided, and deleted in the same way that invoices are. Converting quotes is covered later in this chapter.

Sales Orders

Sales orders have two significant uses. The first use is when customers place one large order with you and the order is sent out in batches under separate invoices. The second is when your company creates documents to be used in your plant or shop for internal use, although this is generally called a work order rather than a sales order. Just like quotes, sales orders do not make changes to your general ledger or your inventory. They are held in a kind of limbo until invoiced or deleted.

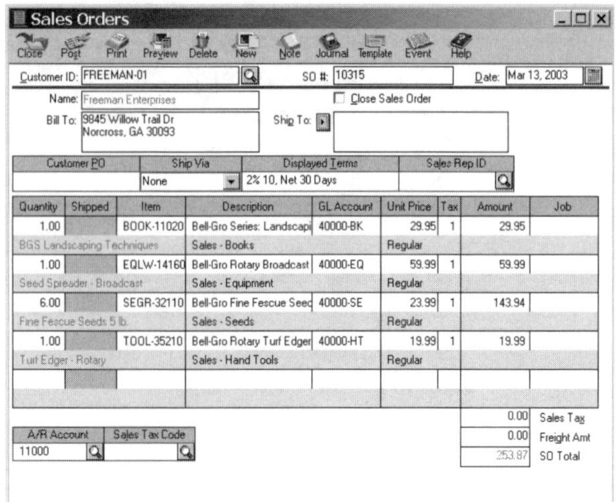

1. Open the Sales Orders form by clicking **Receivables** or **Sales**, **Sales Orders** on the navigation aid or selecting **Tasks**, **Quotes/Sales Order**, **Sales Orders** from the menu bar, or pressing **Alt+K**, **Q**, **O** using the keyboard shortcuts.
2. The sales order is entered just like an invoice or a quote except that you type the sales order number directly in the SO # field. Once the first SO # is typed, Peachtree automatically increments the sales order number by one each time you create a new sales order.
3. Enter the line items for the sales order. You may edit this information if it needs changing later.
4. The sales tax is automatically calculated. Verify the Sales Tax Code field. Depending upon your version of Peachtree and the defaults that have been selected, the A/R Account field may also appear as a field on the form. If it shows, verify the account.
5. Fill in the Freight Amt field if freight is involved.
6. You can check the future journal entry for this sales order, once it becomes an invoice, by clicking the **Journal** button. Notice the message on the Accounting Behind the Screens form.

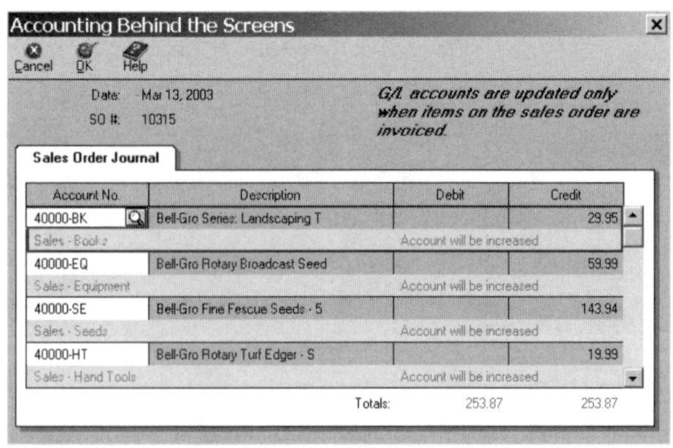

7. Print the sales order by clicking the **Print** button and following the same steps for printing an invoice. The only difference is the forms.

Sales orders are edited and deleted in the same way that invoices are. You do not void sales orders; instead you click on the Close Sales Order check box.

Sales orders are often not printed. That is why the sales order number appears on the form automatically.

Creating an Invoice from a Sales Order

Once a sales order is created, you can use it to create one or more invoices.

1. Open the Sales/ Invoicing form.
2. Fill in the Customer ID field.
3. Select the **Apply to Sales Order #** tab.
4. Click on the **Sales Order** drop-down button. It currently shows <No SO Selected>.

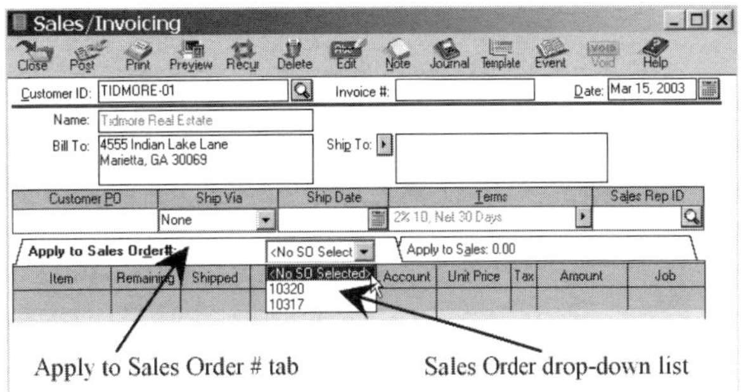

5. Select a sales order from the list. The sales order appears in the line items. Only one sales order may appear on an invoice.

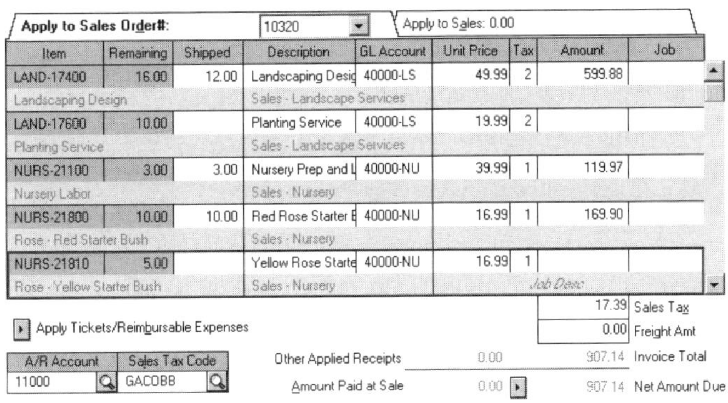

6. The Item and Remaining fields cannot be changed. Enter the quantity of items to be invoiced in the Shipped field. The amount is automatically calculated along with any applicable sales tax.
7. Verify the Sales Tax Code field. Depending on your version, A/R Account may also appear as a field on the form. Verify the account here or by clicking the **Journal** button in the toolbar.
8. Fill in the Freight Amt field if freight is involved.
9. If other items need to be included on this invoice, go to the **Apply to Sales** tab and enter the additional lines.
10. Print the invoice or click **Save** to print later.

Work Orders

Many of my customers use work orders instead of sales orders. These customers need to send a form back to the shop for manufacturing, repair, or assembly. This form tells the shop foreman what needs to be done. Some of my customers use the sales order function to create work orders and some use the quote function. Generally, if you might be shipping partial orders, use the sales order function. I personally prefer the quote function to create work orders when partial shipments are not a problem. Either choice is fine; you should just be consistent and choose one method.

Generally, a shop work order will show quantities, items, and descriptions, but not pricing or total information. You may also want to include a line for sign-off by the person doing the work. Some work orders allow space for a drawing. See Chapter 18 for information on creating your own work orders.

Follow these steps to implement work orders:

1. The first thing you need to create a work order is the work order form to be printed. Two generic work orders are included in the companion files, one for using the sales order function and the other for using the quote function. These forms may be copied to the PEACHW folder on your hard drive if you wish to use them. (Some network installations require you to copy the forms to the network PEACHW folder.) You should also copy the forms to your company folder under the PEACHW folder. This way when you create a backup, you will also be backing up your custom forms. Unfortunately, these forms are only good for the latest versions of Peachtree.
2. Open either the Sales Orders form or the Quotes form and create the work order. Remember that you don't need to enter a quote number with quotes.
3. Print the form using the new form that was copied to the hard drive. I prefer to print these forms on a dot-matrix printer using three-part carbonless paper.
4. File one copy of the work order in the pending file.
5. The two remaining parts go to the shop foreman. When the work is completed, the foreman keeps one copy for the shop records and returns the remaining copy to the accounting department along with any notes or editing that may be required.
6. The accounting person goes into Peachtree and makes any needed changes to the work order and, using the notes, converts the quote to an invoice or opens the sales order in the invoice function.

Tip: If your shop has a secure network station, the shop foreman can make changes directly to the work order. Just be sure that the foreman has adequate computer skills and that other employees do not have access to the machine. (You would be surprised how computer savvy some employees can be — or worse, how their lack of knowledge can cripple your system.) Also make sure that you have good security in place.

Converting Quotes to Sales Orders or Invoices

Use this process to convert a quote to an invoice or a sales order. If you are using work orders through the quotes function, you will use this same process to convert a work order to an invoice.

1. Open the Quotes form.
2. Click the **Edit** button and locate the quote to be converted to an invoice or sales order. Click **OK** to bring it to the Quotes form.
3. Make any necessary changes to the quote before converting it. The most common change is to change the date to the correct invoice date.
4. Click the **Convert** button. 

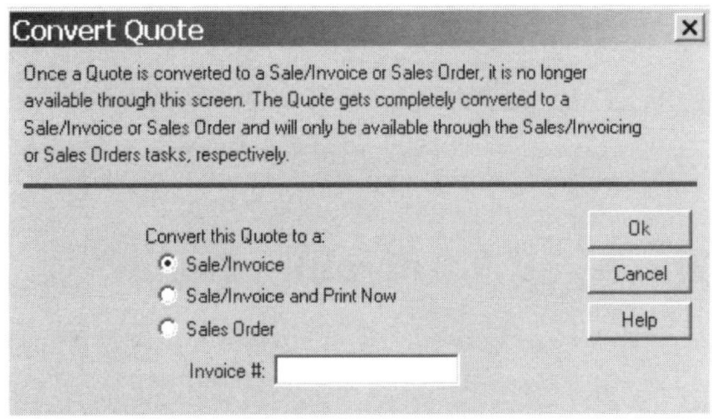

5. The Convert Quote dialog box appears.

   Select a conversion option as follows:

   Sale/Invoice — This option converts the invoice for later printing. You may fill in the Invoice # field or leave it blank. The new invoice will appear in the invoice list without an invoice number or with the entered invoice number. Remember that if you input the invoice number Peachtree will interpret the invoice as already printed.

   Sale/Invoice and Print Now — Use this option to print the invoice now without going to the Sales/Invoicing function. You may fill in the Invoice # field or leave it blank. The invoice printing process will prompt you for an invoice number when the form prints. The new invoice will appear in the invoice list with the entered invoice number.

   Sales Order — The quote is converted to a sales order, not an invoice. The Invoice # field becomes the SO # field with the next sales order number showing. The new sales order will appear in the sales order list with the entered sales order number.

6. Click **OK**.

   The quote disappears from the quotes list.

Packing Slips

Once invoices are created, a packing slip can be printed by bringing the invoice into the Sales/Invoicing form and clicking **Print**. When the Print Forms dialog box appears, select **Packing Slip Plain** as the form to print.

Customer Credit Memos

If you need to send a credit memo to your customer, created either by using the void invoice function or by entering an invoice with a negative balance, then select one of the credit forms when printing the invoice. You can void an invoice and then edit the quantities so that an invoice is only partially voided.

An invoice with a negative balance is created by entering a regular invoice and making either the quantity or the unit price (one or the other, not both) a negative number.

Quick Invoicing Reports

The following quick reports will allow you to view information on your receivables quickly and easily. For information on changing options, exporting, designing, or printing reports, see Chapter 18.

The Aged Receivables Report

This report is a listing of all customers with outstanding balances, showing the aging of the outstanding balances.

1. Click the **Receivables** or **Sales** folder and the **Sales/Receivables Reports** icon on the navigation aid.

   Or select **Reports**, **Accounts Receivable** from the menu bar.

   Or press **Alt+R**, then **R** using the keyboard shortcuts.

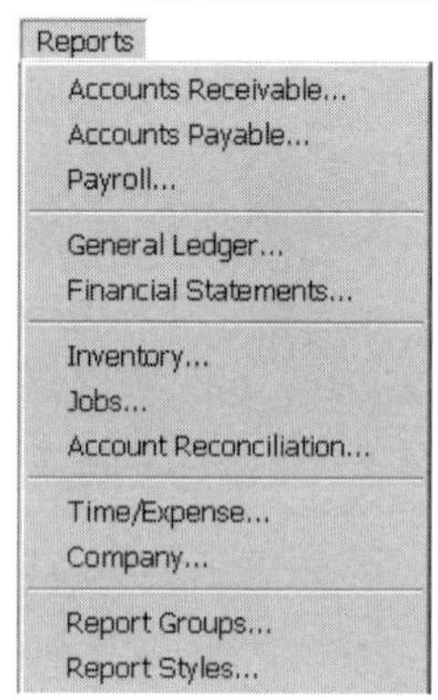

2. The Select a Report window appears.

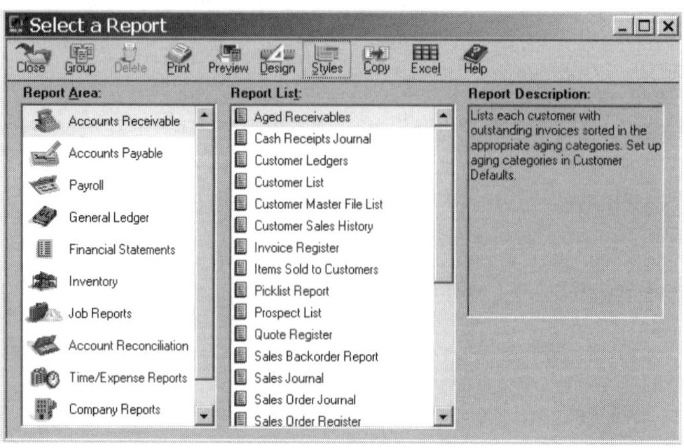

Make sure that **Accounts Receivable** is highlighted in the Report Area list. Select the **Aged Receivables** report from the Report List. Click the **Preview** button on the toolbar.

3. The Aged Receivables dialog box appears.

   Reports are sorted by customer ID or customer name.

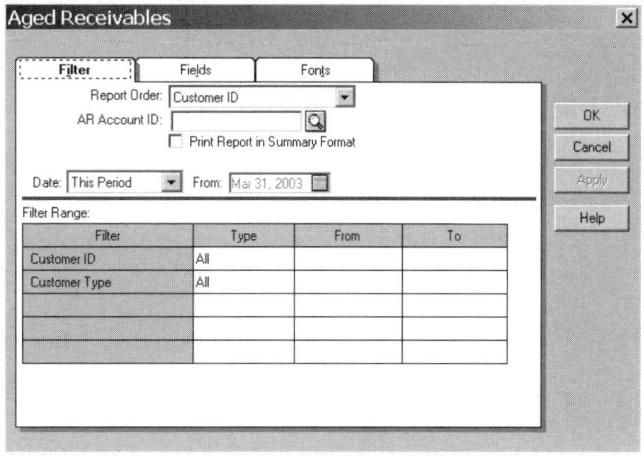

4. If you have more than one accounts receivable G/L account, select the correct G/L account in the AR Account ID field.
5. Checking **Print Report in Summary Format** will give you the totals for customers, not a listing of the individual invoices.
6. To view the report for just one customer, enter the customer ID in the From and To fields. To view the report for a range of customers, such as abccompany to defcompany, enter the IDs in the From and To fields.
7. If you use Customer Type, enter a type in the From and To fields on the Customer Type line.
8. Click **OK** to view the report.

The Customer Ledger Report

This report is a listing of all invoices and payments for a customer during a selected time period.

1. Go to the Select a Report window. (See the previous section.)
2. Select the **Customer Ledgers** report and click **Preview** on the toolbar.
3. The Customer Ledgers dialog box appears.

   The options for Report Order, Customer ID, and Customer Type are the same as for the Aged Receivables report.

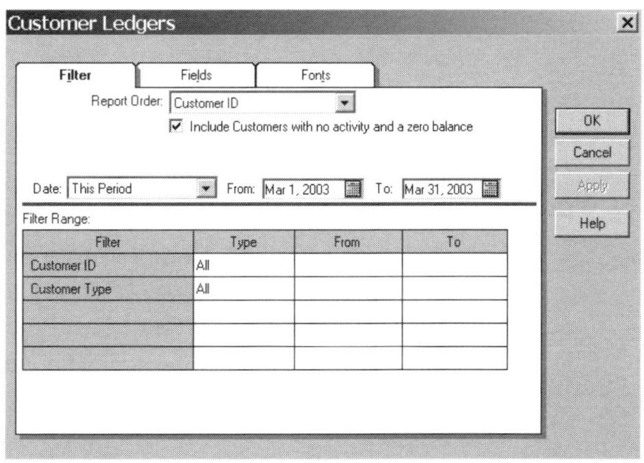

4. Checking **Include Customers with no activity and a zero balance** will show ledgers for all customers.
5. Select the date range for the report using either the Date drop-down list or the mini-calendars in the From and To fields. The report will include the customer's beginning balance, if any, for the range selected.

6. Click **OK** to view the report.

Quickly Viewing Customer Balances

This method is especially useful when a manager or a customer requests a customer's outstanding balance.

1. Go to the Maintain Customers/Prospects form.
2. Select the customer from the Customer ID drop-down list.
3. The customer's current balance shows in the lower right-hand corner.

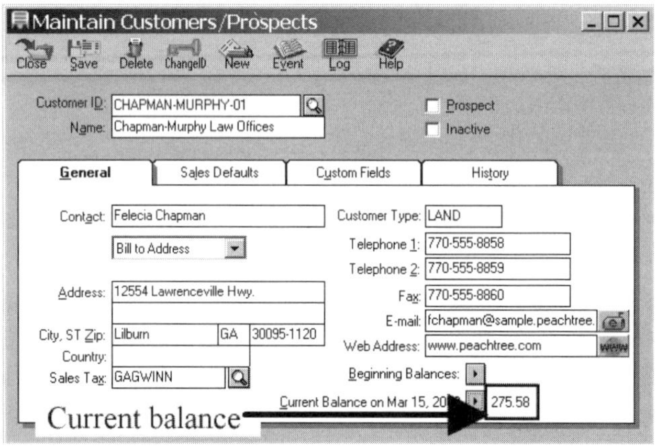

4. Click on the **Current Balance on…** button in the lower right-hand corner to view a recent customer ledger.

Summary

Invoicing is usually one of the first functions a company explores when beginning to use Peachtree. The useful tools can make sending out invoices a quick and easy task.

One of my customers had two data entry people working overtime almost every week to manually put out their invoices. They typed the quote, then the work order, then the invoice, and then the packing slip. If statements had to be sent, those were hand-typed also. Each form required typing everything over and over again — with the opportunity for errors with each rendition. The company was on the point of hiring a third data entry person when Peachtree was installed. Immediately, the data entry people were able to get all the work done without hiring a new person and without any more overtime since the repeated reentry of information was no longer necessary. This obviously represented a huge savings for the company.

Now, get your homework done and get those invoices entered. You will probably want to tackle cash receipts next.

Chapter 6

Cash Receipts

In This Chapter

- Applying receipts to invoices
- Entering receipts without an invoice
- Entering customers' beginning balances
- Credit card and other types of payments
- Quick cash receipts reports

Now that you have invoices entered into the computer, you will want to apply checks to those invoices as soon as they arrive. Receipts are the transactions that allow you to put money in your bank account. There are two types of cash receipts, those with invoices and those without. We will cover applying cash receipts to invoices first. In this chapter we will cover received checks, credit card payments, and cash and how these payments are entered against outstanding invoices or applied directly to a G/L account.

Getting Started

Almost immediately, unless your business is cash only, you will have a check to deposit for an invoice in an earlier month. One way to get these invoices into the computer is to sit down and enter all your customers and their invoices at once. The other way is to enter most of these beginning balance invoices "on the fly" and worry about the remainder in the second month when you have more time.

Entering Beginning Balance Invoices

In Chapters 3 and 4, you were told to get an accurate A/R listing of all customers and the invoices that they owe. Here is where you start using it.

When you have a check for an invoice that is not yet in Peachtree, follow these steps:

1. Verify that the receipt matches an invoice or invoices listed on your accounts receivable ledger. If the amount does not match, you must talk to your CPA to see how she wants to handle the receipt. She may want to have you enter it as new income, she may create a journal entry in the old system to include the amount, or she may use some other method to reconcile the difference.

2. Click the **Receivables** or **Sales** folder in the navigation aid and then click the **Customers** icon in the Maintain section.

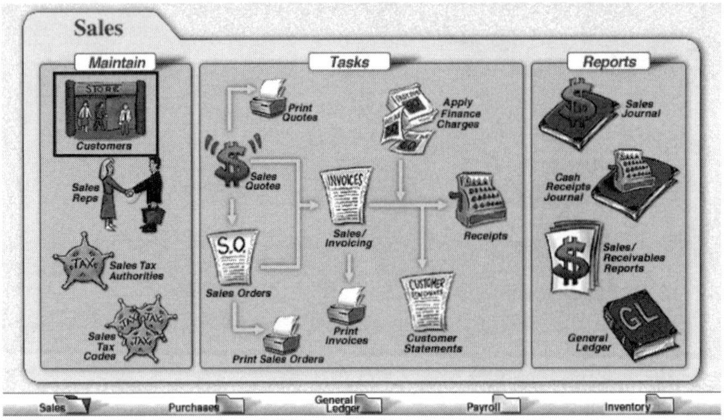

Or select **Maintain, Customers/Prospects** from the menu bar.

Or using the keyboard, press **Alt+M**, then **C**.

The Maintain Customers/Prospects screen appears.

3. Select an existing customer or add a new customer as we showed in Chapter 5.
4. Click the **Beginning Balances** button on the General tab.

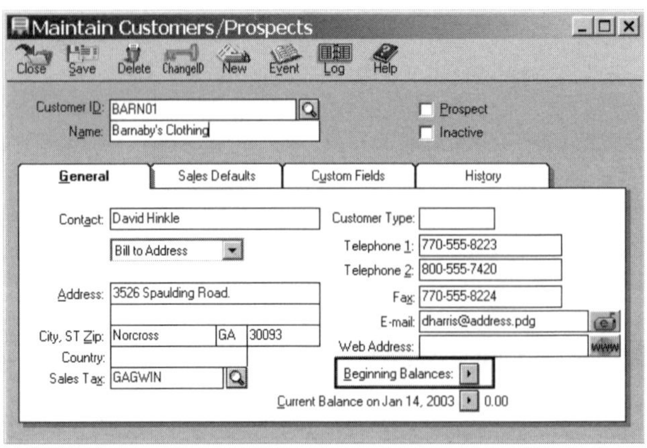

5. The Customer Beginning Balances screen appears.

   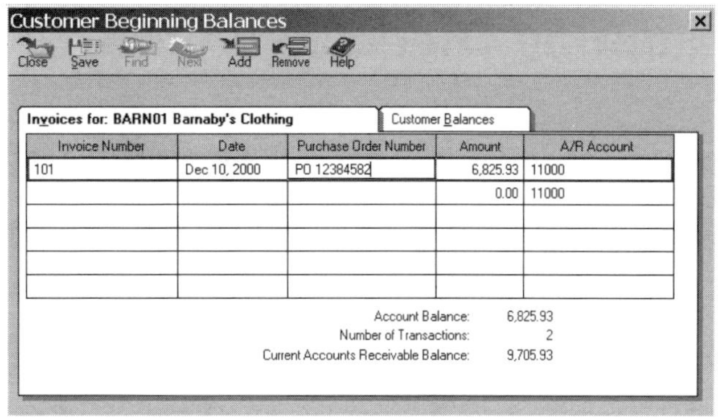

   On the Invoices for tab, you can enter the following:

   Invoice Number — This is your original invoice number.

   Date — The date of the original invoice.

   Purchase Order Number — If the customer has a PO associated with this invoice, enter it here.

   Amount — The total amount of the invoice, including any taxes.

   A/R Account — The accounts receivable G/L account number. If you have more than one A/R account, be sure to select the correct one.

6. Click **Save** in the toolbar.

7. After the information is entered, you can click on the **Customer Balances** tab. The total of all invoices will show on the line for the customer. To see the total of all invoices entered in the customers' beginning balances, change the accounting period (see Chapter 2) to the period before your company's Begin Transactions date. The total will show as the Current Accounts Receivable Balance.

   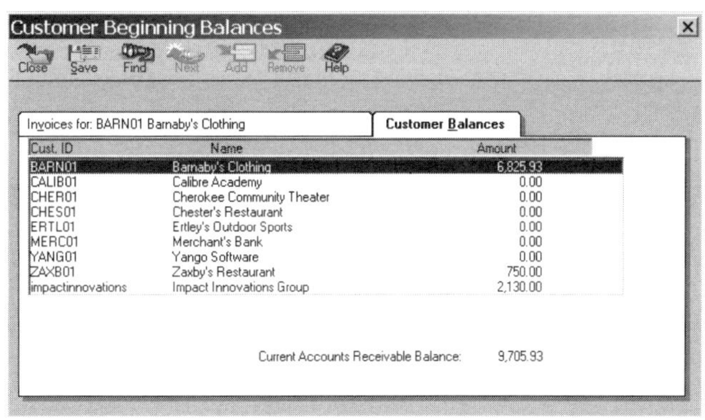

8. Click **Close** to leave this screen.

Adding the invoices to the beginning balances is the best way to process checks arriving that need to be applied to invoices created in your old system. After the beginning invoice is entered, you can process the receipt just as you will new invoices.

Entering Checks and Cash

Check entry and cash entry are almost identical. The only difference is what you put in the Reference field and where you place the information on your deposit slip.

Applying a Receipt Against an Invoice

Once invoices are in your system, you can apply receipts to them as follows:

1. Go to the **Receivables** or **Sales** folder in the navigation aid and select **Receipts** in the Tasks area.

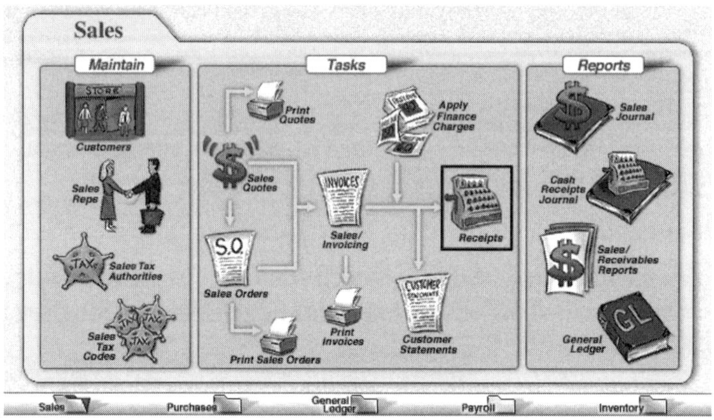

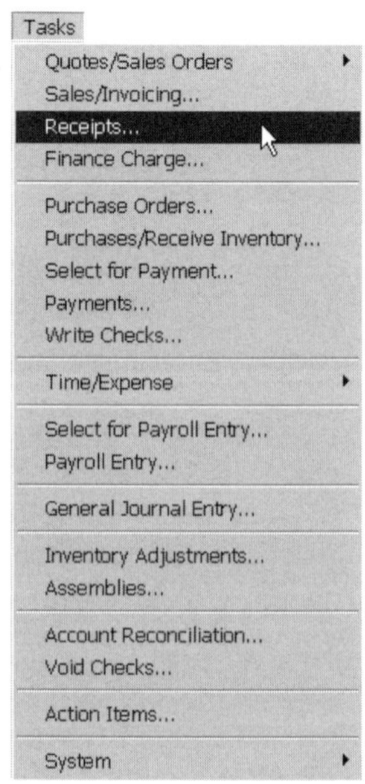

Or select **Tasks**, **Receipts** from the menu bar.

Or using the keyboard, press **Alt+K**, then **R**.

2. The Receipts form appears.

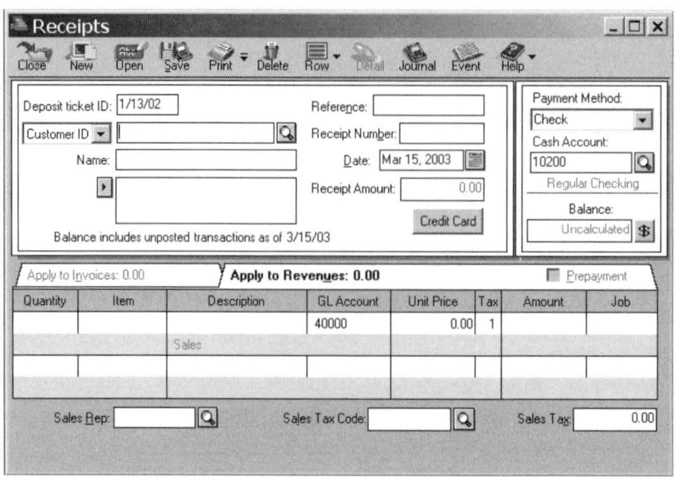

The first field to fill in on this screen is Deposit ticket ID. The deposit ticket ID is directly related to the physical deposit ticket that you give to the bank. Many users use the current date as the ID, but I have found that it is best to number your deposit tickets (if they are not preprinted with numbers) and use this number as the deposit ticket ID. Using sequential numbers starting with 1 or 2003-1 works best. All checks deposited together on the same day into the bank must have the same deposit ticket ID to make balancing the checking account easier, even if they are entered into Peachtree on different days. Simply using this procedure could save you a major headache when it comes time to balance your checking account.

3. Select an ID from the Customer ID drop-down list. If needed, you can add the customer by clicking the **New** button in the drop-down list.
4. The Reference is the check number on the customer's check. This field will accept letters. If you are depositing cash, put the date or "CASH" in the Reference field.
5. Ignore the Receipt Number field for now. It is new to 2002. If you need it, you will be prompted for it the same way as when you print invoices.
6. Enter the date of this deposit, not the date you received the check, in the Date field. It is important to use the same date on all checks deposited on the same deposit ticket. You can use the calendar function to select a date.
7. The Receipt Amount will be calculated automatically.
8. Ignore the Credit Card button for now.
9. Select the Payment Method from the drop-down list. Generally you will use **Check**.
10. The next field asks for the cash account. This is the G/L account of the bank account that you are depositing money into.
11. The Balance field is also calculated automatically. This is your bank balance. Sometimes Balance will show ???????? or Uncalculated. This happens when you have selected to hide the bank balance in the Global Options or, occasionally, when Peachtree gets confused. It is simple to refigure the bank balance by clicking the **$** button. Note that during this first month your bank balance will be incorrect. We will fix the bank balance in the second month when we cover balancing the checking account in Chapter 11.
12. If the customer has invoices in the system, the Apply to Invoices tab will appear with the invoices listed.

    Find the correct invoice in the list. If the total of the invoice is being paid, check the **Pay** column by clicking in the check box. The Amount Paid field will automatically be filled in.

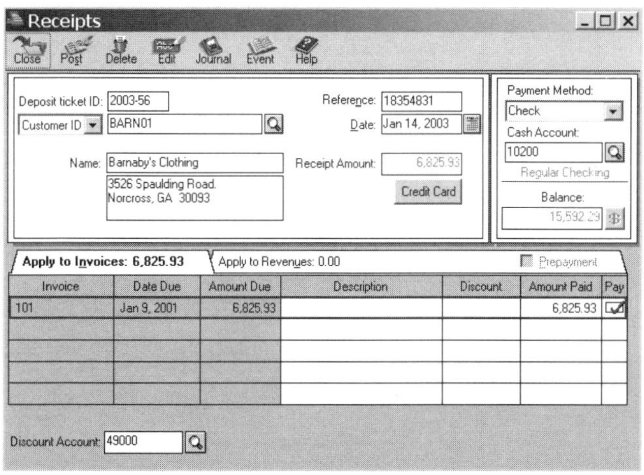

If there is an entry in the Discount field, that amount will be deducted.

13. For a partial receipt, enter the amount directly into the Amount Paid field.
14. As each amount is added, the total appears in the Receipt Amount field at the top. Verify that the total matches the receipt amount.
15. If you do not need to give your customer a receipt, click the **Save** or **Post** button to save this transaction.

    If your customer needs a receipt, such as at a cash register, click **Print**. The ability to print receipts is new to Peachtree 2002. In older versions you had to create an invoice and then put in the payment information (two steps) before you could print an invoice with payment information. Now all that can be accomplished from the Receipts screen. After clicking the **Print** button the Print Forms: Receipts dialog box appears.

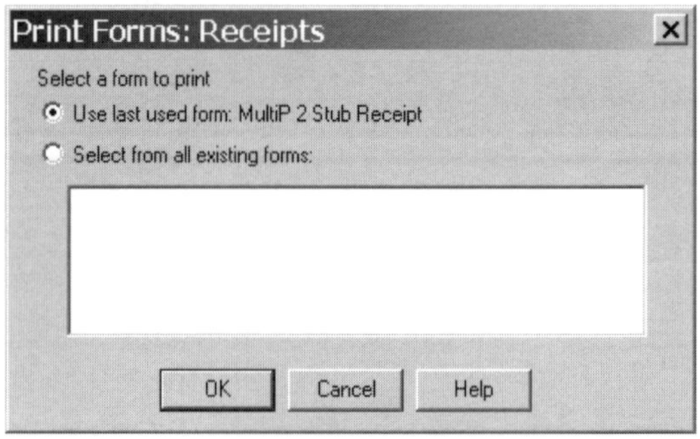

16. Select the correct form to print, either Use last used form or one from the Select from all existing forms list. Click **OK** and the second Print Forms dialog box appears.

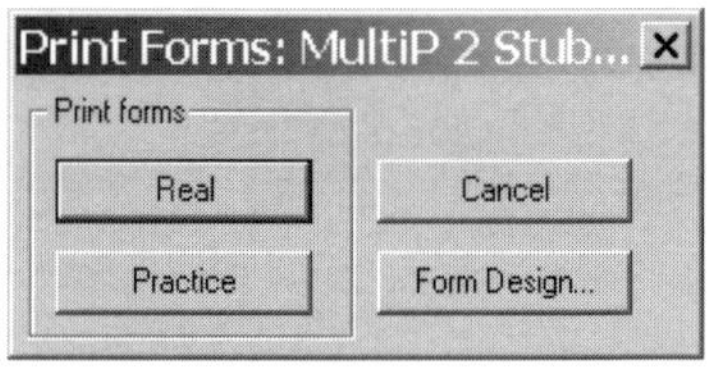

17. Click **Real**. The About to Print Receipt dialog box appears.

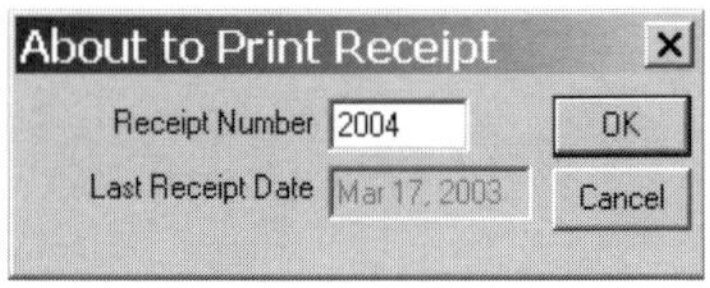

18. Enter or verify the Receipt Number. Click **OK**. The receipt will print to the default printer.

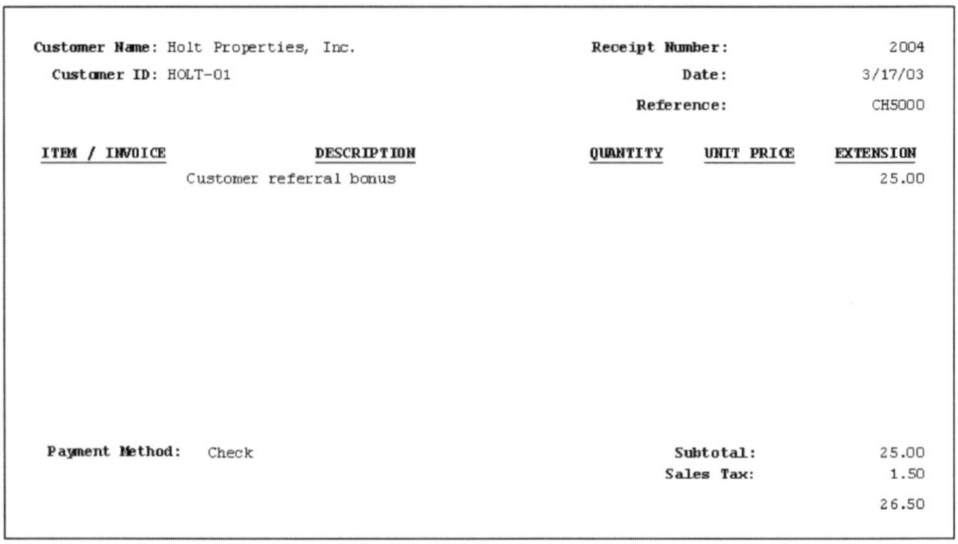

Customer Name: Holt Properties, Inc.
Customer ID: HOLT-01

Receipt Number: 2004
Date: 3/17/03
Reference: CH5000

ITEM / INVOICE	DESCRIPTION	QUANTITY	UNIT PRICE	EXTENSION
	Customer referral bonus			25.00

Payment Method: Check

Subtotal: 25.00
Sales Tax: 1.50
26.50

Making Deposits for Receipts without an Invoice

Occasionally, you will need to enter a receipt that does not have an invoice. These transactions could include refunds, small one-time purchases by walk-in customers, or other miscellaneous receipts. They should not be invoices that should be in the customer's beginning balance. If you run a retail operation, most of your receipts may not use invoices and you will print the receipt for the customer.

1. Open the Receipts screen as shown earlier.
2. Fill in the Deposit ticket ID field.
3. If the receipt is from a customer, select the customer ID from the drop-down list. If the receipt is a refund from a vendor, click the drop-down button on **Customer ID** and change it to **Vendor ID**.

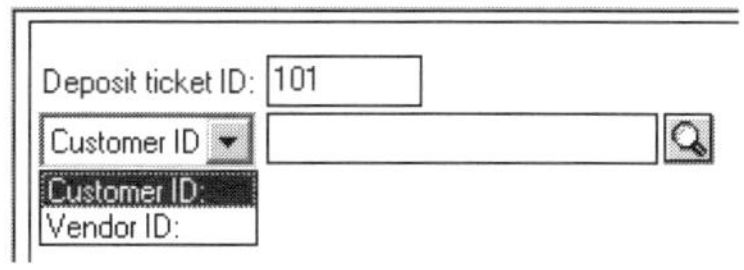

4. If the receipt is from someone else, leave this field blank and tab to the Name field. Enter the name of the payer.

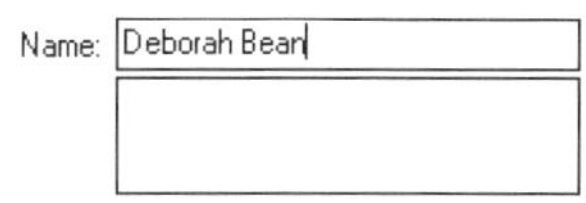

Tip: If this is a walk-in customer and you do a lot of cash business, you may want to create a customer called Cash and apply all your walk-in customers to this customer ID. If you want to capture names from cash customers to send them promotional materials, don't use a cash account. Instead, add them as a customer from the Receipts form so you can later extract the names to send letters directly from Peachtree. If you do decide to create a mailing list of cash customers, I suggest you use the customer's ten-digit phone number as the customer ID for quick and easy entry and locating.

5. Fill in the Reference, Date, Payment Method, and Cash Account fields as explained earlier. Many walk-in customers use cash as the Payment Method, so verify that it is correct.
6. Notice that the Apply to Revenues tab is showing and is the only tab into which data can be entered. The Apply to Invoices tab is hidden and grayed out.

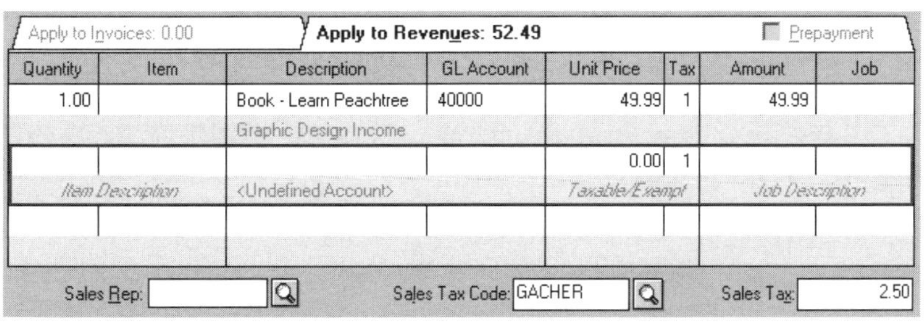

7. The Apply to Revenues tab works similarly to the invoicing screen. Enter information into the Quantity, Description, GL Account, and Unit Price fields. Generally, the G/L account should be a sales account but if this is a refund of an expense, you will want to apply the amount to the correct expense account (such as Telephone expense for a refund on a phone deposit). Deposits made to expense accounts will be allocated as negative expenses.

If you selected a vendor ID, some of the fields will be disabled. You can only enter information into the Description, GL Account, and Amount fields. The GL Account will accrue to the default sales account, which you will have to change to the correct account.

8. If the item is taxable, enter the correct sales tax code in the Tax column. Verify that the correct Sales Tax Code shows in the field at the bottom of the screen. The sales tax will be calculated automatically.
9. The total of the sale, including tax, will appear on the tab and in the Receipt Amount field.

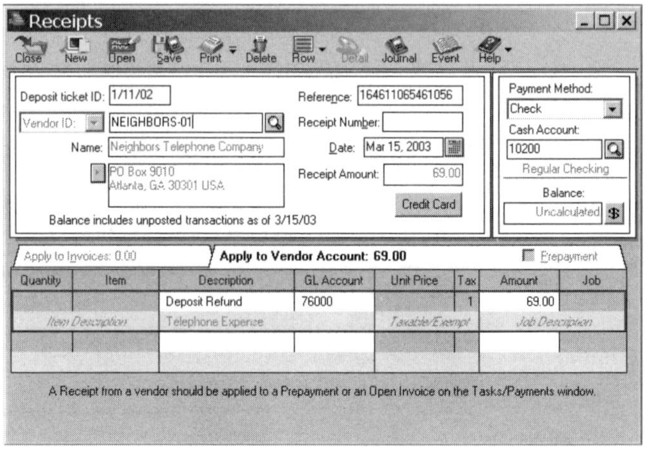

10. The Prepayment check box will be discussed later in this chapter.
11. Click **Save** or **Post** in the toolbar to save the receipt. Click **Print** to print the receipt for a customer.

    You can mix receipts and enter information in both of the Apply tabs.

Entering Receipts Homework

After your first receipt is entered, you need to locate all receipts from earlier in this month and enter them here. The goal this month is to enter all receipts for this month in Peachtree, in addition to adding them to your old accounting system.

As you make deposits, make sure that the split between the previous month and the current month is very clear. If a check is to be applied to an invoice in the previous month, the invoice should be in the customer's beginning balance, for this month only. If the check is to be applied to an invoice in the current month or future months, the invoice will have been entered into Peachtree through the Sales/Invoicing function.

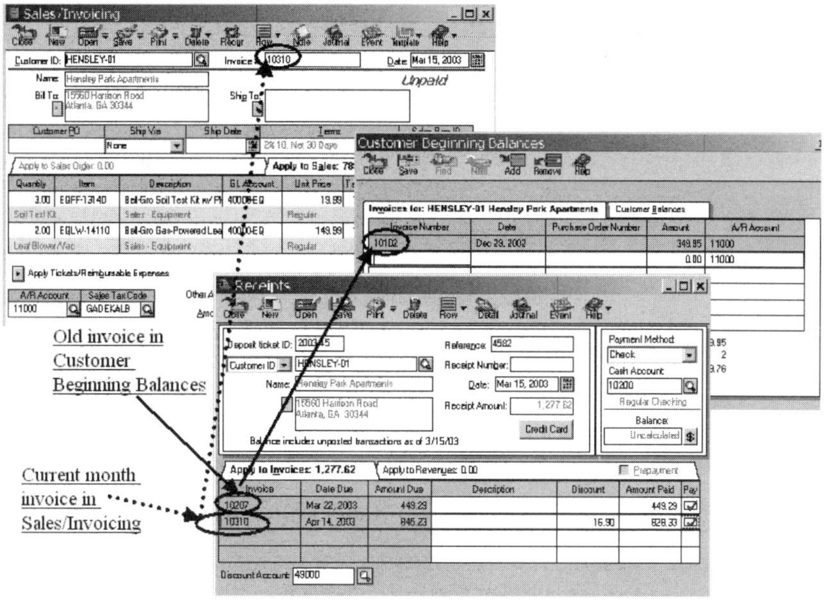

Once you have the knack of entering receipts, go on to the next task.

Other Types of Receipts

In addition to check and cash receipts from customers, you can also show credit card receipts and prepayment or down payment receipts.

Credit Card Receipts

Peachtree now has a credit card service that allows you to set up an online merchant account and authorize credit card receipts right over the Internet. This service is provided through Chase Merchant Services, LLC, although other online merchant services can be used. The service does not require a credit card swipe machine or an additional phone line, although a separate line is recommended if you do a lot of credit card business. If your computer has Internet access (either through a dial-up connection or with a high-speed connection) you can use the service while you are connected to the Internet and while you are in Peachtree.

To set up an online merchant account, select **Online**, and then **Credit Card Authorization Center** from the Peachtree menu bar and follow the instructions. In 2002, select **Services** and then **Credit Card Authorization**.

If you already have a merchant account through the traditional swipe machine, that information may be manually recorded in Peachtree.

Credit Cards Accepted

Before accepting credit cards, you need to enter the types of payments your company uses.

1. Select **Maintain**, **Default Information**, and then **Customers** from the menu bar.
2. The Customer Defaults window appears. Select the **Pay Methods** tab.

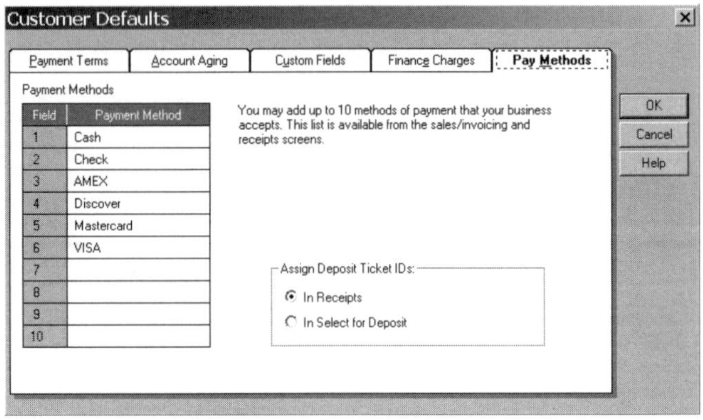

3. Always leave the Cash and Check entries where they are. You may change or add additional entries as needed. Enter the descriptions in the Payment Method column. Enter the most-used credit cards at the top of the list and less-used credit cards towards the bottom. This will speed up processing in the future when you need to extract the information from drop-down menus.
4. Click **OK** to save the information.

Processing Fees Account

Credit card companies charge merchants processing fees and discounts. You need to set up a general ledger account to track these fees. I suggest one account for each credit card that you accept unless the cards are processed together with the same discounts and fees (such as VISA and MasterCard). To set up a new general ledger account, see "Adding an Account" in Chapter 3. Make sure that the Account Type field is set to **Expenses**.

Entering Credit Card Receipts

You start entering a credit card receipt the same way that a check is entered.

1. Open the Receipts form and select a customer ID to bring up the correct customer.
2. Enter a Reference for this customer. Since this is not a check, you will not have a check number. Instead, you might consider using the last four digits of the credit card number followed by the date or some other format.
3. Fill in the Date field.
4. Select the payment method in the Payment Method field. This should be the credit card.
5. In the Cash Account field, select the account that the credit card company will transfer the money to.
6. Enter the receipt information with the invoices to be paid or other receipt data.

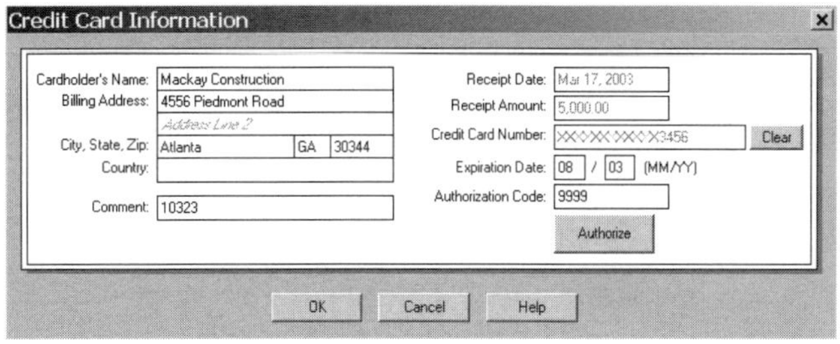

7. Click the **Credit Card** button. The Credit Card Information form appears.
8. If the cardholder's name is different than the customer name, enter the corrected information in the Cardholder's Name field.
9. The Receipt Date and the Receipt Amount fields will automatically be filled in from the Receipts form.
10. Enter the credit card number and the expiration date in the proper fields. You can clear the Credit Card Number field if you make an error by clicking the **Clear** button. Once the processing takes place, the credit card number is encrypted with only the last four digits visible.

Warning!! After authorization you cannot change or clear the Credit Card Number field.

11. The Comment field can be used to hold information regarding this authorization. Peachtree includes the field on processing reports, so you may want to record the invoice number or customer name in this field.
12. Click the **Authorize** button.
13. Peachtree will connect to the online processing site and authorize the transaction. If you are using Peachtree's Credit Card Service, the authorization code will be entered automatically. If some other method of authorization is used, you will need to enter the authorization code manually.
14. Click **OK** to return to the Receipts form.

Prepayments

Another type of receipt is the prepayment. A prepayment occurs when you require a deposit on work to be completed and the invoice has not yet been created. The prepayment is then applied to the customer's invoice at some later time. Prepayments do not appear as a line item on the invoice; they are only applied against the invoice. Prepayments are handled as follows:

1. Open the Receipts form and select a customer ID to bring up the correct customer.
2. Fill in the Reference field for this customer.
3. Enter the date.
4. Select the payment method. Prepayments can be any type of payment that your company receives.
5. Select the account in the Cash Account field.

6. Click on the **Apply to Revenues** tab.
7. Check the **Prepayment** check box. The line items change so that only a few fields are available.

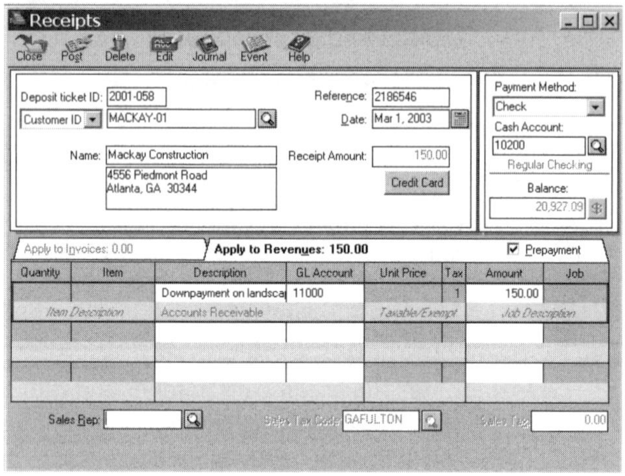

8. Enter the description of this down payment.
9. The GL Account field defaults to the accounts receivable general ledger account.
10. Enter the amount of the prepayment in the Amount field.
11. Click **Save** or **Post** to save the transaction.
12. Later, when the invoice is created, you can apply the prepayment to the invoice. This is generally done when the next, or final, payment is made. When you are ready to apply the prepayment, go back to the Receipts form.

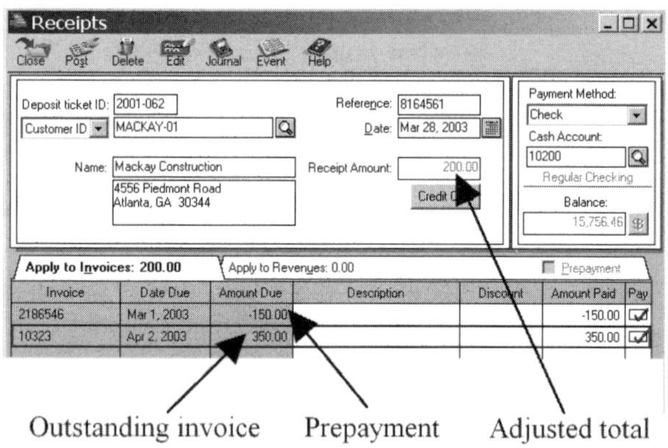

13. The prepayment will show as a negative invoice with the Invoice column containing the receipt's reference number and the Date column containing the receipt date.
14. If the current receipt is for the difference between the prepayment and the invoice amount, click the **Pay** check boxes for both items. Peachtree automatically calculates the adjusted total in the Receipt Amount field.

    If the current receipt is for a lesser amount, enter the amount paid on the outstanding invoice line as the total of the payment and the prepayment.

    If the prepayment was for the full amount of the invoice, or the final payment is going to be far enough in the future that you want to apply the prepayment now, enter the amount paid or check the **Pay** check boxes for both lines. In this case, the receipt amount will be $0.00. If there is no check number to put in the Reference field, you can enter **Apply Prepayment** or **Write-off** as the reference.
15. Click **Save** or **Post** to record this transaction.

Applying Credits for Customers

Customer credits show up in three ways. The first occurs when you void an invoice from the Sales/Invoicing window. The second occurs when you have created a credit memo (negative invoice) for the customer and need to apply it to outstanding invoices. The third is when the amount paid on an invoice is greater than the original invoice. The overpayment will show up with that invoice number as a negative amount.

When an invoice is voided, Peachtree generally applies the voided invoice to the original invoice automatically so that you don't have to worry about those transactions anymore. This is the simplest transaction with all processing taking place automatically in Peachtree. The other two occurrences require manual interaction, since the negative amounts show up on the Receipts form and must be applied in some manner.

1. Open the Receipts form and select a customer ID to bring up the correct customer. Enter the header information as needed.
2. Click on the **Apply to Invoices** tab.

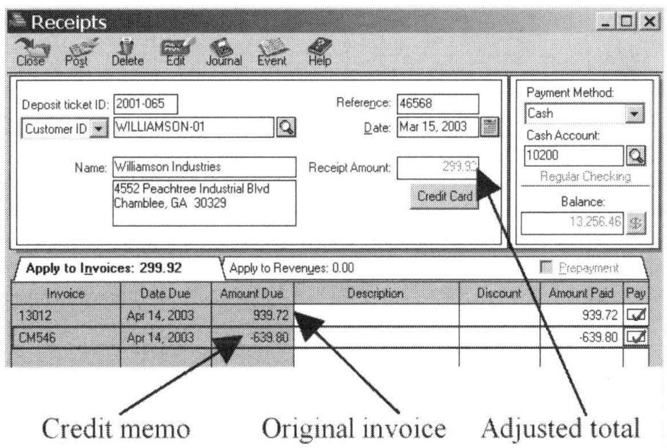

3. In our case, the customer requested landscaping work, and after the design and prep work was done, he backed out of the job. He still owes for the design and prep work, but we sent a credit memo (negative invoice) for the items that were not delivered. When we printed the credit memo, we gave it an invoice number that is different from our normal sequence of numbers. The customer has applied the credit memo to the original invoice and sent you the remaining balance.
4. Apply the credit memo to the original invoice just as you would a prepayment. If the Receipt Amount field totals $0.00, then use a reference for the transaction such as **Write-off** to indicate what has occurred.

Quick Cash Receipts Reports

Cash receipts reports help you verify that all receipts and customer credits have been allocated to the correct general ledger accounts.

The Cash Receipts Journal

This is the journal showing the receipts applied through the receipts function in journal entry format. It includes all debits and credits to all general ledger accounts, including applied credit memos, prepayments, and adjustments. The total on this report is not always the total of the bank deposits.

This report's options can significantly affect the appearance of the report. If one meets your needs especially well, be sure to save the settings.

1. Click the **Cash Receipts Journal** icon in the Receivables or Sales folder on the navigation aid.

   Or select **Reports**, **Accounts Receivable** from the menu bar.

   Or press **Alt+R**, then **R** using the keyboard shortcuts.

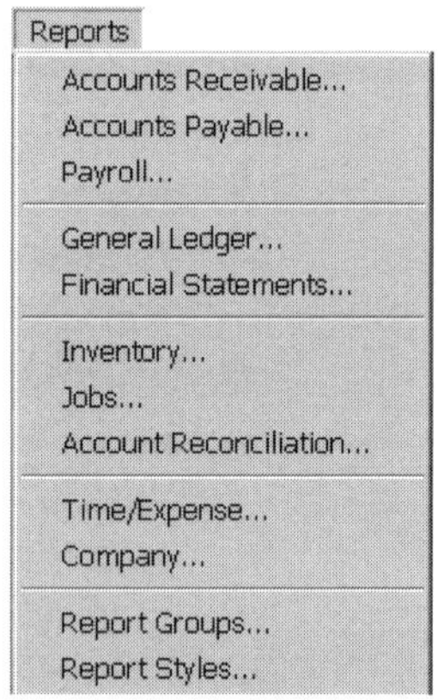

2. The Select a Report window appears.

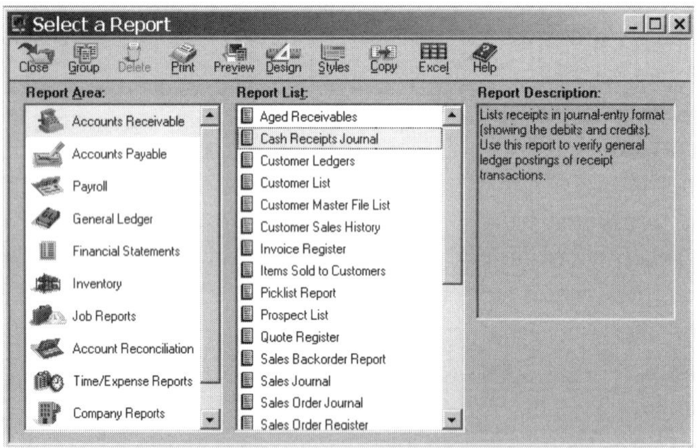

   Select the **Cash Receipts Journal** report and click the **Preview** button.

3. The Cash Receipts Journal dialog box appears.

   Select a **Report Order**. Choices include Check Date, GL Account, and Reference.

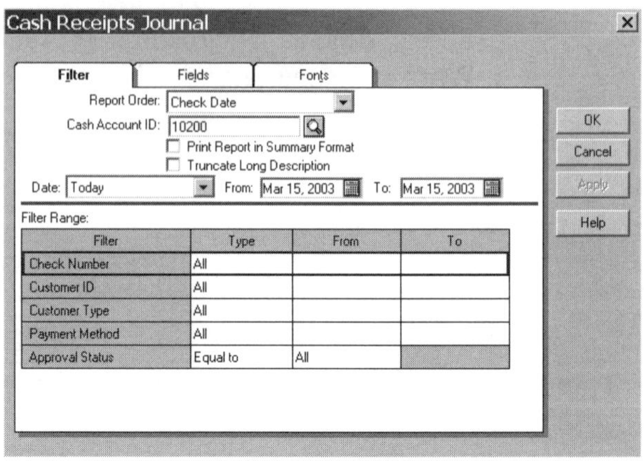

4. Select the correct account in the Cash Account ID field. If none is selected, the report will print the deposits for all of your cash accounts.
5. The Print Report in Summary Format option means that the report will be summarized so that there is only one debit or credit amount for each item. Depending upon the report order, this may mean for each general ledger account or each customer. This feature takes some experimentation to understand. Try the various possibilities.
6. The Truncate Long Description check box removes descriptions that take more than one line.
7. Select the date range for the report using either the Date drop-down list or the mini-calendars in the From and To fields. For some companies, the Today option can be very beneficial, although many companies will use the Current Period option.
8. In the Filter column, Check Number is actually the Reference from the Receipts form. Remember that the field uses an alphabetic rather than a numeric sort so that check numbers entered From 100 To 200 will include 10386.
9. To view the report for just one customer, enter the customer ID in the From and To fields. To view the report for a range of customers, such as abccompany to defcompany, type the IDs in the From and To fields.
10. If you use Customer Type, you may enter a type in the From and To fields.
11. The Payment Method field allows you to request payments of a specific type such as Cash, Check, or AMEX. These must be typed exactly as used on the Receipts form. There should be a drop-down list here; I don't know why there is not one.
12. The Approval Status field is for credit cards. The choices are All, Approved, and Pending.
13. Click **OK** to view the report.

The Bank Deposit Report

The Bank Deposit Report is not located in the Accounts Receivable report section, but in the Account Reconciliation report section. This is a great report for reconciling your deposits because the report is grouped by the Deposit ticket ID. Remember earlier in this chapter when I discussed that all deposits on the same physical deposit slip needed the same deposit ID? This report is one of the reasons that procedure is so important. If done correctly, each deposit is totaled separately and should match the total on the physical deposit slip.

1. To get to the Bank Deposit Report, click the **General Ledger** folder and the **Account Reconciliation** icon on the navigation aid.

Or select **Reports**, **Account Reconciliation** from the menu bar.

Or press **Alt+R**, then **O** using the keyboard shortcuts.

2. The Select a Report window appears.

   Verify that **Account Reconciliation** is highlighted in the Report Area list and that **Bank Deposit Report** is highlighted in the Report List. Click **Preview**.

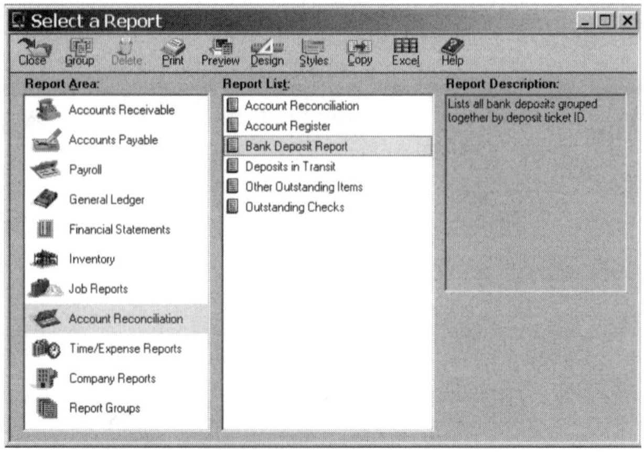

3. The Bank Deposit Report dialog box appears.

   The Report Order field only has Deposit Ticket ID as a choice.

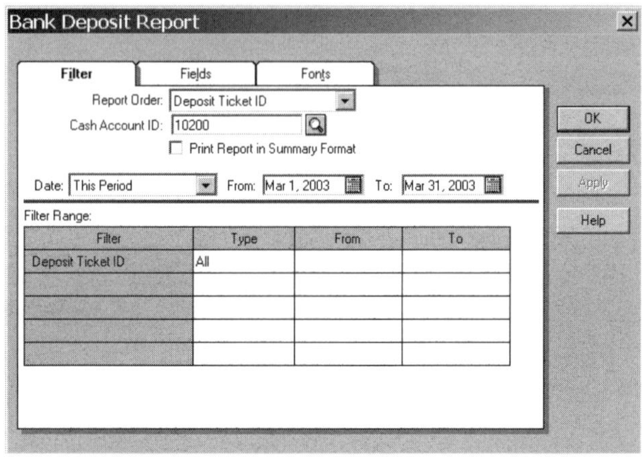

4. Select the correct account in the Cash Account ID field. If none is selected, the report will print for the deposits to all accounts.
5. The Print Report in Summary Format option means that the report will be summarized so that only the total for each deposit ID is shown.
6. Select the date range for the report using either the Date drop-down list or the mini-calendars in the From and To fields. The Today option will give the details of today's deposit and can help you to reconcile it.
7. In the Filter Range section there is only one filter. You may select a specific deposit ticket ID or a range of IDs by typing the desired IDs in the From and To fields. You may want to use this method to get the details of today's deposit instead of the date range.
8. Click **OK** when you are done.

Summary

In this chapter you should have learned the necessary steps to apply customer receipts to your invoices, to apply miscellaneous receipts, to handle credit cards and prepayments, and to apply credit memos. These steps, along with invoicing, will help you to maintain your account receivables. In the next month, you will learn to reconcile your accounts receivable and to make adjustments.

Chapter 7

Purchases

In This Chapter

- Adding vendors
- Entering, editing, and deleting bills
- Creating purchase orders
- Applying purchase orders to bills
- Closing purchase orders
- Vendor credit memos
- Aged payables and other reports

The purchases function is how bills are entered into the system and paid. It is also the way that inventory is added into the system. If you need to keep strict track of inventory, you will want to go to the instructions on inventory, found in Chapter 10, before you start entering bills.

Getting Started

Before you can pay bills and print checks using Peachtree's computerized system, you need to get computer checks. Your Peachtree box will have information on ordering checks specifically designed for Peachtree, or you can contact one of the check distributors, such as Deluxe or Checks in the Mail, and order Peachtree checks. If you need computer checks, order them immediately because you will be using them before this month is out.

It is also possible to change the existing Peachtree forms to accommodate your existing checks. Modifying existing Peachtree forms is verrrrrrrrrry tedious. You should only consider modifying the existing forms if you have some experience in desktop publishing or graphic form design and you also understand how computers read line items through the use of commands. If the preceding sentence made no sense to you — order new checks. It will be simpler, result in fewer problems, and lead to far less aggravation!

Entering Bills from Vendors

Every company receives bills from its vendors. These bills need to be entered into the system. In this chapter we will cover the basic bills that you receive. Other types of payments including information on bank payments, credit card accounts, and other special payments will be covered in Chapter 8.

For starters, pull a bill from your desk and get ready to enter it. If the bill does not have address information on it, you will need that also.

1. Go to the **Purchases** folder on the navigation aid and click on the **Purchases/ Receive Inventory** icon.

   Or select **Tasks, Purchases/Receive Inventory** from the toolbar.

   Or using the keyboard, press **Alt+K**, then **C**.

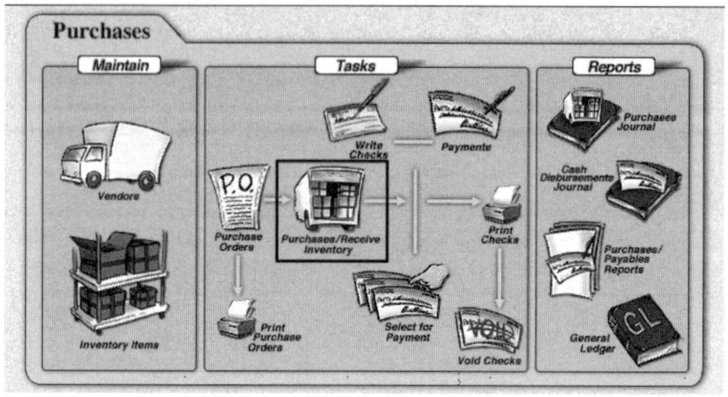

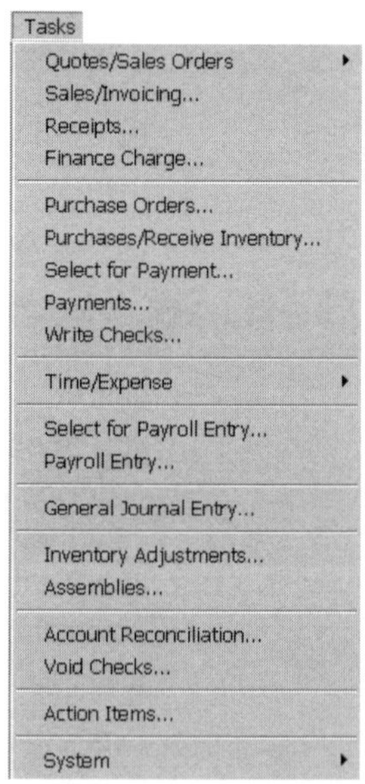

2. The Purchases/Receive Inventory screen appears.

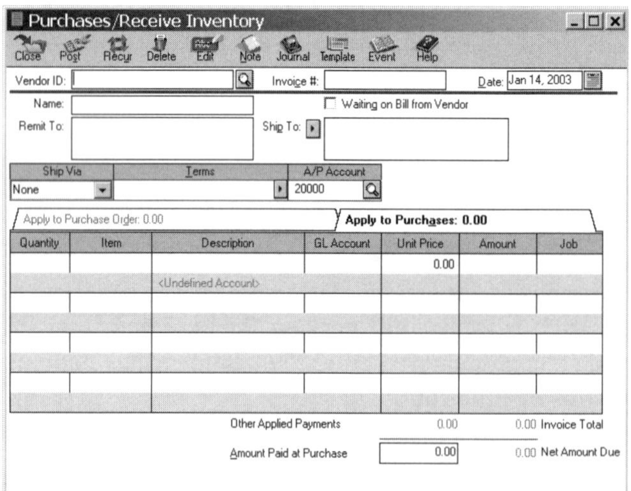

Take a look at the screen. Notice that it is similar in some ways to the Invoicing screen.

3. The first thing we want to do with the invoice is select a vendor. Click on the **Lookup** button in the Vendor ID field and select a vendor. You can also type a ? in the field to bring up the vendor list.

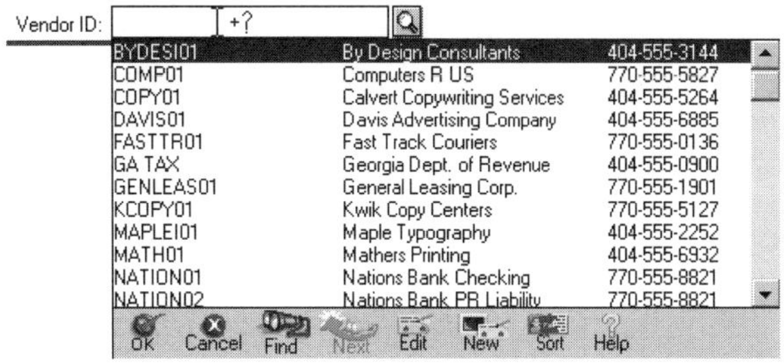

There is a good chance that you haven't entered any vendors as yet. We can add vendors directly from the Purchases form. The program does not require us to back out of this screen and go to another part of the program. To add vendors on the fly, skip ahead to the following section. If you already have vendors, continue with Step 4.

4. In Purchases/Receive Inventory form, enter the vendor in the Vendor ID field. The Name and mailing address (Remit To) fields are automatically entered.

5. Tab to the Invoice # field. Enter the customer's invoice number in this field. This accepts any alphanumeric entry. If a number is not available, use a scheme such as the year and month (2003-04) for the invoice number or make up one on your own. If the invoice number has already been entered into the system, the program will give you a warning message when you go to save the bill. This will help keep you from double-entering bills.

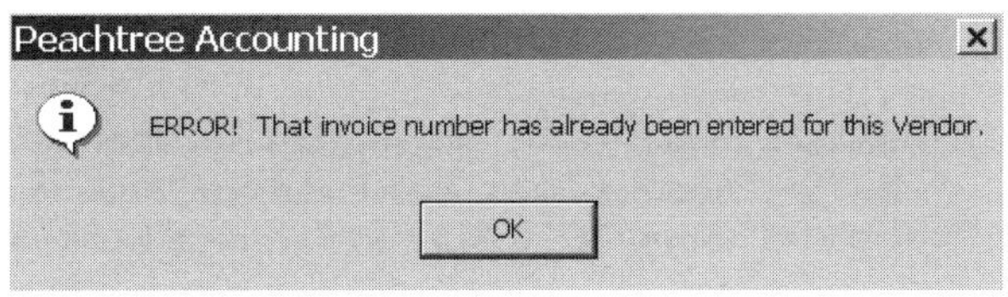

6. Fill in the Date field for this bill. This is the customer's invoice date, not the due date. The due date is calculated by applying the selected payment terms to the invoice date.

7. The next field is the Waiting on Bill from Vendor check box. Use this when you want to show that you have received inventory or parts but have not yet received the bill. If you check the box, you don't have to enter the invoice number. Later, when the bill arrives, edit the transaction and enter the missing information.

8. Clicking the button attached to the Ship To field causes the Ship To Address dialog box to appear.

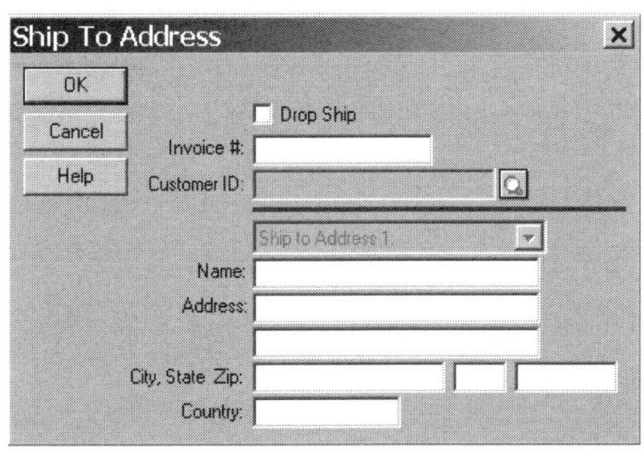

You may enter an address directly or you may enable the Customer ID field by clicking the Drop Ship check box. Ship to addresses are entered using the following fields.

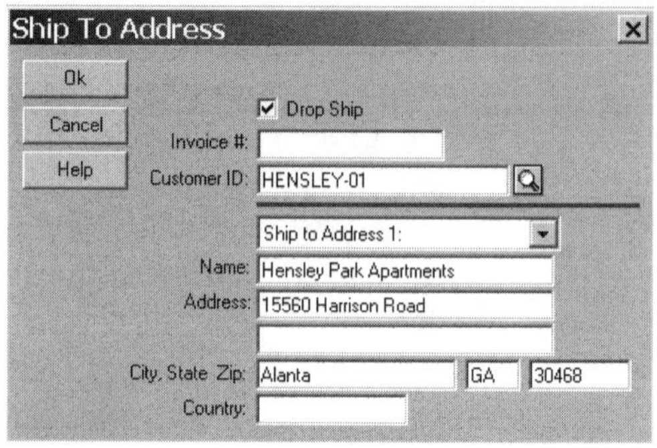

Drop Ship — The check box indicates that the items purchased are being sent directly to an address other than your billing address.

Invoice # — If the shipping address is for a customer that you have billed, this is the invoice number that is being sent to the customer.

Customer ID — Again, if a customer is involved, this is the associated customer ID number.

To Address — This field has no name, but it is a drop-down box that determines which billing or shipping address for the customer should be used.

Name (and all remaining fields) — Peachtree automatically enters this based on the customer's billing and shipping addresses. If this shipment is to go to another location, you must enter the new name and address.

Warning!! Be very careful after entering the information in the Name and Address fields. Peachtree can lose the typed information if you click the **Customer ID** or **Ship to Address** button after the name and address are entered.

9. Click **OK** to return to the Purchases form.
10. The Ship Via field defaults to the customer's default setting that you entered when you added the customer. Click on the drop-down list to change the setting for this bill.
11. The customer's default terms appear in the Terms field. Click the arrow button to the right of this field to bring up the Terms Information dialog box.
12. Change the information, including the due date, as needed and click **OK**.

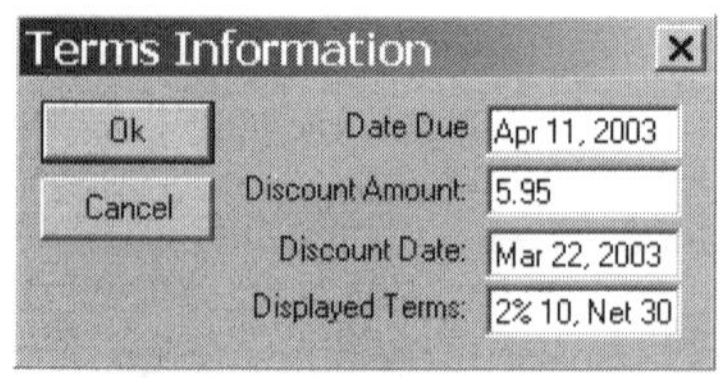

13. The next field, A/P Account, is very important. This is the G/L account number for your accounts payable. Unless you have multiple A/P accounts, this account should not change. A common mistake is to change this to the expense account that the bill is to be charged to. I often have to go to clients to repair a month's worth of invoices that have used the wrong account in this field.
14. Go to the **Apply to Purchases** tab. We will cover the Apply to Purchase Order tab later.
15. The line item fields require some thought and practice in entering. If you are recording inventory to be tracked, you must enter each separate item individually showing

the actual quantity and item. When you use inventory items, the Description, GL Account, Unit Price, and Amount fields are entered automatically.

Apply to Purchase Order: 297.60 | **Apply to Purchases: 4,778.30**

Quantity	Item	Description	GL Account	Unit Price	Amount	Job
65.00	AVRY-10100	Assembled Redwood 12-Room	12000	55.90	3,633.50	
Bird House Kit		Inventory				
144.00	AVRY-10140	Catalog #B11255: Thistle Bird	12000	7.95	1,144.80	
Thistle Bird Seed Mix-6 lb.		Inventory				

Or if you are entering a bill from a vendor, such as the office supply place, all items that belong to the same G/L account can be entered on the same line. As an example, assume you get this bill for office supplies:

OFFICE SUPPLY COMPANY

4/10/2001		1:58 PM
265526		
	SAN Perm Markers Red	
	12 @ 2.97	35.64
233222		
	GP Laser Prt Ppr Case	
	1 @ 48.99	48.99
653285		
	YLW #2 Pencils Case	
	6 @ 2.99	17.94
893529		
	MX CD-R Disks 5PK	
	3 @ 5.99	3.59
	Subtotal	106.16
*******	Sales Tax @ 8.25%	8.76
	TOTAL DUE	**114.92**

Thank you for shopping
Office Supply Company

You have one G/L account for Office Supplies and a second G/L account for Laser and Computer Supplies. Your line items may look like the following:

Apply to Purchase Order: 297.60 | **Apply to Purchases: 114.92**

Quantity	Item	Description	GL Account	Unit Price	Amount	Job
		Red markers, #2 pencils	75500	0.00	58.01	
		Supplies Expense				
		Laser paper, Writable CD's	75600	0.00	56.91	
		Printer & Computer Supplies				

Notice several things about this example. We did not fill in the Quantity, Item, or Unit Price fields. The Description was simple and short and included more than one line item from the bill. The Amount includes any associated sales tax for each item on the bill.

Line items should be entered in one of the two ways shown. Most companies use both types of entries, depending upon what type of bill is being paid.

16. The Apply to Purchases tab shows the total to be paid to the vendor. It should be compared to the bill and corrections should be made if the two amounts do not match.
17. The Job field will not be covered in this book because of space constraints.
18. When all line items have been entered and verified, click **Save** or **Post** on the toolbar to save the bill until it is ready to be paid.
19. The next step is procedural only and does not concern the Peachtree program but can help you greatly in deterring the double-entry of bills — a common error for smaller companies with less-trained individuals. After the bill is entered into

Peachtree, put a very large "E" on the receipt part of the bill (not the remittance) to show that it has been entered. I use a bright-colored highlighter for the task and generally make the "E" about five inches tall. This process quickly, simply, and very obviously shows what has been entered and what hasn't. Sometimes a low-tech solution can be as useful as a high-tech one!

Adding a Vendor "On the Fly"

1. If adding invoices, click on the **Lookup** button in the Vendor ID field and click the **New** button in the Vendor List toolbar.

   Or enter + in the Vendor ID field.

2. The Maintain Vendors form appears.

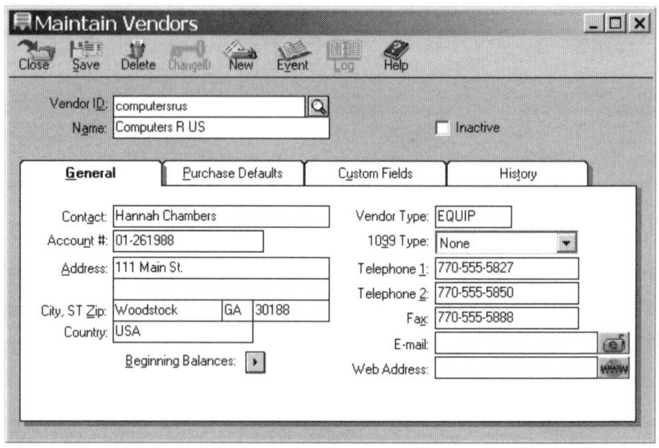

   Enter a unique ID in the Vendor ID field. Remember the discussion on IDs and enter an ID that suits your company's standards.

3. Enter the vendor name just as you want it to appear on the check.
4. Enter the contact name, if you have one.
5. If you have an account number, enter it in also. This is not the purchase order number for any specific purchase but is the general account number. Purchase orders are covered later in this chapter.
6. You have two lines for the address. Do not use the second line for the information that goes into the City, ST, and Zip fields. Peachtree uses the two-digit abbreviation for the state. Although not in the list, you can enter the two-digit Canadian province abbreviation and they will be accepted. The Zip field will also take U.S. 5+4 zip codes and Canadian postal codes. If the address is in the U.S., you may ignore the Country field.
7. Ignore the Vendor Type field for now.
8. If the vendor should be mailed a 1099 at the end of the year, click the drop-down next to 1099 Type and select either **Independent Contractor** or **Interest**.
9. You have two Telephone fields for voice phone numbers and a Fax field. These are free-form and can be entered in any manner.
10. The next two fields are for e-mail and web addresses. If you have an e-mail program installed on your system, clicking on the **E-mail** button will open the e-mail program and display a message form with the recipient (the To field) filled out with the

contents of the E-mail field. If you have an Internet connection, the indicated web page will appear after initial connection messages are displayed.

11. Select the **Purchase Defaults** tab.

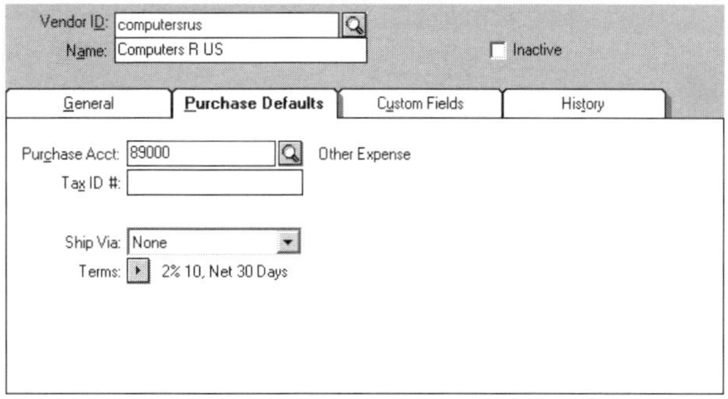

12. Select an account from the Purchase Acct field drop-down list. This is the general ledger account number to charge with the expenses applied to this vendor. You may leave it as a miscellaneous expense account or you can use the account these bills are generally applied to. For example, if the vendor is the phone company, use the Telephone Expenses G/L number.
13. Enter the vendor's tax ID number in the proper field. This will save you lots of effort when it is time to send out 1099s at the end of the year.
14. Select a shipping method from the Ship Via drop-down list. These are the same methods as used in invoicing.

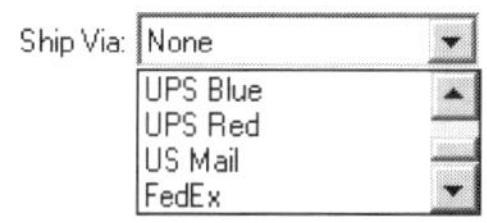

15. To change the terms, click the button next to the Terms field. The Vendor Terms dialog box appears. Unclick the **Use Standard Terms** check box and then change the terms to a different number of days or click the **C.O.D.** or **Prepaid** check boxes. If discounts are not available, put zeros in the Discount in and Discount % fields. Peachtree automatically places the correct wording on the vendor form. We discuss more about terms in Chapter 13.

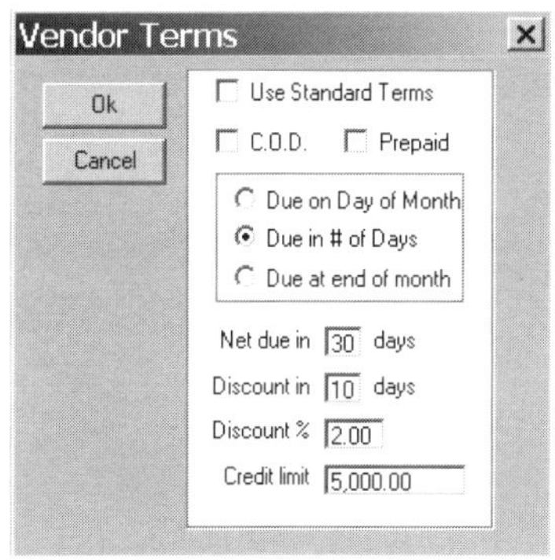

16. Once all information is entered, click the **Save** or **Post** button and then **Close** to return to the Purchases form.

If you added vendors on the fly while entering bills, return to Step 4 in the previous section.

Purchases and Accounting Behind the Scenes

The latest versions of Peachtree allow you to view the actual entry of a purchase. On the Purchases/Receive Inventory form, click the **Journal** button on the toolbar. The Accounting Behind the Screens form appears.

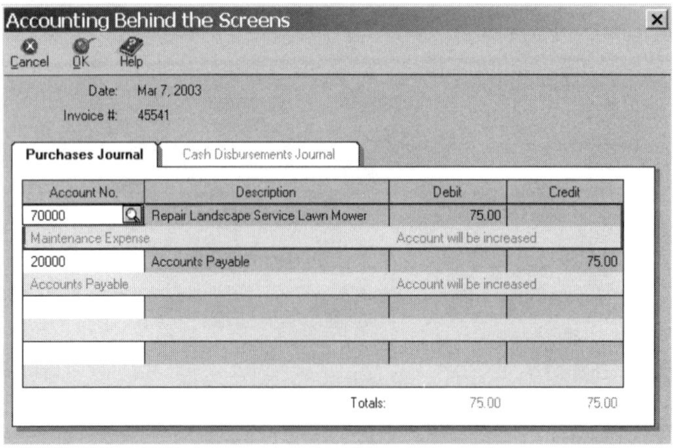

The Purchases Journal will be selected and the journal entry for this transaction will appear. It is possible to change the expense account and the accounts payable account on this form, but that is all. Also, the debits and credits must balance.

Editing Bills

Sometimes, you will need to make a change to an existing bill. Peachtree makes it very easy to change the original document. To edit an existing bill, follow these steps:

1. On the Purchases/Receive Inventory form, click the **Edit** button. 

2. The Select Purchase window appears.

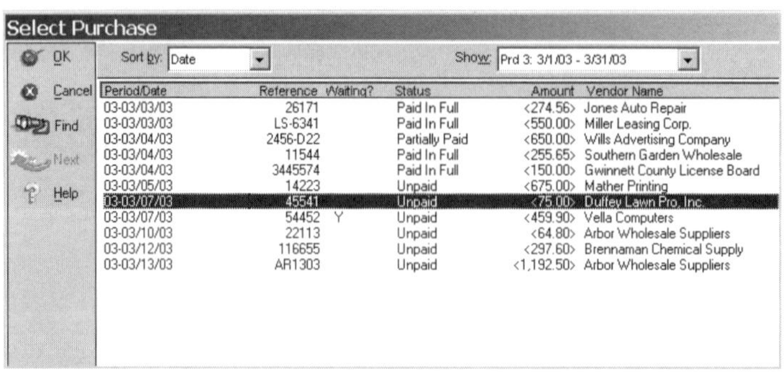

Purchases may be sorted by Date, by Reference (the invoice number), or by ID (vendor ID). The current accounting period transactions show in the window. You may select another period from the Show drop-down list. If you use batch posting, the Status drop-down will also be available.

3. Locate the desired invoice and click **OK** to return to the Purchases/Receive Inventory form.
4. Edit the bill as needed. For those bills that cannot be edited, the locked information will be grayed out and you will need to create a vendor credit memo.

5. Click **Save** or **Post** when you are done.

Deleting a Bill

Bills are only deleted, not voided.

1. Select the bill to be deleted and bring it up on the Purchases/Receive Inventory form.
2. Click the **Delete** button. 

3. A confirmation message box appears.

   Click **Yes** to delete.
4. Go to the Select Purchase window and notice that the original bill is no longer in the system.

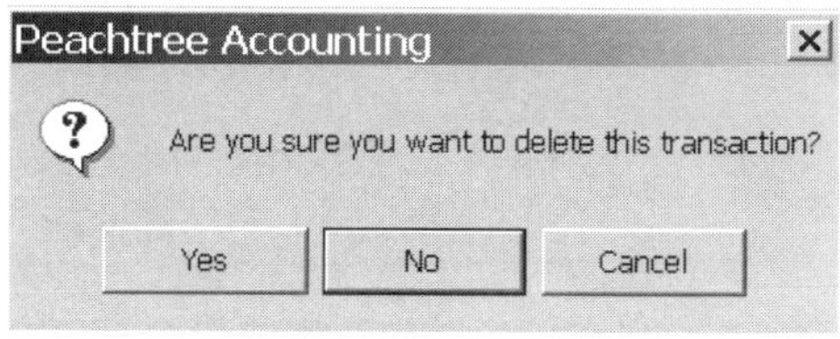

Some bills, such as those that have already been paid, cannot be deleted. In these cases, the Delete button will be grayed out.

Entering Bills Homework

After your first few bills are entered, you need to locate all bills from earlier in this month, whether paid or not, and enter them. The goal this month is to enter all bills into Peachtree that had not been entered into your old system on the first of the month, in addition to adding them to your old accounting system. Bills added to your old system before the first of the month will be entered in the vendors' beginning balances and will appear on the aged payables listing. We will cover beginning balances in Chapter 8.

If you use accrual accounting and enter bills into a previous month, those should be entered into the earlier month in your old accounting system and into Peachtree as beginning balances.

Once you have the knack of entering bills, you may go on to another task.

Other Types of Purchase Documents

In addition to entering purchases into the system, you also need to be able to enter vendor credit memos. Many companies also make use of purchase orders when ordering supplies.

Purchase Orders

Many companies try to control their costs and discourage employee abuse through the use of purchase orders (POs). If employees often pick up items from your suppliers, requiring purchase orders can reduce the chances of an employee picking up something for himself.

If you decide to implement purchase orders, be consistent. Have specific procedures for issuing and tracking the POs. Also consider that the purchases data entry person should not be the person to issue purchase orders; leave that task to the office manager or shop foreman. Otherwise you will be circumventing all the controls you want to put into place!

To enter a PO, follow these steps:

1. Click the **Purchase Orders** icon in the **Purchases** folder on the navigation bar.

   Or select **Tasks**, **Purchase Orders** from the menu bar.

   Or press **Alt+K**, then **U** using the keyboard shortcuts.

2. The Purchase Orders form appears.

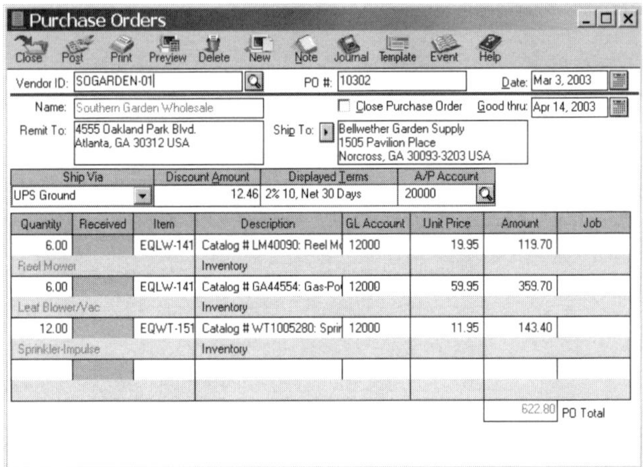

   Enter the vendor ID or select one from the drop-down list. If this is a new vendor, you may add it on the fly. The vendor name and address will appear automatically.

3. If you want Peachtree to track sequential purchase order numbers, leave the PO # field blank and the number will be requested when you print the PO. If this is a manual purchase order, enter the PO number here.

4. Enter the date the purchase order is issued.

5. Just like sales orders, POs are good for a certain length of time. Enter a date in the Good thru field provided.

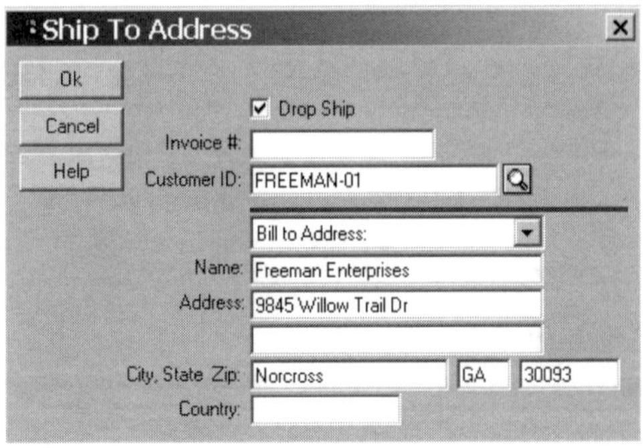

6. The Ship To address field is filled with your company's address. If the purchase is to go to another site, click the **Ship To** button to bring up the Ship To Address form.

7. If the order is to be sent to another location, click the **Drop Ship** check box.

8. If the drop ship is for a customer who is to be invoiced, you may enter the

invoice number in the space provided. Generally, you will not have an associated invoice number yet, so you can leave the field blank for now and edit it later.

9. Enter the address or select one of the shipping addresses or the billing address for the customer.
10. Click **OK** to return to the Purchase Orders form.
11. Select a shipping method from the Ship Via drop-down list.
12. The Discount Amount, if available, will be calculated when items are entered for the purchase order.
13. The vendor's default terms appear in the Displayed Terms field. This field should not be changed here, but on the purchases form.
14. The A/P Account field is the accounts payable general ledger account used for this purchase. Unless you have more than one account, this number should not change.
15. Enter the line items, as follows:

    Quantity — If this PO is for a job, enter **1**; if hours, sets, pieces, etc., enter the number.

    Received — This column is grayed out and unavailable. The number received is filled in when the purchase order is opened in the Purchases/Receive Inventory screen.

    Item — If you purchase a lot of the same services or items or you are tracking inventory, you will want to enter the item ID here. The item ID will automatically complete the Description, GL Account, and Unit Price fields. Items can be used for inventoried product or parts so that when you purchase an item, it is added to the inventory. You can also use items to speed up your data entry. Inventory items are discussed in Chapter 10.

    Description — Type the full description. There is a limit on the information that you can enter of about 160 characters, or 5½ lines. To go to a new line within the field, press **Ctrl+Enter**.

    GL Account — This should be a G/L expense account unless this is an unusual item. A default account will populate this field from the default GL Purchase Acct field on the vendor's record if an item was not entered. Change this to another account by clicking on the Lookup button and finding the account number in the list or by typing the number into the field directly.

    Unit Price — If you know the price per unit (and there is a number in Quantity), type it here. When you tab from the field, the Amount is calculated.

    Amount — The Amount is calculated from the Quantity and Unit Price. You can also work the calculations backward by leaving either the Quantity or the Unit Price blank. If you enter the Unit Price and Amount, the Quantity is calculated. If you enter the Quantity and Amount, the Unit Price is calculated.

    Job — This field is not covered due to space constraints.

16. Enter other line items on this invoice as needed.
17. You can check the future journal entry for this purchase order, once it becomes a bill, by clicking the **Journal** button. Notice the message on the Accounting Behind the Screens form.

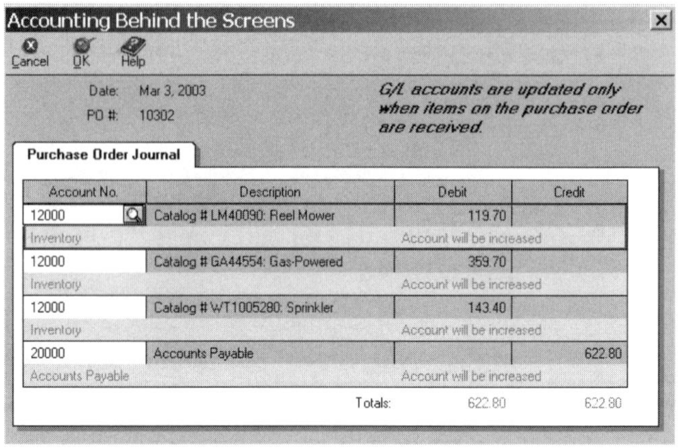

Printing and Saving a Purchase Order

Now that the PO information has been entered, we need to save it and print it. Both tasks are accomplished by clicking the Print button, or you can click Post or Save to save the purchase order for later printing.

1. Click the **Print** button on the toolbar. 

2. The Print Forms dialog box appears.

   Select the appropriate form to use, such as **PO Plain**. You may want to preview some of the different forms before choosing a form to use. You can preview a form by clicking the **Preview** button on the Purchase Orders form.
3. Click **OK**.
4. Another, smaller, Print Forms dialog box appears.

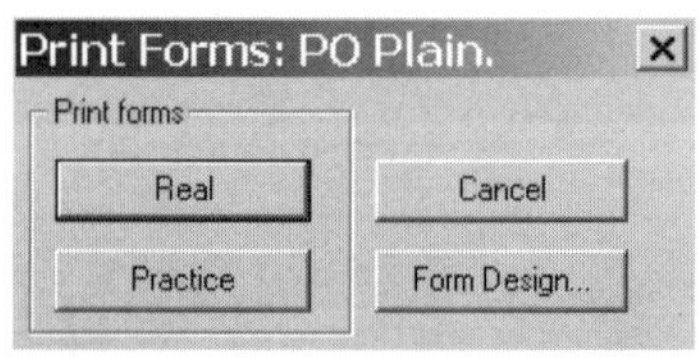

   Click the **Real** button.
5. The About to Print Purchase Order dialog box appears.

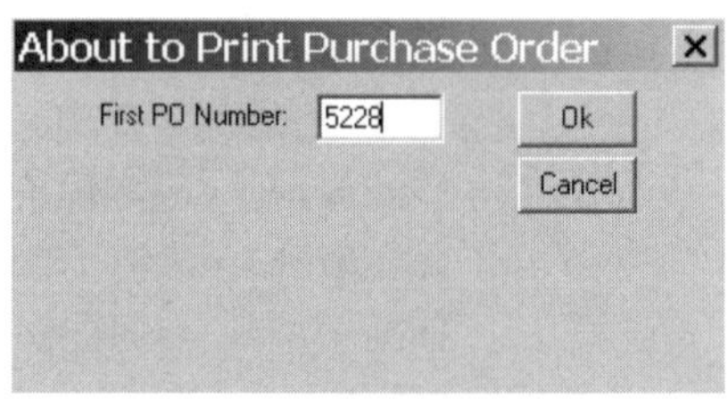

   Fill in the First PO Number field. If you use preprinted, prenumbered POs, the PO number should match the current form. If you use plain paper and generate purchase order numbers, you can use any number, either following your current sequence or beginning a new one.

Luckily, once the first PO number is created, the program remembers the last number used and simply adds one to the current number for the next PO. Peachtree also handles purchase order numbers with letters in them, although there is a chance the program might get confused on some of the sequencing.

6. Click **OK**.

   The PO prints to the computer's current default printer.

Applying Purchase Orders to Bills

When your vendors' bills arrive, they should have the purchase order number on them so that you can apply a PO to the bill. A purchase order can be used against multiple bills if products or services are billed separately.

Follow these steps to apply a PO to a vendor bill:

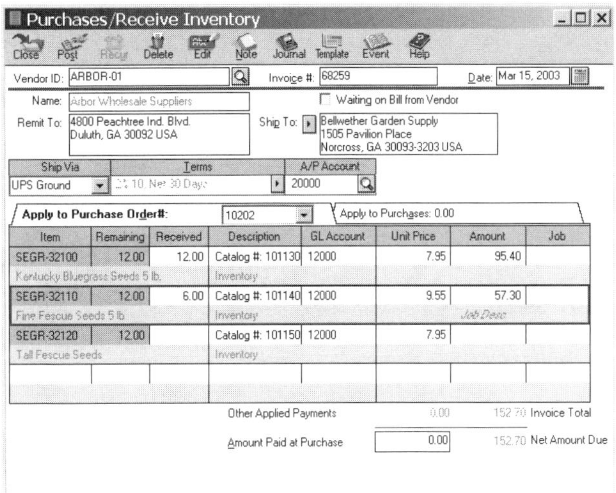

1. Open the Purchases form by clicking on the **Purchases/ Receive Inventory** icon in the **Purchases** folder on the navigation aid or by selecting **Tasks, Purchases/Receive Inventory** on the menu bar or by pressing **Alt+K, C** using the keyboard shortcuts.
2. Select a vendor from the Vendor ID drop-down list.
3. Enter the vendor's **Invoice #**. If you are entering the items from a packing slip, leave the Invoice # field blank and click the **Waiting on Bill from Vendor** check box.
4. Enter the date of the bill or the packing slip.
5. If this was a shipment to another location, click on the **Ship To** button and enter the correct shipping address.
6. Change the shipping method in the Ship Via field, if needed.
7. Change the Terms field, if needed.
8. Verify that the correct A/P account is being used.
9. Click on the **Apply to Purchase Order #** tab.
10. Select a purchase order from the drop-down list that shows <No PO Selected>. A bill can only have one PO applied to it. You can also add non-purchase order lines to the bill in the Apply to Purchases tab, although those should not be listed on another PO.

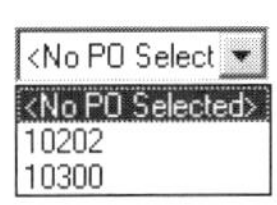

11. When a PO is selected, the line items show in the Item column with the Remaining quantities. Type the number of items Received in that column. The Amount is automatically calculated.
12. Click **Save** or **Post** to save the bill.

Closing Purchase Orders

Once a purchase order is in the system, you usually do not want to delete it because it will be linked to the vendor and you will want the information to remain in your company ledgers. Instead of deleting the PO, you should just close it. This removes it from the list of available purchase orders and from reports showing open POs, but it leaves a record so that if the vendor later bills you on that PO you will have a trail to follow. You can also close a purchase order that has only been partially applied.

If you need to close a purchase order, just bring the PO into the Purchase Orders form and click the Close Purchase Order check box, then click Save or Post to save the transaction.

Vendor Credit Memos

In order to record changes to your bill made by your vendor, you should receive a credit memo from the vendor to be applied to the bill. A vendor credit memo is simply a negative bill. It should be entered in the same way as a bill, except you will enter a negative quantity or amount as shown.

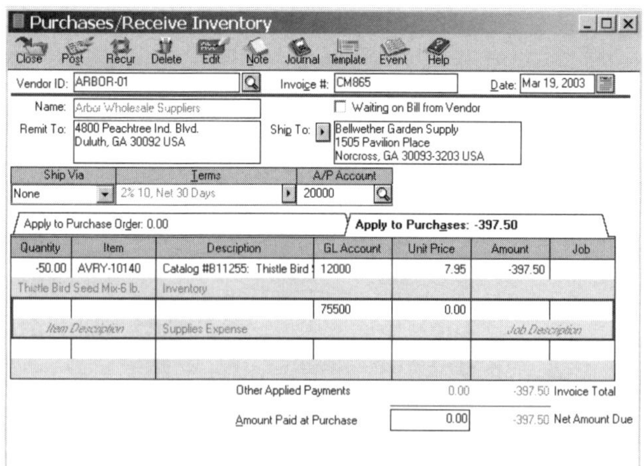

Applying vendor credit memos to outstanding bills will be shown in the next chapter.

Quick Purchase Reports

These reports will help you to see what bills are outstanding and what purchases should be forthcoming.

The Aged Payables Listing

This report is a listing of all vendors with outstanding bills, showing the aging of the outstanding balances.

1. Click the **Purchases/Payables Reports** icon in the **Receivables** or **Sales** folder on the navigation aid.

   Or select **Reports**, **Accounts Payable** from the menu bar.

   Or press **Alt+R**, then **P** using the keyboard shortcuts.

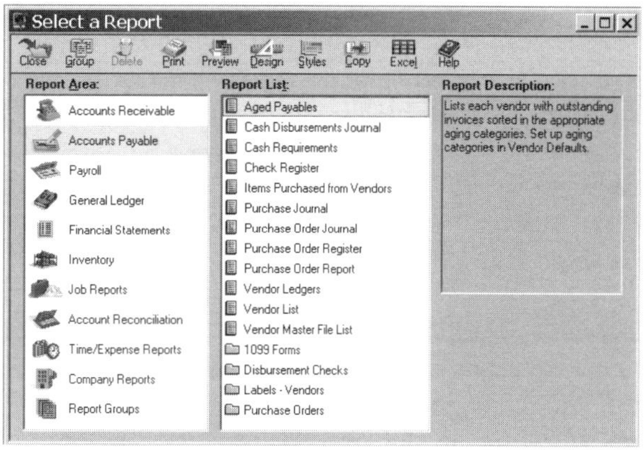

2. The Select a Report window appears.

   Make sure that Accounts Payable is highlighted in the Report Area list. Select the **Aged Payables** report from the Report List. Click the **Preview** button on the toolbar.

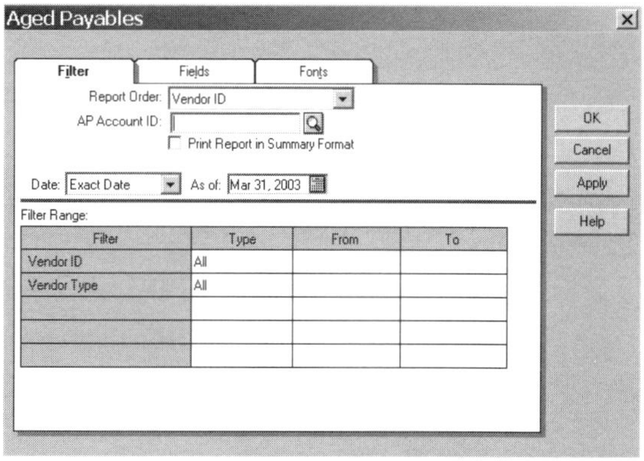

3. The Aged Payables dialog box appears.

   Select either **Vendor ID** or **Vendor Name** in the Report Order field.
4. If you have more than one accounts payable G/L account, select the correct G/L account in the AP Account ID field. Leaving this field blank will print payables from all AP accounts.
5. Checking Print Report in Summary Format will give you the totals for vendors, not a listing of the individual bills.
6. To view the report for just one vendor, enter the vendor ID in the From and To fields. To view the report for a range of vendors, such as abccompany to defcompany, enter the IDs in the From and To fields. Leave these fields blank to view all vendors.
7. If you use Vendor Type, you may enter a type in the From and To fields.
8. Click **OK** to view the report.

The Vendor Ledgers Report

This report is a listing of all bills and payments for a customer during a selected time period.

1. Go to the Select a Report window.
2. Select the **Vendor Ledgers** report and click **Preview** on the toolbar.
3. The Vendor Ledgers dialog box appears.

   The options for the Report Order, Vendor ID, and Vendor Type fields are the same as on the Aged Payables report.

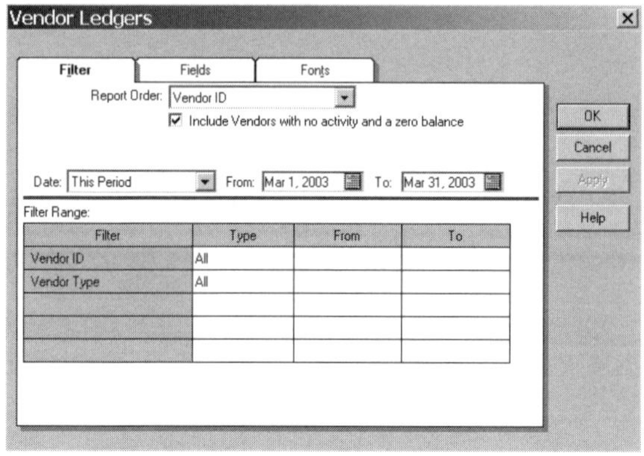

4. Checking Include Vendors with no activity and a zero balance will show ledgers for all vendors, not just those with outstanding bills.
5. Select the date range for the report using either the Date drop-down list or the mini-calendars in the From and To fields. The report will include the vendor's beginning balance, if any, for the range selected.
6. Click **OK** to view the report.

The Cash Requirements Report

This report is similar to the Aged Payables report except that the aging is not split into columns. Instead, the actual age in days is listed as a separate column. Also shown on this report are the bill's due date and any available discounts. This makes this report a great tool in planning cash flow to take advantage of offered discounts.

1. Go to the Select a Report window.
2. Select the **Cash Requirements** report and click **Preview** on the toolbar.
3. The Cash Requirements dialog box appears.

   The options here are the same as those on the Aged Payables report.
4. Click **OK** to view the report.

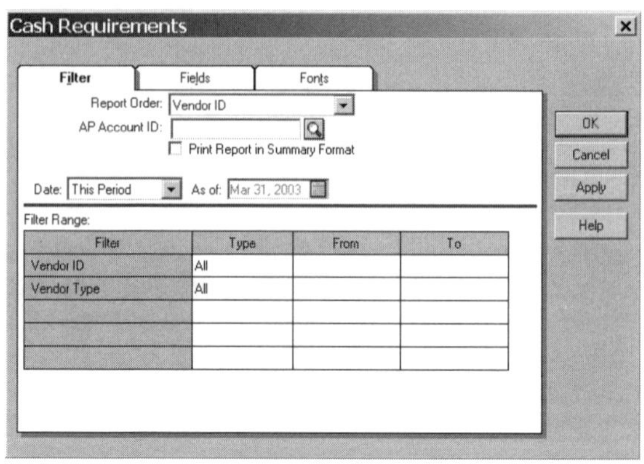

Quickly Viewing Vendor Balances

This method is especially useful when a manager or a customer requests a customer's outstanding balance.

1. Go to the Maintain Vendors form.
2. Select an ID from the Vendor ID drop-down list.
3. The vendor's current balance shows in the lower left-hand corner.

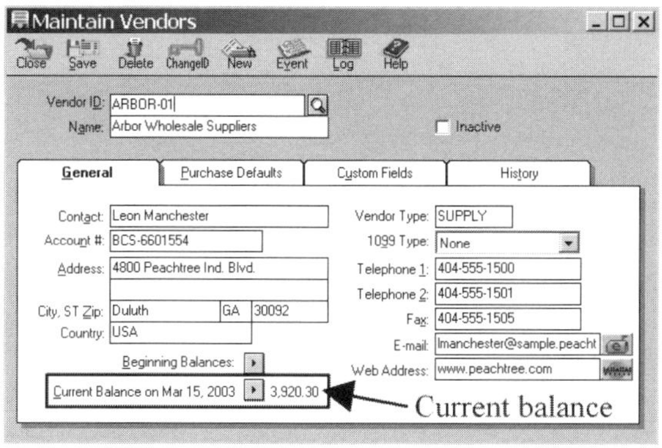

4. Click on the **Current Balance on...** button to view a recent customer ledger.

Summary

In this chapter you should have learned the necessary steps to apply customer bills to your purchases including entering, editing, and deleting bills. You should also have learned the steps in creating a purchase order and applying the purchase order to the bills. These steps will help you to maintain your account payables. In the next chapter, you will learn to pay your account payables.

Chapter 8

Payments

In This Chapter

- Paying bills
- Making payments without a bill
- Making payments with a credit card
- Voiding checks
- Getting a check register

The nicest part about computerized accounting is that checks do not have to be hand written any more. This labor-saving device is worth countless dollars and hours in aching hands. While computerized accounting has simplified and made the process much easier, unfortunately it has not yet figured out a way to eliminate the paying of the bills and the subsequent depletion of the bank account!

Getting Started

There are only two tasks to take care of before you can start paying bills. The first is to have computer checks that you can print. This was discussed in Chapter 7. The second task is to enter the vendor beginning balances.

Entering Vendor Beginning Balances

In all probability, soon after beginning the practice month you will need to pay a bill for a vendor that is not yet in the system. If the bill was entered in the old system in the previous month, you do not want to enter it into the Peachtree system as a purchase. Instead you need to enter it as a vendor beginning balance. If you had entered the bill in the previous month, then it would appear in the A/P general ledger balance. If you then added the purchase to the new system, it would also appear in the A/P balance. That means that you would have double-entered the bill and would not be able to reconcile the accounts payable.

This is why the A/P listing of all outstanding bills that you were told to get in Chapters 3 and 4 is so important. Have this list available when you follow these steps to enter a purchase in the vendor's beginning balance.

1. Verify that the bill matches an invoice or invoices listed on your A/P ledger. If the amount does not match, you must talk to your CPA to see how she wants to handle

the purchase. She may want to have you enter it as a new bill, she may create a journal entry in the old system to include the amount, or she may use some other method to reconcile the difference.

2. Click the **Purchases** folder on the navigation aid and then click the **Vendors** icon.

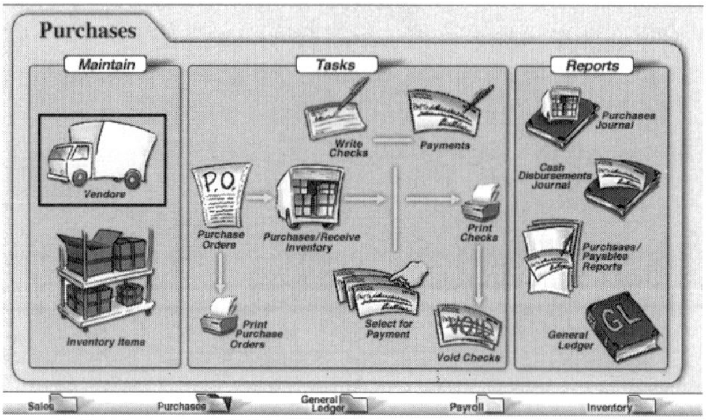

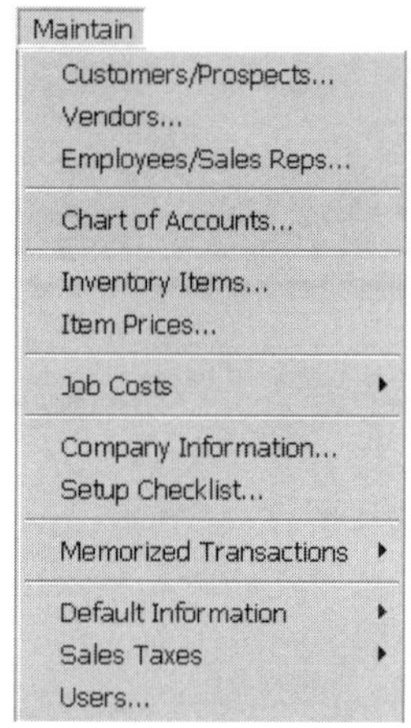

Or select **Maintain**, then **Vendors** from the menu bar.

Or press **Alt+M**, then **V**.

3. The Maintain Vendors form appears.
4. Select an existing vendor from the Vendor ID drop-down list or add a vendor as shown in Chapter 7.
5. Click the **Beginning Balances** button in the lower left-hand corner.

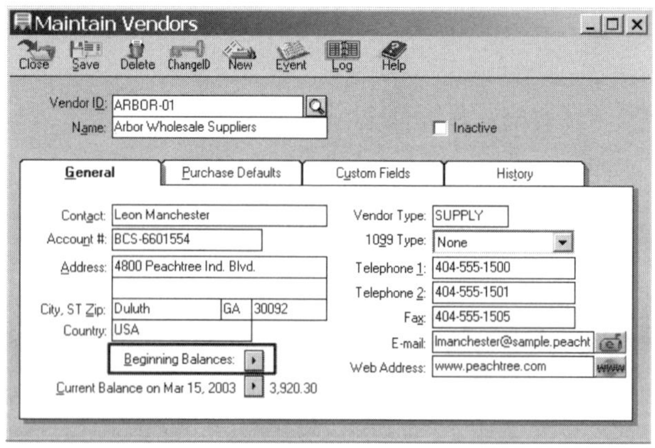

6. The Vendor Beginning Balances screen appears.

   Click on the **Purchases from** tab if it is not showing.

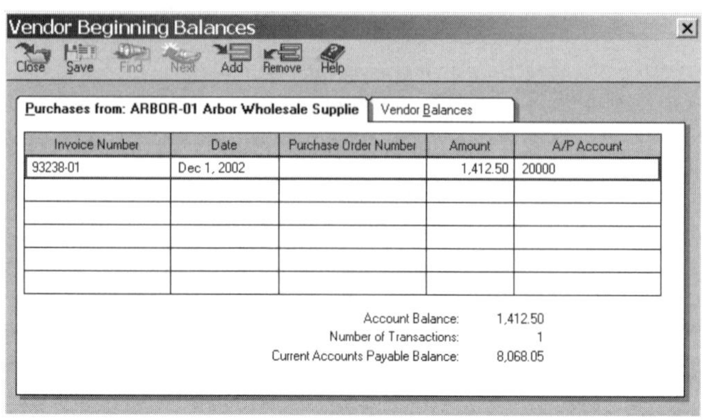

7. Enter a line for each outstanding bill for this vendor in the following columns.

   Invoice Number — This is the vendor's invoice number.

   Date — The date of the original bill.

   Purchase Order Number — If you have a purchase order associated with this bill, enter the number here.

   Amount — The total of the bill, including tax and freight. This should match the total on your A/P listing.

   A/P Account — This should be the accounts payable general ledger account. Most companies only have one A/P account. If you have more than one, verify that this is the correct account.

8. Click **Save** to save the entered bills.

9. Click on the **Vendor Balances** tab to see the listing of all entered vendors with their current balances.

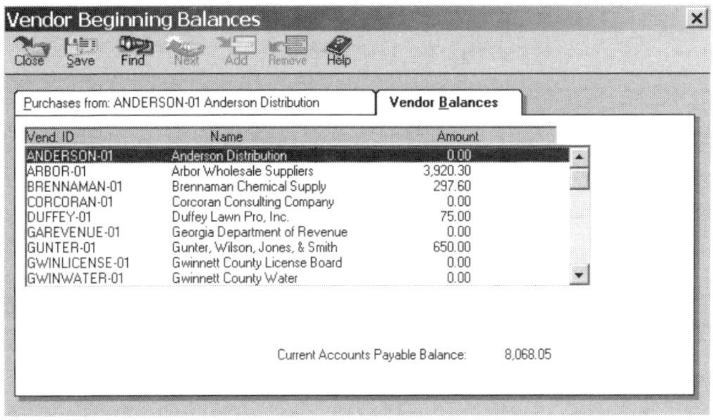

10. To see the total of all vendor beginning balances, you need to change the accounting period (see Chapter 2) to the month before the Begin Transactions date. The amount of the Current Accounts Payable Balance should then match your A/P listing.

11. Click **Close** to leave this screen.

Paying Bills

After entering bills, you will want to pay those bills. (Actually you probably will not want to pay them but the hassles of not paying generally are greater than the pain of just paying the fool things.) Here we will cover paying individual bills and batch printing bills.

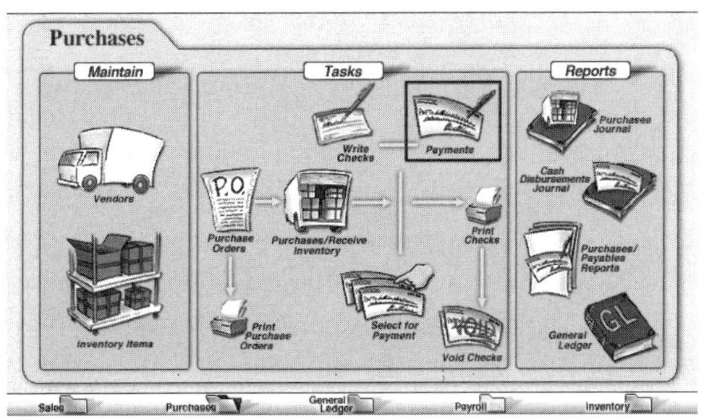

1. Go to the **Purchases** folder on the navigation aid and click on the **Payments** icon.

Or select **Tasks**, **Payments** from the toolbar.

Or press **Alt+K**, then **Y** using the keyboard shortcuts.

2. The Payments form appears.

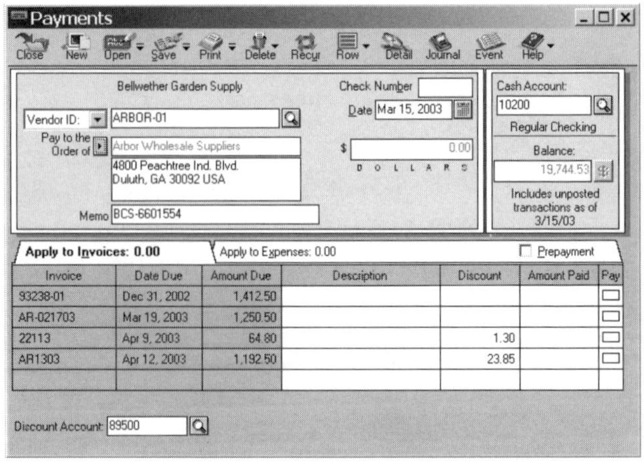

   Enter the vendor ID or select it from the drop-down list. Because there is a bill associated with this payment, there must be a vendor already in the system.

3. If the address that the check is to be sent to is different from the one shown, click the **Pay to the Order of** button.

4. The Pay To Address dialog box appears.

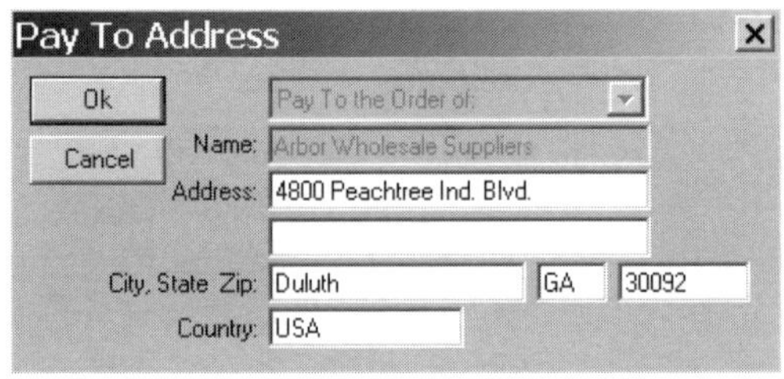

   Change the address if you need to. Click **OK** to return to the Payments form.

5. Leave the Check Number field blank; it will be filled in when the check is printed. Peachtree uses the Check Number field to determine if the check has been printed. If the field is blank, the check is considered to not have been printed.

6. The Date field should contain the date the check is printed, generally today or a date in the near future.

7. If you entered an account number on the vendor form, it will show in the Memo field. You may type other information in here as well.

8. The next field is the Cash Account field. This is the bank account that this payment will be taken from. If you only have one bank account, this number should not be changed. If you have more than one bank account, verify that the correct account is being used. There are also other types of payment that you can enter here, such as a payment from petty cash or credit card payments. Be sure to select the correct general ledger account.

9. Ignore the Balance field for now. The bank balance will be covered in the next month.

10. There are two tabs in the lower section of the Payments form — Apply to Invoices and Apply to Expenses. Because this vendor has bills to be paid, the Apply to Invoices tab should be showing.

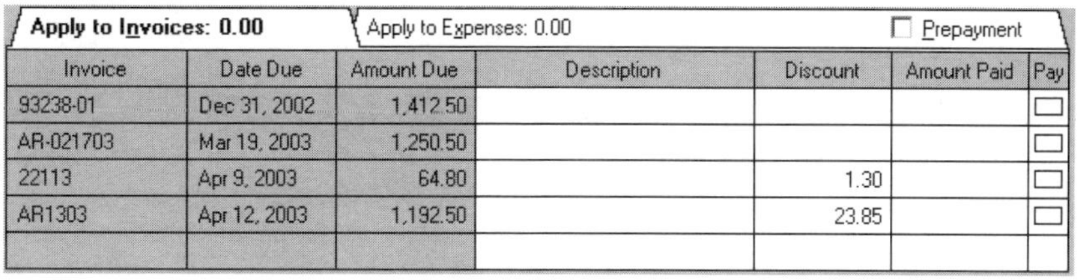

Apply to Invoices: 0.00 | Apply to Expenses: 0.00 | Prepayment

Invoice	Date Due	Amount Due	Description	Discount	Amount Paid	Pay
93238-01	Dec 31, 2002	1,412.50				☐
AR-021703	Mar 19, 2003	1,250.50				☐
22113	Apr 9, 2003	64.80		1.30		☐
AR1303	Apr 12, 2003	1,192.50		23.85		☐

11. The Apply to Invoices tab shows the list of outstanding bills (the vendor Invoice Number column), the due date of the bill, and the amount due.
12. To pay a bill in full, click the check box in the **Pay** column. The total, less any applicable discount, will appear in the Amount Paid column. To make a partial payment, enter the amount you want to pay in the Amount Paid field.
13. You can enter a description if you desire. The description will appear on the check but it will not appear in any of the basic reports.
14. The total of all bills to be paid shows on the tab and in the Dollars field in the upper section of the form.
15. At the bottom of the form is the Discount Account field. This is the G/L account that discounts are allocated to. Generally, you will have just one discount account. Verify that this is the correct account.

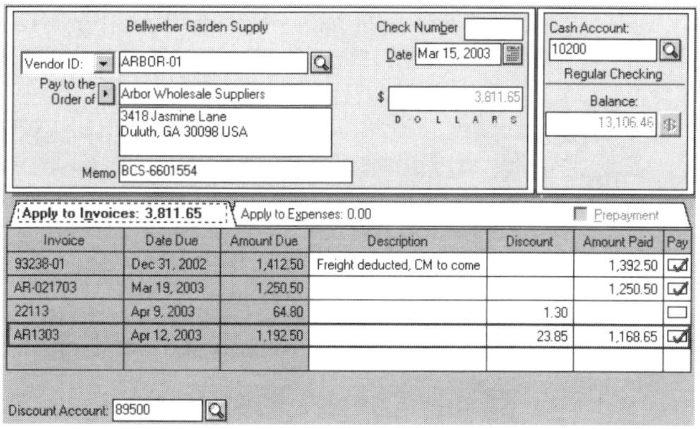

16. From here you can print the check or you can save it for later batch printing. To print the check now, go to the section titled "Printing a Check from the Payments Form." For batch printing, click **Save** or **Post** and skip to the "Batch Printing Checks from the Reports Window" section.

Printing Checks

There are several ways to print checks. In this book we will cover printing a check from the Payments form and batch printing checks from the Reports window.

Printing a Check from the Payments Form

You can print a single check directly from the Payments form either when it is entered or at some later time.

1. If it isn't currently displayed, bring up the payment on the Payments form. The Check Number field should be blank.

2. Print the check by clicking the **Print** button to save and print the check.
3. The Print Forms: Disbursement Checks dialog box appears.

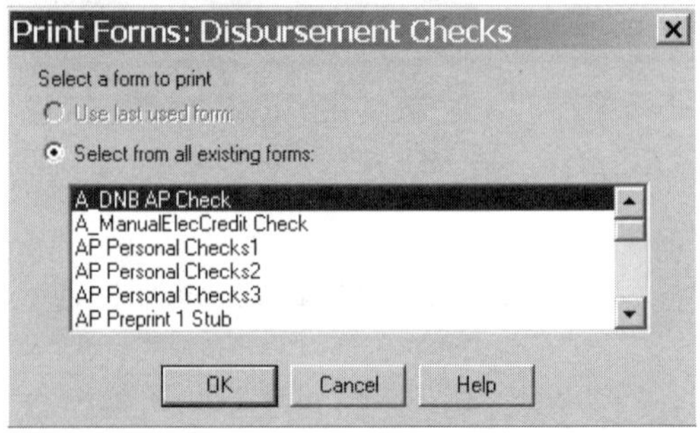

   If you know which check you have, you can select it here. You may need to try a few different checks to find the one to fit your form. I prefer the MultiP AP Chks 2 Stub, which prints on standard Peachtree checks that you can order from any computerized check supplier. Select a check from the Select from all existing forms list and click **OK**.
4. The Print Forms dialog box appears.

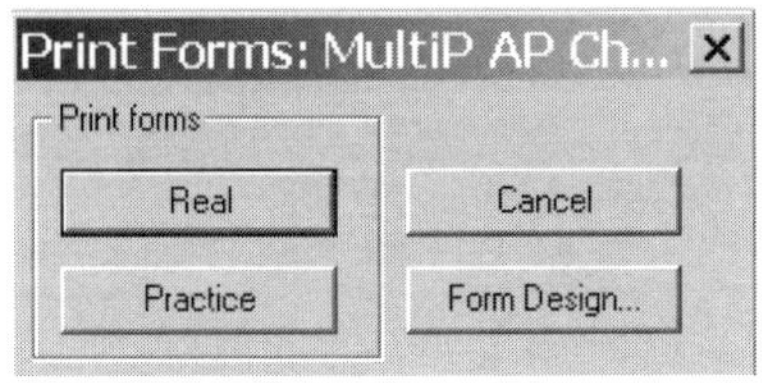

   Click the **Practice** button for this first check so that the program can let you do a test print and align the check to match your printer. Use a blank piece of paper for this test, not a real check.

Note: This is one of the big reasons why I prefer laser checks to continuous forms. Unlike single-page checks, you cannot use a blank piece of paper to set up a continuous form test print. You have to use a good check which you will then need to destroy. The overhead in this operation is extremely time-consuming, annoying, and increases exponentially if you only have one printer that is used for everything.

5. The Windows Print dialog box will appear.

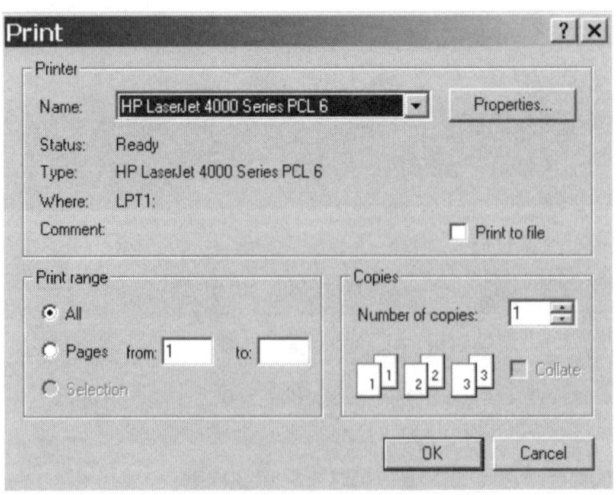

   Select a printer and click **OK**.

6. The Peachtree Accounting printing message box appears, followed by the Did the form align properly message box.

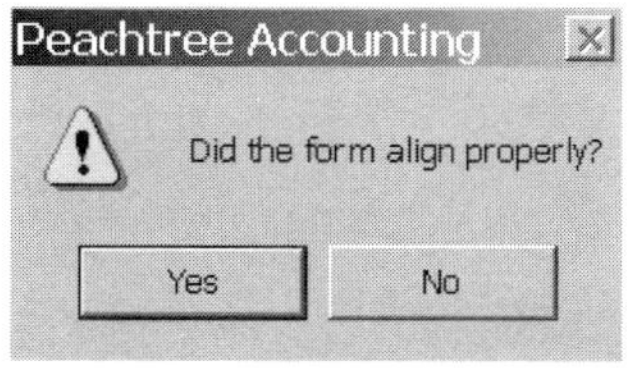

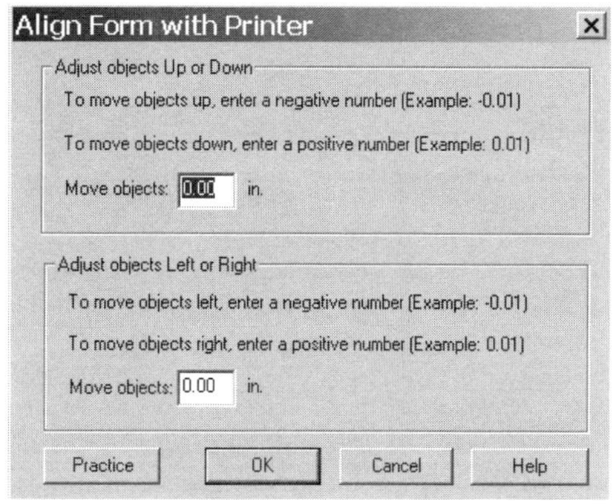

7. Look at the test check that printed and hold it up to a blank real check. If the forms align properly, click **Yes**. If not, click **No** to open the Align Form with Printer dialog box.
8. Read the instructions to move the fields on the check up or down and left or right. Type the number of inches, in hundredths, in the Move objects fields. Click the **Practice** button to test. Repeat the alignment feature until you have the check set up correctly. Click **OK** to save the alignment. You are returned to the Print Forms dialog box.

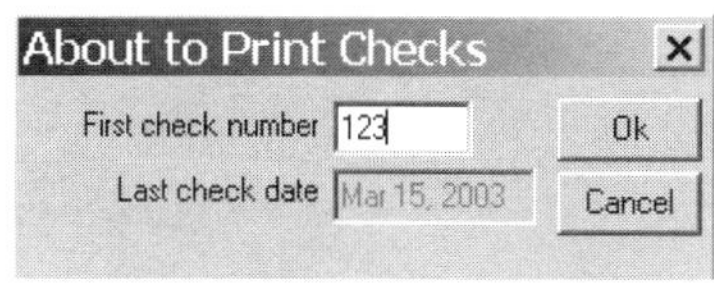

9. Now that you are ready to print the check, click **Real**. The About to Print Checks dialog box appears.

   If this is the first time you have printed a check, type the check number in the First check number field. Verify that the check number matches the check in the printer. Be sure to place the check in the printer and, if this is a shared printer, warn coworkers that you are printing a check.
10. Verify that the check will go to the correct printer. See the section on changing printers in Chapter 2 if you need help.
11. Click **OK**. A message box will appear showing that the check is printing.

Batch Printing Checks from the Reports Window

Another way to print checks is to save all the payments without printing and then print all the checks at once. This is especially helpful if you share a printer with others. By doing this, you only have to load the checks once.

1. Create payments as you normally would, but instead of clicking the **Print** button on the toolbar, click the **Save** or **Post** button.

2. Close the Payments form.
3. Click the **Purchases** folder on the navigation aid and then click the **Purchases/Payables Reports** icon.

   Or select **Reports** and then **Accounts Payable** from the menu bar.

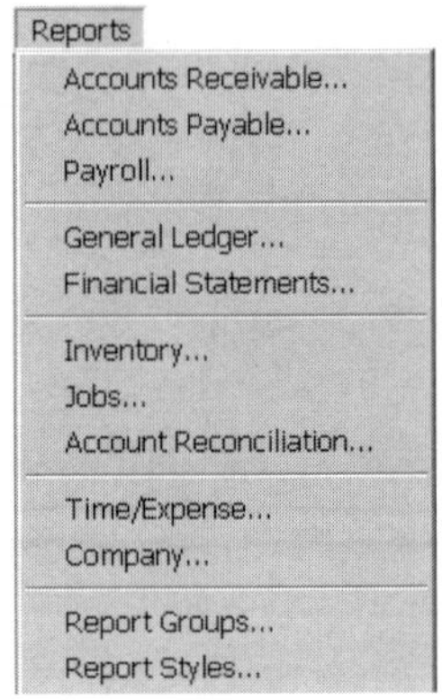

   Or press **Alt+R**, then **P** using the keyboard shortcuts.
4. The Select a Report window appears.

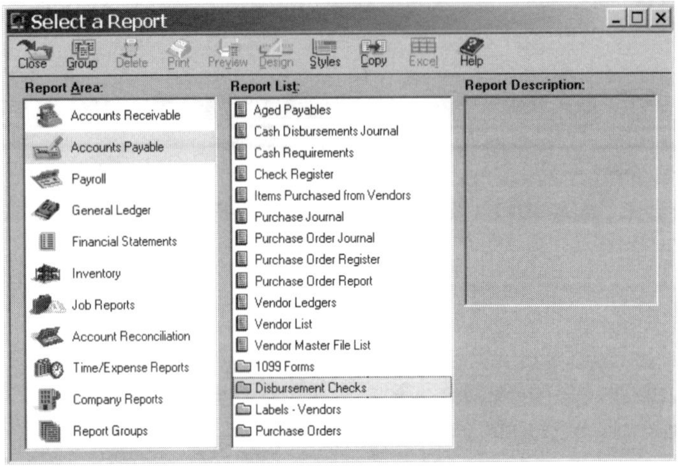

   Verify that **Accounts Payable** is selected in the Report Area list. Click on the **Disbursement Checks** folder in the Report List. Some versions of Peachtree require you to double-click.
5. A list of the check forms appears under Disbursement Checks. Any customized checks will be included with a red arrowhead on the icon.

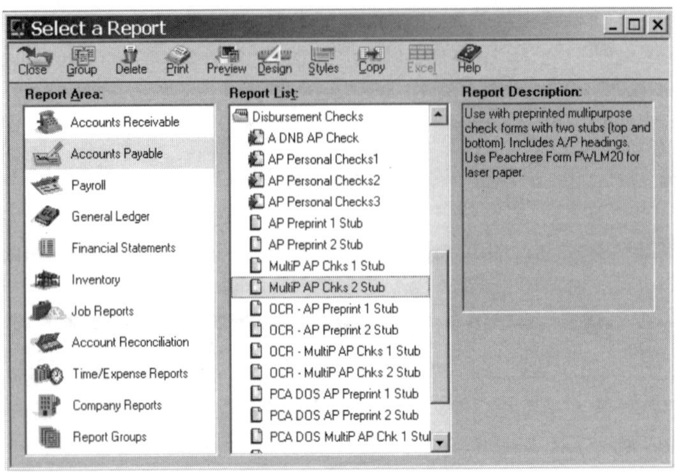

Select the desired check and click the **Print** button in the toolbar.

6. The Forms to Print dialog box appears.

   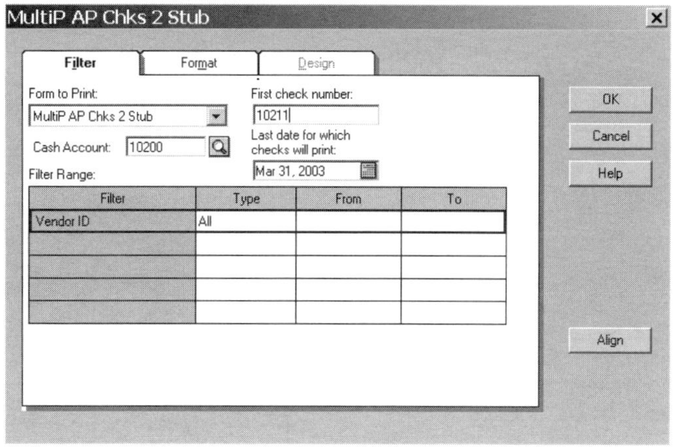

   From this form you may actually change the form you want to print in the Form to Print drop-down box. The First check number field holds the first number on the batch of checks that you will be printing. Verify that it matches the first check to be put in the printer.

7. Select the correct account from the Cash Account drop-down list. When you created the payments, you selected this account. Only payments allocated to this cash account will print.

8. In the Last date for which checks will print field, select the date to print checks through. If a check is dated after the date in this field, it will not print.

9. You can select a range of vendors by typing the vendor IDs in the From and To fields on the Vendor ID line.

10. If you have changed paper in a continuous form printer, you will probably want to print a practice check. If you have already tested your checks with a single-form printer (like most laser and dot-matrix printers) you will not need to do this.

    To align the printer, click the **Align** button.

11. The Align Form with Printer dialog box appears.

    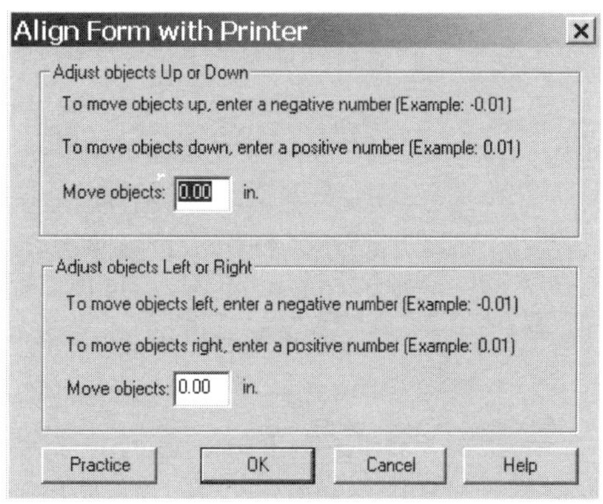

    You may change the alignment of the form by typing the amount to move checks up or down and left or right in the Move objects fields.

12. Click the **Practice** button to print a sample on blank paper. Hold the practice check up to a real check to see if it matches. You are returned to the Align Form with Printer dialog box and can make more adjustments as needed. Continue printing practice checks until the forms align.

13. Click **OK** to return to the Forms to Print dialog box.

14. Place the checks in the printer. Make sure they are in correctly and in the right order. If you share a printer, warn your coworkers that you have loaded checks.
15. Click **OK**.
16. A Print dialog box will appear. Its appearance may vary based upon your printer configuration.

    Make sure that the correct printer is selected. If you are using a laser printer and need additional copies of each check, type the amount in the Number of copies field. Generally, this means that the laser forms have additional pages between each check copy.

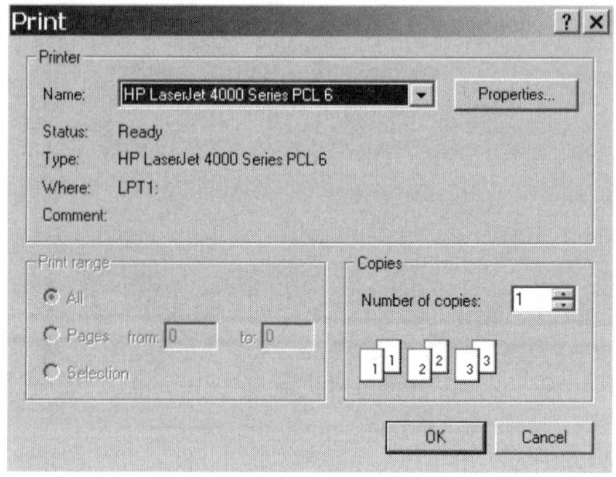

17. Click **OK**.
18. The checks will print. Verify that they are correct and that the Peachtree check numbers match the actual check numbers. A message box will appear asking if the checks printed properly.

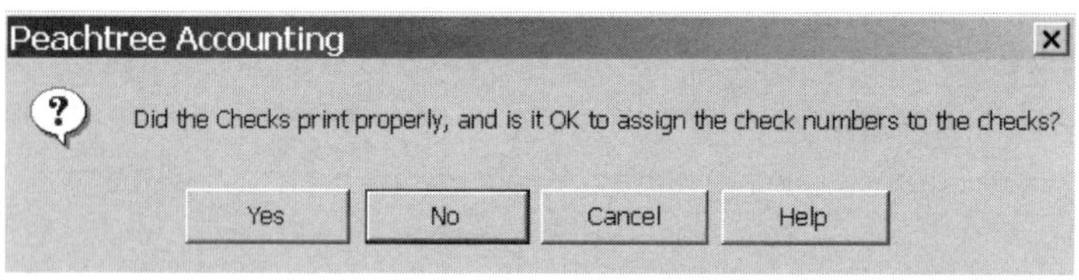

I have had many customers make a mistake here and click the wrong button. The buttons perform the following actions when clicked:

Yes — Peachtree assigns the check numbers to the checks. If you go to the Select Payment window, you will see the payments with numbers as assigned.

No — The entire printing process is cancelled and ignored. Check numbers are not assigned to the checks and you are taken back to the Select a Report window. The program even cancels the use of the check numbers that were assigned so that the next time you print checks the original check number appears.

Cancel — This works exactly like the No button.

Help — This brings up the Peachtree Help window to explain your choices for this message box.

Tip: If you make a mistake and update the checks when some or all have printed incorrectly, you can fix it. Go to the Select Payments window and bring up each incorrect check and remove the check number. Then go through the print process again. All checks without a check number will be reprinted.

Other Types of Payments

Making Payments without a Bill

Sometimes you will need to write a check for which you do not have a bill or you will have to add additional expenses to a check while paying bills. The process is very similar to entering a bill except you will enter the purchase information on the check as opposed to entering it on a bill and then paying the bill.

Making payments without a bill should not be a standard procedure because these bills are not tracked through the accounts payable function. These payments are generally used for C.O.D.'s or when you order cash-and-carry supplies from a company and you want an employee to go pick up the order.

1. Go to the Payments form.
2. Select a vendor ID. Add a new vendor if this vendor is not yet in the system. If this is a one-time payment, you may skip this field.
3. Change the Pay to the Order of address if needed by clicking the associated button. If this is a one-time payment, you may add the payee name in the Name field of the Pay To Address dialog box also. Click **OK** when you are done with the dialog box.

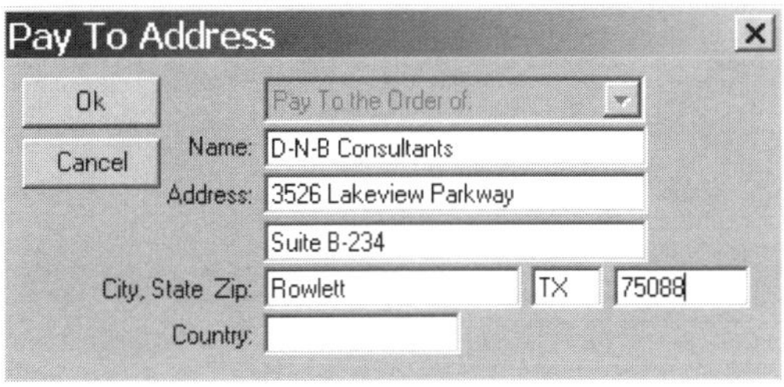

4. Enter information in the Memo field.
5. Leave the Check Number field blank to print the check.
6. Enter the date of the check.
7. Verify that the correct cash account is being used.
8. Select the **Apply to Expenses** tab.
9. Enter the line item information the same way as you would on the Purchases/Receive Inventory form. Remember that you can combine similar items as long as you are not recording inventory that you are also tracking. Inventory must always be entered using the correct ID in the Item column.

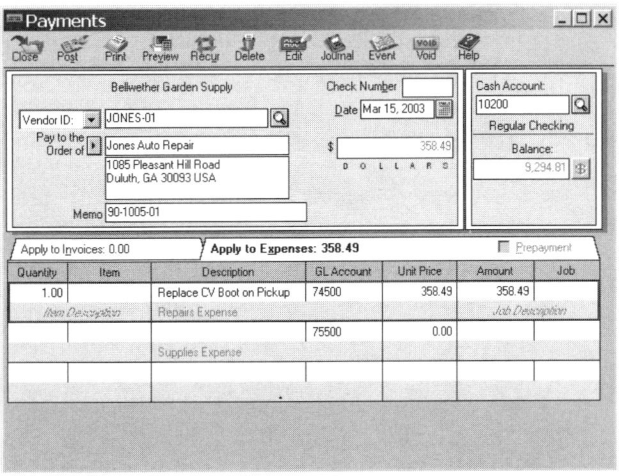

10. Print the check as shown earlier in this chapter.

Entering Manual Checks

In many businesses the owner or manager may carry an ordinary company checkbook with them to pay for all types of expenses. Peachtree can handle this situation easily.

Tip: For businesses that need the flexibility of one or more people writing checks while out at job sites or when buying parts for projects that have immediate needs, you can use Peachtree's strengths to your advantage. Get a separate set of checks — I prefer duplicate checks — for each regular checkwriter. Each set of checks should have a distinct set of check numbers, such as 1001–3999 for the owner, 4001–9999 for the site boss, and 10001+ for the office's laser checks. This way you can tell in an instant who wrote the check based upon the reference in your reports. With the low cost of checks from on-line check companies, there is no reason not to take advantage of this flexibility. Just make sure the check-writers are trustworthy and you have in writing that the check-writer is responsible for any expenses determined to be personal in nature.

1. Open the Payments form.
2. Enter the manual check just as you do other checks.
3. Type the check number in the Check Number field.
4. When everything is entered, click the **Save** or **Post** button in the toolbar. There is no need to print the check.

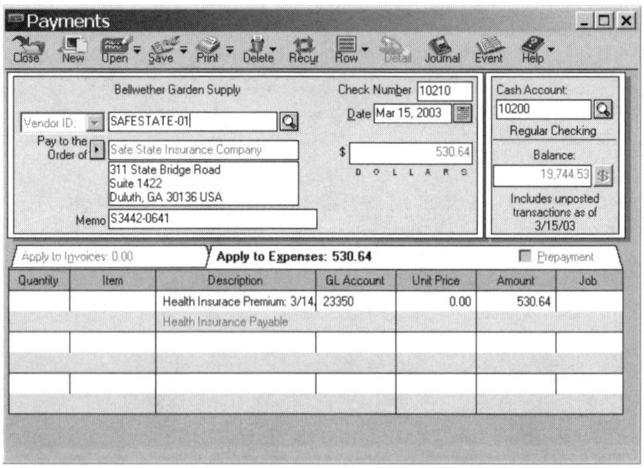

I order duplicate checks for my manual checks so that I can attach the dupe to the receipt or bill instead of a laser check stub.

Automatic Payments

An automatic payment is one that is taken directly from your bank. It requires an authorization by you and is generally a regular monthly payment for such things as insurance payments, Internet access payments, or loan payments. These are entered the same way that manual checks are entered. Because a check is not actually issued for this type of payment you will not be issuing a check number for the automatic payment. Instead, enter an easily recognizable reference that will refer to the automatic payment. For example, use InternetWD03-22 for a regular withdrawal to pay for Internet access that is taken out on the 22nd of the month.

Prepayments

Another type of payment that you may need to handle are prepayments. A prepayment occurs when you need to place a deposit on an order for goods or services. You will not have the bill yet and will want to apply the prepayment to the bill when it arrives. Prepayments can be written on any type of check, printed or manual.

1. Open the Payments form and select the vendor ID.
2. Fill in the Memo and the Date fields. Verify the account in the Cash Account field.
3. Select the **Apply to Expenses** tab.
4. Click the **Prepayment** check box. The details section changes so that only the Description, GL Account, and Amount fields are enabled.

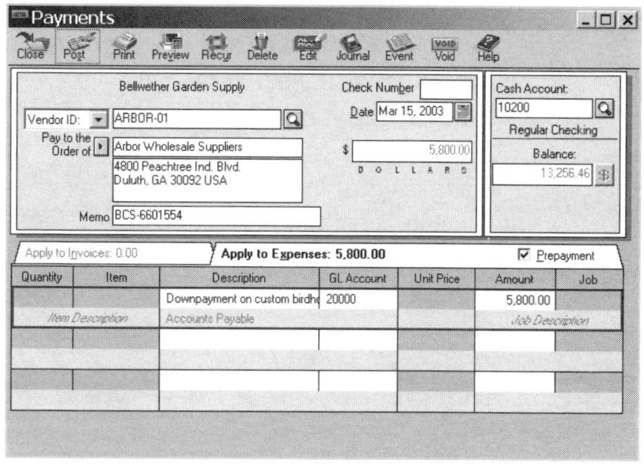

5. Fill in the Description and the Amount fields. The GL Account field should be left as the A/P general ledger account unless you have more than one accounts payable.
6. If this is a manual check, enter the check number and click **Save** or **Post**. If this check needs to be printed, click the **Print** button.

Applying a Prepayment

After you have made the prepayment, the bill will eventually arrive. Enter it in the Purchases section as you do other bills. When you are ready to pay the balance of the bill you can apply the prepayment.

1. Open the Payments form and select the vendor ID.
2. Fill in the Memo and the Date fields. Verify the account.
3. Click the **Apply to Invoices** tab.

   Notice that the prepayment shows as a negative invoice. Your original check number will be in the Invoice column and the check date will be in the Date Due column.

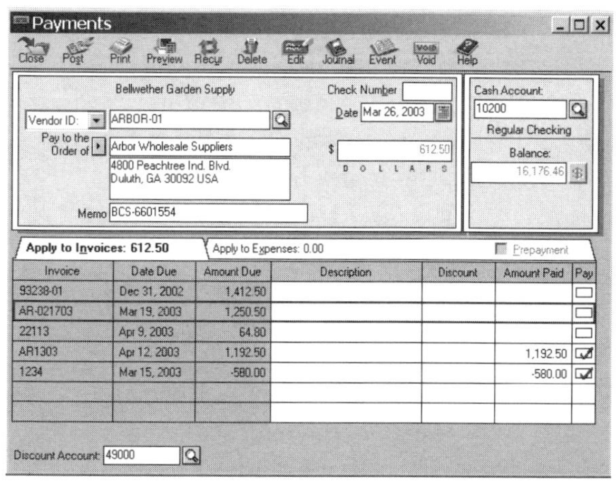

4. Click the **Pay** check box for the bill to be paid along with the prepayment. Alternately, type the amounts in the Amount Paid field. The prepayment should be typed as a negative number. The adjusted total will be calculated in the Dollars field.
5. Print the payment as you normally do.

Applying Vendor Credit Memos

Vendor credit memos are handled the same way as applying prepayments. Once the vendor credit memo is entered (see Chapter 7), it can be applied to any outstanding bill. If the bill and the credit memo cancel each other out (the Dollars field is equal to $0.00), you should enter something like **Write-off** or **Apply CM** in the Check Number field.

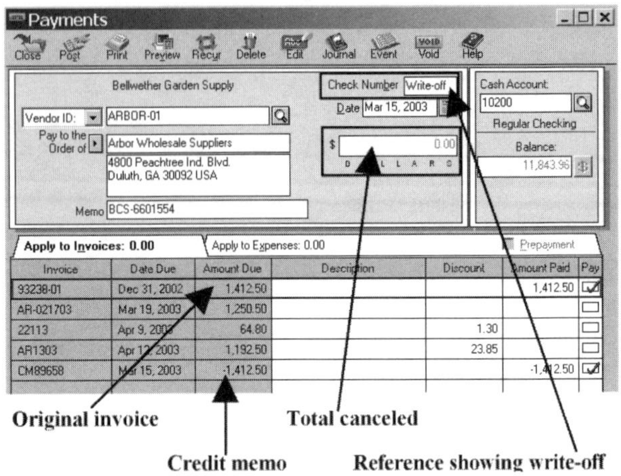

Using Credit Cards to Make Payments

Credit cards make life simpler in many ways. They also make the accounting process of trying to track all the charges and credits far more difficult. Up until recently, I used my own method of tracking credit cards. Recently, I discovered a new method that makes it much easier.

In my old method, I created a bill for each credit card purchase. I applied it to the credit card company and used the purchase invoice number and description to show who the bill was actually for. I added all finance charges and interest in the same way. Then when I went to pay the credit card company I would have all these charges that I had to apply my payments to — some of them going back months. As you can see in the adjacent figure, it could become quite confusing. (Some of the information is marked out for privacy issues.)

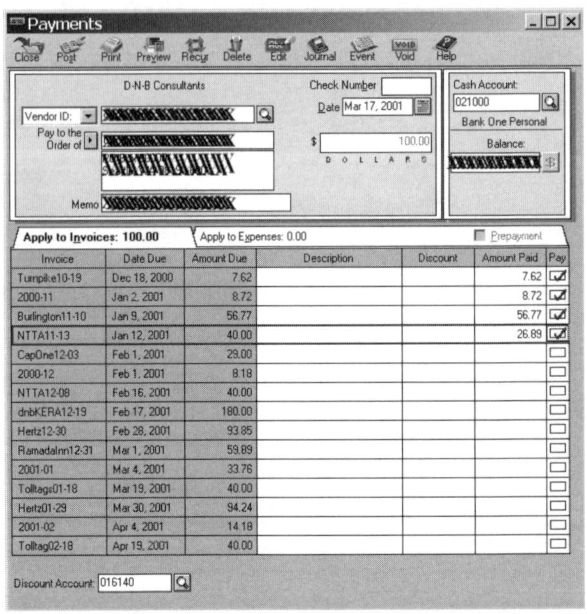

Peachtree handles the problem of credit cards in a totally different way. I recently discovered this new method when I was researching this book. Boy, was I surprised!

Setting Up the Credit Card Liability Account and Vendor Account

In order to make credit card payments, you must first set up a credit card liability account, followed by setting up the vendor. You will need a separate liability account and vendor for each credit card.

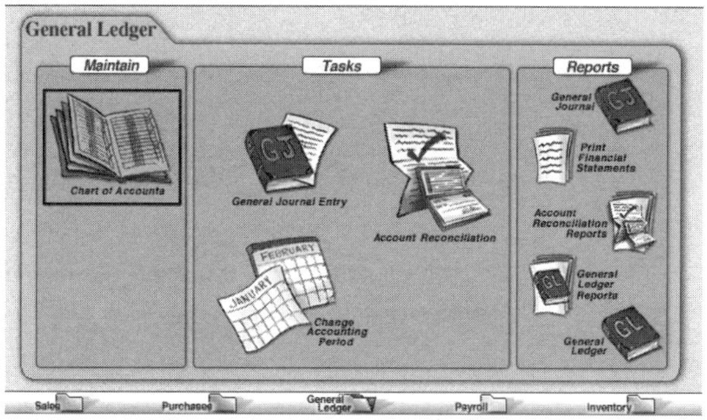

1. Click on the **Chart of Accounts** icon in the **General Ledger** folder on the navigation aid.

   Or select **Maintain**, **Chart of Accounts** from the menu bar.

   Or press **Alt+M**, then **A** using the keyboard shortcuts.

2. The Maintain Chart of Accounts window appears.

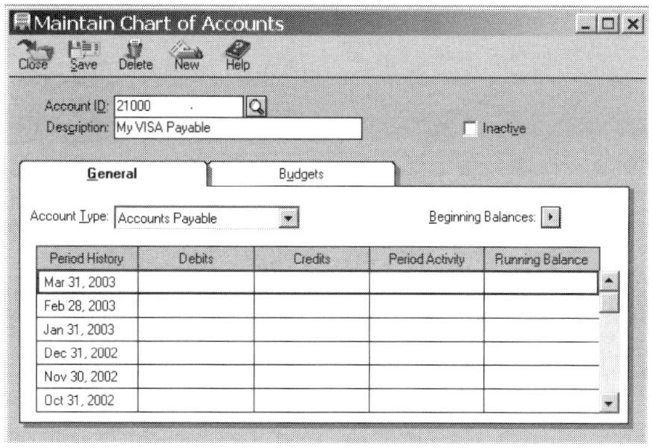

   Enter a new account number in the Account ID field. Be sure to put it in the correct sequence with other accounts payable general ledger accounts. If you use a Peachtree general ledger, the accounts payable account is 20000 and the next G/L account is 23000, so you may want to use a number like 21000. Check with your CPA as to the actual account number to use.

3. Enter a description of the credit card.
4. Select **Accounts Payable** from the Account Type drop-down list.
5. Click **Save** in the toolbar to record the new G/L account.

   Next we want to set up the vendor account for this credit card.

1. Open the Maintain Vendors window as shown in the previous chapter.
2. Fill in the Vendor ID, Name, Address, and other fields as you would normally. Be sure to put the credit card number in the Account # field on the General tab.

3. Click on the **Purchase Defaults** tab.

   In the Purchase Acct field, select the liability account that you just set up.

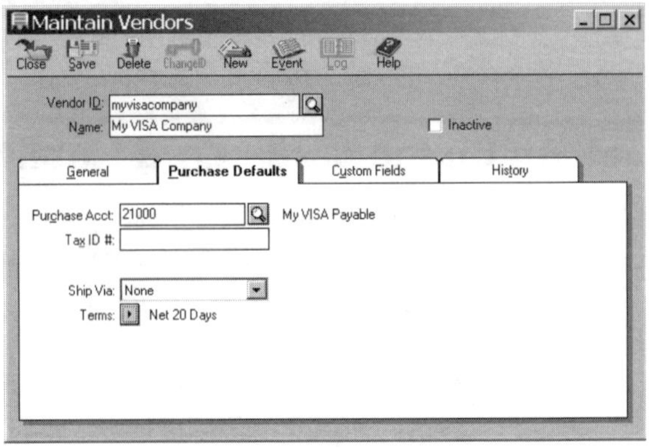

4. Click the **Terms** button.

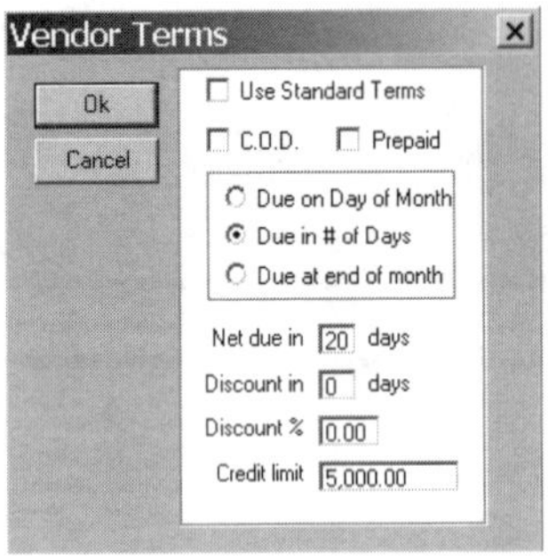

5. Change the terms for the credit card. In the Credit limit field, enter your card's credit limit.
6. Click **OK** to return to the Maintain Vendors window.
7. Click **Save** to record the credit card vendor.

   It is likely that you will have a credit card balance when you begin using Peachtree. Add this to the beginning balance as we showed earlier in this chapter. You can put everything in as a lump sum; just be sure to select the credit card liability account rather than the accounts payable account.

Entering Credit Card Purchases

Once the liability account and the vendor account have been created, you can start entering payments made by credit card. Notice that credit card purchases are not handled through the purchases/receive inventory function, but through the payments function. This is because you are paying one of your creditors with a form of payment that is not a check but a credit card.

1. Open the Payments form.
2. Enter the payment information as you normally would. The vendor is not the credit card, but the actual company that you paid. We pay the credit card company later.

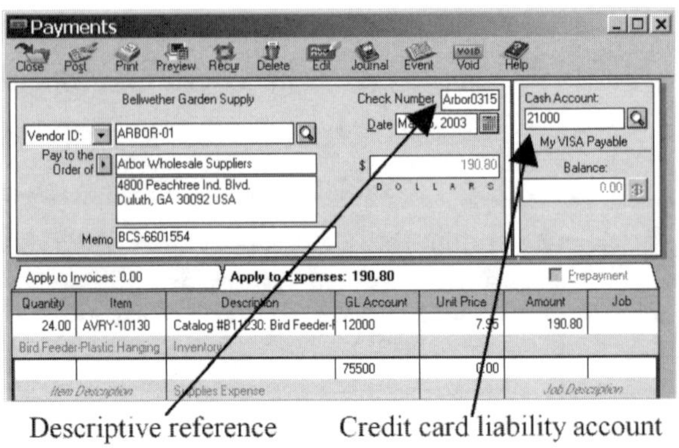

3. In the Check Number field, enter a descriptive reference for this payment. I typically use the vendor name and the month and date. You want something descriptive so that you can recognize this transaction from others when you reconcile the credit card account.
4. In the Cash Account field, enter the credit card liability account rather than a checking account.
5. Click **Save** or **Post** to record the credit card payment. You can print a fake check copy on plain paper if you want an extra document for your files.

> **Tip:** Printing a fake check copy can be a very good idea. That way you can file the original receipt in your vendor file so that if you are questioned about the payment later you won't have to go searching for the receipt in a credit card file or some other place (if you can remember where you filed it). Then save the fake paper copy in the credit card pending file to help you reconcile this later.

Paying Credit Cards

Unfortunately, that credit card statement (like some of the bills mentioned earlier) is going to show up eventually and you will need to pay it. Paying your credit card bill is just like making any other payment. Generally, you will want to reconcile the credit card statement before you make the payment. We will cover balancing the credit card account and entering finance charges in Chapter 13. Here we will cover the payment.

1. Open the Payments form and select the credit card vendor ID.
2. Enter the check date.
3. Verify that the Cash Account field has the correct account.
4. Enter the payment on the Apply to Expenses tab. GL Account must contain the credit card liability account.
5. Print the check according to your normal procedures.

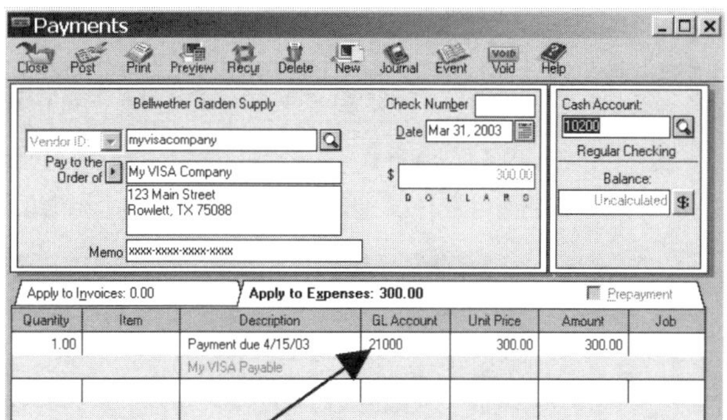

Credit card liability account

Making Payments Homework

After your first few bills are paid, you need to locate all payments against bills and manual checks from earlier in this month and enter them here. The goal this month is to enter all payments into Peachtree that have not yet been entered into your old system as of the first of the month, in addition to adding them to your old accounting system. Most of these can be added as manual checks. You should go ahead and print the check on plain paper so that it can be attached to the original check copy. That way you can readily see which checks have already been entered.

Once you have the knack of paying bills and entering payments, you may go on to another task.

Quick Payment and Check Reports

Payment reports will let you see what bills have been paid.

The Cash Disbursements Journal

This is the journal showing the payments applied in journal entry format. It includes all debits and credits to all general ledger accounts, including applied credit memos, prepayments, and adjustments. The total on this report is not always the total of the checks paid.

This report's options can significantly vary the look of the report. If one particular set of options produces a report that meets your needs especially well, save the settings. It is much easier to save the preferred settings than it is to remember them each time!

1. Click the **Cash Disbursements Journal** icon in the **Purchases** folder on the navigation aid to go directly to the report.

   Or select **Reports**, **Accounts Payable** from the menu bar.

   Or press **Alt+R**, then **P** using the keyboard shortcuts.

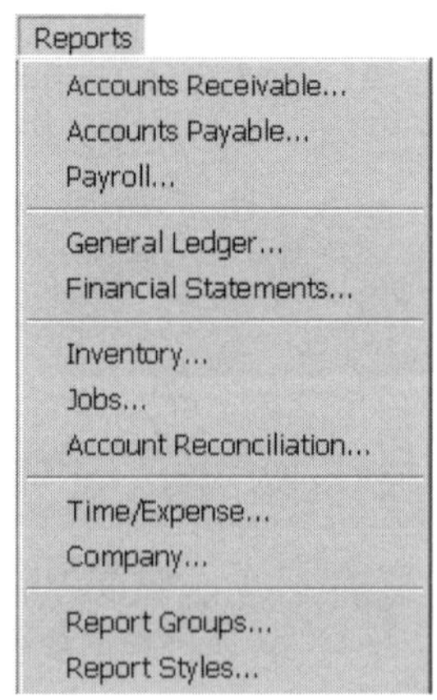

2. The Select a Report window appears.

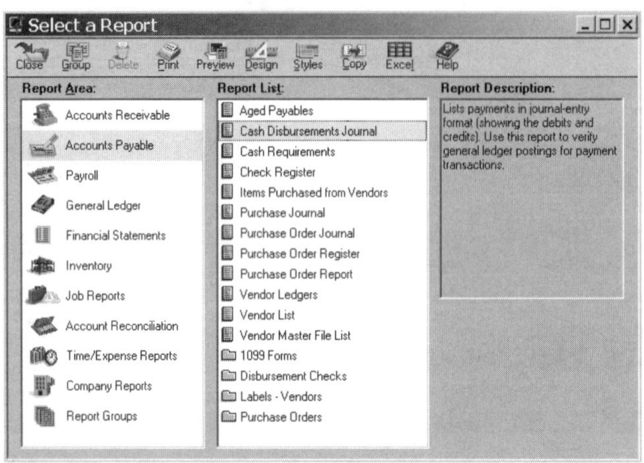

Select the **Cash Disbursements Journal** report and click the **Preview** button.

3. The Cash Disbursements Journal dialog box appears.

   Select a report order. Choices include Check Number, Date, and Account ID.

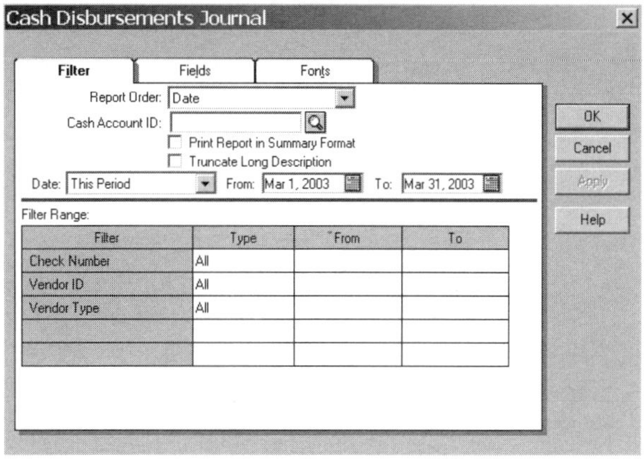

4. Select the correct account in the Cash Account ID field. If none is selected, the report will print for the payments from all accounts.
5. The Print Report in Summary Format option means that the report will be summarized so that there is only one debit or credit amount for each item. Depending upon what was selected in the Report Order field, this may mean that the report is summarized for each general ledger account or for each vendor. This feature takes some experimentation.
6. The Truncate Long Description check box removes descriptions that take more than one line.
7. Select the date range for the report using either the Date drop-down list or the mini-calendars in the From and To fields. For some companies the Today option can be very beneficial, although companies will also use the Current Period option.
8. In the Filter column, the Check Number is a text value, not a numeric value. This means that a filter From 1000 To 2000 will include 10386.
9. To view the report for just one vendor, enter the Vendor ID in the From and To fields of the Filter Range section. To view the report for a range of vendors, such as abccompany to defcompany, enter the IDs in the From and To fields.
10. If you use Vendor Type, you may enter a type in the From and To columns.
11. Click **OK** to view the report.

The Check Register

This report is a simple listing of checks and their total. You can also use it to print a listing of checks about to be printed.

1. Go to the Select a Report window.
2. Select **Check Register** in the Report List and click the **Preview** button.

3. The Check Register dialog box appears.

   Select **Date** or **Check Number** in the Report Order drop-down list.

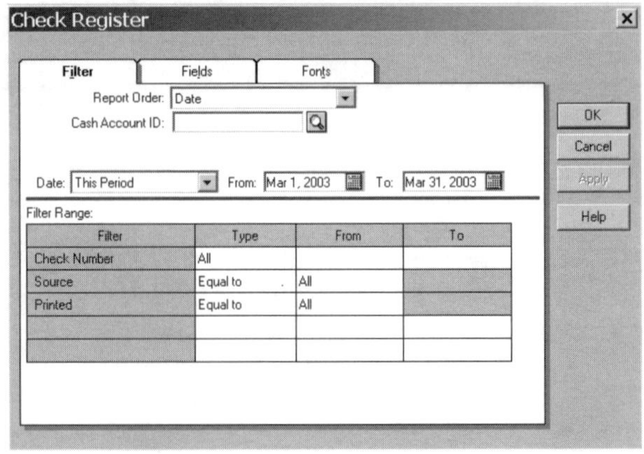

4. Select the correct account in the Cash Account ID field. If none is selected, the report will print for the payments from all accounts. This includes your payroll checking account.
5. Select the date range for the report using either the Date drop-down list or the mini-calendars in the From and To fields. If you have just printed a batch of checks, the Today option can be very beneficial since it will list the checks just printed.
6. In the Filter Range section you can select a Check Number range. Remember that Peachtree does not sort check numbers numerically.
7. Source lets you determine if you only want to show Accounts Payable checks, Payroll checks, or All.
8. The Printed filter lets you select between Printed, Unprinted, or All checks. This is a good filter because you can use it before printing checks to verify the payments to be made by selecting the Unprinted option.
9. Click **OK** to view the report.

Summary

There are many different types of payments to understand in getting Peachtree up and running. Each has its own unique purposes and lets you track your expenditures in an easy-to-use format. Many accounting programs cannot handle payments such as credit cards and manual checks, but Peachtree does it with flair.

Now that sales and payables are covered, it is time to turn to other tasks this month.

Chapter 9

Payroll

In This Chapter

- Using the Payroll Setup Wizard
- Editing pay types and deductions
- Adding employees
- Adding payroll beginning balances
- Employee advances, tips, expenses, vacation, sick leave, and health insurance

The Peachtree payroll function is really robust and will let you pay many types of salaried and hourly employees. In this chapter, I will show you how to personalize your payroll so that it will meet your company's needs. In addition, we will briefly look at employee advances, expenses, and different types of deductions. Payroll taxes will not be covered here, but will be a featured topic in the third month. If you need to make payroll tax deposits before then, you will not encounter any problems since you will still be entering all payroll information in the old program or manual system for all three months of the setup process.

Allow at least one extra day to set up payroll initially, more if you want to use electronic payroll, and to complete your first payroll. Thereafter, depending upon the number of hourly employees, I have seen payroll preparation time drop as much as 80% over what was previously spent. The average decrease in time appears to be at least half.

There are many methods of paying employees. Most companies use the standard salary and hourly time payroll methods. Other companies pay by the piece or billable hour. Some companies use a combination of methods. In this chapter we will show different methods of paying employees.

First though, let me grandstand a little and tell you my opinion of pay methods. I feel that employees ought to be rewarded when they work hard. Companies that offer incentives to employees are more likely to retain those employees. I firmly believe that every dollar spent to retain an employee is many dollars saved in training a new employee. So stop and think about how you can reward your employees.

When I had customer service technicians going out to job sites, I found that they could waste a lot of hours traveling to and from customers' sites and gabbing with the customers on non-billable time. These employees were paid by the hour and some of them did not seem to care very much about how little they accomplished. I also found that warranty work was a problem. If the employee did an incomplete or inadequate job and then later had to return to finish the job, the client could not be billed under the company warranty policy. On the other hand, the employee was paid for that time since he was working. In addition, because I required my employees to attend a certain amount of continuing training, some employees were trying to take advantage of that and spend an inordinate number of hours in seminars and classes.

So I began to think about the problem and decided to work "out of the box." It was then that I discovered a way to pay them that made them want to stuff as many billable hours into the week as possible.

I decided that all techs who worked at customer sites would be paid a small hourly rate. It was at the very lowest end of what was industry standard for entry-level computer techs. So low, that if that was all the employees received, they would soon be looking for new jobs. But it meant that if they were doing paperwork or in training classes, they would still be paid for their time. This rate also covered vacation and sick leave. I only paid a maximum of 40 hours per week and no overtime.

Then I instituted a billable bonus schedule. For the first 20 hours of billable time in a week, employees received a bonus per hour. This bonus was still on the low end, though, so that if employees worked 40 hours with only 10 billable, they received a so-so paycheck, and if they billed 20 hours, the paycheck was better and averaged out to about what the industry standard was in the area.

For 21 to 30 billable hours, I doubled the billable bonus. In this range paychecks rose and the employees were much happier. This payroll amount is what I would have been paying to keep really good employees anyway, but with the bonus system I guaranteed my billable hours, which were the lifeblood of my company. The employees could see the advantage of the additional billable hours since they were benefiting from it.

For more than 30 hours I tripled the billable bonus. Obviously, my go-getters were really hustling to get this many hours in. Because of travel time, it was hard to bill this many hours, but with some overtime they made it. Of course, I was not paying overtime because the employee was getting the bonus instead. This way only good employees received extra pay. At this rate, my employees were competing wage-wise with the top-paid techs in the area.

Interestingly enough, my warranty work decreased. Because warranty hours were not billable, my techs took a few extra minutes to check their work so they wouldn't have to go back out to fix a problem that was not going to pay them. This meant that my customers were happier since once the technician left, the customer's system was almost always going to be solid.

If this idea seems really radical to you, let me remind you how many car mechanics are paid. The car repair industry has huge books telling repair shops how many hours of labor each job should take. This is what the repair shop charges you. So if you have a 2002 Ford Taurus, you will always be charged one hour of labor to replace an alternator. A car that is more difficult to work on would have a different scale, but the number of hours would be constant for all similar jobs on all similar cars. Many shops pay the mechanic according to the books. But if a mechanic can get the job done in half the time, he is still paid for the full time. Therefore, the mechanics who hustle get paid extra.

So if you are looking for a way to motivate your employees, think about what I have said.

Moving off the soapbox and back into teaching mode, it doesn't matter whether you pay team bonuses, hourly bonuses, or job bonuses, Peachtree can make it easy to implement pay methods that are unique to your industry.

Getting Started

The first thing to do before paying employees is to set up the payroll function. You need to set up pay levels, deductions, and other types of payroll accounts. Then you need to enter your employees.

The Payroll Setup Wizard

Peachtree has a wizard to assist in setting up payroll. Follow these steps:

1. Select the **Payroll** folder on the navigation aid and click the **Payroll Setup Wizard** icon.

   Or select **Maintain**, **Default Information**, **Payroll Setup Wizard** from the menu bar.

   Or press **Alt+M**, then **D**, then **P** using the keyboard shortcuts.

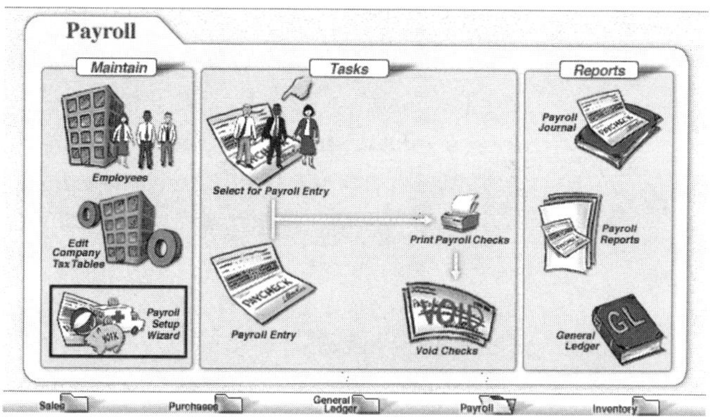

2. The Payroll Setup Wizard appears.

   The wizard shows the current payroll year, which should be this year if you have recently installed Peachtree. Click **Next**.

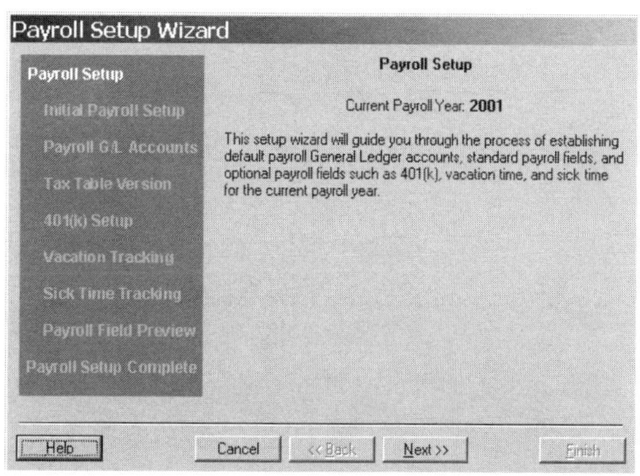

3. The Initial Payroll Setup screen appears.

   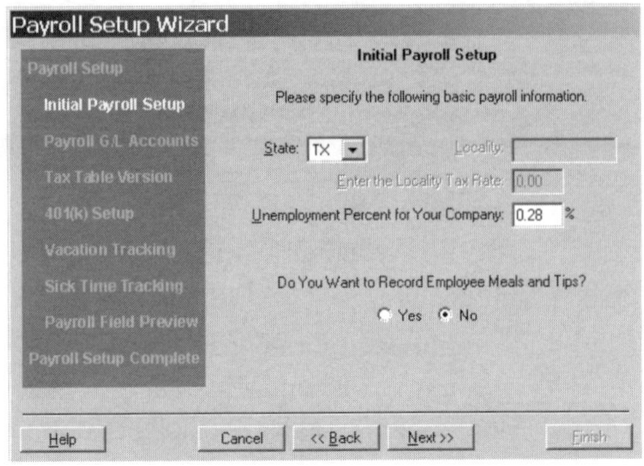

   Select your state from the State drop-down list. Most states luckily do not have local taxes so you will generally skip the Locality fields. If your state does have local taxes, enter the name of the local tax in the Locality field and the rate, as a percentage, in the Enter the Locality Tax Rate field.

4. In the Unemployment Percent for Your Company field, enter your state unemployment rate.
5. Answer the question on employee meals and tips either **Yes** or **No**.
6. Click **Next** to continue.
7. The Default Payroll G/L Accounts screen appears.

   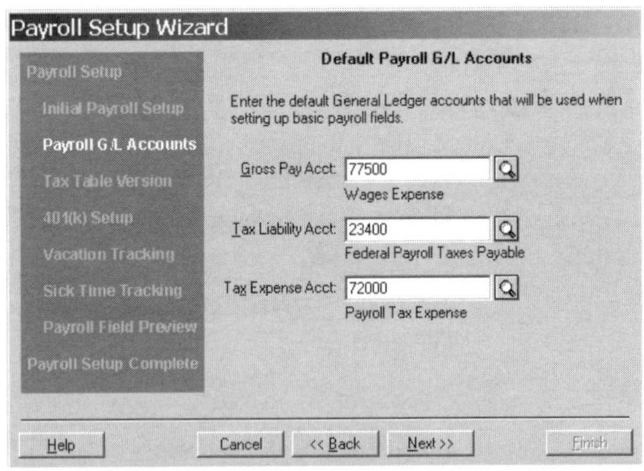

   The Gross Pay Acct field is the salaries or wages account that you use. If you have more than one account, select the main one.

8. The Tax Liability Acct field is for the federal withholding liability account. You should only have one.
9. The Tax Expense Acct field is the G/L expense account where the employee portion of payroll taxes is charged. If you have more than one account, select the main one.
10. Click **Next**.
11. The Payroll Tax Table Information screen appears.

    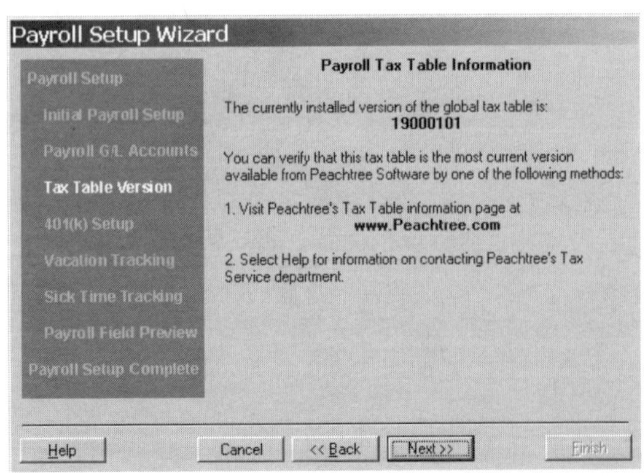

    The installed version of the Peachtree tax table is shown here. Go to the Peachtree.com web site to verify that you have the latest version. A new version was scheduled to be released in April 2002. If you have an older version, you will need to order or download the latest version.

Tip: If you don't have the latest version of the tax table and you purchased Peachtree after the first of the year, call Peachtree. Sometimes they will update your tax table free of charge.

12. Click **Next**.
13. The 401(k) Setup Information screen appears.

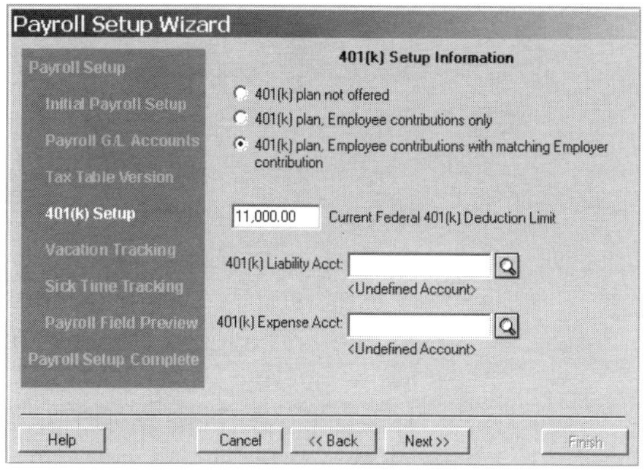

The 401(k) plan is a great way for employers to encourage employees to put money into a pension and profit sharing plan. Most employers match contributions to some extent. If employees contribute to a plan, an employer has legal responsibilities to care for the plan. Discuss your 401(k) situation with your CPA carefully. If you already have a plan, you will want to enter the plan information here.

14. Select the appropriate 401(k) option in the upper portion of the window.
15. Verify the amount in the Current Federal 401(k) Deduction Limit field.
16. Select the correct account in the 401(k) Liability Account field. This is the account that tracks what employees and the employer have accrued.
17. Select the correct account in the 401(k) Expense Account field. This is the account for the employer's contributions to be expensed against.
18. Click **Next**.
19. If you selected to match contributions, Part II of the 401(k) setup will appear. Otherwise, you will skip this window and move to Step 21.

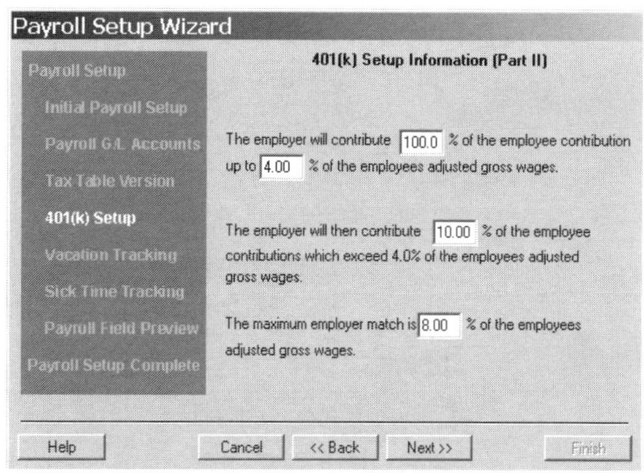

This window has three contribution limits. The first is how much your company matches for each dollar that an employee contributes at the beginning of the year. Some companies match dollar-for-dollar up to a specific percentage of the employee's wages. In that case you would enter 100 in The employer will contribute field and the percentage you are matching in the up to field. Some employers only match a percentage of the employee's contributions. Remember to use whole numbers, not decimals (4.00 equals 4%, .04 equals 0.04%).

Once the initial percentage is met, some employers continue to match a portion. On the first 4% of wages, the employer may match 100%; after that point the match may drop. The match for later contributions should be entered in The employer will then contribute field.

The maximum employer match is field is the limit of all employer matching.

Click **Next** to continue.

20. The Tracking Vacation Time window appears.

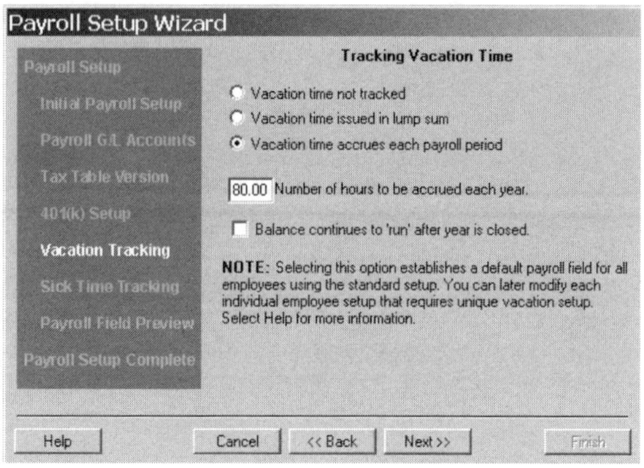

    There are three options in the upper portion of this window. If you do not offer or track vacation, select the first option. The second option is for companies that assign payroll accumulations on a calendar or annual basis. These companies assign vacation when the employee's hiring anniversary comes up or they assign it at the first of the year for all employees based upon the number of months the employee has worked.

    The last option accrues one period's worth of vacation each time the employee is paid. Many employers use this method because once it is set up there is very little maintenance.

21. The Number of hours to be accrued each year field contains the standard vacation time that you offer to employees. If you type 80 hours in the field, and you selected to accrue vacation each period, and you pay twice a month, the per period accrual will be 3.33 hours.
22. The Balance continues to 'run' field is for companies that allow employees to use vacation and save it up past the end of the year. If employees must use their vacation in the current year, do not select this check box.
23. Click **Next** to continue.
24. The Tracking Sick Time window appears.

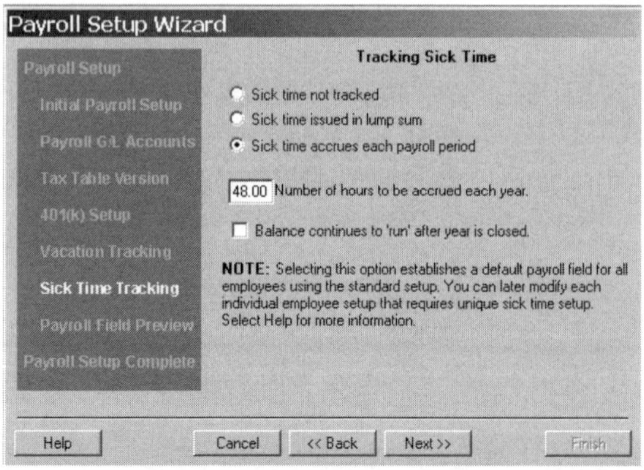

    Tracking sick leave is exactly like vacation. If you do not track sick time, select the first option. If sick time is assigned annually, select the second option. If sick time is accrued each pay period, select that option.

25. Fill in the Number of hours to be accrued each year field.
26. If sick time can be carried over to the next year, click the **Balance continues** check box. This means that all sick time will be carried over.
27. Click **Next** to continue.
28. The Payroll Field Preview appears.

    If this is the first time that you have run the payroll wizard, the EmployEE Fields tab will show all of the added payroll expense G/L account and the liability G/L accounts for the employee's portion of payroll. The EmployER Fields tab shows both the liability and the payroll taxes expense G/L accounts that have been added. Peachtree uses the EE and ER in these fields so that you can quickly distinguish between the employee's deductions and the employer's deductions.

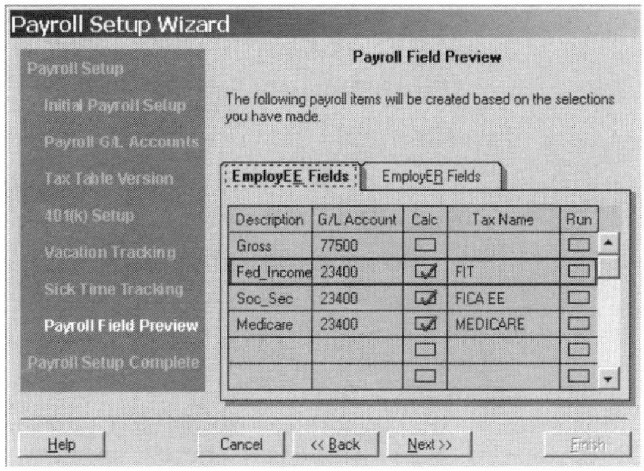

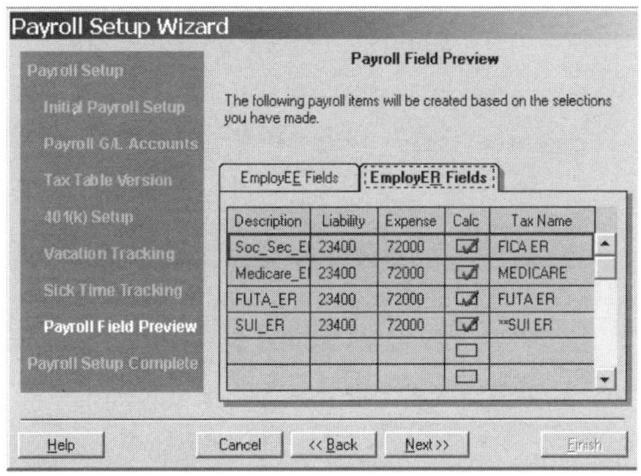

29. If you are modifying payroll fields, only the new fields will show on these tabs.

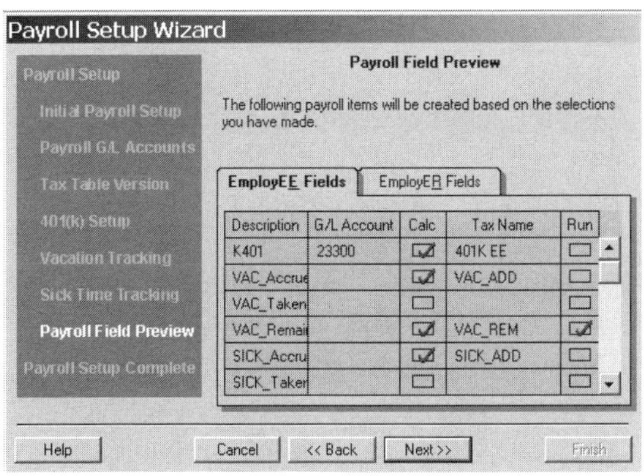

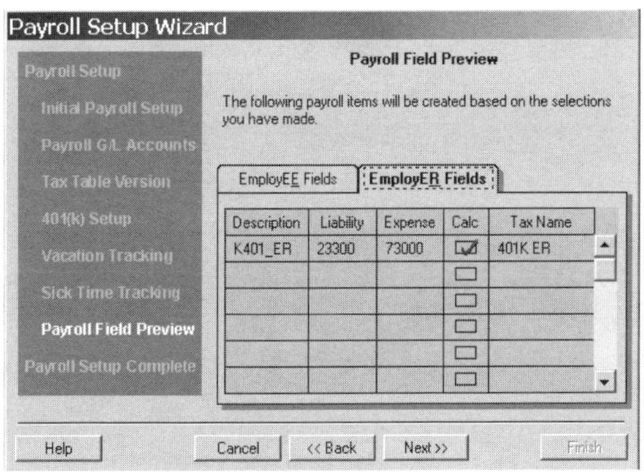

30. Click **Next** to see the Payroll Setup Complete screen. Click **Finish** to close the wizard.

Entering Payroll

Now it is time to enter payroll. This is so easy that you will be sorry that you haven't used Peachtree before now to do this.

1. Select the **Payroll** folder in the navigation aid and click the **Payroll Entry** icon, or select **Task**, **Payroll Entry** from the menu bar, or press **Alt+K**, then **E** using the keyboard shortcuts.
2. If this is the first time you have opened payroll, the Select a Cash Account message box appears. After you have entered payroll, this message box sometimes continues to appear. Select the account you will be paying payroll from and click **OK**. If the message box does not appear or you make a mistake, the account can be changed on the Payroll Entry form.

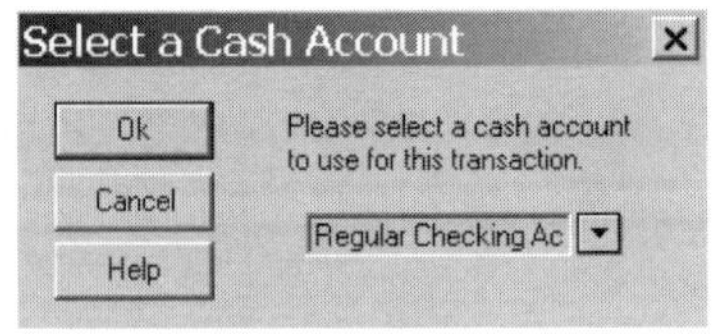

3. The Payroll Entry form appears.

   You probably do not have any employees in the system yet. Employees can be added directly from the Payroll Entry screen. To add an employee, see the following section. If you already have employees entered, continue with Step 4.

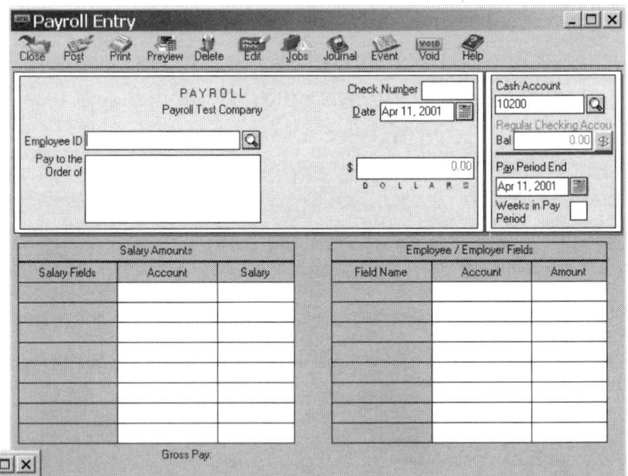

4. Select an employee in the Employee ID field.

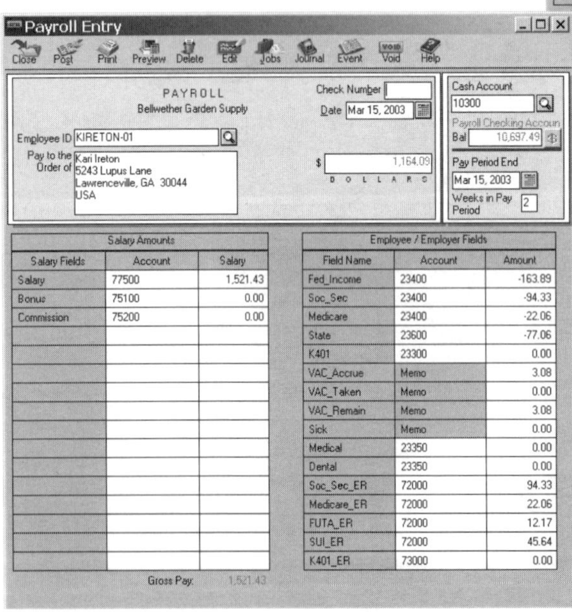

Several things happen when the employee is entered. The system already knows what type of pay is due this employee and enters the salary for the period in the Salary Amounts columns. Then the deductions are calculated and shown in the Employee/Employer Fields columns for Fed_Income (federal withholding), Soc_Sec, Medicare, and State withholding. It also figures the 401(k), medical and dental insurance, and vacation amounts, and any other deductions that you have set up.

5. The employer portion of deductions is also calculated and shown at the bottom of the Employee/Employer Fields columns. These fields are shown with _ER at the end of the field names. They show up as positive amounts.
6. If the employee is paid hourly, the Salary Amounts columns change to Hours Worked. The hours per pay period entered on the employee form is automatically entered in the Regular field.

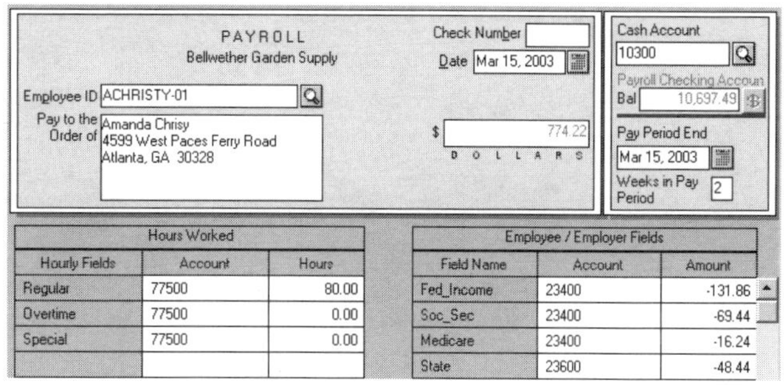

7. You may change the number of hours. If you do so, the Gross Pay and deductions fields will be recalculated.

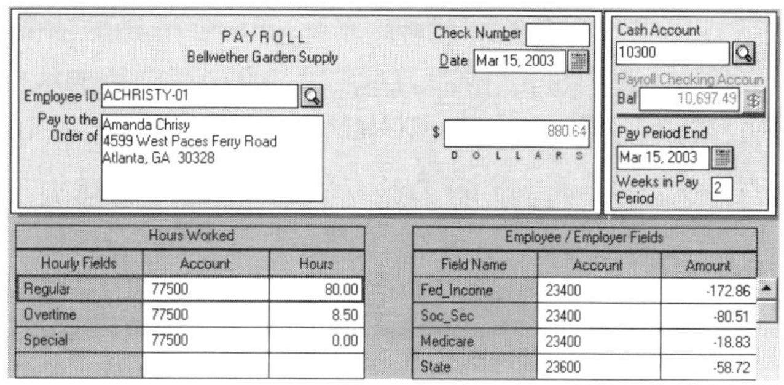

8. In the upper section of the payroll record, leave the Check Number field blank. It works just like the check numbers for accounts payable.
9. Enter the date of the payroll check.
10. The Dollars field is the net pay for this employee.
11. Verify the account in the Cash Account field.
12. The Pay Period End field contains the closing day for the pay period. For some companies it may be the same day as the paycheck and for others it may be weeks earlier.
13. The Weeks in Pay Period field is filled in automatically.
14. Click **Print** to print the payroll check. It is printed in the same manner as accounts payable checks.

Adding an Employee "On the Fly"

1. Click the **Lookup** button in the Employee ID field and then click the **New** button.
2. The Maintain Employees/Sales Reps form appears.

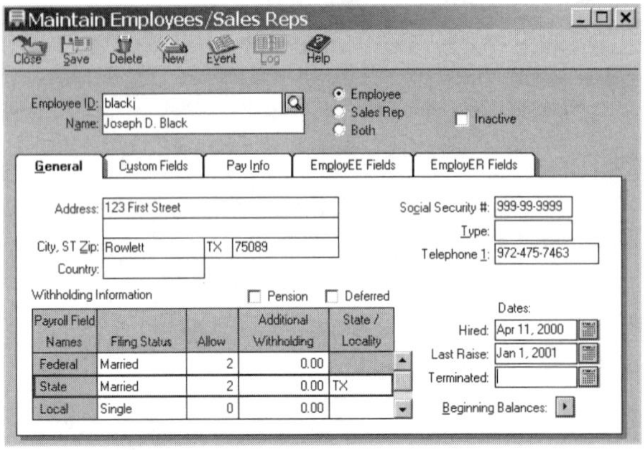

Enter a unique employee ID. I prefer using the last name followed by the first initial. If I have two employees with similar names, I might also use a middle initial or add something to the ID to distinguish between the two.

3. In the Name field, enter the name of the employee as it will appear on the check, the W-2, and government payroll reports.
4. Fill in the Address, Social Security #, and Telephone 1 fields, and the Hired and Last Raise fields below Dates.
5. Ignore the Type field and Pension option for now. Select the **Deferred** check box if the employee participates in a 401(k) plan.
6. In the Withholding Information section, fill in the Filing Status, Allow (for W-2 allowances), and Additional Withholding fields according to the information on your employee's W-4. If your W-4s are not current, this is a good time to get them updated. Also enter the information for the State and Local lines, if used.
7. We will ignore the Beginning Balances button for now. This will be addressed later in this chapter.
8. Select the **Pay Info** tab.

   Here you determine how this employee is to be paid. In the Pay Method field, you can select Salary, Hours per Pay Period, and Time Ticket Hours. For now we will concentrate on the first two methods. Time ticket hours will not be covered in this book.

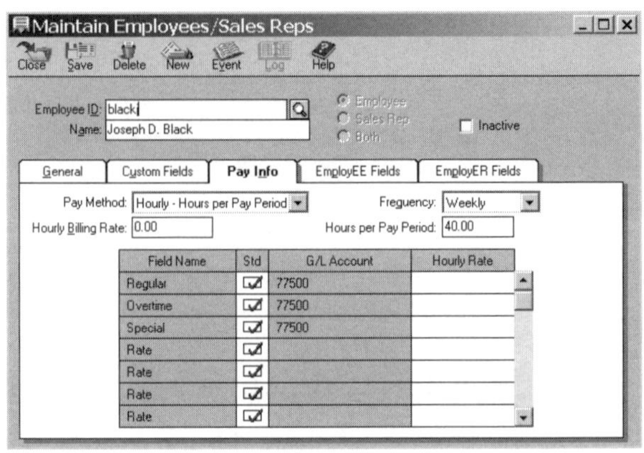

Note: If you use ADP payroll processing, a fourth method is also available — Electronic time. We will not cover this method in this book. You need to contact ADP if you are using this method.

9. Select how often you pay in the Frequency field.

10. The Hours per Pay Period field is automatically filled in when you select the payroll frequency. When you get to biweekly and monthly, the hours could vary from period to period. This can be changed during payroll entry. If this is a part-time employee, you can change this entry.
11. If you chose Salary, the lower section has a Salary Rate column for each of the salary field names. This is the salary per pay period. Enter only the regularly paid amounts and leave occasional payments, such as Bonus and Special as 0.00, unless those amounts are to be paid on all checks. If the payments are only paid occasionally, you may type the actual amount on the paycheck.

    If this is an hourly employee, fill in the hourly rate for Regular hours, Overtime hours, or any other type of pay for this employee only. If the employee does not receive one of the pay types, leave it blank.

Tip: If you need to occasionally pay amounts to hourly employees using the Special rate, type **1.00** into the Hourly Rate column. This way you can type the actual number of dollars you want to pay the employee, instead of a calculated number of hours.

12. You may look at the EmployEE Fields and the EmployER Fields tabs, but we will not make any changes to these fields at this time.
13. Click **Save** to save this employee. Click **Close** to return to the Payroll Entry form. After adding an employee, continue with Step 4 in the previous section.

Payroll Homework

The amount of homework you have with payroll depends upon how accurate you want your end-of-year records to be for this payroll year. If you are near the end of the year, you may want to figure year-end reports manually. If you are near the beginning of the year, you will want to get the entire year's payroll information into the system for quarterly and annual reports.

Regardless, you need to enter all payroll checks between now and the first of this month.

Payroll Beginning Balances

To get previous months into the system for reporting purposes, follow these steps:

1. Click the **Payroll** folder and the **Employees** icon on the navigation aid or select **Maintain**, **Employees/Sales Reps** from the menu bar or press **Alt+M**, then **E** using the keyboard shortcuts. The Maintain Employees/Sales Reps form appears.
2. Click the **Beginning Balances** button on the General tab.

3. The Employee Beginning Balances form appears.

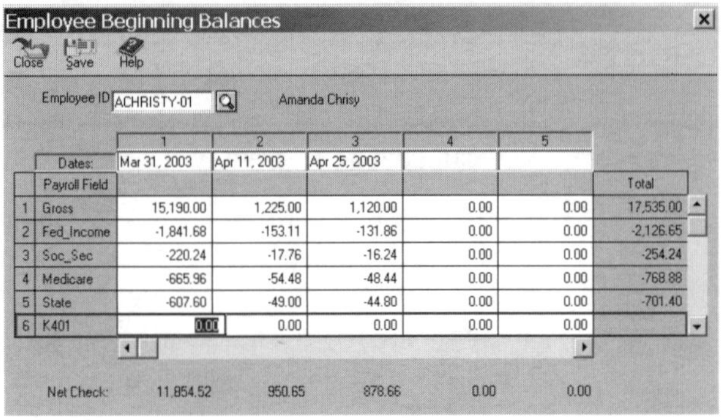

You may enter previous payroll information in any way that you want for payroll periods previous to the current month. One of the best ways is to enter previous quarters as entire quarters and then each check for the current quarter, not counting the current month. For example, if I paid payroll biweekly and I were beginning my Three-Month Plan in May, I would enter the first quarter, ended March 31, in the first column. I would then enter the two pay periods in April in the next two columns. All of my May payroll would be entered through the regular payroll function.

4. Enter the gross pay and all of the deductions as shown.
5. Click **Save** to record the beginning payroll balances.

Other Types of Payroll

There are few tasks in Peachtree as varied as payroll. There are so many different ways to pay employees, so many deductions, and so many records to keep. We have already covered the basics of calculating a paycheck; now we will cover some of the constant tasks and worries of the payroll specialist.

Employee Advances

Many employers allow their employees to receive part of their pay as an advance or a loan on occasion. These might be used for such diverse things as helping an employee pay the rent or post bail, for an employer-sponsored employee computer purchase program (one of my personal favorites since I have a computer services company), or for educational reimbursement. All may be good reasons to loan money to your employees to retain their services.

Creating an Employee Loan Receivables Account

In order to make employee advances, you must first set up an employee advances receivables account. If you want to distinguish between regular employee advances and another type of advance, say employee computer purchases, car loans, or even mortgage loans, you will need a receivables general ledger account for each different type of receivable. If you have used one of the Peachtree standard charts of account, an employee advances account may already exist.

1. Click on the **General Ledger** folder and the **Chart of Accounts** icon on the navigation aid.

   Or select **Maintain**, **Chart of Accounts** from the menu bar.

   Or press **Alt+M**, then **A** using the keyboard shortcuts.

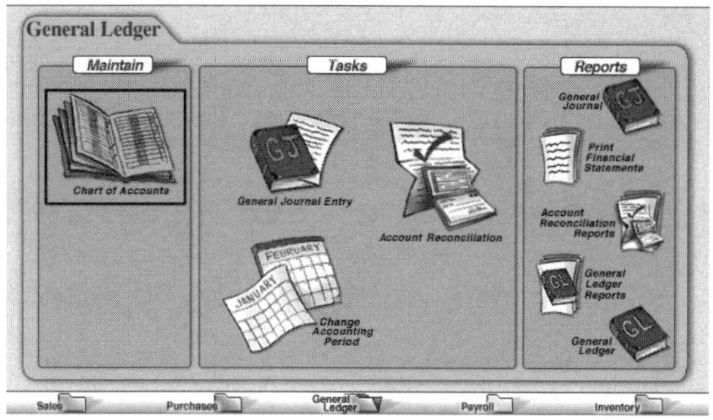

2. The Maintain Chart of Accounts window appears.

   Enter a new account number in the Account ID field. Be sure to put it in the correct sequence with other account payable general ledger accounts. Check with your CPA for the actual account number to use.

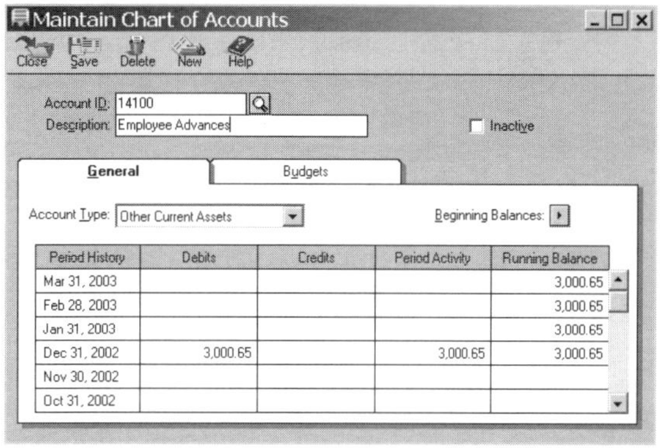

3. Enter a description of the receivables account.
4. Select **Other Current Assets** from the Account Type drop-down list.
5. Click **Save** in the toolbar to record the new G/L account.

Creating the Employee Loan Default Field

The next task is to create a line item on your paychecks to pay and receive loan payments.

1. Select **Maintain**, **Default Information**, then **Employees** from the menu bar.

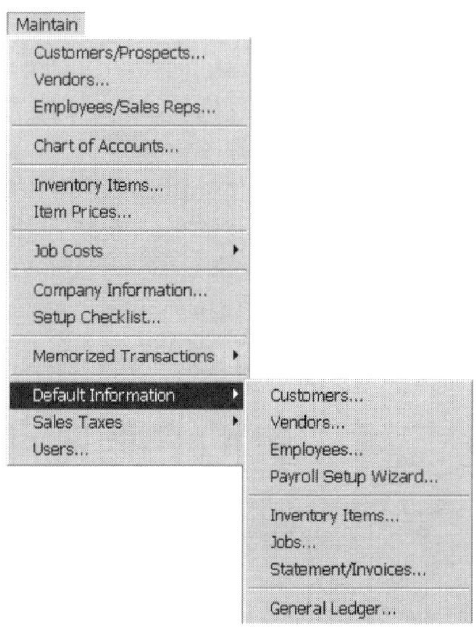

2. The Employee Defaults window appears. Click on the **EmployEE Fields** tab.

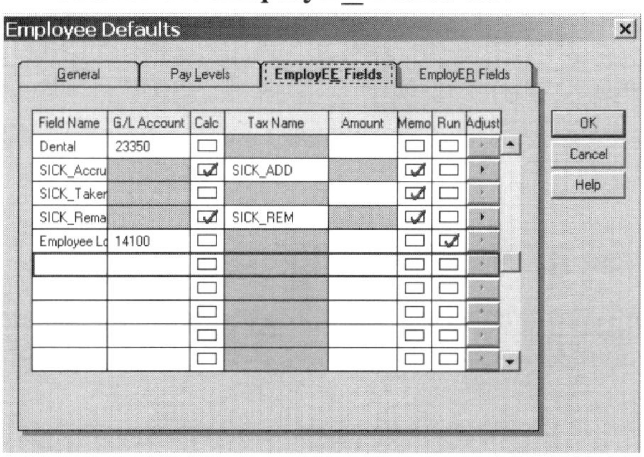

3. Add a line at the bottom of the list. The Field Name should be **Employee Loans** or some similar name. The G/L Account is the general ledger account that we just created. Leave the rest of the fields alone for now, except the Run check box. Select **Run** so that loans will not be zeroed out at the beginning of the next year.
4. Click **OK** to save the information.

Making an Employee Advance

Now that the receivables account and the pay field have been set up, you may create an advance check.

Tip: Before giving out any employee advance, you should get a signed promissory note regarding repayment of the debt. This note should state that if the employee is terminated or quits for any reason, the balance of the debt may be deducted from any remaining payments to be made to the employee. In many states, without such a notice you can be required, by law, to pay the employee without deducting anything. Be smart — all employers know that relationships with employees can degenerate very quickly and for no apparent reason. You may want to see your CPA or attorney about this if you have any questions and to prevent future regrets.

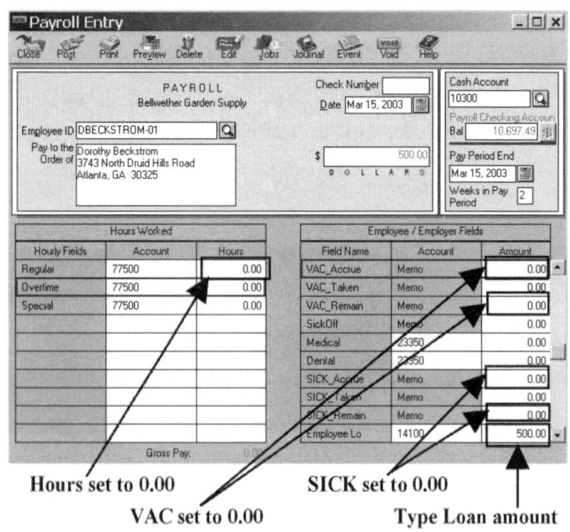

1. Open the Payroll Entry form.
2. Select the employee from the Employee ID field.
3. Set the Regular hours to **0.00** or, if this is a salaried employee, set the Salary to **0.00**.
4. In the Employee/Employer Fields section, go to the Employee Loans line and enter the amount of the advance.
5. Change the VAC_Accrue, VAC_Remain, SICK_Accrue, and SICK_Remain fields, or any other similar fields, to **0.00**. If you change these fields before you fill in the Employee Loans field, these fields will recalculate themselves and have to be reset again later.
6. Print the check.

Getting an Employee Advance Repaid

Obviously, employee loans should be repaid. With Peachtree, you can schedule a lump sum payment or regular payments.

For a lump sum repayment, simply type the amount to be deducted from the employee's paycheck in the Employee Loans field. Be sure to enter it as a negative number.

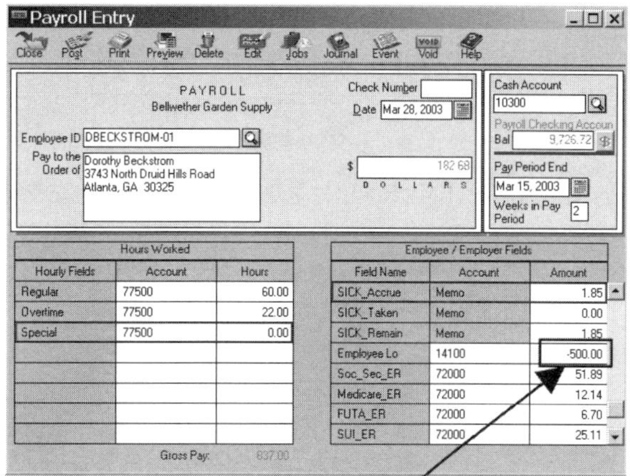

Type repayment amount as negative

To set up regular payments, follow these steps:

1. Open the Maintain Employees form and select the employee ID.

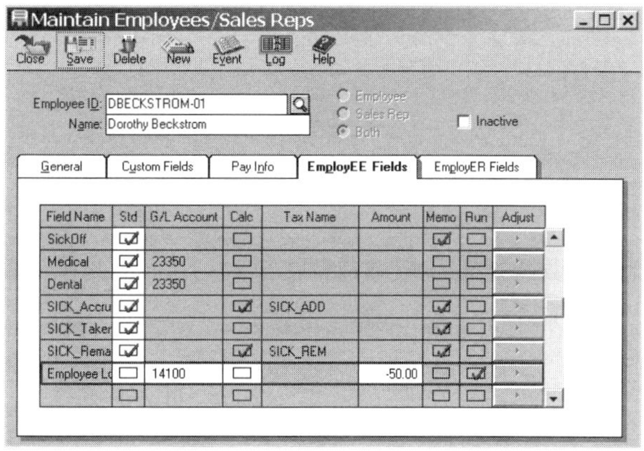

2. Select the **EmployEE Fields** tab.

   On the line for Employee Loans, uncheck the **Std** check box — for Standard deduction.
3. In the Amount column, enter the amount of the regular payment to be made. If payments are not going to be made in equal amounts, you can still put a minimum in here and change it on the Payroll Entry form.
4. Click **Save**.
5. Open the Payroll Entry form.

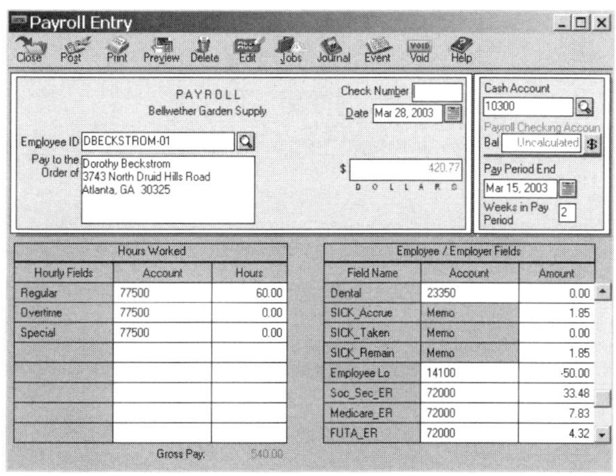

6. Select the employee ID.
7. For hourly employees, enter their hours as usual.
8. Verify the Employee Loans payment amount. It may be increased or decreased, as needed; just be sure that the amount is a negative number.

9. To track the payment and verify where the employee is in repaying the loan, click the **Preview** button in the toolbar and select one of the payroll checks.

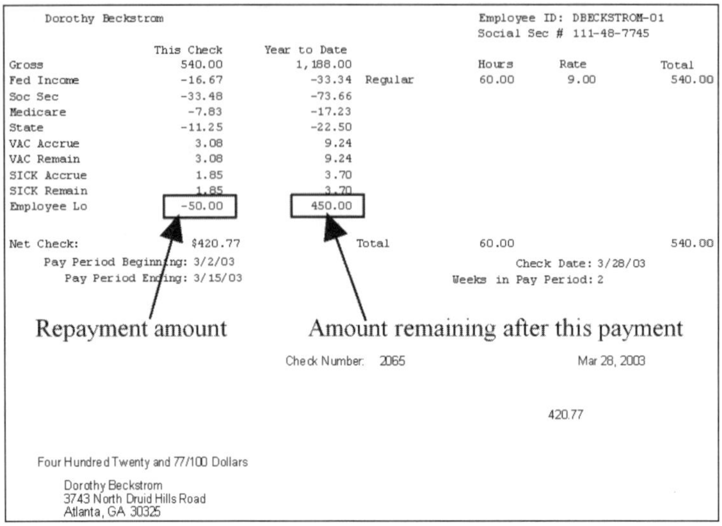

Dorothy Beckstrom

Employee ID: DBECKSTROM-01
Social Sec # 111-48-7745

	This Check	Year to Date		Hours	Rate	Total
Gross	540.00	1,188.00				
Fed Income	-16.67	-33.34	Regular	60.00	9.00	540.00
Soc Sec	-33.48	-73.66				
Medicare	-7.83	-17.23				
State	-11.25	-22.50				
VAC Accrue	3.08	9.24				
VAC Remain	3.08	9.24				
SICK Accrue	1.85	3.70				
SICK Remain	1.85	3.70				
Employee Lo	-50.00	450.00				
Net Check:	$420.77		Total	60.00		540.00

Pay Period Beginning: 3/2/03
Pay Period Ending: 3/15/03

Check Date: 3/28/03
Weeks in Pay Period: 2

Check Number: 2065 Mar 28, 2003

420.77

Four Hundred Twenty and 77/100 Dollars

Dorothy Beckstrom
3743 North Druid Hills Road
Atlanta, GA 30325

10. Print the paycheck as normal.

Employee Expenses

Employee expenses may be paid through Peachtree's Time & Billing function, but that method will not be discussed in this book due to space constraints. Employee expenses may also be paid through the accounts payable function, using your regular checking account rather than the payroll account, which is what we will show here. I like this method because it gets the expenses into the Cash Disbursements Journal with minimal fuss and with less reconciliation effort.

1. Set up an employee expense payment schedule, such as employees turning in all expenses by five days before payroll will receive an expense check with their paycheck.
2. Employees should turn in the approved expense check form. There are forms available for sale through your local office supplier, or you may want to create something as simple as the one on the following page created in Microsoft Excel.

Expense Report
D-N-B Consultants

Employee Name Deborah Bean

Date	Description	Account	Amount
2/20/2003	Flight to Scotts Bluff, Nebraska	76500	862.95
2/20/2003	Car Rental - one week	76500	265.48
2/20 - 27	Holiday Inn Express, 6 nights	76500	485.36
2/20 - 27	Meals	76500	168.02
2/21 & 2/26	Take clients (Jim Jones &	70500	158.29
	Chris Blackhurst) to dinner		
2/24/2003	Treat office staff to late-night pizza	70500	75.00
2/27/2003	Airport parking	76500	68.00
2/21/2003	Purchase Writable CD &	50000	252.32
	10 CD's for backups		
		Total	2,335.42

Signature Approval

3. Verify the expense report. Be sure that all amounts are correct and all receipts are attached according to your policies. You may or may not require your employees to enter account numbers.
4. Open the Purchases/Receive Inventory form.
5. If the employee does not have a vendor ID, create one by adding a new vendor.
6. Enter the expenses as you do any other purchase.
7. Print the expense check for the employee.
8. File the expense report in the A/P files, not the employee files. This way it is easy to refer back to the expenses without the red tape of opening a confidential employee file.

Employee Tips

There are two types of tips that employees receive. First, there are tips that the employees receive directly. The second type of tips are those that are paid by you from charge slips or tip pools. These are handled separately in Peachtree. You may or may not have selected to include tip income when you initially ran the payroll setup. If you did not, we will cover the steps to do these tasks manually.

Reporting Unpaid Tips

Unpaid tips are tips that employees receive directly from customers. In many situations, these are reported to the employer so that employees may have additional amounts withheld from their paychecks to cover the taxes on the tips.

Warning!! Changing pay levels and deductions should only be done at the beginning of a payroll (calendar) year. Changes at any other time may cause serious repercussions when calculating W-2s. Although it is possible to add new items during the year, you should never change the name or G/L account of an existing item during the year.

1. Select **Maintain**, **Default Information**, then **Employees** from the menu bar.
2. The Employee Defaults window appears. Select the **EmployEE Fields** tab.

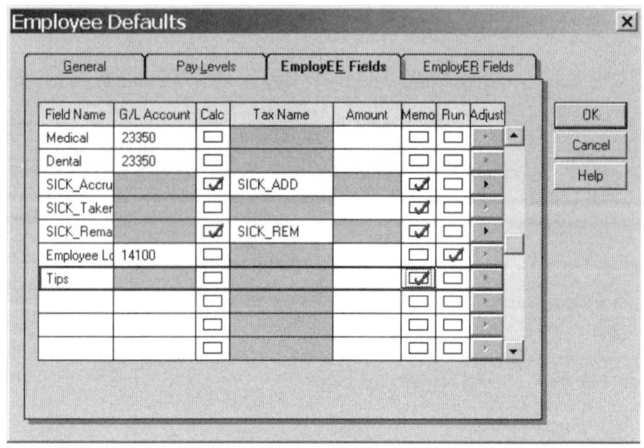

3. Enter a new line called **Tips**.
4. Select the **Memo** check box. This means that the amount will not be added to the paycheck when it is calculated.
5. The G/L Account field will become grayed out when you select the Memo check box. Ignore the Calc and Run check boxes. Leave Amount blank. It will be filled in when the paycheck is created.
6. To add the tips to the income, go to Fed_Income in the Field Name column and click the **Adjust** button.
7. The Calculate Adjusted Gross dialog box appears.

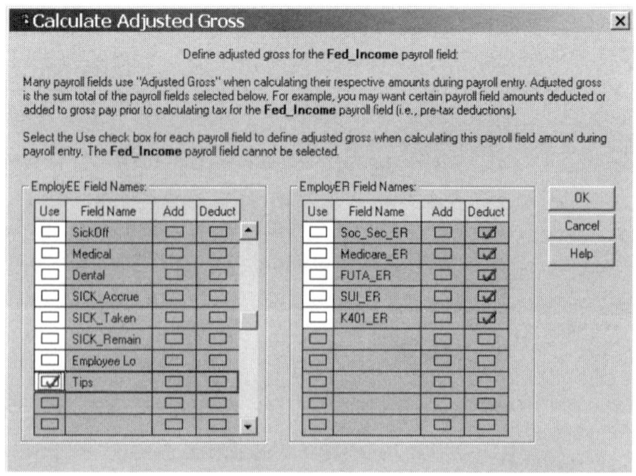

8. Select the **Use** check box for the Tips line.
9. Click **OK**.
10. In the Employee Defaults window, go to the Adjust buttons for the Soc_Sec and Medicare fields in both the EmployEE Fields and the EmployER Fields tabs. Also add Tips to any other tax fields, including state and local taxes, that need to include the tip income.
11. Click **OK** to save the information and then go back into the Employee Defaults window.
12. Select the **General** tab.
13. Click the **W-2s** button in the Assign Payroll Fields for section.

14. The Assign Payroll Fields for W-2s dialog box appears.

    Select **Tips** from the FICA Tips drop-down list.

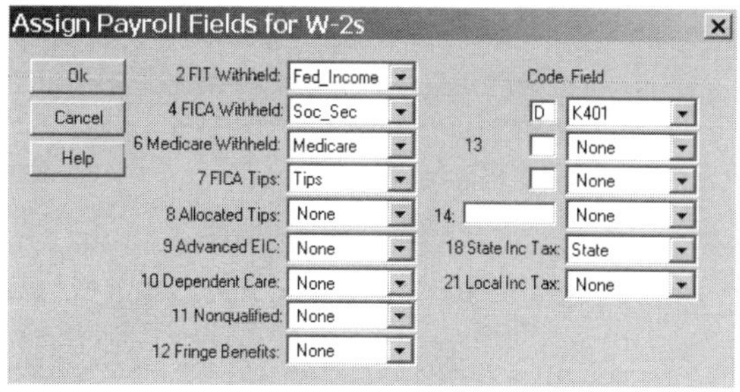

15. Click **OK** to return to the Employee Defaults window.
16. Click **OK** to save the tip information.

On a regular basis, your employees must inform you of their tip income. Then, when you go to create a paycheck for that employee, you can add the tips as follows:

1. Open the Payroll Entry form and select an employee in the Employee ID field.
2. Enter the hours or the salary in the left side of the form.
3. In the Employee/Employer Fields section, add the tips on the Tips line in the Amount field. When you do this, you will notice that additional taxes are taken from the gross pay.
4. Print the check as usual.

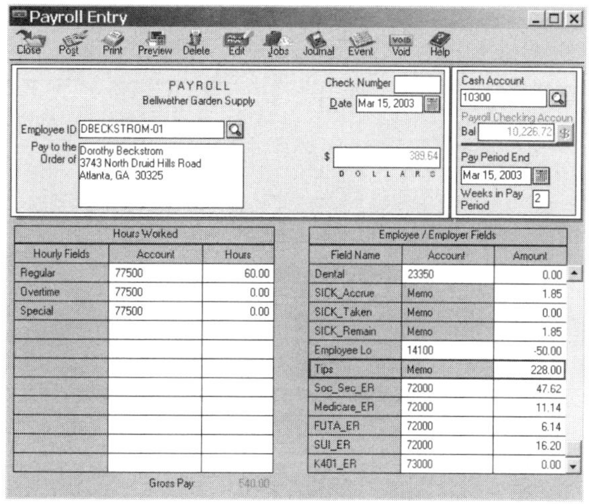

Paying Tip Income

If you regularly cash out your employees' tips that are paid on credit cards, you may not need to create a separate credit card tips line. Cashing out tips means that you give the employees the cash, and that amount along with other tips they have collected are reported as tips as we discussed above.

On the other hand, if you do not cash out credit card tips but distribute them on the paychecks, you need a way to record that income as tip income.

Warning!! Changing pay levels and deductions should only be done at the beginning of a payroll (calendar) year. Changes at any other time may cause serious repercussions when calculating W-2s. Although it is possible to add new items during the year, you should never change the name or G/L account of an existing item during the year.

1. Set up a credit card tips liability account by opening the Maintain Chart of Accounts form (see Chapter 3).

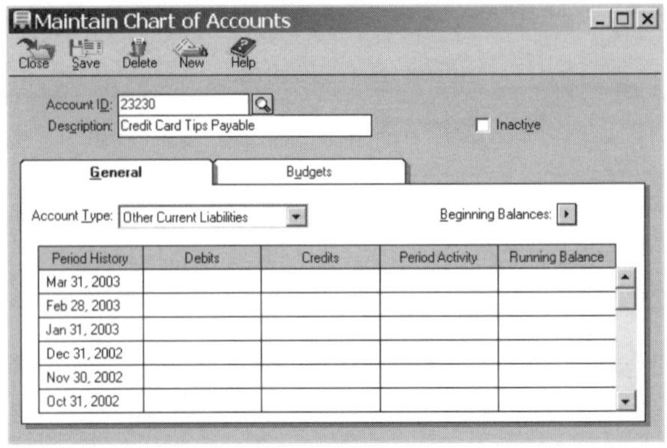

2. Make sure the account fits in with other general ledger accounts. Select **Other Current Liabilities** in the Account Type field.
3. Click **Save** to record the account.
4. Open the Employee Defaults window and select the **EmployEE Fields** tab.

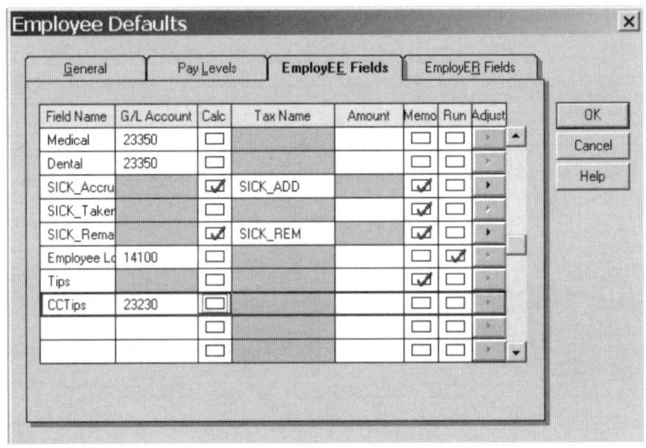

5. Enter a new line called **CCTips**.
6. Select the new account that you just created from the G/L Account drop-down box.
7. Do not select the Memo, Calc, or Run check boxes. Leave the Amount field blank. It will be filled in when the paycheck is created.
8. Add the credit card tips to the income for the Fed_Income, Soc_Sec, and Medicare fields in both the EmployEE Fields and the EmployER Fields tabs by selecting the Use check box in the Calculate Adjusted Gross dialog box. Also add CCTips to any other tax fields that need to include the tip income.

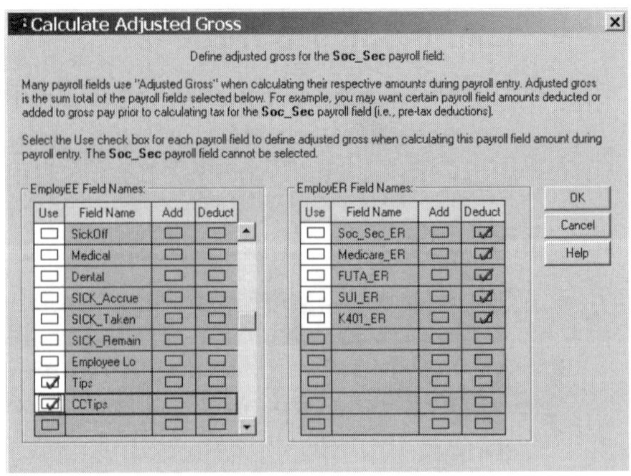

9. If you record both regular tips and credit card tips, you must combine the two fields to be able to report the information on your employees' W-2s. To do this, select **File**, then **Payroll Tax Tables**, then **Edit Company** from the menu bar.

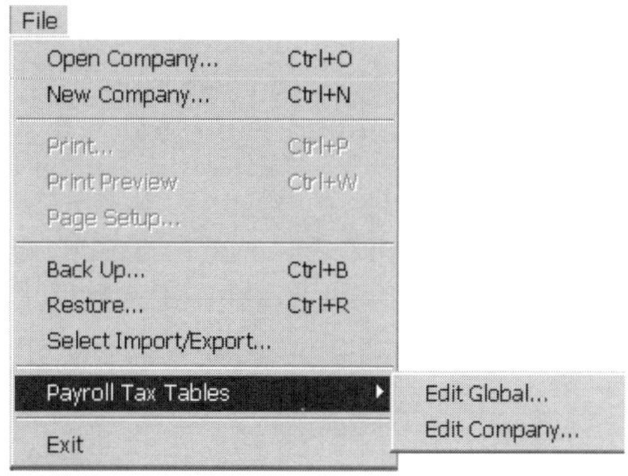

10. The Maintain Company Payroll Tax Tables dialog box appears.

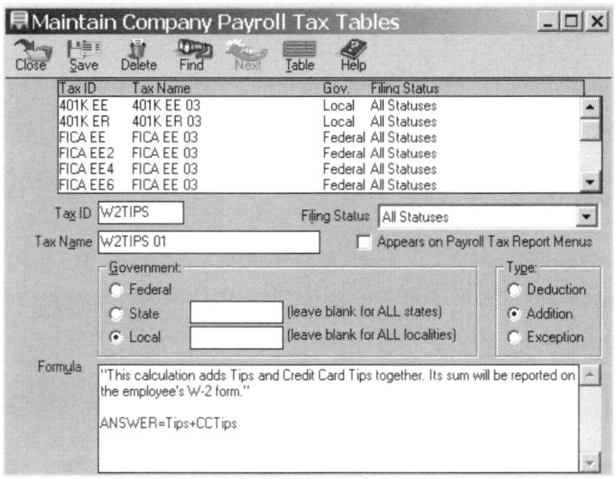

In the Tax ID field, enter **W2TIPS**.

11. Enter **W2TIPS 01** in the Tax Name field where 01 indicates the last two digits of the current year. Be sure to leave a space before the year.
12. Select **All Statuses** from the Filing Status drop-down list.
13. The Appears on Payroll Tax Report Menus check box should be unselected.
14. Select **Local** as the Government option.
15. Select **Addition** as the Type option.
16. In the Formula field, type the following information, using Ctrl+Enter to go to a new line. The information at the beginning in quotes is a comment describing the formula.

    "This calculation adds Tips and Credit Card Tips together. Its sum will be reported on the employee's W-2 form."

    ANSWER=Tips+CCTips

17. Click **Save** in the toolbar to record the tax table. Close the dialog box.

18. Reopen the Employee Defaults window and select the **EmployEE Fields** tab.

    Enter a new line for **W2Tips**.

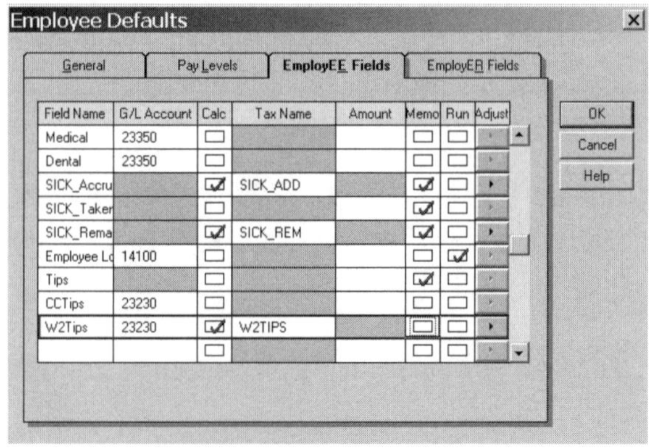

19. Select the credit card tips liability account in the G/L Account field.
20. Check the **Calc** check box. This will enable the Tax Name field.
21. Select the **W2Tips** tax table from the drop-down list.
22. Leave Memo and Run unselected.
23. Click **OK** to save the information, then go back into the Employee Defaults window and select the **General** tab.
24. Click the **W-2s** button in the Assign Payroll Fields for section.
25. The Assign Payroll Fields for W-2s dialog box appears.

    Select **W2Tips** from the FICA Tips drop-down list.

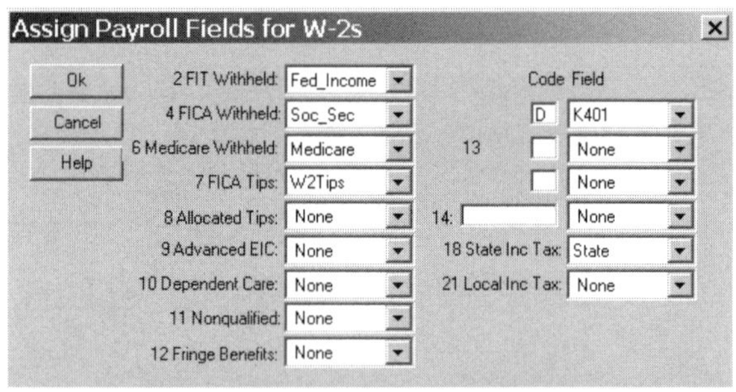

26. Click **OK** to return to the Employee Defaults window.
27. Click **OK** to save the tip information.

Now when you pay your employees, you can add the amount of credit card tips to the gross pay and include the cash tips in the employee's W-2 as follows:

1. Open the Payroll Entry form and select an employee ID.

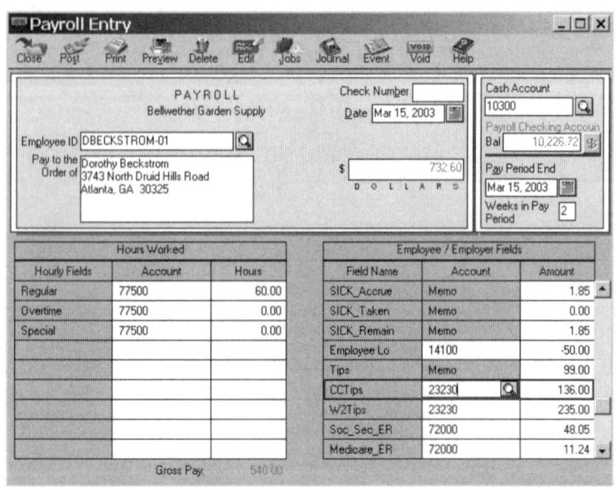

2. Enter the hours or the salary in the left side of the form.
3. In the Employee/Employer Fields section, add the credit card tips on the CCTips line and the cash tips on the Tips line in the Amount field. The total of the two amounts will be shown in the W2Tips line. The CCTips will be added to the paycheck and both fields will deduct additional taxes from the gross pay.

4. Print the check as usual.

401(k) Contributions

Earlier in this chapter, we set up the 401(k) plan for the company. Here we will set up the employee contributions. Employees contribute a percentage of their gross pay, not a specific dollar amount.

1. Open the Maintain Employees form and select an employee from the Employee ID field.
2. Select the **General** tab.
3. In the Withholding Information section, scroll down until you reach the 401k% line in the Payroll Field Names column.
4. In the Additional Withholding column, type the percentage to be withheld from the employee's gross pay.

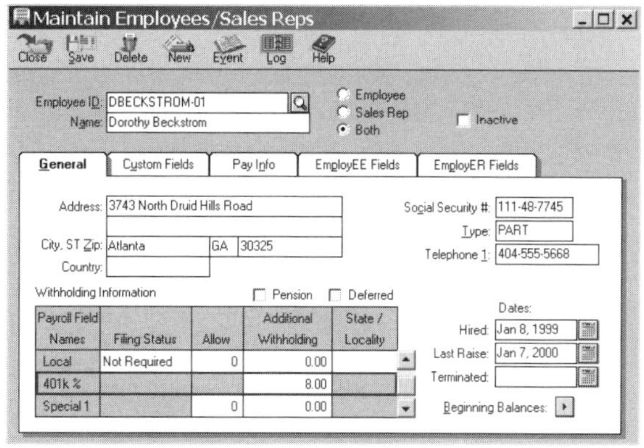

5. Click **Save** to record the information.
6. When a paycheck is created for the employee, the percentage will be deducted from gross pay.
7. The employer's portion, if any, will also be shown lower down in the list.

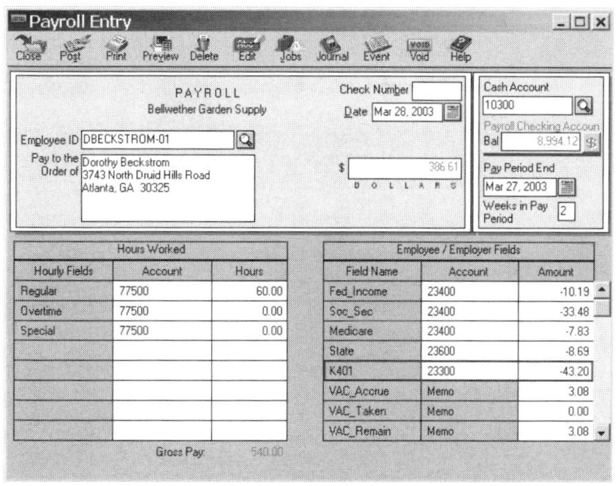

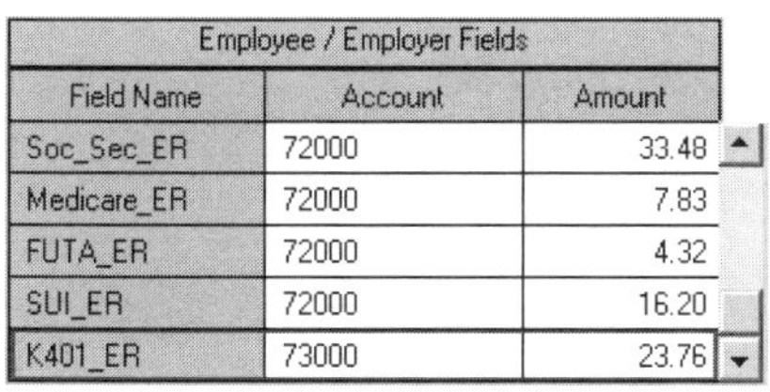

Employee / Employer Fields		
Field Name	Account	Amount
Soc_Sec_ER	72000	33.48
Medicare_ER	72000	7.83
FUTA_ER	72000	4.32
SUI_ER	72000	16.20
K401_ER	73000	23.76

8. Process the check as usual; there is no need to make any changes to the 401(k) fields.

Vacation and Sick Time

Vacation and sick time are part of the benefits that we pay to employees to encourage them to stay with our company. Tracking the hours associated with these benefits can be a headache if you do not have a system set up. Fortunately, Peachtree provides several ways to manage this problem. How you set up vacation and sick time in the Payroll Setup Wizard will determine how you track the hours used. Also, you do not have to track vacation and sick time in the same way. You can do one as a lump sum and the other as an accrual.

Warning!! Changing how time is issued should <u>only</u> be done at the beginning of a payroll (calendar) year. Changes can cause serious repercussions to employee records if done at any other time.

Time Accrued Each Payroll Period

With the accrual method, employees start receiving vacation and sick time as soon as they receive their first paycheck. It may only be as little as a part of an hour per period, but those amounts will add up so that after one year — if no time has been taken — they will have an amount of time equivalent to what they would have had if you issued time in a lump sum at the beginning of the year. The advantage to this approach is that you don't have to do any additional work, especially if the employee wants to take some time before that first calendar year is up.

Although we use the vacation accrual as an example, the same procedure may be used for sick time by selecting the appropriate sick time fields.

1. Use the Payroll Setup Wizard to set the vacation as accruing each pay period.
2. The standard vacation accrual is based upon a two-week vacation per year and a 40-hour work week. You may want to offer other vacation periods to some employees, such as 120 hours for employees who have worked more than three years or 40 hours for part-time employees. Open the Maintain Company Payroll Tax Tables dialog box to add a new vacation option.

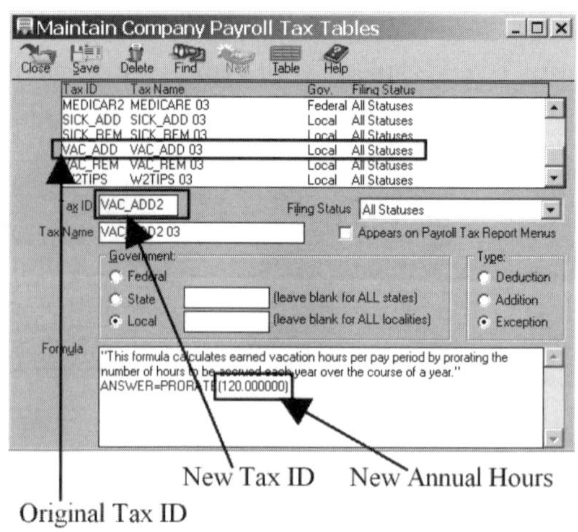

3. Select one of the time add tables, either **VAC_ADD** or **SICK_ADD**. Change the tax ID so that the ID now has a 2 at the end, such as **VAC_ADD2**.
4. Change the Tax Name field in the same manner, before the digits representing the year.
5. Change the Formula field to reflect the new number of hours per year for this tax table.
6. Click **Save** to record the new tax table.
7. To change the accrual for an employee, open the Maintain Employees form.

8. Select an employee in the Employee ID field and click on the **EmployEE Fields** tab.
9. Go to the VAC_Accrue line and unselect the **Std** check box. Std stands for the standard deduction or calculation. We are going to change it.
10. In the Tax Name column, select the new vacation tax table for this employee.

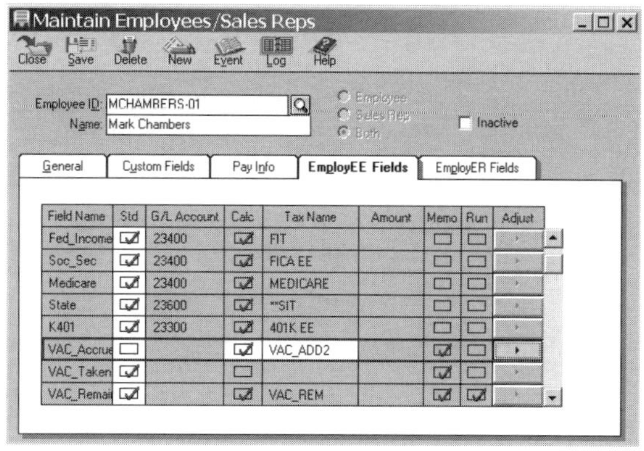

11. Click **Save** to record the changes to this employee's record.
12. The next time a check is calculated, the new accrual will appear. For other employees, the accrual is 3.8 hours per pay period using a biweekly payment method. For our employee with the new vacation package, the accrual is 4.62 hours per pay period.
13. An employee's accrued vacation will show on his pay stub. In order to use the vacation, you must enter the number of hours taken in the correct field.

    Type the number of hours in the VAC_Taken column as a positive number, not negative. The program subtracts the vacation taken from the vacation accrual and shows the net change to the employee's remaining vacation time in VAC_Remain.

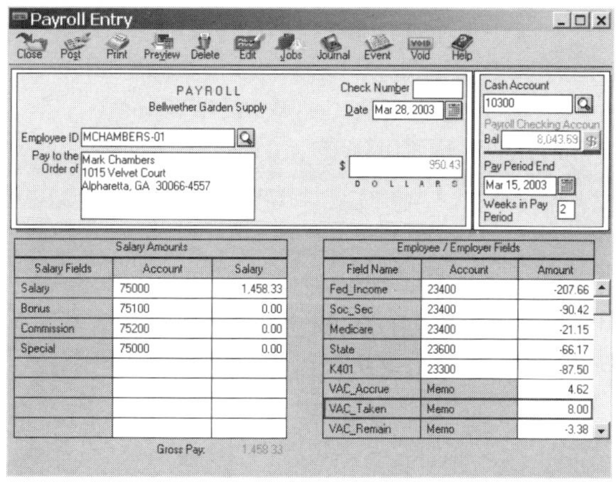

14. The changes appear on the employee's pay stub.

Mark Chambers

	This Check	Year to Date
Gross	1,458.33	4,374.99
Fed Income	-207.66	-622.98
Soc Sec	-90.42	-271.26
Medicare	-21.15	-63.45
State	-66.17	-198.51
K401	-87.50	-262.50
VAC Accrue	4.62	12.32
VAC Taken	8.00	8.00
VAC Remain	-3.38	4.32

Time Issued in Lump Sum

For vacation and sick time that is issued in a lump sum, you will need to enter hours at specific times during the year. One common way of doing this is to add the hours on the employee's anniversary. Unfortunately, this means you will have to track each employee's anniversary date. The other way to add vacation and sick time is to do it for all employees at the beginning of each year. In this section we will assume that both vacation and sick time are set up the same.

1. Use the Payroll Setup Wizard to set the time as issued in a lump sum.
2. Open the Maintain Employees form and select an employee in the Employee ID field.
3. Click the **Beginning Balances** button to open the Employee Beginning Balances window.

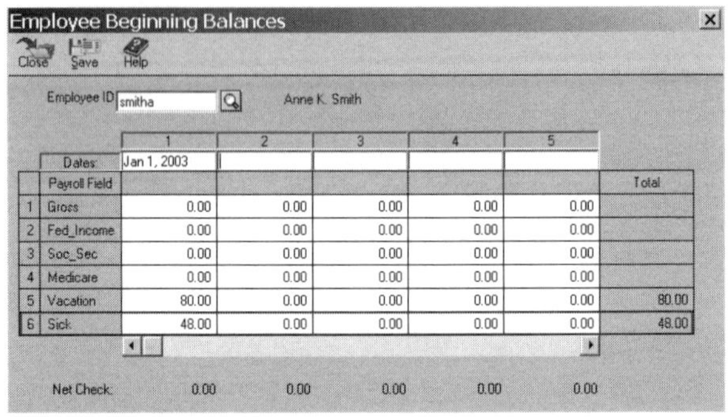

4. In an empty column in the Dates row, enter the date that the payroll will be entered, such as the first of the year or the month that you will begin calculating vacation for first-time users.
5. On the Vacation line, enter the number of hours to be allocated to the employee for the coming year.
6. Click **Save** to record the beginning balances.

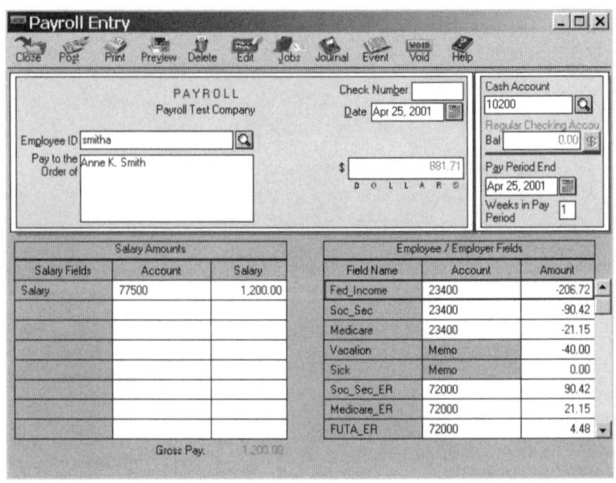

7. Used vacation is entered at the time of payroll entry. Open the Payroll Entry form and select the employee.

   Notice that instead of three lines for vacation, there is only one.
8. Type the vacation used in the Vacation field as a negative number (you are deducting the number of vacation hours).
9. The program subtracts the amount of vacation from the vacation entered in the beginning balance and reports it on the pay stub. The Year to Date column shows the vacation remaining.

Anne K. Smith

	This Check	Year to Date
Gross	1,200.00	1,200.00
Fed Income	-206.72	-206.72
Soc Sec	-90.42	-90.42
Medicare	-21.15	-21.15
Vacation	-40.00	40.00
Sick		48.00

10. When the year is over, you can add new vacation amounts directly to the first check of the new year as a positive number indicating the total number of hours for the coming year.

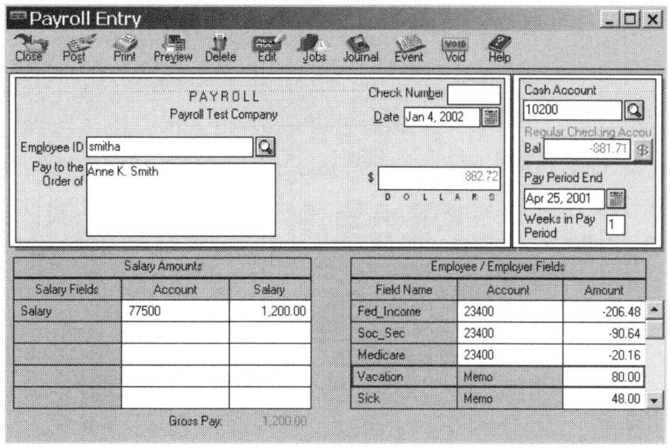

Instead of adding hours to the first payroll, you could run a vacation accrual for all employees on plain paper. Just be sure that the gross pay and the net pay are both equal to 0.00. Instead of using your regular check numbers, make the check number something like VAC2001-01. If you put that in as the first check number, Peachtree will increment each additional check.

Health Benefits and Other Deductions

Many companies offer health benefits, dental insurance, life insurance, and other benefits to their employees. Some of these benefits may be free and some you may charge back to your employees. Other deductions may be for specific types of employees, such as uniform or tool costs. Another type of deduction is a state or federal withholding for past-due taxes or child support. All of these are handled in a very similar manner.

To begin a deduction, you must first decide where the collected money will go. Is it to be allocated to a liability account, which will later be distributed to the courts or an insurance company? Or is this a reduction of an expense where your costs are being subsidized by the employee's payments? Talk to your CPA about the allocation of the deduction.

1. If necessary, create the liability or contra-expense general ledger account using the Maintain Chart of Accounts function.
2. Open the Employee Defaults window and select the **EmployEE Fields** tab.
3. Create a new line with the name of the new deduction, such as **Health Ins** or **Child Support** in the Field Name column.
4. Select the liability or other general ledger account that the deduction is to be allocated to in the G/L Account field.
5. If this is a standard deduction for all employees, such as a uniform expense, type the deduction in the Amount column. Otherwise, leave it blank and fill in the amount on the employee records. Remember that positive numbers will be added to the check and negative numbers will be subtracted.
6. Click **OK** to save the information.
7. Open the Maintain Employees window and select an employee.

8. Select the **EmployEE Fields** tab.
9. Go to the line with the deduction. Click the **Std** column to uncheck the check box if the Amount column is not the correct amount.
10. Type the correct amount. Remember that positive numbers will be added to the check and negative numbers will be subtracted.
11. Click **Save** to save the employee record.

    The deduction will appear the next time you create a paycheck for the employee. The amount may still be changed before printing the check.

Transfers to the Payroll Checking Account

Most larger companies have a separate payroll checking account. Only the gross payroll amount, including the employer taxes, is placed in this account. Between payrolls, the balance is at or near a zero balance. When your payroll date arrives, you need to deposit money into this account from your regular checking or savings account. There are two methods of doing this. The first is to create a general journal entry to show the transfer. The second is to use the receipts function to perform the same operation. How comfortable you feel about using the journal entry function will have a bearing on which method you use.

Transfers Using a Journal Entry

This method requires that you understand how journal entries are created. You should also understand what debiting and crediting a cash account does to the account's balance.

1. Open the journal entry function by selecting the **General Ledger** folder and clicking on the **General Journal Entry** icon in the navigation aid.

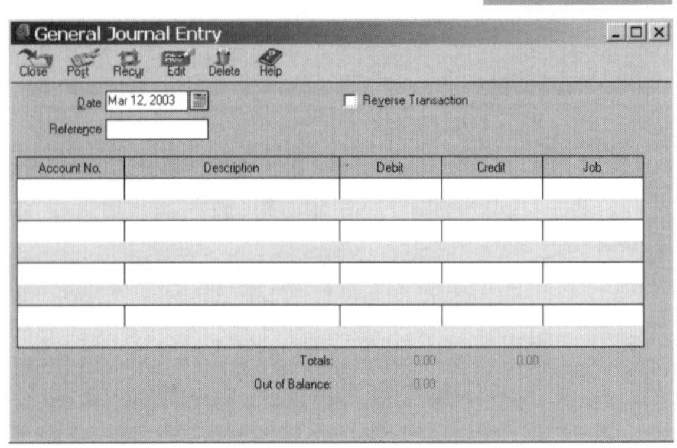

   Alternately, select **Tasks, General Journal Entry** from the menu bar or press **Alt+K**, then **G** using the keyboard shortcuts. A blank General Journal Entry form will appear.

2. In the Date field, enter the date of this journal entry. This is the date that the money is transferred.

3. In the Reference field, enter a unique ID for this journal entry. Since this transaction occurs regularly, you might want to make the reference show that the entry is for a payroll transfer along with the date, for example, PYRL031203.
4. The Reverse Transaction option will be covered in Chapter 16.
5. In the first Account No. field, select the payroll account number from the drop-down list.
6. Enter a description of the transaction.
7. In the Debit column, type the amount to be transferred to this account. This is a debit because cash accounts are debited to increase them. This amount should be the total gross payroll and all employer taxes if taxes are paid directly from the payroll account. If taxes are paid from the checking account, this amount will be the net payroll.
8. Tab to the next line and enter the checking account number in the Account No. field. Use the same description. Enter the amount in the Credit column.

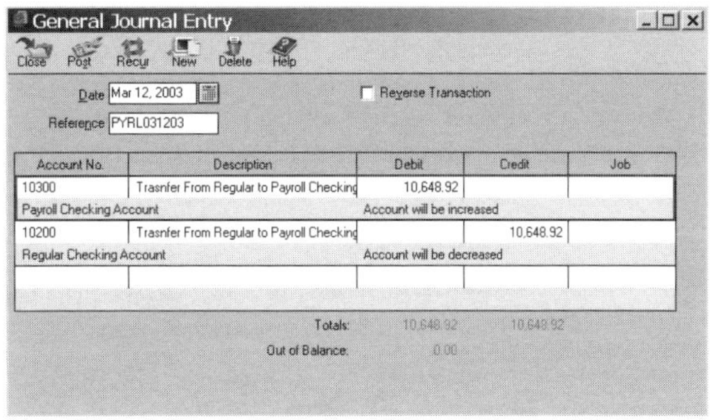

9. If debits and credits are entered correctly, the Totals at the bottom will be equal and the Out of Balance amount will be 0.00.
10. Click **Save** or **Post** to save the journal entry.

Transfers Using the Receipts Function

Some people are more comfortable using the receipts function to make transfers between accounts. The method is just as easy as creating a journal entry.

1. Create a customer in the Maintain Customers form for the payroll transfer. Use something similar to the one shown. For the GL Sales Acct field, use the checking account general ledger account.

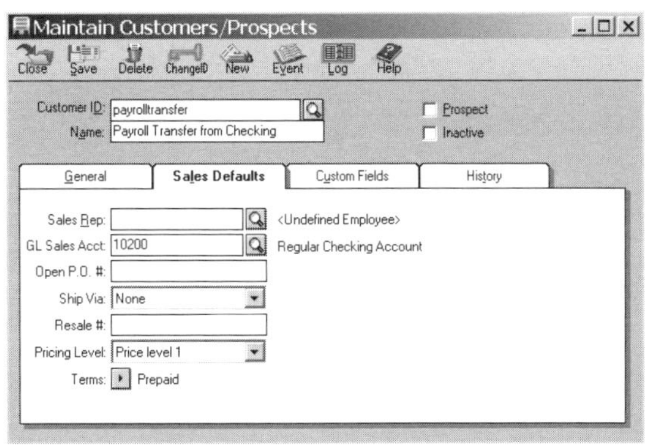

2. Open the Receipts form. Enter the new customer ID.
3. The Deposit ticket ID field should be descriptive to show that this is a payroll transfer, for example, **PR031203**.

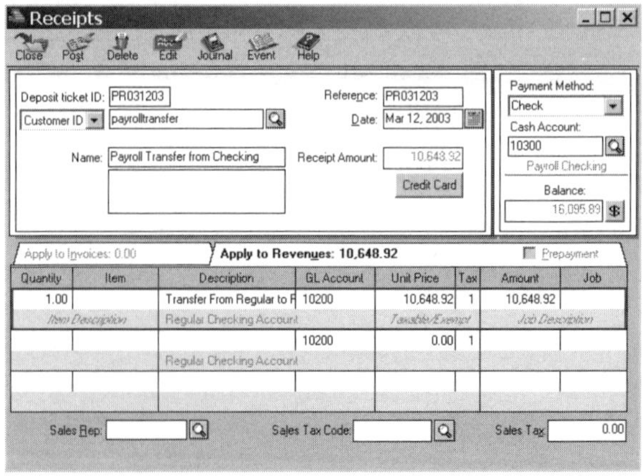

4. The Reference field can contain the same code, or if your bank gives you a confirmation number, use that as a reference.
5. Enter the date of the transfer in the Date field.
6. The Cash Account field should be set to the payroll checking account. As a receipt, this is the account that is receiving the money.
7. In the Apply to Revenues tab, enter **1.00** in the Quantity field. The Description field is the transfer description. The Unit Price and Amount fields hold the amount of the transfer. The GL Account is the checking account from which the money is being transferred.
8. Click **Post** or **Save** to record the transaction.

Quick Payroll Reports

The main purpose of the payroll reports is to determine that all employees have been paid correctly. Not only do we need to verify hours for which they are to be paid, but also all deductions, loans, and benefits.

The Payroll Register

The Payroll Register can be printed before or after payroll checks have been printed. If there is a chance that you might have to make changes or if you are by nature a pessimist and know something is going to go wrong, it is strongly suggested that you do it before the checks are printed. It is far easier to not have to void printed checks than it is to have never printed them in the first place.

This report shows all types of pay, deductions, and employer payments regarding each employee's check.

1. From the Select a Report window, choose **Payroll** from the Report Area list and **Check Register** from Report List.

2. Click the **Preview** button to open the Payroll Register dialog box.
3. Select an order. For this report, Check Date seems to work well. The order will affect the printing of subtotals on the report. If you select Employee ID, a summary will be printed after each employee and can make it more difficult to locate information.

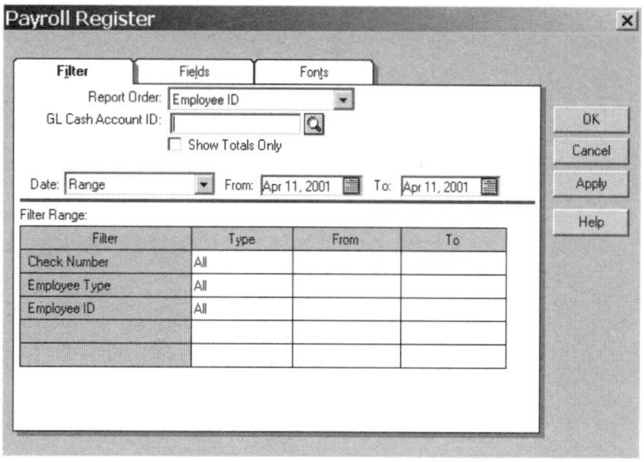

4. If you have other checks in the system, you may want to fill in the GL Cash Account ID field.
5. I generally ignore the Show Totals Only option for this report.
6. Select the date range for the checks. I often use the date the checks are printed.
7. You may also select to filter the information shown by Check Number, Employee Type, or Employee ID.
8. Click **OK** when you are done.

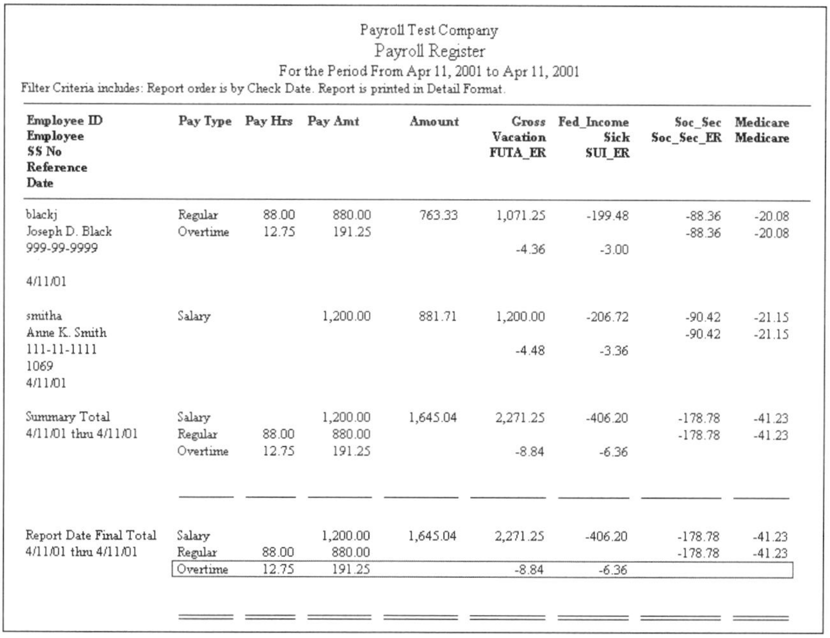

Payroll Test Company
Payroll Register
For the Period From Apr 11, 2001 to Apr 11, 2001
Filter Criteria includes: Report order is by Check Date. Report is printed in Detail Format.

Employee ID Employee SS No Reference Date	Pay Type	Pay Hrs	Pay Amt	Amount	Gross Vacation FUTA_ER	Fed_Income Sick SUI_ER	Soc_Sec Soc_Sec_ER	Medicare Medicare
blackj	Regular	88.00	880.00	763.33	1,071.25	-199.48	-88.36	-20.08
Joseph D. Black	Overtime	12.75	191.25				-88.36	-20.08
999-99-9999					-4.36	-3.00		
4/11/01								
smitha	Salary		1,200.00	881.71	1,200.00	-206.72	-90.42	-21.15
Anne K. Smith							-90.42	-21.15
111-11-1111					-4.48	-3.36		
1069								
4/11/01								
Summary Total	Salary		1,200.00	1,645.04	2,271.25	-406.20	-178.78	-41.23
4/11/01 thru 4/11/01	Regular	88.00	880.00				-178.78	-41.23
	Overtime	12.75	191.25		-8.84	-6.36		
Report Date Final Total	Salary		1,200.00	1,645.04	2,271.25	-406.20	-178.78	-41.23
4/11/01 thru 4/11/01	Regular	88.00	880.00				-178.78	-41.23
	Overtime	12.75	191.25		-8.84	-6.36		

9. Notice that the report shows both printed checks (with a reference number) and unprinted checks. Salaried and hourly employees are shown with easily read hours. Also, both the employees' deductions and the employer's portion are shown.

The Tax Liability Report

The Tax Liability Report can assist you in determining your 941 deposits.

1. From the Select a Report window, choose **Payroll** from the Report Area list and the **Tax Liability Report** from Report List.
2. Click the **Preview** button to open the Tax Liability Report dialog box.

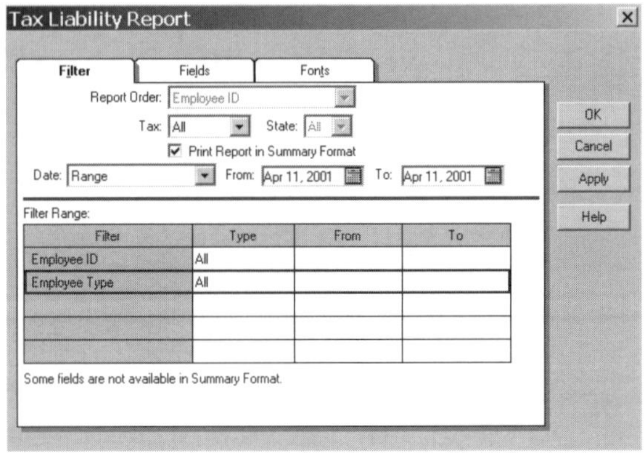

3. If you click the **Print Report in Summary Format** check box, the Report Order field becomes unavailable. I like this report to be summarized because of the quick information available that way. If the report is not summarized, it becomes too much like some of the other payroll reports where I have to dig for the tax amounts.
4. You may select **All** for the Tax drop-down, or limit the report to **Federal**, **State**, or **Local** taxes. If **State** is chosen, you may select from the State drop-down list.
5. Select the date range for the report. Generally, I use the report for only one pay period.
6. In the Filter Range section, you may choose to filter the report by Employee ID or Employee Type.
7. Click **OK** to view the report.
8. Notice in this report that all federal liabilities are listed, including the taxable gross amounts. This report makes it easy to prepare your deposit in a timely manner.

Payroll Test Company
Tax Liability Report
For the Period From Apr 1, 2001 to Apr 30, 2001
Filter Criteria includes: Report order is by Employee ID. Report is printed in Summary Format.

Tax Description	Gross	Taxable Gross	Tax Liability
FUTA	4,351.25	4,351.25	16.38
940 Total			16.38
FIT	4,351.25	4,351.25	781.84
FICA EE	4,351.25	4,351.25	355.68
FICA ER	4,351.25	4,351.25	355.68
Medicare EE	4,351.25	4,351.25	78.77
Medicare ER	4,351.25	4,351.25	78.77
941 Total			1,650.74
Report Total			1,667.12

Summary

Payroll can be a very complicated function for many companies. There are so many ways to pay employees and so many headaches to deal with where deductions and taxes are concerned. Unfortunately, it is impossible to cover every contingency in this chapter. Hopefully, what we have covered here will help you to get started with this function.

Chapter 10

Inventory

In This Chapter

- Adding inventory items
- The difference between inventory classes
- Using inventory items in different ways
- Customizing the Sales Journal to show inventory items
- Quick inventory reports

Using inventory items in your data entry of invoices and bills has two main purposes. The first purpose is that this function will allow you to track inventory that you keep on your shelf and account for in your financial statements. The second purpose is that it will allow you to greatly reduce your data entry time for commonly used items or descriptions. This includes items you buy for clients or labor descriptions. Both types of inventory may be used together or separately.

Adding an Inventory Item

1. Go to the **Inventory** folder on the navigation aid and click on the **Inventory Items** icon.

   Or select **Maintain**, **Inventory Items** from the menu bar or press **Alt+M**, then **I** using the keyboard shortcuts.

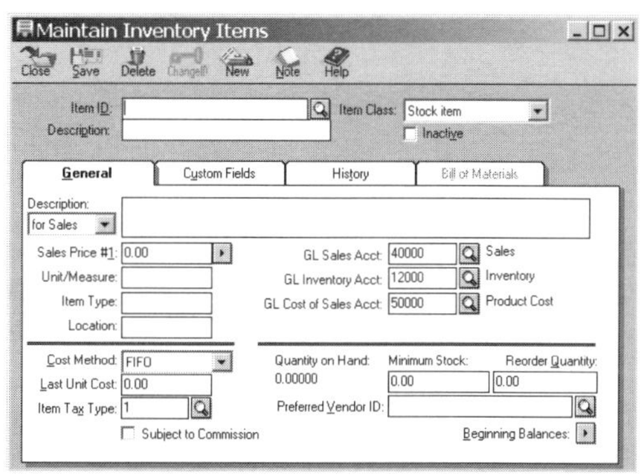

2. The Maintain Inventory Items form appears.

   We will cover the two main types of inventory separately. First we cover physical inventory that is tracked and then we discuss inventory items for things that are not counted.

Adding Stock Inventory

When large amounts of inventory are regularly purchased and then put on the shelf until used, it has a value that should be tracked. This is especially true if you need to know how many are left or when it is time to reorder. The inventory will also have to be physically counted at some point, especially at year-end, so that you can record adjustments due to breakage, pilferage, or some other circumstance.

1. Open the Maintain Inventory Items form.
2. Enter a unique ID for this inventory item. The ID should be easy to remember to speed up data entry. Because this is a physical thing that you are going to sell from off the shelf, you might use a manufacturer's preprinted SKU or product code that is already on the box. Alternately you may have your own stickers with codes on them. You might also consider using your vendor's item ID if you always get the items from the same place. Just remember that these numbers are used for both invoicing and purchases. If the ID is available for one function but not the other, it may not be a good ID.
3. Enter a description for the item. This is a very short but easily recognized description that is seen in lists.
4. Item Class is a vital field for inventory. This field tells Peachtree how to handle the inventory item. For items that are physically counted, you must use **Stock item** for the class.

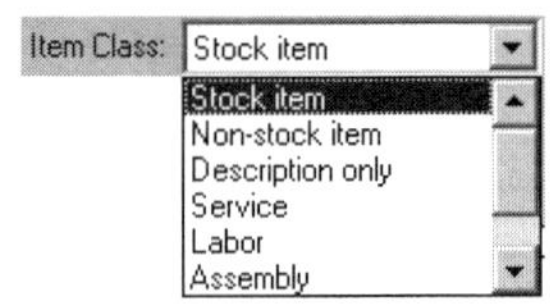

Warning!! Once the item class is set and saved, it cannot be changed.

5. The next field is also a description field with two choices: Description for Sales and Description for Purchases.

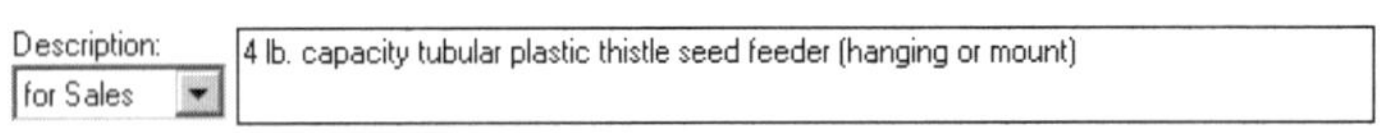

You may type different text for each choice. The Description for Sales appears on invoices. The Description for Purchases appears on purchase orders and bills.

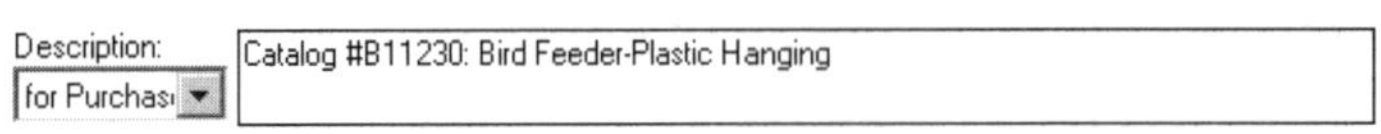

6. The next field is Sales Price #1. This is the main price level for all customers. Peachtree allows multiple pricing of items. Enter the price in dollars and cents, without sales tax.
7. Next fill in the Unit/Measure field. This is a free-form field and can be anything. Just remember that the unit of measure must match for sales and purchases. You cannot buy by the case and sell by the bottle. If that is how merchandise is received and sold, work out a procedure to handle this situation. One way is to track everything in cases so a purchase would be one case (12 bottles) and a sale would be expressed in .0833 cases (single bottles). The other way is to multiply your inventory receipts by the number of bottles so that 12 bottles are received and single bottles are sold.
8. The Item Type field is also a free-form field. In it you can enter the type of inventory that the item is, such as hair care, software, computers, power tools, or whatever. Or

you could use this field to describe items used in various parts of your business, such as networking projects, computer repairs, and training materials. Determine how, and if, you want your inventory subdivided, and then use those divisions. The Item Type field is used in reports.

Warning!! The Item Type field is case sensitive so that if you enter the type as **Computers** in one record and **COMPUTERS** in a second record, Peachtree will count those as different types. Standardize on a single format and stick to it.

9. Location is another free-form field and allows you to show where the items are located. Unfortunately, Peachtree only allows one location for each item.
10. The next three fields are taken together for stock items and are used to help track the inventory and cost of goods sold. The first field, GL Sales Acct, is the general ledger revenue account charged on invoices when a sale of this item is made. This should be a sales account on your income statement.
11. The GL Inventory Acct field contains the general ledger asset account that this inventory is allocated to for purchases.
12. The GL Cost of Sales Acct field holds the general ledger asset account that this inventory is allocated to when the items are sold.

The inventory process works so that when you purchase inventory and enter it into the Purchases form showing the correct quantity and using the correct item ID, the transaction is allocated to an inventory account.

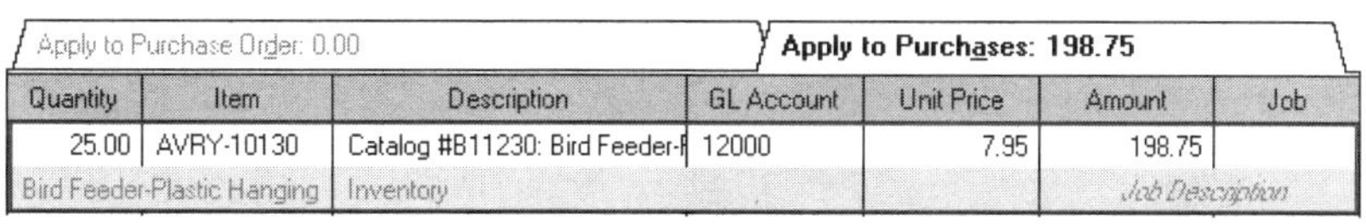

On the Purchases form, if you click the **Journal** button on the toolbar you can see the journal entry for this transaction on the Accounting Behind the Screens form.

When the item is sold, you enter the items sold to the customer, also using the item ID, and the revenue account is charged with the sales amount.

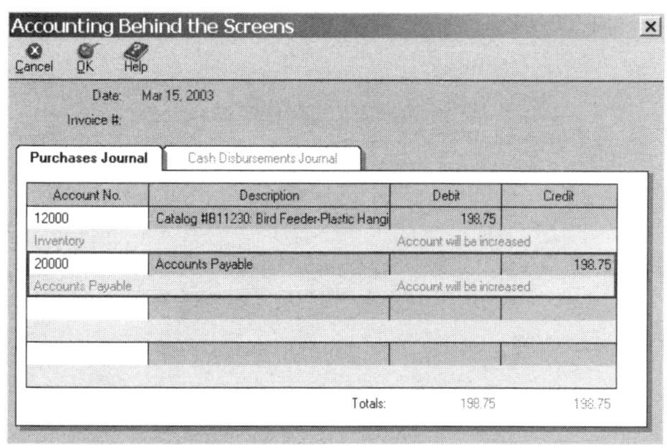

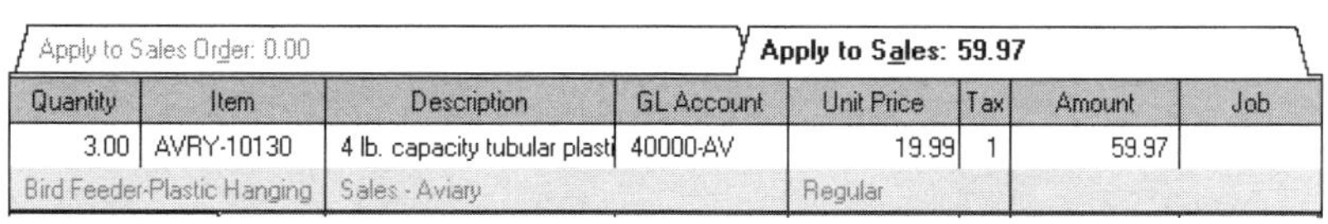

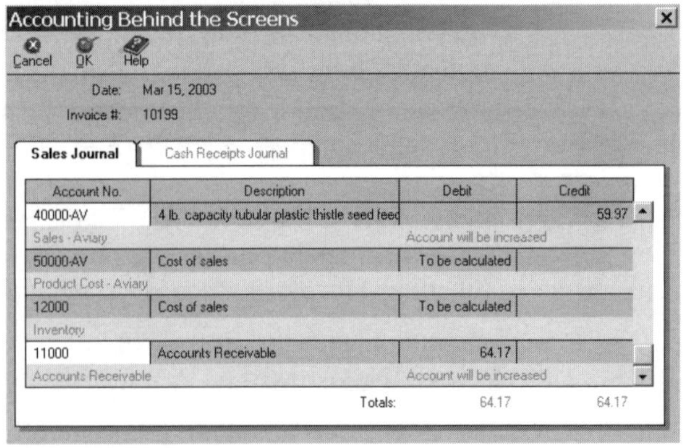

If you click on the **Journal** button on the Sales form, you can see on the Accounting Behind the Screens form that when items are removed from the inventory account they are charged to a cost of sales account.

13. Going back to the Maintain Inventory Items form, the next fields deal with costing information. In the Cost Method field, select the type of costing that you use: LIFO, FIFO, or Average. Most companies use FIFO (first in, first out), but if you do not know what method you use, speak with your CPA.
14. You may enter the Last Unit Cost for this item. This is the last price you paid when buying inventory. Remember that if you buy in cases and sell in units, you must use the per unit cost here. The next time you purchase inventory, Peachtree will update this field with the latest cost. Peachtree will also update this field when a beginning balance is entered.

Warning!! Once the costing method is set and the item is saved, the costing method cannot be changed!

15. If an item is taxable when you sell it, select the tax type from the Item Tax Type list.
16. If you pay commissions to salespeople and this is a item on which commission is paid, check the **Subject to Commission** check box.
17. The Quantity on Hand amount is calculated by the system.
18. Minimum Stock is the number of items in inventory at which, when reached, you will need to reorder stock.
19. The Reorder Quantity is the amount of this item that is normally ordered when the minimum Stock amount is reached.
20. The Preferred Vendor ID field is a drop-down list of vendors. If you usually buy this item from one particular vendor, you can enter that information.
21. Click **Save** to record the inventory item.

Adding Inventory Beginning Balances

Once the inventory item is saved, you can add the beginning balance for the item. This is the number of items that were in your inventory on the date that you began transactions. Any sales or purchases will be added through the appropriate function.

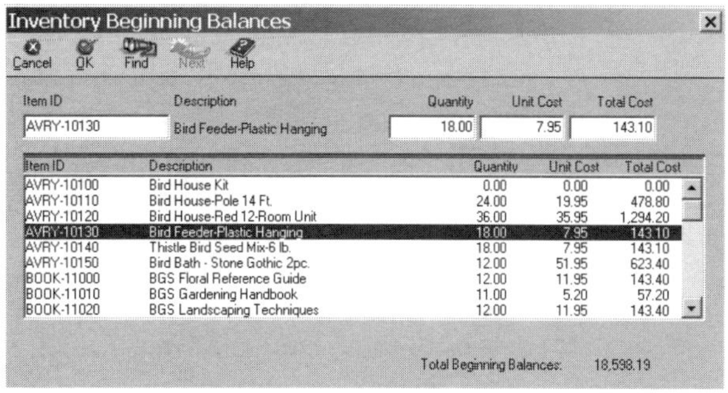

1. Click the **Beginning Balances** button to open the Inventory Beginning Balances window.
2. If not already selected, enter the item's ID. Enter the Quantity from your physical inventory listing that we discussed in Chapter 4. This is the number of items for the date you begin transactions. The Unit Cost should be entered and the Total Cost is automatically calculated. The Total Cost must match your valuation of this inventory from your list; you may need to adjust the Unit Price to accommodate this need.
3. Click **OK** to record the beginning balance. Click **Cancel** to return to the previous form.
4. Click on the **Custom Fields** tab.

   Use the fields provided to enter additional information on this item.
5. Click **Save** to record all information.

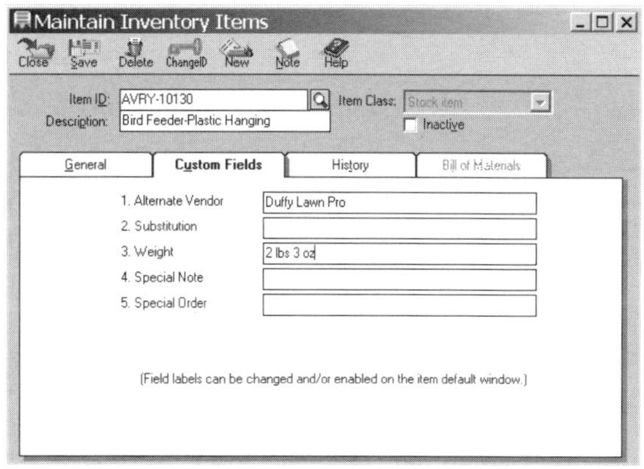

Adding Other Types of Inventory

Other types of inventory include those items that do not need tracking. These include items you buy or use constantly for clients, but do not keep a physical count of. These also include items charged to clients regularly, such as labor or a service. Peachtree has added to the list of classes over the years, so that some classes are almost identical to others.

Add these items the same way as you do stock items, but be sure to notice where some fields disappear or are unavailable. Also, the costs of sales may be handled differently with some classes. None of these classes will show up in inventory reports with any costing information.

Types of inventory, not including stock items, are listed below.

General inventory items that can be used by any company include the following:

Non-stock item — This inventory class allows you to assign quantities, descriptions, and unit prices, which are printed on invoices but are not tracked. A cost of goods general ledger account can be assigned to this class, but it is not affected by a costing method. I tend to use this class for most of my inventory items that are not Descriptions or Stock items because the class allows you to enter quantities. I do not always add the sales price because some items may be so generic that pricing may vary greatly from invoice to invoice. See the sample invoice later in this chapter for Non-stock items.

When using this item, note that the general ledger account used for entering purchases is the GL Salary/Wages Acct, not the GL Cost of Sales Acct, as you would think. Examples of this class could include service, hardware (generic), weekly mowing, and diagnostic fee.

Description only — This class is simply a description that can be used for comments for both invoices and purchases. These might include standard warranty information or setup information. There is no price or cost associated with this class on the inventory form, but you can still add quantity and unit price on the invoice. Examples of this class could include warranty comments or a thank you.

Labor — This item class is used in the same way that the next one, Service, is used. Peachtree suggests you use Labor for outside labor that you use for projects. Cost can be entered but is not tracked, although you can export information to Excel and run calculations there.

Service — This item class is the same as Labor. Peachtree suggests you use this for labor performed by your own employees.

Inventory items used with Peachtree's Time & Billing function include the following types:

Activity — This item class is used in the Time & Billing function to indicate how time is spent when performing services for a customer or job.

Charge — This item class is also used with the Time & Billing function for those items that are expenses incurred by an employee or purchased from a vendor that will be charged to a client. These items are recorded on employee or vendor expense tickets when you plan on billing customers for expenses

The final inventory item is for companies that make items from other items:

Assembly — This class is for items that are made up of other items, either Stock or other classes. An example would be a fruit basket that consists of a basket, three bananas, four oranges, two apples, a bow, grass filling, and half an hour of labor. The components of the assembly are listed in the Bill of Materials tab. Costing information for assembly item shows up in the inventory reports.

Month 1

Using Inventory Items

Items are used when creating invoices for customers, entering purchases, or making payments.

1. When you are creating an invoice, fill in the Quantity field and then select the item from the Item drop-down list.

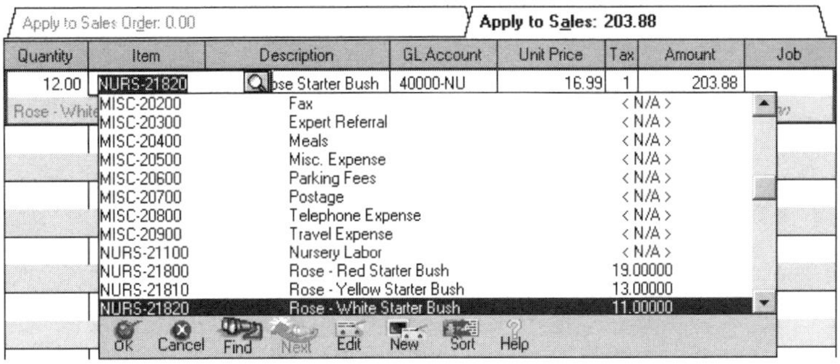

2. Notice in the Item list that the Item ID, the Item Short Description, and the Quantity are shown. If the item is not a stock item, <NA> will show in the Quantity column. If you need to sell more than is in stock, Peachtree will warn you if you selected that option (see Chapter 2).

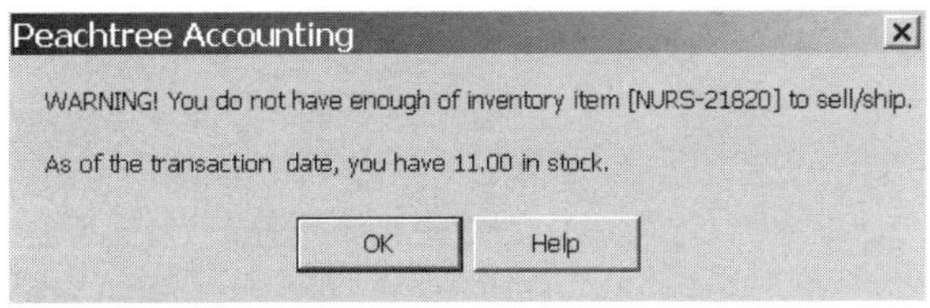

3. Peachtree will still let you save the invoice, even if you have depleted or oversold your inventory.
4. Once the item is selected, the Description for Sales appears in the Description field and the Unit Price and the Amount are calculated. The Tax field is also set to the correct Item Tax Type from the Maintain Inventory Items form.

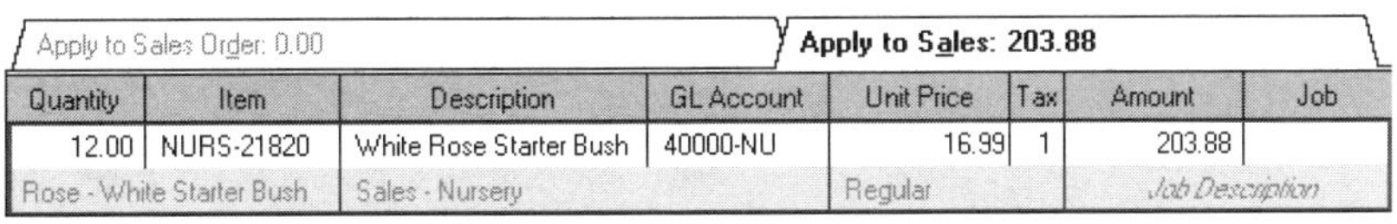

When you purchase items, either from the Purchase Orders, Purchases/Receive Inventory, or Payments forms, the same method is used.

1. From the Purchases form, fill in the Quantity field and then select the item from the Item drop-down list.

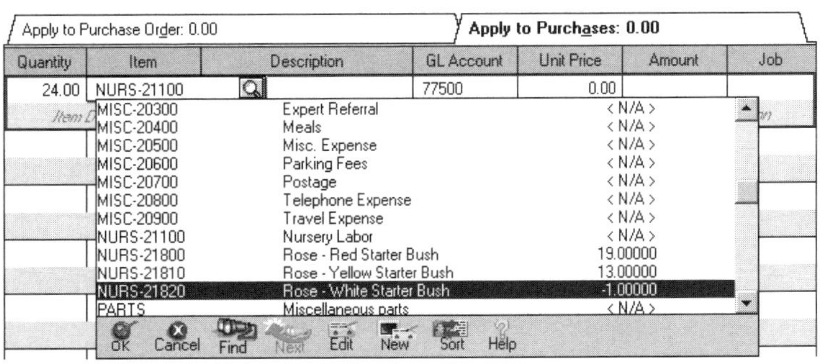

2. Notice in the Item list that the Item ID, the Item Short Description, and the Quantity are shown. If the item is not a stock item, <NA> will show in the Quantity column.
3. Once the item is selected, the Description for Purchases appears in the Description field. If the item is a stock item, the Unit Price is shown and the Amount is calculated. If it is not a stock item, you must enter a Unit Price before the Amount is calculated.

Common Inventory Questions and Answers

Depending upon your company, you may have just a handful or hundreds of items. Although the inventory tracking is very good, there are some distinctive lacks in the program. I find I am asked several questions over and over regarding the inventory. These are the solutions I have implemented with some success:

- *My inventory is in more than one location. How do I distinguish the items?* — In this case, there are two options. The first alternative is to not distinguish the location and to include in the number of items the count for all locations. The second alternative is to include the location in the item identification so you will have IDs such as AVRY-10130-DNTN and AVRY-10130-RWLT. The first identification is for items in the first location, the second identification is for the items in the second location. Each is tracked separately. If items are moved from one location to another, you must make an adjustment.
- *I get the same items, but in different colors so that I have one brown, one gold, one green, etc. How do I track these?* — The answer to this question is very similar to the answer above; either combine them all in the AVRY-10130 item or create different items such as AVRY-10130-BRN, AVRY-10130-GLD, and AVRY-10130-GRN.
- *I constantly buy parts to repair clients' machines. I don't want to keep an inventory because each part is specific for the job, but I want to track the number of items that I sell and purchase. Is there a way to accomplish this?* — The solution to this problem is to create a non-stock item called PARTS, HARDWARE (or a similar name), and make the sales price equal to 0.00. When you purchase an item for the client, use the item ID and then use the same ID again when you list it on the invoice. Although the item will not show up in the inventory reports, it will show up in the A/R report, Items Sold to Customers, and the A/P report, Items Purchased from Vendors. You can then compare the two to track profitability.
- *I need to track service contracts and I'd like to know how many hours a client has left on the contract when I invoice them. Also, I don't want to claim the income until the hours are used, not when they are sold. How can I do this?* — I have handled this problem several ways and have come up with a procedure that works for my own company and others. Follow these steps to track service contracts:

1. Create a Service Contracts Liability or Deferred Income general ledger account. Set the Account Type as **Other Current Liabilities**.
2. Determine the unit of measure for the service contract. It could be hours, visits, or months, or some other unit. It must be measurable in some way.
3. Set up three inventory items to be used to track service contracts: **contractstart**, **usecontract**, and **remaincontract**. Each of these has a unique description that will show on the invoice. The first two have pricing information. The Item Class for all is **Non-stock item** so that I can enter quantities on invoices.

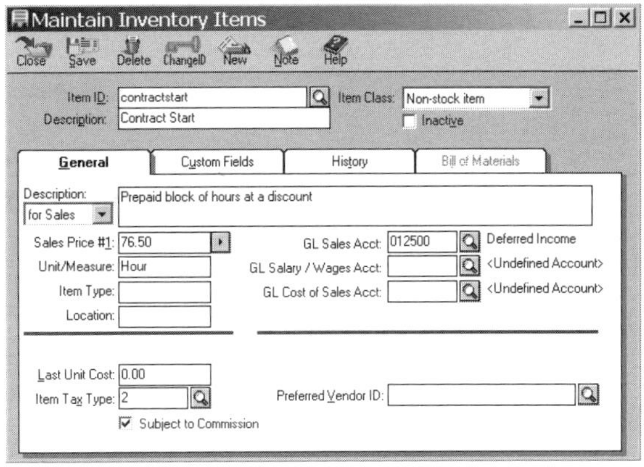

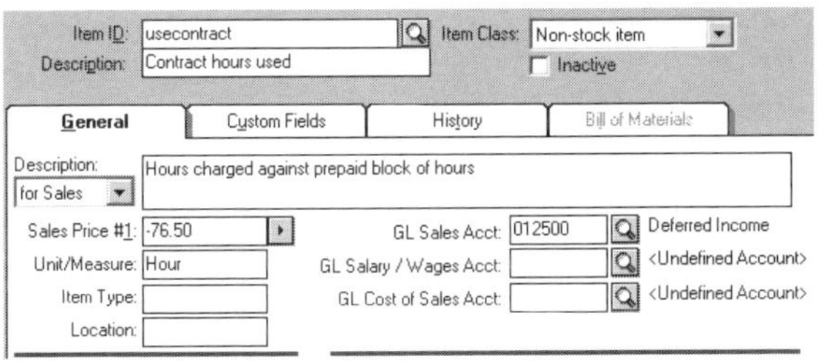

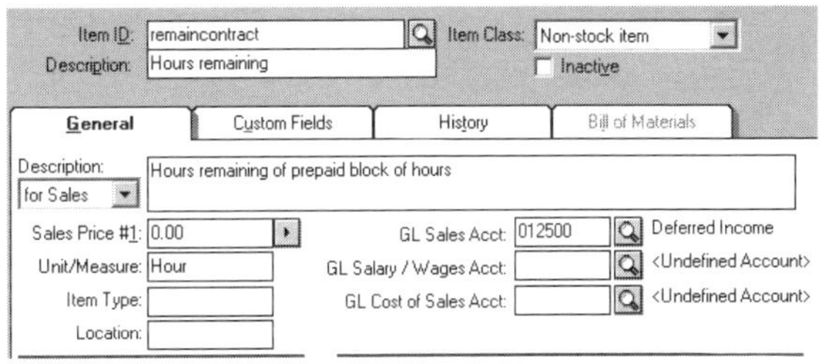

4. Notice that the Sales Price for usecontract is a negative number. Also notice that there is no Sales Price for remaincontract.
5. When a service contract, or prepaid block of hours as described in the Description for Sales field, is sold, the hours are allocated to the Deferred Income G/L account.

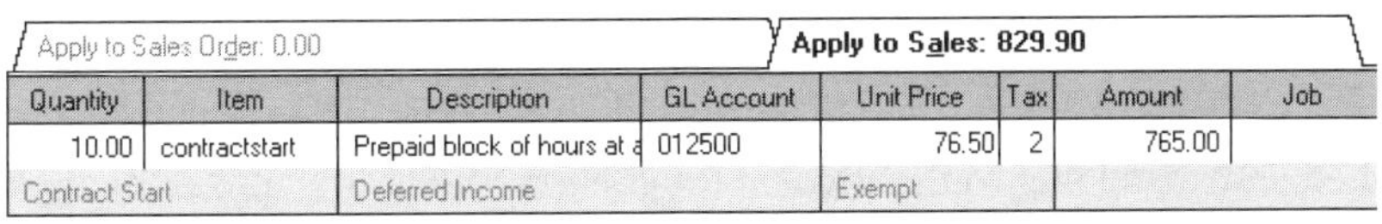

6. When a customer is serviced, the hours are charged to the inventory item Service, which is allocated to the Sales G/L account so that the hours are claimed as income now.

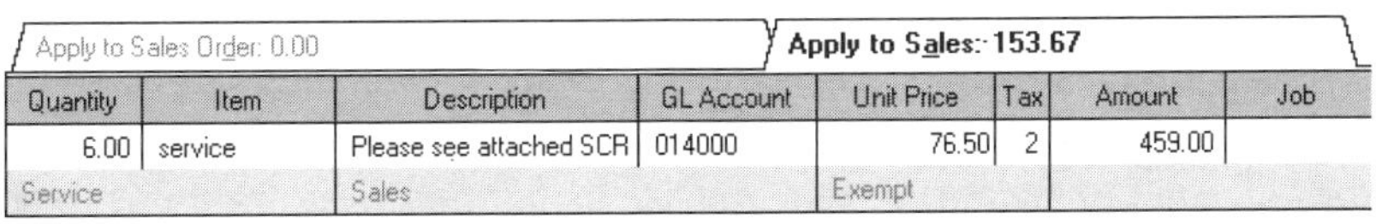

7. On the same invoice, the hours to be charged against the service contract are also entered. Because Unit Price is negative, Amount is deducted from the invoice and from the Deferred Income account.

Apply to Sales Order: 0.00 — **Apply to Sales: 153.67**

Quantity	Item	Description	GL Account	Unit Price	Tax	Amount	Job
6.00	usecontract	Hours charged against pre	012500	-76.50	2	-459.00	
Contract hours used		Deferred Income		Exempt			

8. All that is left is to show the remaining hours on the service contract. Unfortunately, these have to be hand-calculated. Although a GL Account is shown, there is no allocation made to it, because the Unit Price is 0.00.

Apply to Sales Order: 0.00 — **Apply to Sales: 153.67**

Quantity	Item	Description	GL Account	Unit Price	Tax	Amount	Job
2.00	remaincontract	Hours remaining of prepaid	012500	0.00	2		
Hours remaining		Deferred Income		Exempt			

9. The body of a typical invoice, with other charges, will end up looking like the following.

Quantity	Item	Description	Unit Price	Extension
8.00	remaincontract	Hours remaining of prepaid block of hours		
6.00	service	Please see attached SCR for details	76.50	459.00
6.00	usecontract	Hours charged against prepaid block of hours	76.50	-459.00
2.00	remaincontract	Hours remaining of prepaid block of hours		
1.00	hardwarereimb	Reimbursement for hardware/software purchased - Receipt attached for RadioShack	18.38	18.38
1.00	hardwarereimb	Reimbursement for hardware/software purchased - Receipt attached	135.29	135.29

10. Notice that the first line shows the initial remaining hours. This is added so that both you and the client can see a clear-cut use of the hours. The service hours are then shown, adding to the invoice total. Next, the hours applied against the service contract are deducted. The final remaining hours are shown on the next line.

Inventory Homework

Now that you have a better understanding of inventory, you should look over the invoices and bills that you have entered to see which ones can be edited to include the appropriate inventory items. This is especially true of your stock items. Then you will want to make sure that you are using the inventory items to create new invoices and bills.

Quick Inventory Reports

There are several reports that assist you in tracking physical inventory and in analyzing what services or non-stock items are sold to customers. While some of these reports are located with the inventory reports, unfortunately several are not. The problem with Peachtree's inventory reports is that most of them only report on stock or assembly items. Peachtree needs to realize that many companies would like the same reports for all item classes.

A Customized Sales Journal

The Sales Journal, from the A/R reports, can be modified to include some useful information if most of your inventory items are not stock items.

1. From the Select a Report window, select **Accounts Receivable** and **Sales Journal**. Click the **Preview** button. The Sales Journal dialog box appears.

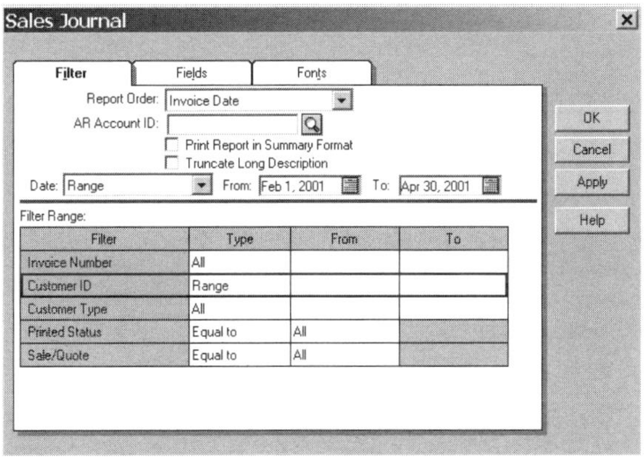

2. Select a Date range for this report. For now, leave all other fields as they are. Click on the **Fields** tab.

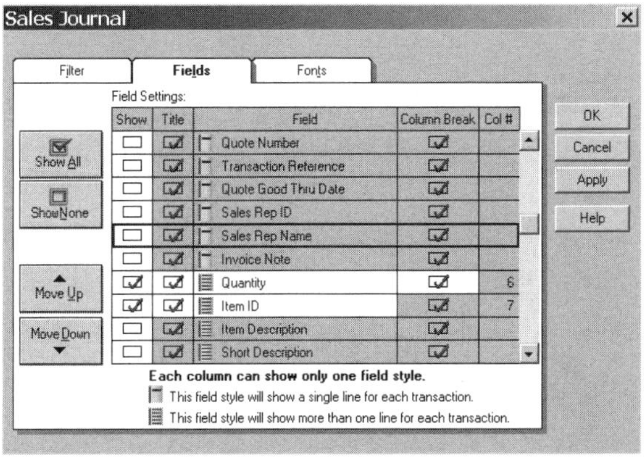

3. Scroll down the Field Settings list until you come to **Quantity** and **Item ID**. Click the **Show** column of both lines.
4. Select one of the lines and click the **Move Up** button. The line will move up the list. Do this until the line is above Line Description.
5. Repeat the procedure for the other line. Quantity should now show as number 4 in the Col # field. Item ID should be Col # 5.
6. Click **OK** to view the report.

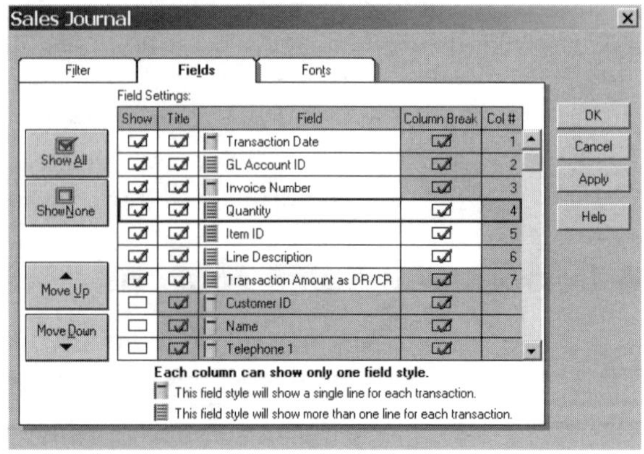

D-N-B Consultants
Sales Journal
For the Period From Feb 1, 2001 to Apr 30, 2001
Filter Criteria includes: 1) Customer IDs from rdsinc to rdsinc. Report order is by Invoice Date. Report is printed in Detail Format.

Date	Account ID	Invoice No	Qty	Item ID	Line Description	Debit Amnt	Credit Amnt
2/28/01	012500	01006	6.00	remaincontract	Hours remaining of prepaid block of hours		
	014000		2.50	service	1/15 & 1/17 - Please see attached SCR for details		191.25
	014000		1.00	service	Fax server rebuilt		76.50
	014000		0.50	service	Fax server installed		38.25
	014000		2.00	service	Repair system after Garland power surge		153.00
	014000		2.00	service	Cleanup of user machines/run antivirus/rundisk Norton disk utilities		153.00
	012500		8.00	usecontract	Hours charged against prepaid block of hours	612.00	
	012500		-2.00	remaincontract	Hours remaining of prepaid block of hours		
	012500		10.00	contractstart	Prepaid block of hours at a discount		765.00
	012500		8.00	remaincontract	Hours remaining of prepaid block of hours		
	014400		1.00	hardwarereimb	Reimbursement for hardware/software purchased -		64.90

7. The report will include the Qty and Item ID as columns in the report. If the report is too spread out, click the **Design** button and move the columns as needed.
8. Click **Preview** to return to view mode.

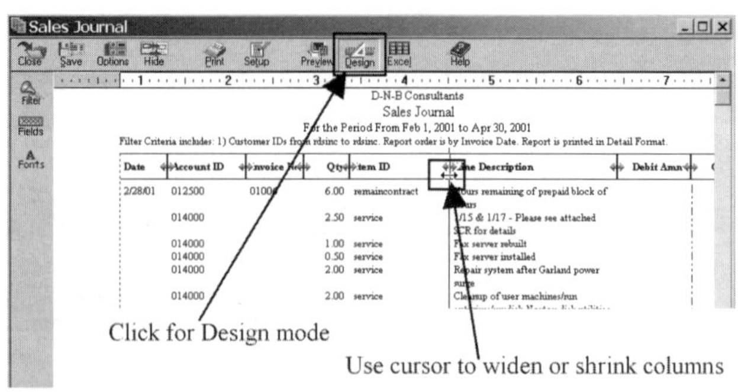

9. A recently added feature to Peachtree is the ability to export the report to Excel. This provides the power of a spreadsheet to analyze the data within the report.

   I find that this process works best if you open Excel first. Otherwise the process appears to take an extra long time as the Windows overhead determines that Excel needs to be loaded, loads the program, and moves the data to the program.

First open Excel. Next go back to the Peachtree report and click the **Excel** button in the toolbar. A Copy Report to Excel dialog box appears.

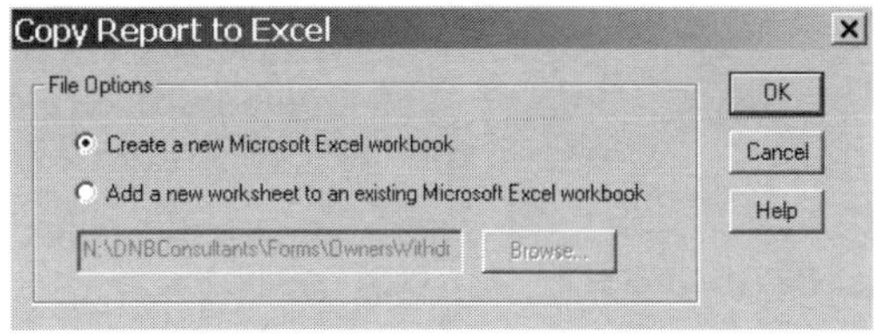

10. You may select to create a new workbook or to add a worksheet to an existing workbook. To add a worksheet, click the **Browse** button to locate the workbook.
11. Click **OK**. Peachtree will spend a few seconds copying the report. A status window will display during the copy procedure.

12. After the copy procedure is complete, the Excel button on your Windows taskbar should start to flash. Click on **Excel** to open the report.

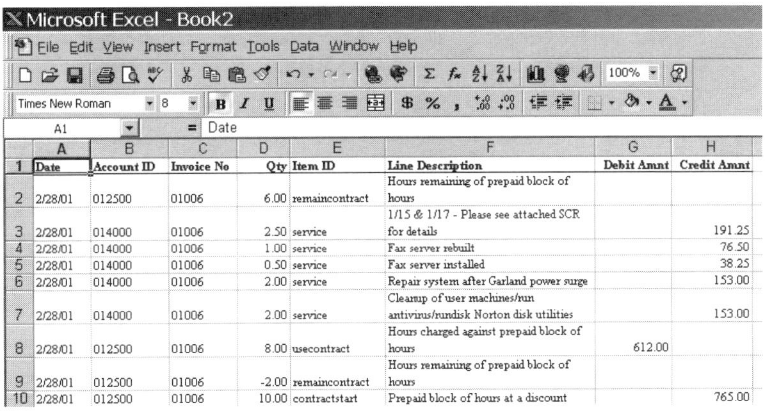

	A	B	C	D	E	F	G	H
1	Date	Account ID	Invoice No	Qty	Item ID	Line Description	Debit Amnt	Credit Amnt
2	2/28/01	012500	01006	6.00	remaincontract	Hours remaining of prepaid block of hours		
3	2/28/01	014000	01006	2.50	service	1/15 & 1/17 - Please see attached SCR for details		191.25
4	2/28/01	014000	01006	1.00	service	Fax server rebuilt		76.50
5	2/28/01	014000	01006	0.50	service	Fax server installed		38.25
6	2/28/01	014000	01006	2.00	service	Repair system after Garland power surge		153.00
7	2/28/01	014000	01006	2.00	service	Cleanup of user machines/run antivirus/rundisk Norton disk utilities		153.00
8	2/28/01	012500	01006	8.00	usecontract	Hours charged against prepaid block of hours	612.00	
9	2/28/01	012500	01006	-2.00	remaincontract	Hours remaining of prepaid block of hours		
10	2/28/01	012500	01006	10.00	contractstart	Prepaid block of hours at a discount		765.00

13. Notice that fields that were not repeated on the Peachtree report are repeated on the Excel report. From here you may sort and subtotal the data to get the information in the format that you need.
14. When you go to close the report in Peachtree, a message box appears. This is a result of your changing the layout of the original report.

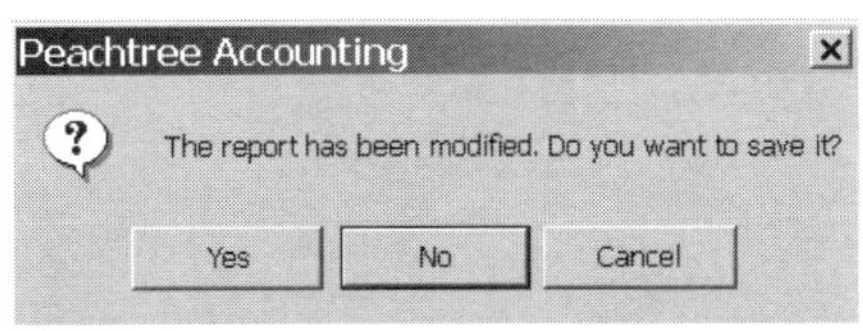

15. If you want to use this report regularly and not have to recreate it, click **Yes**. A Save As window appears.
16. Enter the new name and a description. Click **Save**. The report will appear in the Select a Report window.

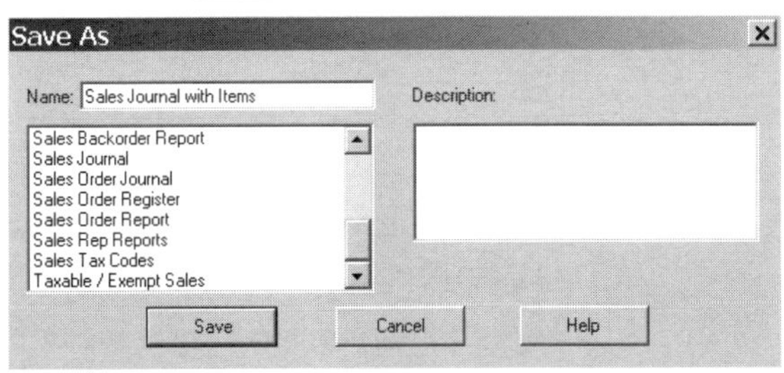

Tip: Always save custom reports under a different name than the original report. If you have to restore a backup or upgrade Peachtree, the original report may be overwritten with a default version of the report

Items Sold to Customers

This report lists all items sold to customers. The report includes quantities and costs of sales. Unfortunately, the report is limited since it cannot be filtered or sorted by Item ID.

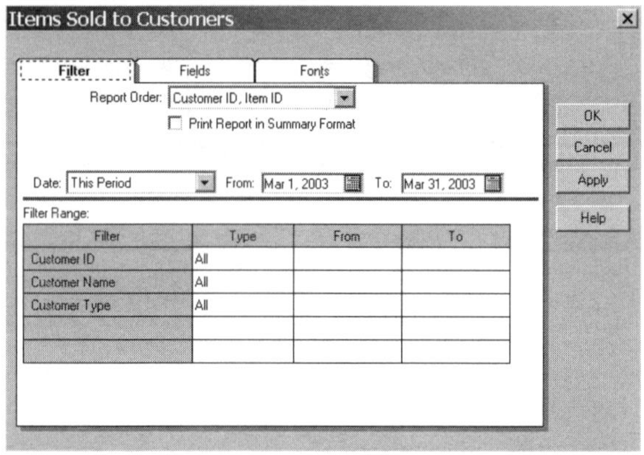

1. Open the Items Sold to Customers dialog box.
2. Choices for the Report Order field include Customer ID, Customer Name, Customer ID, and Item ID.
3. Do not select Print Report in Summary Format. If summarized, the report totals by customer and the item IDs are lost.
4. You may select a date range. The report may also be filtered by the Customer ID, Customer Name, and Customer Type in the Filter Range section.
5. Click **OK** to view the report.

Bellwether Garden Supply
Items Sold to Customers
For the Period From Mar 1, 2003 to Mar 31, 2003
Filter Criteria includes: Report order is by Customer ID, Item ID. Report is printed in Detail Format.

Customer ID Name	Item ID	Qty	Amount	Cost of Sales	Gross Profit	Gross Margin
HOLT-01 Holt Properties, Inc.	FERT-16120	6.00	53.94	21.90	32.04	59.40
	FERT-16160	10.00	99.90	39.50	60.40	60.46
	SEFL-31110	2.00	2.78	1.10	1.68	60.43
	SEFL-31150	2.00	2.78	1.10	1.68	60.43
		20.00	159.40	63.60	95.80	60.10
MACKAY-01 Mackay Construction			5,000.00		5,000.00	100.00
			5,000.00		5,000.00	100.00
MASON-01 Mason Office Park	AVRY-10130	20.00	399.80	159.00	240.80	60.23
	LAND-17800	3.50	69.97		69.97	100.00
		23.50	469.77	159.00	310.77	66.15

6. For stock inventory items, the quantity, amount, cost of sales, gross profit, and gross margin are shown.

   For other items, quantity is included if a quantity was entered on the invoice. There is no cost of sales and gross margin will always show as 100%.

You may want to export this report to Excel to allow sorting and subtotaling of the items.

Items Purchased from Vendors

This report shows what items have been purchased, including the quantities and amounts.

1. Open the Items Purchased from Vendors dialog box and select the criteria to print the report. The filters and report order are very similar to the Items Sold to Customers report.

Bellwether Garden Supply
Items Purchased from Vendors
For the Period From Mar 1, 2003 to Mar 31, 2003
Filter Criteria includes: Report order is by Vendor ID, Item ID. Report is printed in Detail Format.

Vendor ID Name	Item ID	Qty	Amount
ANDERSON-01			1,000.00
Anderson Distribution	PARTS	1.00	29.68
		1.00	1,029.68
ARBOR-01	AVRY-10130	24.00	190.80
Arbor Wholesale Supplier	AVRY-10140	150.00	1,192.50
	BOOK-11030	6.00	31.20
	NURS-21820	24.00	122.40
	POTS-30210	12.00	28.20
	SEVG-33100	12.00	5.40
		228.00	1,570.50

2. Quantities and amounts show for both stock and other items, if available. Amounts are also shown for purchased items that do not have an item ID.

   You may want to export this report to Excel to allow sorting and subtotaling of the items.

Inventory Unit Activity Report

The Inventory Unit Activity Report only shows listings for stock and assembly inventory items. The information that is shown is very good, but, personally, I wish it would include non-stock items also.

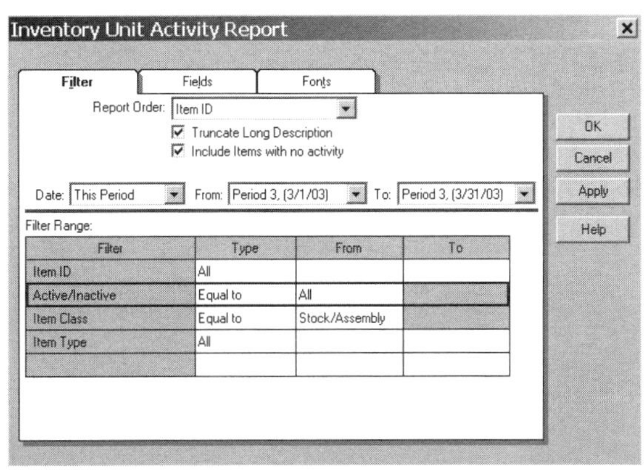

1. Open the Inventory Unit Activity Report dialog box.
2. Select an option in the Report Order field.
3. Select the **Truncate Long Description** check box to keep the report from printing descriptions longer than one line.

4. Unselect the **Include Items with no activity** check box to only print inventory items that show sales, purchases, adjustments, or assembly.
5. Enter the date range.
6. Limit the items in the list by only selecting a group of items using the Item ID filter.
7. Notice the Active/Inactive line in the Filter Range section. By selecting **Active** in the From column, you can exclude items that are no longer used.
8. Unfortunately, Item Class will only let you select Stock item, Assembly, or Stock/Assembly.
9. Enter an Item Type, if needed. Remember that the Type field is case sensitive and must be entered exactly.
10. Click **OK** to view the report.

Bellwether Garden Supply
Inventory Unit Activity Report
For the Period From Mar 1, 2003 to Mar 31, 2003
Filter Criteria includes: 1) Stock/Assembly. Report order is by ID. Report is printed with Truncated Long Descriptions.

Item ID Item Description Item Class	Beg Qty	Units Sold	Units Purc	Adjust Qty	Assembly Qty	Qty on Hand
AVRY-10120 Bird House-Red 12-Room Unit Stock item	36.00				-6.00	30.00
AVRY-10130 Bird Feeder-Plastic Hanging Stock item	12.00	20.00	24.00			16.00
AVRY-10140 Thistle Bird Seed Mix-6 lb. Stock item	8.00	156.00	150.00			2.00
AVRY-10150 Bird Bath - Stone Gothic 2pc. Stock item	6.00					6.00
BOOK-11000 BGS Floral Reference Guide Stock item	6.00					6.00
BOOK-11010 BGS Gardening Handbook Stock item	5.00	3.00				2.00
BOOK-11020 BGS Landscaping Techniques Stock item	6.00			1.00		7.00

Summary

Inventory is a very complex subject for some businesses. We have only scratched the surface in this book due to space constraints. Unfortunately, as I have noted several places in the chapter, inventory is still one of the weaker areas of the Peachtree program. We have tried to explain some workarounds for these limitations, but some things cannot be worked around in the program.

One of the most difficult conversions I ever worked on had problems with the inventory. The company was a custom drapery and furniture shop. The inventory was split so many ways due to color and pattern differences that the listing of inventory items was over 200 pages long. The shop was closed for three days just to count the inventory and then the data entry turned out to be very poor. We discovered that numerous items that were dispersed throughout the shop were actually duplicates. We finally managed to get everything but the conversion took an extra month and we kept discovering for several months that a few items had been overlooked or entered more than once.

Later, in Month 3, we will learn how to reconcile the inventory when a physical count is taken. Adjustments to inventory will be covered in the same month, in Chapter 17.

Month 2

The Balancing Month

- Balancing Checking and Credit Card Accounts
- Balancing Accounts Receivable
- Balancing Accounts Payable
- Sales Taxes
- Balancing Payroll

Chapter 11

Balancing Checking and Credit Card Accounts

In This Chapter

- Starting the balancing month
- Entering the checking account beginning balance
- Reconciling the bank account
- Clearing checks individually or through a range
- Locating missing checks
- Clearing deposits and automatic payments
- Entering service charges, interest, and adjusting transactions
- Correcting adjustments through the General Journal entry function

Your Three-Month Plan — The Balancing Month

At the end of your first month you should have a good understanding of entering the different types of day-to-day transactions in Peachtree. Your employees should have implemented procedures to make this data entry go smoothly. Now comes the harder part of putting Peachtree all together. As the employees continue to enter transactions in both the old and the new systems, the balances for many of your accounts will need to be reconciled. Don't be discouraged; you are on your way to having accurate books.

Before you start this part of the book, you should verify that all invoices, receipts, bills, and payments have been entered into the system.

Changing the Accounting Period

Peachtree is designed so that you cannot enter data into previous accounting periods. If you try to enter a transaction into a period that has been closed, you will get this error message.

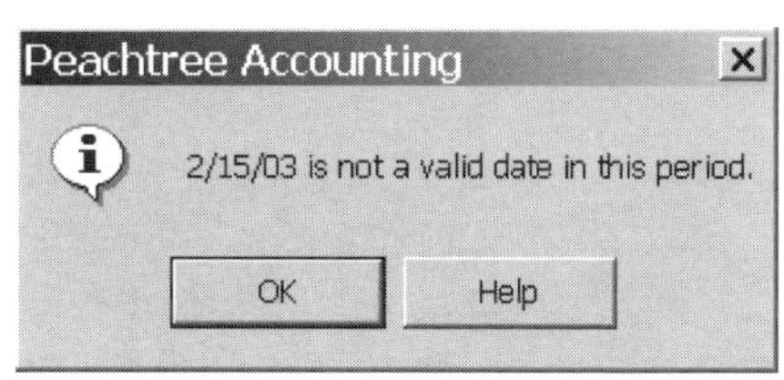

If you need to enter the transaction into the closed period, you will need to change the current accounting period to the previous one, and then enter the transaction into the correct period. See Chapter 2 for information on changing the accounting period.

It is possible to edit transactions in previous accounting periods. If you bring up the transaction and then click Save or Post, the following message will appear.

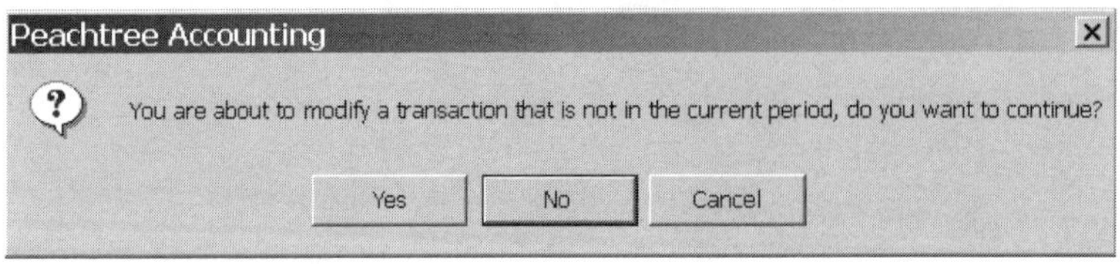

If you click Yes, the changes will be saved and your financial statements for the previous month, and subsequent months, could be affected. Create a policy for your employees on changing records in previous months and whether it is to be allowed or not.

Tip: If you don't want to allow your employees to add records in previous months, or you are a one-person operation, there is a way to add a record to a previous month without changing the accounting period and forcing everyone out of the system. Enter the transaction in the current month and then save the transaction. Then call up the record and change the date to the earlier month. You will get a warning message, but the system will accept the transaction. I wouldn't tell your employees about this ability. Just let them think that you have "super access."

You will need to decide when you close a month. Some companies will decide to do this immediately on the first business day of the month and only allow managers to go back to the previous month. Others will decide to leave the old month open for a few days or weeks. It is even okay to leave the current month open until all entries are completed for a month and it is considered officially closed on the books.

You must be careful when your accounting period does not match the current calendar month, for example if you have February as your current accounting period and it is now March 10, because when the system date is outside the current period, the date on an open form will show as the first date in the current accounting period.

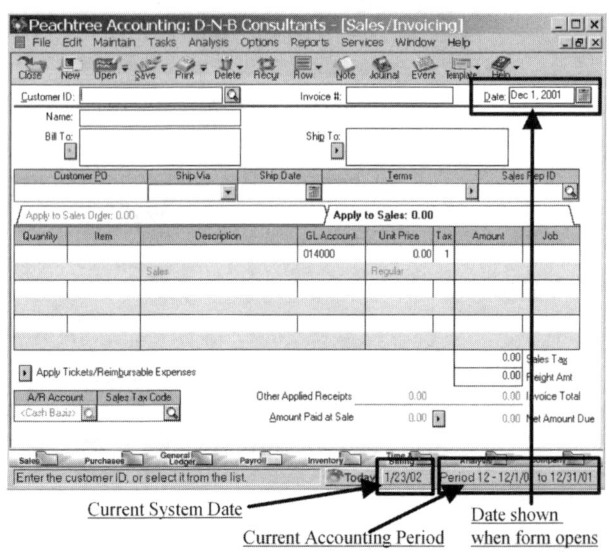

I have worked with numerous companies that handled the open accounting period in a variety of ways. If you are a small organization, how you handle the periods is totally up to you. For larger organizations, you will want to have a standard policy that is followed throughout the year, and may be governed by your industry or auditing procedures. For companies with more than three people in the accounting department, I often suggest that the old accounting period is held open until the fifth business day after the start of the month. By that time the bank reconciliation should have been completed and any old bills or sales can also be included in that month if needed. At that point the reports, files, and preliminary financial statements are run for the CPA and the accounting period is changed to the new month. By the end of the month the CPA will return corrections and needed journal entries. The accounting period is reset to the old month, the changes are made, and the final financial statements are run. The accounting period is again set to the current month and the old month is considered closed until the end of the year when the CPA may decide on additional changes.

Getting Started on the Bank Reconciliation

There is probably no task in accounting that can be more annoying than trying to balance a checkbook manually. A simple addition error can cause hours of searching. Many experts feel that if the checkbook is balanced to within $100.00 that there is no problem. But those small adjustments add up so that soon your A/R and A/P balances are out of balance and you have no idea if some of the older checks were actually paid or not. Peachtree's account reconciliation function is very good for an accounting program. It will let you make adjustments, add service charges and interest easily, and, best of all, you can leave the function without losing your work.

Before you can balance your bank account, you must be sure that all receipts and payments have been recorded in A/R and A/P. Go over your check copies and deposit slips and verify that all are entered. This includes any manual checks or ATM withdrawals. Once that is done, you are ready to enter your beginning bank balance.

The Beginning Bank Balance

In entering the beginning bank balance, you have to be very careful that the balance includes all checks and deposits written in the previous month. The beginning balance is not the amount that is shown on your bank statement for last month; it is the amount that the general ledger shows for the Begin Transactions date (see Chapter 4). Your CPA should be able to provide this balance for you with your trial balance for last month if you cannot determine it yourself. This amount should also match the G/L balance in your old accounting system.

If you regularly reconcile your bank account, this amount is the bank balance, plus any deposits in transit, less outstanding checks. If your bank statement is not dated for the end of the month, you still need to calculate the balance to the end of the month before the Begin Transactions date.

To enter the beginning bank balance, follow these steps:

1. Open the Maintain Chart of Accounts form.

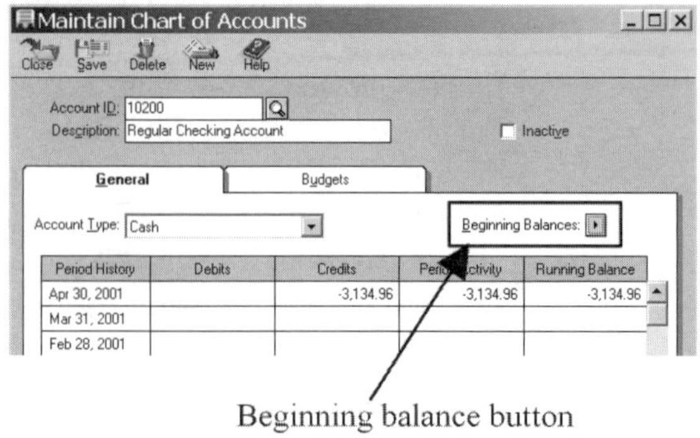

2. Click the **Beginning Balances** button. The Select Period dialog box appears.

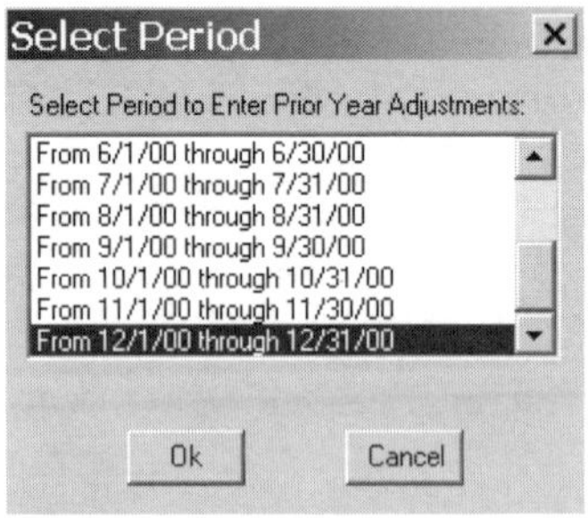

3. Depending upon how you set up the company, you should be able to select the month previous to your Begin Transactions date. If it is not available, select the last month of the previous financial year. Click **OK**. The Chart of Accounts Prior Year Adjustments screen appears.

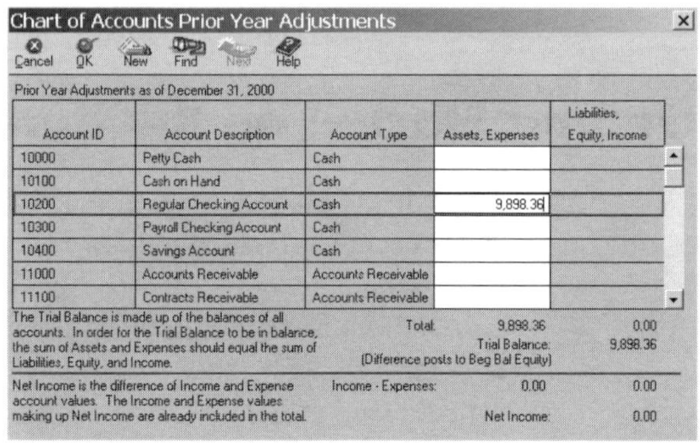

4. Locate the checking account. Enter the balance in the Assets, Expenses field. If, by chance, your bank account was overdrawn on this date, enter a negative number.

5. Scroll down the list until you get to the lines in the list where the Account Type is Equity. Depending on your company type — corporation, proprietorship, or partnership — your equity accounts will have different names. For now, choose the Retained Earnings account and enter the balance from the previous step in the Liabilities, Equity, Income column. The Retained Earnings entry is not permanent and will be changed later next month.

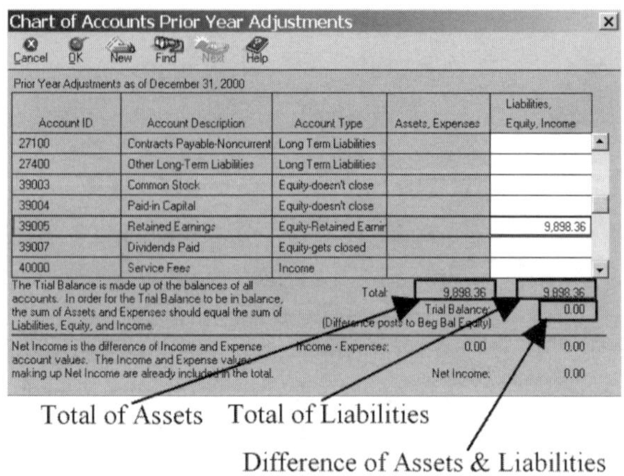

6. Once both entries are made, the Total field for both columns should be equal and the Trial Balance amount should be 0.00. Click **OK**.
7. Close the Maintain Chart of Accounts form.

Reconciling a Bank Account

Sometime after the first of the month, you will receive a statement from your bank. Once it has arrived, you can reconcile the account. The following example is partially based on data in the Bellwether Garden Supply sample company that accompanies Peachtree. I have had to add some additional transactions to be able to show some of the features and problems of reconciling a bank account. The sample bank statement and an adjusted copy of the sample company are included in the downloadable files for you to follow.

1. The current accounting period shown on the status bar should be set to the same month as the statement. If the accounting periods do not match, you will need to change it. Changing the accounting period was covered in Chapter 2.
2. From the navigation aid, click on the **Account Reconciliation** icon in the **General Ledger** folder.

Alternately, select **Tasks**, **Account Reconciliation** from the menu bar or press **Alt+K**, then **O** using the keyboard shortcuts.

3. A blank Account Reconciliation screen appears.

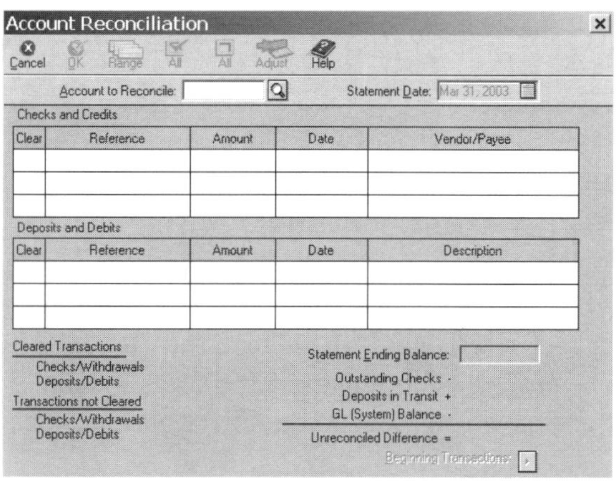

In the Account to Reconcile field, select the account for this statement.

4. The Statement Date field defaults to the last day of the current accounting period. If your statement ending date is different, change the date here.

5. Now, you want to look at your bank statement. A simple sample bank statement is shown here.

Statement Date: Mar 1 to Mar 31, 2003

Beginning Balance:		**20,281.37**
Checks Paid:	-	**8,265.01**
Other Withdrawals	-	**10,074.82**
Deposits	+	**14,445.86**
Balance as of Mar 31		**16,387.40**

Checks Paid

Dt Paid	Ck #	Amt	Dt Paid	Ck #	Amt
3/3	10199	289.68	3/24	10204	335.50
3/10	10200	431.40	3/24	10205	147.00
3/14	10201	124.68	3/25	10203	550.00
3/18	10207	550.00	3/28	10206	274.56
3/19	10208	250.54	3/28	10211	3,811.65
3/21	10209	500.00	3/31	10212	1,000.00

Other Withdrawals including charges and fees

Date	Description	Amt
3/18	Wire Transfer Ref PYRL031203	10,000.00
3/24	ACH Debit 0322 Internet National	64.82
3/31	Service Fee	10.00

Deposits and other additions

Date	Description	Amt
3/3	Deposit	645.72
3/4	Deposit	7,913.49
3/6	Deposit	220.31
3/10	Deposit	97.57
3/17	Deposit	715.44
3/19	Deposit	763.82
3/24	Deposit	3,178.41
3/28	Deposit	826.74
3/31	Interest Earned	84.36

6. Get the ending balance for the bank statement, shown here as the Balance as of Mar 31. Enter this amount in the Statement Ending Balance field.

7. During the entry of these fields, your screen will be populated with the transactions for the selected account.

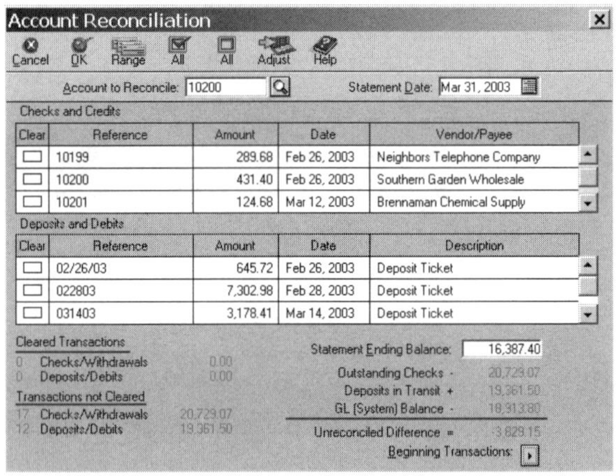

There are two lists on the screen. The upper is the Checks and Credits section. It contains checks, withdrawals, and other items posted as credits to the account. The lower section is for Deposits and Debits. Remember, we are talking about your general ledger here, not the bank's records. What the bank says is a credit to your account, you classify as a debit to increase your bank account.

There are several totals in the lower half of the screen that may assist you in verifying the accuracy of your reconciliation. On the left are the Cleared Transactions. As you clear a transaction by putting a check mark in the Clear column of the two lists, the amount of the transaction will be added to the Checks/Withdrawals or the Deposits/Debits totals.

Below the Cleared Transactions are the Transactions not Cleared. These totals will decrease as transactions are cleared. The Checks/Withdrawals total and the Deposits/Debits total are transferred to the Outstanding Checks and Deposits in Transit totals on the right.

In the lower right corner of the screen is the Unreconciled Difference total. As we clear transactions this amount will go up and down. It is the difference between the Statement Ending Balance less the Outstanding Checks plus the Deposits in Transit less the GL (System) Balance. If all transactions are cleared correctly, this amount will become zero.

Note: Unfortunately, Peachtree has used the same setup for this screen forever and there is no way to see more than three lines in the list, no matter what your monitor resolution. The screen cannot be resized or maximized at all. This makes it more difficult to perform the account reconciliation procedure. Hey, Peachtree, give us a break!

8. Going back to the bank statement, we first want to clear the Checks Paid. Some bank statements show checks in date paid order, some in check number order, and some mix all transactions (checks, withdrawals, and deposits) in date order for the period. As you can see, this statement is divided into three sections. We will follow the format of showing the transactions in the three sections in date order. Depending upon your statement format, you may need to make some slight adjustments to these procedures, but overall the steps are the same.

   The first check listed on our bank statement is Ck # 10199. Locate that check in the Checks and Credits list on the Account Reconciliation form. Although the date on the check is shown as Feb 26, 2003, the check did not clear the bank until 3/3/2003.

   You may also notice the way that Peachtree sorts the list of checks in the Reference column. Although the top of the list appears to be sorted numerically, it is actually sorted alphabetically. The digits 0-9 come before the letters A-Z, which come before the letters a-z.

9. Click in the **Clear** column. A red check mark will appear in the check box. We can continue the process for the next couple of checks.

Tip: As I clear transactions on my bank statement, I use a pencil and mark the same transaction on the actual statement with a tiny dot, dash, or check mark to show that is has been cleared. In our example, there are not that many transactions, but if your statement is several pages long, marking it will help you to keep track of what has been cleared and what has not. If I have to redo the reconciliation, I will change to a different color. As we all know, sometimes statements can be very difficult to balance.

10. If you look at the statement carefully, you will see that check numbers 10203 through 10209 have all cleared, even though they are not shown in order. You can clear a range of checks all at once by clicking the **Range** button in the toolbar.

11. The Clear Range window appears.

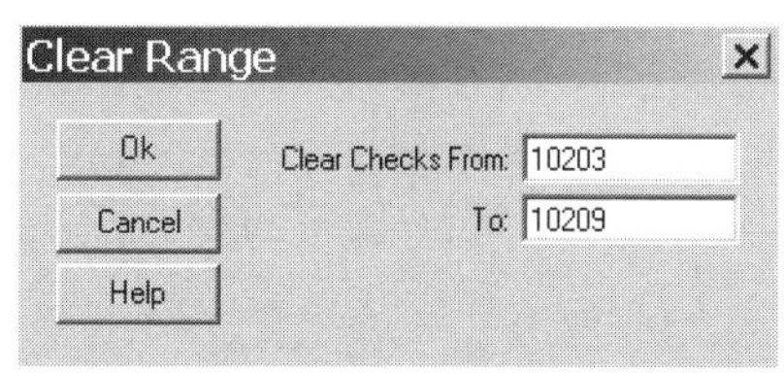

   Enter the beginning and the ending check numbers in the Clear Checks From and To fields. Click **OK** to return to the Account Reconciliation screen.

12. The selected checks will be cleared. We can next clear check number 10211. When we get to the last check, you will notice that check number 10212 is not in the list. It may have been a manual check that was not entered at the time that it was printed.

If you receive copies of your checks, you can find that check to see who the payee is. You will need to track down any backup or receipts relating to the check to discover where the check is to be allocated. Going back to the check copy and the documentation can help you discover potential fraud by your employees.

13. After the documentation on the check is located, you need to leave the Account Reconciliation screen to go look in the Payments form for the check to discover why it is missing. To leave the screen and save the reconciliation, click the **OK** button in the toolbar. Peachtree will show a quick status bar to show that the reconciliation is being saved.

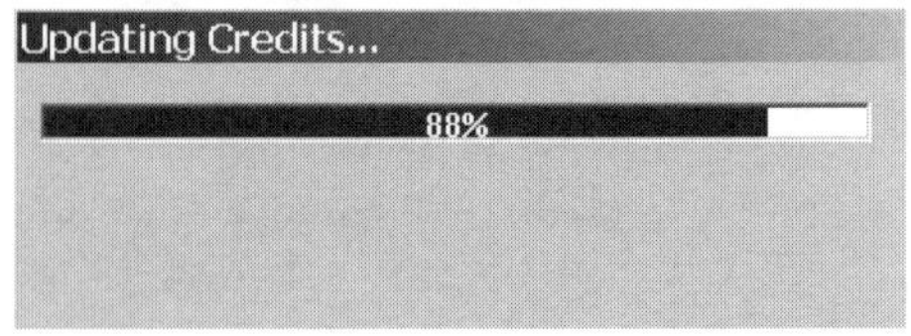

    Then the Account Reconciliation screen will close.

14. Go to the Payments screen and look to see if the check is in the Select Payment list but was entered incorrectly. Remember that the check may be from a previous month, so you may need to look at other periods by changing the period in the Show drop-down list.

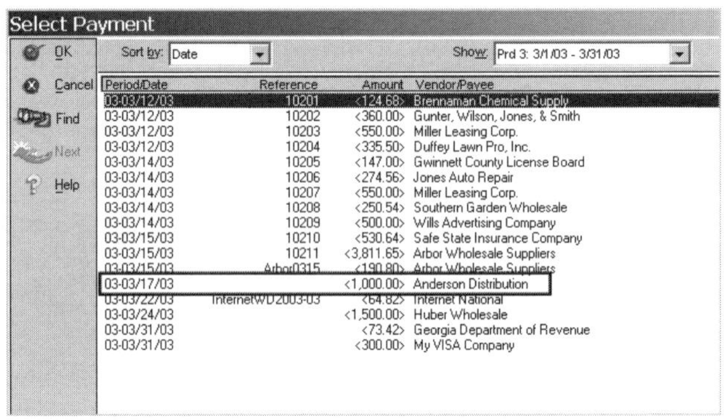

15. In our case, we discover that the check was for Anderson Distribution. It is in the Select Payment list, but does not have a check number assigned for some reason. Select the payment and enter the check number into the Reference field, then save the transaction again.

    If the check does not appear in the list, click **Cancel** to return to the Payments form and enter the check as a manual check.

> **Note:** You can also enter a check by making an adjustment to the account reconciliation, but I prefer to enter the check on the Payments form because the check may have a bill involved. Entering an adjustment check will not allow you to pay an outstanding bill; therefore the bill will remain in the outstanding A/P.

16. Once the payment has been entered, return to the Account Reconciliation screen. When it appears, it will be blank. Choose the account in the Account to Reconcile field and all the information that you have saved will appear. Notice that check number 10212 now appears.

Checks and Credits

Clear	Reference	Amount	Date	Vendor/Payee
☐	10210	530.64	Mar 15, 2003	Safe State Insurance Company
☑	10211	3,811.65	Mar 15, 2003	Arbor Wholesale Suppliers
☐	10212	1,000.00	Mar 17, 2003	Anderson Distribution

17. Clear that check, and all the checks in this section of the bank statement are now cleared.
18. If you go further down the list of Checks and Credits, you will notice that checks numbered 10213 and 10214 are already cleared. There are cleared because they are actually voided checks. If you scroll down the Deposits and Debits section, you will notice that 10213V and 10214V, the reversals to void the checks, are also cleared.

Checks and Credits

Clear	Reference	Amount	Date	Vendor/Payee
☑	10212	1,000.00	Mar 17, 2003	Anderson Distribution
☑	10213	450.00	Mar 16, 2003	Parr Brothers Tree Surgeons
☑	10214	50.00	Mar 15, 2003	Morgan Enterprises

Deposits and Debits

Clear	Reference	Amount	Date	Description
☐	031403	3,178.41	Mar 14, 2003	Deposit Ticket
☑	10213V	450.00	Mar 17, 2003	Parr Brothers Tree Surgeons
☑	10214V	50.00	Mar 17, 2003	Morgan Enterprises

Month 2

19. Next, we want to go to the Other Withdrawals section on the bank statement. These transactions are also located in the Checks and Credits section of the Account Reconciliation form.

Checks and Credits

Clear	Reference	Amount	Date	Vendor/Payee
☑	10212	1,000.00	Mar 17, 2003	Anderson Distribution
☐	InternetWD2003-03	64.82	Mar 22, 2003	Internet National
☐	PYRL031203	10,000.00	Mar 12, 2003	Transfer From Regular to Payro

20. The first transaction is for a wire transfer (discussed in Chapter 9) from the checking account to the payroll account (entered in the General Journal). The second transaction is an automatic withdrawal (discussed in Chapter 8) from your checking account for Internet service. Both these transactions can be cleared.
21. The last transaction is for the bank's monthly service fee. It is probably not yet in the system. This type of transaction can easily be entered as an adjustment. Click the **Adjust** button 

in the toolbar.

22. The Additional Transactions screen appears.

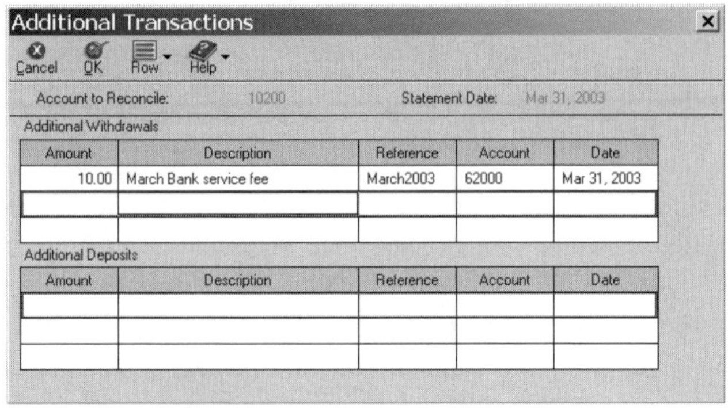

23. The service fee will go into the Additional Withdrawals section. Fill in the Amount, Description, Reference, the associated general ledger Account, and Date fields for the transaction. Click **OK** to return to the reconciliation screen and then clear the service fee transaction.

24. If you now look at the lower part of the screen, you can see some changes that have occurred because of the items that have been cleared.

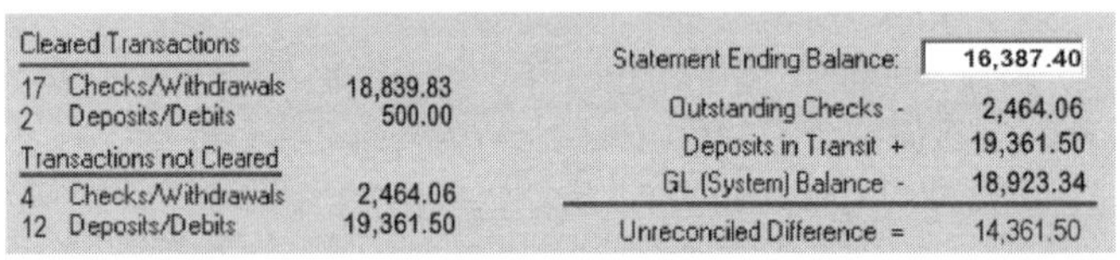

In the Cleared Transactions section, the amount of all cleared Checks/Withdrawals is $18,839.83. This is the total of the Checks Paid and Other Withdrawals sections on the bank statement. The number of Checks/Withdrawals is 17, which matches the 12 checks, two voids, and three withdrawals.

The amount of Checks/Withdrawals in the Transactions not Cleared section has been reduced to $2,464.06. This amount also shows on the right for the amount of the Outstanding Checks.

25. Next, we want to look at the deposits section of the bank statement and the Deposits and Debits listing. In the Account Reconciliation dialog, you will notice the sorting of the deposit ticket IDs in the Reference column. It appears a bit confusing with dates being shown in several formats. In fact, the Reference 030303 comes before 2/28/03, and 3/18/03 comes before 3/4/03. Because Peachtree sorts the Reference field alphabetically, it can become very difficult to locate individual deposits. For this reason alone, it is important to use a standardized system for numbering your deposit slips. See Chapter 6 for more information on numbering deposit ticket IDs. We will show how these confusing deposit ticket IDs are displayed in the listing here. Hopefully, you will see from this example how not to number these items.

26. The first deposit in the listing is for $645.72. It is easily located and cleared on the reconciliation screen.

Deposits and Debits

Clear	Reference	Amount	Date	Description
☑	02/26/03	645.72	Feb 26, 2003	Deposit Ticket
☐	022803	4,881.80	Mar 15, 2003	Deposit Ticket
☐	030303	220.31	Mar 3, 2003	Deposit Ticket

The date that the deposit was created was Feb 26, 2003. Because the owner of this company makes the deposits, and he sometimes takes several days to do so, the deposit was not given to the bank until 3/3/2003, which is noted on the bank statement. Deposits may not match the dates that they are created.

27. The next deposit on the bank statement is for $7,913.49. That amount cannot be located in the listing of the deposits. If you do some detective work, you will notice that there are two deposits that were created on Feb 28, 2003. One has a Reference of 022803, the other has a Reference of 2/28/03 (the second one is located quite a ways down the list). The total of these two match the amount of the bank statement deposit on 3/4/03, so you can clear both of these.

28. During the month of March, you voided or wrote off some invoices using the receipts function.

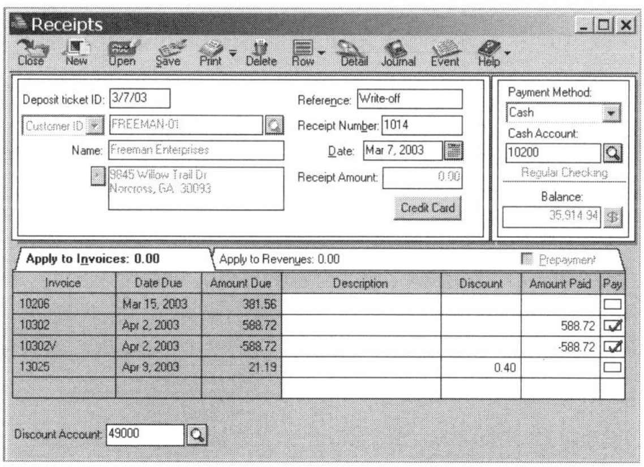

There are two of these for March and they will appear in the deposits listing as blank deposits. You will want to clear these also.

Clear	Reference	Amount	Date	Description
☐	3/17/03		Mar 17, 2003	Deposit Ticket

29. You can clear the rest of the deposits the same way. Notice that the voided checks, which we discussed earlier, have already been cleared. Also notice that Reference 033103, for $5000.00, does not show up on the bank statement and, therefore, should not be cleared.

30. The last transaction on the bank statement is for the interest earned on this account. Just like the service fees, it can be added through the adjustments function. Click the **Adjust** button to open the Additional Transactions screen.

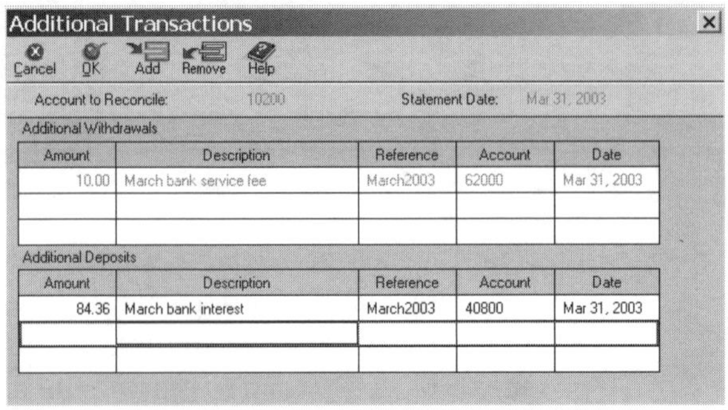

31. Enter the information in the Additional Deposits section. Be sure to select the correct general ledger account for this transaction. When you are done, click the **OK** button.
32. The interest deposit now appears in the list of deposits and can be cleared.

    Once all deposits are cleared, you can see the results in the lower part of the screen.

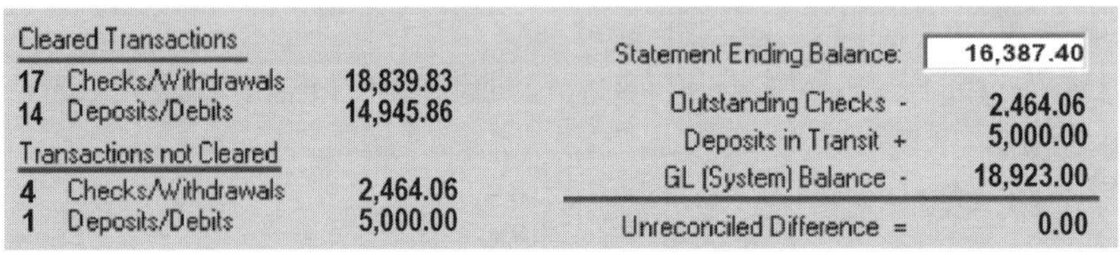

33. In this case, the total of the Deposits/Debits matches the Deposits total on the bank statement, but the number of Deposits/Debits does not. This is because one of the statement deposits is listed as two different deposits on the reconciliation screen and because the listing also contains several invoice write-offs.

    The listing also shows $5,000 for the Deposits/Debits in the Transactions not Cleared section. The reason for the uncleared deposit is that, although the deposit was recorded in March, the bank has not yet received it. You will want to investigate the reason, which could be because the deposit is sitting in the owner's car or, in this case, it was a credit card payment that has not yet been acknowledged by the bank.

    If you now look at the Unreconciled Difference total, you will see that it is equal to 0.00. Congratulations, your bank statement has balanced!
34. Click the **OK** button to save the bank reconciliation.

Solutions for Bank Reconciliation Problems

When trying to reconcile your bank statement, you can often run into problems and find it difficult to get the Unreconciled Difference to equal zero. The following are potential problem areas and possible solutions.

- Problems sometimes occur when balancing your bank statement because you lose track of where you are in the reconciliation and miss clearing some items. Use a pencil or pen to mark the cleared transactions on the statement so that you can keep track. You may also need to start over from scratch in clearing the items. You can mark all items as not cleared by clicking the **All** blank check mark button  on the toolbar. Another trick is to get a coworker to go over the list of checks and deposits with you.

- Your check amount and the check amount on the bank statement do not match. Even with computer-generated checks, your vendors and the banks sometimes misread a check amount and show $97.11 instead of $97.17. If it is a large amount, contact the bank to get them to correct the error. For an inconsequential amount, save the reconciliation-to-date and go into the Payments form. Change the amount paid to reflect the difference. If the payment is against a bill, enter the difference in the Discount field. Return to the Account Reconciliation screen and continue.
- The bank deposit amount and the deposit amount do not match. First, verify the total of the deposit slip. Did you make an addition error? Next verify the actual amounts of the checks received. Your files should have remittances or check copies of the deposit to help find the error. If the error is a large one, you will want to contact the bank to get the deposit amount corrected. For a small amount, save the reconciliation-to-date, go into the Receipts form, and change the amount paid the same as way as shown to change checks. Any small differences can be entered into the Discount column to resolve the invoice and the receipt amount.

Making an Adjusting Entry

Occasionally, you will never find the error that you are looking for and you will need to make an adjustment to finish the reconciliation.

1. First note the amount of the Unreconciled Difference, in this case a positive 98 cents.

2. Go to the Additional Transactions screen.
3. Because the difference is positive, we need to add a transaction to the Additional Deposits section. If the difference were negative, we would need to add a transaction to the Additional Withdrawals section.

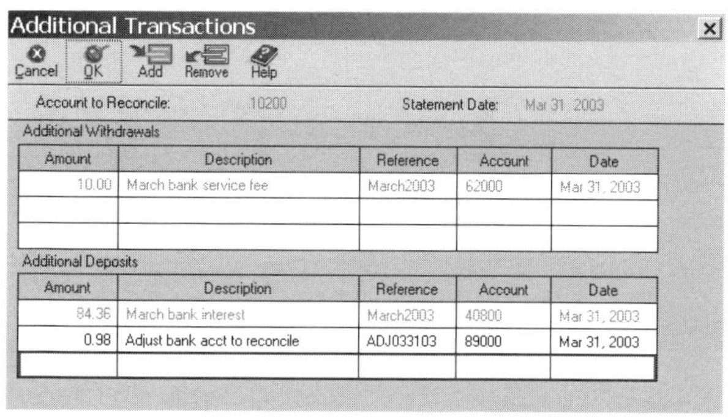

4. Type the adjusting entry with enough information to show why the adjustment is being created. The account should be an appropriate account such as Other Income, Other Expense, Cash Over and Short, etc. Click **OK** to record the entry.
5. Clear the adjusting transaction and verify that the difference is now zero.

Correcting Adjustments

Everyone makes an error occasionally on an adjusting entry. These cannot be corrected on the Additional Transactions screen. You will notice in the earlier figures that once an adjustment has been saved, the entry becomes grayed out on the Additional Transactions screen. There is a Remove button on the screen's toolbar, but it only applies to entries that have not yet been saved. To delete or edit an adjusting entry, follow these steps:

1. Go to the General Journal Entry form by clicking the **General Journal Entry** icon in the **General Ledger** folder on the navigation aid.
2. Click the **Open** button (Edit button in earlier versions) on the toolbar.
3. The Select General Journal Entry screen appears.

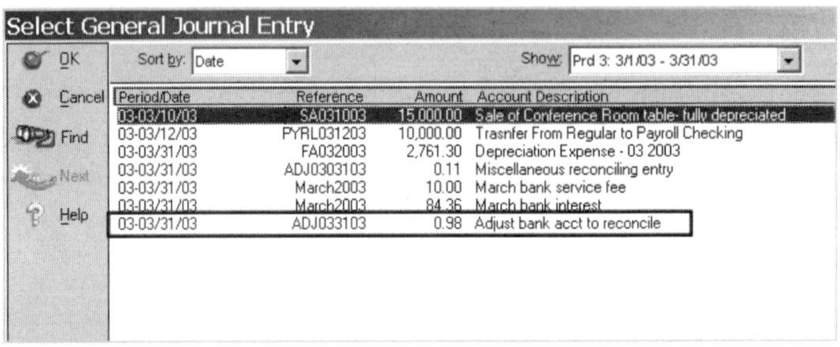

Select the entry to be corrected and click **OK**.

4. The entry will appear in the General Journal Entry form.

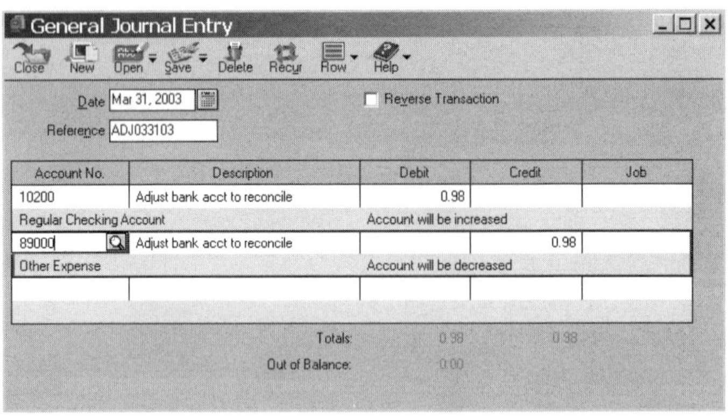

Make the changes as needed. Anything can be changed here, including the account number, description, and debit or credit amounts. You can even change the entry so that the Regular Checking Account is credited and the Other Expense account is debited.

5. Click **Save** or **Post** to record the changes to the transaction.

In the earlier mentioned adjustment, if we discovered that the difference was a negative 98 cents, not a positive, and we switched the debit and credit amounts, we would discover a change to the Account Reconciliation screen. The adjustment would now appear in the Checks and Credits section. On the Additional Transactions screen the adjustment would also have moved.

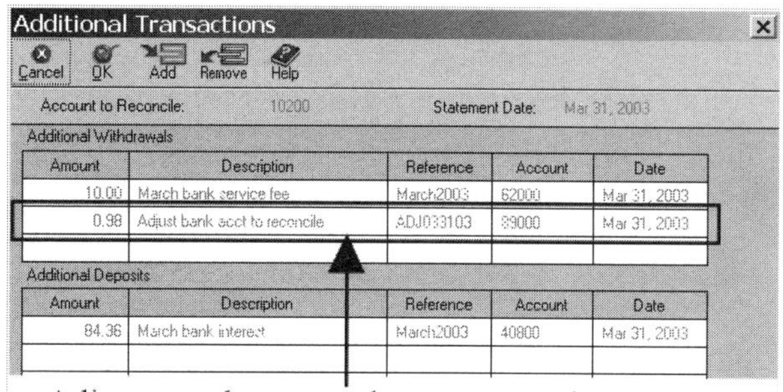

Adjustment has moved to upper section

Reconciliation Reports

There are several reports that will assist you in your reconciliation and some that will be important to your CPA.

The Bank Deposit Report

This report was discussed in Chapter 6 to help you verify the amount of your deposits. The same report can be printed on a monthly basis, in detail, to help you clear the individual deposits.

The Check Register

This report was discussed in Chapter 8. This report can be printed for the full month to verify that all checks have been entered. The Check Register is accessed by clicking the **Purchases/Payables Reports** icon in the **Purchases** folder in the navigation aid or by selecting **Reports**, **Accounts Payable**.

The Account Register

The Account Register is a listing of all transactions for a specific cash account. It includes all checks, withdrawals, and deposits, along with adjusting entries and a running balance for the account.

The Account Register is accessed by clicking the **Account Reconciliation Reports** icon in the **General Ledger** folder in the navigation aid or by selecting **Reports**, **Account Reconciliation**.

1. Select **Account Register** from the Report List in the Select a Report window.

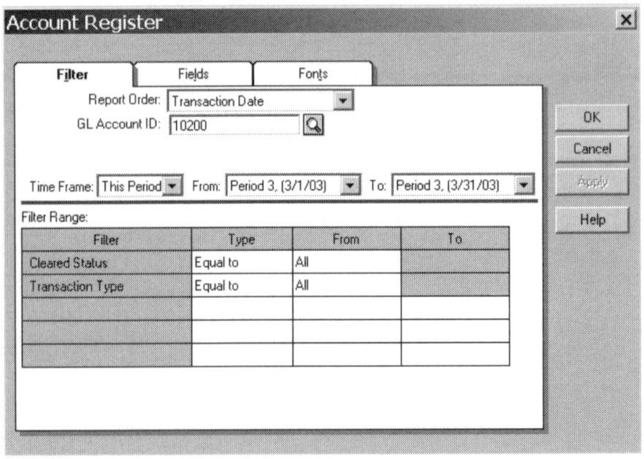

2. The Account Register dialog box appears.

   Generally, you will want to select **Transaction Date** in the Report Order field.

3. The GL Account ID field contains the general ledger cash account to be reported on.
4. Select the range in the Time Frame field, using the From and To date fields, if needed. Only complete months may be chosen, either **This Period** or a range of periods.
5. In the Filter Range section, you may select Cleared Status. Cleared, Uncleared, and All may be chosen in the From field.

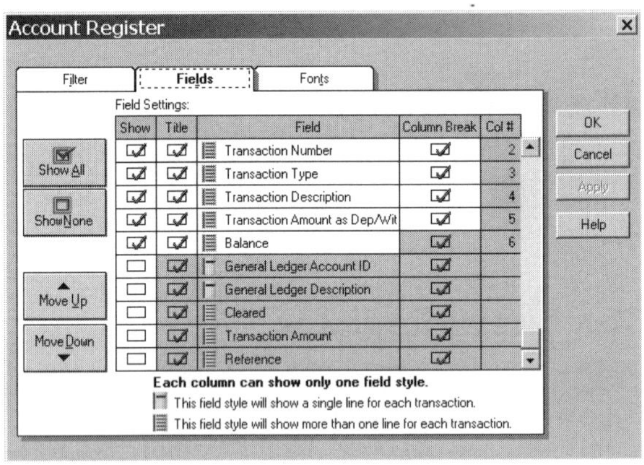

6. You may also limit the Transaction Type to Check, Deposit or Other.
7. On the Fields tab, you may choose to add additional fields to this report.
8. Click the check box in the **Show** column to add any of the fields.
9. Click **OK** to view the report.

The Account Reconciliation Report

This report takes the form of a normal bank reconciliation and shows the beginning and ending general ledger balances; the totals of checks, deposits, and other transactions; and the outstanding checks and deposits in transit.

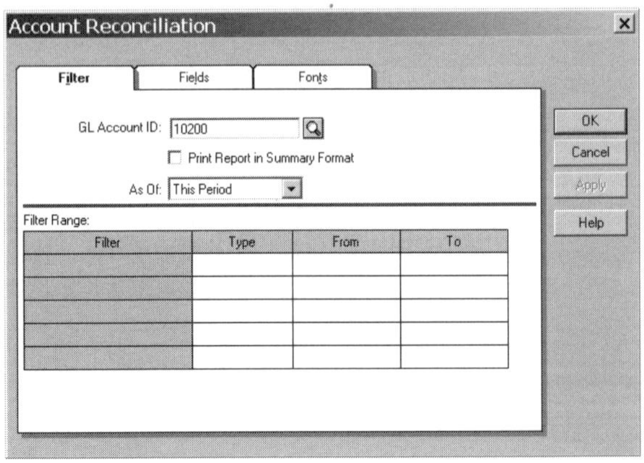

This report is available through the Account Reconciliation Reports and is listed as the Account Reconciliation.

Select the bank account and the period for the report. You may also select to show the report in summary format.

Bellwether Garden Supply
Account Reconciliation
As of Mar 31, 2003
10200 - Regular Checking Account
Bank Statement Date: March 31, 2003
Filter Criteria includes: Report is printed in Detail Format.

Beginning GL Balance				28,119.50
Add: Cash Receipts				15,684.09
Less: Cash Disbursements				<10,072.81>
Add <Less> Other				<9,925.64>
Ending GL Balance				18,923.34
Ending Bank Balance				16,387.40
Add back deposits in transit				
	Mar 31, 200	033103	5,000.00	
Total deposits in transit				5,000.00
<Less> outstanding checks				
	Mar 24, 200		<1,500.00>	
	Mar 31, 200		<73.42>	
	Mar 12, 200	10202	<360.00>	
	Mar 15, 200	10210	<530.64>	
Total outstanding checks				<2,464.06>
Add <Less> Other				
Total other				
Unreconciled difference				0.00
Ending GL Balance				18,923.34

Summary

As you can see, reconciling the bank account can go very easily if all transactions are recorded correctly. Mistakes can become very time-consuming, so it is important that you and your employees understand the steps involved in entering deposits and payments. Getting all transactions into the system is 90% of the bank reconciliation function. If not entered correctly, the work involved in getting the checking account to balance can become overwhelming.

Over the years, I have personally reconciled dozens of companies' checking accounts and, in almost every case, I have been able to balance to the penny. These accounts ranged from the very small of only a few thousand dollars in transactions to multimillion dollar bank balances.

Once your main checking account is balanced, you can use these same procedures to balance other types of cash accounts. Just be sure that you have the beginning balance for each of the accounts.

Chapter 12

Balancing Accounts Receivable

In This Chapter

- Verifying the customer beginning balances
- Balancing accounts receivable
- Finding accounts receivable errors
- Adjusting accounts receivable for errors and inaccurate balances
- Accounts receivable default information
- Statements, finance charges, and deposit slips

Once your bank account is balanced, it is time to start looking into the balance of the accounts receivable account. Accounts receivable are created when you sell to a customer and they promise to pay you at a later date. Each sale to a customer is recorded through the Sales/Invoicing form. When invoices are created, your Sales general ledger account is increased, as is your accounts receivable general ledger account. In double-entry accounting we would say that Sales is credited and A/R is debited. If you don't understand the difference between a debit and a credit, talk to your CPA or pick up an accounting book for non-accountants to gain an understanding. Luckily, Peachtree can tell whether a debit or credit will increase your G/L accounts.

The reason behind keeping your accounts receivable accurate is that it will help you to analyze the performance of customers and determine which ones should be assisted in reducing their balances and which ones you might be better off without. I know that in my own business I have "fired" about 5 to 10% of my customers per year. You know these customers. They are the ones who nitpick every line item on their invoice in an effort to get their bills reduced or who always pay you 60 to 90 days late and never pay a late charge. As a business owner, it is sometimes easier to replace these customers than deal with them. Hopefully, this chapter will assist you in taking a better look at your own customers from month to month.

Customer Beginning Balances

In your first month of working with Peachtree, you were told to get an accurate A/R listing of all customers and the invoices that they owe. In Chapter 6 you were shown how those invoices should be entered into the customers' beginning balances. Before we can balance last month's A/R, we must first reconcile the beginning balances.

1. Pull out your beginning A/R listing. It should list every invoice that was owed you before your Begin Transactions date. If you started entering transactions on March 31, it would be the balances as of February 28. It may look something like this:

Pavilion Design Group
Accounts Receivable Listing
As Of February 28, 2003

Customer ID	Customer	Invoice No	Invoice Date	Amount
CRAW01	Crawford Bridal Designs	7467	02/01/03	1,600.00
HAUC01	DBH Enterprises	7470	02/02/03	650.00
GUAP01	Guapo Computadores, Inc.	7469	02/04/03	47.70
OLIV01	Oliver's Army Surplus	7468	02/02/03	175.00
ZAXB01	Zaxby's Restaurant	7465	01/06/03	750.00
Report Total				3,222.70

2. If any of these invoices are not yet entered into the beginning balances, enter them now by first changing the accounting period to the month before you began entering transactions. Then bring up the Customer Beginning Balances form by clicking the **Receivables** or **Sales** folder on the navigation aid, the **Customers** icon, and then the **Beginning Balances** button on the Maintain Customers/Prospects form.
3. Verify that the total of your beginning A/R listing matches the total on the form. (Be sure that you are in the right accounting period.) It is absolutely imperative that these balances match. If they do not, talk to your CPA to see where the adjustment should be made. Remember that this A/R listing will be the basis for your new accounts receivable ledger and should be entered correctly.

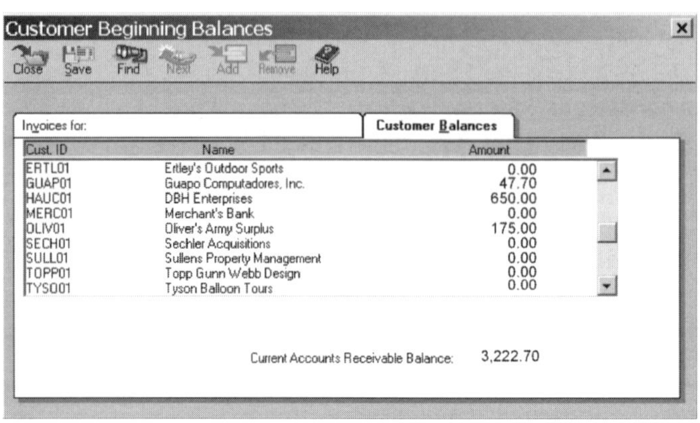

4. These amounts, the beginning A/R listing and the Customer Beginning Balances form, should also match the balance of the Accounts Receivable general ledger account for your beginning Trial Balance which should have been provided to you by your CPA. Click the **Chart of Accounts** icon in the **General Ledger** folder on the navigation aid. The Maintain Chart of Accounts form appears.

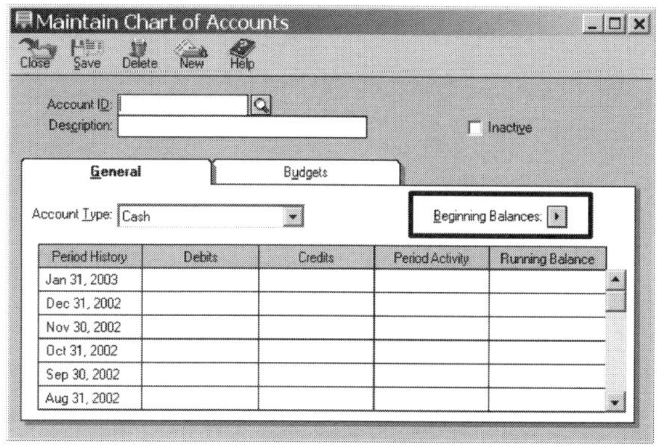

5. Click the **Beginning Balances** button on the form. The Select Period dialog box appears.

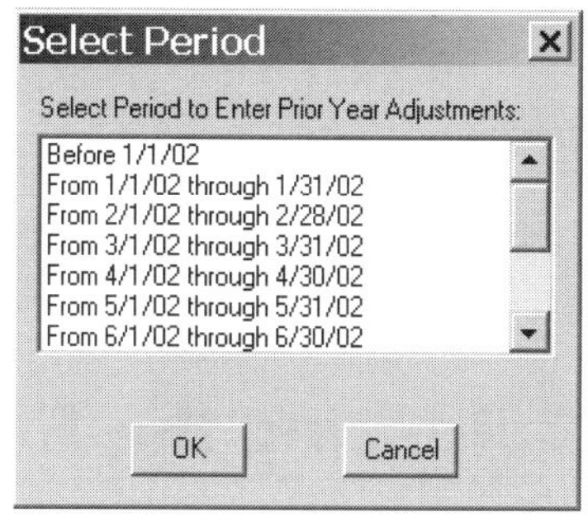

6. Again, be sure that you are in the correct period to enter the account balances. You should be able to select the month previous to your Begin Transactions date. If it is not available, select the last month of the previous financial year. Click **OK** to open the Chart of Accounts Prior Year Adjustments screen.

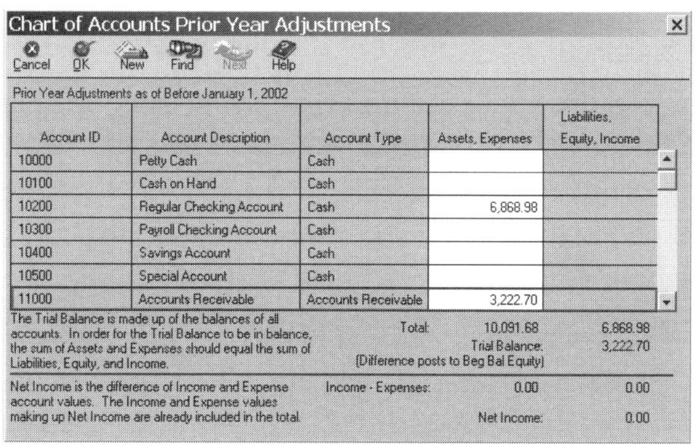

7. Enter the amount of your A/R in the Assets, Expenses column on the correct Accounts Receivable line. If you have more than one A/R account, enter the correct amount on each of the lines. Then go down the list to the Retained Earnings account (or another account, such as Beginning Balance Equity, if your CPA recommends it).

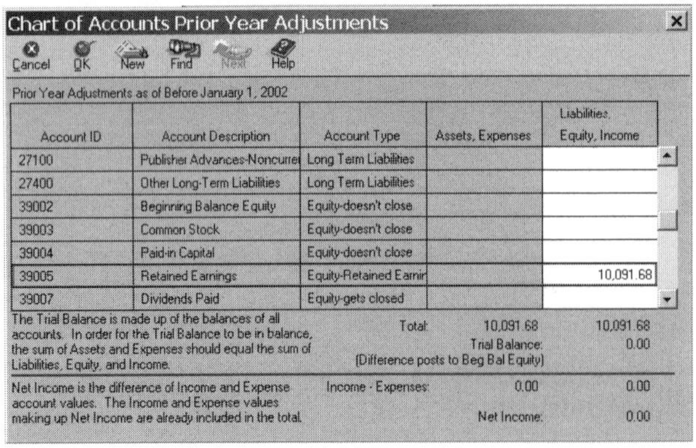

8. Add the A/R amount to any other amounts in the Liabilities, Equity, Income column. The Trial Balance field should be 0.00 when you are done.
9. Click **OK** to save and close the form. Appropriate journal entries will be created to store the information.

Balancing the A/R

From month to month when you balance your A/R, you follow a very simple formula. You take the previous month's ending balance, add in the net total of all invoices for sales on-account, subtract the net total of all receipts, and the result should match this month's ending balance.

The A/R reconciliation shown in this section is calculated using the Pavilion Design Group company backup provided with the downloadable files and follows these steps:

1. Go to the Select a Report screen. Select **Accounts Receivable** in the Report Area and select **Aged Receivables** in the Report List.

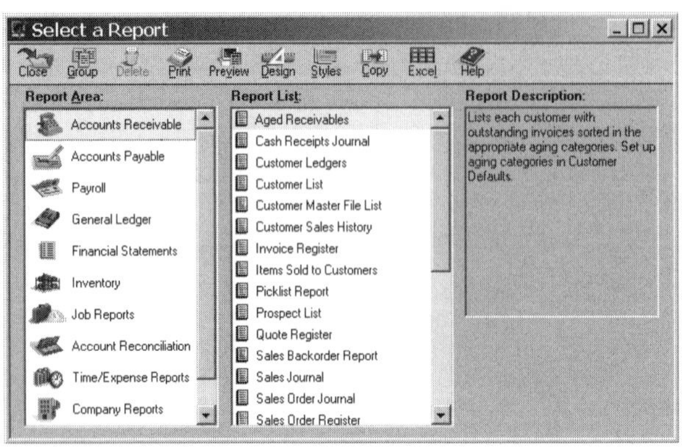

2. Click the **Preview** button and the Aged Receivables filter appears.

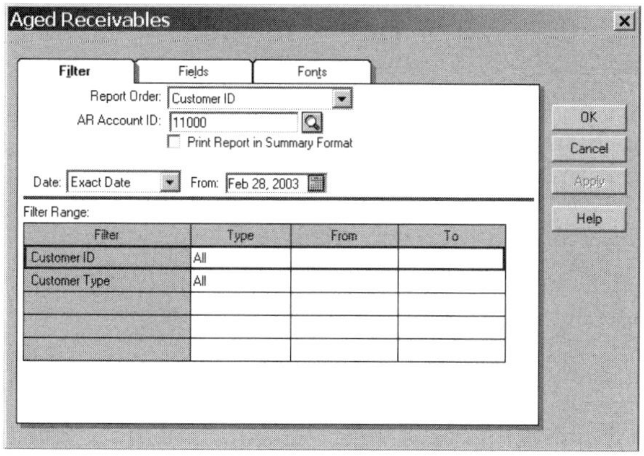

3. You may choose a report order, either **Customer ID** or **Customer Name**. Choose the correct general ledger account for the AR Account ID that you are balancing. In the Date field, select **Exact Date.** In the From field, select the last day of the previous month. We will ignore the Fields and Fonts tabs at this time. Click **OK**. The Aged Receivables report will appear.

Pavilion Design Group
Aged Receivables
As of Feb 28, 2003
Filter Criteria includes: Report order is by ID. Report is printed in Detail Format.

Customer ID Customer Contact Telephone 1	Invoice No	0 - 30	31 - 60	61 - 90	Over 90 days	Amount Due
ZAXB01 Zaxby's Restaurant Mr. Bill Zaxby 770-555-8564	7465	750.00				750.00
ZAXB01 Zaxby's Restaurant		750.00				750.00
Report Total		3,222.70				3,222.70

4. Go to the Total line for the report. In our example, the total for all outstanding invoices on February 28, 2003, is $3,222.70. This is the beginning balance of our reconciliation. In our example, and the first time that you balance your accounts receivable, this amount should also match the beginning A/R listing. In later months, the beginning balance amount will be the ending balance for the previous month. Note this amount on your worksheet or in a spreadsheet program.
5. Now we get the additions to accounts receivable for the month. Close the previous report and select **Accounts Receivable** in the Report Area and **Invoice Register** in the Report List. Click the **Preview** button. The Invoice Register filter form will appear.

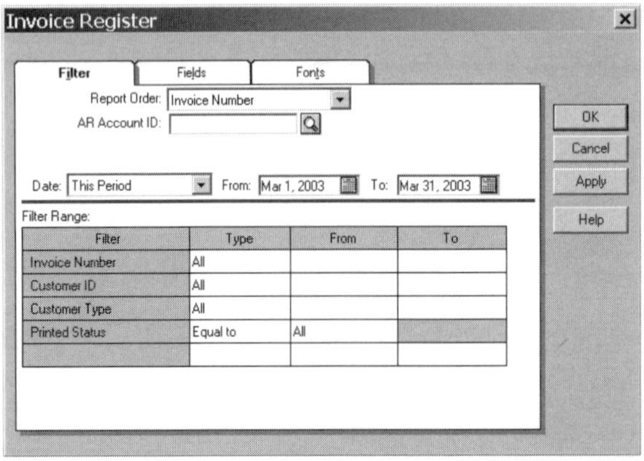

6. Select **Invoice Number** in the Report Order field. Leave the AR Account ID field blank for now. Select **This Period** in the Date field. The From and To fields are automatically filled in. Click **OK** to see the report.

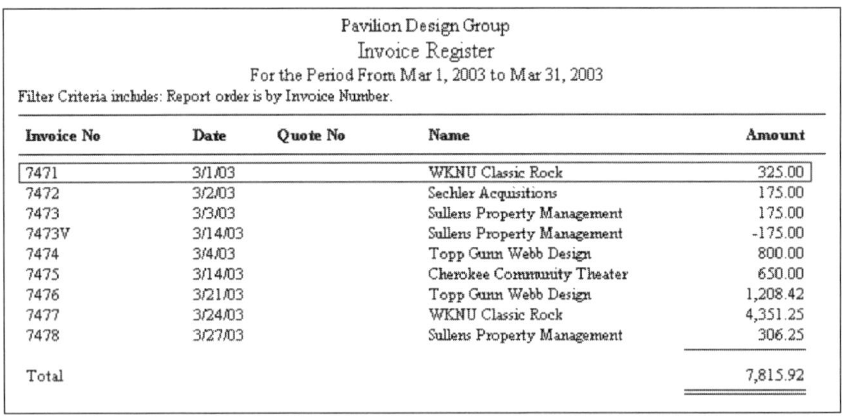

Pavilion Design Group
Invoice Register
For the Period From Mar 1, 2003 to Mar 31, 2003
Filter Criteria includes: Report order is by Invoice Number.

Invoice No	Date	Quote No	Name	Amount
7471	3/1/03		WKNU Classic Rock	325.00
7472	3/2/03		Sechler Acquisitions	175.00
7473	3/3/03		Sullens Property Management	175.00
7473V	3/14/03		Sullens Property Management	-175.00
7474	3/4/03		Topp Gunn Webb Design	800.00
7475	3/14/03		Cherokee Community Theater	650.00
7476	3/21/03		Topp Gunn Webb Design	1,208.42
7477	3/24/03		WKNU Classic Rock	4,351.25
7478	3/27/03		Sullens Property Management	306.25
Total				7,815.92

7. Make a note of the Total of the Invoice Register, in this case $7,815.92. We want to verify this number against the Sales Journal.

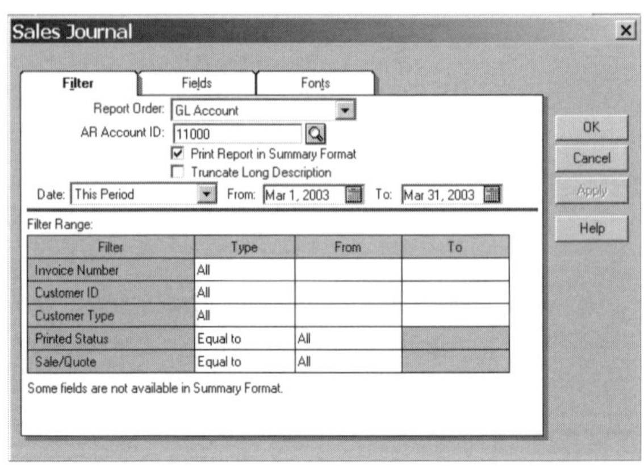

8. Close the Invoice Register. Next, we will select another report from the Accounts Receivable Report Area. Select **Sales Journal** from the Report List and click the **Preview** button. The Sales Journal filter form will appear.

9. Here the Report Order field gives us a choice of Invoice Date, GL Account, or Invoice Number. Select **GL Account**. Select the appropriate account in the AR Account ID field. If you leave this field blank, it will

give you the report for all accounts receivable accounts, but we want to verify the invoice register so we will enter the actual A/R account. Check the **Print Report in Summary Format** check box so the report will print only a summary of all transactions, not each individual one. The date for this report is **This Period** because we want the sales journal for the current open accounting period. The From and To dates are pre-entered from the Date selection.

10. Click the **Fields** tab.

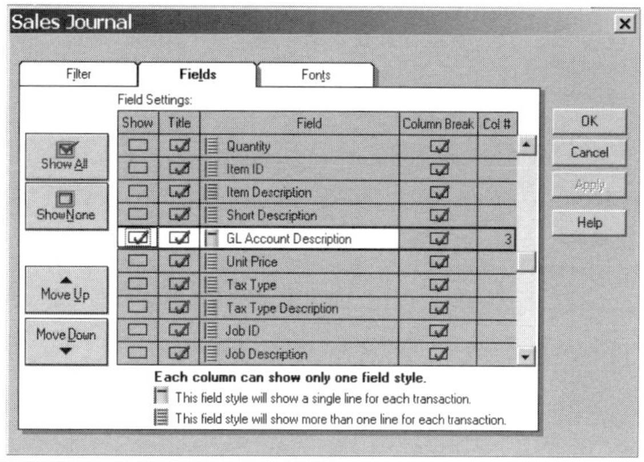

11. Go down the Field Settings list and check the **Show** column for GL Account Description. If you like, you can move it up the list so that the account description becomes the first or second column. Click **OK** and the report will appear.

Pavilion Design Group
Sales Journal
For the Period From Mar 1, 2003 to Mar 31, 2003
Filter Criteria includes: Report order is by GL Account. Report is printed in Summary Format.

Account ID	Debit Amnt	Credit Amnt	Account Description
11000	7,990.92	175.00	Accounts Receivable
23100		6.42	Sales Tax Payable
40000	175.00	2,863.25	Graphic Design Income
40800		4,875.00	Photo Income
41000		56.25	Printing Income
41200		90.00	Production Income
41600		100.00	Other Income
	8,165.92	8,165.92	

12. In our report, you will take the amounts for all sales made on accounts for your customers, which in this case appears to be $8,165.92 — which does not match the Sales Journal. Upon further looking, notice that there is a debit of $175.00 on the Graphic Design Income line — this is a reduction of the income. Also notice that there is a credit amount of $175.00 on the Accounts Receivable line — this amount is not to be included in our calculation. Both these amounts must be subtracted from the total to reach $7,815.92, which does match the invoice register. We take this number and add it to the ending balance of the previous month on your worksheet.

Note: Because all sales were made on-account, the total sales amount also matches the debit to A/R. If any sales were made as cash sales, the cash sales would also be deducted from the total. The total should include all sales made on-account and all sales taxes and discounts. If you have more than one A/R account, you will need to run the report for each account separately. The total of all accounts should match the invoice register.

13. Close this report. The next report needed is the Cash Receipts Journal. It is also shown in the Accounts Receivables reports. Click the **Preview** button to bring up the filter.

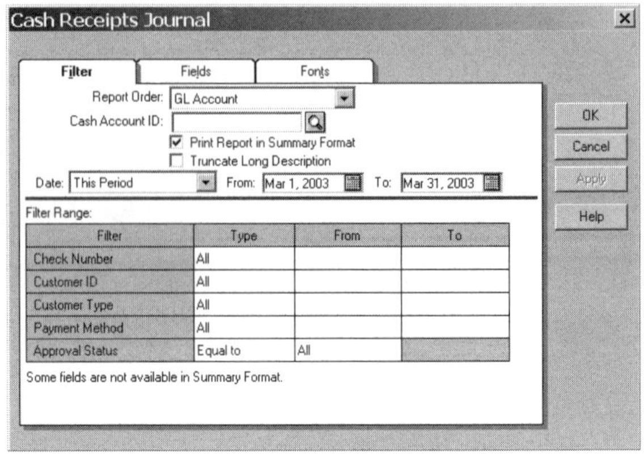

14. The order for this report should also be **GL Account**, although Check Date and Reference (customer check number) are also available. We will not select anything in the Cash Account ID field because we do not care where the money went; we are only concerned with transactions in the A/R account. Check the **Print Report in Summary Format** check box. The date for this report is **This Period** with the associated From and To dates. On the Fields tab, you will want to check the **Show** column for the GL Account Description also. Click **OK**.

Pavilion Design Group
Cash Receipts Journal
For the Period From Mar 1, 2003 to Mar 31, 2003
Filter Criteria includes: Report order is by GL Account. Report is printed in Summary Format.

Account ID	Debit Amnt	Credit Amnt	Account Description
10200	2,376.38		Regular Checking Account
11000	175.00	2,525.00	Accounts Receivable
23100		1.38	Sales Tax Payable
40800		25.00	Photo Income
	2,551.38	2,551.38	

15. The amount of cash received against invoices can be calculated as the deposits to the checking account, $2,376.38, less the amounts received for cash sales, $25.00 for Photo Income and $1.38 for Sales Tax Payable. The result, $2,350.00, matches the Accounts Receivable net amount of $2,350.00. This amount is the net deduction to A/R and should be noted on the worksheet.

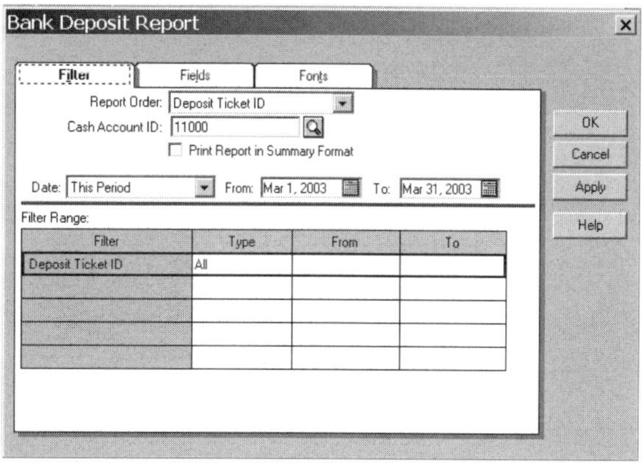

16. We can run a verifying report by going back to the Select a Report window and selecting **Account Reconciliation** in the Report Area and **Bank Deposit Report** in the Report List. Click **Preview** to bring up the Bank Deposit Report filter form.
17. We will use this report in a slightly different manner than we normally would. In the Cash Account ID field, select the accounts receivable general ledger account ID — not a cash account as you normally would. The Report Order field should be left as **Deposit Ticket ID** and the date should be **This Period**. Click **OK**.

Pavilion Design Group
Bank Deposit Report
For the Period From Mar 1, 2003 to Mar 31, 2003
11000 - Accounts Receivable
Filter Criteria includes: Report order is by Deposit Ticket ID. Report is printed in Detail Format.

Deposit Ticket ID	Date	Reference	Description	Amount
20030310	3/10/03	89163	Crawford Bridal Designs	-800.00
			Total Deposit	-800.00
20030314	3/14/03	4568	Zaxby's Restaurant	-750.00
			Total Deposit	-750.00
20030324	3/24/03	8654325	Crawford Bridal Designs	-800.00
			Total Deposit	-800.00
			Total Deposits for the Period	-2,350.00

18. This report differs from a normal bank deposit report because it only shows deposits that are made against A/R. The total of the report is $2,350.00, which matches the cash receipts report.
19. On our worksheet, we should now show the following figures. The ending balance for last period (which this month is the A/R beginning balance listing total) is found from the total of last month's aged receivables — $3,222.70. To that we add the net invoices for A/R, which is the Accounts Receivable line from the Sales Journal — $7,815.92. From that we subtract the net receipts, which is the Accounts Receivable line from the Cash Receipts Journal — $2,350.00. The total of these amounts is $8,688.62. This amount represents the A/R ending balance for the current period.

Pavilion Design Group
Accounts Receivable Reconcilion
March 31, 2003

A/R Ending Balance 2/28/03		$ 3,222.70
Sales Journal Income (includes sales tax)	7,990.92	
less Credit memos	(175.00)	
Additions to A/R for March		$ 7,815.92
Cash Receipts Journal	(2,376.38)	
less Cash Sales	26.38	
Deductions to A/R for March		$ (2,350.00)
A/R Ending Balance 3/31/03		**$ 8,688.62**

20. We check the A/R ending balance by running the Aged Receivables report for the current period.

Pavilion Design Group
Aged Receivables
As of Mar 31, 2003
Filter Criteria includes: Report order is by ID. Report is printed in Detail Format.

Customer ID Customer Contact Telephone 1	Invoice No	0 - 30	31 - 60	61 - 90	Over 90 days	Amount Due
WKNU Classic Rock Darren Knudsen 770-555-4596	7477	4,351.25				4,351.25
WKNU01 WKNU Classic Rock		4,676.25				4,676.25
Report Total		8,688.62				8,688.62

If these amounts match, your A/R is in balance. This reconciled amount can now be accurately used when discussing assets with your CPA, the bank, or your other creditors.

Adjustments to A/R

One of the reasons that we balance the accounts receivable to verify their accuracy is to ensure that the amount reported on our financial statements reflects the true state of our business. It is not difficult for the accounts to get out of balance if proper care is not taken during the data entry process. Other circumstances that may also affect the account balance include power failures that occur during the posting process, conversions from an older to a newer version of Peachtree, apathy or even deliberate malice on the part of an employee, and the posting of unbalanced transactions. I have seen every one of these cause major headaches for my clients.

Invoice Errors

A typical error that occurs is posting invoices to the wrong account. For instance, if you were running the reconciliation used in the previous example and the Invoice Register showed the same total of $7,815.92, the sales journal could show a different total as shown in the following figure.

Pavilion Design Group
Sales Journal
For the Period From Mar 1, 2003 to Mar 31, 2003
Filter Criteria includes: Report order is by GL Account. Report is printed in Summary Format.

Account ID	Debit Amnt	Credit Amnt	Account Description
11000	7,190.92	175.00	Accounts Receivable
23100		6.42	Sales Tax Payable
40000	175.00	2,863.25	Graphic Design Income
40800		4,075.00	Photo Income
41000		56.25	Printing Income
41200		90.00	Production Income
41600		100.00	Other Income
	7,365.92	7,365.92	

The on-account sales total we calculate on this report is $7,015.92.

1. To check the problem, we should go back to the Invoice Register and rerun it for the specific A/R general ledger account rather than all accounts. That report will show the following data.

Pavilion Design Group
Invoice Register
For the Period From Mar 1, 2003 to Mar 31, 2003
Filter Criteria includes: Report order is by Invoice Number.

Invoice No	Date	Quote No	Name	Amount
7471	3/1/03		WKNU Classic Rock	325.00
7472	3/2/03		Sechler Acquisitions	175.00
7473	3/3/03		Sullens Property Management	175.00
7473V	3/14/03		Sullens Property Management	-175.00
7475	3/14/03		Cherokee Community Theater	650.00
7476	3/21/03		Topp Gunn Webb Design	1,208.42
7477	3/24/03		WKNU Classic Rock	4,351.25
7478	3/27/03		Sullens Property Management	306.25
Total				7,015.92

2. Notice that this report does not match the original invoice register. Look through the list and you will see that the invoice numbered 7474 is missing. Go to the Sales/Invoicing form and open the invoice.

Month 2

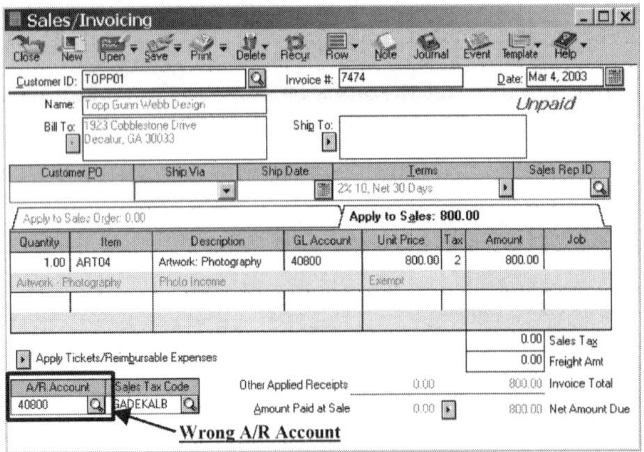

3. A common error for data entry people is to enter the wrong general ledger ID in the A/R Account field. Once the number is entered incorrectly, Peachtree will remember the number until it is changed again. Usually when this error occurs there will be more than one invoice that has been applied to the wrong account. By regularly balancing accounts, this type of error will not go uncorrected for very long. I had one client that had over two months of invoices applied to a miscellaneous expense account. Enter the correct ID number in the field and click **Save**. The Sales Journal will now show the corrected amount.

   Another way the invoice could be wrong is if the line item GL Account field is allocated to the A/R account, not a sales account.

4. If you are having problems locating the actual error, run the Sales Journal again. Change the Report Order field to **Invoice Date**. Make sure that the AR Account ID field is blank. Uncheck **Print Report in Summary Format** and click **OK**.

Pavilion Design Group
Sales Journal
For the Period From Mar 1, 2003 to Mar 31, 2003
Filter Criteria includes: Report order is by Invoice Date. Report is printed in Detail Format.

Date	Account ID	Account Description	Invoice No	Line Description	Debit Amnt	Credit Amnt
3/4/03	40800	Photo Income	7474	Artwork: Photography		800.00
	40800	Photo Income		Topp Gunn Webb Design	800.00	
3/14/03	40000	Graphic Design Income	7475	Artwork: Graphic Design		650.00
	11000	Accounts Receivable		Cherokee Community Theater	650.00	

5. You can go through each transaction to locate any errors. Notice that Invoice No. 7474 has two entries for Photo Income and does not have an entry for Accounts Receivable. From here, you can double-click on the transaction to bring up the Sales/Invoicing form and then verify or correct the information.

Cash Receipts Errors

A similar mistake can happen on the cash receipts side where the A/R account ID is entered into the Cash Account or the Discount Account field.

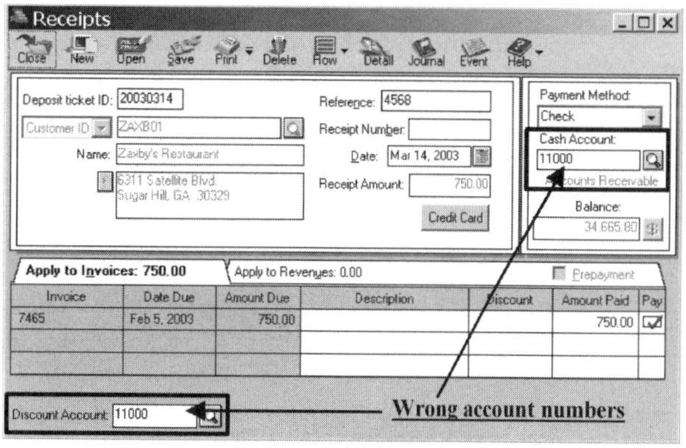

Finding this error is a little more difficult.

1. As you can see in the Cash Receipts Journal and the Bank Deposit Report, the net amounts applied to the Accounts Receivable line and the Total Deposits for the Period line, $1,600.00, match each other.

Pavilion Design Group
Cash Receipts Journal
For the Period From Mar 1, 2003 to Mar 31, 2003
Filter Criteria includes: Report order is by GL Account. Report is printed in Summary Format.

Account ID	Debit Amnt	Credit Amnt	Account Description
10200	1,626.38		Regular Checking Account
11000	925.00	2,525.00	Accounts Receivable
23100		1.38	Sales Tax Payable
40800		25.00	Photo Income
	2,551.38	2,551.38	

Pavilion Design Group
Bank Deposit Report
For the Period From Mar 1, 2003 to Mar 31, 2003
11000 - Accounts Receivable
Filter Criteria includes: Report order is by Deposit Ticket ID. Report is printed in Detail Format.

Deposit Ticket ID	Date	Reference	Description	Amount
20030310	3/10/03	89163	Crawford Bridal Designs	-800.00
			Total Deposit	-800.00
20030324	3/24/03	8654325	Crawford Bridal Designs	-800.00
			Total Deposit	-800.00
			Total Deposits for the Period	-1,600.00

But the subsequent calculation (3,222.70 + 7,815.92 – 1600.00 = 9,438.62) does not match the Aged Receivables balance (8,688.62). There is a difference of $750.00. This error requires additional work.

2. Go back to the Cash Receipts Journal filter and change the Report Order to **Check Date.** Make sure that the Cash Account ID field is blank. Uncheck **Print Report in Summary Format** and click **OK.**

Pavilion Design Group
Cash Receipts Journal
For the Period From Mar 1, 2003 to Mar 31, 2003
Filter Criteria includes: Report order is by Check Date. Report is printed in Summary Format.

Date	Account ID	Transaction Ref	Debit Amnt	Credit Amnt	Account Description
3/10/03	11000	89163		800.00	Accounts Receivable
	10200		800.00		Regular Checking Account
3/14/03	11000	4568	750.00	750.00	Accounts Receivable
3/14/03	11000	7473	175.00	175.00	Accounts Receivable
	10200				Regular Checking Account
3/24/03	11000	8654325		800.00	Accounts Receivable
	10200		800.00		Regular Checking Account
3/27/03	23100	21186		1.38	Sales Tax Payable
	40800			25.00	Photo Income
	10200		26.38		Regular Checking Account
			2,551.38	2,551.38	

3. Go down the list. Notice that each item listed has an entry for either Accounts Receivable or an Income account. Each also has an entry for the Regular Checking Account except the item with the Transaction Ref of 4568. That transaction amount is $750.00, which is the same amount as the difference. Double-click on the line item to bring up the transaction and correct the Cash Account. Rerun the reports to get the A/R to balance.

Adjusting Journal Entries

Sometimes, despite all your efforts, you will not find an error in the A/R. At that point, you will have to decide whether the error lies in the transactions or the aged receivables balance. If the aged receivables balance is wrong, you will need to make the correction by creating a new transaction or editing an existing one. You would need to determine which customer had the wrong balance and correct it.

Aged Receivables
As of Mar 31, 2003
Filter Criteria includes: Report order is by ID. Report is printed in Detail Format.

Customer ID Customer Contact Telephone 1	Invoice No	0 - 30	31 - 60
GUAP01 Guapo Computadores, Inc. Thomas A. Gonzalez 770-555-4726	7469		47.70

Here you have a small invoice amount that should not appear on your aged receivables. You know that all the invoices have been paid and your bank account balanced also. We just need to remove this small amount.

1. Open the Receipts form.

2. You can write off the invoice by assigning it to a different cash account, in this case **Other Income**. Another way is to put the entire amount in the Discount column and increase your discount expense.

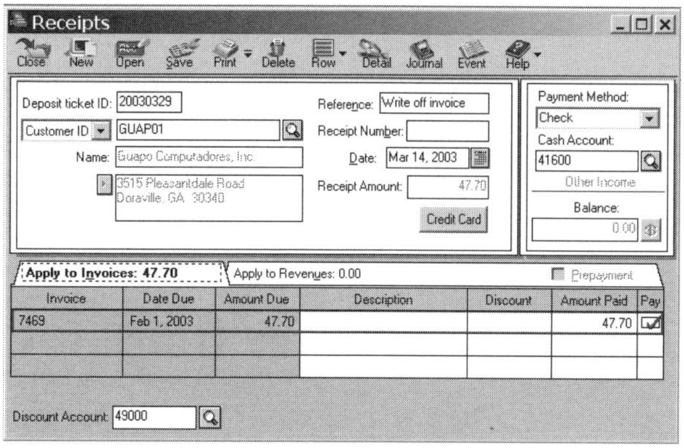

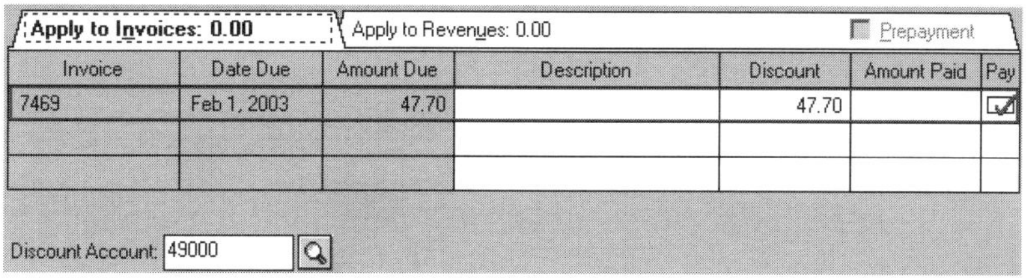

If you are sure that your aged receivables is correct and it is your accounts receivable balance that is incorrect, you will need to make a journal entry as follows:

1. Open the Journal Entry form by selecting the **General Ledger** folder on the navigation aid and then clicking the **General Journal Entry** icon.
2. Enter a date for the entry, usually the last day of the month.
3. Enter a descriptive identifier for the journal entry in the Reference field.

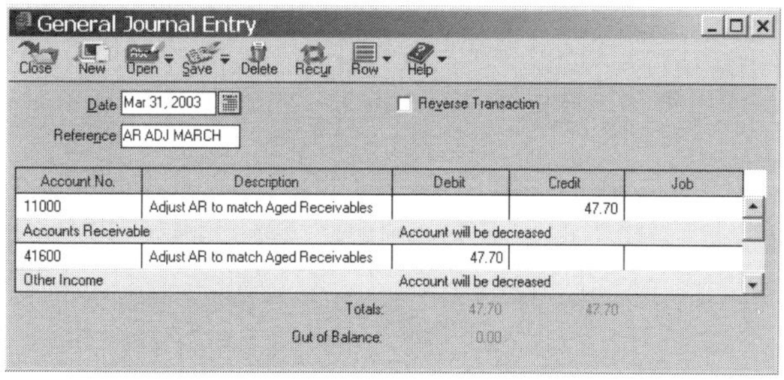

4. The journal entry line item fields are entered as follows.

Account No. — This is the general ledger account ID that the adjustment is to be made to. In our case, one line is for the A/R account and the second line is the offset. It could be allocated to an income account, discount account, or other type of account. You may even decide that the offset should go to several accounts and would therefore enter more than the second line.

Description — Enter the reason for the adjustment.

Debit — This column and the next control whether your journal entry will increase or decrease the AR account and any other accounts. Luckily, a hint appears when an amount is entered into one of these columns telling you whether the selected account is being increased or decreased.

Credit — This column is for the other side of the transaction.

Job — Job costing is not covered in this book due to size constraints.

5. Once all lines of the journal entry are entered, the Totals line should show that debits equal credits. This means that the Out of Balance line will be equal to 0.00.
6. Click **Save** or **Post** to save the journal entry.

A/R and Customer Default Information

When your company was originally set up we accepted the accounts receivable and customer defaults. In this section we will cover how to customize those defaults.

Customer Defaults

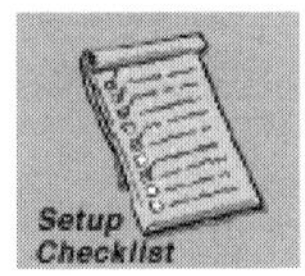

The defaults are accessed in several ways.

1. Click on the **Setup Checklist** icon in the **Company** folder on the navigation aid. Then select the **Customer Defaults** item in the list.

   Or select **Maintain**, **Default Information**, **Customers** from the menu bar.

   Or press **Alt+M**, then **D**, then **C** using the keyboard.

2. The Customer Defaults screen appears.

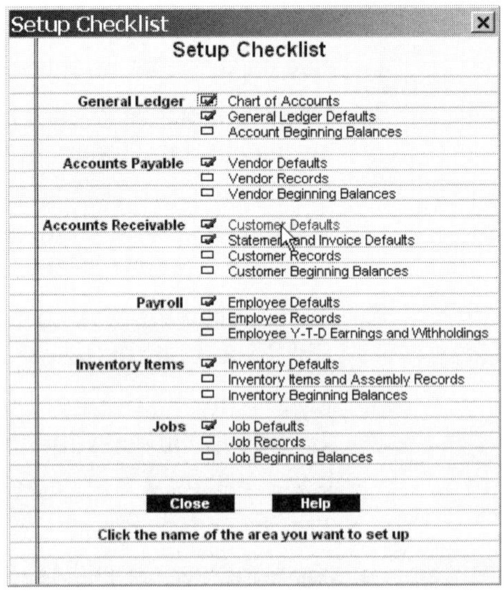

Payment Terms

The first tab on the Customer Defaults screen is the Payment Terms tab.

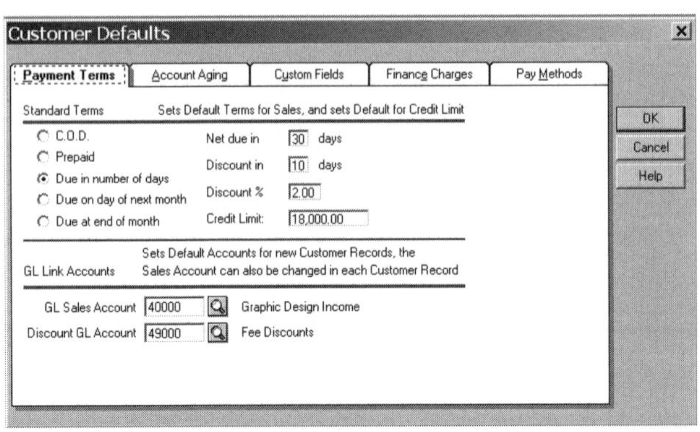

This tab controls how you want your customers to pay you. Remember that these are the defaults. The payment terms can be customized to suit each customer's needs and your requirements by using the following instructions.

1. The Standard Terms section sets your normal sales procedures. If you normally sell on-account then you will want to choose either the Due in number of days, Due on day of next month, or Due at end of month option. These three options allow you to manage when you receive most of your cash receipts. The options also control when you start counting the number of days past due and, if you charge them, when finance charges are accrued.

   The Due in number of days option is for those companies that expect to be paid within a certain length of time, which could be anywhere from 10 to 90 days. The actual number of days is set in the next section.

   Companies that choose to make their invoices Due on day of next month want to assure themselves of payments on a day next month. The day of the month is set in the next section. This means that if you want your check by April 30 and you send the invoice on March 1, you will wait almost 60 days for the payment. If you want to get paid on April 10 and the invoice is sent on March 30, the customer will have less than two weeks to get the payment to you. Few companies use this method unless they only have a cash receipts person entering data and making deposits about one week a month.

   The last on-account option is Due at end of month. This method means that whether the invoice is sent on March 1 or March 30, it is still due on March 31.

   The other two options in this section are C.O.D., for those companies that want payment when merchandise or services are delivered, like lawn care or water delivery, and Prepaid, for those companies that do mostly retail sales.

2. The next section, Sets Default Terms for Sales and sets Default for Credit Limit, is related to the previous section.

   If you chose Due in number of days, then the Net due in days field is the number of days in which the invoice should be paid. If you offer discounts, the number of days that the invoice should be paid in is typed in the Discount in days field. If no discounts are offered, enter **0** in this field. If you offer discounts, you will also want to type the percentage in the Discount % field. This can also be changed to 0.00 if discounts are not offered.

   If your invoices are Due on day of next month, the fields change. The first field becomes Due on the next month. Enter the day of the month that invoices are due. The discount fields are still available for this option.

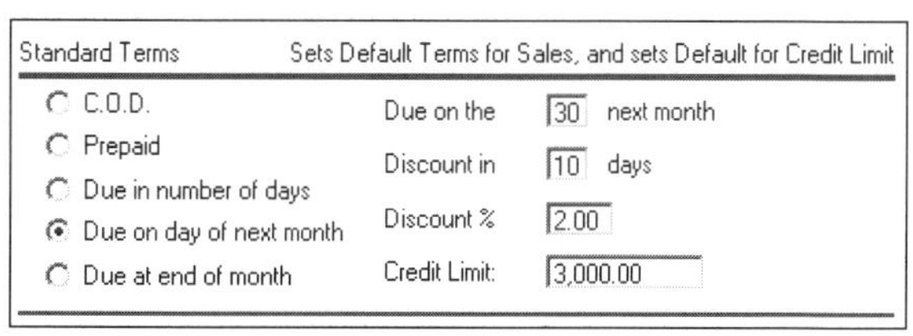

For the Due at end of month option, the Due on the next month field becomes disabled, but you may still offer discounts.

3. The last field in this section is Credit Limit. Enter the standard amount of credit that you allow customers. If a customer goes over the credit limit a message appears when you create an invoice that will take them over that limit.

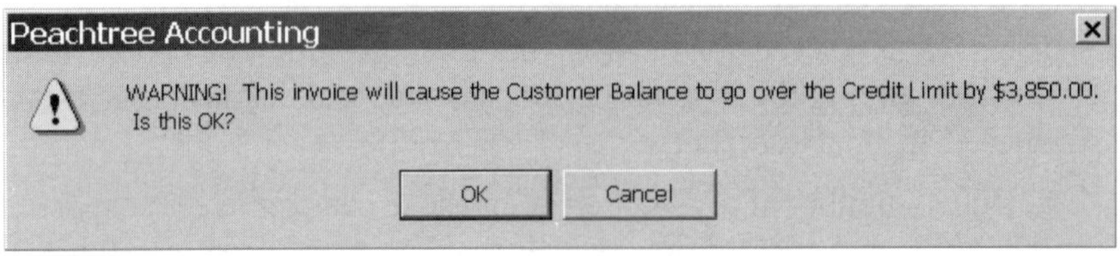

4. The next section of the Payment Terms tab, GL Link Accounts, controls the general ledger accounts that sales are assigned to. When a customer is added to the system, you can assign a specific sales account to their record. For one customer it could be Programming Fees and for another it might be Service Calls. If you do not assign an account or if a payment is received for someone who is not a customer in the system, Peachtree defaults the income and any potential discounts to the accounts displayed in the GL Sales Account and the Discount GL Account fields.

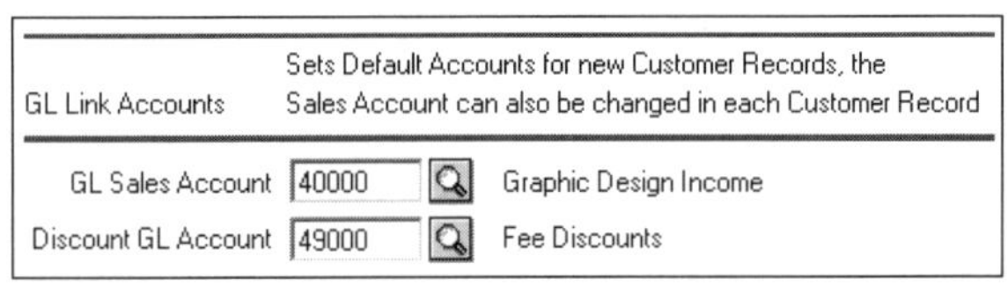

Account Aging

The second tab of the Customer Defaults window is Account Aging. It controls how the age of your invoices is displayed in the Aged Receivables and other reports.

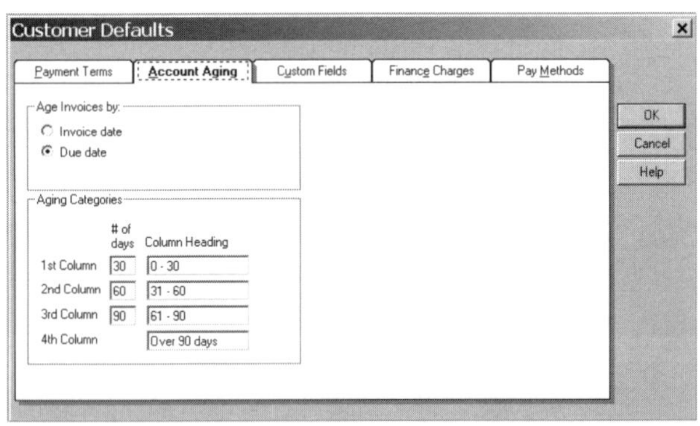

1. In the top section, Age Invoices by, you have two options — Invoice date and Due date. If you have an invoice that is dated April 5 and the invoice is unpaid on May 15, you can count the age of the invoice in one of two ways. Aging by invoice date will make the invoice 40 days old because you start counting from the first date of the invoice, April 5. If you choose the other option, by due date, the invoice is only considered to be 10 days old because you didn't start counting the age until May 5. Most companies choose to age their invoices by invoice date.

2. The lower section, Aging Categories, controls how your Aged Receivables report looks. The Column Heading field shows the heading for each column across the top, described as 0-30, 31-60, 61-90, and Over 90 days. The # of days column shows the

maximum age that can appear in each column. Obviously there is not a # of days field for the 4th Column line because it contains all invoices that are not in the other columns.

Pavilion Design Group
Aged Receivables
As of Mar 31, 2003
Filter Criteria includes: Report order is by ID. Report is printed in Summary Format.

Customer ID Customer Contact Telephone 1	0 - 30	31 - 60	61 - 90	Over 90 days	Amount Due
Report Total	8,640.92	47.70			8,688.62

Each column lists the appropriate invoices and totals in its column based upon the age of the invoices that we have set.

Be aware that if you select Due date to age your invoices, and you accept the default aging on your A/R, then when your Aged Receivables report prints, it will show the invoices in the column for their age based on the date the invoices are due. This means that some invoices in the 0-30 column will have a negative age. A customized Aged Receivables report is shown here to illustrate how the invoice and due date affect the age.

Pavilion Design Group
Aged Receivables
As of Mar 31, 2003
Filter Criteria includes: Report order is by ID. Report is printed in Detail Format.

Customer ID Customer Contact Telephone 1	Invoice No	Date	Age	0 - 30	31 - 60	61 - 90	Over 90 days	Amount Due
CHER01 Cherokee Community Theater Mrs. Tracy Dee 770-555-5598	7475	3/14/03	-13	650.00				650.00
CHER01 Cherokee Community Theater				650.00				650.00
GUAP01 Guapo Computadores, Inc. Thomas A. Gonzalez 770-555-4726	7469	1/2/03	58		47.70			47.70
GUAP01 Guapo Computadores, Inc.					47.70			47.70

Invoice Date

Age according to Due Date

Custom Fields

Custom Fields, the third tab, allows you to add some customization to your customer records. These fields can be referred to by office staff or even printed on invoices or reports.

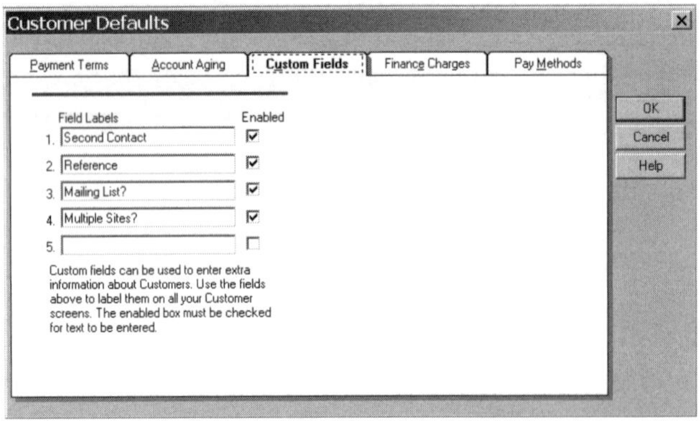

When your company is created, these fields are not enabled and do not have field labels. You may add any type of information that you desire. The labels for the sample company, Pavilion Design Group, are shown here.

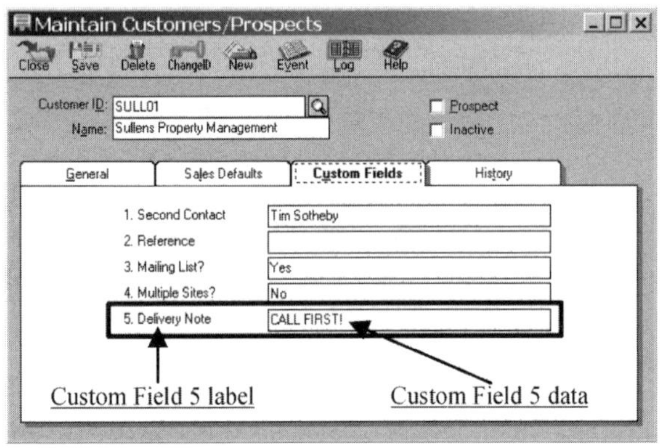

1. To insert and use your own custom fields, select the **Enabled** check box and then enter the name of the custom field in the Field Labels fields. On the Customer form you can enter the customer's information in the appropriate field.
2. As I noted earlier, this information can be added to reports and forms. An example would be the Delivery Note for Custom Field 5 shown in the example here. You could add the note to the Packing Slip or Invoice to instruct your employees. See Chapter 18 on customizing forms to add a field to a form.

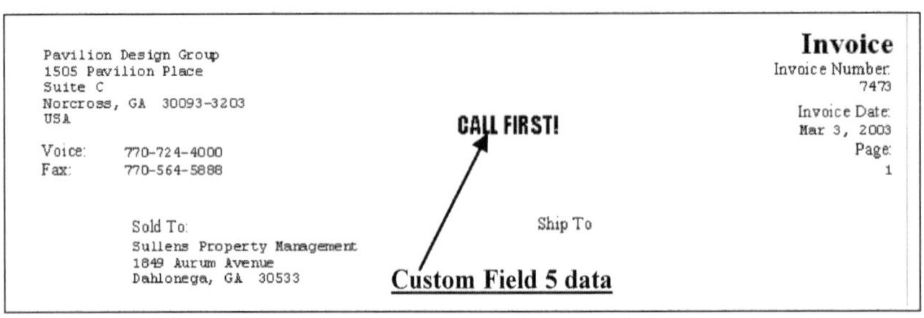

Finance Charges

The fourth tab, Finance Charges, deals with interest and late fees that should be charged to customers with past due invoices.

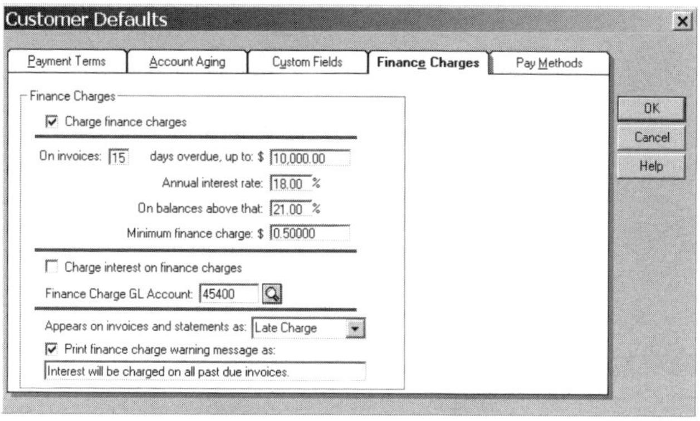

1. The top check box, Charge finance charges, must be checked in order to charge finance charges on customer accounts. In the second section, you determine how those finance charges are calculated. Finance charges are only charged when the age of the invoice is greater than the On invoices field. If you select to age invoices by invoice date, finance charges will apply when the invoice is this many days old. If you select to age invoices by due date, the invoice will be this many days past due before finance charges will apply. The Annual interest rate field controls the rate charged.
2. For companies that charge a higher, or lower, interest rate for customers with higher balances, enter the dollar amount subject to the first rate in the Up to $ field. The rate on higher balances is entered in the On balances above that field.
3. Many companies have a minimum finance charge that is entered in the Minimum finance charge field.
4. In the next section you can select to charge interest on finance charges by checking the check box. The Finance Charge GL Account field contains the general ledger account that this income is allocated to — usually Interest Income or Finance Charges Revenue.
5. In the bottom section you can determine the appearance of finance charges or any warnings. The Appears on invoices and statements as field lets you set the description of the invoice. You may select **Finance Charge** or **Late Charge**, or you can type a custom description such as **Late Fee** or **Interest**.
6. You may also check the **Print finance charge warning message as** box to add a custom description of how finance charges are determined. The custom warning is typed in the blank field below the check box.

Pay Methods

The last tab is Pay Methods.

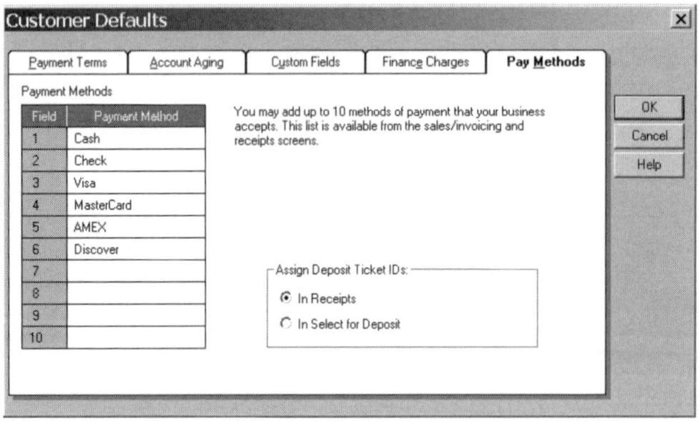

1. The Payment Methods list that appears on the left can be adjusted with as many or as few payment types that you receive. You will want to put the most used types at the top of the list. The credit card types do not have to be listed separately and you may decide to only use Credit Card as a payment type instead of listing each one.

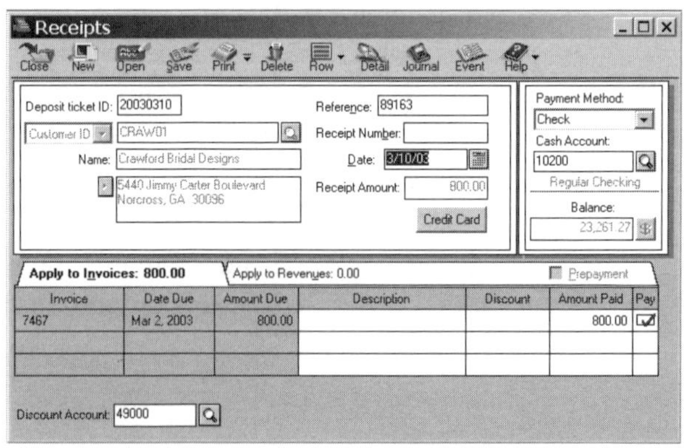

2. The Assign Deposit Ticket IDs area relates to your bank deposits. When you enter a receipt, you may want to enter the deposit ticket number directly. In that case, select **In Receipts.**

   If you receive a lot of checks and want to assign them to specific deposits, choose **In Select for Deposit.** See the A/R Reports section in this chapter for more information on selecting receipts for deposit.

Statement/Invoices Defaults

How statements and invoices are printed can also be customized in Peachtree. Open the Statement/Invoices defaults this way.

1. Select the **Setup Checklist** icon from the **Company** folder and click the **Statement and Invoice Defaults** line.

   Or select **Maintain**, **Defaults**, **Statements/Invoices** from the menu bar.

   Or using the keyboard, press **Alt+M, D, T.**

2. The Statement/Invoices Defaults screen appears.

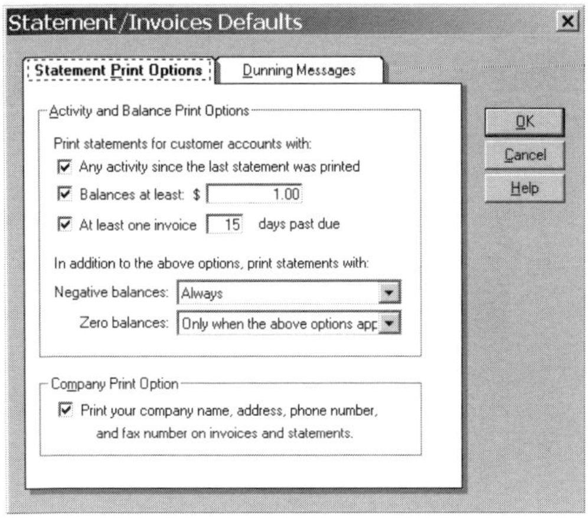

Statement Print Options

The first tab has several sections that control how invoices and statements are printed. The top section determines which customer accounts are printed when statements are run.

1. If the Any activity since the last statement was printed option is checked, statements will run for all customers with any payment or invoice activity since the last statement was run.
2. The Balances at least option allows you to set the minimum dollar balance for which to print statements. If a customer has a balance of only $.50, a statement would not print in the example shown. Enter the minimum dollar amount in the field.
3. The At least one invoice check box should only be selected if you do not want to print invoices for customers who have up-to-date accounts. Set the number of days past due for when you want statements to appear. This field could be set to 1 to show all past due invoices.
4. The Negative balances drop-down allows you to choose when statements for customers with negative balances should be printed. The options are Always, Never, and Only when the above options apply.
5. The Zero balances drop-down allows you to choose when statements for customers without a balance should be printed. The options are also Always, Never, and Only when the above options apply.
6. The Company Print Option area is for statements and invoices. If unselected, invoices and statements will not show your company information. This is helpful if you print these forms on your company letterhead.

Dunning Messages

Dunning messages appear on statements and give the customer a message based upon the age of their oldest invoice.

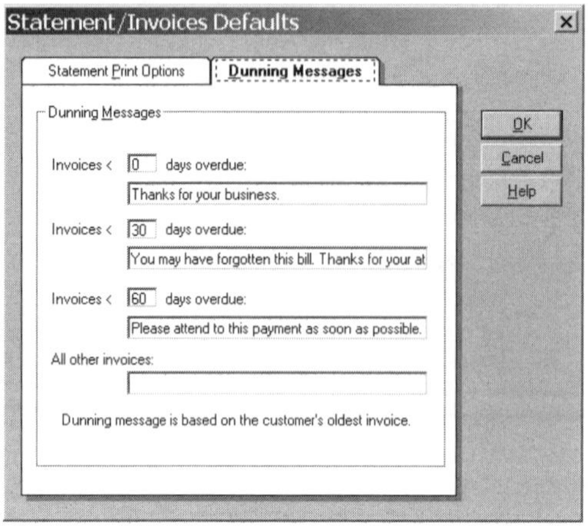

You may enter the message that you want to appear in the appropriate field and change the number of days overdue when the message should appear.

A/R Reports and Month-End Functions

Finance Charges

Generally, finance charges are applied before statements are run. Here are the instructions to calculate finance charges after you have set the defaults shown earlier in this chapter.

1. Click on the **Apply Finance Charges** icon in the **Receivables** or **Sales** folder on the navigation aid.

   Or select **Task**, **Finance Charge** from the menu bar.

   Or press **Alt+K**, **F** using the keyboard.

2. The Calculate Finance Charges dialog box appears.

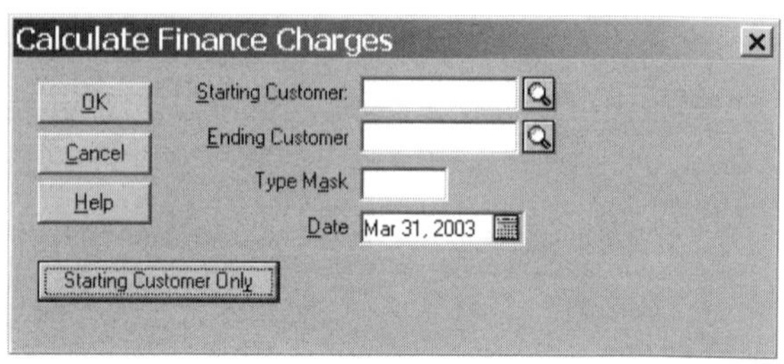

   If you want to calculate finance charges for all customers, leave the Starting Customer and Ending Customer fields blank. For a single customer, enter the customer ID in the Starting Customer field and when other fields are entered, click the **Starting Customer Only** button.

3. On the Maintain Customers/Prospects form is a field called Customer Type. If you want to print statements only for those customers with a specific type, such as MOWING, you can enter the customer type in the Type Mask field. Remember that the Type Mask and the Customer Type fields are both case specific. This means that MOWING does not equal Mowing or mowing.
4. In the Date field, enter the date through which to calculate finance charges.
5. Click **OK** or **Starting Customer Only** to calculate the charges.
6. The Apply Finance Charges dialog box appears.

   By choosing **No** under Apply Finance Charges, you can view the report without creating finance charge invoices. Choosing **Yes** will create the report and apply the charges to the customers' balances.

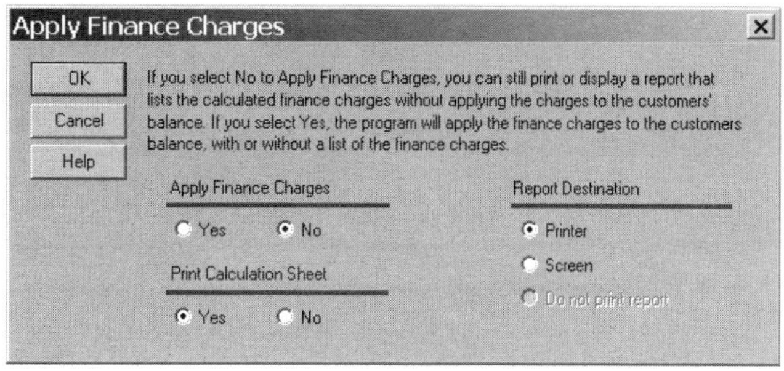

7. Select to send the report to the Printer or the Screen or, if Yes is chosen in the Apply Finance Charges option, you can select to skip the report with the Do not print report option.
8. The report can show you how finance charges are calculated if you choose **Yes** under Print Calculation Sheet.
9. Click **OK** to continue.
10. If you selected to view the report, the Finance Charge Report Selection dialog box appears.

    Select the Report Style and the Report Order. Click **OK** to print the report.

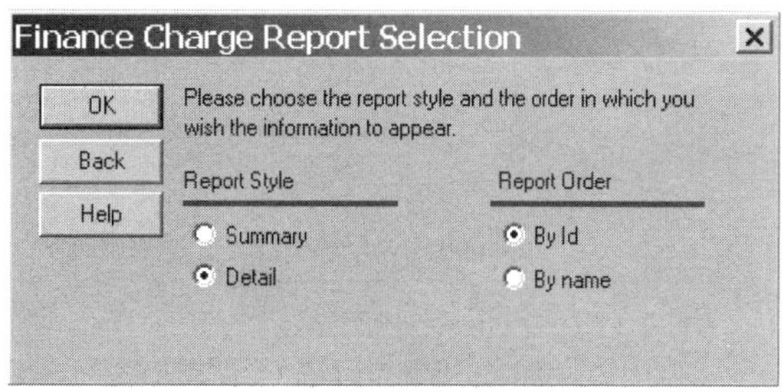

Pavilion Design Group
Finance charges
March 31, 2003

Customer	Name		Ref #	Overdue Amount	Finance Charge
CHER01	Cherokee Community Theater		FC3VX00001	650.00	5.45
	Invoice#	Due Date	Balance Due		
	7475	4/13/03	650.00		
GUAP01	Guapo Computadores, Inc.		FC3VX00002	47.70	2.07
	Invoice#	Due Date	Balance Due		
	7469	2/1/03	47.70		
HAUC01	DBH Enterprises		FC3VX00003	650.00	17.63
	Invoice#	Due Date	Balance Due		
	7470	3/5/03	650.00		
OLIV01	Oliver's Army Surplus		FC3VX00004	175.00	3.88
	Invoice#	Due Date	Balance Due		
	7468	3/16/03	175.00		
SECH01	Sechler Acquisitions		FC3VX00005	175.00	2.50
	Invoice#	Due Date	Balance Due		
	7472	4/1/03	175.00		

The Calculation Sheet will appear at the bottom of the report.

The finance charges show up as invoices and can be edited, voided, deleted, or even paid.

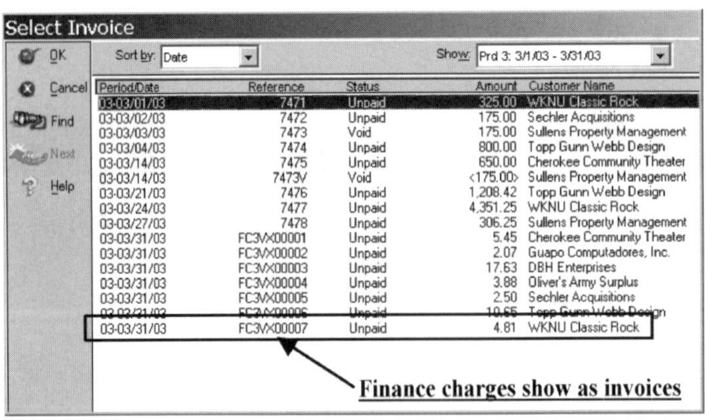

Statements

Statements can be run at any time. Some companies, such as an office supply company or a lawn service company, run them every month for all of their customers, because their customers only pay from statements. Other companies run statements rarely and only because a customer has become past due. In this case, the statement is sent as a reminder.

Follow these steps to run statements:

1. If you charge late fees, run the finance charges function before running statements.
2. Click on the **Customer Statements** icon in the **Receivables** or **Sales** folder.

   Or select **Reports**, **Accounts Receivable** from the menu bar, or press **Alt+R**, then **R.**

3. The Select a Report dialog box appears with the Customer Statements folder highlighted in the Report List.

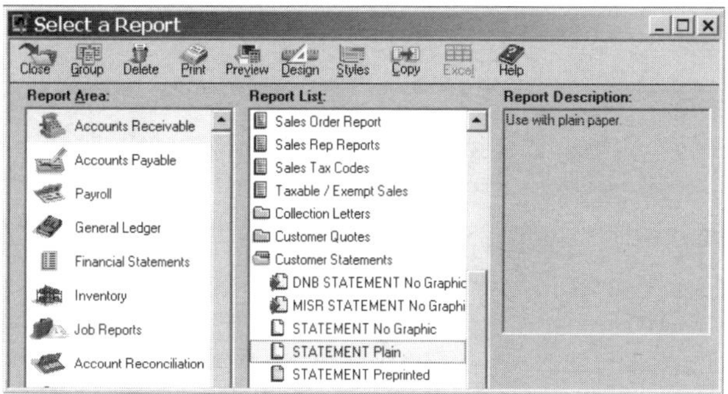

   Select a statement from the list and click **Preview.**

4. The Statement filter appears.

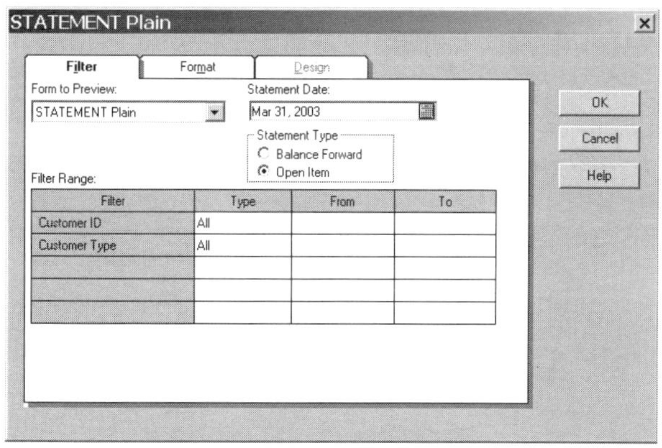

   You may select another form in the Form to Preview field — which turns to Form to Print if you click **Print** on the previous screen.

5. In the Statement Date field, enter the through date for the statements.
6. The Statement Type field has two options. Balance Forward will give the previous statement's balance and then show invoices and receipts for the customer. Open Item shows only unpaid invoices and unapplied credits.
7. In the Filter Range section you may select a specific customer or a range of customers by filling in the From and To boxes in the Customer ID line.
8. Using the Customer Type line, you can print statements for those customers that have specific information located in the associated Customer Type field on the customer's record. On the Customer Type line, enter the customer type desired in the From and To columns. The Type column will change to Range when you enter data in the From and To fields. Remember that the Customer Type line is case specific. This means that NORTH DISTRICT does not equal North District or north district.
9. Click **OK** to view the statements.

Deposit Tickets

If you have deposits with numerous items or daily cash that needs balancing, you may decide to withhold assigning information in the Deposit ticket ID field until you are ready to write up the bank deposit slip.

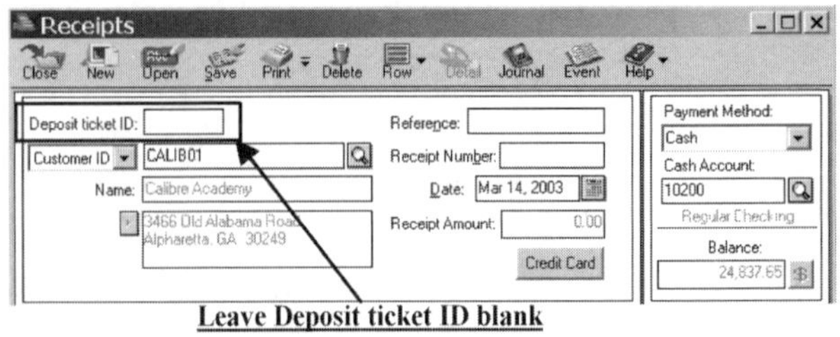

1. Select **Tasks**, **Select for Deposit** from the menu bar.
2. The Select for Deposit window appears.

   All receipts that do not show an entry in the Deposit ticket ID field will show on this screen. In the Account ID field, select the bank account that this deposit is for.

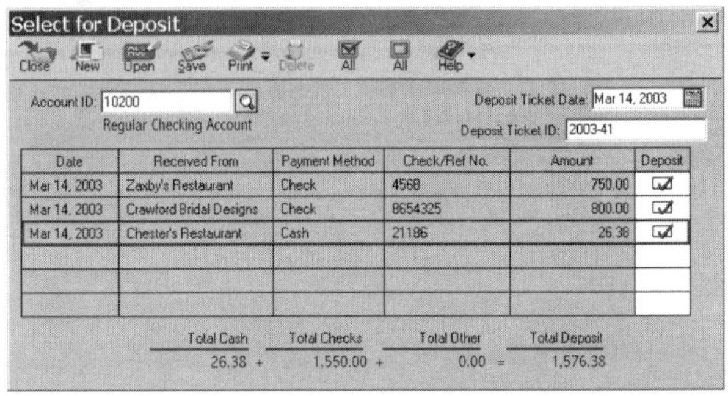

3. The date of the deposit goes in the Deposit Ticket Date field.
4. Fill in the Deposit Ticket ID field. After the first ID is entered, Peachtree will try to increment the ID by one automatically.
5. In the Deposit column, click the check box for each receipt that is to go into the bank on this deposit.
6. Once all receipts have been checked, verify the amount of the deposit against the Total Deposit shown at the bottom of the screen. There are individual totals for Total Cash, Total Checks, and Total Other (credit cards).
7. Click the **Print** or **Preview** button for the Print/Preview Forms window to appear.

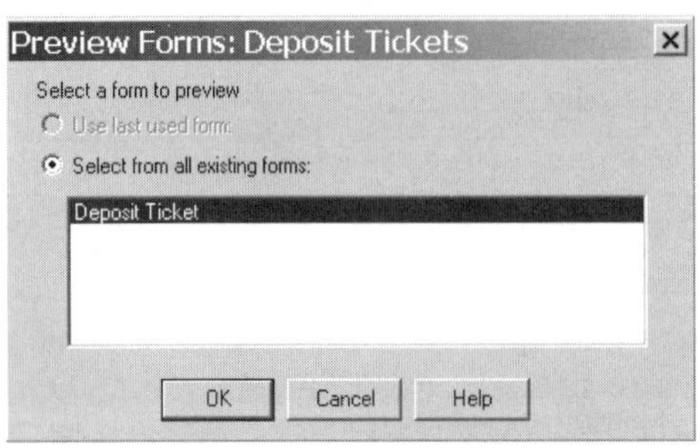

8. Select a form and click **OK**. The Deposit Report appears.

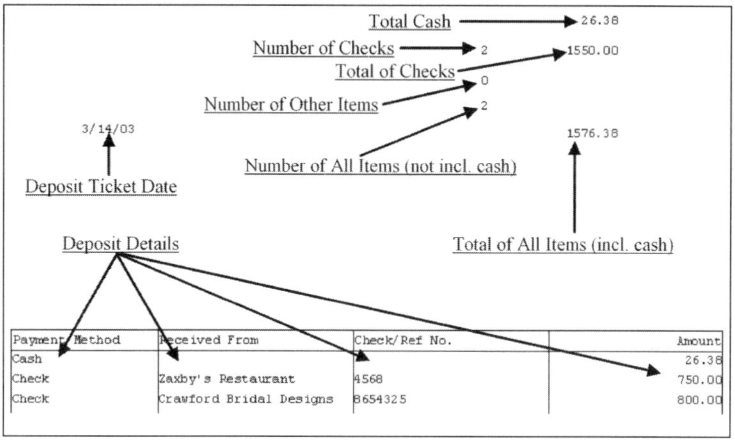

The report is a little difficult to read because it does not have descriptions on the top portion where I have labeled what shows there. Our deposit did not include any credit card items, so the number of other items is zero as is the total.

Summary

At this point you should now feel capable of balancing your accounts receivable and printing reports for your company and your customers. The additional functions and features described in this chapter are to increase your ability to control your accounts receivable and to speed up the payment of customer invoices.

Chapter 13

Balancing Accounts Payable

In This Chapter

- Verifying the vendor beginning balances
- Balancing accounts payable
- Finding accounts payable errors
- Adjusting accounts payable for errors and inaccurate balances
- Accounts payable default information
- Reconciling credit card statements

Accounts payable balances are created when you buy goods and services from a vendor and you owe them an amount that you promise to pay at a later date. Purchases may be recorded through the Purchases/Receive Inventory form or directly through your payments function. When these debts are incurred, your A/P general ledger account is increased, as is your expense or inventory accounts. In double-entry accounting we would say that A/P is credited and an expense or inventory is debited. If you don't understand the difference between a debit and a credit, talk to your CPA or pick up an accounting book for non-accountants to gain an understanding. Luckily, Peachtree can tell whether a debit or credit will increase your G/L accounts.

The reason for keeping your accounts payable accurate is that it will help you to analyze your cash flow and determine how to keep expenses to a minimum and paid within terms. This should increase your credit rating and your ability to fund your company.

Vendor Beginning Balances

In your first month working with Peachtree, you were told to get an accurate A/P listing of all vendors and the bills that you owe. In Chapter 8 you were shown how those bills should be entered into the vendors' beginning balances. Before we can balance last month's A/P, we must first reconcile the beginning balances.

1. Pull out your beginning A/P listing. It should list every bill that you owed before your Begin Transactions date. If you started entering transactions on March 31, it would be the balances as of February 28. It may look similar to the following figure.

Pavilion Design Group
Accounts Payable
As of February 28, 2003

Vendor ID	Vendor	Invoice No	Date	Amount Due
COMP01	Computers R US	656580	1/3/03	650.00
DAVIS01	Davis Advertising Company	960124	2/5/03	200.00
FASTTR01	Fast Track Couriers	223652	1/5/03	15.85
FASTTR01	Fast Track Couriers	223936	1/25/03	24.69
GENLEAS01	General Leasing Corp.	665992	2/3/03	3,750.00
MAPLEI01	Maple Typography	875154	2/6/03	256.00
MATH01	Mathers Printing	654686	2/4/03	55.00
PETE01	Peter's Photography Lab	88779	1/31/03	59.50
Report Total				5,011.04

2. If any of these bills are not yet entered into the beginning balances, enter them now by first changing the accounting period to the month before you began entering transactions. Then bring up the Vendor Beginning Balances form by clicking the **Purchases** folder on the navigation aid, the **Vendors** icon, and then the **Beginning Balances** button on the Maintain Vendors form.

3. Verify that the total of your beginning A/P listing matches the total of the form. (Be sure that you are in the right accounting period.) It is absolutely imperative that these balances match. If they do not, talk to your CPA to see where the adjustment should be made. Remember that this A/P listing will be the basis for your new accounts payable ledger and should be entered correctly.

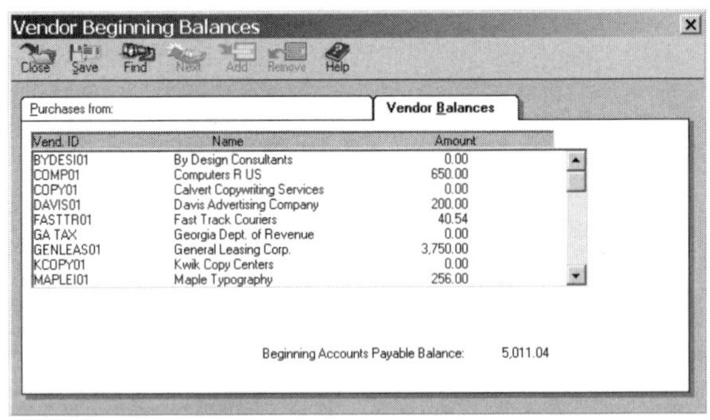

4. These amounts, the beginning A/P listing and the Vendor Beginning Balances form, should also match the balance of the Accounts Payable general ledger account for your beginning Trial Balance which should have been provided to you by your CPA. Click the **Chart of Accounts** icon in the **General Ledger** folder on the navigation aid. The Maintain Chart of Accounts form appears.

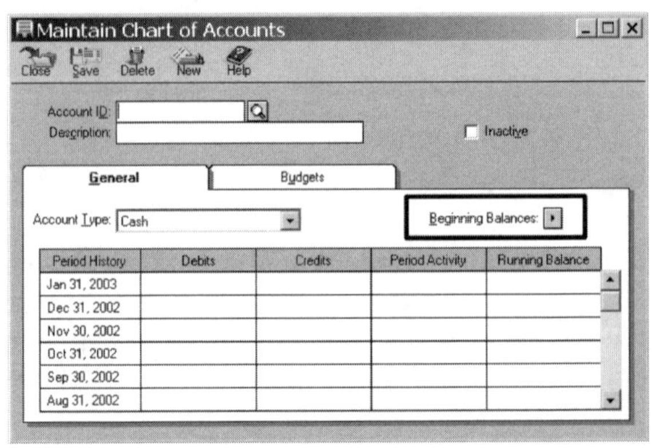

5. Click the **Beginning Balances** button on the form. The Select Period dialog box appears.

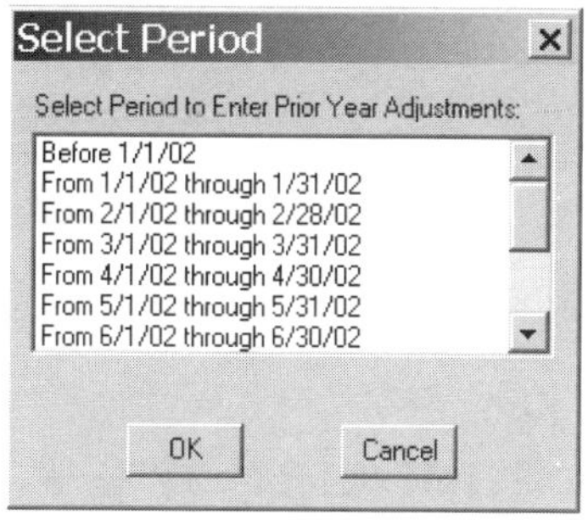

6. Again, be sure that you are in the correct period to enter the account balances. You should be able to select the month previous to your Begin Transactions date. If it is not available, select the last month of the previous financial year. Click **OK** and the Chart of Accounts Prior Year Adjustments screen appears.

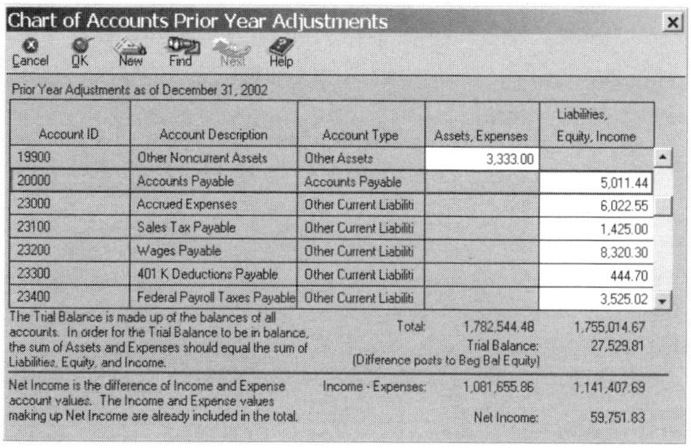

7. Enter the amount of your A/P in the Liabilities, Equity, Income column on the correct Accounts Payable line. If you have more than one A/P account, enter the correct amount on each of the lines. Then go down the list to the Retained Earnings account (or another account, such as Beginning Balance Equity, if your CPA recommends it).

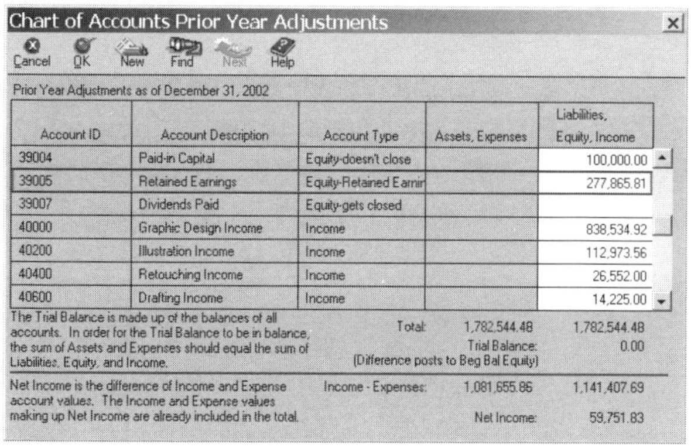

8. Add the A/P amount to the correct account in the Liabilities, Equity, Income column. The Trial Balance field should be 0.00 when you are done.

Note: By this time you may already have much of your trial balance entered and may need to add or subtract part of the Retained Earnings, or other account, to reconcile the beginning balances.

9. Click **OK** to save and close the form. Appropriate journal entries will be created to store the information.

Note: If you have selected to use Cash Basis as your accounting method, you will not have an accounts payable general ledger account and will not be able to run some of the reports that require a specified account. Because you cannot change the account number on the Purchases/Receive Inventory form, it is also difficult to put bills to the wrong A/P account. The same is true for the accounts receivable balance also.

Balancing the A/P

From month to month when you balance your A/P, you follow a very simple formula: You take the previous month's ending balance, add in the net total of all bills for purchases on-account, subtract the net total of all payments, and the result should match this month's ending balance.

The A/P reconciliation shown here is calculated using the Pavilion Design Group company backup included with the companion files and can be completed following these steps.

1. Go to the Select a Report screen. Select **Accounts Payable** in the Report Area and select **Aged Payables** in the Report List.

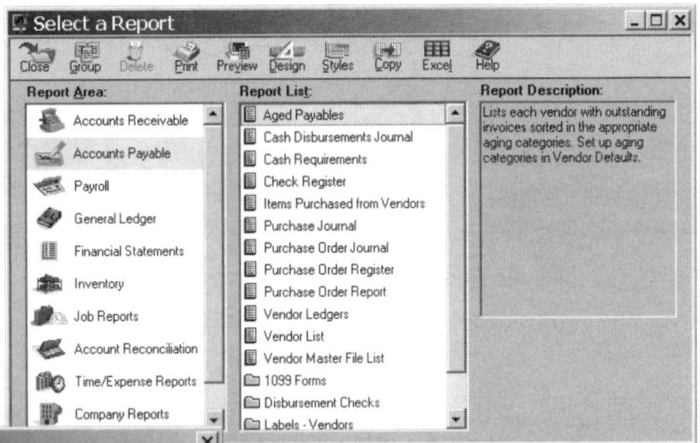

2. Click the **Preview** button and the Aged Payables filter appears.

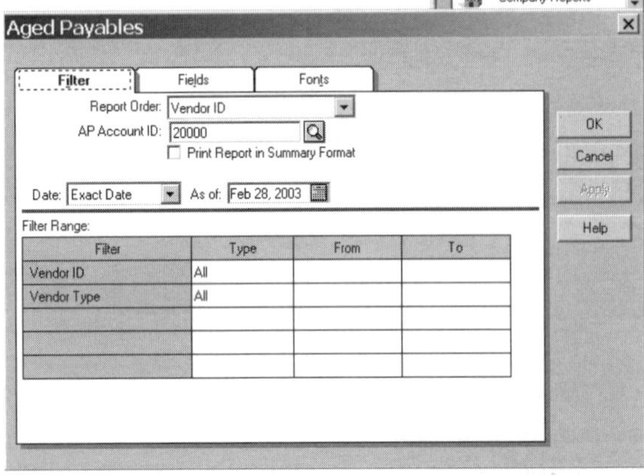

3. You may choose a report order, either **Vendor ID** or **Vendor Name**. Choose the correct general ledger account for the AP Account ID that you are balancing. In the Date field, select **Exact Date**. In the From field, select the last day of the previous month. We will ignore the Fields and Fonts tabs at this time. Click **OK**. The Aged Payables report will appear.

Pavilion Design Group
Aged Payables
As of Feb 28, 2003
Filter Criteria includes: Report order is by ID. Report is printed in Detail Format.

Vendor ID Vendor Contact Telephone 1	Invoice No	0 - 30	31 - 60	61 - 90	Over 90 days	Amount Due
MATH01 Mathers Printing		55.00				55.00
PETE01 Peter's Photography Lab Peter Strong 770-555-2365	88779	59.50				59.50
PETE01 Peter's Photography Lab		59.50				59.50
Report Total		5,011.04				5,011.04

4. Go to the Total line for the report. In our example, the total for all outstanding bills on February 28, 2003, is $5,011.04. This is the beginning balance of our reconciliation. In our example, and the first time that you balance your accounts payable, this amount should also match the beginning A/P listing. In later months, the beginning balance amount will be the ending balance for the previous month. Note this amount on your worksheet or in a spreadsheet program.

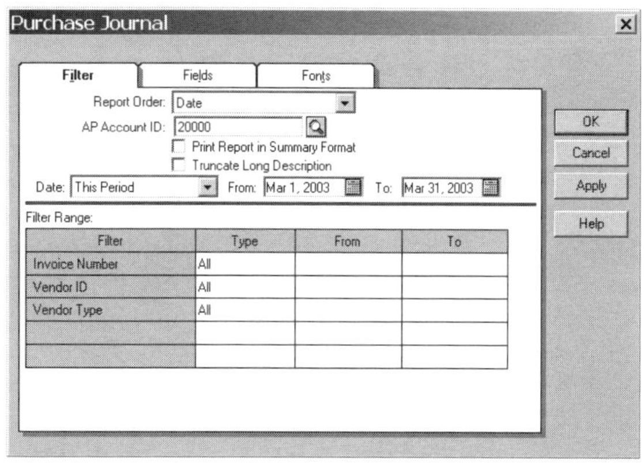

5. We now need to get the amount of the new bills added to accounts payable for the month. Close the previous report and select **Accounts Payable** in the Report Area and **Purchase Journal** in the Report List. Click the **Preview** button. The Purchase Journal filter will appear.
6. Select **Account ID** in the Report Order field. Enter the correct accounts payable account in the AP Account ID field. Select **This Period** in the Date field. The From and To fields are automatically filled in. Click **OK** to see the report.

Pavilion Design Group
Purchase Journal
For the Period From Mar 1, 2003 to Mar 31, 2003
Filter Criteria includes: Report order is by Account ID. Report is printed in Summary Format.

Account ID	Account Description	Debit Amount	Credit Amount
20000	Accounts Payable	190.00	5,880.08
60000	Advertising Expense	749.68	190.00
64200	Courier Delivery Expense	47.40	
71000	Maintenance and Repairs Ex	650.00	
73000	Outside Services Expense	665.00	
78500	Rent-Office	3,750.00	
89000	Other Expense	18.00	
		6,070.08	6,070.08

7. The Total of the purchase journal is $6070.08. Look carefully at the amounts allocated to expenses and to the A/P account. The debits include an amount on the Accounts Payable line that will have to be subtracted from the total expenses. There is also a credit on the Advertising Expense line, which will also have to be deducted. This gives us a net total of $5,690.08 ($6,070.08 less $190.00 less $190.00).

   Unfortunately, there is not another report that we can run this total against.

8. Close this report. The next report needed is the Cash Disbursements Journal. It is also shown in the Accounts Payable reports. Click the **Preview** button to bring up the filter.

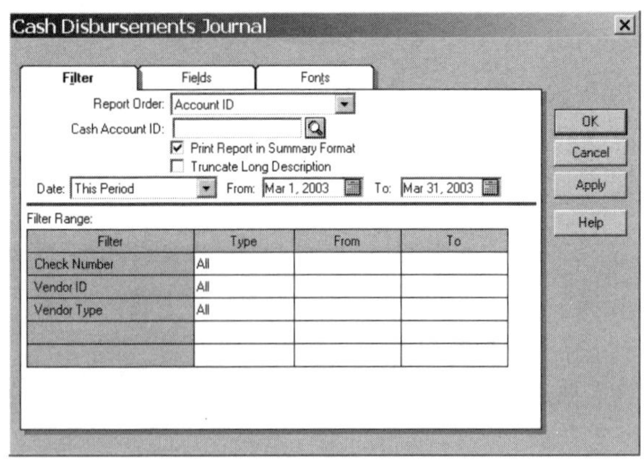

9. The Report Order field for this report contains Account ID, although Date or Check Number are also available. We will leave the Cash Account ID field blank. Select **This Period** in the Date field with the associated From and To dates. Click **OK**.

Pavilion Design Group
Cash Disbursements Journal
For the Period From Mar 1, 2003 to Mar 31, 2003
Filter Criteria includes: Report order is by Account ID. Report is printed in Summary Format.

Account ID	Account Description	Debit Amou	Credit Amo
10200	Regular Checking Accoun	465.50	12,646.39
15100	Equipment	6,999.95	
20000	Accounts Payable	5,416.54	475.00
49000	Fee Discounts		9.50
49000	Fee Discounts	9.50	
75000	Photostats Expense	239.40	
		13,130.89	13,130.89

10. The payments made against bills can be calculated by taking the net amount of the line for Accounts Payable, which is $4,941.54. This amount is the net deduction to A/P and should be noted on the worksheet.
11. On our worksheet, we should now show the following figures. The ending balance for the last period (which this month is the A/P beginning balance listing total) is found from the total of last month's aged payables — $5,011.04. To that we add the net amount of the bills that were entered in A/P — $5,690.08. From that we subtract the checks that went against the Accounts Payable, which is the net A/P line in the Cash Disbursements Journal — $4,941.54. The total of these amounts is $5,759.58. This amount represents the A/P ending balance for the current period.

Pavilion Desion Group
Accounts Payable Reconciliation
March 31, 2003

Beginning Balance - Feb 28, 2003		$	5,011.04
Bills added to A/P	5,880.08		
less Credit Memos	(190.00)		
Total Additions		$	5,690.08
Bills paid	(5,416.54)		
less Voided Checks	475.00		
Total Withdrawals		$	(4,941.54)
Ending Balance - Mar 31, 2003		**$**	**5,759.58**

12. We check the A/P ending balance by running the Aged Payables report for the current period.

Pavilion Design Group
Aged Payables
As of Mar 31, 2003
Filter Criteria includes: Report order is by ID. Report is printed in Detail Format.

Vendor ID Vendor Contact Telephone 1	Invoice No	0 - 30	31 - 60	61 - 90	Over 90 days	Amount Due
Peter's Photography Lab Peter Strong 770-555-2365						
PETE01 Peter's Photography Lab		59.50				59.50
Report Total		5,759.58				5,759.58

If these amounts match, your A/P is in balance. This reconciled amount can now be accurately used when discussing liabilities with your CPA, the bank, or your other creditors.

Adjustments to A/P

One of the reasons that we balance the accounts payable to verify their accuracy is to ensure that the amount reported on our financial statements reflects the true state of our business. Many circumstances can affect the account balance if proper care is not taken during the data entry process. Other problems can include power failures that occur during the posting process, conversions from an older to a newer version of Peachtree, apathy or even deliberate malice on the part of an employee, and the posting of unbalanced transactions.

Bill Errors

A typical error that occurs when posting bills is to enter the wrong account in the wrong field. For instance, if you were running the reconciliation used in the previous example, the A/P ending balance would be $5,284.58, which would not match the aged payables. Because we don't have the kind of matching reports that are found in the Accounts Receivable, we will have to do some detective work to find the problem.

1. When we ran the Purchase Journal as shown earlier, we entered the accounts payable ID into the AP Account ID field. Using that method we calculate the addition to A/P to be $5,215.08 on the following report.

Pavilion Design Group
Purchase Journal
For the Period From Mar 1, 2003 to Mar 31, 2003
Filter Criteria includes: Report order is by Account ID. Report is printed in Summary Format.

Account ID	Account Description	Debit Amount	Credit Amount
20000	Accounts Payable	190.00	5,405.08
60000	Advertising Expense	749.68	190.00
64200	Courier Delivery Expense	47.40	
71000	Maintenance and Repairs Ex	650.00	
73000	Outside Services Expense	190.00	
78500	Rent-Office	3,750.00	
89000	Other Expense	18.00	
		5,595.08	5,595.08

2. We can verify this amount by rerunning the report. To locate any differences between the two reports, print the Purchase Journal again, but this time select **Invoice Number** for Report Order and again leave the AP Account ID field blank. Uncheck **Print Report in Summary Format** and click **OK**.

Pavilion Design Group
Purchase Journal
For the Period From Mar 1, 2003 to Mar 31, 2003
Filter Criteria includes: Report order is by Invoice Number. Report is printed in Summary Format.

Date	Account ID	Account Description	Invoice #	Debit Amount	Credit Amount
3/24/03	73000	Outside Services Expense	P-4606	475.00	475.00

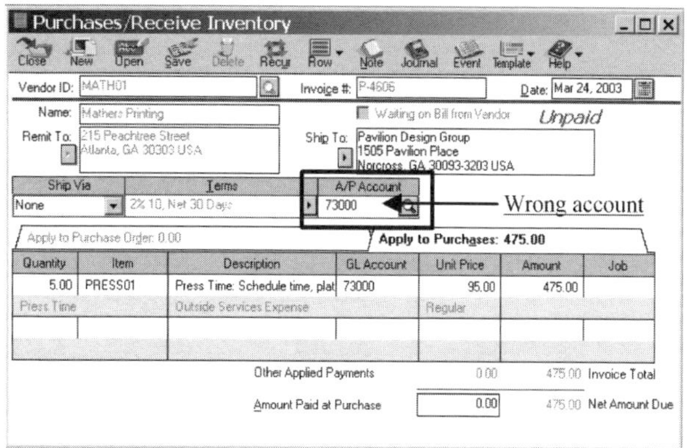

3. Look through the report and you will see that Invoice # P-4606 has both the Debit Amount and Credit Amount allocated to Account ID 73000. Double-click the line on the report to go to the Purchases/Invoicing form and open the invoice.
4. A common error for data entry people is to type the wrong general ledger ID in the A/P Account field. Once the number is entered incorrectly, Peachtree will remember the number until it is changed again. Usually when this error occurs there will be more than one invoice that has been applied to the wrong account. Regularly balancing your account means this error will not go uncorrected for very long.
5. Enter the correct ID number in the field and click **Save**. The Purchase Journal will now show the corrected amount.

Another way the invoice could be wrong is if the line item GL Account field is allocated to the A/P account, not a Purchases account.

Payment Errors

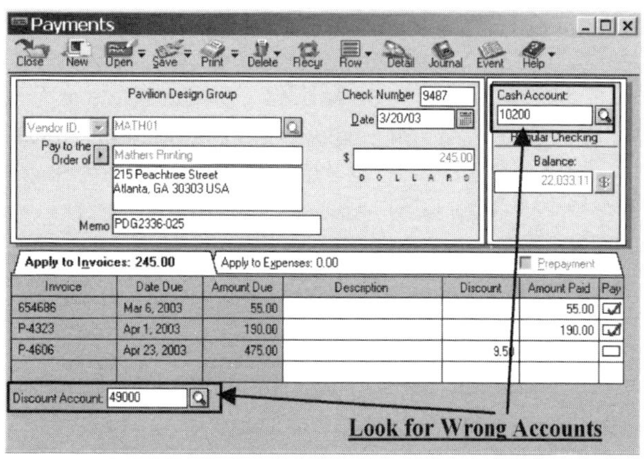

A similar mistake can happen on the payments side where the A/P account ID is entered in the Cash Account or the Discount Account field.

Finding this error is more difficult than finding an error entered into the purchases. Payments made against items made against purchases and items paid as manual checks show up in the same report and there is not a report in the Accounts Reconciliation area that will let us get this number by the A/P account ID.

1. Go back to the Cash Disbursements Journal filter and change Report Order to **Check Number.** Make sure that the Cash Account ID field is blank. Uncheck **Print Report in Summary Format** and click **OK.**

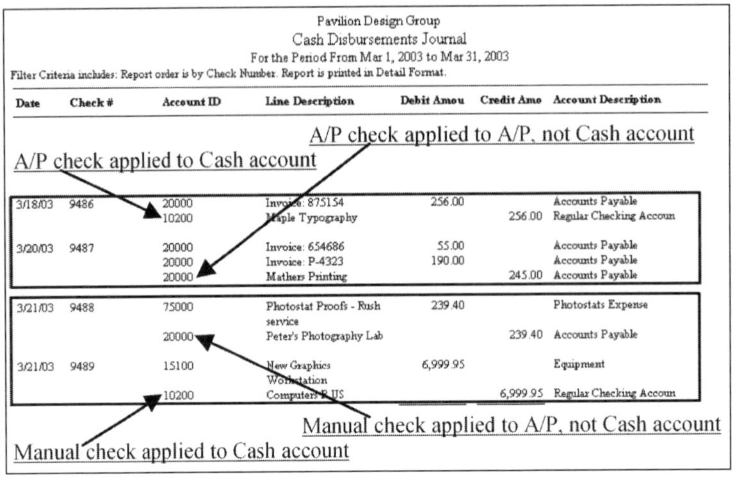
Pavilion Design Group
Cash Disbursements Journal
For the Period From Mar 1, 2003 to Mar 31, 2003
Filter Criteria includes: Report order is by Check Number. Report is printed in Detail Format.

Date	Check #	Account ID	Line Description	Debit Amou	Credit Amo	Account Description
3/18/03	9486	20000	Invoice: 875154	256.00		Accounts Payable
		10200	Maple Typography		256.00	Regular Checking Accoun
3/20/03	9487	20000	Invoice: 654686	55.00		Accounts Payable
		20000	Invoice: P-4323	190.00		Accounts Payable
		20000	Mathers Printing		245.00	Accounts Payable
3/21/03	9488	75000	Photostat Proofs - Rush service	239.40		Photostats Expense
		20000	Peter's Photography Lab		239.40	Accounts Payable
3/21/03	9489	15100	New Graphics Workstation	6,999.95		Equipment
		10200	Computers R US		6,999.95	Regular Checking Accoun

2. Go down each item in the list. Notice that items showing an invoice number in the Line Description fields also have Account IDs for the Cash and A/P accounts. Items for manual checks show a Line Description for the products purchased and the Account IDs are for an Expense account and the Cash account.

3. In our report we show two types of errors. The first shows all sides of a transaction applied to the same general ledger account. The second shows the A/P account appearing where we would expect the Cash account to be.

   Double-click on the line items that appear to be in error to bring up the transaction and correct them. Rerun the reports to get the A/P to balance.

Adjusting Journal Entries

Sometimes, despite all your efforts, you will not find an error in the A/P. At that point, you will have to decide whether the error lies in the transactions or the aged payables balance. If the aged payables balance is wrong, you will need to make the correction by creating a new transaction or editing an existing one. You would need to determine which vendor had the wrong balance and then correct it.

If you have a small bill amount that should not appear on your aged payables, you just need to remove the bill by writing it off or putting the entire amount to the Discounts account.

If you are sure that your aged payables is correct and it is your accounts payable balance that is incorrect, you will need to make a journal entry. See Chapter 16 for information on creating a journal entry.

Vendor Default Information

When your company was originally set up we accepted the accounts payable and vendor defaults. In this section we will cover how to customize those defaults.

The defaults are accessed in several ways.

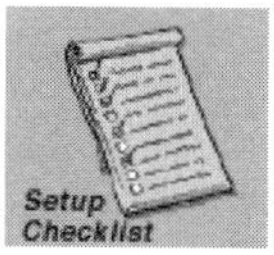

1. Click on the **Setup Checklist** icon in the **Company** folder.

   Then select the **Vendor Defaults** item in the list.

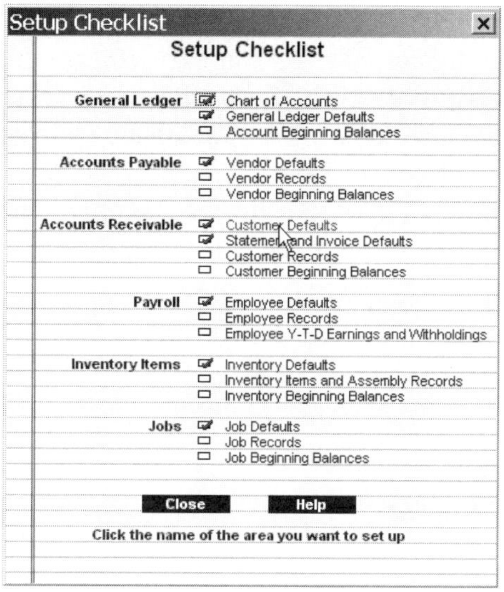

   Or select **Maintain**, **Default Information**, **Vendors** from the menu bar.

   Or press **Alt+M**, then **D**, then **C** using the keyboard.

2. The Vendor Defaults screen appears.

Payment Terms

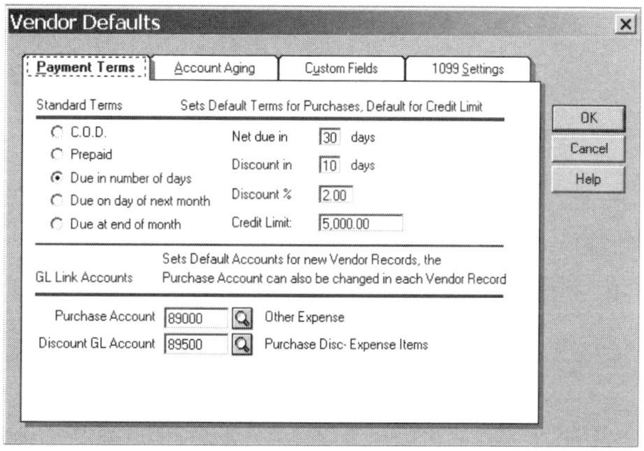

The first tab on the Vendor Defaults screen is the Payment Terms tab.

This tab controls how you want to pay your vendors. Remember that these are the defaults and each vendor can be customized to the specific payment terms on the Maintain Vendors screen. To set the defaults, follow these directions:

1. The Standard Terms section sets your normal purchases procedures for those vendors that extend you credit. If you normally pay by invoice or statements then you will want to choose either the Due in number of days, Due on day of next month, or Due at end of month option. These three options allow you to manage your payables for when you receive cash from your clients. The options also control when you start counting the number of days past due.

   Bills that are Due in number of days are for those companies that expect to pay bills within a certain length of time, which could be anywhere from 10 to 90 days. The actual number of days is set in the next section.

   If you choose to make your bills Due on day of next month you can control when the payments will be sent on a day next month. The day of the month is set in the next section. This means that if you want to pay on April 30 and you were sent the bill on March 1, you will wait almost 60 days to send the payment. If you want to pay on April 10 and the bill was sent on March 30, you will have less than two weeks to get the payment off. Many companies use this method when they only want to pay bills once a month.

   The last option is Due at end of month. This method means that whether the bill was sent on March 1 or March 30, it is still due on March 31.

   The other two options in this section are C.O.D., for those companies that want or need to pay when merchandise or services are delivered, like lawn care or water delivery, and Prepaid, for those companies that send employees to make purchases for products needed to complete jobs.

2. The next section, Sets Default Terms for Purchases, Default for Credit Limit, is related to the previous section.

   If you chose Due in number of days, then the Net due in days field is the number of days in which the bill should be paid. If you are offered discounts, the number of days in which the bill should be paid to receive the discount is entered in the Discount in days field. If no discounts are offered, enter **0** in this field. Enter the percentage offered in the Discount % field. This can also be changed to 0.00 if discounts are not offered.

   If your bills are Due on day of next month, the fields change. The first field becomes Due on the next month. Enter the day of the month that bills are due. The discount fields are still available for this option.

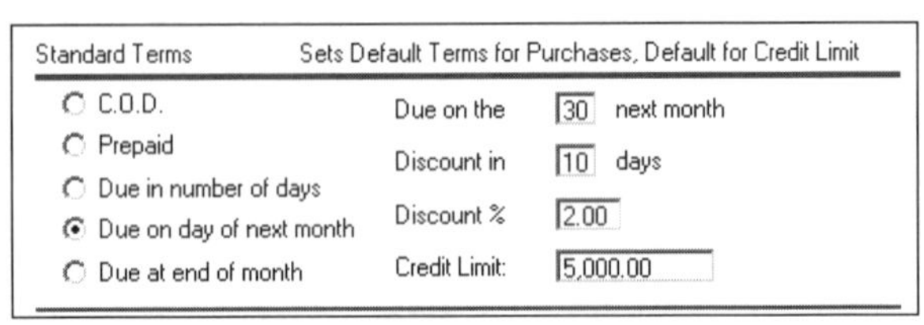

   For the Due at end of month option, the Due on the next month field becomes disabled but you may still be offered discounts.

3. The last field in this section is Credit Limit. Enter the standard amount of credit that you are allowed by vendors. If you go over the credit limit, a message does not

appear when you create a bill that will take you over that limit, unlike the customer defaults.

4. The next section of the Payment Terms tab, GL Link Accounts, controls the general ledger accounts that purchases are assigned to. When a vendor is added to the system, you can assign a specific expense, inventory, or cost of sales account to their record. For one vendor it could be Supplies Expense and for another it might be Production Inventory. If you do not assign an account or if a payment is created for someone who is not a vendor in the system, Peachtree defaults the income and any potential discounts to the accounts displayed in the Purchase Account and the Discount GL Account fields.

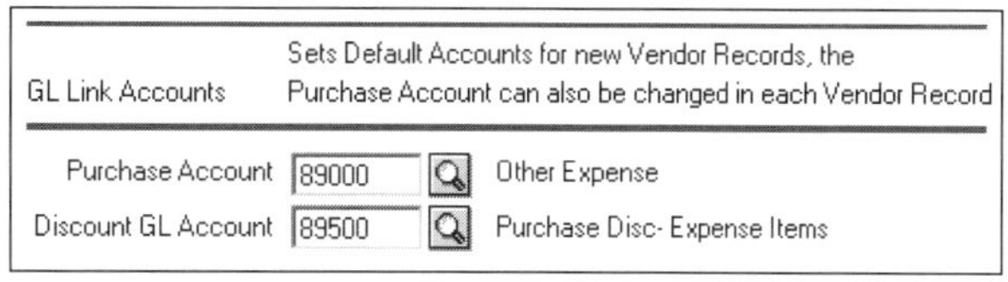

Account Aging

The second tab of the Vendor Defaults window is the Account Aging tab. It controls how the age of your bills is displayed in the Aged Payables and other reports.

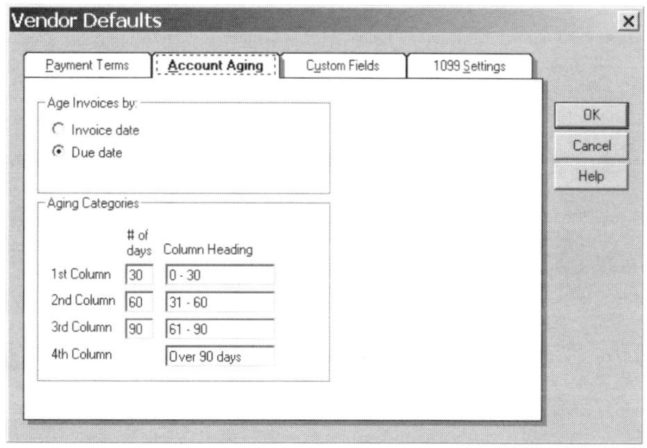

1. In the top section, Age Invoices by, you have two options — Invoice date and Due date. If you have a bill that is dated April 5 and the bill is unpaid on May 15, you can count the age of the bill in one of two ways. Aging by invoice date will make the bill 40 days old because you start counting from the date of the bill, April 5. If you choose the other option, by due date, the bill is only considered to be 10 days old because you didn't start counting the age until May 5. Most companies choose to age their bills by due date, even though they age their customer invoices by invoice date.

2. The lower section, Aging Categories, controls how your Aged Payables report looks. The Column Heading field shows the heading for each column across the top, described as 0-30, 31-60, 61-90, and Over 90 days. The # of days column shows the maximum age that can appear in each column. Obviously there is not a # of days field for the 4th Column line because it contains all bills that are not in the other columns.

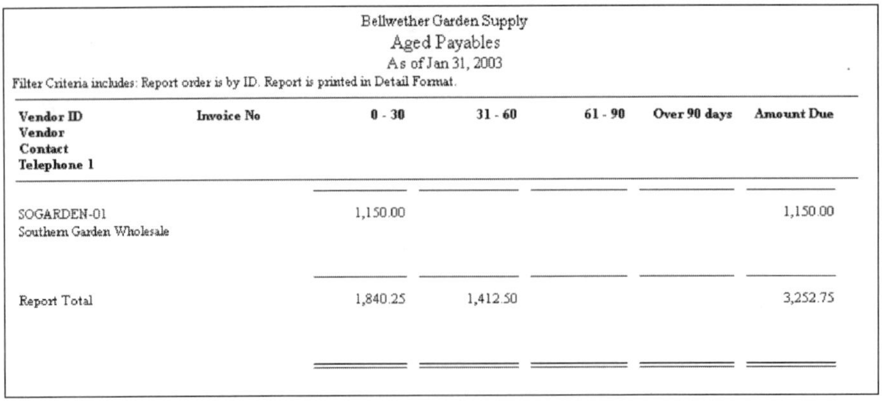

Bellwether Garden Supply
Aged Payables
As of Jan 31, 2003
Filter Criteria includes: Report order is by ID. Report is printed in Detail Format.

Vendor ID Vendor Contact Telephone 1	Invoice No	0 - 30	31 - 60	61 - 90	Over 90 days	Amount Due
SOGARDEN-01 Southern Garden Wholesale		1,150.00				1,150.00
Report Total		1,840.25	1,412.50			3,252.75

Each column lists the appropriate bills and totals in its column based upon the age of the bills that we have set.

Be aware that if you select Due date to age your bills, and you accept the default aging on your A/P, the Aged Payables report will show the bills in the column for their age based on the date the bills are due. This means that some bills in the 0-30 column will have a negative age. A customized Aged Payables report is shown here to illustrate how the invoice and due date affect the age.

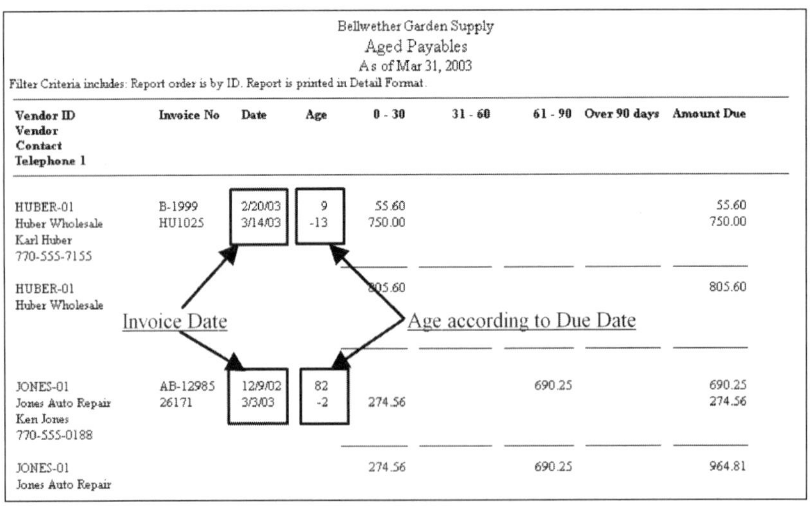

Bellwether Garden Supply
Aged Payables
As of Mar 31, 2003
Filter Criteria includes: Report order is by ID. Report is printed in Detail Format.

Vendor ID Vendor Contact Telephone 1	Invoice No	Date	Age	0 - 30	31 - 60	61 - 90	Over 90 days	Amount Due
HUBER-01 Huber Wholesale Karl Huber 770-555-7155	B-1999 HU1025	2/20/03 3/14/03	9 -13	55.60 750.00				55.60 750.00
HUBER-01 Huber Wholesale				805.60				805.60
JONES-01 Jones Auto Repair Ken Jones 770-555-0188	AB-12985 26171	12/9/02 3/3/03	82 -2	274.56		690.25		690.25 274.56
JONES-01 Jones Auto Repair				274.56		690.25		964.81

Custom Fields

Custom Fields, the third tab, allows you to add some customization to your vendor records. These fields can be referred to by office staff or even printed on bills or reports.

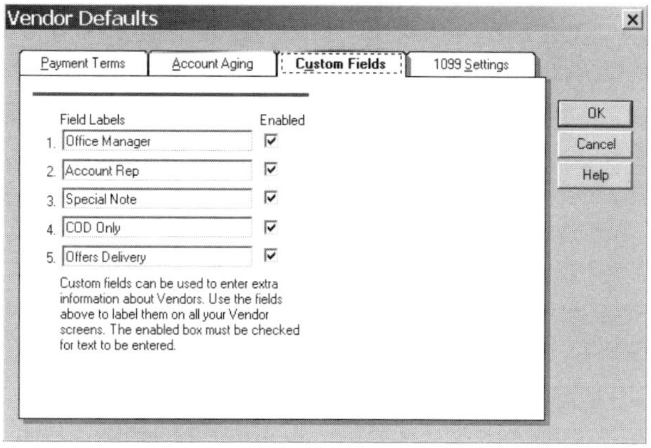

When your company is created, these fields are not enabled and do not have field labels. You may add any type of information that you desire. Simply select the **Enabled** check box and then enter the name of the custom field in the Field Labels fields. On the Vendor form you can enter the vendor's information in the appropriate field.

1099 Settings

The 1099 Settings tab lets you add specific general ledger accounts to your 1099 vendors.

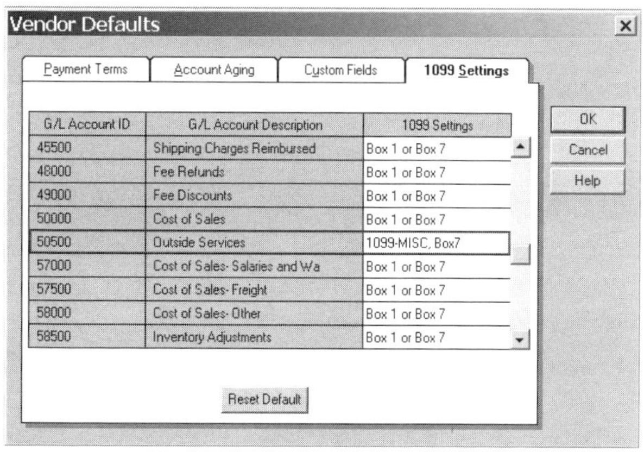

The 1099 Settings tab allows you to limit the G/L Account IDs that print in specific boxes on your 1099-MISC and 1099-INT. For instructions on who to send a 1099-MISC to, go to the web site http://www.irs.gov/pub/irs-pdf/i1099m02.pdf. For instructions on who to send a 1099-INT to, go to http://www.irs.gov/pub/irs-pdf/i1099i02.pdf.

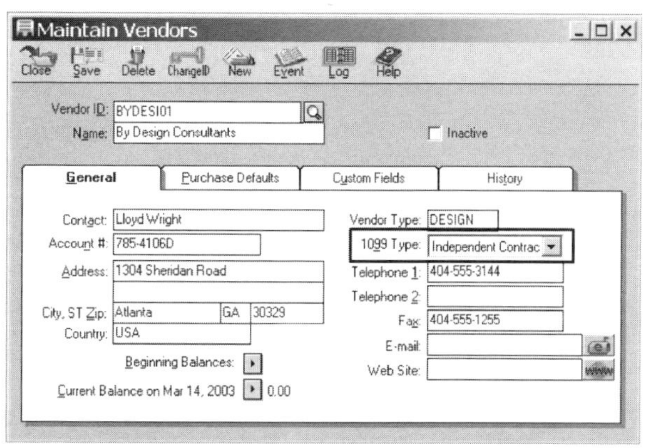

The following steps show how to set up vendors for 1099 forms and how to use the 1099 Settings tab:

1. In the Maintain Vendors screen, the General tab has a 1099 Type field.

Select the type of 1099 that is to be sent to the vendor. Choices include Independent Contractor, Interest, and None.

2. Select the **Purchase Defaults** tab and enter the vendor's tax ID number in the field provided. This number could be the vendor's federal tax ID number or social security number. The information is found on the IRS form W-9 that should be provided by any vendors who meet the criteria for using this form. If you do not know the criteria or need more information on W-9s, go to the web site http://www.irs.gov/pub/irs-pdf/iw9.pdf for instructions. The form itself can be printed from the Internet by going to http://www.irs.gov/pub/irs-pdf/fw9.pdf.

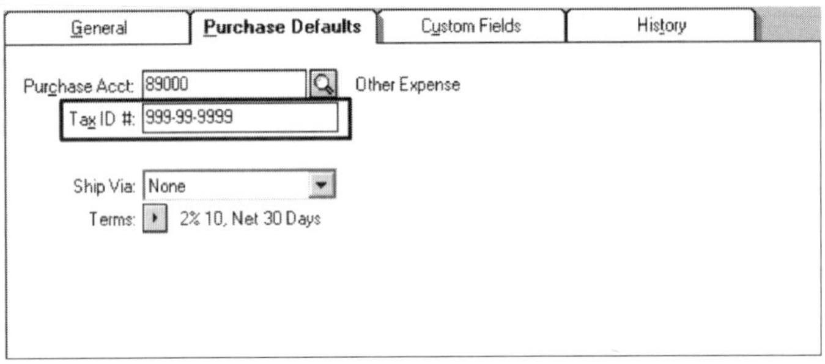

3. Once you have determined which of your vendors need 1099s, return to the 1099 Settings tab on the Vendor Defaults screen (see the figure on the previous page).

   The first column of the tab is for the G/L Account ID and contains a listing of all of your general ledger accounts. The second column is the G/L Account Description. The third column, 1099 Settings, is where the general ledger accounts are summarized in a field on the 1099.

4. When bills are entered and paid, the line items are allocated to one or more G/L accounts, usually expense accounts or outside labor costs.

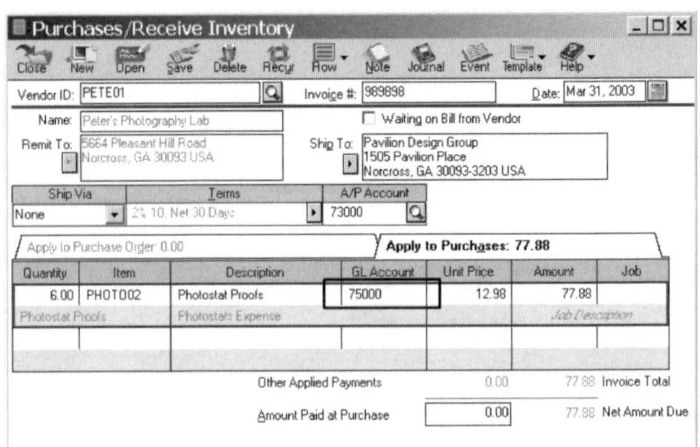

5. When 1099s are run, the amounts paid on the general ledger accounts are added up and printed in either the Box 1 field of a 1099-INT or the Box 7 field of a 1099-MISC.

6. Some types of payments are not included in a 1099, such as merchandise or rent. If a G/L Account ID should not appear on a 1099, select **None** from the 1099 Settings drop-down list. If the account should only appear on a 1099-INT, select **1099-INT, Box 1**. If the account should only appear on a 1099-MISC, select **1099-MISC, Box**

7. If an account can appear on either type of 1099, select **Box 1 or Box 7** from the list.

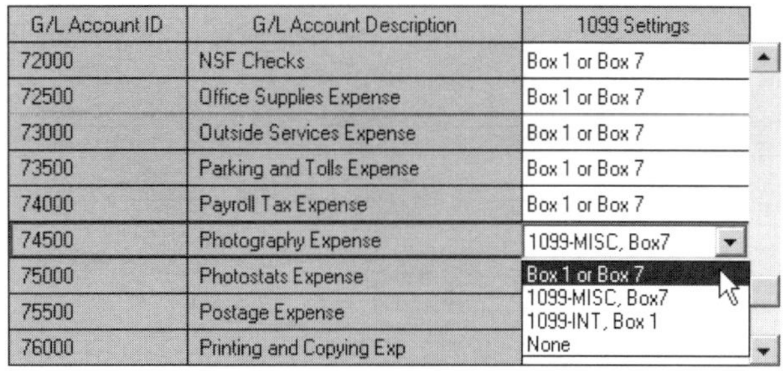

7. Make payments throughout the year as you normally would. If we look at an example of how these fields work for a 1099-MISC, you can see the results of the selections. We will look first at three G/L accounts in Pavilion Design Group. Account ID 73000, Outside Services, is set to the default choice of Box 1 or Box 7. Account ID 74500, Photography Expense, is set to 1099-MISC, Box 7. Account ID 75000, Photostats Expense, is set to None. (These are not representative of actual payments included in a 1099 and are for instruction purposes only.)

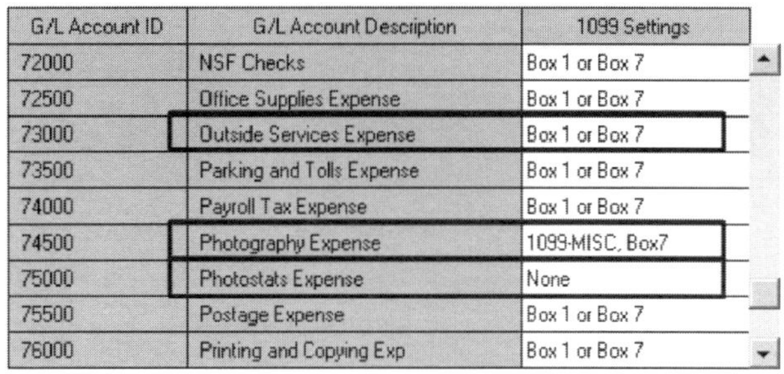

8. During the year payments are made to Pete's Photography Lab. The payment details are allocated to different G/L accounts.

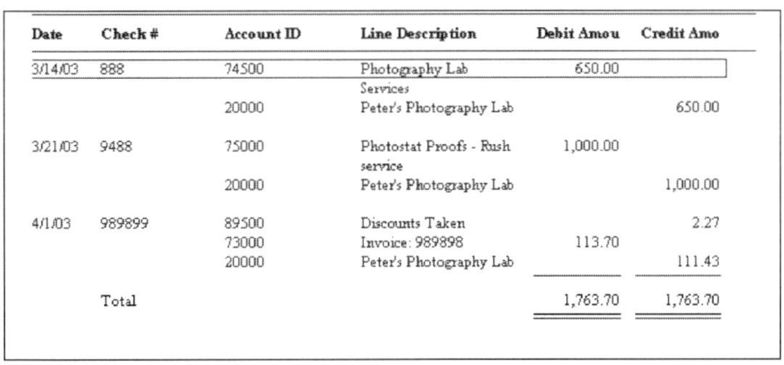

Date	Check #	Account ID	Line Description	Debit Amou	Credit Amo
3/14/03	888	74500	Photography Lab Services	650.00	
		20000	Peter's Photography Lab		650.00
3/21/03	9488	75000	Photostat Proofs - Rush service	1,000.00	
		20000	Peter's Photography Lab		1,000.00
4/1/03	989899	89500	Discounts Taken		2.27
		73000	Invoice: 989898	113.70	
		20000	Peter's Photography Lab		111.43
	Total			1,763.70	1,763.70

9. When it is time to run 1099s, go to the Select a Report screen and select **Accounts Payable** in the Report Area. Double-click on the **1099 Forms** folder in the Report List.

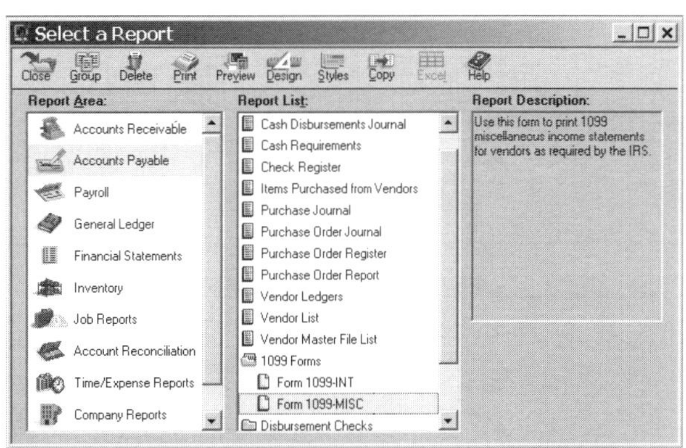

Month 2

10. Select **Form 1099-MISC**, insert the forms into the printer, and click **Print**. The following form will print.

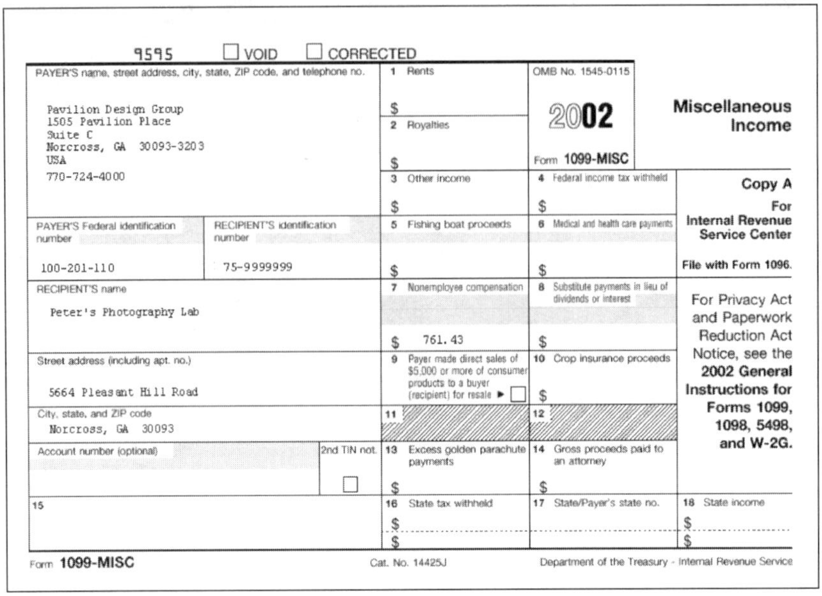

9595 ☐ VOID ☐ CORRECTED

PAYER'S name, street address, city, state, ZIP code, and telephone no.

Pavilion Design Group
1505 Pavilion Place
Suite C
Norcross, GA 30093-3203
USA
770-724-4000

1 Rents $
2 Royalties $
3 Other income $
4 Federal income tax withheld $
5 Fishing boat proceeds $
6 Medical and health care payments $
7 Nonemployee compensation $ 761.43
8 Substitute payments in lieu of dividends or interest $
9 Payer made direct sales of $5,000 or more of consumer products to a buyer (recipient) for resale ▶ ☐
10 Crop insurance proceeds $
11
12
13 Excess golden parachute payments $
14 Gross proceeds paid to an attorney $
15
16 State tax withheld $ $
17 State/Payer's state no.
18 State income $ $

OMB No. 1545-0115

2002

Form 1099-MISC

Miscellaneous Income

Copy A For Internal Revenue Service Center

File with Form 1096.

For Privacy Act and Paperwork Reduction Act Notice, see the 2002 General Instructions for Forms 1099, 1098, 5498, and W-2G.

PAYER'S Federal identification number: 100-201-110

RECIPIENT'S identification number: 75-9999999

RECIPIENT'S name: Peter's Photography Lab

Street address (including apt. no.): 5664 Pleasant Hill Road

City, state, and ZIP code: Norcross, GA 30093

Account number (optional)

2nd TIN not. ☐

Form 1099-MISC Cat. No. 14425J Department of the Treasury - Internal Revenue Service

Notice that the total, $761.43, for the 1099 is not the same as the total for the payments, $1,761.43. Because one of the payments was allocated to an account set to **None**, it did not show on the 1099.

A/P Reports and Month-End Functions

Check Register

At the end of each month you may desire a listing of all checks printed from each checking account during the month for your CPA or your own files.

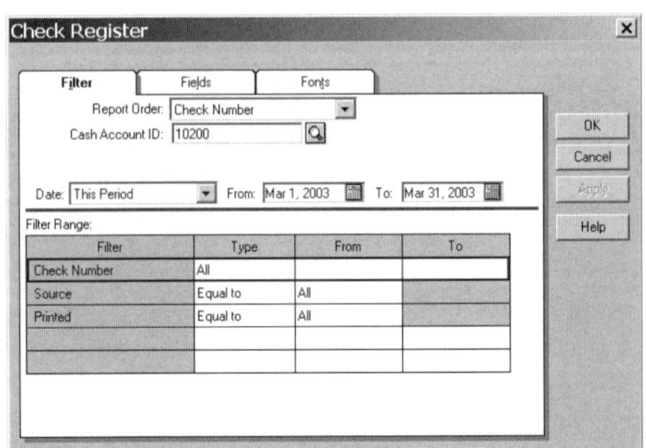

1. From the Select a Report screen, select **Accounts Payable** in the Report Area and **Check Register** in the Report List. Click the **Preview** button and the Check Register filter appears.
2. Select the order from the Report Order drop-down, either **Date** or **Check Number**.
3. In the Cash Account ID field, enter the checking account number.

4. In the Date field, select either **This Period** or **Range**.
5. Verify the dates in the From and To fields.
6. Click **OK** to see the report.

Pavilion Design Group
Check Register
For the Period From Mar 1, 2003 to Mar 31, 2003
Filter Criteria includes: Report order is by Check Number.

Check #	Date	Payee	Cash Account	Amount
9482	3/3/03	Mathers Printing	10200	465.50
9482V	3/7/03	Mathers Printing	10200	-465.50
9483	3/5/03	General Leasing Corp.	10200	3,750.00
9484	3/14/03	Computers R US	10200	650.00
9485	3/14/03	Fast Track Couriers	10200	40.54
9486	3/18/03	Maple Typography	10200	256.00
9489	3/21/03	Computers R US	10200	6,999.95
Total				11,696.49

Reconciling Credit Card Accounts

In Chapter 8 we learned how to set up and pay credit cards from the Payments window. When a credit card bill is received, you will want to reconcile the bill before you pay it.

A bill received from a credit card company will generally look something like the following.

My Credit Card Company

V/MC Account
9999-9999-9999-9999

FEB 04, 2003 - MAR 03, 2003
Page 1 of 1

Account Summary

Previous Balance	$	966.35
Payments, Credits, and Adjustments	$	822.69
Transactions	$	873.87
Finance Charges	$	15.43
New Balance	$	1,032.96
Minimum Amount Due	$	125.00
Payment Due Date		April 3, 2003
Total Credit Line	$	12,000.00
Total Available Credit	$	10,967.04
Credit Line for Cash	$	12,000.00
Available Credit for Cash	$	10,967.04

Customer Service
Call to report a lost or stolen card
999-999-9999

Send Payments To:
My Credit Card Company
123 Main Street
Anytown, US

Payments, Credits, and Adjustments

1	22 FEB	PAYMENT RECEIVED	$ -800.00
2	28 FEB	CREDIT OFFICE PLACE #9999 ROWLETT, TX	-22.69

Transactions

1	6 FEB	OFFICE PLACE #9999 ROWLETT, TX	$ 86.98
2	9 FEB	BRANDYBERRYS #8888	48.67
3	13 FEB	MOXXEN GAS #999999 DALLAS, TX	15.00
4	16 FEB	HOLIDAY HOTEL #888 SAN ANTONIO TX	69.89
5	16 FEB	OLIVE TREE 00094599 SANTONIO TX	136.24
6	16 FEB	SOUTH TX AIR 30195895686 DFW-SAN	248.00
7	17 FEB	LENNYS 8989 ROUNDROCK TX	12.51
8	28 FEB	MOXXEN GAS #999999 DALLAS, TX	10.00
9	2 MAR	H AND D Internet #30689898989 MPLS, MN	234.59
10	2 MAR	OFFICE PLACE #9999 ROWLETT, TX	11.99

Finance Charges *Please see revese side for important information*

	Balance rate applied to	*Periodic Rate*	*Corresponding APR*	**FINANCE CHARGE**
PURCHASES	$ 1,119.35	.04447% F	16.23%	$ 15.43
CASH	$ .00	.04447% F	16.23%	$ .00

The current accounting period shown on the status bar should be set to the same month as the statement. If the accounting periods do not match, you will need to change it. Changing the accounting period was covered in Chapter 2.

1. From the navigation aid, click on the **Account Reconciliation** icon.

   Alternately, select **Tasks**, **Account Reconciliation** from the menu bar or press **Alt+K**, then **O** using the keyboard shortcuts.

2. A blank Account Reconciliation screen appears.

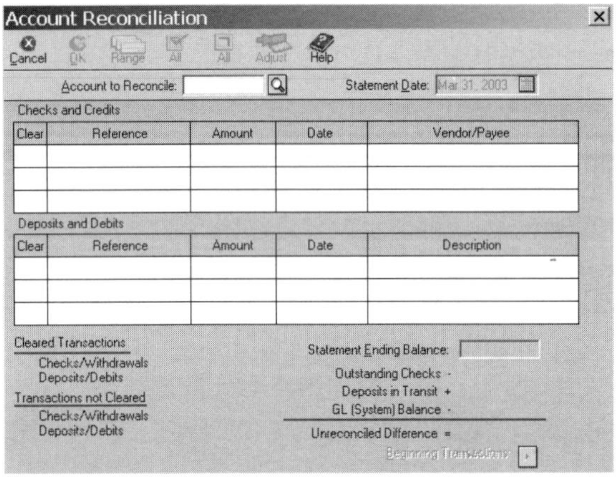

   In the Account to Reconcile field, select the account for this statement.

3. The Statement Date field defaults to the last day of the current accounting period. If your statement ending date is different, change the date here.
4. Enter the ending balance from the credit card statement in the Statement Ending Balance field. Remember to make the number a negative.
5. Credit card charges are in the Checks and Credits section, and payments on your account and credits are in the Deposits and Debits section.
6. When you need to add the finance charge, click on the **Adjust** button to bring up the Additional Transactions screen.

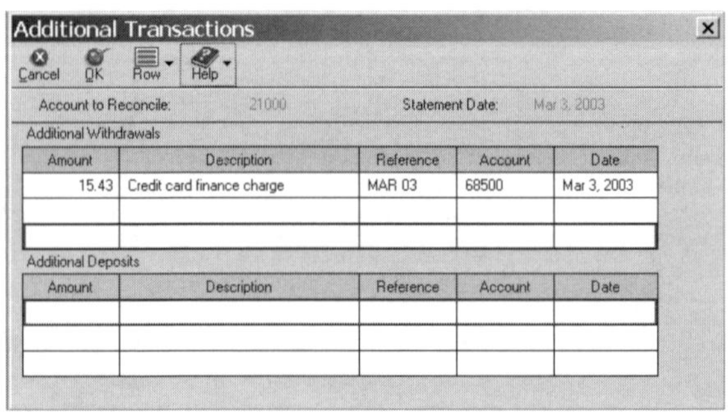

7. Finance charges are added the same way that bank statement service charges are. The finance charges go into the Additional Withdrawals section. If you have any annual fees, this is a good place for them also.
8. When you are done, click **OK** to return to the reconciliation screen.

9. When the transactions on your statement are cleared and your Unreconciled Difference is equal to 0.00, then the statement is complete. Click **OK** to save the reconciliation.

   You can click OK at any time to save your work and leave the screen in order to make corrections to existing transactions or to add new ones. You may also print a Reconciliation Report if needed.

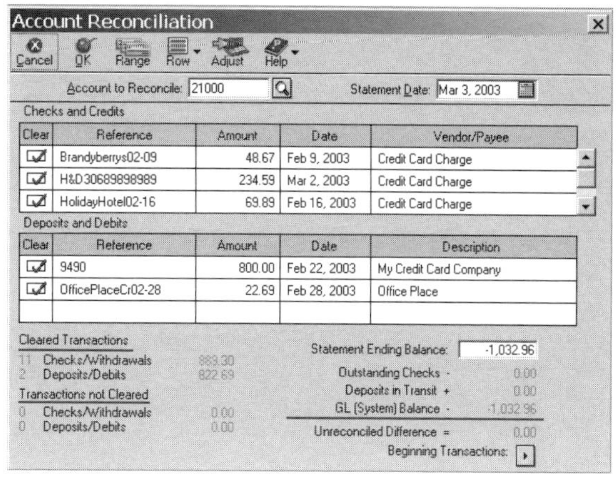

Summary

At this point you should now feel capable of balancing your accounts payable and your credit card statements. The additional functions and features described in this chapter are to increase your control of vendor bills and to prepare 1099s for independent contractors.

Chapter 14

Sales Taxes

In This Chapter

- How sales taxes work
- The sales tax liability account
- Creating sales tax authorities and sales tax codes
- Deciding how to set up tax rates — using one or many
- Customers with multiple sales tax rates
- Sales tax beginning balances
- Paying sales taxes

Unless you and your company are lucky enough to be located in a state that does not charge sales taxes or you have a company whose services are totally untaxed, you will have to determine the amount of sales taxes that are owed to the different taxing authorities on a regular basis. A *taxing authority* is an organization that assesses sales taxes. Taxing authorities include the state, local entities, metropolitan transportation authority (MTA), or special purpose district (SPD). When the term "sales taxes" is used it refers to any type of percentage tax assessed on a type of transaction and includes use taxes, fuel taxes, transaction taxes, and service taxes.

There are several ways to calculate sales taxes. How yours are set up will determine the effort needed to fill out your state's forms. Luckily, many states have a state-wide tax collection organization that collects and distributes all taxes to the different taxing authorities.

Sales Taxes in Peachtree

In older days when accounting was done manually, trying to keep all the sales tax amounts accounted for and distributed to the proper taxing authorities was rather involved. A tax audit was a major nightmare for many small businesses that lacked the manpower to track and pay these amounts in a timely and accurate manner. With the advent of computerized accounting, the sales tax function has been greatly simplified. Where once tax ledgers had to be manually updated and errors were rampant and where taxes could be easily sent to the wrong agency and credits were slow in returning, we now have reports and codes that can easily be transferred to the correct form. The tax audit is no longer a blow that sends us running to a tax professional but instead is dealt with quickly and easily because the information is close at hand in the computer system.

Here's an example of the differences between the old and new sales tax methods: One of my clients was audited for sales taxes the year after converting her manual accounting system to Peachtree. She had been audited almost ten years earlier and recounted the nightmare that took almost two months to complete. The time spent was the result of having to go through and verify a year's worth of sales — many of which were charged incorrect tax amounts or allocated to the wrong taxing authorities. This latest audit took less than two days because all the information could be tracked through the system from the customers' records to the sales to the payments to the taxing authorities. This is the power that Peachtree can bring to your company.

A Brief Overview of the Sales Tax Function

In order to decide the most effective method of handling your sales taxes, you should first have an understanding of how the sales tax function operates in Peachtree. The information provided here mostly reflects tax laws in Texas, although I have tried to make allowances for other states. You should be able to translate the processes to your own circumstances.

When you create a new customer, the record contains a field called Sales Tax. In this field you enter the name of a sales tax code that applies to this customer. A sales tax code includes all the information needed to calculate the different sales taxes on taxable items including what type of tax it is, such as a state, local, metropolitan transportation authority, or special district tax. The sales tax code also determines where the taxes are sent, such as the State of Texas, the City of Rowlett, or the Dallas Area Rapid Transit. A sales tax code can contain multiple types of taxes and destinations, not just one.

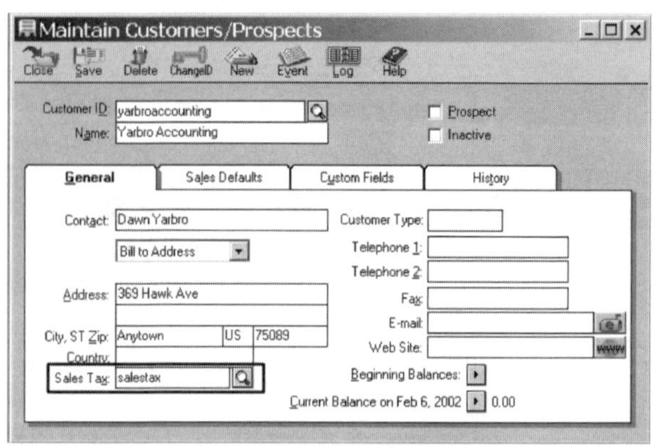

If the customer is exempt from sales taxes, such as a nonprofit organization or a customer that buys items from you for resale, you can either add the sales tax code that you have created for nontaxable organizations or leave the Sales Tax field blank.

When an invoice is input for this customer, the Sales Tax Code field on the Sales/Invoicing form is filled with the customer's sales tax information. If the customer is tax exempt, the field on the Sales/Invoicing form remains blank. Peachtree takes the total of taxable items and calculates the amounts that are due to the taxing authorities for the various types of taxes included in the sales tax code. Although not shown in this chapter, the same computations are true for the Receipts form.

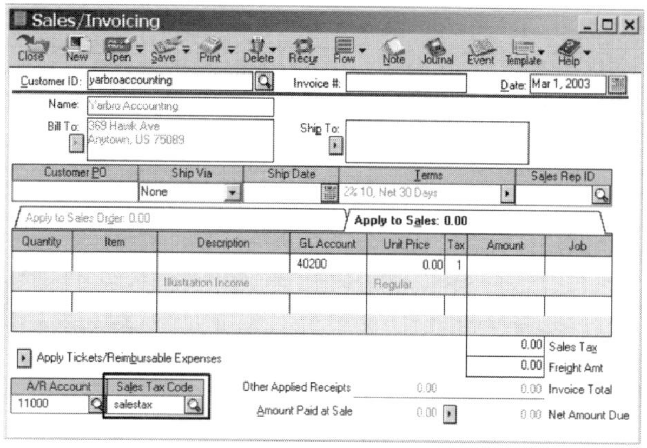

When an item record is added to inventory, regardless of its class, you catalog the item as a taxable or exempt product or service in the Item Tax Type field. Most companies only have two types of taxable items — Regular (1) or Exempt (2). If you need to distinguish between these types for reporting purposes, such as alcohol taxes, gasoline taxes, or rent taxes, you can add more tax types. Item tax types will be covered later in this chapter.

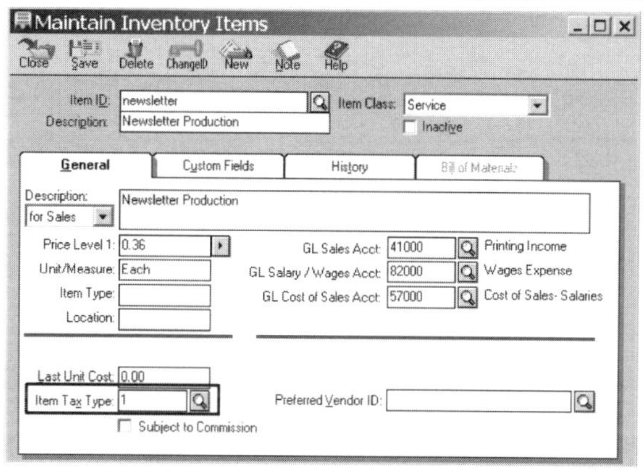

When an inventory item is entered on the Sales/Invoicing form, the tax type appears automatically in the Tax column for that line. If the item is taxable and the customer is a taxable customer, the sales taxes will be calculated using the percentages that are attached to the taxing authorities included in that sales tax code. If an item is not from inventory but is typed in manually, the tax type defaults to taxable but can be changed to exempt if needed. In this invoice, there is both a taxable and an exempt sales item.

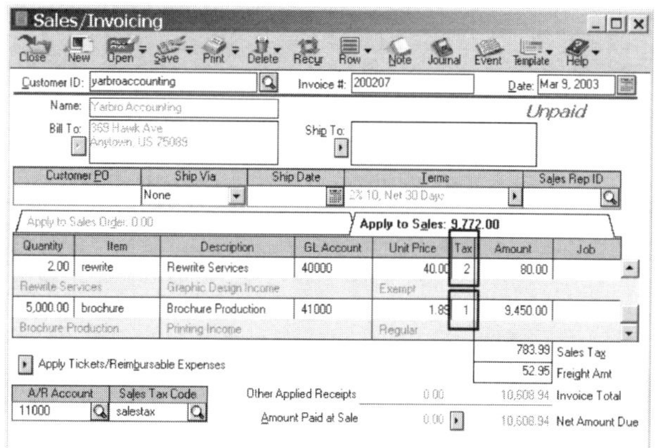

For each invoice the sales tax is added up on the invoice but is actually distributed in the Sales Journal according to the different taxing authorities.

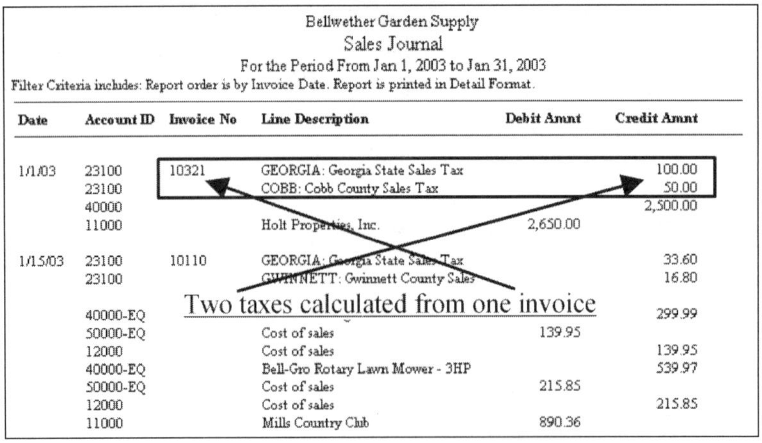

Bellwether Garden Supply
Sales Journal
For the Period From Jan 1, 2003 to Jan 31, 2003
Filter Criteria includes: Report order is by Invoice Date. Report is printed in Detail Format.

Date	Account ID	Invoice No	Line Description	Debit Amnt	Credit Amnt
1/1/03	23100	10321	GEORGIA: Georgia State Sales Tax		100.00
	23100		COBB: Cobb County Sales Tax		50.00
	40000				2,500.00
	11000		Holt Properties, Inc.	2,650.00	
1/15/03	23100	10110	GEORGIA: Georgia State Sales Tax		33.60
	23100		GWINNETT: Gwinnett County Sales		16.80
	40000-EQ				299.99
	50000-EQ		Cost of sales	139.95	
	12000		Cost of sales		139.95
	40000-EQ		Bell-Gro Rotary Lawn Mower - 3HP		539.97
	50000-EQ		Cost of sales	215.85	
	12000		Cost of sales		215.85
	11000		Mills Country Club	890.36	

All collected sales taxes are applied to a general ledger account. Usually this is a liability account and is called Sales Taxes Payable. You may have more than one sales tax liability account, but most companies do not require more than one. Different taxes can be collected and paid from the same liability account.

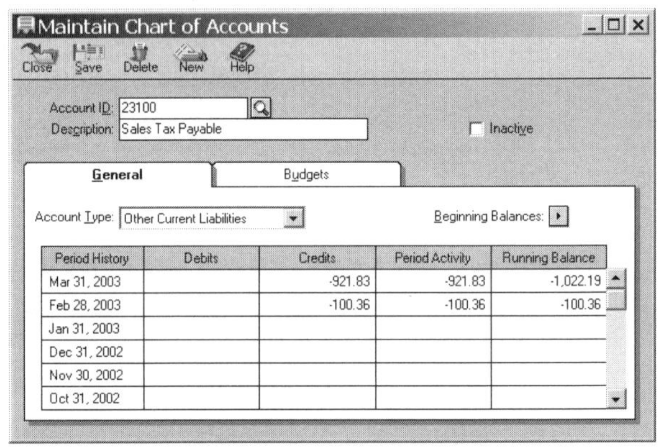

At the end of the tax collection period, which could be monthly, quarterly, or annually, all collected sales taxes are paid to the proper taxing authority.

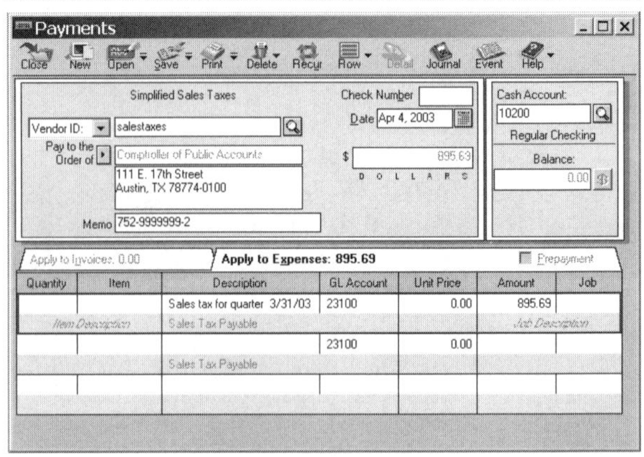

Setting Up Sales Taxes

The procedures for setting up sales taxes can get quite complex and there are a lot of decisions to make along the way. I will try to cover some possible circumstances well enough that you can make the decisions for your company correctly the first time so you do not have to go back and change records at a later date.

Sales taxes are amounts that are calculated by companies as a percentage of a sales transaction that are then remitted to an organization. The taxes are levied by government agencies for the public's benefit and the rates are set by the agencies and ratified by voters. These taxes can be used to support states, counties, cities, and areas needing mass transit systems, school systems, or community hospitals. Not all states and communities are subject to the same types of taxes. Sales taxes, like all taxes, can be very complicated in what is taxable and at what rate, and what is tax exempt. For information on what types of products and services are taxable, how or when the taxes are paid, and what kinds of taxes must be paid, you will need to contact your taxing authority. Only the most generic circumstances are covered in this chapter.

The Sales Tax Liability Account

If you must charge sales tax to your customers, you must create a sales taxes liability account in Peachtree before you can enter invoices or customers. If you used one of Peachtree's charts of accounts, the general ledger account is already included. The G/L Account ID is 23100, as seen in this partial COA.

Simplified Sales Taxes
Chart of Accounts
As of Mar 31, 2003
Filter Criteria includes: Report order is by ID. Report is printed with Accounts having Zero Amounts and in Detail Format.

Account ID	Account Description	Active	Account Type
19200	Notes Receivable- Noncurrent	Yes	Other Assets
19900	Other Noncurrent Assets	Yes	Other Assets
20000	Accounts Payable	Yes	Accounts Payable
21000	My Credit Card Liability	Yes	Accounts Payable
23000	Accrued Expenses	Yes	Other Current Liabilities
23100	Sales Tax Payable	Yes	Other Current Liabilities
23200	Wages Payable	Yes	Other Current Liabilities
23300	401 K Deductions Payable	Yes	Other Current Liabilities
23400	Federal Payroll Taxes Payable	Yes	Other Current Liabilities
23500	FUTA Tax Payable	Yes	Other Current Liabilities
23600	State Payroll Taxes Payable	Yes	Other Current Liabilities
23700	SUTA Tax Payable	Yes	Other Current Liabilities
23800	Local Payroll Taxes Payable	Yes	Other Current Liabilities
23900	Income Taxes Payable	Yes	Other Current Liabilities
24000	Other Taxes Payable	Yes	Other Current Liabilities

If you have created your company from scratch or are using an existing COA, you will need to add the G/L account yourself. Generally, a sales tax account is considered part of the Other Current Liabilities, although your CPA may wish to classify it as an Accounts Payable type.

Most companies only need one sales tax liability account because they pay all their sales taxes at the same time to one tax collection organization. If you pay to several different tax collection organizations, such as different states, or you pay your taxes at different times, such as state taxes monthly and local taxes quarterly, you may decide to use more than one sales tax liability account. Another instance in which more than one account might be necessary is if your industry, such as oil and gas, has an abundance of federal, state, and locally regulated taxes.

The Sales Tax Vendor

Once you have established your sales tax liability account, you need to create vendor records for your tax collection organizations. If all of your taxes are paid to a state organization, such as the Texas State Comptroller of Public Accounts, only one vendor record is required.

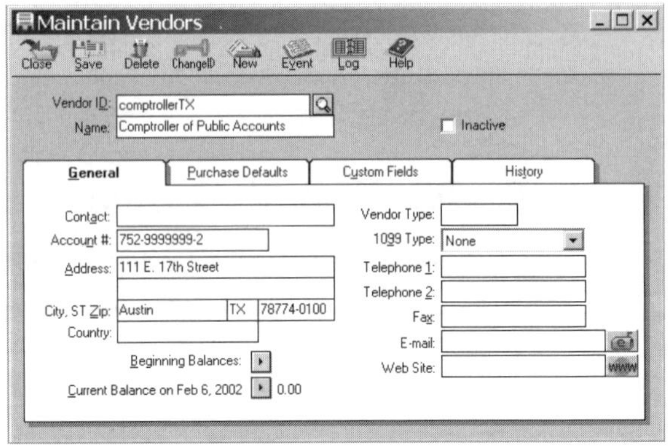

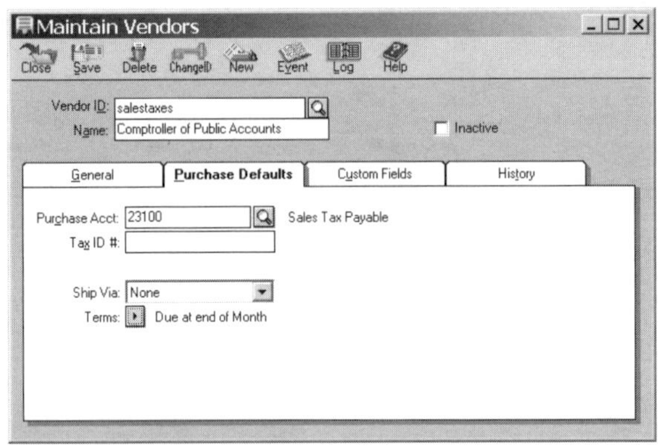

1. Open the Maintain Vendors form.
2. In the Vendor ID field, enter an ID that you will easily remember. If you only have one tax authority, it can even be something as simple as **salestax.** Fill in the Name and Address fields as needed. The Account # field is your taxpayer number. Enter other information as needed.
3. Select the **Purchase Defaults** tab.
4. In the Purchase Acct field select the sales tax liability account from the drop-down. You can ignore the Tax ID # and Ship Via fields. The Terms field can be set as needed, although if you pay quarterly or annually there is no selection for those. Also, some states use discounts to encourage prompt payment of taxes. Do not use the Terms discount fields to calculate your discount. Tax discounts are covered later in this chapter.
5. Click **Save** to save the record. Add more records if needed.

Sales Tax Authorities

A sales tax authority represents an organization that collects taxes on the sales of goods and services as part or all of its budget and then uses those taxes for the benefit of a community. Most taxing authorities are based upon your location and the type of community services that you receive, such as transportation and hospital services. Even if you only pay one sales tax vendor (tax collection organization), your tax bill may reflect a combination of several tax authorities, such as state, local, and transportation tax districts, or your tax authority may represent just a single entity.

Sales taxes can be set up in several ways. Examples of some different types of tax authorities and different ways to set them up are shown in the next several sections.

Multiple Locations, Multiple Tax Authorities

Even though this is the most complicated method of setting up tax authorities, we will start with this one because it is the one demonstrated in Peachtree's sample companies. Texas has several main types of sales taxes in the Dallas area, including the suburban cities of Rowlett and Mesquite. These include the state sales tax of 6.25%, the 1% city tax that both cities charge, and the 1% MTA tax for Dallas and Rowlett for DART. The downtown Dallas area has an additional tourist tax of 3% for hotels, meals, and car rentals. If you had stores in two locations, such as Rowlett and Mesquite, Texas, you would need to set up several tax authorities to distinguish between the sales taxes for each location.

1. Open the Maintain Sales Tax Authorities window by clicking the **Sales Tax Authorities** icon in the **Receivables** or **Sales** folder.

   Or select **Maintain**, **Sales Taxes**, **Sales Tax Authorities** from the menu bar.

   Or press **Alt+M**, **X**, **A** using the keyboard.

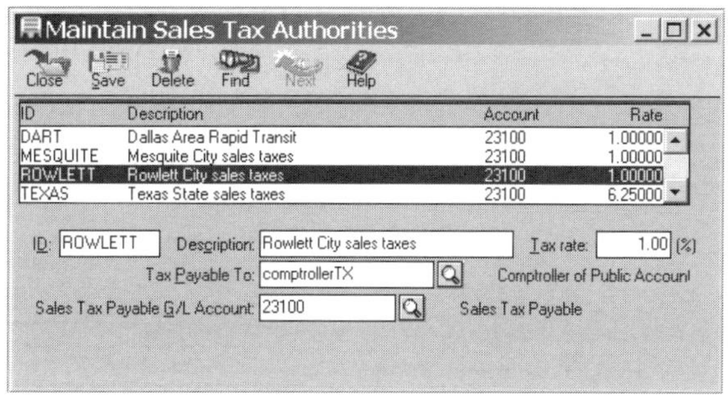

2. Enter a sales tax authority ID in the ID field. Use something simple to describe the type or location of the tax, like **ROWLETT**.
3. Enter a description for this authority, such as **Rowlett City sales taxes**.
4. Enter the tax rate as a percentage. If the taxing authority's rate is 6¼% or, if you multiply your taxable sales by .0625 to determine your sales tax, enter **6.25**.
5. Click the **Lookup** button in the Tax Payable To field and select the sales tax vendor from the drop-down.
6. Select the general ledger account for the Sales Tax Payable G/L Account field.
7. Click **Save** to record the sales tax authority.
8. Sales tax authorities are used to create a sales tax code, which is described in the next section. The sales tax code for the Rowlett store will include the ROWLETT, DART, and TEXAS sales tax authorities. The sales tax code for the Mesquite office will include the MESQUITE and TEXAS sales tax authorities. Mesquite does not use the area's bus service and, therefore, does not collect or pay transportation taxes.

   When you create an invoice for a sale from the Rowlett store, you will select the correct sales tax code to be applied to the invoice, and the invoice will determine the amounts to be collected for the different sales tax authorities, as you can see in the Sales Journal for invoice number 200207.

Simplified Sales Taxes
Sales Journal
For the Period From Mar 1, 2003 to Mar 31, 2003
Filter Criteria includes: 1) Customer IDs from yarbroaccounting to yarbroaccounting. Report order is by Invoice Date. Report is printed in Detail Format.

Date	Account ID	Invoice No	Line Description	Debit Amnt	Credit Amnt
3/9/03	23100	200207	ROWLETT: Rowlett City sales taxes		94.50
	23100		DART: Dallas Area Rapid Transit		94.50
	23100		TEXAS: Texas State sales taxes		590.63
	40000		Grahic Design Services		192.00
	40800		Photographic Services with proofs		50.00
	40000		Rewrite Services		80.00
	41000		Brochure Production		9,450.00
	45500		Freight Amount		52.95
	11000		Yarbro Accounting	10,604.58	
		Total	Total Taxes = 779.63	10,604.58	10,604.58

When you go to fill out your sales tax forms it is easy to determine the amounts that should be allocated to each taxing authority. The amounts for Rowlett, DART, and Texas are shown separately.

If the invoice is out of the Mesquite office, the MESQUITE sales tax code is applied and a different amount of tax is collected.

Simplified Sales Taxes
Sales Journal
For the Period From Mar 1, 2003 to Mar 31, 2003
Filter Criteria includes: 1) Invoice Numbers from 200211 to 200211; 2) Customer IDs from to . Report order is by Invoice Date. Report is printed in Detail Format.

Date	Account ID	Invoice No	Line Description	Debit Amnt	Credit Amnt
3/28/03	23100	200211	MESQUITE: Mesquite City sales taxes		94.50
	23100		TEXAS: Texas State sales taxes		590.63
	40000		Grahic Design Services		192.00
	40800		Photographic Services with proofs		50.00
	40000		Rewrite Services		80.00
	41000		Brochure Production		9,450.00
	45500		Freight Amount		52.95
	11000		Yarbro Accounting	10,510.08	
		Total	Total Taxes = 685.13	10,510.08	10,510.08

In addition to your normal tax authorities, I suggest that you create an additional one called NONTAX. This tax authority should be used for customers who are nontaxable such as nonprofit organizations. The tax rate will be 0.00. If you have a tax authority like this it will make your tax period processing easier as will be shown at the end of the chapter.

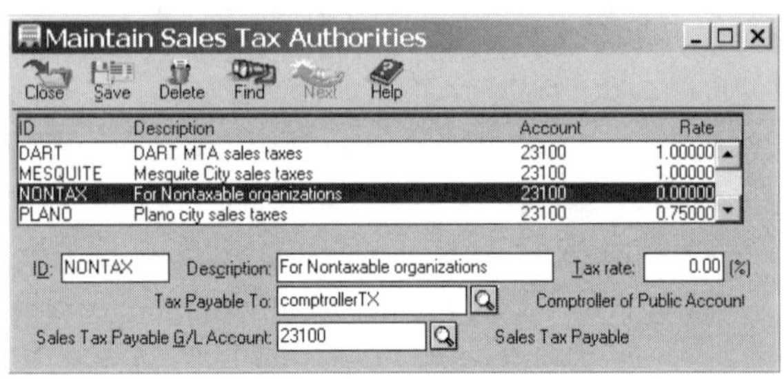

Multiple Locations, Single Tax Authorities

Another way to handle tax authorities is to combine the taxes for each location into a single record with the total percentage. If you use this method, you will have to calculate the separate taxing authorities' amounts from the total taxes for each sales tax authority in Peachtree. This is similar to the method described in Chapter 5, but names each taxing authority by the location. This method should only be used if you can easily determine the different taxing authorities' percentages when it is time to report the taxes.

1. Open the Maintain Sales Tax Authorities window.
2. Enter a sales tax authority ID in the ID field, using something simple to describe the tax by location, like **ROWLETT** or **ROWLETTTX**.
3. Enter a description for this authority, such as **Rowlett, TX sales taxes**.
4. Enter the tax rate as a total percentage for the location. Include the state sales tax of 6.25%, the city taxes of 1% that both cities charge, and the 1% MTA tax for DART for the Rowlett store.

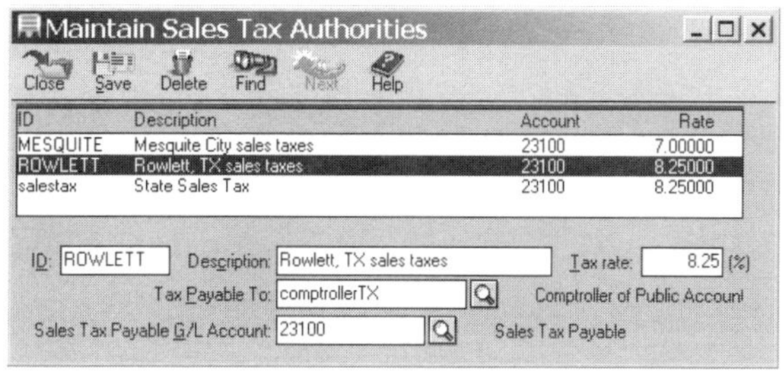

5. Fill in the Tax Payable To field and the Sales Tax Payable G/L Account field. Click **Save** to record the sales tax authority. You will also want to include a NONTAX tax authority as was mentioned earlier.

When you create an invoice you choose the sales tax based on the location, but rather than showing multiple lines on the report only one line is shown.

Simplified Sales Taxes
Sales Journal
For the Period From Mar 1, 2003 to Mar 31, 2003
Filter Criteria includes: 1) Customer IDs from yarbroaccounting to yarbroaccounting. Report order is by Invoice Date. Report is printed in Detail Format.

Date	Account ID	Invoice No	Line Description	Debit Amnt	Credit Amnt
3/9/03	23100	200207	ROWLETT: Rowlett, TX sales taxes		779.63
	40000		Grahic Design Services		192.00
	40800		Photographic Services with proofs		50.00
	40000		Rewrite Services		80.00
	41000		Brochure Production		9,450.00
	45500		Freight Amount		52.95
	11000		Yarbro Accounting	10,604.58	
		Total		10,604.58	10,604.58

Notice here that there is only one line for the total amount of taxes shown on the earlier report. If the same invoice had taxes paid for Mesquite and not Rowlett, the sales tax amount would show the total tax amount as $685.13.

At the end of the tax period, you can determine the amounts for the separate tax authorities very easily. In the case of the Rowlett office, take the total taxes of $779.63. Divide the total taxes by the total sales tax rate of 8.25, which gives you the 1% tax amount, in this case $94.50. (It actually comes out to 94.5006061, but we will round.) Multiply this amount by the tax rate for each taxing authority — 1% for ROWLETT, 1% for DART, and 6.25% for TEXAS — for taxing authority amounts of $94.50, $94.50, and $590.63. You can check the amounts by adding them back together to get the original total of $779.63.

Sales Tax Calculation

	Example	Worksheet
Type the total of the taxes for the location.	779.63	
Type the total sales tax rate	8.25	
This is the 1% rate	94.50	#DIV/0!
Type the 1st Tax Authority Rate	1.00	
This is the total taxes due for the 1st Tax Authority	**94.50**	**#DIV/0!**
Type the 2nd Tax Authority Rate	1.00	
This is the total taxes due for the 2nd Tax Authority	**94.50**	**#DIV/0!**
Type the 3rd Tax Authority Rate	6.25	
This is the total taxes due for the 3rd Tax Authority	**590.63**	**#DIV/0!**
Type the 4th Tax Authority Rate	-	
This is the total taxes due for the 4th Tax Authority	-	**#DIV/0!**
Type the 5th Tax Authority Rate	-	
This is the total taxes due for the 5th Tax Authority	-	**#DIV/0!**
Check calculations - TOTAL TAXES FOR THE LOCATION	779.63	#DIV/0!

Note: I have included the worksheet in the companion files with the calculations to use this method. It includes a sample calculation using the numbers in the above example. The #DIV/0! errors show because numbers have not yet been entered into the Worksheet column.

Single Location

If you only have one location, you can use the method described above and have only one simplified tax authority, or you can add all the tax authorities for your location. The sales tax authority can be named for each of your locations or can be named something simple like salestax for a single tax authority.

Sales Tax Codes

When I explained the sales tax authorities previously, I briefly described the sales tax code. The tax codes are covered more thoroughly in this section. A sales tax authority is based upon a type of tax such as state, city, or MTA. A sales tax code is the combination of sales tax authorities that are required to be paid on any sale. Each taxable customer has a sales tax code applied to their invoices that is entered on their record. If they have more than one location, each location can have its own tax code. If the customer purchases items from you at one of your locations other than the one he normally purchases from, the sales tax code can be changed on the Sales/Invoicing form.

To create sales tax codes and assign taxing authorities to them, follow these instructions:

1. Click the **Receivables** or **Sales** folder in the navigation aid to open it and then click the **Sales Tax Codes** icon.

2. The Maintain Sales Tax Codes screen appears.

   In the Sales Tax Code field, enter the ID for this code for the current location such as **SalesTax**, **ROWLETT**, or **DALLASCO**. You are limited to eight digits.

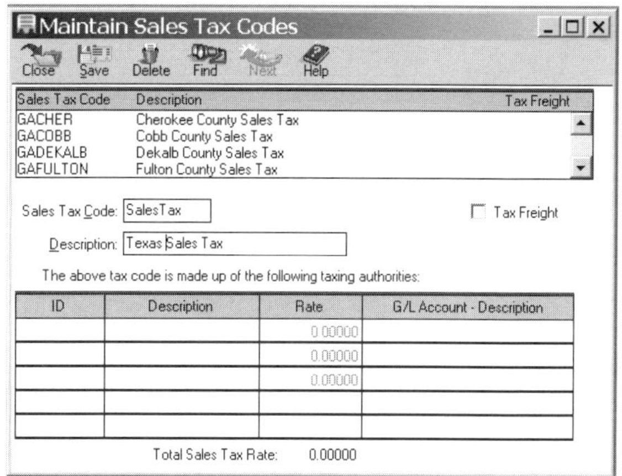

3. Enter a description, such as **Sales Tax**, **Rowlett City Sales**, or **8.25% Taxes** in the Description field.
4. If freight is taxed at this location, check the **Tax Freight** check box. If you have both taxed and untaxed freight, check the Tax Freight box only if most of your freight is taxed. We will discuss having both taxed and untaxed freight in Chapter 17.
5. Right-click the mouse when the lookup keys are showing in the first ID field for the section that begins The above tax code.
6. Select a Sales Tax Authority ID to be included in this tax code. It will appear on the line and will also show the Description, Rate, and G/L Account Description.
7. Tab to the next line and add any additional tax authorities needed. The Total Sales Tax Rate for this tax code can be seen at the bottom of the form.

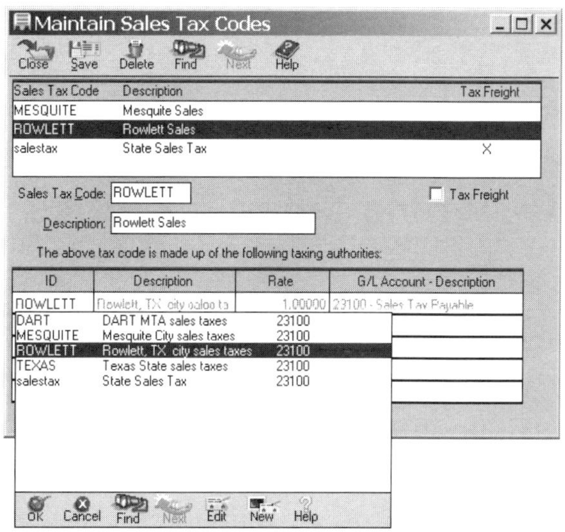

Month 2

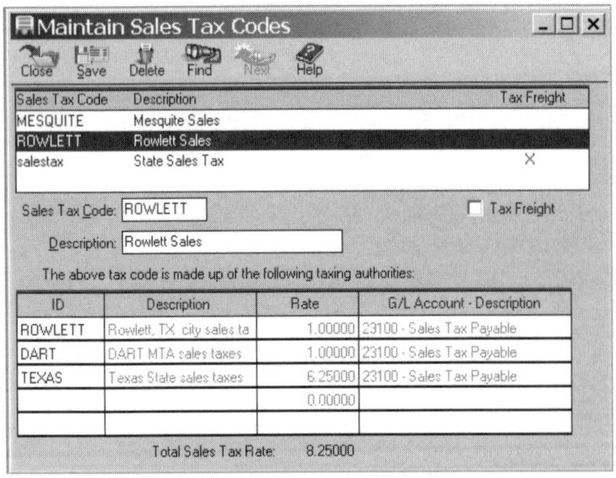

8. Click **Save** to finish creating the sales tax code. Add other sales tax codes as needed.

As with the tax authorities, you will also want to have a tax code named NONTAX. It will be added the same way as other tax codes; just include the NONTAX tax authority in the appropriate line.

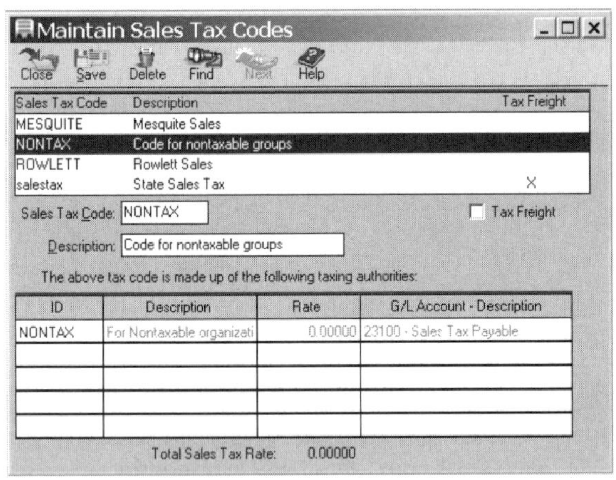

Assigning Sales Tax Rates to Customers

Now that your sales tax codes are entered, you can apply the codes to customer records as follows.

1. Open the Maintain Customers screen and select a customer record.

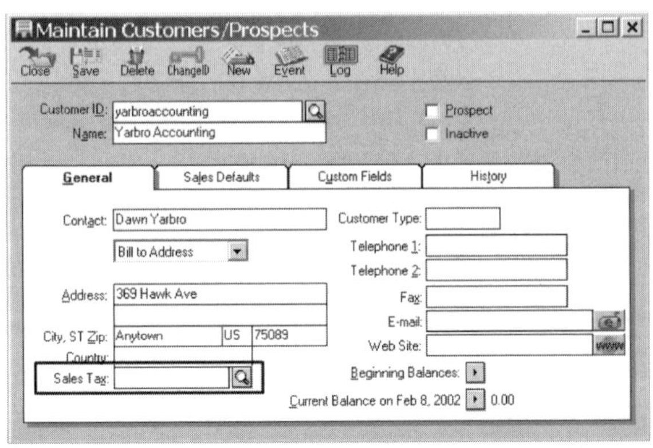

2. Click the **Lookup** button on the Sales Tax field to show the list of sales tax codes.

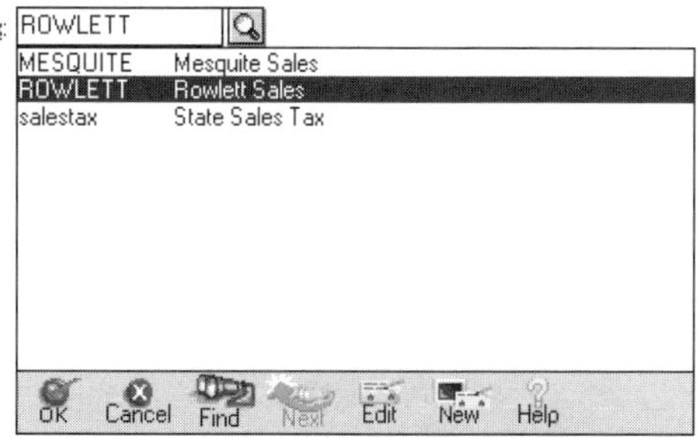

3. Select a tax code from the list and click **OK**. If the customer is a nontaxable organization, you will want to select the appropriate tax code for them also. Click **Save** to record the information.
4. Verify that the selected tax code is the correct one for this customer. This can be a good time to make sure that you have the required documentation in your records for the tax status and tax ID numbers.
5. When you create an invoice for this customer, the Sales Tax Code field will be automatically populated with the correct tax code.

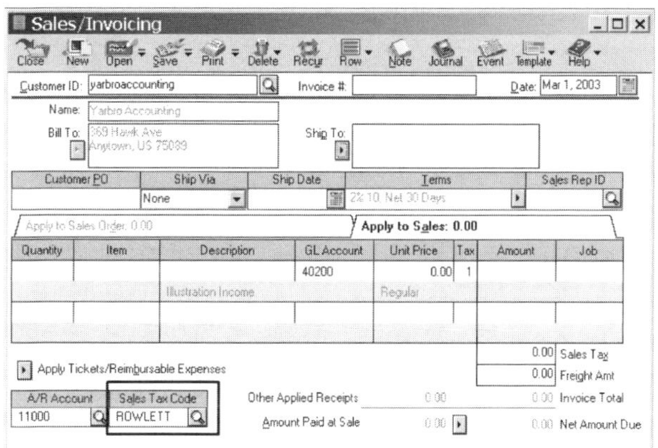

Customers with Multiple Rates

If your company has multiple locations with different tax codes and your customer purchases from different offices, you will need to apply more than one tax code to the customer. This method also works if you need to apply different tax codes to customers' invoices because the product or service performed is in a location that requires you to use a different tax rate, such as out of state. There are two ways to do this. The first method applies the different tax code to the customer record.

1. Open the customer record and select the **Lookup** button on the Bill To Address field.

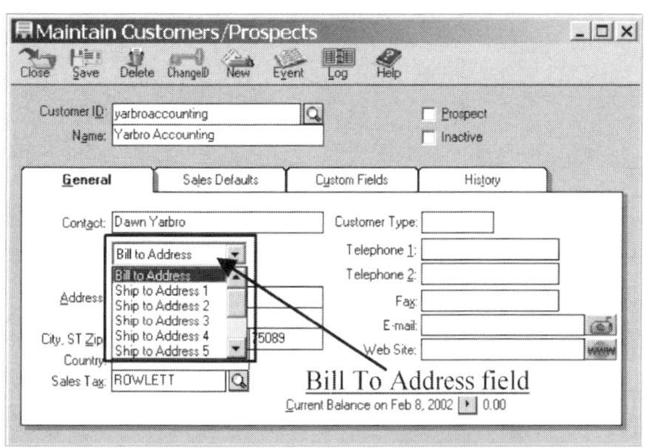

Month 2

2. Select **Ship To Address 1** in the list.
3. In the Ship Name field, enter a description like **Purchases from Mesquite Office** or **Shipments to Minnesota**. Enter the associated shipping address in the appropriate fields.
4. In the Sales Tax field, select the tax code for purchases from this location.
5. Click **Save** to record the information.
6. When it is time to create a new invoice you have to be a little observant at data entry because the Ship To Address 1 information automatically appears in the Ship To field, along with the associated Sales Tax Code.

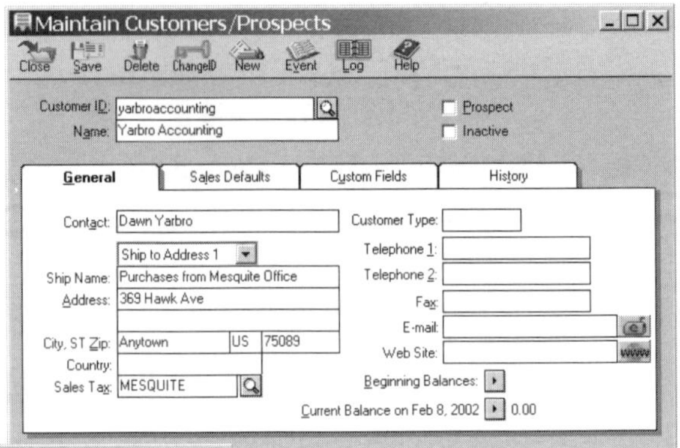

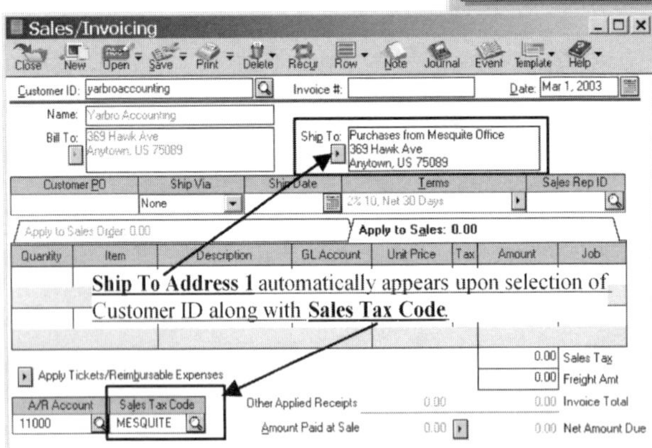

7. If you need to use the Sales Tax Code for the billing address, you must click the **Ship To** button and select the **Bill To Address** from the list.

   The appropriate Sales Tax Code will automatically appear.

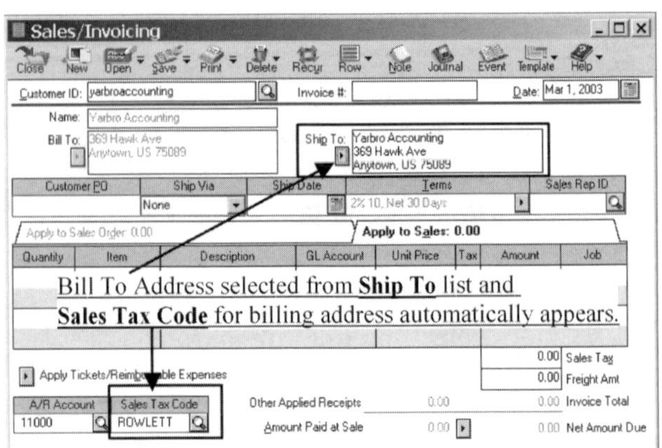

Tip: If your customer usually buys from one location and only occasionally buys from another, you can use the Ship To Address 1 for the most-used tax code and add ship to addresses (up to nine) for the other locations. When the invoice is created the most-used tax code will appear with the first ship to information.

The second method of applying different tax rates to the same customer is to manually change the Sales Tax Code field on the Sales/Invoicing form when you create an invoice for the customer. This will apply the correct sales tax rate to all taxable items on the invoice. You must be careful that you are applying the correct rate on each invoice because errors will be time-consuming.

Note: Unfortunately, only one sales tax rate can be applied to an invoice. If you need to apply different rates, you must create separate invoices for the items with the different rates.

Tax Types

Now that we have covered sales tax codes we need to discuss taxable and nontaxable items. Whether an item is taxed on an invoice is controlled by the tax type. If the customer is taxable and an item is tax exempt, the customer will not be charged sales tax for that item. If a customer is nontaxable and an item is taxable, the customer will still not be taxed on the taxable item because of their status. Tax types control whether tax is calculated on an item and tax codes control whether the taxable item is actually taxed for the customer on their invoices. Tax types are set up as a company default.

1. Select the **Company** folder and the **Setup Checklist** icon from the navigation aid. Click on **Inventory Defaults** in the Setup Checklist.

   Or select **Maintain**, **Default Information**, **Inventory Items** from the menu bar.

   Or using the keyboard, press **Alt+M**, then **D**, then **I**.

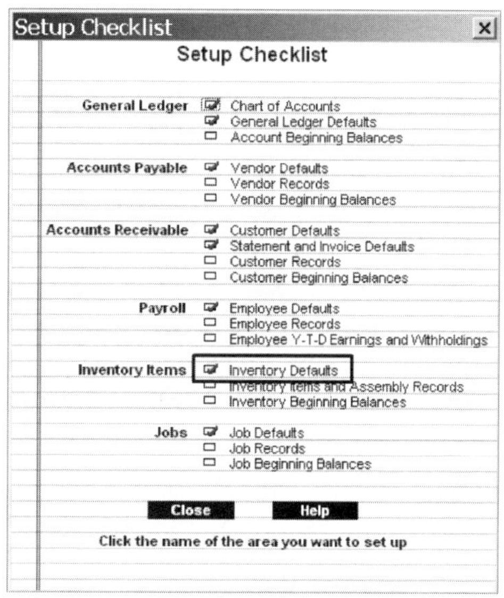

2. The Inventory Item Defaults window appears. Click the **Taxes/Shipping** tab.

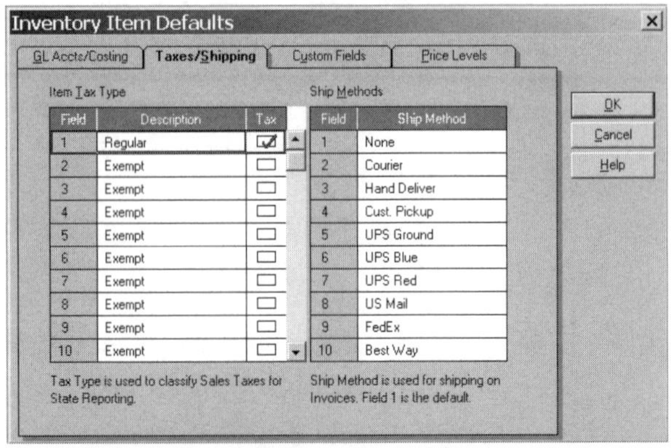

3. Most companies will use the standard Peachtree defaults shown in the Item Tax Type section. The Field column has a number in it. On the Field 1 line the Description is Regular and the Tax column is checked. This means that any item with a tax type of 1 will be charged sales tax at the rate shown by the customer's sales tax code. As you can see in this example, any line item without an inventory item listed in the Item column defaults to a tax type of 1 in the Tax field and the customer is charged sales tax.

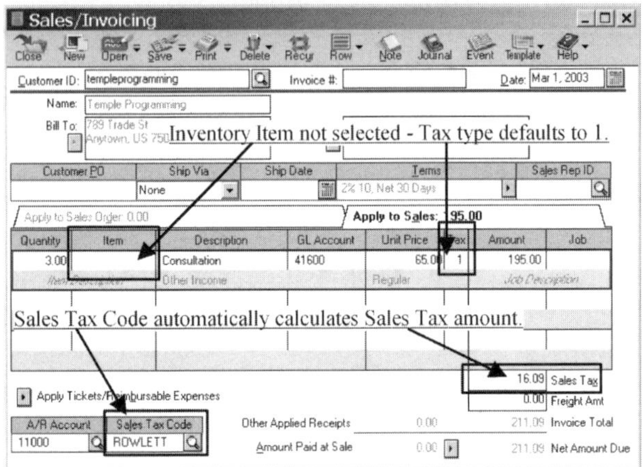

4. The Field 2 line has a description of Exempt and the Tax column is unchecked. This means that any item with a tax type of 2 is not taxed.

Tip: If most of your sales are not taxable, you can make the Field 1 line the Exempt line and the Field 2 line the Regular taxable line. Be sure to verify that the Tax column is checked or unchecked correctly.

5. If you have more than one type of sales tax that you pay, you can add them to the list. For example, if you were required to charge regular sales tax on most items, but needed to separate liquor sales, you could add an Alcohol tax type.

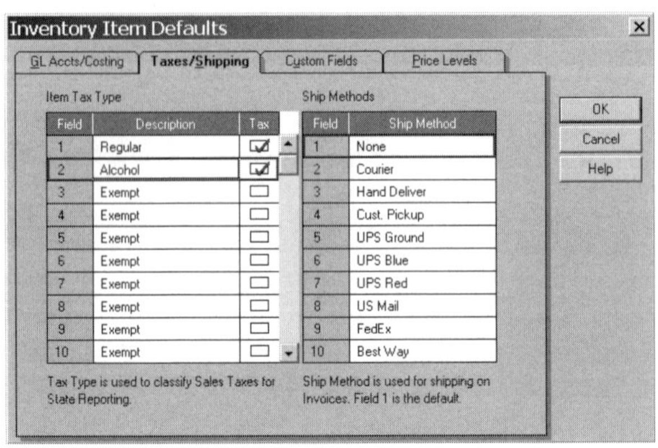

The one downside to this method is that you cannot use more than one tax type, except for Exempt, on an invoice — unless both types are taxed at the same rate. This means that a customer who buys something like souvenirs (tax type 1 — Regular) at a shop and also buys a bottle of wine (tax type 2 — Alcohol), must have their purchases entered on different invoices or receipts rather than just one.

Adding Tax Types to Inventory

Once you have your tax types set up, you need to set up your inventory items with them.

1. Open the Maintain Inventory Items form by clicking the **Inventory Items** icon in the **Inventory** folder on the navigation aid.

   Or select **Maintain**, **Inventory Items** from the menu bar.

   Or press **Alt+M**, **I** on the keyboard.

2. When entering an item in inventory, select the **Item Tax Type** from the list by clicking the **Lookup** button.

3. Click **Save** to record the tax type.

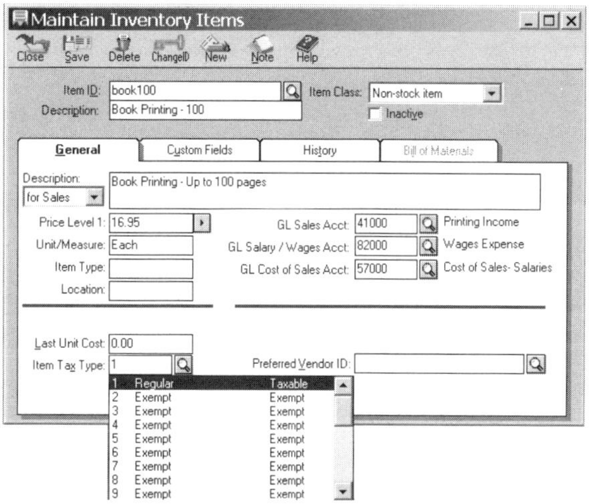

4. When an invoice is created and an inventory item is chosen in the Item field, the Tax field will show the associated tax type.

   Sales tax is then calculated on the taxable items according to the tax rate shown in the Sales Tax Code field.

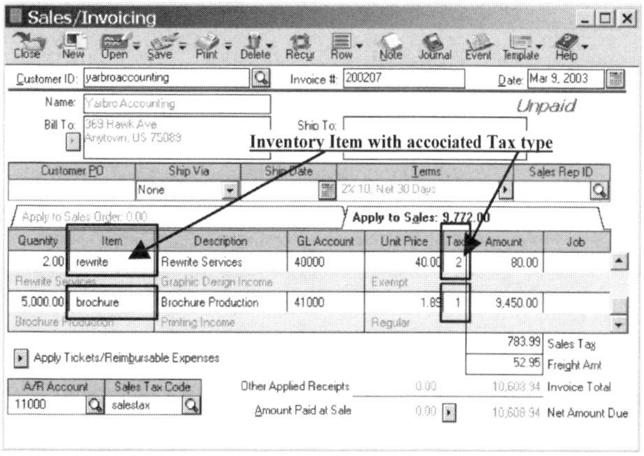

Reporting and Paying Sales Taxes

Now that you have an understanding of how sales taxes are calculated, you need to learn how to calculate the different amounts that go to the different tax collection agencies. We also want to set up the taxes to reflect any previous activity that needs to be reported on your next tax report.

Warning!! You are remembering that you need to keep entering all data in your old accounting system, aren't you? You must keep the old system up to date until the end of the Three-Month Plan. The continued operation of running systems in parallel is critical to guarantee the success of your Peachtree conversion.

Sales Tax Beginning Balances

The sales tax beginning balance is very easy to set up regardless of your tax accounting period. A tax accounting period is the length of time over which taxes are collected, reported, and then paid. This length of time may be a month, a quarter, or a year. The balances of the tax liability general ledger account in the beginning trial balance will enable you to track the sales taxes for your tax accounting period and the amount needs to be included in your trial balance.

To record the beginning balance sales tax liability, follow these steps:

1. If you have more than one taxing authority, you will need to calculate how much sales tax is allocated between each of the taxing authorities. This could be a spreadsheet calculation that you keep in a file or it could be information from your previous accounting system.
2. Open the Maintain Chart of Accounts form and click the **Beginning Balance** button. Select the month prior to your Begin Transactions date in the Select Period dialog box and click **OK**. The Chart of Accounts Prior Year Adjustments screen appears.

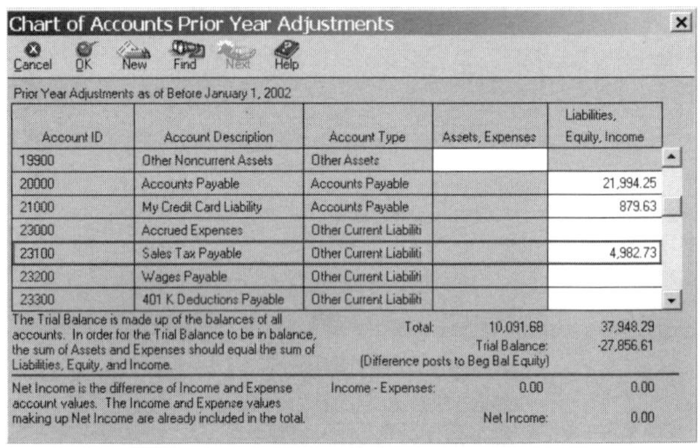

3. Go down the list to the **Sales Tax Payable** line. In the Liabilities, Equity, Income column enter the total amount of taxes that were due as shown on your trial balance. If you had a credit, the amount should be entered as a negative number.

   As I said earlier, there is no good way to track the individual balances for each of your taxing authorities.
4. Go down to the **Retained Earnings** line and subtract the amount paid from the number there so that the Trial Balance at the bottom is equal to 0.00.

Tip: A quick way to determine the Retained Earnings amount is to delete the previous line and press **Tab** or **Enter**. Then take the amount that now appears for the Trial Balance and enter it on the Retained Earnings line.

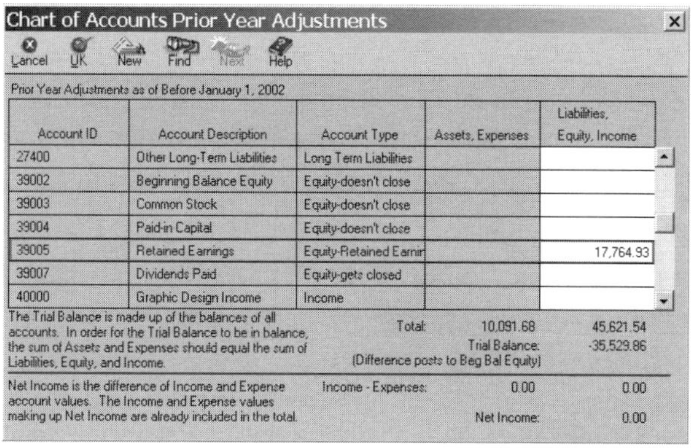

Account ID	Account Description	Account Type	Assets, Expenses	Liabilities, Equity, Income
27400	Other Long-Term Liabilities	Long Term Liabilities		
39002	Beginning Balance Equity	Equity-doesn't close		
39003	Common Stock	Equity-doesn't close		
39004	Paid-in Capital	Equity-doesn't close		
39005	Retained Earnings	Equity-Retained Earnir		17,764.93
39007	Dividends Paid	Equity-gets closed		
40000	Graphic Design Income	Income		

5. If you have paid sales taxes since your Begin Transactions date, the checks will appear in your Cash Disbursements report and should have been allocated to the Sales Tax Payable general ledger account. The check will reduce the amount owed that you show in the beginning balances so that the amount in the G/L account now reflects the amount currently owed.

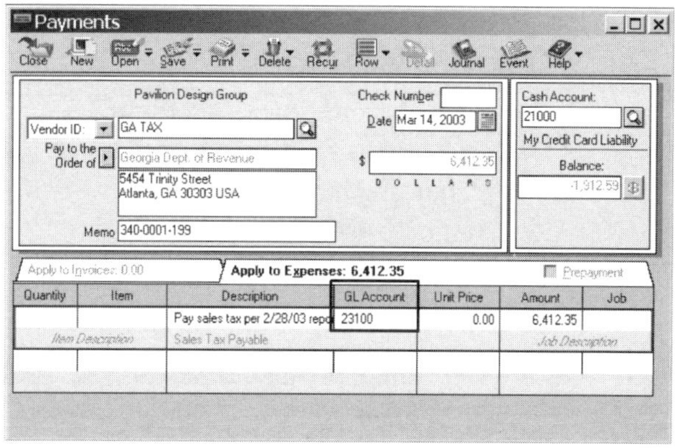

The next time you pay your taxes, you will need to divide the taxes among the different tax authorities using the single tax authority method and the accompanying worksheet included with the companion files as we discussed earlier in this chapter. If you have more than one location, separate the amounts due for each sales tax code and create a separate worksheet for each location.

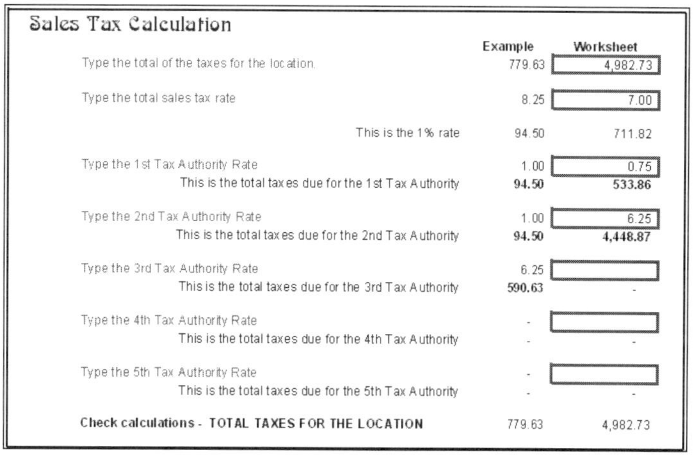

	Example	Worksheet
Type the total of the taxes for the location.	779.63	4,982.73
Type the total sales tax rate	8.25	7.00
This is the 1% rate	94.50	711.82
Type the 1st Tax Authority Rate	1.00	0.75
This is the total taxes due for the 1st Tax Authority	**94.50**	**533.86**
Type the 2nd Tax Authority Rate	1.00	6.25
This is the total taxes due for the 2nd Tax Authority	**94.50**	**4,448.87**
Type the 3rd Tax Authority Rate	6.25	
This is the total taxes due for the 3rd Tax Authority	**590.63**	-
Type the 4th Tax Authority Rate	-	
This is the total taxes due for the 4th Tax Authority	-	-
Type the 5th Tax Authority Rate	-	
This is the total taxes due for the 5th Tax Authority	-	-
Check calculations - TOTAL TAXES FOR THE LOCATION	779.63	4,982.73

The total of all locations should match the sales total for the company, after you add in sales to nontaxable organizations. Determining sales to nontaxable organizations is discussed in the next section.

The Sales Tax Report

At the end of the tax period you need to determine certain numbers for your sales tax report. Most states have you list your gross sales, your tax exempt sales, and your net taxable sales. These can be determined from the Taxable/Exempt Sales report.

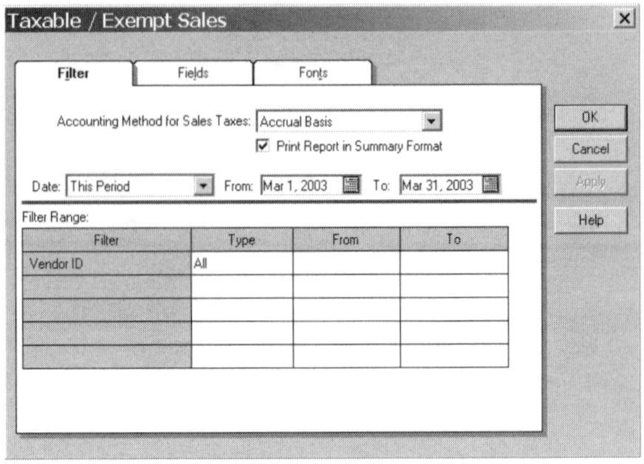

1. From the Select a Report screen, select **Accounts Receivable** in the Report Area and **Taxable/Exempt Sales** in the Report List. Click the **Preview** button. The Taxable/Exempt Sales filter appears.
2. In the Accounting Method for Sales Taxes field, select the accounting method that your company uses, either **Accrual Basis** or **Cash Basis**.
3. Check the **Print Report in Summary Format** check box.
4. The Date field should probably be set to **Range** and the From and To fields should encompass your tax accounting period.
5. Click on the **Fields** tab and check the **Show** column for the Taxable Type line.

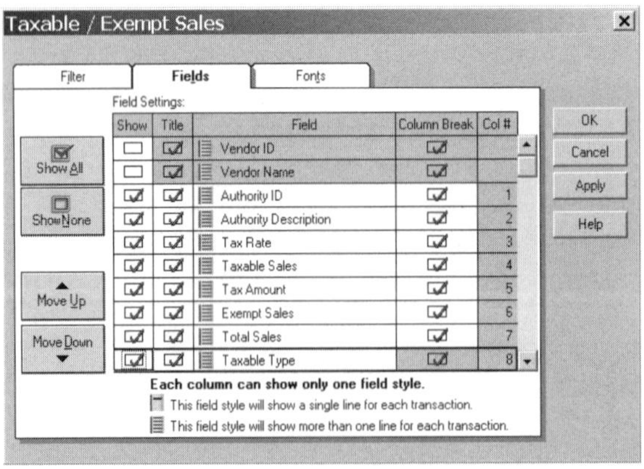

6. Click **OK** to view the report.

Simplified Sales Taxes
Taxable / Exempt Sales
For the Period From Mar 1, 2003 to Mar 31, 2003
Filter Criteria includes: Report is printed in Summary Format.

Authority ID	Authority Description	Tax Rate	Taxable Sale	Tax Amount	Exempt Sales	Total Sales	Taxable Type
DART	DART MTA sales taxes	1.00	20,548.35	205.49		20,548.35	Total for Regular
DART	DART MTA sales taxes				894.00	894.00	Total for Exempt
DART	DART MTA sales taxes				105.90	105.90	Total for Exempt
DART	Total DART MTA sales taxes		20,548.35	205.49	999.90	21,548.25	
MESQUITE	Mesquite City sales taxes	1.00	260.00	2.60		260.00	Total for Regular
MESQUITE	Mesquite City sales taxes				2,400.00	2,400.00	Total for Exempt
MESQUITE	Total Mesquite City sales taxes		260.00	2.60	2,400.00	2,660.00	
NONTAX	For Nontaxable organizations		131.40			131.40	Total for Regular
NONTAX	For Nontaxable organizations				150.00	150.00	Total for Exempt
NONTAX	Total For Nontaxable organizatio		131.40		150.00	281.40	
ROWLETT	Rowlett, TX city sales taxes	1.00	20,548.35	205.49		20,548.35	Total for Regular
ROWLETT	Rowlett, TX city sales taxes				894.00	894.00	Total for Exempt
ROWLETT	Rowlett, TX city sales taxes				105.90	105.90	Total for Exempt
ROWLETT	Total Rowlett, TX city sales tax		20,548.35	205.49	999.90	21,548.25	
TEXAS	Texas State sales taxes	6.25	20,808.35	1,300.53		20,808.35	Total for Regular
TEXAS	Texas State sales taxes				3,294.00	3,294.00	Total for Exempt
TEXAS	Texas State sales taxes				105.90	105.90	Total for Exempt
TEXAS	Total Texas State sales taxes		20,808.35	1,300.53	3,399.90	24,208.25	

It is important to remember that this report is divided into sales tax authorities — not sales tax codes. For each sales tax authority on the report there is a total for each tax type, such as regular and exempt. You will notice that some of the authorities have two lines for exempt on the report. That is because the second exempt line is for non-taxable freight.

This report does not have any other totals except for those shown for each tax authority. There is no total regular sales or total exempt line. Each taxable and exempt line can include sales for other lines because the same sales item can include more than one tax authority. If you look at the report in detail format and include the Reference field you can see where the same invoice is included in two different taxing authorities.

Authority ID	Authority Description	Tax Rate	Taxable Sale	Tax Amount	Exempt Sales	Reference	Total Sales	Taxable Type
ROWLETT	Rowlett, TX city sales taxes	1.00	9,450.00	94.50		200207	9,450.00	Regular
ROWLETT	Rowlett, TX city sales taxes	1.00	1,410.75	14.11		200208	1,410.75	Regular
ROWLETT	Rowlett, TX city sales taxes	1.00	237.60	2.38		200212	237.60	Regular
ROWLETT	Rowlett, TX city sales taxes	1.00	11,098.35	110.99			11,098.35	Total for Regular
ROWLETT	Rowlett, TX city sales taxes				192.00	200207	192.00	Exempt
ROWLETT	Rowlett, TX city sales taxes				50.00	200207	50.00	Exempt
ROWLETT	Rowlett, TX city sales taxes				80.00	200207	80.00	Exempt
ROWLETT	Rowlett, TX city sales taxes				250.00	200208	250.00	Exempt
ROWLETT	Rowlett, TX city sale				572.00		572.00	Total for Exempt
ROWLETT	Rowlett, TX city sale				52.95	200207	52.95	Exempt
ROWLETT	Rowlett, TX city sale				52.95		52.95	Total for Exempt
ROWLETT	Total Rowlett, TX ci			110.99	624.95		11,723.30	
TEXAS	Texas State sales taxe			16.25		200206	260.00	Regular
TEXAS	Texas State sales taxe			88.17		200208	1,410.75	Regular
TEXAS	Texas State sales taxe			590.63		200211	9,450.00	Regular
TEXAS	Texas State sales taxe			14.85		200212	237.60	Regular
TEXAS	Texas State sales taxe			709.90			11,358.35	Total for Regular
TEXAS	Texas State sales taxes				250.00	200208	250.00	Exempt
TEXAS	Texas State sales taxes				2,400.00	200210	2,400.00	Exempt
TEXAS	Texas State sales taxes				192.00	200211	192.00	Exempt
TEXAS	Texas State sales taxes				50.00	200211	50.00	Exempt
TEXAS	Texas State sales taxes				80.00	200211	80.00	Exempt
TEXAS	Texas State sales taxes				2,972.00		2,972.00	Total for Exempt
TEXAS	Texas State sales taxes				52.95	200211	52.95	Exempt
TEXAS	Texas State sales taxes				52.95		52.95	Total for Exempt
TEXAS	Total Texas State sales taxes		11,358.35	709.90	3,024.95		14,383.30	

Amounts for the same Reference appear in both Rowlett and Texas tax authorities

This is the reason that I like to use the Multiple Locations, Single Tax Authority method for calculating taxes as I showed earlier. It is also the reason that I create a nontaxable tax code and tax authority. Notice that in the first Taxable/Exempt Sales report there is a section for the NONTAX tax code. This information will become valuable as we calculate our sales taxes.

Some earlier versions of Peachtree do not have a report that is as easy to read or as functional as the one shown here. If you have an older version, there is an easy method to determine taxable and nontaxable sales. I will discuss this method at the end of the "Short Form" section of this chapter.

The Sales Tax Reporting Form

So now we need to determine the information that should be entered on our sales tax forms that we send to the collector of our sales taxes. Because most states have a state-wide collecting agency, we will assume that all collected taxes will go to one sales tax vendor.

For the purposes of our example, we will use the following Invoice Register which has been modified to show the sales tax amount. All sales were for Texas locations.

Simplified Sales Taxes
Invoice Register
For the Period From Mar 1, 2003 to Mar 31, 2003
Filter Criteria includes: Report order is by Invoice Number.

Invoice No	Date	Quote No	Name	Amount	Sales Tax
200206	3/5/03		Texscape, Inc.	278.85	18.85
200207	3/9/03		Yarbro Accounting	10,604.58	779.63
200208	3/23/03		Dallas Singles Association	1,777.14	116.39
200209	3/23/03		North Texas Pro Golfers Academy	281.40	
200210	3/24/03		Texscape, Inc.	2,400.00	
200211	3/28/03		Yarbro Accounting	10,604.58	779.63
200212	3/31/03		RDS Metals	257.20	19.60
Total				26,203.75	1,714.10

The Short Form

Texas has two basic tax reporting forms. The first is the short form. The short form can be used by companies that have one location and only make sales from that location. That includes many small businesses. A similar form is used by other states also.

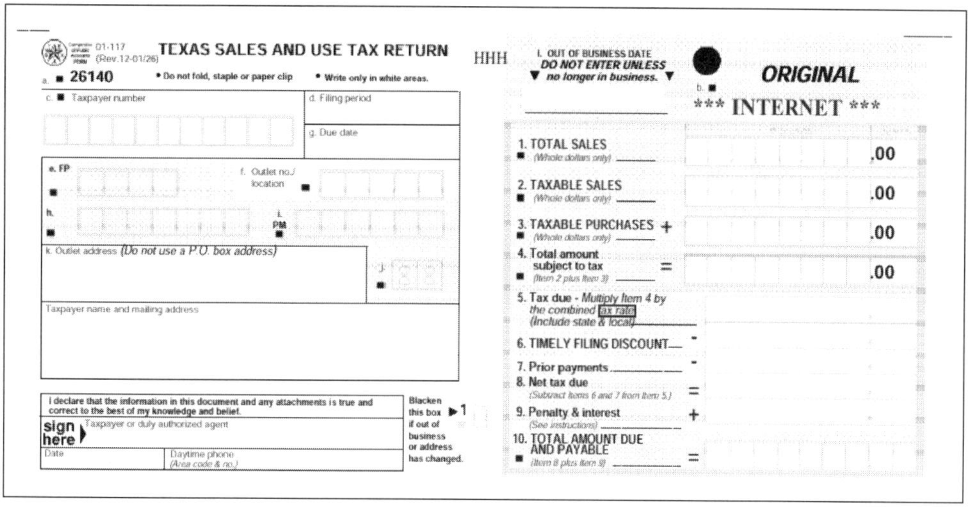
01-117 (Rev.12-01/26) TEXAS SALES AND USE TAX RETURN HHH

a. ■ 26140 • Do not fold, staple or paper clip • Write only in white areas.

c. ■ Taxpayer number

d. Filing period

g. Due date

e. FP

f. Outlet no./location

h.

i. PM

k. Outlet address (Do not use a P.O. box address)

j.

Taxpayer name and mailing address

I declare that the information in this document and any attachments is true and correct to the best of my knowledge and belief.

sign here ▶ Taxpayer or duly authorized agent

Date

Daytime phone (Area code & no.)

Blacken this box ▶ 1 if out of business or address has changed.

l. OUT OF BUSINESS DATE DO NOT ENTER UNLESS ▼ no longer in business. ▼

b. ■

ORIGINAL

*** INTERNET ***

1. TOTAL SALES ■ (Whole dollars only) .00
2. TAXABLE SALES ■ (Whole dollars only) .00
3. TAXABLE PURCHASES + ■ (Whole dollars only) .00
4. Total amount subject to tax = ■ (Item 2 plus Item 3) .00
5. Tax due - Multiply Item 4 by the combined tax rate (Include state & local)
6. TIMELY FILING DISCOUNT -
7. Prior payments -
8. Net tax due (Subtract Items 6 and 7 from Item 5.) =
9. Penalty & interest (See instructions) +
10. TOTAL AMOUNT DUE AND PAYABLE ■ (Item 8 plus Item 9) =

The short form requires you to track total sales, sales subject to tax, and taxable purchases.

1. Run the Taxable/Exempt Sales report. It will show the tax authorities in your sales tax code. If all sales were for the ROWLETT tax code, it would include taxing authorities for ROWLETT, DART, and TEXAS. The NONTAX sales will also show on the report.

Simplified Sales Taxes
Taxable / Exempt Sales
For the Period From Mar 1, 2003 to Mar 31, 2003
Filter Criteria includes: Report is printed in Summary Format.

Authority ID	Authority Description	Tax Rate	Taxable Sale	Tax Amount	Exempt Sales	Total Sales	Taxable Type
DART	DART MTA sales taxes	1.00	20,808.35	208.09		20,808.35	Total for Regular
DART	DART MTA sales taxes				3,294.00	3,294.00	Total for Exempt
DART	DART MTA sales taxes				105.90	105.90	Total for Exempt
DART	Total DART MTA sales taxes		20,808.35	208.09	3,399.90	24,208.25	
NONTAX	For Nontaxable organizations		131.40			131.40	Total for Regular
NONTAX	For Nontaxable organizations				150.00	150.00	Total for Exempt
NONTAX	Total For Nontaxable organizatio		131.40		150.00	281.40	
ROWLETT	Rowlett, TX city sales taxes	1.00	20,808.35	208.09		20,808.35	Total for Regular
ROWLETT	Rowlett, TX city sales taxes				3,294.00	3,294.00	Total for Exempt
ROWLETT	Rowlett, TX city sales taxes				105.90	105.90	Total for Exempt
ROWLETT	Total Rowlett, TX city sales tax		20,808.35	208.09	3,399.90	24,208.25	
TEXAS	Texas State sales taxes	6.25	20,808.35	1,300.53		20,808.35	Total for Regular
TEXAS	Texas State sales taxes				3,294.00	3,294.00	Total for Exempt
TEXAS	Texas State sales taxes				105.90	105.90	Total for Exempt
TEXAS	Total Texas State sales taxes		20,808.35	1,300.53	3,399.90	24,208.25	

2. To determine the Total Sales for the state, you need to compare the reports shown earlier. On the Invoice Register, the total of the Amount column is $26,203.75. This amount includes sales tax, so we must subtract the sales tax ($1,714.10) shown on the report from the total, for a total amount of sales of $24,489.65. This can be verified by the Taxable/Exempt Sales report by taking the amount due to the Texas tax authority (because all taxable sales are subject to state tax regardless of location) of $24,208.25 and adding in the NONTAX sales of $281.40, for a total amount of sales of $24,489.65. This is the amount entered on the Total Sales line on the form.

Note: If you have not set up a NONTAX tax code and tax authority, then sales to nontaxable organizations will not appear on this report. You will have to determine the total sales from the Invoice Register only.

3. To get the total amount of Taxable Sales, take the total sales ($24,489.65) and subtract both the Texas Exempt Sales ($3,399.90) and the NONTAX Exempt Sales ($281.40) for a total of $20,808.35 for Taxable Sales.

4. The next line is Taxable Purchases. This line is the amount of any items you purchased that were subject to sales tax but that you did not pay. An example would be a computer services company that buys parts from a supplier and does not pay sales tax because the items they purchase are for resale. One day they buy parts for a computer in the office that has broken. That purchase should be subject to sales tax but because the supplier has you set up as a nontaxable vendor, they did not charge the sales tax on the purchase. You are still liable for paying sales tax to the state for that merchandise. This line is where that purchase should be recorded.

   Another transaction that is subject to sales tax is when you purchase inventory for your company. No tax is paid because inventory purchases for resale are not taxable. One day, to repair an office computer, you pull parts from your inventory for the company's use in the office computer. The items pulled are also subject to tax and should be reported here.

   For our example we will assume Taxable Purchases of $100.00.

5. The next line in our sales tax form is the Total amount subject to tax. Take the total taxable sales ($20,808.35) and add the taxable purchases ($100.00) for the taxable amount of $20,908.35.

6. For the Tax due line, you will need to multiply the taxable amount ($20,908.35) by your sales tax rate, which is 8.25% in this example. The Tax due calculated is $1,724.94.

   You can check that amount by adding the total tax amount for each tax authority and then calculating the tax amount on the Taxable Purchases line and adding that to the previous total. The amount should match the Tax due line on the form. There are slight differences in the examples shown due to Peachtree's calculations always rounding up rather than to the nearest dollar.

TAX DUE				
	Calculate			
		Total Subject to Sales Tax		20,908.35
		Tax Rate		0.0825
			Total Tax Due	**1,724.94**
CHECK TAX DUE				
	Taxes due on Sales			
		DART Tax Amount		208.09
		NONTAX Tax Amount		0.00
		ROWLETT Tax Amount		208.09
		TEXAS Tax Amount		1,300.53
			Total Taxes due on Sales	1,716.71
	Taxes due on Purchases			
		Taxable Purchases		100.00
		Tax Rate		0.0825
			Total Taxes due on Purchases	8.25
	Total Taxes due on Sales			1,716.71
	Total Taxes due on Purchases			8.25
			Total Tax Due	**1,724.96**

If your form requires you to divide the taxes between the different taxing authorities, the tax for each authority is equal to the total tax amount for each authority. Any taxable purchases will need to be multiplied by the tax authority rate to get the tax due. That amount will then be added to the Total Tax amount for the tax authority.

The previous example will also work for companies with a tax code with only a single tax authority. All calculations for determining the sales taxes in the above example are included with the companion files.

Tip: If you have an older version of Peachtree, there is a simple method for calculating taxable and nontaxable sales totals. This method assumes that the taxes collected over the tax period are correct and that taxes are fully paid at the end of every tax period. Take the ending balance of your Sales Tax Payable account ($1,716.71) and divide it by the tax rate for the location (0.0825). This gives you the Taxable Sales Total ($20,808.71). The Nontaxable Sales Total ($3,681.04) is calculated by subtracting the Taxable Sales Total from the Total Sales ($24,489.65), which is determined using the Invoice Register. Add the taxes for Taxable Purchases ($8.25) to get the Total Sales Tax Due ($1,724.96).

The Standard Form

The standard form is for companies with multiple locations or multiple tax codes. Some states require you to break out taxes by location, others require you to break them out by taxing authority, and some require both. We will cover sales taxes broken out by taxing authority.

Run the Taxable/Exempt Sales report. This report is based upon the same Invoice Register that we ran earlier in this chapter.

Simplified Sales Taxes
Taxable / Exempt Sales
For the Period From Mar 1, 2003 to Mar 31, 2003
Filter Criteria includes: Report is printed in Summary Format.

Authority ID	Authority Description	Tax Rate	Taxable Sale	Tax Amount	Exempt Sales	Total Sales	Taxable Type
DART	DART MTA sales taxes	1.00	11,358.35	113.59		11,358.35	Total for Regular
DART	DART MTA sales taxes				2,972.00	2,972.00	Total for Exempt
DART	DART MTA sales taxes				52.95	52.95	Total for Exempt
DART	Total DART MTA sales taxes		11,358.35	113.59	3,024.95	14,383.30	
MESQUITE	Mesquite City sales taxes	1.00	9,450.00	94.50		9,450.00	Total for Regular
MESQUITE	Mesquite City sales taxes				322.00	322.00	Total for Exempt
MESQUITE	Mesquite City sales taxes				52.95	52.95	Total for Exempt
MESQUITE	Total Mesquite City sales taxes		9,450.00	94.50	374.95	9,824.95	
NONTAX	For Nontaxable organizations		131.40			131.40	Total for Regular
NONTAX	For Nontaxable organizations				150.00	150.00	Total for Exempt
NONTAX	Total For Nontaxable organizatio		131.40		150.00	281.40	
PLANO	Plano city sales taxes	0.75	260.00	1.95		260.00	Total for Regular
PLANO	Plano city sales taxes				2,400.00	2,400.00	Total for Exempt
PLANO	Total Plano city sales taxes		260.00	1.95	2,400.00	2,660.00	
ROWLETT	Rowlett, TX city sales taxes	1.00	11,098.35	110.99		11,098.35	Total for Regular
ROWLETT	Rowlett, TX city sales taxes				572.00	572.00	Total for Exempt
ROWLETT	Rowlett, TX city sales taxes				52.95	52.95	Total for Exempt
ROWLETT	Total Rowlett, TX city sales tax		11,098.35	110.99	624.95	11,723.30	
TEXAS	Texas State sales taxes	6.25	20,808.35	1,300.53		20,808.35	Total for Regular
TEXAS	Texas State sales taxes				3,294.00	3,294.00	Total for Exempt
TEXAS	Texas State sales taxes				105.90	105.90	Total for Exempt
TEXAS	Total Texas State sales taxes		20,808.35	1,300.53	3,399.90	24,208.25	

The following examples are based on a company with three locations — Mesquite, Plano, and Rowlett. Both Rowlett and Plano include DART taxes and all locations include Texas tax. As you can see, a nontaxable tax code is included for nontaxable organizations.

To fill out a report like the State of Wyoming report shown in the following figure, use these instructions.

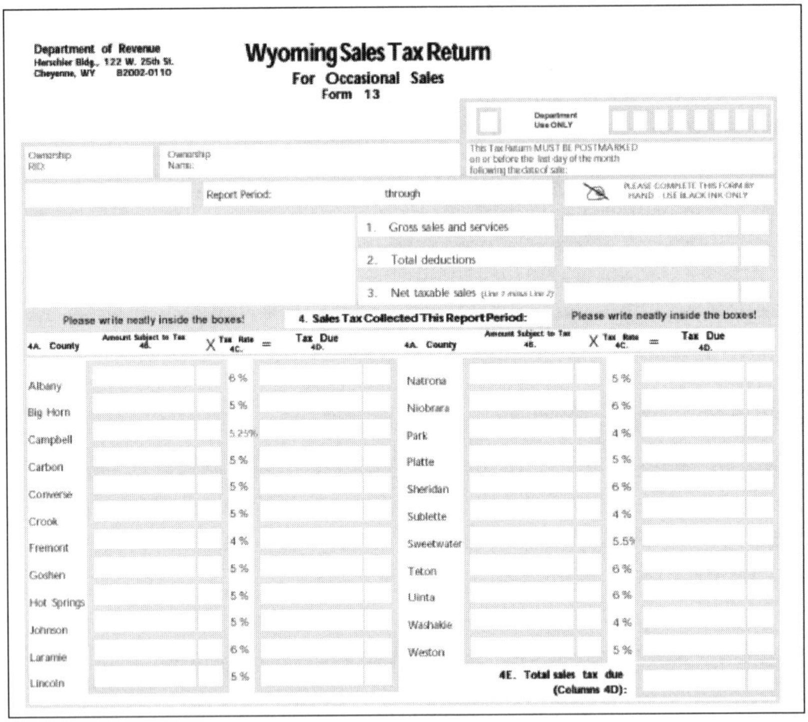
Department of Revenue
Herschler Bldg., 122 W. 25th St.
Cheyenne, WY 82002-0110

Wyoming Sales Tax Return
For Occasional Sales
Form 13

Department Use ONLY

Ownership RID:
Ownership Name:
This Tax Return MUST BE POSTMARKED on or before the last day of the month following the date of sale:

Report Period: through
PLEASE COMPLETE THIS FORM BY HAND - USE BLACK INK ONLY

1. Gross sales and services
2. Total deductions
3. Net taxable sales (Line 1 minus Line 2)

Please write neatly inside the boxes! **4. Sales Tax Collected This Report Period:** Please write neatly inside the boxes!

4A. County	Amount Subject to Tax 4B.	X Tax Rate 4C. =	Tax Due 4D.	4A. County	Amount Subject to Tax 4B.	X Tax Rate 4C. =	Tax Due 4D.
Albany		6 %		Natrona		5 %	
Big Horn		5 %		Niobrara		6 %	
Campbell		5.25%		Park		4 %	
Carbon		5 %		Platte		5 %	
Converse		5 %		Sheridan		6 %	
Crook		5 %		Sublette		4 %	
Fremont		4 %		Sweetwater		5.5%	
Goshen		5 %		Teton		6 %	
Hot Springs		5 %		Uinta		6 %	
Johnson		5 %		Washakie		4 %	
Laramie		6 %		Weston		5 %	
Lincoln		5 %		**4E. Total sales tax due (Columns 4D):**			

1. Calculate the Gross sales and services. The total amount of sales that we calculated from the Invoice Register was $24,489.65. The amount matches the Total Sales we can calculate from the Taxable/Exempt Sales report.
2. Subtract the Total deductions. This amount is the Texas Total Exempt Sales and the NONTAX Total Exempt Sales and equals $3,681.30.
3. Subtract Total deductions from Gross sales and services for Net taxable sales of $20,808.35.
4. For each line on the form that matches, enter the Amount subject to tax and the Tax due. Both entries come from the Taxable/Exempt Sales report.
5. To check the amounts, take the Taxable Amount for each location, in our case, Mesquite, Rowlett, and Plano, and multiply it by the corresponding tax code rate. The Total sales tax due on the form should match. Remember that Peachtree rounds up, so there may be slight differences in these examples.

TAXES DUE				
	Authority	**Taxable Amount**	**Tax Rate**	**Tax Due**
	DART	11,358.35	1.00%	113.59
	MESQUITE	9,450.00	1.00%	94.50
	NONTAX	131.40	0.00%	0.00
	PLANO	260.00	0.75%	1.95
	ROWLETT	11,098.35	1.00%	110.98
	TEXAS	20,808.35	6.25%	1,300.52
			Total Taxes Due	**1,621.54**
CHECK TAXES DUE				
	MESQUITE	9,450.00	7.25%	685.13
	PLANO	260.00	8.00%	20.80
	ROWLETT	11,098.35	8.25%	915.61
			Total Taxes Due	**1,621.54**

Paying Sales Taxes

Once your sales taxes are determined for the individual tax codes and taxing authorities, it is easy to pay your taxes.

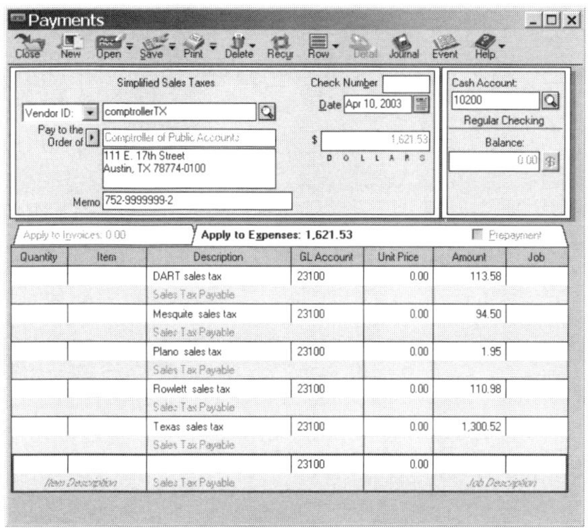

1. Bring up the Payments form.
2. Select the tax vendor from the **Vendor ID** drop-down list. If you have more than one tax collection agency, you will need to create a separate check for each vendor.
3. Enter the date of the payment in the Date field.
4. Select your normal cash account.
5. On the Apply to Expenses tab, enter the amounts to pay for the taxes. You can enter a lump sum or you can divide the amounts due by location or taxing authority. Be sure to use the Sales Tax Payable general ledger account for the GL Account field.
6. Have Peachtree memorize the payment so you do not have to type all the lines in again. Click the drop-down arrow next to the **Save** button.
7. Click the **Memorize** button.

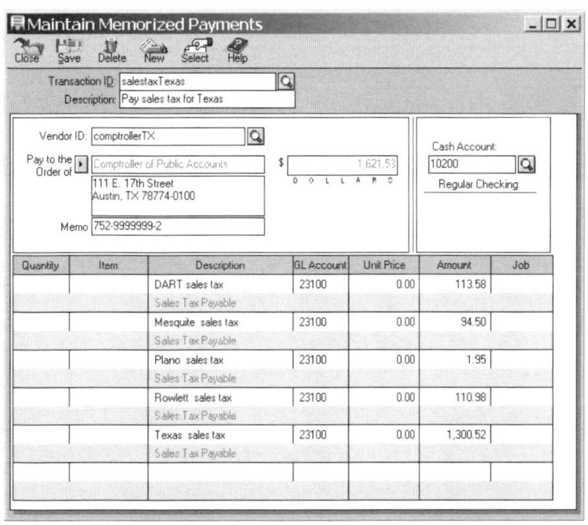

8. Enter a transaction ID that will help you to remember this payment, and enter a description.
9. Verify that the Vendor ID appears correctly. Also verify the cash account and the line items. The amounts will be changed each time you select the memorized transaction.
10. Click **Save** to record the memorized payment.
11. Click **Print** to print and record the payment.

    To use the memorized payment at a later date, click the **Open** drop-down arrow and then the **Select** button. Select the transaction from the list.

Summary

Sales taxes can be a very complicated part of Peachtree, and the repercussions of incorrect payments can add up for the smaller business owner. Penalties and overpayments of sales taxes both cost you dollars. Over the years, Peachtree has fine-tuned the sales tax reporting function and the sales tax report to better reflect real-world situations. This improvement makes it much easier for small businesses to calculate, track, and pay sales taxes without resorting to heavy manpower or CPA costs.

Chapter 15

Balancing Payroll

In This Chapter

- Payroll Setup Wizard revisited
- Creating a payroll field
- Employee defaults
- State and locality taxes
- Global and company tax tables
- Installing a Payroll Tax Service Update
- Balancing payroll
- Payroll reports, including the 941

In this chapter we will look at entering employee information and employee defaults, and we will balance the payroll. Payroll is a function that can be easily balanced as long as the paychecks and beginning balances have been entered correctly. There are many details to track in creating paychecks, but the program works very well if data is entered correctly.

Payroll Setup Wizard

In Chapter 9 we showed how to use the Payroll Setup Wizard to begin using payroll. Once the wizard is used, certain types of information cannot be changed. We will not go through the entire Payroll Setup Wizard here because it was covered in Chapter 9. I know that the following warning has been reiterated many times, but I cannot stress the importance of it enough.

Warning!! Changing any of the payroll information should only be done at the beginning of a payroll (calendar) year. Changes at any other time may cause serious repercussions when calculating W-2s and other reports. Although it is possible to add new items during the year, such as tips, vacation, or sick leave, you should never change the name or G/L account of an existing item during the year and you should never delete an existing payroll field.

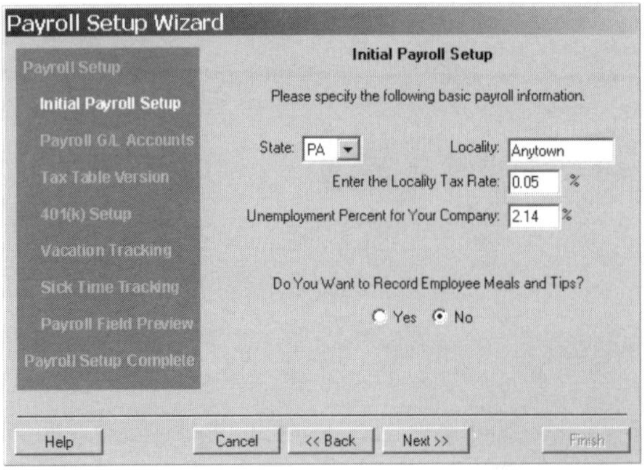

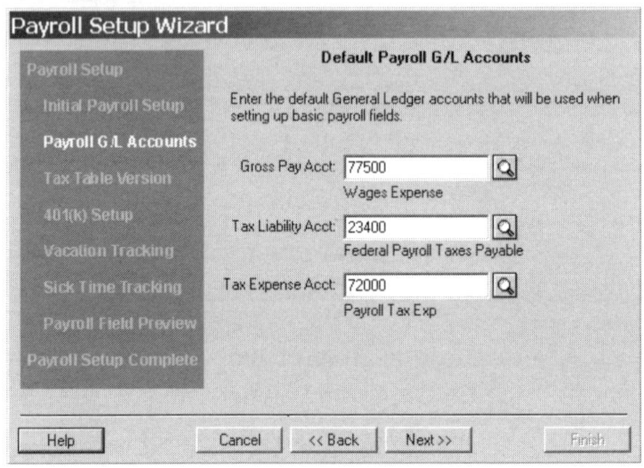

The Initial Payroll Setup screen asks for your state so that the program can use information stored in the tax tables for employee and employer state deductions. If needed, you can also fill in the Locality and Locality Tax Rate fields. On this screen you also need to enter your Unemployment Percentage for the current year. I will show how to change this rate later in this chapter.

The next screen for the wizard is for the Default Payroll G/L Accounts. Choose these accounts carefully. If you are copying your company from another Peachtree company, you will not want to copy the employee defaults because I have heard from other consultants, though my clients have never experienced it, that these default payroll accounts can come across incorrectly. I have also heard that converting or upgrading a company can occasionally, though very rarely, cause the same problem, so if you do either of these, make sure that these accounts transfer correctly.

The 401(K), Vacation, and Sick time screens in the payroll wizard can be changed at the end of any payroll year. Return to the Payroll Setup Wizard to make the changes. If you need to add or make changes to other payroll fields, some general instructions are included in this chapter.

Employee Defaults

Employee defaults control the calculation, tracking, and reporting of payroll information. New employee defaults can be added to Peachtree when your company adds new types of additions or deductions to employees' paychecks. Employee defaults can be edited after you create a new company, although there should be no real reason to do so unless you want to subdivide pay types such as one account for regular hourly wages and a second for overtime wages.

Warning!! Changing pay levels and deductions should only be done at the beginning of a payroll (calendar) year. Changes at any other time may cause serious repercussions when calculating W-2s. Although it is possible to add new items during the year, you should never change the name or G/L account of an existing item during the year and you should especially never delete an existing payroll field.

The employee defaults will be described here in the order that they appear in the Peachtree menu. The steps for adding new payroll fields will be shown later in the chapter because those steps are not in the same order as the defaults.

General

The general defaults control which state and local taxes are calculated on your payroll. If, for any reason, your company moves and needs to change these fields, it is better to create a new company and transfer the balances rather than make the changes on this page. To access these defaults, follow these steps:

1. Open the Employee Defaults window by clicking the **Company** folder on the navigation aid, clicking the **Setup Checklist** icon, and clicking **Employee Defaults** on the list.

   Or select **Maintain** from the menu bar and then select **Default Information** and **Employees.**

   Or press **Alt+M**, **D**, and then **E** using the keyboard.

2. The Employee Defaults window opens to the General tab.

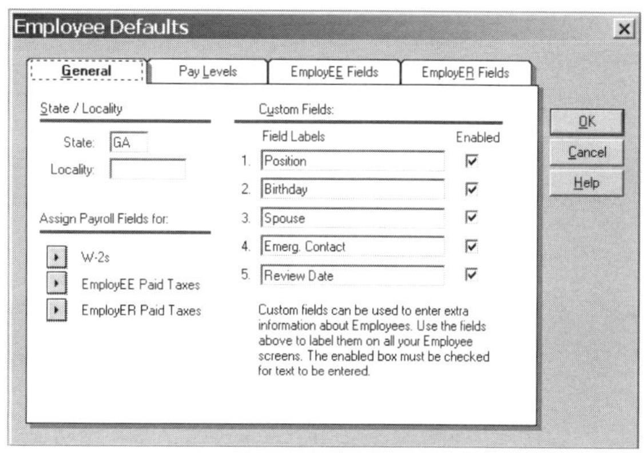

State/Locality

You can change the state and local tax tables here although those should have been created the first time you ran the payroll wizard. If you did not set up the locality and the locality tax rate in the payroll wizard, you will need to add a new payroll field and a tax table.

Assign Payroll Fields For

This section of the General tab controls what information appears on the employee's W-2 at the end of the year. The section also determines what taxes should be calculated for employees and employers. Click the arrow next to the payroll tax name to access the corresponding dialog boxes.

W-2s — When W-2s are printed at the end of each year, payroll information such as federal and social security withholding go into specific boxes on the form.

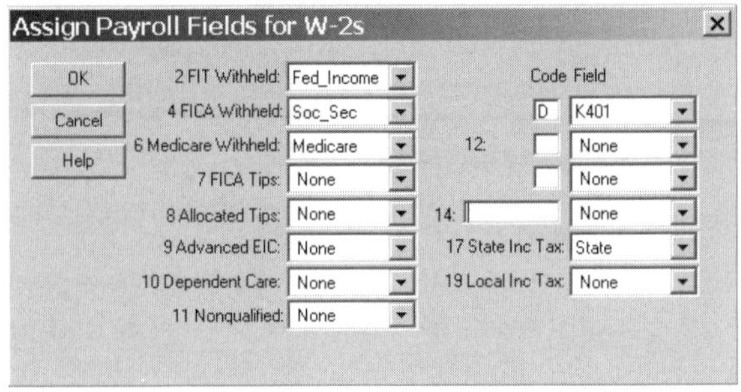

The number of the W-2 box along with its name appears next to a drop-down field. If you add a type of income or tax to your company you need to verify that it will print correctly on the W-2. In Chapter 9 you were shown how to assign payroll fields for such things as tips. Box 14 has a space for a customized label. Adding new payroll fields is covered later in this chapter.

EmployEE Paid Taxes — Some states or localities require extra taxes to be paid by employees.

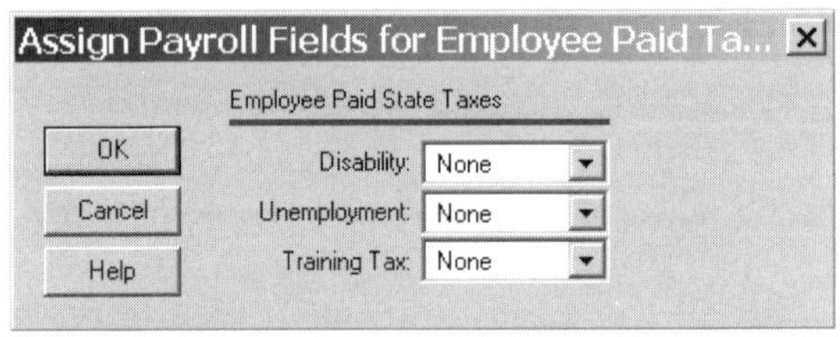

From the drop-down list select the appropriate payroll field for the corresponding employee deduction.

EmployER Paid Taxes — Just as employees may have extra deductions, so can employers.

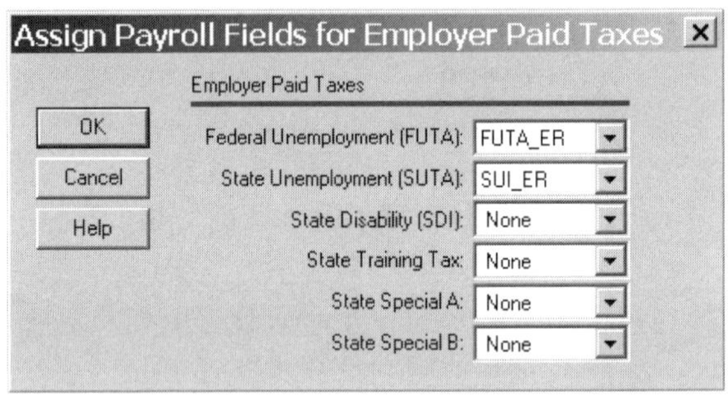

The most common of these are the Federal Unemployment (FUTA) and the State Unemployment (SUTA) taxes. Peachtree normally creates the FUTA_ER and SUTA_ER payroll fields when the other standardized payroll fields are produced.

Custom Fields

Custom fields work the same way as they do in the customer and vendor records. You are given five fields to label and use as you need. Standard fields for Position, Birthday, Spouse, Emergency Contact, and Review Date are already filled in and enabled. These fields can be printed on reports, if needed.

Pay Levels

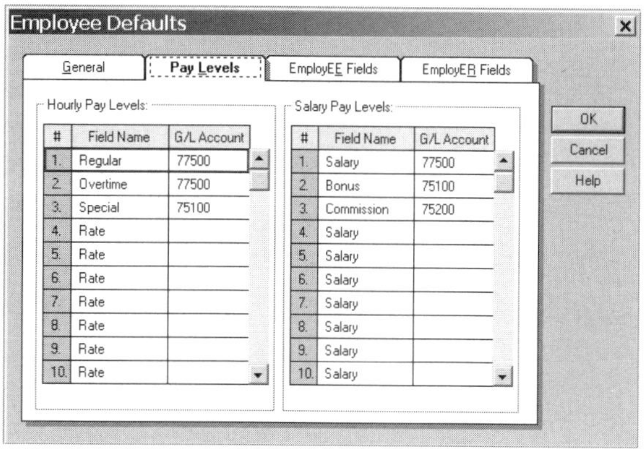

Next we want to look at the Pay Levels tab.

The fields in the pay levels tables control the types of income that are paid to employees. Each table controls either the hourly or the salaried employees. Both types of employees can receive up to 10 types of income. Pay rates and salaries are assigned on the employee records.

To add or change a pay level, enter the name on a Field Name line or select an existing one. In the G/L Account field, select the general ledger account associated with this type of income.

Warning!! Changing pay levels and deductions should only be done at the beginning of a payroll (calendar) year. Changes at any other time may cause serious repercussions when calculating W-2s. Although it is possible to add new items during the year, you should never change the name or G/L account of an existing item during the year and you should especially never delete an existing payroll field.

EmployEE Fields

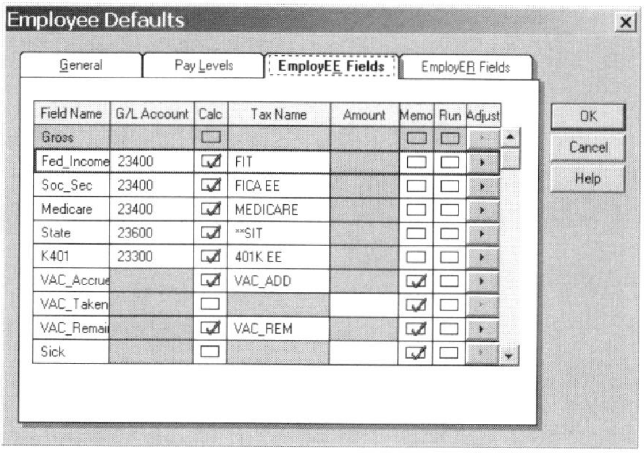

In Chapter 9 you were shown how to add EmployEE fields for such things as tips, vacation hours, and loans.

You may add new payroll fields using these instructions:

1. Go to a new line and enter the name of the deduction or data to be tracked. We will look at a deduction for dental insurance and for a payroll field called Bill Hours that will track an employee's billable hours over the calendar year.
2. If the field is for data that needs to be posted to the general ledger, you will assign the G/L Account number from the drop-down. If a new general ledger account needs to be created for this field, you should create the account first. This field cannot be used if the Memo field is checked.

3. The Calc field is for amounts that are calculated using a tax table. Tax tables are discussed elsewhere in this chapter. If Calc is checked, the name of the table must be entered in the Tax Name field.
4. The Amount field holds the dollar amount to be deducted from or added to an employee's paycheck if a calculation is not used. For example, all employees selecting dental insurance will be charged $9.95 per paycheck.
5. Check the Memo box for data, like Bill Hours, that you want to track but do not want to affect income or deductions. When Bill Hours are added on the Payroll Entry form, they accumulate in this field so that you can see the total Bill Hours for a month or year.
6. The Run check box is for data that you do not want to be set to zero at the end of the payroll year. This would include employee loans because you want the loan amount to remain after the new year starts. You would not check the box for a payroll field like Dental because that amount is tracked on an annual basis.

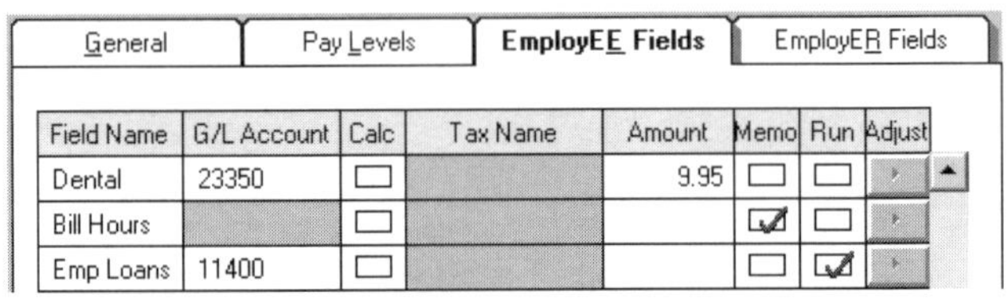

7. The last column, Adjust, contains a button that takes you to the Calculate Adjusted Gross dialog box.

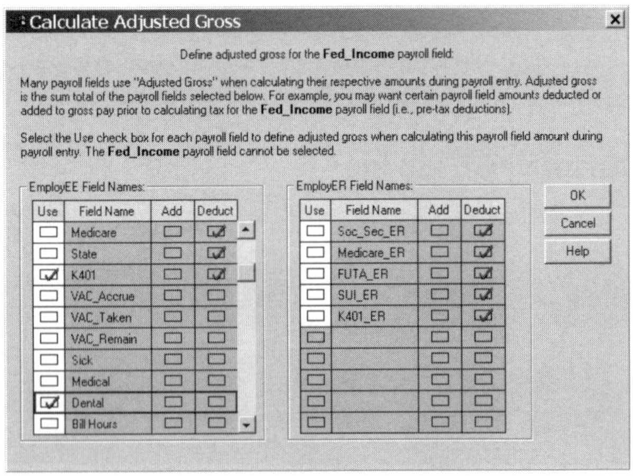

If our dental insurance deduction was a qualified deduction and we used a tax table to calculate the amount of the deduction, we could remove the amount of the insurance from the employee's calculated gross pay when determining the amount of federal taxes to be withheld. Click the **Use** column for the Field Name to include the calculation in the determination of gross income for taxation purposes. You need to do this for all fields on the above screen, such as Fed_Income, Soc_Sec, and Medicare, that are affected by this new calculated payroll field.

Note: I have had some problems getting the Adjust function to work the way that Peachtree says it should, and I could not get access to the Add and Deduct fields no matter what I did.

EmployER Fields

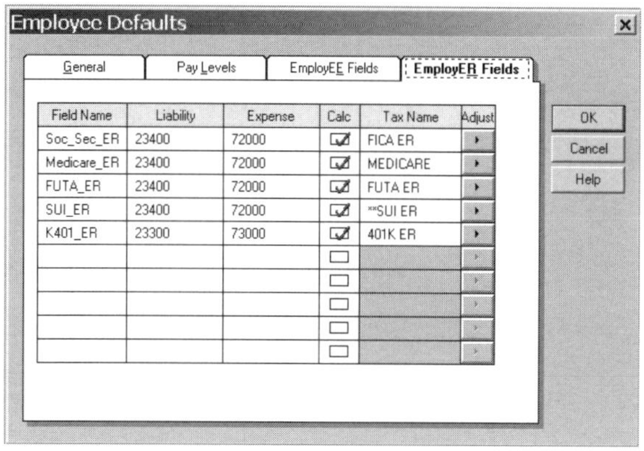

On the EmployER Fields tab you are setting up the payroll fields the same as you do for the EmployEE Fields tab except that these fields are for those taxes that are your responsibility.

Each Field Name has an associated Liability and Expense G/L account that is selected from the drop-down. They are also based on tax tables so the Calc column is checked and the Tax Name field has the name of the table. The Adjust button is used to add or deduct the amounts to adjusted gross income.

Tax Tables

Tax tables control the calculations that determine the employee deductions and payroll taxes for both employees and employers that are based upon government-mandated taxes and deductions requiring an equation to determine.

There are two classes of tax tables. Global tax tables are developed and updated by Peachtree and are sold to Peachtree users on an annual basis as part of the Payroll Tax Service. These include federal and state income tax withholding. Company tax tables are set up for individual Peachtree companies and may be edited according to the individual needs of your payroll. Company tables include formulas for state unemployment taxes and vacation calculations.

Installing a Payroll Tax Service Update from Peachtree

In earlier versions of Peachtree there were ways to create tax tables using the previous year's tax tables. This was extremely beneficial to very small companies or those companies that had not yet received their tax updates from Peachtree. In Peachtree 2002, the tax tables must be registered before they can be used. I guess that Peachtree is now determined to get its $150 from companies every single year, regardless of a company's size or financial status.

To install and register a tax update once it is received, follow these steps:

1. Close all programs on your desktop, including Peachtree.
2. Place the Payroll Tax Service Update CD received from Peachtree in your CD-ROM drive. The Peachtree Payroll Tax Service menu should appear.

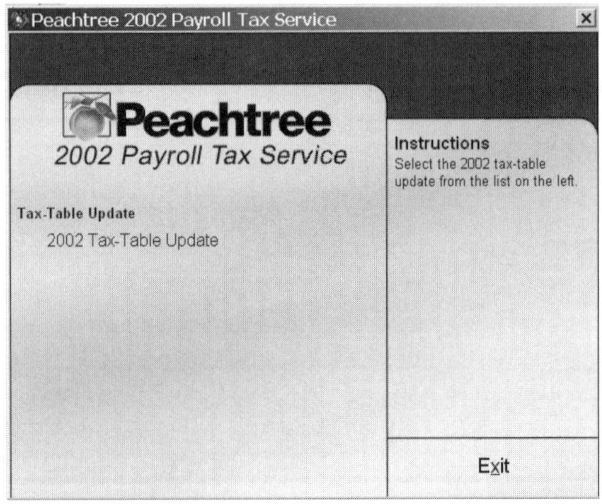

If the menu does not appear, go to the Windows taskbar and click **Start**, **Run**. Click the **Browse** button and select **AUTORUN.EXE** file from the CD drive folder.

3. If your Peachtree program is not up to date, there will be a program update listed here. You must install the update before you install the tax update. Click on the program update and follow the directions. You will most likely be asked to reboot the computer after the update is finished. Leave the CD in the drive during the reboot and the computer will return to this menu to continue with the tax table update.
4. Click the **Tax-Table Update** item in the menu. The Tax Service window and the Welcome screen appears.

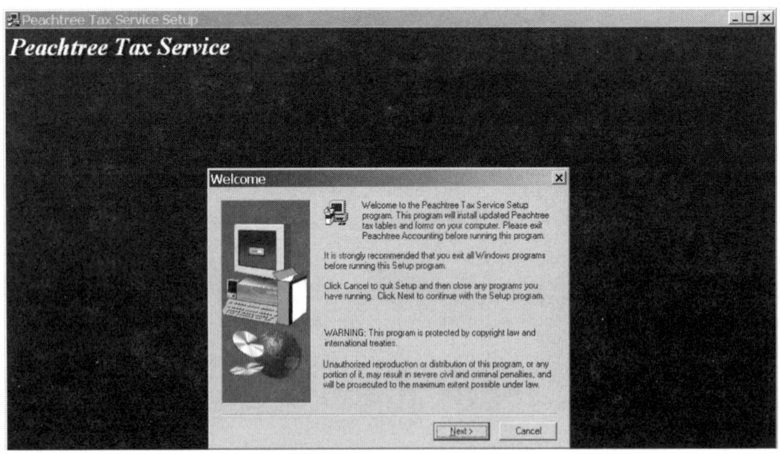

5. Click the **Next** button after you read the screen.
6. The Software License Agreement screen appears.

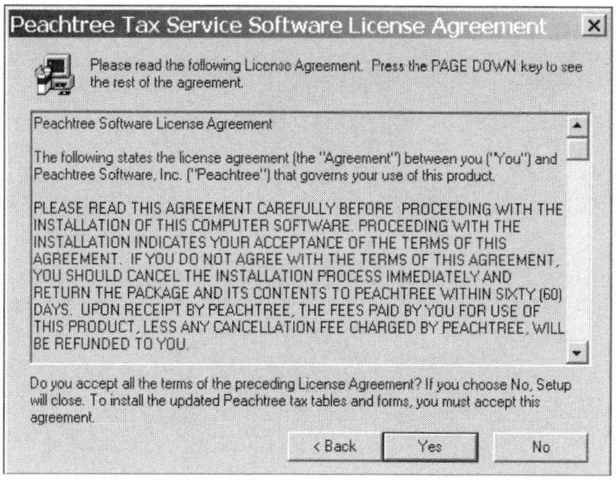

You must click **Yes** to continue with the update.

7. The Tax Service Information screen appears.

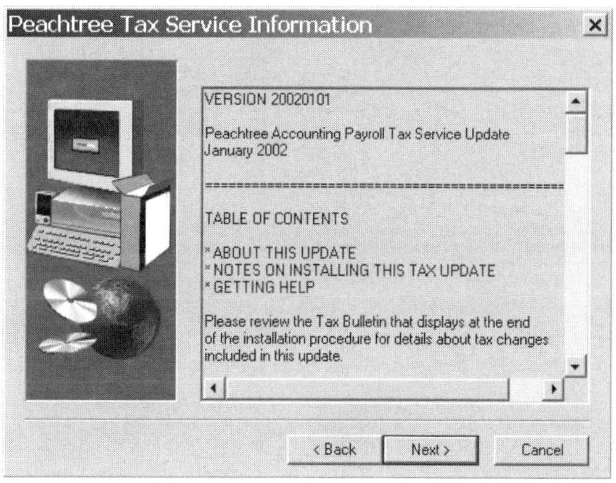

Click **Next**.

8. In the Choose Destination Location screen, Peachtree will try to locate the files for your computer.

   If you want to change the destination, click the **Browse** button and select the new location. Click **Next**.

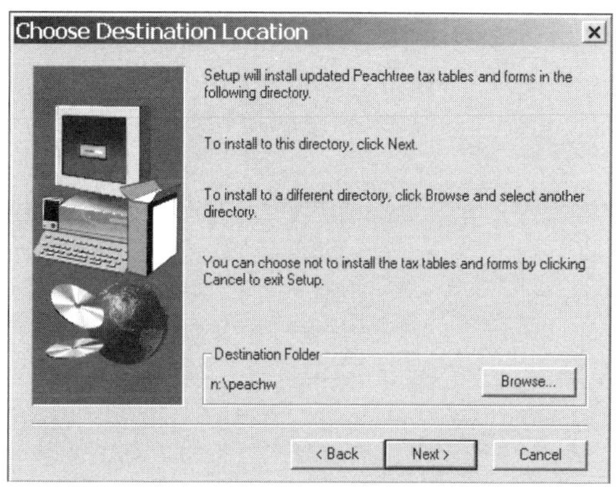

9. The files will be copied to the selected destination.

10. When the process is complete, the Setup Complete screen will appear.

    Peachtree includes a help file with information for all of its tax updates. If you want to view the file, check the **Yes** check box.

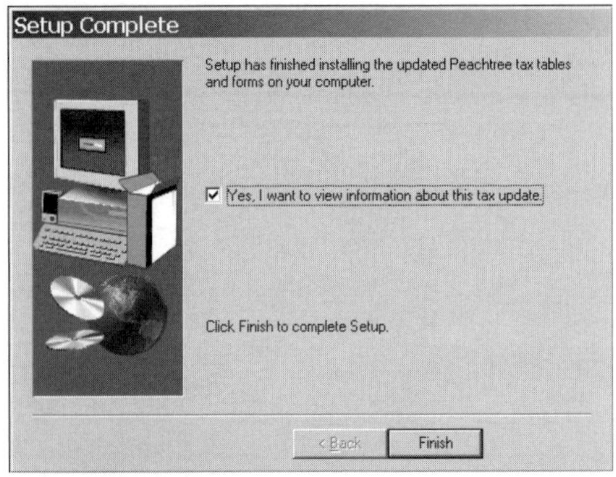

11. To complete the tax update, click **Finish**. If you selected to view the update it will appear; otherwise you will be taken back to the Windows desktop.
12. Once a tax update is installed, it is still not ready to use. When you open Peachtree and look at the tax tables, the new tables will not show; instead you will be taken to the Register Tax Service screen. For obvious reasons, the Serial Number shown is phony.

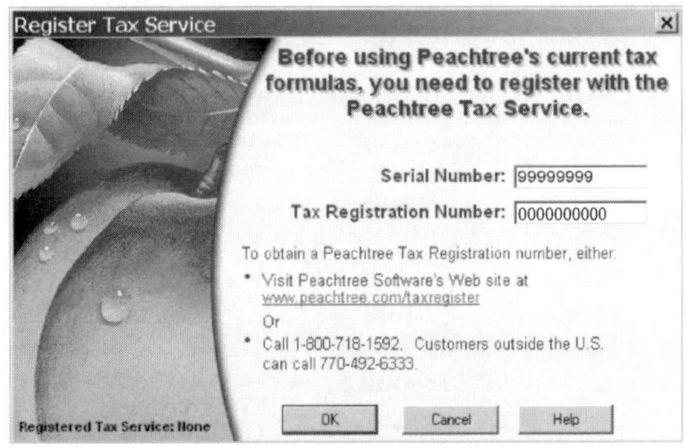

    It is also possible that you may receive the following warning at some point during the update or registration process. You must call Peachtree at the number shown to get help with the update or registration before it can be used. Write down the phone number (currently 1-800-336-1420) and click **Yes** to close the warning.

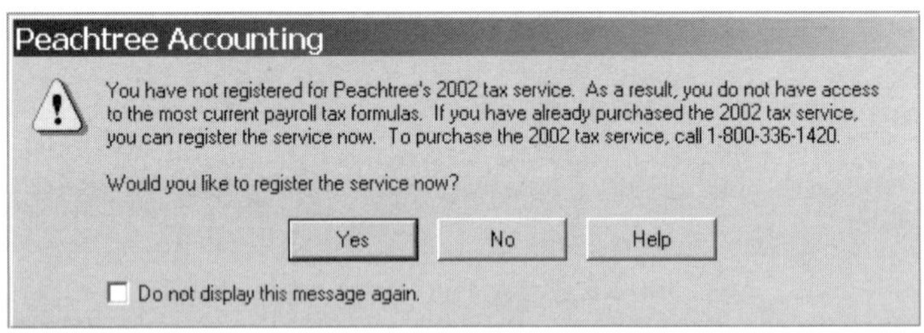

13. If you click **OK** on the Register Tax Service screen, the screen will close. You must either call the displayed phone number, or go to the web site shown on the form to register online. If you click on the hyperlink shown, the Register Product window will appear.

14. Select **Payroll Tax Service** and click **Continue.**
15. An Information window appears.

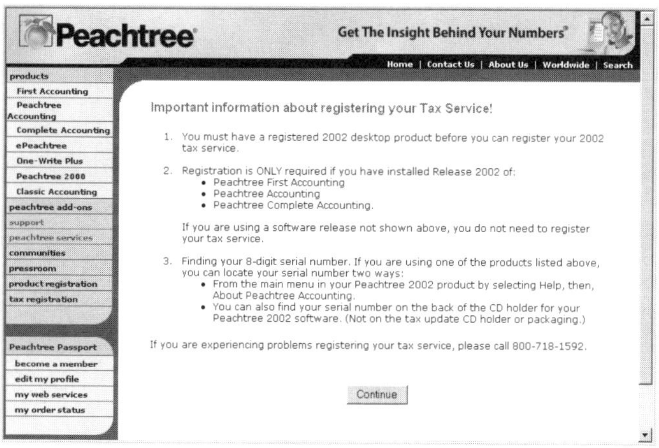

Click **Continue** to go to the Passport Login Page.

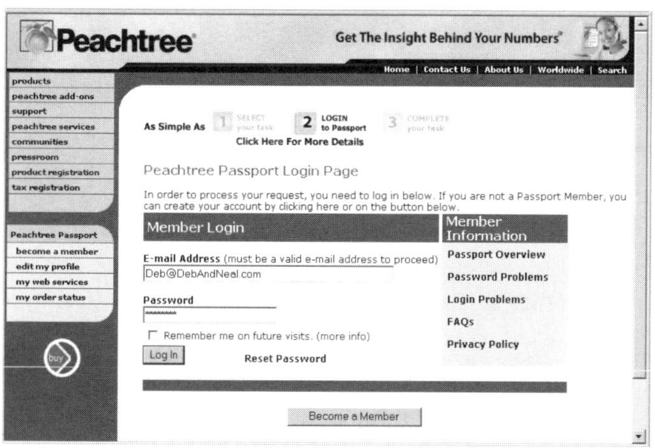

16. If you do not yet have a Passport login, you will need to click the **Become a Member** button and get a Passport account. Otherwise, enter your e-mail address and your password in the fields provided. Click **Log In.**
17. In the Online Registration window, verify the information, which includes your Serial Number and the Tax Registration Year.

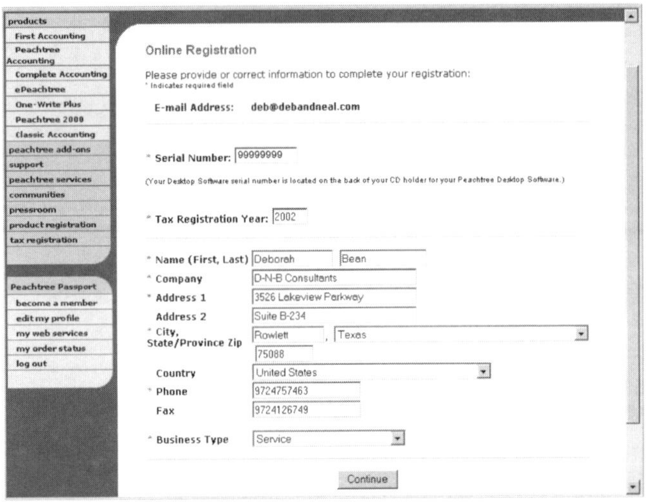

Change these numbers if needed, then click **Continue.**

18. The Review Registration window appears.

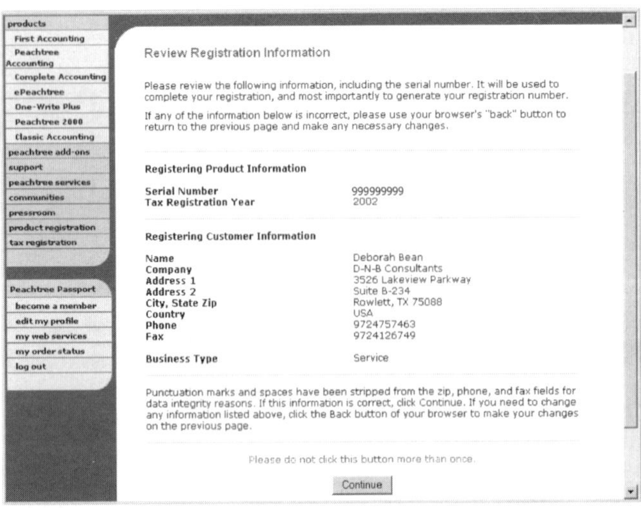

Review the information and notice the warning just above the Continue button. If you find any errors on this window, use the browser's Back button to return to the previous window to make changes. Click the **Continue** button.

19. The program may take several moments to register you. At that point, you can make a note of the number that appears on the next screen, which is not displayed here, so it can be entered into your Peachtree.

Note: I had trouble at this time and received an error message that told me to call Peachtree Customer Service to register. It took several tries, but we finally came up with a tax registration number that worked. If you receive an error, you can still register the tax update in Peachtree; you do not have to continue the online registration.

Note: A special thanks to Peachtree employees Felecia Thomas, Customer Service, and Aimee Weaver, Public Relations, for their help in getting my Peachtree program and my Tax Service Update registered. They were both courteous, knowledgeable, and understanding of the special problems that Peachtree consultants, like myself, sometimes run into with multiple serial numbers and versions.

20. Once you get the registration number for the tax update, you need to close your Internet connection and go back to the Register Tax Service window in Peachtree.

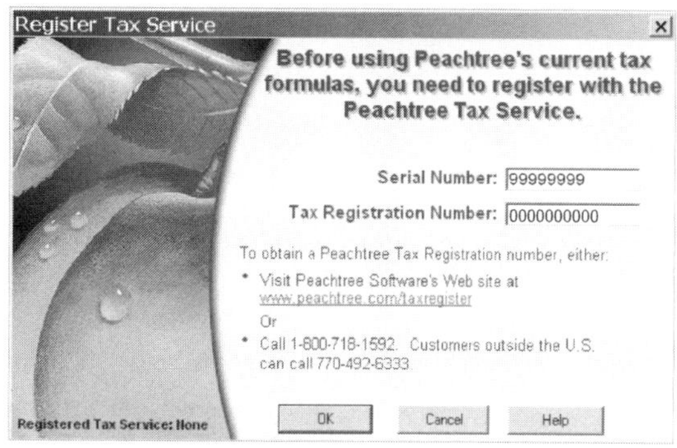

21. Enter the number you were given in the Tax Registration Number field. Click **OK**.

You are now registered for the service and can use the tax tables to generate payroll. Don't forget that you will need the tax service next year also.

Global Tax Tables

Global tax tables control all of the major withholdings that an employee and an employer are required to pay at the state level. Global tax tables also affect all companies that are created in Peachtree, so if you have companies with the same locality taxes, you will want to maintain them in this area. To maintain tax tables for multiple companies with their own specific rates, you will want to use the company tax tables.

1. Select **File**, **Payroll Tax Tables**, **Edit Company** from the menu bar to see the global tax tables.

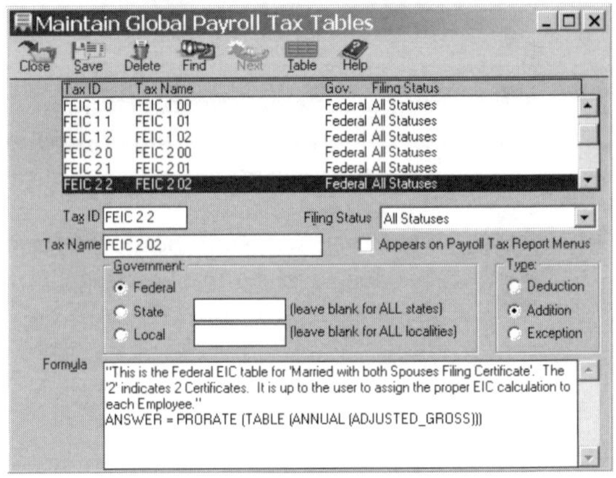

2. The tables include all information necessary to calculate a specific type of tax. The one shown is for the Earned Income Credit for the year 2002. The Tax ID and Tax Name are used to identify this table when you select a tax table in the EmployEE and EmployER Fields tabs on the Employee Defaults form. Notice that there are two tax tables for the EIC for 2002 — FEIC 2 2 and FEIC 1 2. The difference between the two is based on whether the employee is filing as "Married with both Spouses Filing Certificate" or "Single or Married without Spouse Filing."

3. The Filing Status can be All Statuses or can be for a specific status for an employee. The filing status for the employee is determined from the information on the Maintain Employees/Sales Reps form. For instance, the FIT M2 tax table is only for employees who are married.

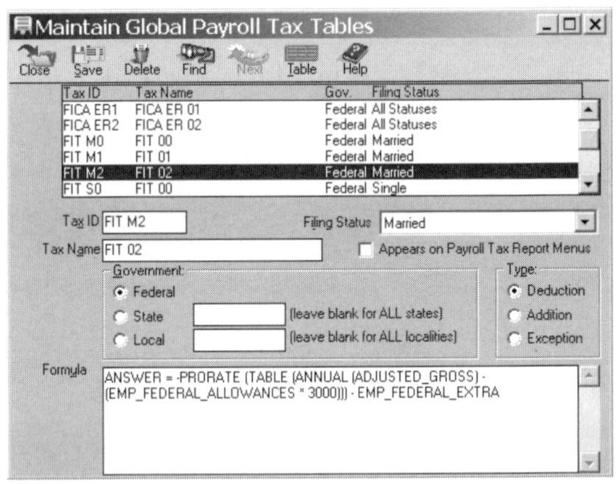

4. The Type section of the tax table record displays whether the amount calculated on the employees paycheck is an Addition to gross income, a Deduction from gross income, or an Exception, such as vacation or sick time, which can be both.

5. In the Government section, taxes are specified as Federal, State, and Local. All states with income taxes, and Puerto Rico, are included in the tax tables. You can see in the Local tax table for Phil that it is tax for persons living in Philadelphia, Pennsylvania. Again, the employee's record will determine if this tax is calculated for the employee's paycheck.

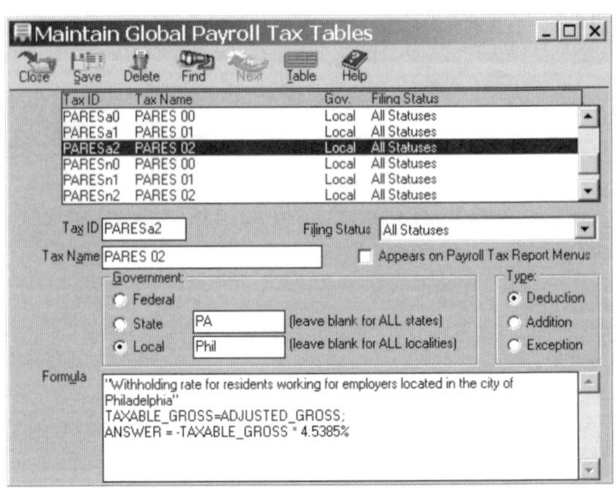

6. The Appears on Payroll Tax Report Menus check box determines whether the tax calculated is included on the Payroll Tax Report.
7. The PARESa2 tax shown uses a formula, or equation, to calculate the amount that appears on the paycheck. The formula has a specific syntax and makes TAXABLE_GROSS of an employee's pay for the period equal to the adjusted gross income. It then multiplies TAXABLE_GROSS by 4.5385% to determine the amount of the Locality payroll field on the paycheck. If the employee earned $500 of adjusted gross income, the Locality payroll field would be equal to $22.69 of tax. Changing a single character in any way can destroy the formula.

   The FIT M2 tax has a formula also. In the equation the related table is called. It provides the calculation used to determine the amount of the associated tax. Click the **Table** button in the toolbar to view the table.

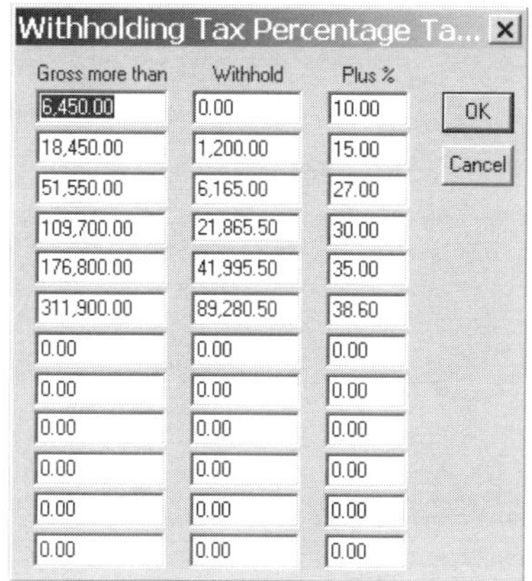

   The information contained in the Peachtree table is based upon annual income. The current information in the table should always match the IRS Circular E that you receive from the government. Slight differences on a paycheck, of a penny or two, from the Circular E table amounts are due to rounding differences.

Company Tax Tables

Company tax tables are the tax tables for each individual company. They include the tax tables for the payroll fields that are unique to each company, such as 401(k) contributions and vacation and sick leave calculations.

1. Company tax tables are accessed by selecting **File**, **Payroll Tax Tables**, **Edit Company** from the menu bar.

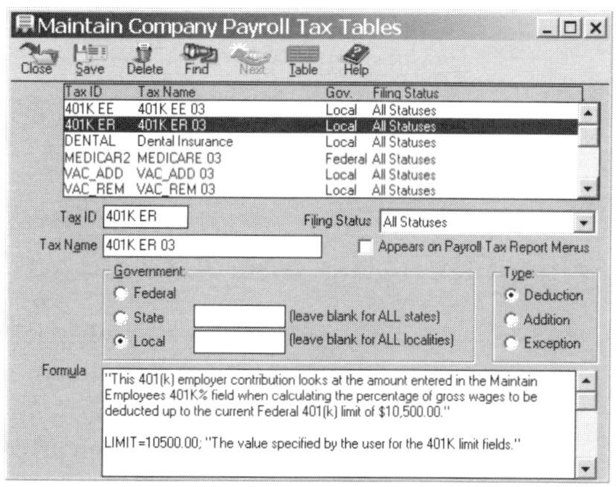

2. The screen is set up the same way as the global tax tables are. Adding new company tax tables without formulas was described in Chapter 9.
3. To add a new formula, I find it is best to copy an existing formula and make the changes needed. Peachtree tax formulas appear to be based on one of the numerous versions of the BASIC computer language.

In the company tax tables, you should be able to locate your unemployment tax information for both the LIMIT and the PERCENT. The tax tables will have names such as GASUI ER 03 or **SUI ER 03. If you cannot locate the tax tables, copy the sample company table and change the limit and percent fields to your company's amounts. Then follow the steps for adding the deduction (employEE or employer) as a payroll field.

Creating a New Payroll Field

When payroll checks are created for employees, certain amounts are withheld and additional amounts may be included in the employees' taxable income at the federal, state, or local level. These withholdings and additions are assigned payroll fields so that they will show up on payroll reports. A standard earnings report showing these different payroll fields is displayed here.

Bellwether Garden Supply
Current Earnings Report
For the Period From Mar 1, 2003 to Mar 31, 2003
Filter Criteria includes: Report order is by Employee ID. Report is printed in Detail Format.

Employee ID Employee SS No	Date Reference	Amount	Gross State VAC_Remain Soc_Sec_ER K401_ER	Fed_Income K401 Sick Medicare_E	Soc_Sec VAC_Accrue Medical FUTA_ER	Medicare VAC_Taken Dental SUI_ER
SPRATT-01 Samuel Pratt 111-47-3336	3/31/03 999	1,148.62	1,583.33 -73.22 3.08 -98.17	-145.36 -95.00 -22.96	-98.17 3.08 -12.67	-22.96 -47.50
Total 3/1/03 thru 3/31/03		2,231.71	3,166.66 -146.44 6.16 -196.34 -79.17	-290.72 -190.00 -45.92	-196.34 6.16 -48.75 -25.34	-45.92 -16.78 -95.00

For each employee paycheck, the employee and employer taxes, vacation and sick pay amounts, health insurance deductions, and many other possible payroll benefits and deductions are tracked. In Chapter 9 you were shown how to create payroll fields for different types of tips and employee loans. Here we will cover the basic steps for adding a new type of payroll field for companies that have fringe benefits and additional deductions.

Fringe Benefits and Additional Deductions

Fringe benefits are additional payments, services, or items given to an employee. These benefits are often tax deductible and must be included in an employee's income for tax purposes. Examples of fringe benefits include a car allowance, company contest winnings such as trips or game tickets, or organization memberships. Fringe benefits that are not issued on a regular basis do not need to be set up until the end of your payroll year.

Additional deductions are amounts that are charged to the employee that may or may not affect the employee's withholdings.

To track a fringe benefit or an additional deduction, follow these steps:

1. Add the name of the fringe benefit or deduction as a new line in the EmployEE Fields tab of the Employee Defaults screen. The Field Name field is limited to 11 characters.
2. If you are reporting information but not adding or subtracting from the employees' paychecks, and you do not want to affect the general ledger accounts, click the **Memo** check box. If the amounts are tracked through a G/L account, enter the fields as shown in Chapter 9.
3. If the field does not affect taxable income, go to Step 8. If the field affects any employee taxes, go up the list of payroll field names to the Fed_Income line and click the **Adjust** button. You should not click the OK button yet.
4. Check the **Use** check box for the new field that you have created. Click **OK.** Repeat Steps 2 and 3 for each tax that needs to include the benefit, such as social security and Medicare taxes.
5. Without clicking OK, go to the **General** tab.
6. For taxable items, click the **W-2s** button in the Assign Payroll Fields for section.
7. Fringe Benefits are currently assigned to Box 12 on W-2s. Select the new field name from the drop-down list in the 12 field.
8. Click **OK.**
9. If all information has been entered correctly, click **OK** to leave the Employee Defaults screen.
10. For deductions, add the deduction amount to the employee record in the appropriate line for the deduction on the EmployEE Fields tab, or leave the amount blank and add the deduction as needed on the employee's paycheck.
11. To add the amount of a fringe benefit for the year, open the Payroll Entry form and select the correct employee.

    Enter the amount of a fringe benefit in the associated line in the Employee/Employer Fields section. The amount will affect net pay on a check so you should enter the amount on a regular paycheck in the correct payroll (calendar) year. If the taxes are greater than the net pay, you may need to divide the benefit between several paychecks.

Tip: For fringe benefits that are received regularly, you can add an amount to the fringe benefits field on the employee's record in the Maintain Employees/Sales Reps form. Go to the EmployEE Fields tab and unclick the **Std** check box. Then enter the amount to be added for each payroll period. The taxes will be calculated on the smaller amount rather than in a lump sum.

Balancing Payroll

Balancing payroll is fairly easy as long as you have continued to use your old accounting system according to the Three-Month Plan. Most of the effort of balancing goes into verifying that the payroll checks in Peachtree match the gross pay, net pay, and withholdings amounts of the paychecks in the old accounting system. Use the Current Earnings Report each month to verify that the amounts allocated to each of the payroll fields match the old fields. If you study the Peachtree and the old accounting system reports here, you will notice that the payroll for March 23, 2003, shows a difference between the two systems for Susan Peachy. The lines in the report for Susan Peachy are italicized for better identification.

Peachtree Accounting System

Employee	Ref	Date	Pay Type	Pay Hrs	Pay Amt	Net Pay	Fed_ Income	Soc_Sec	Medicare	State	K401	Vacation	Sick	Medical	Dental	Emp Loans
Amanda Chrisy	2051	3/14/03	Regular	14.00	196.00	108.89	-28.73	-12.15	-2.84	-0.55	-7.84			-28.50	-6.50	
Alex Kornylak	2052	3/14/03	Regular	25.00	350.00	173.92	-45.92	-21.70	-5.08	-4.38	-14.00	3.08	-8.00	-28.50	-6.50	-50.00
Dorothy Beckstrom	2053	3/14/03	Regular	12.00	108.00	99.73		-6.70	-1.57							
Derrick Grohs	2054	3/14/03	Salary		1,346.15	934.99	-111.92	-78.45	-18.35	-59.85	-80.77	3.08		-48.95	-12.87	
Elliot Adams	2055	3/14/03	Regular	16.00	192.00	158.40	-18.29	-11.90	-2.78	-0.63						
Mark Chambers	2056	3/14/03	Salary		1,458.33	950.43	-207.66	-90.42	-21.15	-66.17	-87.50	3.08		-28.50	-6.50	
Melvin Foster	2057	3/14/03	Salary		1,458.33	950.18	-207.66	-90.42	-21.15	-66.17	-87.50	3.08		-28.50	-6.75	
Marianna Markely	2058	3/14/03	Regular	23.00	207.00	130.16		-12.83	-3.00		-8.28	3.08	-8.00	-36.95	-15.78	
Mitchell Tamburrino	2059	3/14/03	Regular	35.00	385.00	226.32	-58.48	-23.87	-5.58	-5.79	-15.40	3.08		-36.78	-12.78	
Michelle Wang	2060	3/14/03	Regular	35.00	315.00	253.14	-36.36	-19.53	-4.57	-1.40		3.08				
Steve Barton	2061	3/14/03	Regular	37.50	412.50	246.09	-49.25	-25.58	-5.98	-7.88	-16.50	3.08		-48.75	-12.47	
Susan Peachey	*2062*	*3/14/03*	*Regular*	*40.00*	*360.00*	*289.86*	*-2.26*	*-22.32*	*-5.22*	*-6.08*		*-5.08*		*-28.50*	*-6.50*	
Samuel Pratt	2063	3/14/03	Salary		1,583.33	1,083.09	-145.36	-98.17	-22.96	-73.22	-95.00	3.08		-48.75	-16.78	
3/1/03 thru 3/31/03			Salary		2,525.50	*1,686.51*	-911.89	-514.04	-120.23	-292.12	-412.79	22.64	-16.00	-362.68	-103.43	-50.00
3/1/03 thru 3/31/03			Regular	237.50	5,846.14	3,918.69										

Old Accounting System

Salaried Employees	Check#	Date	Pay Type	Pay Amt	Fed_ Income	Soc_Sec	Medicare	State	K401	Vacation	Sick	Med	Dental	Emp Loans	Net Pay
Derrick Grohs	2054	3/14/03	Salary	1,346.15	-111.92	-78.45	-18.35	-59.85	-80.77	3.08		-48.95	-12.87		934.99
Mark Chambers	2056	3/14/03	Salary	1,458.33	-207.66	-90.42	-21.15	-66.17	-87.50	3.08		-28.50	-6.50		950.43
Melvin Foster	2057	3/14/03	Salary	1,458.33	-207.66	-90.42	-21.15	-66.17	-87.50	3.08		-28.50	-6.75		950.18
Samuel Pratt	2063	3/14/03	Salary	1,583.33	-145.36	-98.17	-22.96	-73.22	-95.00	3.08		-48.75	-16.78		1,083.09
3/1/03 thru 3/31/03			Salary	5,846.14	-672.60	-357.46	-83.61	-265.41	-350.77	12.32	0.00	-154.70	-42.90	0.00	3,918.69

Hourly Employees	Check#	Date	Pay Type	Pay Hrs	Pay Amt	Fed_ Income	Soc_Sec	Medicare	State	K401	Vacation	Sick	Medical	Dental	Emp Loans	Net Pay
Amanda Chrisy	2051	3/14/03	Hourly	14.00	196.00	-28.73	-12.15	-2.84	-0.55	-7.84			-28.50	-6.50		108.89
Alex Kornylak	2052	3/14/03	Hourly	25.00	350.00	-45.92	-21.70	-5.08	-4.38	-14.00	3.08	-8.00	-28.50	-6.50	-50.00	173.92
Dorothy Beckstrom	2053	3/14/03	Hourly	12.00	108.00		-6.70	-1.57								99.73
Elliot Adams	2055	3/14/03	Hourly	16.00	192.00	-18.29	-11.90	-2.78	-0.63							158.40
Marianna Markely	2058	3/14/03	Hourly	23.00	207.00		-12.83	-3.00		-8.28	3.08	-8.00	-36.95	-15.78		130.16
Mitchell Tamburrino	2059	3/14/03	Hourly	35.00	385.00	-58.48	-23.87	-5.58	-5.79	-15.40	3.08		-36.78	-12.78		226.32
Michelle Wang	2060	3/14/03	Hourly	35.00	315.00	-36.36	-19.53	-4.57	-1.40		3.08					253.14
Steve Barton	2061	3/14/03	Hourly	37.50	412.50	-49.25	-25.58	-5.98	-7.88	-16.50	3.08		-48.75	-12.47		246.09
Susan Peachey	*2062*	*3/14/03*	*Hourly*	*40.00*	*360.00*	*-24.58*	*-22.32*	*-5.22*	*-6.08*		*-5.08*		*-28.50*	*-6.50*		*266.80*
3/1/03 thru 3/31/03			Hourly	237.50	2,525.50	-261.61	-156.58	-36.62	-26.71	-62.02	10.32	-16.00	-207.98	-60.53	-50.00	*1,663.45*

By looking at the deductions and net pay you can see that the federal income withholding is off for Susan Peachy. By going into your old records, you discover that Ms. Peachy was recently married and the old system still has her as single and is therefore taking out more of her pay for taxes.

If you are using the old system to distribute checks instead of the new Peachtree system, you can open up that check in Peachtree and make the adjustments in the correct payroll fields to match the original system. For companies that are handing out the Peachtree checks instead of the old checks, you will need to make the changes to the check in your old system or contact your CPA to determine what journal entries are needed.

At the end of each month, if you have a separate account, you must balance the payroll checking account. Use the instructions in Chapter 11 to add the general ledger beginning balance for the payroll checking account and for the steps for balancing the account. The Check Register and the Account Reconciliation reports should both match the old accounting system. The report shown here is for demonstration purposes only and is to show final balance errors only.

Peachtree Payroll Account Registration	
Beginning GL Balance	6,566.66
Add: Cash Receipts	
Less: Cash Disbursements	<10,322.84>
Add <Less> Other	10,000.00
Ending GL Balance	6,243.82
Ending Bank Balance	4,892.49
Add back deposits in transit	
Total deposits in transit	
<Less> outstanding checks	
Total outstanding checks	<5,430.35>
Add <Less> Other	
Total other	
Unreconciled difference	16,566.66
Ending GL Balance	6,243.82

Old Accounting System	
Beginning GL Balance	6,566.66
Add: Cash Receipts	10,000.00
Less: Cash Disbursements	(10,345.90)
Ending GL Balance	6,243.82
Ending Bank Balance	14,892.49
Total outstanding checks	(5,453.41)
Unreconciled difference	16,589.72
Ending GL Balance	6,220.76

Again, if these do not match, you must go through the checks to determine where the errors are located and make the changes to the old or the Peachtree accounting system.

Peachtree Payroll Check Register

Reference	Date	Employee	Amount
2051	3/14/03	Amanda Chrisy	137.62
2052	3/14/03	Alex Kornylak	269.84
2053	3/14/03	Dorothy Beckstrom	99.73
2054	3/14/03	Derrick Grohs	934.99
2055	3/14/03	Elliot Adams	176.69
2056	3/14/03	Mark Chambers	950.43
2057	3/14/03	Melvin Foster	950.18
2058	3/14/03	Marianna Markely	130.16
2059	3/14/03	Mitchell Tamburrino	284.80
2060	3/14/03	Michelle Wang	289.50
2061	3/14/03	Steve Barton	295.34
2062	***3/14/03***	***Susan Peachey***	***266.80***
2063	3/14/03	Samuel Pratt	1,083.09
		3/1/03 thru 3/31/03	5,869.17

Old Accounting System

Reference	Date	Employee	Amount
2051	3/14/03	Amanda Chrisy	137.62
2052	3/14/03	Alex Kornylak	269.84
2053	3/14/03	Dorothy Beckstrom	99.73
2054	3/14/03	Derrick Grohs	934.99
2055	3/14/03	Elliot Adams	176.69
2056	3/14/03	Mark Chambers	950.43
2057	3/14/03	Melvin Foster	950.18
2058	3/14/03	Marianna Markely	130.16
2059	3/14/03	Mitchell Tamburrino	284.80
2060	3/14/03	Michelle Wang	289.50
2061	3/14/03	Steve Barton	295.34
2062	***3/14/03***	***Susan Peachey***	***289.86***
2063	3/14/03	Samuel Pratt	1,083.09
		3/1/03 thru 3/31/03	5,892.23

In this process, you should also look at the general ledger balances for the payroll taxes payables reports to verify that they match between the old and new systems. Errors for these amounts are detected in the same way, by searching the individual paychecks for discrepancies. Also check that the beginning balances for each system are correct. Running general ledger reports is covered in Chapter 16.

Bellwether Garden Supply
General Ledger
For the Period From Mar 1, 2003 to Mar 31, 2003
Filter Criteria includes: Report order is by ID. Report is printed with Truncated Transaction Descriptions and in Summary By Journal Format.

Account ID Account Description	Date	Jrnl	Trans Description	Debit Amt	Credit Amt	Balance
23400	3/1/03		Beginning Balance			-1,586.85
Federal Payroll Taxes Pa		PRJ	Payroll Totals		3,795.17	
			Current Period Change		3,795.17	-3,795.17
	3/31/03		Ending Balance			-5,382.02
23500	3/1/03		Beginning Balance			-258.20
FUTA Tax Payable						
	3/31/03		Ending Balance			-258.20
23600	3/1/03		Beginning Balance			-985.33
State Payroll Taxes Paya		PRJ	Payroll Totals		510.00	
			Current Period Change		510.00	-510.00
	3/31/03		Ending Balance			-1,495.33

Once all of your G/L balances and checks match, then your payroll is balanced. After finishing the Three-Month Plan, you do not need to check the payroll balances with the same intensity. Before payroll checks are run, print the Payroll Register and go over the amounts to see if they are reasonable and that all deductions have been calculated. Double-check that payroll amounts, like employee loans and medical insurance, are being deducted and that the hours are correct.

Tip: Use the Payroll Register for the last payroll period and see if employees' records for the current payroll period are a close match; that way you don't have to rely on your memory to recall all of the amounts.

At the end of each month you will balance the payroll checking account. The tax liability report and the general ledger report will be used when required to create your 941 and other tax deposits. If year-end reports and forms are run from Peachtree at the end of the payroll (calendar) year, the amounts should then be correct.

Payroll Reports

In Chapter 9 the Payroll Register and the Tax Liability reports were shown. The Payroll Register is best used to determine actual payments and withholdings for an individual payroll period. It includes pay type (salary, regular, overtime), pay hours broken down by pay type, and the associated pay amount. The Tax Liability report can be run for any period and helps you calculate the taxes due for federal, state, and federal unemployment. Printing W-2s is covered in Chapter 18.

The Current Earnings Report

This report is usually run for the current period. It does not show the beginning balances for the payroll fields but does include them in the year-to-date totals. The report does not show the pay type and hours but does include the check date and check number. The report filter is identical to the Payroll Register report filter.

Bellwether Garden Supply
Current Earnings Report
For the Period From Mar 1, 2003 to Mar 31, 2003
Filter Criteria includes: Report order is by Employee ID. Report is printed in Show Totals Only Format.

Employee ID Employee SS No	Date Reference	Amount	Gross State VAC_Remain Bill Hours FUTA_ER	Fed_Income K401 Sick Emp Loans SUI_ER	Soc_Sec VAC_Accrue Medical Soc_Sec_ER K401_ER	Medicare VAC_Taken Dental Medicare_ER
Report Date Total for		740.47	880.00	-40.56	-54.56	-12.76
Tyler Riddle			-31.65		3.08	
			3.08			
					-54.56	-12.76
			-7.04	-26.40		
YTD Total for		740.47	880.00	-40.56	-54.56	-12.76
Tyler Riddle			-31.65		3.08	
			3.08			
					-54.56	-12.76
			-7.04	-26.40		
Summary Total		10,322.84	14,034.97	-1,172.95	-855.25	-200.03
3/1/03 thru 3/31/03			-510.00	-507.79	58.52	
			58.52		-362.68	-103.43
					-848.46	-198.44
			-109.50	-410.54	-354.34	
Report Date Final Total		10,322.84	14,034.97	-1,172.95	-855.25	-200.03
3/1/03 thru 3/31/03			-510.00	-507.79	58.52	
			58.52		-362.68	-103.43
					-848.46	-198.44
			-109.50	-410.54	-354.34	

The Quarterly Earnings Report and the Yearly Earnings Report

The only difference between these reports and the Current Earnings Report is that the quarterly report defaults to the current quarter and the yearly report defaults to the current year. The reports also include a period beginning balance.

Bellwether Garden Supply
Quarterly Earnings Report
For the Period From Jan 1, 2003 to Mar 31, 2003
Filter Criteria includes: Report order is by Employee ID. Report is printed in Detail Format.

Employee ID Employee SS No	Date Reference	Amount	Gross State VAC_Remain Bill Hours FUTA_ER	Fed_Income K401 Sick Emp Loans SUI_ER	Soc_Sec VAC_Accrue Medical Soc_Sec_ER K401_ER	Medicare VAC_Taken Dental Medicare_ER
ACHRISTY-01	1/1/03					
Amanda Chrisy	BEGBAL					
111-22-1337				40.00		
ACHRISTY-01	3/14/03	137.62	196.00		-12.15	-2.84
Amanda Chrisy	2051		-0.55	-7.84	3.08	
111-22-1337			3.08		-28.50	-6.50
					-12.15	-2.84
			-1.57	-5.88	-7.84	
		137.62	196.00		-12.15	-2.84
Total 1/1/03 thru 3/31/03			-0.55	-7.84	3.08	
			3.08	40.00	-28.50	-6.50
					-12.15	-2.84
			-1.57	-5.88	-7.84	

941 Report

Most small companies use a standard 941 report and can print the report onto the form directly from Peachtree. Print the report following these steps:

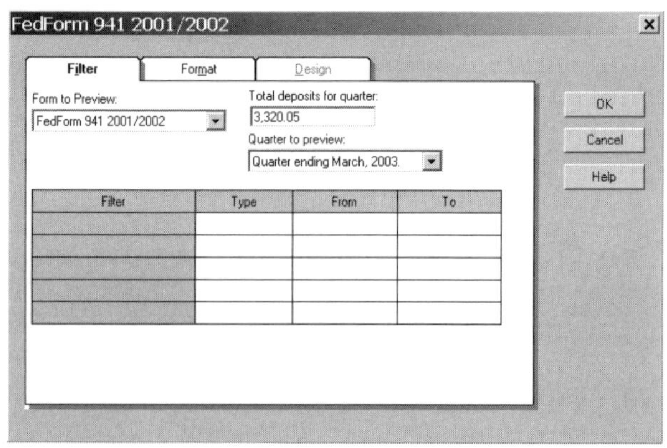

1. On the Select a Report screen, select **Payroll** in the Report Area and the current 941 form, such as **FedForm 941 2001/2002**, from Report List. Click **Preview** or **Print**.
2. Verify that the appropriate quarter is selected in the Quarter to preview (print) drop-down field.
3. On the filter, enter the amount paid for the quarter in the Total deposits for quarter field.
4. Click **OK** to view the report.

```
Bellwether Garden Supply          Mar 31, 2003

                                  100-201-110

1505 Pavilion Place
Norcross, GA  30093-3203
USA

                                       18
                                                          13423.75
                                                           1172.95

                                                           1172.95
                              14034.97                     1740.34

                              14034.97                      407.04

                                                           2147.38


                                                           2147.38
                                                           3320.33


                                                           3320.33

                                                           3320.05

                                                              0.28
```

5. Verify the report, place the 941 in the printer, and print the report. You will probably want to print the report on plain paper first to verify the alignment.

Summary

Adding new fields to Peachtree is one of the few areas that can be very confusing. Between this chapter and the information in Chapter 9, most of your concerns should be addressed. Whenever possible, let the Payroll Setup Wizard handle the creation of new payroll fields. If your company is small, you do not need to worry about a separate payroll checking account, but can print checks from the regular account.

You should have your payroll account and payroll function balanced by the end of the second month to be on target with your Three-Month Plan.

Month 3

The Reconciliation Month

- Reconciling the General Ledger
- Reconciling Inventory
- Reporting
- Finalization and Follow-Up

Chapter 16

Reconciling the General Ledger

In This Chapter

- Starting the reconciliation month
- Your CPA's role
- Understanding general ledger accounts
- General ledger beginning balances
- Creating journal entries, including recurring and memorized entries
- Verifying ending balances
- The balance sheet and the income statement

Your Three-Month Plan — The Reconciliation Month

By this time in your Three-Month Plan, the data entry functions should be at the point that all employees are comfortable with the new procedures, forms, and reports. The checking account, accounts receivable, accounts payable, and sales taxes should be implemented and you should feel confident that the balances and reports accurately report the true state of your company.

In this month we will finish up the final reporting responsibilities, verify the general ledger, and create adjusting journal entries. For this reason, this month is named the reconciliation month because balances will be verified against your CPA's records and the beginning and ending trial balances supplied by your CPA and in the old accounting system. You may need to work with your CPA this month to get all account balances correct.

Some companies complete the second month quickly enough that they can start this month early. Many of my clients who work diligently to follow all steps are able to complete the Three-Month Plan in two months. Regardless, you should have spent all of the first month on data entry procedures and most of the second month reconciling the accounts in the earlier parts of this book.

Warning!! Regardless of whether you complete your Three-Month Plan in two or three months, you must continue to use your old accounting system until the end of your plan. This is absolutely imperative until all balances in Peachtree have been verified against the old system.

In this chapter I will need to explain some basics of accounting to you. I highly recommend that you take a class or seminar if you do not have any accounting training. There are numerous "Accounting for Non-Accountants" seminars around the country. The additional insight that you gain there can only improve your skills in managing your accounting function. It will also assist you in understanding the adjustments that your CPA will occasionally request. This means you will be able to back up your financial statements with real knowledge when discussing them with your banker, creditors, and other financial partners.

If you are already familiar with generally accepted accounting procedures or are an actual accountant in your own right, the next section may be beneath your interest. If you have no understanding of accounting, this next section may be extremely enlightening.

Accounting and the CPA

Although Peachtree does not require you to know anything about accounting, a little knowledge can give you a big understanding of what Peachtree's reports mean, how errors affect the reports, and how errors can be corrected. We will cover some basic knowledge of accounting in the first part of this chapter. We will also discuss the importance of a well-trained and objective CPA.

Accounting is the process of quantifying economic information about an organization. Most information is financial in nature and is used in making decisions that affect the organization. The decisions made are based on questions that can be asked about the information provided. The questions vary according to the person asking them. A manager might ask "How much did we earn?", "What do we owe?", "Are we collecting all the money that we are owed in a timely manner?", and similar questions. A creditor might ask "Does this organization make enough money on a regular basis to pay me back?" or "Does she pay her bills on time?" And then we have all those pesky questions asked by the government.

Despite all of the news headlines to the contrary in 2002, accounting is a profession that is practiced ethically by most of its members. A CPA, certified public accountant, is an individual who has completed a difficult, thorough, and highly disciplined college program and has taken an exhaustive multi-day test that is rigorously managed by the AICPA (American Institute of Certified Public Accountants). In addition, most states require that a CPA have several years of actual work experience in an accounting position before the CPA is licensed.

Some GPAs in private practice only concentrate on what is called "write-up" work. Write-up services are basic data entry services where the CPA takes your checks, deposit slips, invoices, and bills and creates a financial statement from the information at some time in the near future. They also do all of your taxes. Some may do all of your payroll and write the paychecks also. With Peachtree, all of that can be done by you. Peachtree takes you away from the shoebox full of pieces of paper and, instead, gives you the power to know what all of those pieces of paper mean in dollars, and it does it today.

So where does that leave the accountant? Your CPA should be an independent and objective advisor. You should take advantage of the CPA's ability to see the economic standing of your organization from a viewpoint that is both knowledgeable and experienced, who can then offer constructive advice about your operations. With Peachtree, the CPA receives reports and data in electronic format and uses that information to 1) determine final adjustments to monthly and year-end G/L balances so that financial statements are deemed correct and in balance; 2) provide professional tax reporting services for payroll and income taxes, including tax strategies; and 3) offer management advisory services in the processes and procedures of your business to improve the business's economic situation. So take advantage of your CPA and let her help you take your business into the future.

General Ledger Accounts

If accounting is the process of quantifying economic information, then a general ledger account is the tool used to collect the raw data of a transaction in the process. By classifying the activities that occur in your organization by general ledger accounts, certain totals are determined. The amounts of accounts receivable, cash, equity, and other accounts are computed. These amounts can be looked at individually or they can be used in standardized calculations to determine the health of your organization. That is what your creditor does when he asks the amount of your current assets and current liabilities. These amounts are analyzed together and, depending upon your type of business, must fall within a certain range; otherwise your company may be said to be a poor risk.

Many aspects of your company can easily be determined based upon the amounts in your general ledger accounts. That is one of the reasons accounting was invented — not just to torture poor Bob Cratchit and to allow Charles Dickens the chance to write a classic tale.

By now you should have a basic understanding that when you create a transaction in Peachtree, such as paying a bill, you are affecting at least two G/L accounts, in our case the amount cataloged as an expense of the business and the amount of the cash withdrawn from the checking account. The general ledger account is used to summarize the portions of a transaction that apply to the category that the account represents.

Debits and Credits

A general ledger account in its original manual form is called a T-account. Its shape gives the account two sides, each of which can have numbers recorded in it.

General Ledger Account	
Left Side - Debits	Right side - Credits

Numbers recorded on the left side are called *debits*. Numbers recorded on the right side are called *credits*. Forget everything you know about the debits and credits to your checking account and your credit card. Debit and credit do not refer to plus and minus. The terms refer to the side of the account that the transaction is placed. If we look at four accounts, we can see the basics of double-entry accounting and how they relate to Peachtree.

Checking Account

Work performed for D. Smith	500.00		
		Purchase pens and paper	25.00
Work performed for L. Young	850.00		
		A. Miller Accounting services	350.00

Income

		Work performed for J. Smith	500.00
		Work performed for L. Young	850.00

Office Supplies

Purchase pens and paper	25.00		

Accounting Expense

A. Miller Accounting services	350.00		

Each transaction above is recorded as a debit or a credit in two different accounts. "Purchase pens and paper" appears as a credit in the Checking Account and as a debit in the Office Supplies account. In certain accounts the debit (left) side of the transaction increases the account, such as Office Supplies, and in other accounts the credit (right) side of the transactions increases the account, such as the Checking Account.

Using Debits and Credits to Balance Accounts

The double entry of the transaction in two accounts makes it easy to verify that amounts have been entered correctly. Adding up all of the debits and credits of the accounts should give you the same totals for each side.

	Debits	Credits
Checking Account	1,350.00	375.00
Income		1,350.00
Office Supplies	25.00	
Accounting Expense	350.00	
	1,725.00	1,725.00

If the purchase of pens and paper were recorded incorrectly as $35.00 in the Office Supplies account, the debit side would be $1735.00. Our accounts would be out of balance and we would be aware that there was an error someplace. Generally, Peachtree stops you from making unbalanced entries. The same entry in Peachtree would occur on a form.

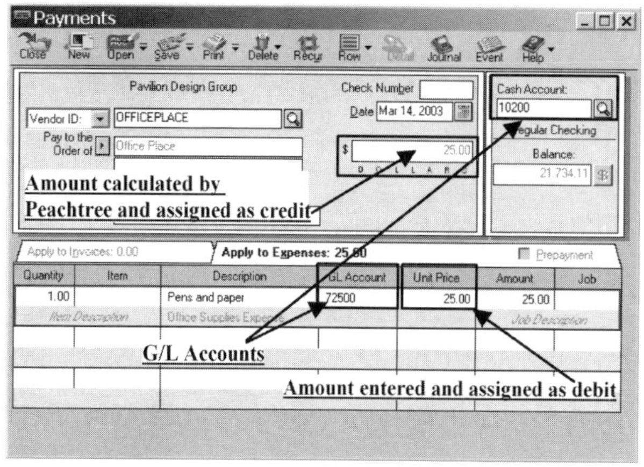

If you enter $25.00 on the transaction line, Peachtree understands that the entry is a debit on the Payments form and adds the total of all lines on the form. The amount calculated is the Dollars field and it is the credit that balances the transaction. If we click the Journal button, we can see the result in the Accounting Behind the Screens window.

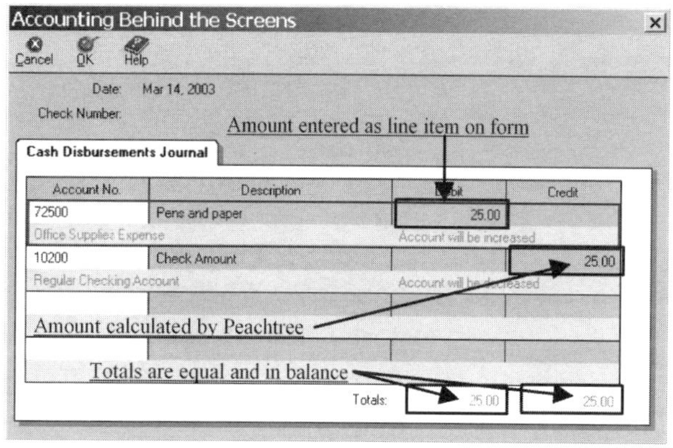

If the purchase were for a variety of items such as office supplies, office equipment, and computer software, the amount of the credit would be the total of the line items. There would not be separate lines in the checking account entry for each entry in the other accounts.

The General Ledger Report

You can view all of the transactions for any or all of the general ledger accounts by running a General Ledger report. To preview a report for a single account, follow these steps:

1. Open the Select a Report screen and select **General Ledger** in the Report Area and **General Ledger** in the Report List.

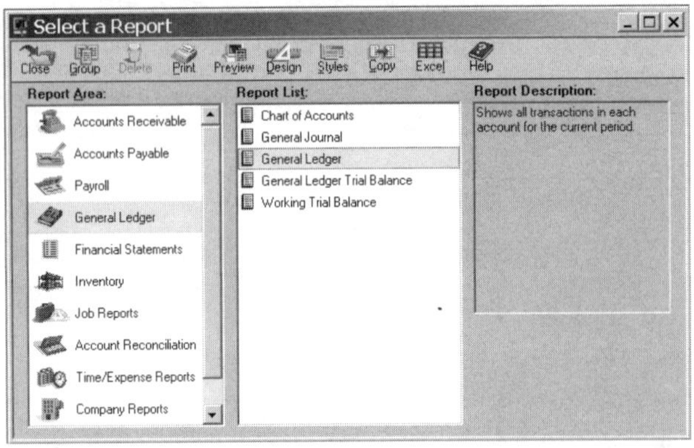

2. Click the **Preview** button on the toolbar to select what portions of the general ledger you want to view. The General Ledger dialog box appears.

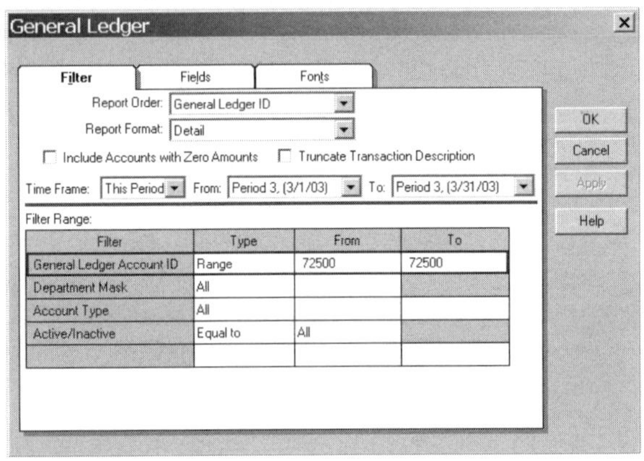

3. The Report Order field can remain set to General Ledger ID, although General Ledger Description is available. When you look at a group of G/L accounts, you will usually want to view them in the order they appear in the chart of accounts (COA) which is by General Ledger ID. The Report Format field allows you to view G/L accounts by Detail or summarized by day, period, journal, or transaction. Depending upon what you need to view, some of the summary formats can greatly reduce the amount of information in the report. We will select **Detail** for now.

4. The Include Accounts with Zero Amounts check box should be selected if you want to see the activity and balances of all accounts, even if the final balance is 0.00. We will leave it unselected.

5. The Truncate Transaction Description option is another mechanism whereby information can be reduced on the report. Some descriptions will carry over to a second, or even third, line and selecting this check box cuts off lines after the first. Uncheck the box so we can view full descriptions.

6. The Time Frame field is called Date in some versions. General Ledger reports are run for a length of time. Selections are This Period, All, and Range. The minimum range is one accounting period. We will use **This Period.**

7. The From and To fields allow you to select period beginning and ending dates, not an actual date. Verify that Period 3, (3/1/03) and Period 3, (3/31/03) are selected from the drop-down lists.

8. Next, in the Filter Range section, on the General Ledger Account ID line, select **Range** in the Type field. In both the From and To fields, enter **72500**. We are going to view the report for a single G/L account.

   Department Mask is not discussed in this book. Leave the associated fields blank.

   Account Type comes from the general ledger record and is used to describe a group of accounts such as Cash, Accounts Receivable, etc. You may select a specific account type from the drop-down. Be aware that if you choose Accounts Receivable in the From field and Cash in the To field that you will also see Accumulated Depreciation accounts on the report. Generally this field is not used because the General Ledger Account ID fields are available.

   The Active/Inactive line allows you to select All, Active, or Inactive accounts for the report from the drop-down. The Type field is always set to Equal to. The default is All.

9. Click **OK** to view the report for the Office Supplies expense G/L account. For this report I have included the complete Peachtree window so that the toolbar, scroll bars, navigation aid, and menu bar are visible.

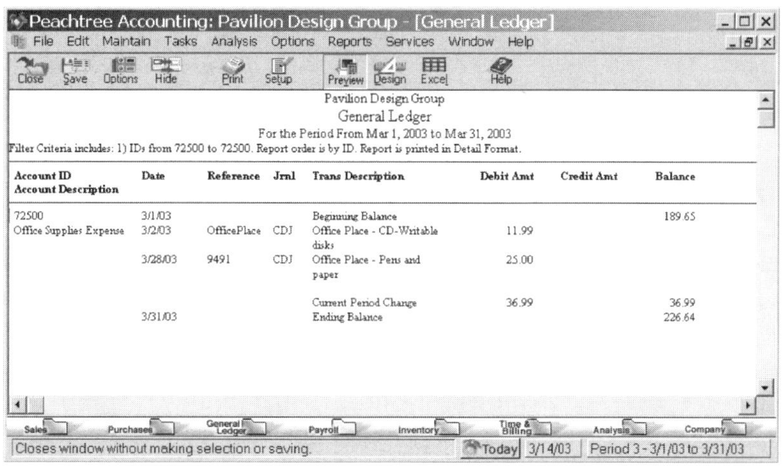

The report shows a lot of information about the transactions that occurred in the Office Supplies Expense account. There is a Beginning Balance line for the account that shows the account balance on 3/1/03 for transactions that occurred during the fiscal year before this period. Each transaction shows the Date, Reference (check number or credit card reference), Jrnl (journal) where the transaction took place, Trans Description, and Debit Amt or Credit Amt.

The Debit Amt and Credit Amt fields on the report retain the T-account format with debits on the left and credits on the right. For this account, all transactions occurring in this period were purchases and debited the expense account.

At the end of the account, on the Change line, the debits and credits are totaled and the net sum of the transactions is shown in the Balance column. This amount is added to the Beginning Balance to calculate the account's Ending Balance on the last day of the period.

If you wanted to look at the details of one of the transactions, you would place your cursor over the transaction until it looks like a magnifying glass.

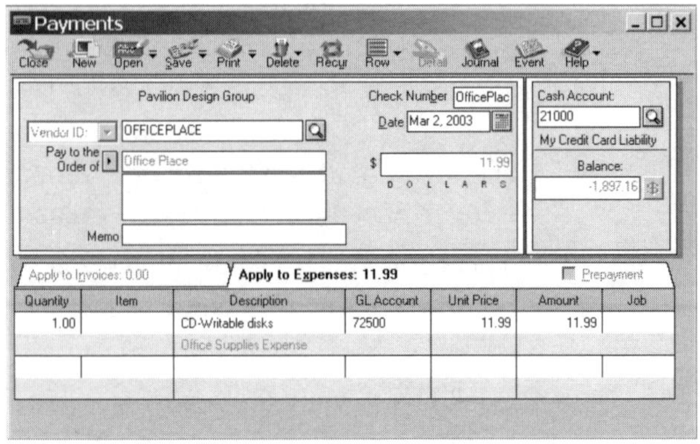

10. Double-click the mouse and the original transaction appears.
11. You can make changes or corrections on the transaction. Click **Save** or **Post** to record the changes and then click **Close** to close the form. The corrections would then appear on the General Ledger report.
12. From the toolbar you can send this report to Microsoft Excel by clicking the **Excel** button. When the button is clicked, the Copy Report to Excel dialog box appears.

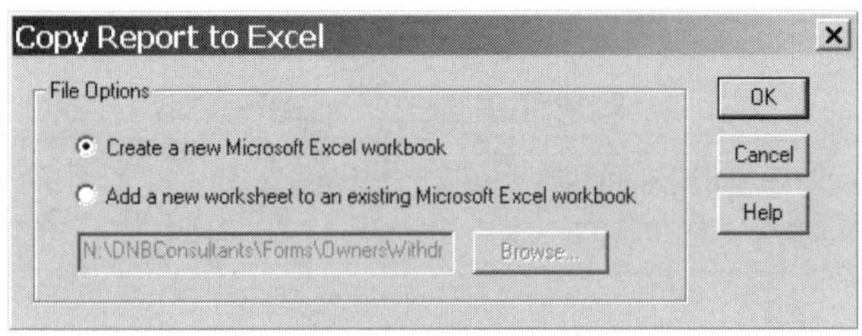

13. You can choose to create a new Microsoft Excel workbook or add a new worksheet to an existing workbook. If you select the second option, use the **Browse** button to locate an existing file. Selecting the first option and clicking the **OK** button starts the copy process. A status bar appears while the process is working.

14. When the copy process is complete, the Excel worksheet appears on the Windows taskbar. Open the Excel report to view the information.

Tip: I have discovered that the copying process is much quicker if you open Excel to a blank workbook or open the existing file to which you are copying before clicking the Excel button.

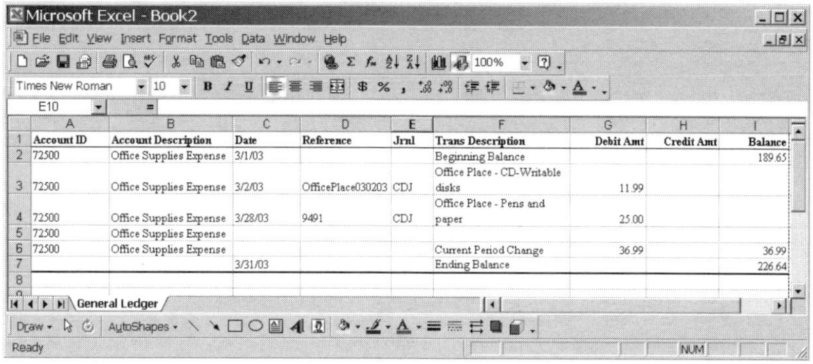

The report does not look exactly like the Peachtree report, but all of the data are included. Any totals on the report are values, not formulas, so if you want to perform any number crunching you will need to make some changes.

Going back to the Peachtree report and the toolbar, the Save button saves all of the filters for the report so that it can be run exactly the same way every time you need the information. This can be very helpful if you add fields to the report. Always save the report under a new name, not with the Peachtree report name, because reinstalling the current version or upgrading to a newer version can cause the report to be overwritten.

The Hide button removes the company name, report name, and other information from the top of the screen. This option is important when viewing longer reports.

Clicking the Print button will allow you to print the report.

The Setup button takes you to the Page Setup dialog box to enable you to change the page orientation to portrait or landscape. It also controls the printer tray used to print the report.

The Design button allows you to change the width of columns on the report. When you are done, click the **Preview** button to return to the report.

15. Click **Close** to close the report.

    If you run a General Ledger report for several accounts, you can see the different debits and credits in the accounts along with the account balances.

Account ID Account Description	Date	Reference	Jrnl	Trans Description	Debit Amt	Credit Amt	Balance
71000	3/1/03			Beginning Balance			
Maintenance and Repairs	3/14/03	656996	PJ	Computers R US - Network Maintenance	650.00		
				Current Period Change	650.00		650.00
	3/31/03			Ending Balance			650.00
72500	3/1/03			Beginning Balance			189.65
Office Supplies Expense	3/2/03	OfficePlace	CDJ	Office Place - CD-Writable disks	11.99		
	3/28/03	9491	CDJ	Office Place - Pens and paper	25.00		
				Current Period Change	36.99		36.99
	3/31/03			Ending Balance			226.64
73000	3/1/03			Beginning Balance			
Outside Services Expense	3/2/03	P-4323	PJ	Mathers Printing - Item: PRESS01 - Press Time: Schedule time, plates, die cut, etc.	190.00		
	3/24/03	P-4606	PJ	Mathers Printing		475.00	
	3/24/03	P-4606	PJ	Mathers Printing - Item: PRESS01 - Press Time: Schedule time, plates, die cut, etc.	475.00		
	3/31/03	989898	PJ	Peter's Photography Lab		113.70	
				Current Period Change	665.00	588.70	76.30
	3/31/03			Ending Balance			76.30

The Trial Balance

Now that you have looked more closely at the general ledger, you need to see how the general ledger balances come together in a report called the trial balance. In earlier times, accountants and bookkeepers with their long lists of ledgers would place the ending balance of each account on a new report with the debit balances and credit balances each in their respective column. If done correctly, according to accounting principles, the debits and credits would equal each other and balance. If the report did not balance, the bookkeepers would go back over the earlier ledgers to locate the error. This trial and error type of verifying the accuracy of accounts is one of the reasons the report is called a trial balance.

In today's computerized accounting system, addition and subtraction errors do not occur. The trial balance is still important because it allows you to quickly see the balance of each general ledger account. The debits and credits will always match because Peachtree should not allow unbalanced transactions in the normal use of the program.

After entering one to two months of data, reconciling accounts receivable and payable, and setting up payroll, a number of general ledger accounts should have balances in the trial balance. The GL Metal Fabricators Company-PreRec.ptb file included with the companion files will be used for most of the rest of this chapter. To load the chapter, use the Restore function and copy over one of the sample companies. You may want to make a backup of the sample company first if you want to use any information in the sample company at a later time.

After loading the G/L Metal Fabricators Company file, you may run the trial balance report following these steps. You may also run the report in this manner for any other sample company.

1. In the Select a Report window, select **General Ledger** in the Report Area and **General Ledger Trial Balance** in the Report List. Click **Preview** and the General Ledger Trial Balance filter will appear.

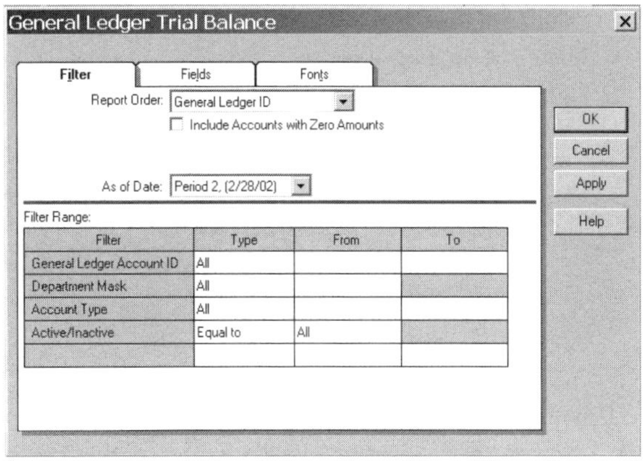

2. Select **General Ledger ID** from the Report Order drop-down. The only other choice for Report Order is General Ledger Description.
3. Verify that **Include Accounts with Zero Amounts** is selected.
4. Select the As of Date from the drop-down. For this report select **Period 2, (2/28/02)**. The trial balance is like a snapshot and shows the balance of selected accounts as of the last day of any given period. The report does not reflect any activity before or after the specified date.
5. In the Filter Range section you may reduce the number of accounts that appear on the report, but doing so will defeat the purpose of the report because, by definition, a trial balance shows all the account balances and also shows that the total of all accounts on the debit side should equal all the accounts on the debit side.
6. We will ignore the filters for now. Click **OK** to see the report.

G/L Metal Fabricators Company
General Ledger Trial Balance
As of Feb 28, 2002
Filter Criteria includes: Report order is by ID. Report is printed in Detail Format.

Account ID	Account Description	Debit Amt	Credit Amt
10200	Regular Checking Account	50,899.96	
10400	Savings Account	50,586.54	
10700	Investments-Cert. of Deposit	100,000.00	
11000	Accounts Receivable	294,129.61	
20000	Accounts Payable		145,483.00
23100	Sales Tax Payable		7,659.41
23400	Payroll Taxes Payable		12,090.76
39005	Retained Earnings		330,382.94
	Total:	495,616.11	495,616.11

7. The accounts shown here are G/L accounts that have been added in the setup of the company when we needed to add account balances for the bank accounts' beginning balances, the A/R invoices, the A/P bills, and other information. Notice how the account balances are set up in a T-account format. Every account with a balance not

equal to zero appears on the report. At the bottom of the report the debits and credits are totaled. The amounts clearly balance each other.

If we look at the trial balance for the first month after adding transactions, we can see more accounts and information.

G/L Metal Fabricators Company
General Ledger Trial Balance
As of Mar 31, 2002
Filter Criteria includes: Report order is by ID. Report is printed in Detail Format.

Account ID	Account Description	Debit Amt	Credit Amt
10200	Regular Checking Account	169,343.84	
10400	Savings Account	50,586.54	
10700	Investments-Cert. of Deposit	100,000.00	
11000	Accounts Receivable	206,451.09	
12000	Materials & Supplies Inventory		544.00
20000	Accounts Payable		99,126.85
23100	Sales Tax Payable		14,689.85
23400	Payroll Taxes Payable		24,468.85
39005	Retained Earnings		330,382.94
40000	Metal Fabrication Income		340,483.67
45500	Shipping Charges Reimbursed		8,819.00
49000	Sales Discounts	2,827.67	
50000	Cost of Goods Sold	123,763.00	
57500	Cost of Sales-Freight	9,316.00	
65500	Freight & Postage Expense	1,426.99	
70000	Maintenance Expense	6,706.00	
71000	Office Expense	661.14	
72000	Payroll Tax Expense	4,641.93	
73500	Rent or Lease Equipment	19,797.18	
74000	Rent or Lease Expense	15,500.00	
75000	Shop Uniforms, Gloves, Goggles	14,694.26	
76000	Telephone Expense	23,776.00	
77000	Salaries Expense	14,030.00	
77500	Wages Expense	36,735.75	
78000	Utilities Expense	19,586.59	
89500	Purchase Disc-Expense Items		1,328.82
	Total:	819,843.98	819,843.98

The numbers here still will not match the records of our CPA, because we postponed entering beginning account balances, which is the next step.

General Ledger Beginning Balances

Now that you have gained an understanding of the way that the accounts are used in Peachtree and how the balances may be viewed, it is time to move on to entering the starting amounts for your account balances so that your trial balance matches your CPA's trial balance. Depending upon which lists you have of those requested back in Chapter 4, your process may go a little differently from the one shown here. Regardless of the Go Live date, your trial balance must agree with your CPA's by the end of the Three-Month Plan.

Using the same company, G/L Metal Fabricators Company, shown above, we can enter the rest of the beginning balances for the general ledger accounts. From the CPA we have determined that the following trial balance is accurate and can be used for the beginning balances.

Tip: If the month prior to your Begin Transactions date is in the previous accounting year, your trial balance should be after all income and expense accounts are closed to retained earnings and all final journal entries have been entered in the CPA's books.

Note: Although the retained earnings account is used in the examples cited, your company may use a different account per your CPA's instructions.

Account ID	Account Description	Debit Amt	Credit Amt
10000	Petty Cash	100.00	
10200	Regular Checking Account	50,899.96	
10400	Savings Account	50,586.54	
10700	Investments-Cert. of Deposit	100,000.00	
11000	Accounts Receivable	294,129.61	
12000	Materials & Supplies Inventory	43,337.74	
15000	Fixed Assets	285,694.34	
17000	Accum. Depreciation		100,440.66
20000	Accounts Payable		145,483.00
23100	Sales Tax Payable		7,659.41
23400	Payroll Taxes Payable		12,090.76
27000	Notes Payable		45,000.00
39003	Common Stock		100,000.00
39004	Paid-in Capital		280,000.00
39005	Retained Earnings		113,241.74
40000	Metal Fabrication Income		360,434.68
40200	Sheet Metal Income		14,784.00
40400	Custom Artwork Income		128,566.00
40600	Interest Income		828.65
45500	Shipping Charges Reimbursed		14,935.26
49000	Sales Discounts		1,845.24
50000	Cost of Goods Sold	141,059.71	
57500	Cost of Sales-Freight	12,868.89	
60100	Advertising Expense	12,060.64	
61000	Auto Expenses	5,654.02	
62000	Bank Charges	120.00	
63000	Charitable Contributions Exp	1,200.00	
63500	Commissions and Fees Exp	6,000.00	
64000	Depreciation Expense	4,756.00	
64500	Dues and Subscriptions Exp	248.00	
65000	Employee Benefit Programs Exp	9,846.00	
65500	Freight & Postage Expense	1,468.52	
67000	Insurance Expense	12,600.00	
67500	Interest Expense	856.39	
68000	Laundry and Cleaning Exp	1,984.76	
68500	Legal and Professional Expense	2,800.00	
69000	Licenses Expense	1,500.00	
70000	Maintenance Expense	13,540.56	
70500	Meals and Entertainment Exp	1,202.30	
71000	Office Expense	1,586.94	
72000	Payroll Tax Expense	9,283.40	
73500	Rent or Lease Equipment	39,594.36	
74000	Rent or Lease Expense	31,000.00	
74500	Repairs Expense	8,865.55	
75000	Shop Uniforms, Gloves, Goggles	24,546.22	
75500	Supplies Expense	4,521.09	
76000	Telephone Expense	44,558.00	
76500	Travel Expense	3,956.54	
77000	Salaries Expense	28,060.00	
77500	Wages Expense	34,576.25	
78000	Utilities Expense	36,888.15	
89500	Purchase Disc-Expense Items	3,358.92	
	Total:	1,325,309.40	1,325,309.40

This report includes the balances for some of the accounts that we have entered previously.

There are two ways to enter the account balances depending on whether you can enter amounts into the period before your Begin Transactions date or into the last period of the previous accounting year. To determine which method is available to you, follow these steps.

From the Maintain Chart of Accounts form, click the **Beginning Balances** button. When the Select Period dialog box appears, see if the accounting period for the month previous to your Begin Transactions date is available or the last month in the previous year.

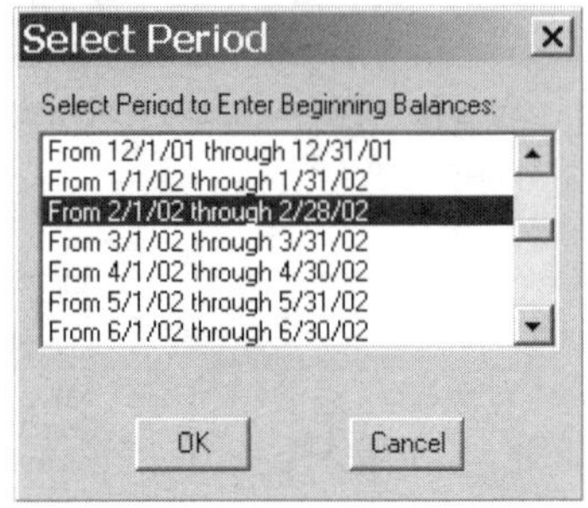

If the previous month is available, follow the instructions in the "Add in Previous Month" section below. If the previous month is unavailable, see the "Previous Month Not Available" section. The G/L Metal Fabricators Company uses the second method.

Add in Previous Month

If you can enter your balances in the previous month using the Beginning Balances button, or your previous month is in the previous accounting year, you may use this method. To enter the beginning balances, use the following instructions:

1. Select the month previous to the Begin Transactions date from the Select Period dialog box. The Chart of Accounts Beginning Balances window appears.
2. The amounts that appear here are ones that have been added as beginning balances in previous chapters to reconcile accounts.

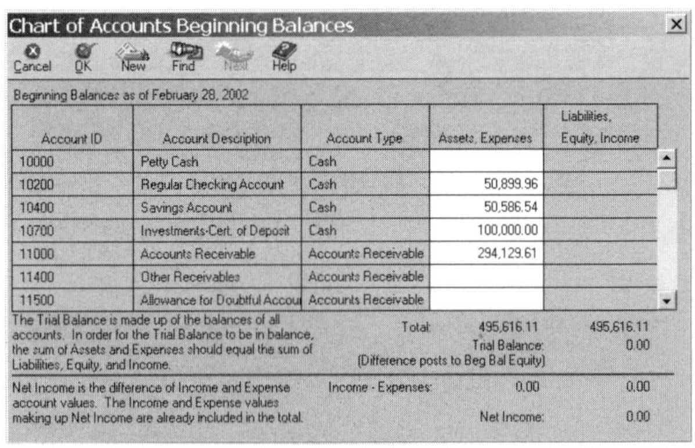

3. Take the CPA's trial balance and look at the first account. It matches the first account, Petty Cash, on the form. Select the Assets, Expenses field and enter the amount, **100.00**.

   The Regular Checking Account, Savings Account, Investments-Cert. of Deposit, and Accounts Receivable lines have already been filled in and the amounts match those on the report, so they can be left alone.

   On the report, the next two accounts, Other Receivables and Allowance for Doubtful Accounts, are missing. These accounts have zero balances and so the Assets, Expenses fields will be left blank.

   The next account is Materials & Supplies Inventory. The company only tracks one type of inventory, sheet metal, using the inventory items in invoicing and purchases. In this company, most work completed has material purchased specifically for the project. At the end of the project any usable materials left are placed on a shelf and used, when required, in other projects. The cost of the material is expensed when purchased for the first project and may increase the cost of that project. New projects are quoted as if all new materials would need purchasing, but are manufactured, whenever possible, with existing materials — which lowers the cost of that project. Over the years, the owner has determined that the overall costs balance out.

Note: I have discovered that many of my clients use this method of inventory. These clients include metal fabricators, electrical contractors, computer service companies, and others. It appears that, for small businesses, the effort of using stored and pulled inventory and job costing is too time-consuming. Even though Peachtree has a good job costing and inventory control module, many of my clients do not make full use of those parts of the program unless they have the extra personnel to devote to the task.

In our case, the company tracks sheet metal because that item is sold to many customers on a walk-in, cash-only, basis. Two to three times a year, especially at year-end, the company performs an inventory valuation and count. At this time, adjustments are made to the inventory account based upon its contents, and obsolete or damaged inventory is disposed of. Inventory adjustments are discussed in the next chapter. On 2/28/02, an inventory valuation and count was conducted and the value of the inventory is included with the trial balance.

The company has only one Fixed Assets account and one Accum. Depreciation account in the program. Fixed Assets are maintained by the CPA, not the company. The company simply makes a journal entry each month for the depreciation amount. If needed, the Peachtree Fixed Assets add-on could be used, although it will not be discussed in this book. Notice that the depreciation account field is in the Liabilities, Equity, and Income column. This is because the account is referred to as a *contra-account*, an account that reduces the value of another account. Another type of contra-account is Allowance for Bad Debts for those companies that use that method of reporting accounts receivable.

The Accounts Payable, Sales Tax Payable, and Payroll Taxes Payable accounts have been discussed in earlier chapters. Those amounts should already be entered in the correct fields.

4. Enter the rest of the liability and equity fields according to the CPA's report. If the amount on the report is different from the amount shown on the form, leave the old amount for now.
5. When you get to the Retained Earnings account, erase the old amount and leave the field blank. Enter the income and expense fields.
6. After all fields but the Retained Earnings field have been filled in, go back to that field.

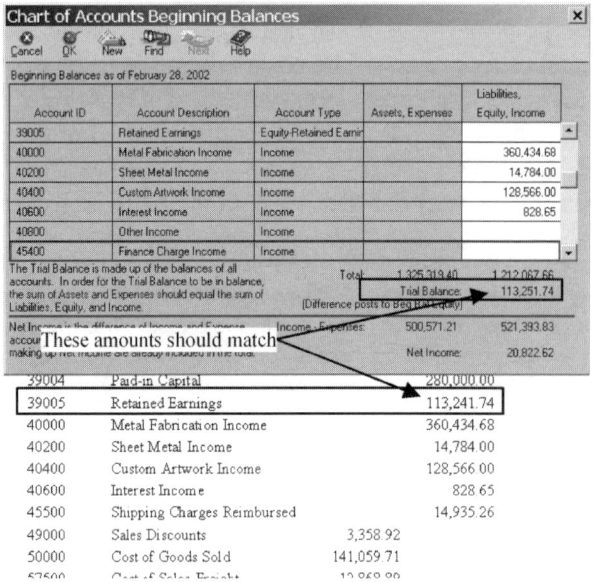

Compare the CPA's Retained Earnings credit amount to the screen's Trial Balance amount. Because the only field left blank at this time is the form's Retained Earnings field, the amounts should match. If they do not match, double-check your entries to see if all the amounts have been entered correctly. In the above case, the error is located in the Employee Benefit Programs Exp account. A data entry error caused the CPA's amount, 9,846.00, to be recorded as 9,856.00. These are the most common types of errors.

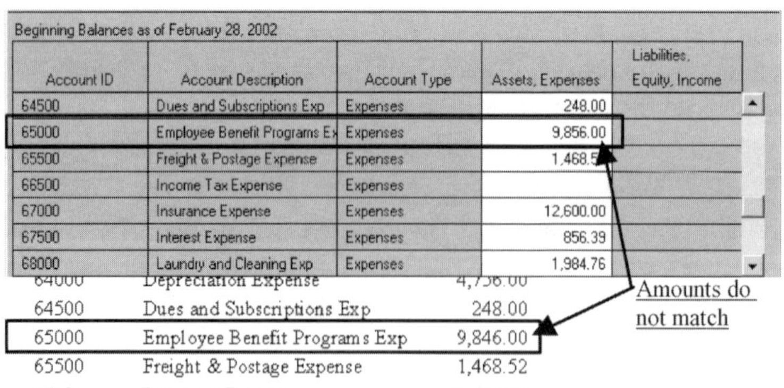

Another error that I have seen is when the CPA's report has been manually typed and one of the accounts has been mistyped. The report will appear to balance, but by entering the error into Peachtree, the totals will not. If your report has come in paper, not electronic, format, run the figures on the calculator and see if the debits and credits actually sum to the corresponding totals shown. I have even seen electronic spreadsheets with typed, not calculated, totals also be wrong. In this case, contact your CPA for the correct amount.

If the above methods do not work, look at the balances for the accounts that were entered when you reconciled cash, A/P, and A/R accounts. Are those accurate according to the CPA's report? If the numbers do not match, and your reconciliations did balance, contact your CPA to determine what needs to be done. If you must change those balances, you will need to go back and redo the reconciliations for each month for the associated accounts.

Regardless of what errors are found, you and your CPA must have trial balances that match at this point. If your old accounting system has an accurate general ledger and trial balance, those amounts must match also.

Note: If you must leave the trial balance without it balancing, you will receive the following error message. Clicking **OK** will add or subtract the difference from your Beginning Balance Equity account. If an account does not exist it will be created. If you click **Cancel**, you will be taken back to the previous screen. I suggest that you go ahead and place the balance in the Retained Earnings account for now so that your balance is zero. When you return to the screen, erase the Retained Earnings amount before making any other changes to keep track of the amount out of balance.

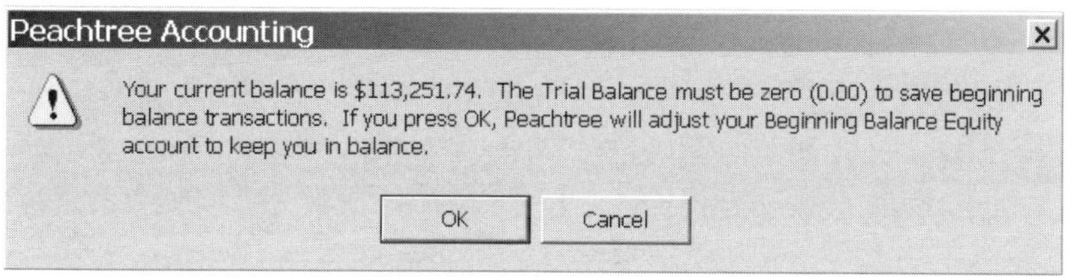

7. Make any necessary changes to the balances until the Trial Balance amount on the screen is zero (0.00).
8. Click **OK** to save the amounts. Peachtree will create the necessary journal entries to record your beginning balances.

Previous Month Not Available

This method is shown using the sample file discussed earlier in the chapter. If the previous month is not available, the beginning balances must be added using a journal entry, not the Chart of Accounts Prior Year Adjustments screen. If your previous month is in the prior accounting year, use the method in the previous section.

Note: I finally determined what appears to make the previous month in the current accounting year available. When you create a new company, you must enter the first month that data will be entered as a month other than January. If your Begin Transactions date is March, but you leave the first month in the Create New Company function as January, the prior months end at the last period of last year. Entering another month in the current year makes all months available. At least this is what appears to be happening. If anyone has a different explanation, let me know!

Account balances are added as beginning balances according to these instructions:

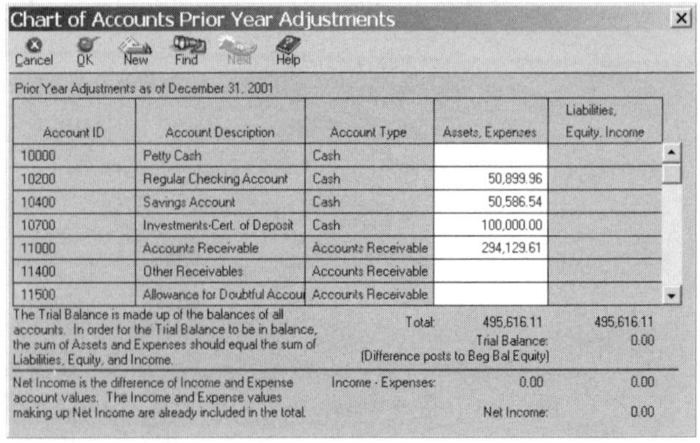

1. Open the Chart of Accounts Prior Year Adjustments form.
2. Verify that the amounts listed in the cash, A/R, A/P, and other accounts with beginning balances match the balances on the CPA's report. Do not worry about the Retained Earnings account — it will definitely not match. If the amounts do not match, you must determine where the error is for those accounts. If your number is in error, the account must be reconciled again with the new number.
3. Once the accounts match and are reconciled, and the account balances on the CPA's trial balance are the correct amounts, delete all amounts on the form. The Total of the Assets, Expenses column and the Liabilities, Equity, Income column will be zero (0.00). The Trial Balance amount will also be zero (0.00).
4. Close the Chart of Accounts Prior Year Adjustments form by clicking **OK**.
5. Change the Accounting Period to the previous month.

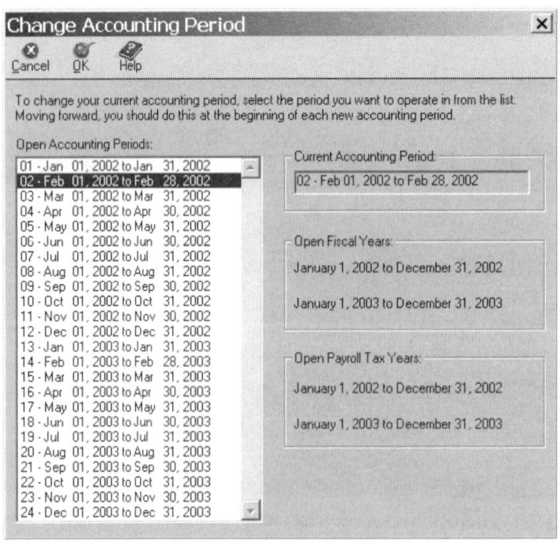

6. Click the **General Journal Entry** icon in the **General Ledger** folder on the navigation aid.

   Or select **Tasks**, **General Journal Entry** from the menu bar.

   Or press **Alt+K** and then **G** using the keyboard.

The General Journal Entry screen appears.

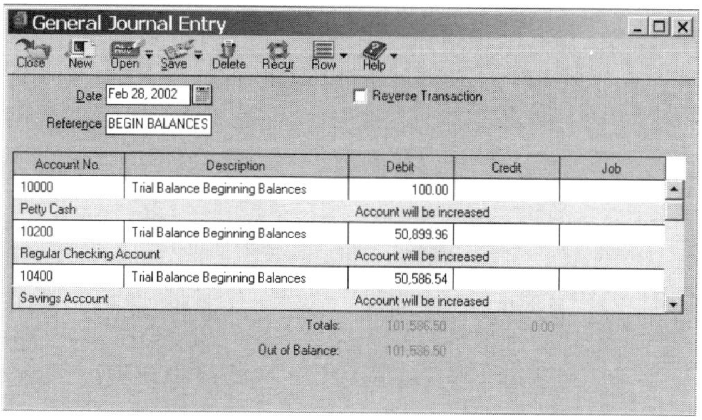

7. Enter the last day of the last month in the Date field. This will be the last day of the current open accounting period.
8. Type a descriptive identifier for this entry in the Reference field. It should be something that clearly defines the entry as a beginning balance entry.

   The Reverse Transaction check box should be left unchecked because we do not need to have a reversing entry for this transaction in the next month.
9. In the first line, type the first account number on the CPA's report in the Account No. field.
10. In the Description field, type a descriptive message for the beginning balance entry.
11. In our example, the first line from the CPA's report is for Petty Cash and it has a debit of 100.00. Enter the amount in the Debit column.
12. Using the Tab key, press twice to go past the Credit and Job fields. Peachtree will not accept an entry in both the Debit and Credit columns for a line at the same time. The Job field is not discussed in this book.
13. After tabbing past these fields, your cursor should now be on the second line. Enter the next account number in that field and tab over to the Debit or Credit column as needed. Notice that the description is automatically copied on each new line.
14. Enter all debit and credit accounts.

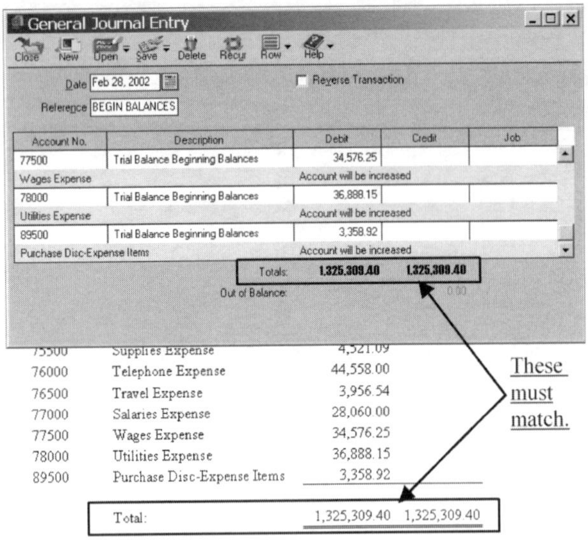

When you have finished the entries, the Totals line of the General Journal Entry form should match the Total of the Debit and Credit columns of the report.

If the amounts do not match, you must verify that all lines were entered correctly on the form. If the amounts still do not match, look at the possible errors described in Step 6 of the "Add in Previous Month" section.

15. Once all amounts match, click **Save** in the toolbar. The journal entry will be saved.

    If you need to leave the screen and the journal entry is not yet complete, you will receive the following message.

An unbalanced journal entry cannot, and should never, be saved. To leave the screen before the completion of the entry, on the last line type an amount that will balance the entry. When you finish the entry, look at that number for the correct amount and proceed from there.

Verifying the Beginning Balances

Once the beginning balances are entered, you should verify that they are correct. Run the Trial Balance report for the last day of the month before the Begin Transactions date, regardless of which method of data entry you used. Verify the totals of the Debit and Credit columns to see that they are correct. If not correct, go through the account lines to locate the errors. Go back to the Beginning Balances form or the General Journal Entry form to locate the errors and make the corrections.

If the beginning balance amounts are correct, you must have a transaction in the month(s) prior to your Begin Transactions date. Print the General Ledger report for all accounts and all months in the current accounting year prior to your Begin Transactions date. Look for any transactions other than the beginning balance entries. Delete the associated transactions after verifying that they do not belong in a subsequent month; for example, a payment that should have been made 03/23/03 that was entered 02/23/03.

Keep up this process until the Trial Balance report is correct.

Verifying the Ending Balances

At the end of each month of the Three-Month Plan, you should compare the trial balance in the old system to the trial balance in the Peachtree system. The balances should match as long as transactions are being handled in the same manner. Verify each general ledger account balance and, if the amounts do not match, go through the transactions to find the differences.

In some cases, the old system does not report all the information that the Peachtree system does. For companies with this situation, the Peachtree trial balance should be sent to the CPA to verify. The CPA will locate any errors and return the corrections to you. Once the corrections are entered, the balances should be correct.

Creating a Journal Entry

Although we discussed journal entries earlier in the chapter, entering one will be covered here to avoid any chance of mistakes. Follow these instructions to create a journal entry:

1. Click the **General Journal Entry** icon in the **General Ledger** folder on the navigation aid.

   Or select **Tasks**, **General Journal Entry** from the menu bar.

   Or press **Alt+K** and then **G** using the keyboard.

   The General Journal Entry screen appears.

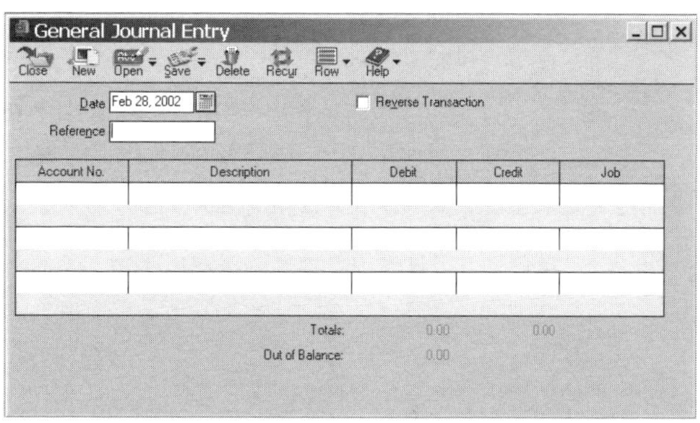

2. Enter the date of the journal entry in the Date field. For most journal entries, this will be the last day of the month for which you are creating the entry.

Month 3

3. Type a descriptive identifier for this entry in the Reference field. It should be something that clearly defines the entry in reports.

   The Reverse Transaction check box should be checked if you want to create a transaction that is opposite to this transaction in the next month. An example of this might be a sale that was dated in the current month that you do not want to be allocated to Sales this month. You would create an entry that debited Sales and credited A/R or Deferred Income.

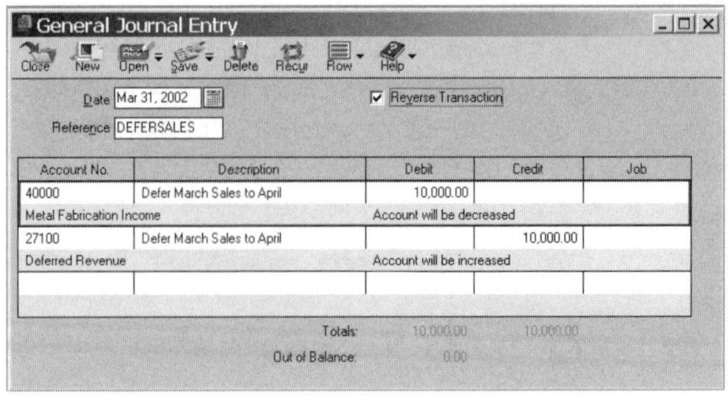

   When the next month rolls around, you want the journal entry so that Sales is credited and A/R or Deferred Income is debited. By checking Reverse Transaction, the journal entry should automatically appear as an entry.

> **Note:** I tried this several different ways using different months, different accounting periods, and different system dates, but could not get the reversing entry to appear. I remember this working in the past, but not in 2002 so far.

4. In the first line, type the general ledger account number in the Account No. field for the first part of your journal entry.
5. In the Description field, type a description for the entry.
6. The associated Debit or Credit should go in the corresponding field. Most journal entries are entered with all of the debits listed first and the credits listed on the latter lines, although that format is not required.

   The Job field is not discussed in this book.
7. Go to the second line. Enter the next account number of the journal entry in the appropriate field and tab over to the Debit or Credit column as needed. Notice that the description is automatically copied on each new line.
8. When all lines are entered and the Totals for the Debit and Credit columns match and the Out of Balance amount is equal to zero (0.00), click **Save** to record the journal entry.

   Existing journal entries may be edited by clicking the Open button on the toolbar and selecting the appropriate record to edit from the Select list.

Recurring Journal Entries

Some journal entries occur every month or for a specific length of time and may be set up as recurring transactions. Follow these instructions:

1. Create the journal entry as you would normally.

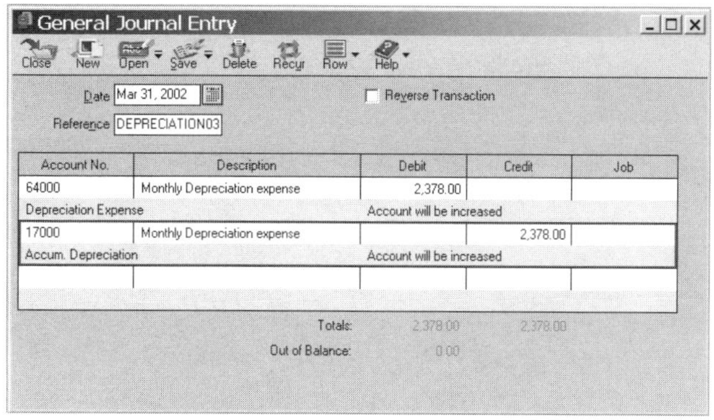

2. Click the **Recur** button in the toolbar. The Create Recurring Journal Entries dialog box appears.
3. In the Number of Times field, enter the number of times that the entry is to appear in the general journal. The first month is included in the count so if you started a journal entry in March and you want it to continue each month until the end of the year you would type **10**, not 9.

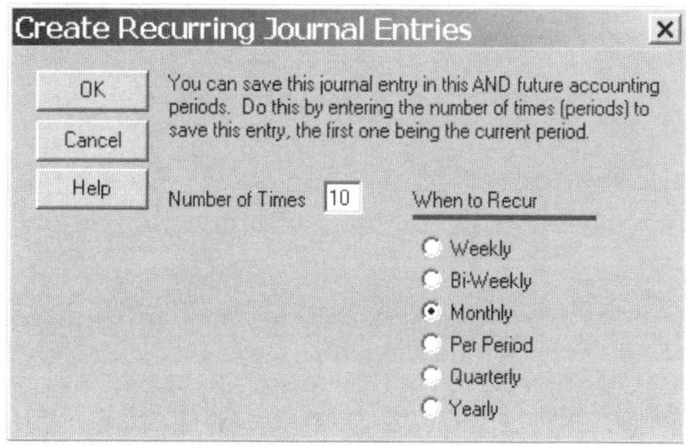

The When to Recur field is the frequency of the journal entry. Most journal entries occur monthly.

4. Click **OK** after selecting the period, and the journal entries will be created.

You may see the results by clicking the Open button and looking in the Select General Journal Entry window.

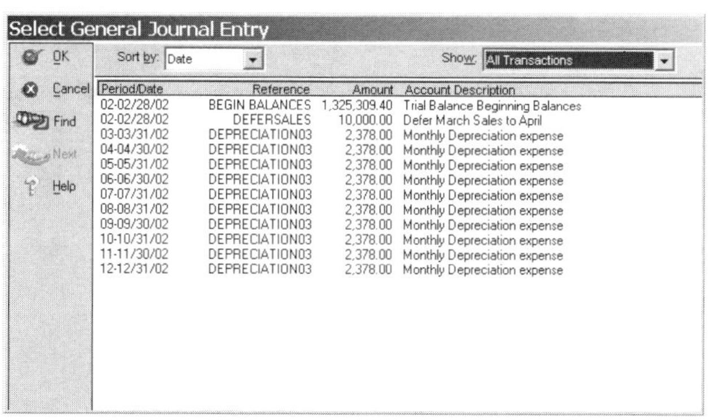

5. If you need to change the amount of the journal entry in later months or for a single month, select the first journal to be changed and make the necessary changes.

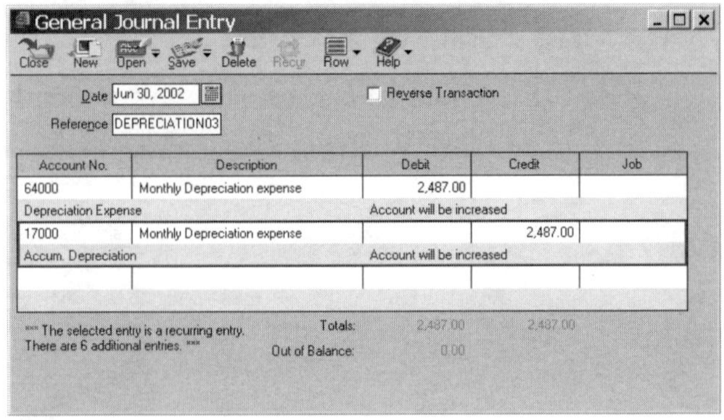

6. Click **Save** and the Change Recurring Journal Entries dialog box appears.

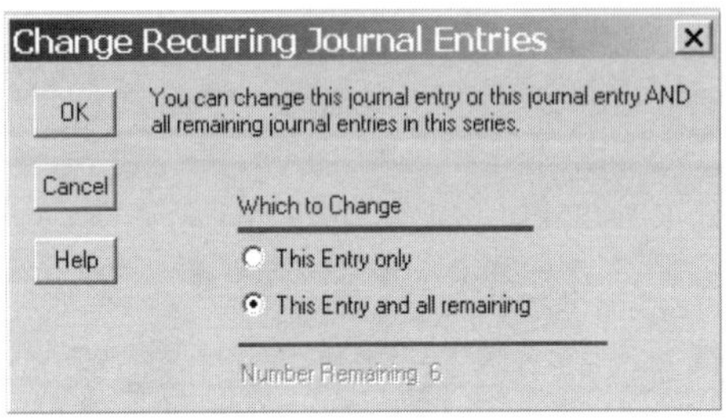

7. Determine whether the change is to be made to this specific entry or this entry and all those remaining.
8. Click **OK** to save the change.

Memorized Journal Entries

Sometimes you need to make a journal entry with the same debits and credits, but it may not be every month or on a regular basis that can be foreseen. A memorized transaction will let the line items be created once and then entered and edited on an as-needed basis.

1. Create the initial journal entry.
2. Click the drop-down arrow next to the Save button and click the **Memorize** button. The Maintain Memorized General Journal Entries window appears.

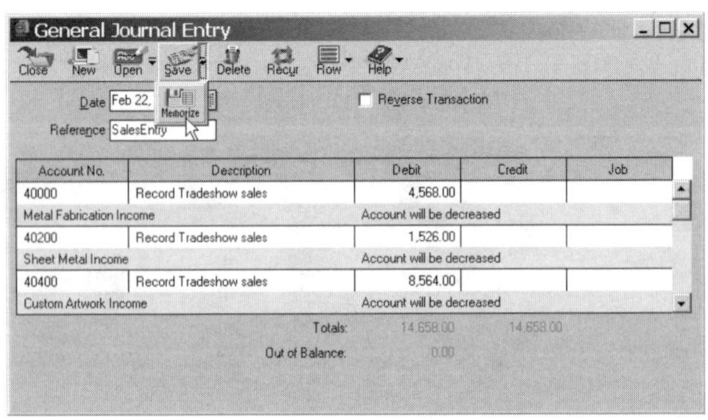

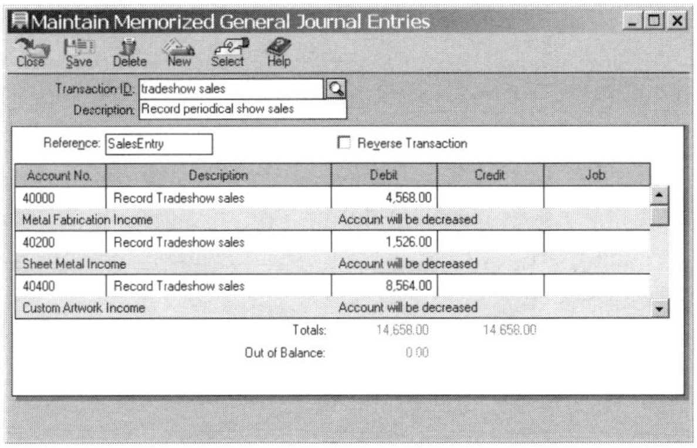

3. In the Transaction ID field, enter a journal entry ID to describe the type of transaction.
4. Type a short message about the journal entry in the Description field.
5. Click **Save** to record the memorized transaction. You are returned to the General Journal Entry screen. To record the transaction on the screen, click **OK**.
6. To use the memorized transaction, open the General Journal screen and click the **Select** button below the Open button.

7. Select the transaction from the list.
8. Change the date or amounts as needed and then click **Save** to record the journal entry.

Financial Statements

The difference between Peachtree and many of the other lower-cost accounting programs is that Peachtree provides true double-entry accounting. Many other programs at this price level only include part of the accounting functions or provide accounting information based upon a single-entry system and then try to convert the information to double-entry format. Peachtree provides the same type of accounting as more expensive systems and also includes many higher types of financial reporting.

Financial statements are the end products of accurate accounting systems. The statements are only as good as the information that is entered. If the data is recorded completely and accurately in a timely manner and if transactions are entered according to standardized procedures with very few exceptions, then the statements derived by the system can be relied upon to provide information that accurately reflects the financial standing of the business.

There are two main statements that each business relies on: the Balance Sheet and the Income Statement. Both are derived directly from the Trial Balance and report information based upon general ledger accounts.

The Balance Sheet

The Balance Sheet is based upon the asset, liability, and equity (owner's equity) accounts. It is based upon the accounting equation A = L + O. This means that the total of the assets equals the total of the liabilities and the owner's equity. Remember in the Trial Balance that the total of all debits equals the total of all credits. The Balance Sheet lists the assets, liabilities, and equity accounts and then rolls up all income and expense accounts into one line on the statement in the owner's equity section called Net Income.

The Balance Sheet is also referred to as a *position statement* because it details information about a company at a specific point in time. It doesn't matter what changes have taken place over a length of time, it only reports the company's financial standing as of a specific moment in time. To view the Balance Sheet, follow these steps:

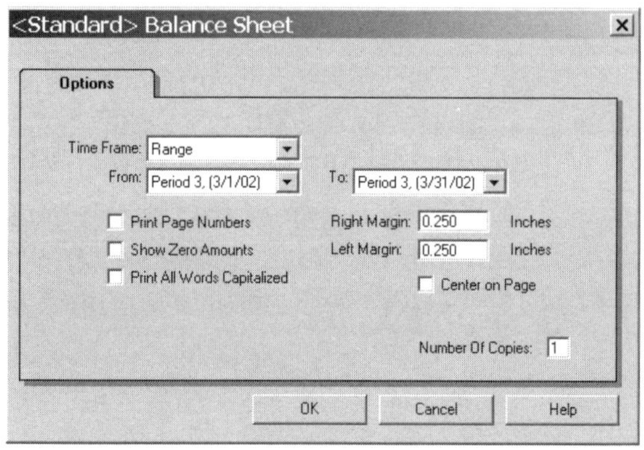

1. From the Select a Report window, select **Financial Statements** in the Report Area and **<Standard> Balance Sheet** from the Report List. The Balance Sheet filter appears.
2. Here you can select the date and some of the printing parameters.

   The Time Frame and From and To fields are a little confusing for anyone with an understanding of balance sheets. Although you select the time period, the balance sheet, by its very nature, should not include From and To fields but only an As Of field. A balance sheet is a snapshot of a company's financial standing and there is no way to view changes over a period of time. For example, if you print a balance sheet for a range of From Period 3, (3/1/02) To Period 4 (4/30/02) or a range From Period 4 (4/1/02) To Period 4 (4/30/02), the resulting report will be exactly the same. Both reports will show the figures as of 4/30/02.

   If you have a multi-page report, you can check **Print Page Numbers**.

   To view asset, liability, or equity accounts with a 0.00 balance, click the **Show Zero Amounts** check box.

   Some companies like to see financial statements with account names all in capital letters. This is especially helpful if you have one account as Regular checking account and another as SAVINGS ACCOUNT. Check **Print All Words Capitalized** to enable this option.

   The Right Margin and Left Margin fields allow you to set the associated margins to assist those companies that print their reports on letterhead with wide margins. These options can also be set by working with your printer properties.

Check the **Center on Page** check box to center the report's data within the selected margins when it is printed. When left unchecked, the report will print aligned along the left margin.

If you need multiple copies of the balance sheet when it is finalized, enter the number in the Number Of Copies field.

3. Click **OK** when the options are set. A sample balance sheet from the G/L Metal Fabricators file is shown here.

G/L Metal Fabricators Company
Balance Sheet
March 31, 2002

ASSETS

Current Assets				
Petty Cash	$	100.00		
Regular Checking Account		169,343.84		
Savings Account		50,586.54		
Investments-Cert. of Deposit		100,000.00		
Accounts Receivable		206,451.09		
Materials & Supplies Inventory		42,793.74		
Total Current Assets				554,617.21
Property and Equipment				
Fixed Assets		285,694.34		
Accum. Depreciation		<102,818.66>		
Total Property and Equipment				182,875.68
Other Assets				
Total Other Assets				0.00
Total Assets			$	737,492.89

LIABILITIES AND CAPITAL

Current Liabilities				
Accounts Payable	$	99,126.85		
Sales Tax Payable		14,689.85		
Payroll Taxes Payable		24,468.85		
Total Current Liabilities				138,285.55
Long-Term Liabilities				
Notes Payable		45,000.00		
Total Long-Term Liabilities				45,000.00
Total Liabilities				183,285.55
Capital				
Common Stock		100,000.00		
Paid-in Capital		280,000.00		
Retained Earnings		113,241.74		
Net Income		60,965.60		
Total Capital				554,207.34
Total Liabilities & Capital			$	737,492.89

4. I suggest that after you have all of the settings for the balance sheet as you want them that you save the report under a new name so the report will print correctly with the changed options. Click **Save**  on the Preview Report toolbar.

   The Save As dialog box appears.

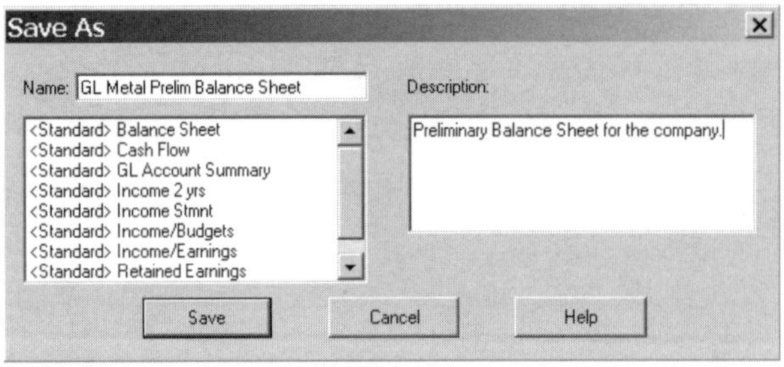

5. Enter a new name for the report in the Name field. Do not use the default name because reinstalling or upgrading Peachtree will overwrite the file.
6. Enter text in the Description field that describes the report.
7. Click **Save** when you are done. The new report will now show in the Select a Report window.

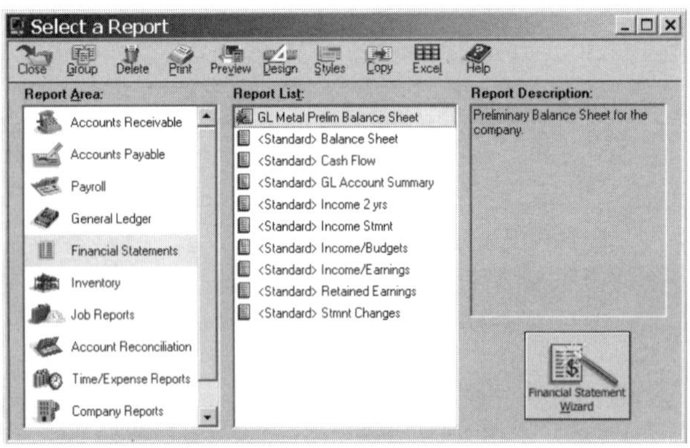

The Income Statement

The Income Statement is often known by other names such as the profit and loss report or the revenue and expense report. This report details all the income received for products and services, the costs of producing the income, and the operating expenses of the company. Some amounts are actual financial transactions, such as the sale of sheet metal or paying the telephone bill, while other amounts may be depreciation or amortization costs from capital expenditures that are not reported on the Income Statement.

Open the income statement in the same way that the balance sheet is opened:

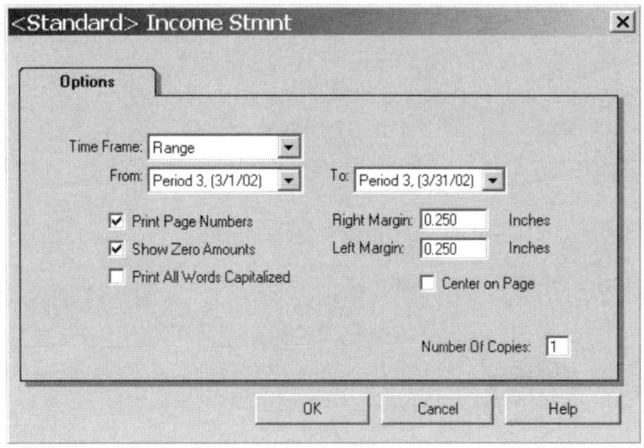

1. From the Select a Report window, select **Financial Statements** in the Report Area and **<Standard> Income Stmnt** from the Report List. The Income Stmnt filter appears.
2. In the Time Frame and From and To fields you select the time period for the report. Many companies regularly print reports for a month, a quarter, or a year.

   If you have a multi-page report, you can check **Print Page Numbers**.

   To view income or expense accounts with a 0.00 balance, click the **Show Zero Amounts** check box.

   Some companies like to see financial statements with account names all in capital letters. This is especially helpful if you have one account as Metal fabrication income and another as SHEET METAL INCOME. Check **Print All Words Capitalized** to enable this option.

   The Right Margin and Left Margin fields allow you to set the associated margins to assist those companies that print their reports on letterhead with wide margins. These options can also be set by working with your printer properties.

   Check the **Center on Page** check box to center the report's data within the selected margins when it is printed. When left unchecked, the report will print aligned along the left margin.

   If you need multiple copies of the income statement when it is finalized, set the number in the Number Of Copies field.
3. Click **OK** when the options are set. A sample income statement from the G/L Metal Fabricators file is shown on the following page.

G/L Metal Fabricators Company
Income Statement
For the Three Months Ending March 31, 2002

		Current Month			Year to Date	
Revenues						
Metal Fabrication Income	$	211,190.67	59.24	$	561,625.35	64.71
Sheet Metal Income		9,248.00	2.59		24,032.00	2.77
Custom Artwork Income		130,045.00	36.48		258,611.00	29.80
Interest Income		0.00	0.00		828.65	0.10
Shipping Charges Reimbursed		8,819.00	2.47		23,754.26	2.74
Sales Discounts		<2,827.67>	<0.79>		<982.43>	<0.11>
Total Revenues		356,475.00	100.00		867,868.83	100.00
Cost of Sales						
Cost of Goods Sold		123,763.00	34.72		264,822.71	30.51
Cost of Sales-Freight		9,316.00	2.61		22,184.89	2.56
Total Cost of Sales		133,079.00	37.33		287,007.60	33.07
Gross Profit		223,396.00	62.67		580,861.23	66.93
Expenses						
Advertising Expense		0.00	0.00		12,060.64	1.39
Auto Expenses		0.00	0.00		5,654.02	0.65
Bank Charges		0.00	0.00		120.00	0.01
Charitable Contributions Exp		0.00	0.00		1,200.00	0.14
Commissions and Fees Exp		0.00	0.00		6,000.00	0.69
Depreciation Expense		2,378.00	0.67		7,134.00	0.82
Dues and Subscriptions Exp		0.00	0.00		248.00	0.03
Employee Benefit Programs Exp		0.00	0.00		9,846.00	1.13
Freight & Postage Expense		1,426.99	0.40		2,895.51	0.33
Insurance Expense		0.00	0.00		12,600.00	1.45
Interest Expense		0.00	0.00		856.39	0.10
Laundry and Cleaning Exp		0.00	0.00		1,984.76	0.23
Legal and Professional Expense		0.00	0.00		2,800.00	0.32
Licenses Expense		0.00	0.00		1,500.00	0.17
Maintenance Expense		6,706.00	1.88		20,246.56	2.33
Meals and Entertainment Exp		0.00	0.00		1,202.30	0.14
Office Expense		661.14	0.19		2,248.08	0.26
Payroll Tax Expense		4,641.93	1.30		13,925.33	1.60
Rent or Lease Equipment		19,797.18	5.55		59,391.54	6.84
Rent or Lease Expense		15,500.00	4.35		46,500.00	5.36
Repairs Expense		0.00	0.00		8,865.55	1.02
Shop Uniforms, Gloves, Goggles		14,694.26	4.12		39,240.48	4.52
Supplies Expense		0.00	0.00		4,521.09	0.52
Telephone Expense		23,776.00	6.67		68,334.00	7.87
Travel Expense		0.00	0.00		3,956.54	0.46
Salaries Expense		14,030.00	3.94		42,090.00	4.85
Wages Expense		36,735.75	10.31		71,312.00	8.22
Utilities Expense		19,586.59	5.49		56,474.74	6.51
Purchase Disc-Expense Items		<1,328.82>	<0.37>		2,030.10	0.23
Total Expenses		158,605.02	44.49		505,237.63	58.22
Net Income	$	64,790.98	18.18	$	75,623.60	8.71

Notice that the income statement has the information for the selected period plus year-to-date information. It also includes percentages based upon income. In the report, the Total Cost of Sales is approximately 37% of income and the Net Income is about 18%. These figures will help you track your costs based upon your income.

When the income statement is set up as you need it, you should save the report under a new name so that the report will print correctly with the changed options.

There are several other types of income statements provided in Peachtree. These include the Income 2 yrs statement which compares this year to last year. Of course, this statement will not be valuable until you have over one year's worth of data in the program. Another report is the Income/Budgets statement which compares budget information against actual amounts. Budgets are not covered in this book but may be entered on the Maintain Chart of Accounts form. The last statement to discuss is the Income/Earnings statement, which is the same as the income statement but includes adjustments to the Retained Earnings account. Because Net Income is rolled up into Retained Earnings, this report will quickly show the changes to the account right where the causes of the changes can be traced.

There are several other reports that you can look at and discuss with your CPA to decide what reports are important to track as your business grows. Some of your company's associates will also want to see reports that are pertinent to their relationship with you.

Periodical Procedures

Over the years as you build your business, each of your accounting and administrative employees will need to develop standardized procedures for the areas under their stewardship. These procedures and policies will allow almost all transactions to be controlled and recorded in an orderly and logical manner. If you are constantly being bombarded with questions on how to handle this customer and that bill, you will not be able to get your own work accomplished. If you are constantly being bombarded, it also means that there is not enough standardization for handling transactions. Get your procedures down on paper on how to handle the regular transactions, and when a real problem appears you will know it because it will be outside the normal range of your policies.

A desk procedures manual should be so complete that if the person were to disappear tomorrow, a new employee with the correct skill sets could come in, pick up the manual, and start working that day. I have seen this actually happen in companies that allowed me to write up their desk procedures manuals. And the manual should not cover just the day-to-day stuff — monthly, quarterly, and annual procedures should also be included. This is what will be discussed in the following section — procedures that occur on a periodical basis.

Month-end Procedures

If you are using 12 accounting periods that are based on the months of the year or you are using 13 accounting periods that are based upon four-week months or 12 months and an adjustment period, you will need to perform certain functions every time an accounting period is closed. These procedures also apply to those with accounting periods longer than one month. The procedures shown here are based upon the duties I performed as a staff accountant where I was responsible for the monthly and annual closings. In setting up numerous companies, these are the procedures that I suggest to my clients. Remember that every company is different and some activities will occur on a more or less frequent basis.

The following procedures are based upon closing the month of March 2002 for the G/L Metal Fabricators file. The activities occur in April — after the end of the month being closed.

1. Starting April 1 through April 5, all work orders, sales orders, and invoices to be written up are entered into Peachtree by the A/R data entry person. The current accounting period is still set to March 2002. During the same time period, the A/P data entry person is collecting all bills and entering those into the system also. The cash receipts person creates the deposits for April, being careful that the correct date of the deposit is entered.
2. On Monday, April 8, the current accounting period is changed to April 2002. Any invoices or bills to be applied to March must now go through the office manager or accounting supervisor.
3. A/R, A/P, payroll, and the checking accounts are all balanced by the appropriate people. General ledger balances are reconciled where necessary and evaluated for appropriateness and sensibility. Changes are made where necessary.
4. By April 12, preliminary reports are printed or exported to files and sent to the CPA for verification and approval. Preliminary reports are also printed for the owner and office manager to verify acceptability.
5. When the CPA's reports return, about April 22, final adjustments made by the CPA, such as the depreciation journal entry, are entered into the computer. Any new adjustments or entries discovered by office personnel are forwarded and approved or denied by the CPA and handled according to her instructions.
6. By the end of the month of April, final financial statements are printed for March and sent to the appropriate parties, such as the owner, banker, factors, and others. At this time, the monthly backup should be created and stored.

This procedure is continued on a regular basis every month of the year.

Quarterly Procedures

Some procedures only need to be completed on a quarterly or semi-annual basis. These procedures include such things as payroll tax reports and sales tax reports. Some of the quarterly procedures will need to be done very quickly after the end of the quarter; others will allow you more time to complete. Balancing and paying taxes are covered in earlier chapters.

You may also wish to reconcile some of your general ledger accounts, like trust fund accounts and other receivables, to verify that all transactions have been allocated correctly over the last few months. Some of these may be reconciled using the account reconciliation function, the same one used to balance your checking account. Others will require you to export the general ledger account to Excel to be reconciled.

Annual Procedures

The procedures for a company to close its books will vary according to the nature of the company. Some companies only need to verify that the books are correct. Others will need to complete an exhaustive audit conducted by an outside public accounting company. Regardless, before the books are finally closed, you will want to be assured that the information contained in your system is correct as you enter a new accounting year.

Annual and year-end procedures are covered in Chapter 18.

Summary

Reconciling the general ledger can be both very simple and extremely complex depending upon the accuracy and the needs of your business. Keeping good records is essential to making this task go well. Keeping a close eye on the trial balance and the associated financial statements can save a lot of trouble. Make sure that the balances from month to month appear reasonable and investigate any drastic changes. Doing so can resolve potential problems before they occur.

Chapter 17

Reconciling Inventory

In This Chapter

- Inventory assemblies
- Inventory tax types
- Taxed and untaxed freight
- Stock (counted) inventory and other inventory methods
- Reconciling and counting inventory
- Adjusting inventory items and general ledger balances

Inventory Assemblies

Inventory items can be added together to form an inventory item that is sold as a unit. Existing items are added to an item to create a new item that can be sold to customers. An example of an assembly item is found in the Bellwether Garden Supply company file, with an Item ID of AVRY-10100, Bird House Kit.

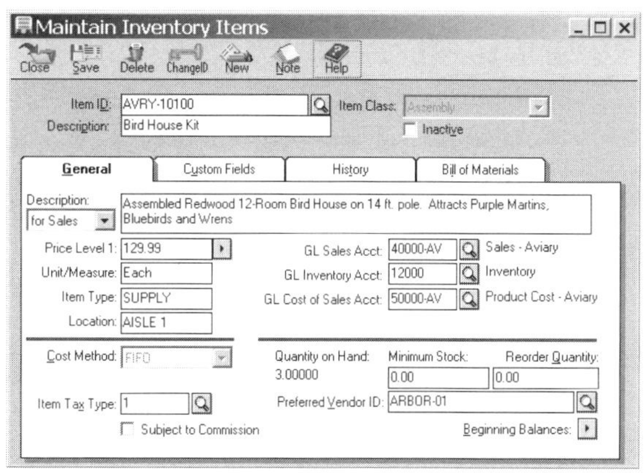

As you can see, the fields on the General tab are similar to other inventory items.

Creating an Assembly Item

Assembly items can be very simple like the one shown here. They can also become quite complex if you were building or manufacturing assemblies using raw and purchased materials. Creating a simple assembly item is very easy following these instructions:

1. Create any inventory items that are included in the assembly and save the items. Set up the beginning balances for the items. Setting up and adding beginning balances to inventory items was covered in Chapter 10.

Month 3

2. Create the new assembly item. Set the Item Class as **Assembly.** Do not save the record yet.
3. Select the **Bill of Materials** tab.

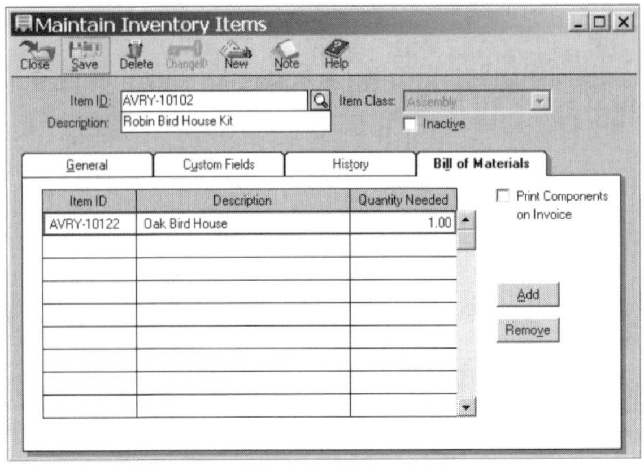

4. In the Bill of Materials list, select the Item ID of one of the inventory items to be included in this assembly.
5. Tab over to the Quantity Needed field and enter the number of items of this inventory item that are required in the assembly.
6. Add other items as needed.
7. If you want the individual items to appear on the customer's invoice, check the **Print Components on Invoice** check box.
8. When all items are added, click **Save.**

Note: Once the inventory item is used, you cannot change the Bill of Materials list, so make sure that the entry is correct before clicking the Save button.

Building an Assembly Item

Once an assembly item is created in the inventory file, you must physically build it and add the built unit to the assembly's quantity on hand. In addition, the items that were used to build the assembly must have their respective quantities on hand reduced.

To build an assembly item, follow these steps:

1. Go to the **Inventory** folder on the navigation aid and click on the **Build/Unbuild Assemblies** icon.

   Or select **Tasks**, **Assemblies** from the menu bar or press **Alt+K**, then **M** using the keyboard shortcuts.

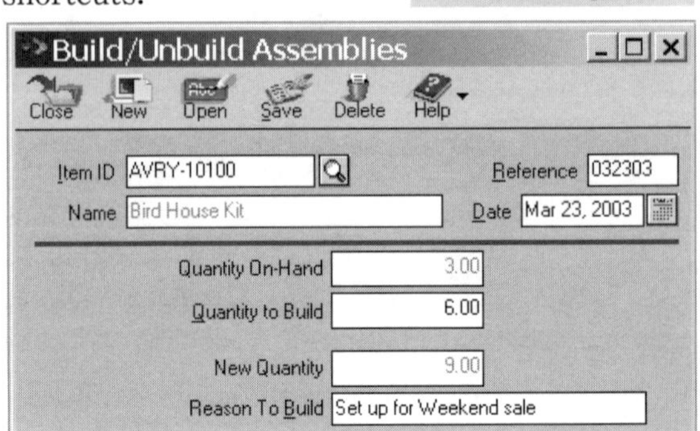

2. The Build/Unbuild Asssemblies form appears.
3. Select the item's ID from the Item ID field. Our example is built from one AVRY-10110 (Bird House-Pole 14 Ft.) and one AVRY-10120 (Bird House-Red 12-Room Unit). Before our transaction, there are 18 poles and 30 12-unit houses in stock.

4. The Name and current Quantity On-Hand will appear. The New Quantity will also be calculated based upon the information shown.
5. Enter a Reference for the transaction.
6. Select the date of the transaction.
7. In the Quantity to Build box, enter the number of new units to be built. The New Quantity will be calculated.
8. Fill in the Reason To Build box, if desired.
9. Click **Save**. The number of new units will be added to the assembly item and the units used to build the assemblies will be deducted from the inventory items used to build the assembly. In our example the number of poles is now 12 and there are now 24 12-unit houses.

   Assemblies are sold as complete units the same way that stock and non-stock items are.

   Assemblies may also be broken down into their individual components when you *unbuild* the assembly. Simply enter a negative number in the Quantity to Build field, and the number of assembled items will be reduced while the individual components are increased.

Inventory Tax Types

When sales taxes were discussed in Chapter 14, the difference between taxable and nontaxable items was explained. Whether an item is taxed on an invoice is controlled by the tax type. If the customer is taxable and an item is tax exempt, the customer will not be charged sales tax for that item. If a customer is nontaxable and an item is taxable, the customer will still not be taxed on the taxable item. Tax types control whether tax is calculated on an item, and tax codes control whether the taxable item is actually taxed for the customer on their invoices. Tax types are set up as a company default; the setup was also explained in Chapter 14.

If you have more than one type of sales tax that you pay, then you can add additional tax types to the default list. But remember that you cannot use more than one tax type, except for Exempt, on an invoice.

Taxed and Untaxed Freight

Due to differing state laws, some companies may find it necessary to apply sales tax to some freight charges and not to others. This can be handled easily by making one or the other type of freight an inventory item. You may decide when setting up sales taxes to leave off taxing freight if it is entered in the Freight field on the Invoice form.

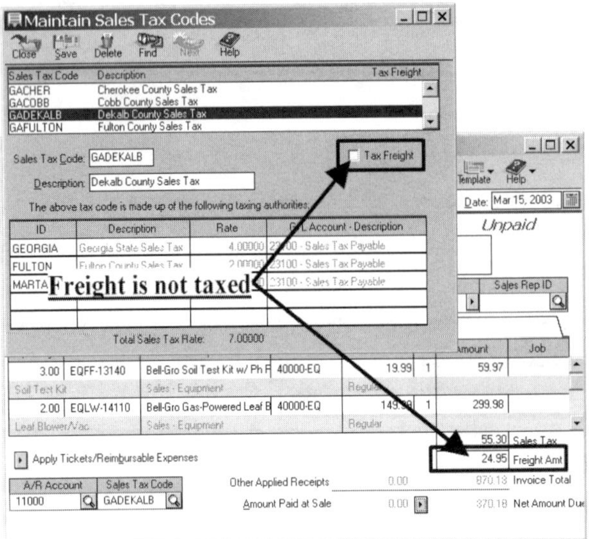

If you then need to tax certain types of freight, you can create an inventory item for freight that is taxable.

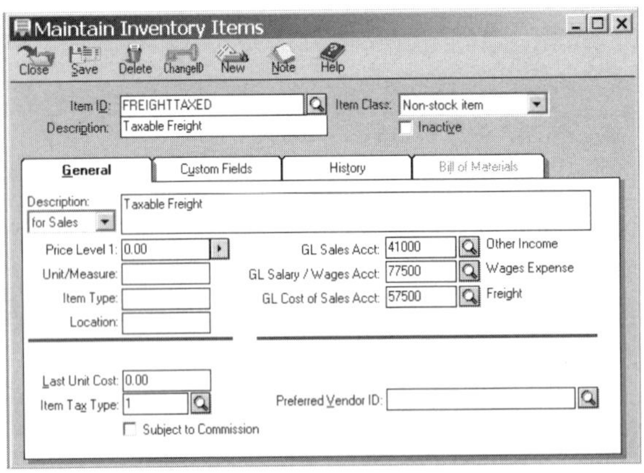

When an invoice is created that needs the taxable freight charge, select the item and enter it on a line in the invoice, rather than in the Freight field on the invoice form.

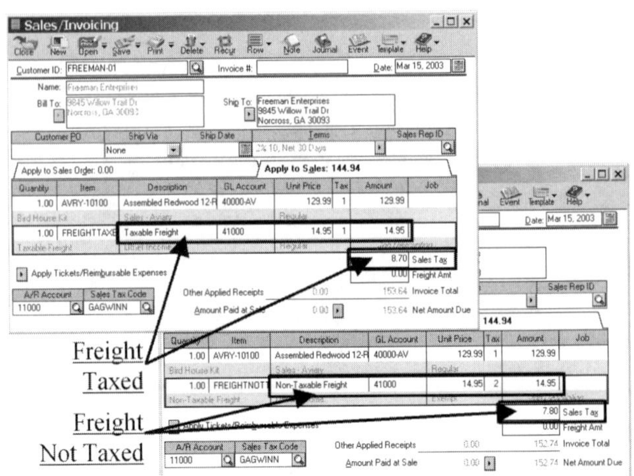

In order to be consistent, some companies delete the Freight line from the printed invoice and enter all freight on the line items of the invoice form. With this scenario, they create both a taxable and a nontaxable freight inventory item.

Methods of Inventory

Companies have physical inventory for two major reasons. The inventory on the shelf allows a company to keep its costs down by buying items, either for resale or assembly, in bulk and, hopefully, at a lower price. Companies then show inventory on the books to spread the cost of purchasing across a number of months and not just as a huge expense in a single month. The expense to cost of sales occurs at the time of the sale that way.

The inventory account balance is based upon determining the value of the inventory that is on the shelves. Inventory may be tracked in several different ways.

Stock Items — All Calculated Quantities

One method tracks the actual number of each item purchased and sold. Inventory items are classified as stock items. When inventory is purchased, using the item ID, the invoice shows a specific number of things, such as network cards, which are added to the quantity on hand. When the inventory is sold, also using the item ID, even as part of an assembly, a specified number of network cards are deducted from the quantity on hand.

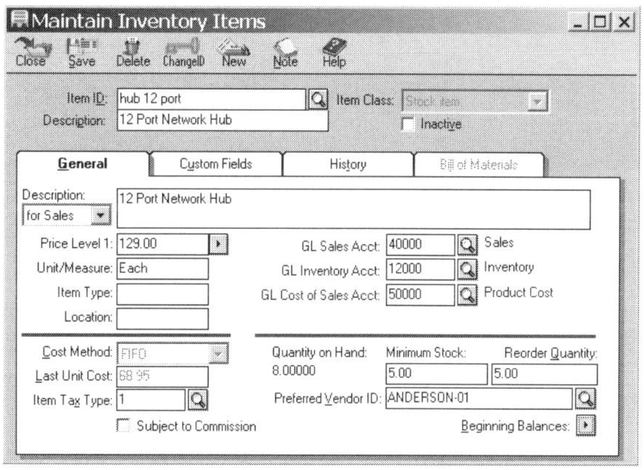

The inventory is valued using one of several costing methods (FIFO, LIFO, or Average) and the sum of all inventory item values is the inventory account balance. This method can be very attractive to companies that sell products for resale or assemblies made of specific items and need to track the number on hand or on the shelf at all times. An example of this is a furniture store with three red couches and six oak tables in the showroom, or a landscape company that plants 12 dwarf hollies and two pecan trees as part of its upgrade landscaping program.

Non-Stock Items — No Calculated Quantities

Another method of tracking inventory is to count the inventory and determine its value using one of the costing methods, and enter the total amount of all inventory in the general ledger account with a journal entry. The inventory items are classified using the non-stock or some other item class. The actual quantities of the items are

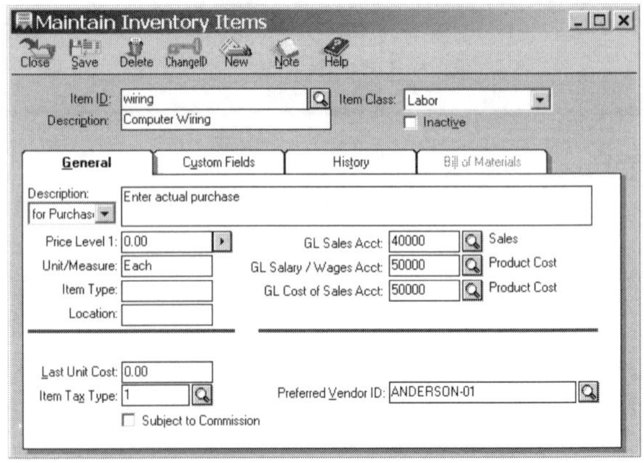

not calculated using the purchases and sales functions, but are evaluated using physical counts and journal entry adjustments.

When inventory is purchased, the purchase goes directly to the cost of sales general ledger account, not inventory. The item ID is not required, or you may use a generic inventory item. When inventory is sold, there is no journal entry from inventory to cost of sales as part of the sales transaction and the item ID may or may not be used. The value of the inventory is evaluated on a regular basis by doing a physical inventory count. A journal entry is used at that time to adjust the value of the inventory. This method is valuable to those companies that provide products using an approximate number of parts. An example of this is a lawn chemical company where a round of spraying may include 2 gallons of pre-emergent and no fertilizer, 1.5 gallons of pre-emergent and 3 gallons of fertilizer, or some other variation of chemicals for the same size lawn.

Note: I once had a baker who wanted to track the flour used to bake a cake using flour as a stock item. He realized the problem when I asked for the exact number of cakes in a bag of flour. He could only give an approximate answer because circumstances might require him to use more flour or less flour in a cake on any given day due to humidity and weather. The solution for him was to calculate the value of the baking ingredients with a physical count and then adjust that amount with a journal entry on a monthly basis.

The downside to this method is that only stock and assembly item classes appear on many inventory reports. If there are a lot of miscellaneous parts that you want to track, it can be difficult to keep up with the different part numbers, types, and sizes of inventory because items not classified as stock or assemblies must be listed separately when taking inventory.

Combination Inventory Method

A third and more common method of inventory valuation is to use a combination of the previous methods. Some inventory items are classified as stock items and others are not. The value of stock items is tracked using the purchasing and sales functions, and other items are only valued when a physical inventory count is made. Generally, this method is used by companies that provide products or services that include both a specific and approximate number of parts. When a combination type of inventory is used, some companies create two separate inventory general ledger accounts, one for stock inventory and the other for non-stock inventory.

An example of a combination inventory method could be the florist who creates arrangements using vases, flowers, and greenery. Each arrangement would consist of just one vase, but the actual number of blooms and leafy stems would come out of a general supply and not be quantified on an invoice because in some arrangements three roses may be too many and in other similar arrangements four may not be enough — depending upon the size and fullness of the blooms. In this case, vases would be stock items and blooms would be non-stock inventory.

Another example of this method of inventory would be a computer networking business that customizes and runs its own network wiring. The number of hubs, routers, and network cards is an exact number based upon the number of computers and servers and is counted as stock inventory. The amount of wire and number of end connectors is generally approximated because some wiring may be damaged or thrown out during the installation, or because measuring out 300 feet versus 306 feet is more time-consuming than it is cost effective. These items are determined to be non-stock items or may not be included as individual inventory items at all, but may be considered part of the installation service. When items are purchased, the stock items are ordered using the inventory item and the exact number purchased is recorded with the per item cost. The non-stock items are allocated to a cost of sales account with or without their own inventory item.

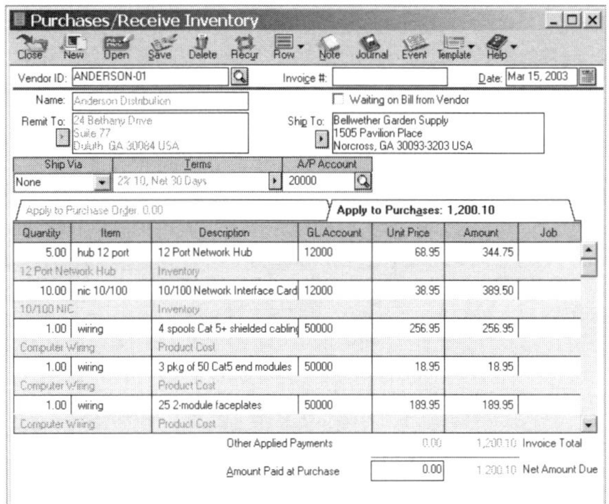

When the items are sold, the sale of stock items reduces the inventory and adds to the cost of sales, but the non-stock items may be included in an associated service or listed separately.

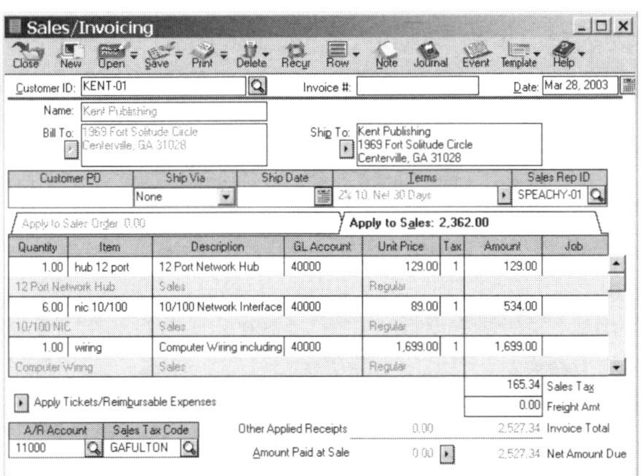

Combination Method — Revised

A second combination method that works better for many companies, and also allows non-stock items to appear on many of the inventory reports, is to create the inventory items with the Stock item class. The amount on hand is set up with a large number, such as 100 or 1,000, but the price and cost are both entered as zero (0.00). Inventory value adjustments are made using journal entries. The items may still be quantified, or not, on invoices and bills. When the quantity of the inventory gets low, the quantity, not value, of the item is adjusted using the inventory adjustment function. This method works especially well for those companies with lots of little parts or ingredients where the quantity can vary tremendously over short periods of time, but for taking inventory need to be seen on reports.

When this method is used, I suggest that the Item Type or one of the inventory custom fields be used to designate this item as a non-stock stock item.

Reconciling Inventory

Although with other general ledger accounts, reconciling may be accomplished by comparing reports and balances, there is only one sure way to determine the balance of an inventory — count it. Purchases and sales are not the only ways that an inventory balance is affected. Some inventory may go bad, such as eggs, roses, or even obsolete computer parts. Sometimes, a part may be sold but not actually used. And some inventory develops legs and walks off your shelves, usually with the help of dishonest customers or employees. Therefore, the only accurate way of determining what is on the shelves is to go and take a look.

You will want to count and reconcile inventory for, at least, the Begin Transactions date. If possible, do it again for the Go Live date. Thereafter, inventory should be reconciled at least once every year.

Counting Inventory

Peachtree has a number of reports that can be used as tools to assist you in taking inventory. The simplest is the Physical Inventory List. This list is best used by modifying the standard report as follows:

1. From the Select a Report window, select **Inventory** in the Report Area and **Physical Inventory List** from the Report List. Click **Preview** and the filter dialog box appears.

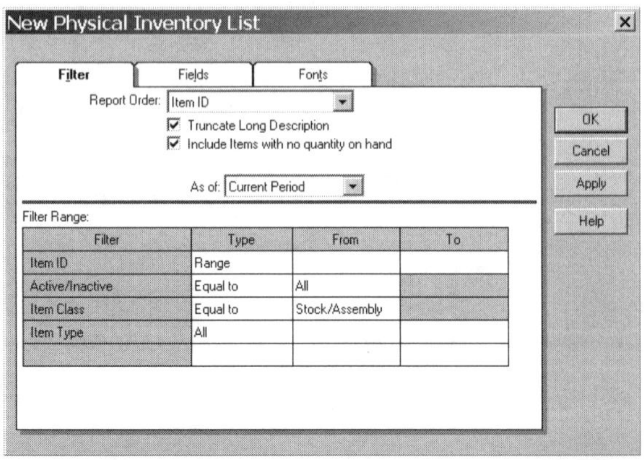

2. Choose the report order from the Report Order drop-down. Item ID and Item Description are available.
3. Check the **Truncate Long Description** check box to keep the report shorter.
4. Generally, you will want to check **Include Items with no quantity on hand** because some items without a quantity showing may actually still have some on the shelves due to data entry errors.
5. The As of field allows you to select the period end date for the report. Generally this will be Current Period, unless you want to select an older period to exclude some new inventory items that were just added to the company. The modified report includes the quantity, so an older period could be confusing because the quantity on-hand will be as of the older date, not the current period.
6. Fields in the Filter Range section allow you to exclude certain items from the list, which is especially helpful if you want to break down the list for numerous inventory takers.
7. Click on the **Fields** tab to add fields for our modified report.

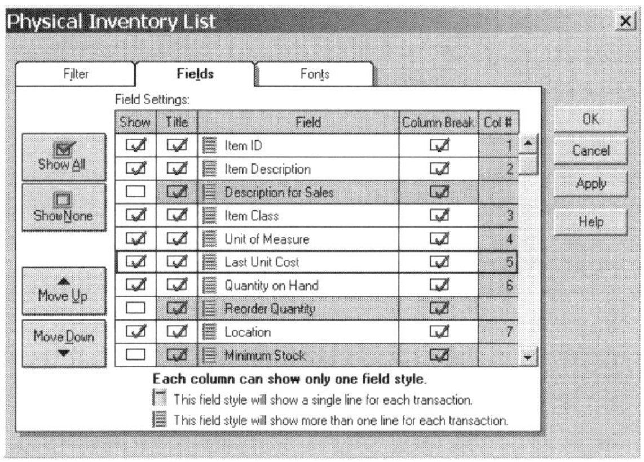

8. Select the Item Class, Quantity on Hand, and Last Unit Cost lines by checking the **Show** check boxes. Using the Move Up button, move the Last Unit Cost line above the Quantity on Hand line. I personally prefer these fields on the report for use later but you may decide to not make these fields available for employees to see for various reasons.
9. Click **OK.**
10. The report will appear. Using the **Design** button, you will need to resize the columns to get the report to fit on the page width.

Bellwether Garden Supply
Physical Inventory List
As of Mar 31, 2003
Filter Criteria includes: 1) IDs from ADMN-01000 to TOPI-40100; 2) Stock/Assembly. Report order is by ID. Report is printed with Truncated Long Descriptions.

Item ID	Item Description	Item Class	Unit	Location	Last Unit Cost	Qty on	Count	By
FERT-16180	All-Purp. Vegetable Fertilizer	Stock item	Bottle	AISLE 4	3.95	22.00		
NURS-21800	Rose - Red Starter Bush	Stock item	Each	NURSER	5.10	24.00		
NURS-21810	Rose - Yellow Starter Bush	Stock item	Each	NURSER	5.10	18.00		
NURS-21820	Rose - White Starter Bush	Stock item	Each	NURSER	5.10	16.00		
POTS-30100	Basket Planter-Wire Hang	Stock item	Each	AISLE 6	0.75	4.00		

As you can see from the portion of the report shown here, there is ample room to note the actual physical count and the name or initials of the person counting the inventory. With the report modifications, the counter can determine if inventory appears to be missing and might be located elsewhere in the store or, if the count is excessively high, whether another inventory item is being mistaken for this inventory item. Once counted, the report can then be given to the accounting department for analysis.

Notice that only stock items appear on the report. If you had a large number of non-stock items that you wanted to count, they would not appear on the report unless you used the method described above. A similar report, with the Item Type field used to denote non-stock stock items, appears here to show how this method may be used when taking inventory.

Item ID	Item Description	Item Class	Item Type	Unit	Last Unit Cost	Qty	Count	By
hub 12 port	12 Port Network Hub	Stock item		Each	68.95	12.00		
misc-l brackets	L brackets	Stock item	NONSTOCK	12/pk		256.0		
misc-phillips screw	Phillips screws	Stock item	NONSTOCK	100/p		99.00		
misc-t brackets	T brackets	Stock item	NONSTOCK	12/pk		899.0		
misc-wire clips	Wire clips	Stock item	NONSTOCK	25/pk		99.00		
misc-wire ties	Wire ties	Stock item	NONSTOCK	50/pk		48.00		
nic 10/100	10/100 NIC	Stock item		Each	38.95	25.00		

Adjusting Inventory

Once inventory is counted and its value is calculated, you may need to make adjustments to either the inventory item quantity on hand or the inventory general ledger account balance. Adjustments may be used to reconcile the new quantity on hand, to remove damaged or obsolete items, or to add new items not recorded in purchases.

Adjusting an Inventory Item

Adjustments to an inventory item are made to a specific inventory stock item or assembly item. These classes determine the value of the inventory by taking the quantity on-hand of the item and multiplying by the unit cost. To adjust the quantity on-hand, use these instructions:

1. Determine what adjustments must be made to reconcile the inventory taken against the inventory shown in the system, by comparing the quantity counted versus the system quantity on hand. The modified Physical Inventory Report can be used as a tool for this purpose.
2. Click the **Inventory Adjustments** icon in the **Inventory** folder on the navigation aid, or select **Tasks**, **Inventory Adjustments** from the menu bar, or press **Alt+K** and then **N** using the keyboard shortcuts.

3. The Inventory Adjustments form appears.

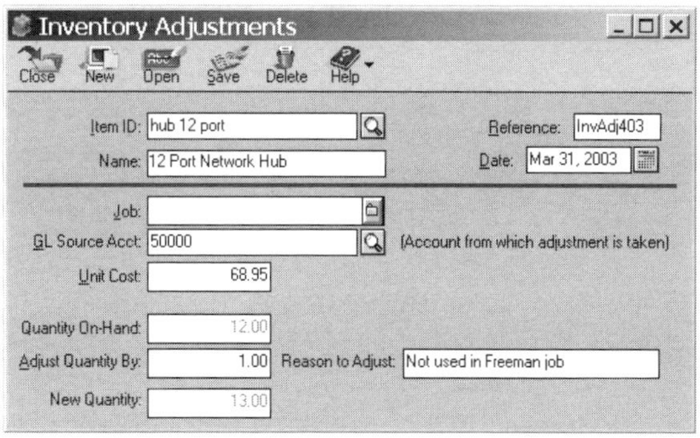

4. Select the ID of the item to be adjusted from the Item ID drop-down list. The Name field will automatically be filled in.
5. Enter a Reference to identify the adjustment transaction. You may want to use a descriptive reference or just number all inventory adjustments.
6. In the Date field, enter the date of the adjustment.
7. If a job is associated with the adjustment, select it from the Job drop-down list. Jobs are not covered in this book due to space constraints.
8. The general ledger source account is automatically entered. The inventory G/L account balance will also be affected by the adjustment, although the Journal button is not available on this form as it is on others. You may change the GL Source Acct field, if needed, to an expense account.
9. The unit cost is also entered automatically, but may be changed by entering a new per unit amount.

10. Quantity on-hand is also entered from Peachtree's records. This amount cannot be changed.
11. In the Adjust Quantity By field, enter the number of units to be added to the amount in the Quantity On-Hand field. A negative number will subtract units from inventory. Fractional units are allowed.
12. The New Quantity box will be automatically filled in by the system.
13. Enter a reason in the Reason to Adjust box if desired.
14. Click **Save** to complete the adjustment.

    Adjustments may be edited or deleted like any other type of transaction.

Adjusting the Inventory General Ledger Account

For inventory items that are not tracked as stock items, the adjustment is made directly to the general ledger inventory account, not the inventory item. Follow these instructions to adjust the inventory G/L account:

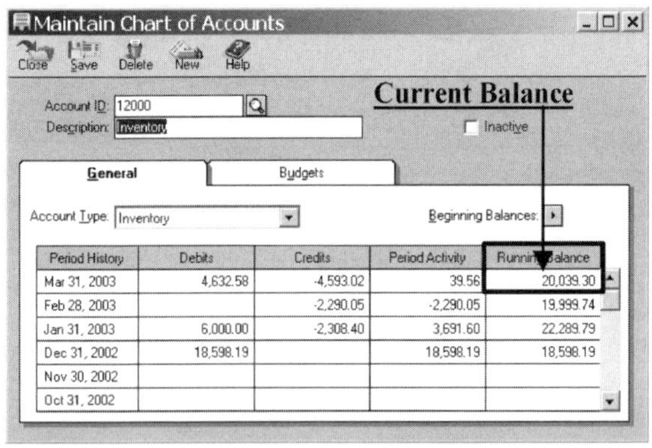

1. In this example, the current balance of the Inventory general ledger account is $20,039.30.
2. If you use a combination inventory method, you must first determine how much of the inventory account balance is made up of actual stock items. Run the Inventory Valuation Report to get the balance of inventory stock and assembly items after all inventory adjustments have been made.

Item ID Item Class	Item Description	Unit	Cost Met	Qty on Hand	Item Value	Avg Cost	% of Inv Valu
Stock item							
TOOL-35600 Assembly	Garden Hoe Kit	Each	FIFO	6.00	93.00		0.55
TOOL-35610 Assembly	Garden Hand Tool Kit	Each	FIFO	3.00	38.10		0.23
hub 12 port Stock item	12 Port Network Hub	Each	FIFO	13.00	896.35		5.32
misc-l brackets Stock item	L brackets	12/pkg	FIFO	256.00			
misc-t brackets Stock item	T brackets	12/pkg	FIFO	899.00			
misc-wire clips Stock item	Wire clips	25/pkg	FIFO	99.00			
nic 10/100 Stock item	10/100 NIC	Each	FIFO	25.00	973.75		5.78
					16,853.30		100.00

3. The stock and assembly inventory value is $16,853.30. Subtracting that from the Inventory account balance will give you the value of the non-stock inventory, $3,186.00.
4. Counting the non-stock inventory gives a balance of $4,985.98. The balance of the Inventory general ledger account is off by $1,799.98.
5. Open the General Journal Entry form. You will need to create a journal entry to increase the Inventory general ledger account.
6. Select the allocation for the other half of the entry. It may be to a cost of sales account, an expense account, or some other account.

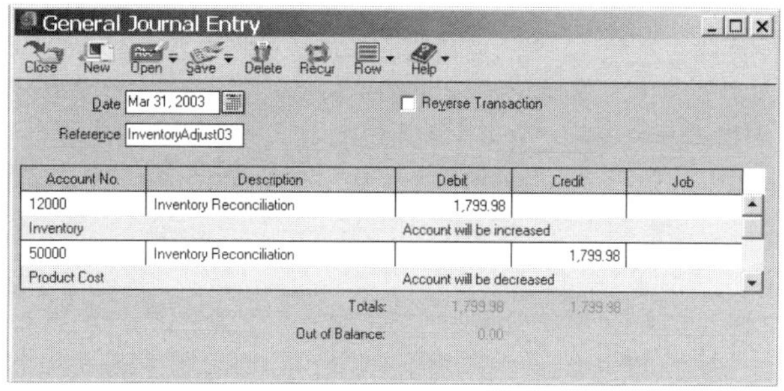

7. Save the journal entry.

   You can see the effect of the journal entry by looking at the Inventory general ledger account again.

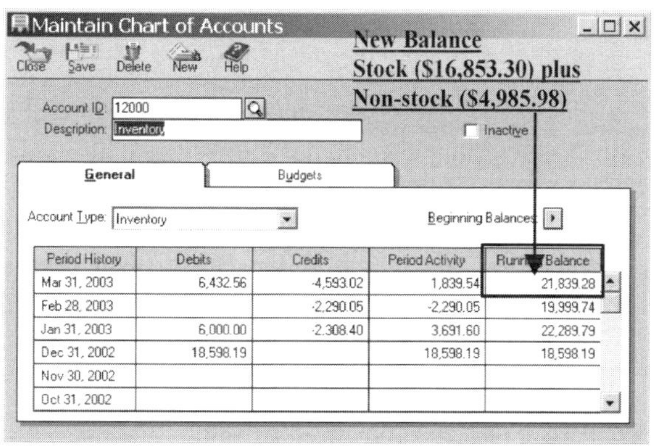

Reconcile your inventory on a regular basis, at least annually, and verify that the inventory count and general ledger account balances are correct.

Summary

For those companies that use the inventory items for more than just a way to reduce typing on invoices, Peachtree provides a mid-level inventory function. The only way the system could really be improved is by providing multiple locations or different color designations under the same inventory ID. The system is simple enough for small businesses to manage and complex enough to handle basic manufacturing needs.

Chapter 18

Reporting

In This Chapter

- Annual procedures
- Closing the payroll and fiscal years
- Purging old data
- Customizing reports, forms, and financial statements

The Three-Month Plan

If you have worked your way through this book to this chapter, you should now have your Peachtree accounting system in order. The day-to-day procedures will be running smoothly. Reconciling the different general ledger accounts will have resulted in the beginning balances and balances-to-date having amounts that will accurately reflect the status of your business.

Once the balancing and reconciliation processes of the second and third months have occurred, your books should match those of your old accounting system. Any differences should be with the full knowledge and consent of your CPA. At this point, you may quit using the old accounting system and "go live" with Peachtree.

CONGRATULATIONS! You are now a complete Peachtree user.

Annual Procedures

Day-to-day, month-end, and quarterly procedures have been covered in earlier parts of this book. Some procedures should only occur on an annual basis. Many of these procedures do not have to occur immediately after the end of the fiscal or calendar year, but may occur months later.

The procedures for a company to close its books will vary according to the nature of the company. Some companies only need to verify that the books are correct. Others will need to complete an exhaustive audit conducted by an outside public accounting company. Regardless, before the books are finally closed, you will want to be assured that the information contained in your system is correct as you enter a new accounting year. The procedures shown in this chapter can be completed using the Bellwether Garden Supply-Annual Procedures.ptb file from the Peachtree CD.

- While you are completing the monthly procedures, you will want to complete final tax reports.
- Although preliminary reports will be sent to the CPA on time, final reports will probably be held off to make sure that all information is accurate before the final reports of the year are created.
- The company file should be backed up to the hard drive so that it can be accessed at a later date.
- Depending upon when the company financial year ends, you will need to close the payroll year and then the fiscal year.

Closing the Payroll Year

Because of government regulations regarding payroll, the following steps will need to be completed within the first 30 days after the end of a payroll year. Requirements will vary depending upon your state and company procedures. Your CPA will have the regulating information on your company's requirements.

1. Verify that all payroll information is accurate and all employee information has been updated before running any payroll forms or final reports. Information can be verified by viewing the Yearly Earnings Report.

2. By the required date, print W-2s for all employees. (W-2 setup was covered in Chapter 15.) From the Select a Report window, choose **Payroll** in the Report Area and **Federal Form W-2** from the Report List.

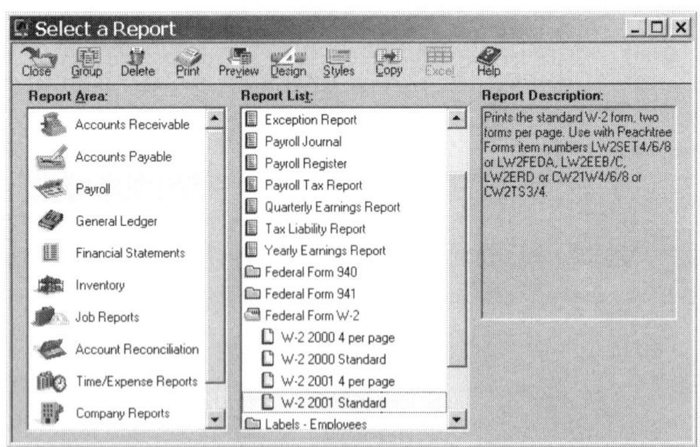

Select the appropriate form from the list and click the **Preview** or **Print** button. The W-2 filter dialog box will appear.

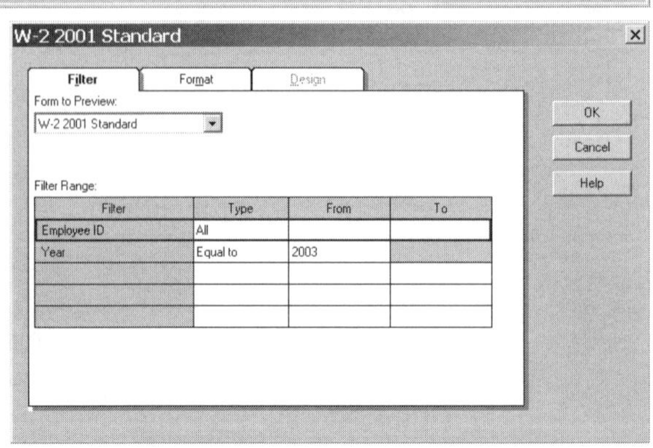

Verify that the correct form appears in the Form to Preview or Form to Print field. In the Filter Range area you may choose to view a range of employees using the Employee ID line. Verify that the correct year appears on the Year line. If printing immediately on the forms, place the forms in the printer. The forms may be reprinted at any time, so you may wish to print them first on plain paper to look over the information. Click **OK**. The forms will print, or appear on your screen, based upon your earlier selection. The forms are preprinted, so the labels do not appear on the report shown here.

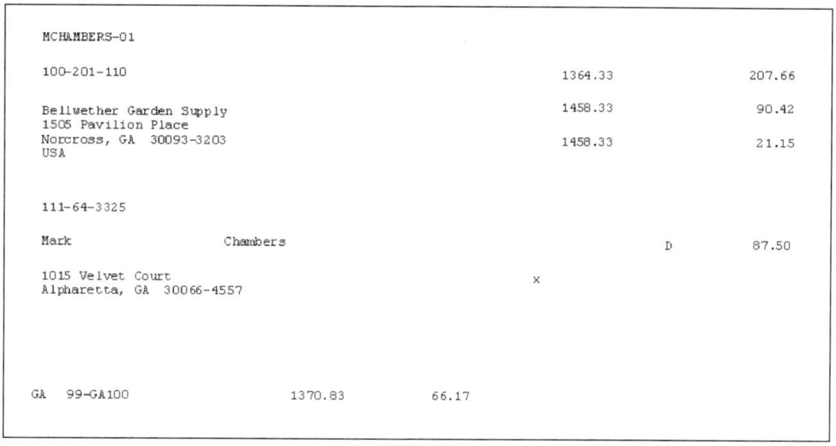
MCHAMBERS-01

100-201-110   1364.33   207.66

Bellwether Garden Supply   1458.33   90.42
1505 Pavilion Place
Norcross, GA 30093-3203   1458.33   21.15
USA

111-64-3325

Mark   Chambers   D   87.50

1015 Velvet Court   x
Alpharetta, GA 30066-4557

GA 99-GA100   1370.83   66.17

The last form printed is a summary of all other forms and includes the company totals.

3. To print a W-3, select the **Federal Form 940** folder and select **Form W-3** to print or preview.

   In the FUTA deposited for the year box, enter the total of your FUTA payments made for this fiscal year. In the SUTA paid this year box, enter those deposits. Verify the other fields and click **OK** to print the W-3.

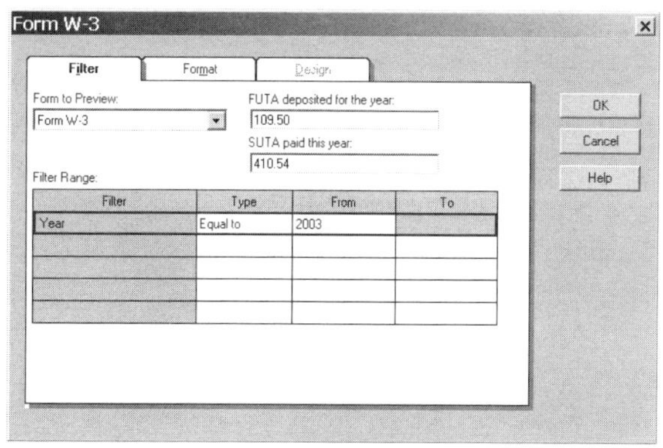

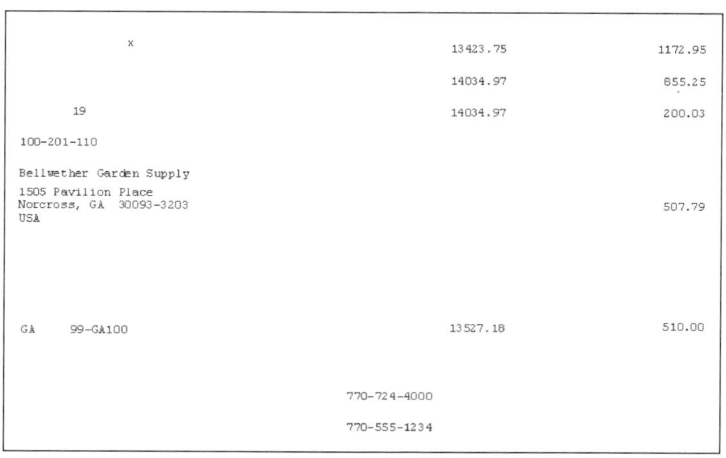
x   13423.75   1172.95

14034.97   855.25

19   14034.97   200.03

100-201-110

Bellwether Garden Supply
1505 Pavilion Place
Norcross, GA 30093-3203   507.79
USA

GA 99-GA100   13527.18   510.00

770-724-4000

770-555-1234

4. In Chapter 13, the settings for 1099s were explained. Verify that all vendors requiring a 1099 are set up correctly. To print or view the forms, select the **1099 Forms** folder from the Accounts Payable reports. Select the appropriate form to view and click **Preview**. The 1099 filter appears.

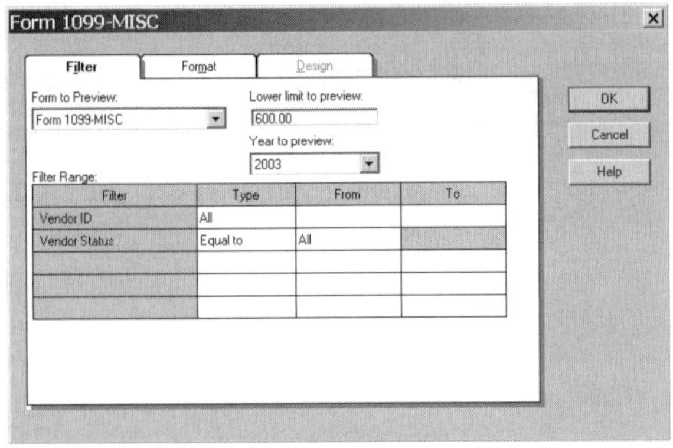

In the Lower limit to preview field, enter the dollar amount to limit the number of forms printed. Regulations require a 1099 for individuals with more than $600.00 in payments, but many companies print the form for all vendors, regardless of the amount. Click **OK**.

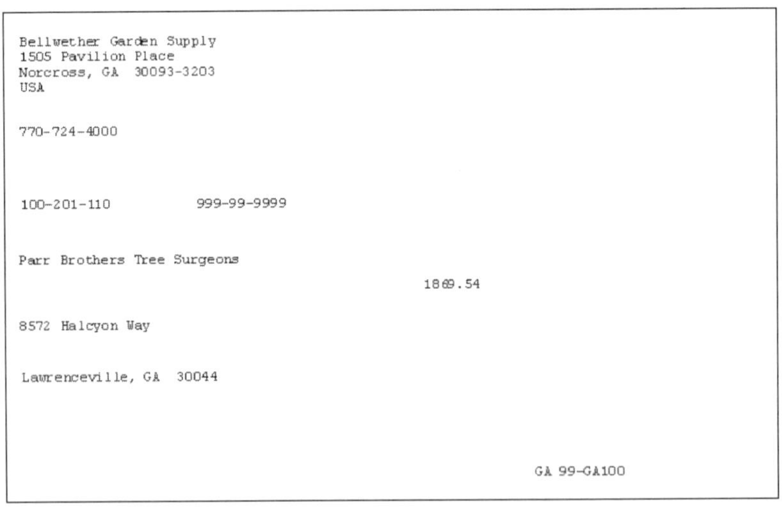

Because this form must also be printed on a form, the labels do not show. You should print the forms on plain paper first to verify the amounts and tax IDs of each vendor before printing on the forms. Sometimes, the alignment or the position of some fields will need to be moved. You will need to print the 1099-MISC and the 1099-INT forms separately. Other 1099 forms are not available.

5. Print any other reports needed regarding payroll for the CPA, management, and any others needing this information.

   Closing the actual payroll year can be held off until later in the new year. Because Peachtree allows two years to be open, you may desire to look at last year's data for some time to come. If you have printed the payroll reports for 2002 and are currently working in 2003, the year 2002 does not have to be closed until right before 2004. If you have a lot of transactions in Peachtree, you may want to close the previous year early to improve Peachtree's performance. When it is time to close the last payroll year, follow these steps:

1. Make a backup of the company file before closing the payroll year. Verify that all users are logged off the system also.

Tip: If the Peachtree program is loaded on a server, I suggest that the close process be performed on the server. Whenever possible, perform the close on the computer on which the company data resides.

Warning!! Once the payroll year is closed, you may not make any more changes to that year. One of the reasons for waiting until later in the year is to verify the accuracy of the data before closing. Any necessary changes will have to be done with beginning balances once the payroll year is closed.

2. From the Tasks menu on the menu bar select **System** and then **Year-End Wizard.** The Year-End Wizard will open.

   Older systems will have two menu selections: Close Fiscal Year and Close Payroll Year; select **Close Payroll Year.** (The screens in this example may not match what is on your screen but they will be similar enough for you to understand the proper procedures.)

3. Notice the current open Payroll Tax Years. We will close the first year, in this case 2003. We will ignore the Fiscal Years for now. Click **Next.**

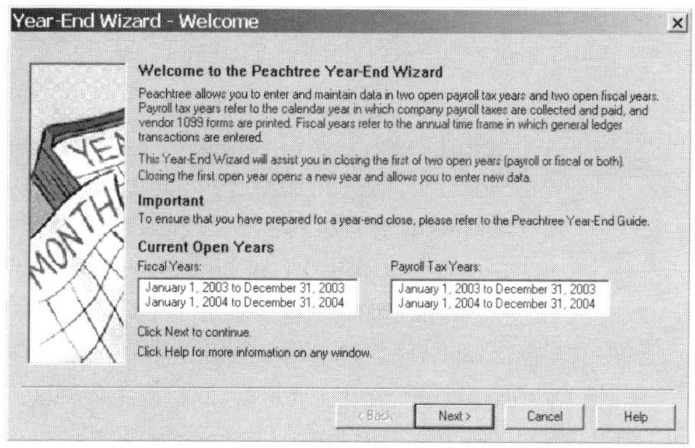

4. The Close Options screen will appear.

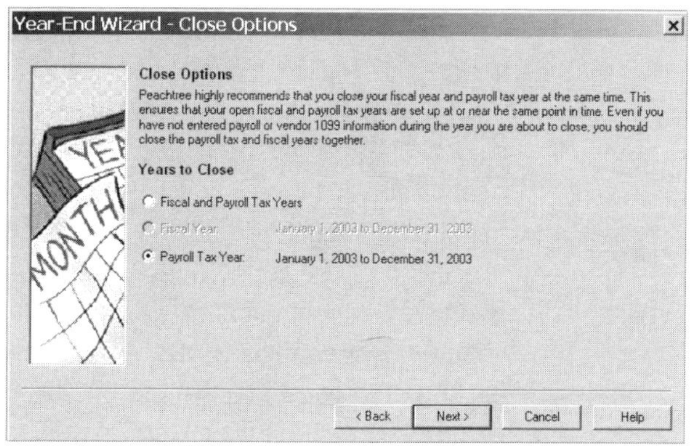

For Years to Close, select **Payroll Tax Year**. In this particular case the Fiscal Year option is disabled, but it may not be on your screen. Click **Next**.

5. Although you should have made a backup before starting this process, the system requires a backup at this point also. I personally make at least three backups (one to CD, one to the server, and one to a local hard drive) before doing any processes of this nature, for safety reasons. I have actually had to go to a second or third backup at times to recover from catastrophic crashes during this, or similar, procedures. Make a new backup; when you return to this screen, click **Next**.

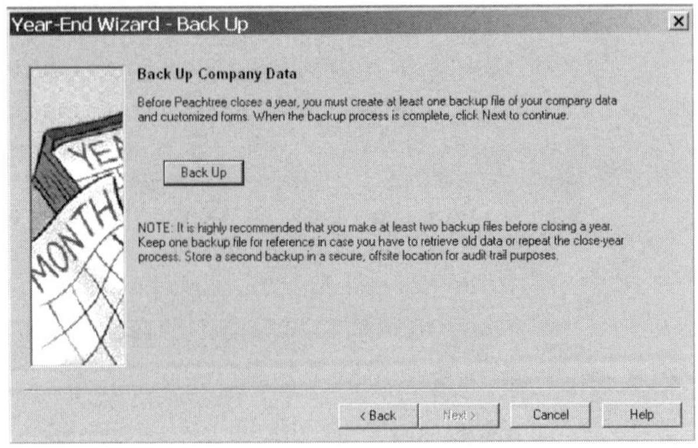

6. When the Confirm Close screen appears, verify that only the payroll tax year is being closed. In the field labeled The following payroll tax year(s) will close, verify the actual year to be closed. Click **Next**.

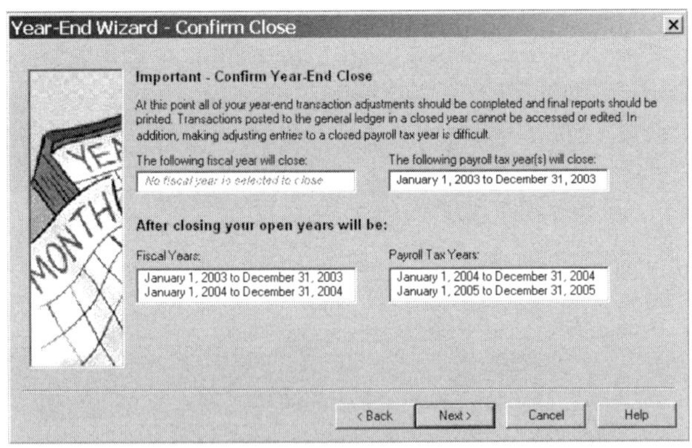

7. The Begin Close screen appears. If you are unsure of what is being closed, you may click the **Back** button to confirm or correct your options. Peachtree suggests that the process to close is run overnight. If your company is smaller (less than an 8 MB backup) and you have fast computers, you may run the close process with little downtime. Click the **Begin Close** button when you are ready.

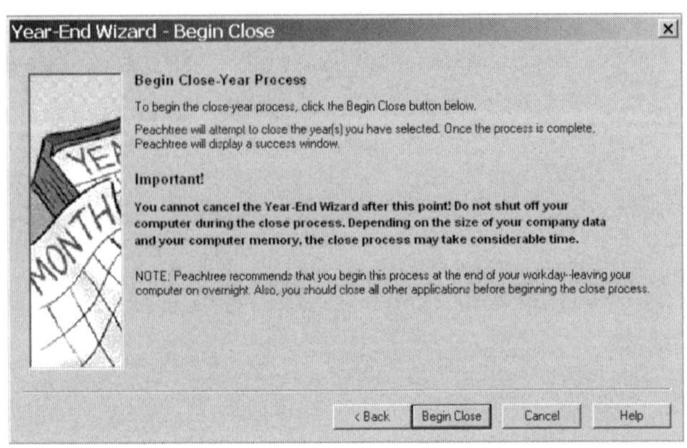

8. When completed (the Bellwether Garden file, with a 1.9 MB backup on a 1 GHz processor, took less than one minute to process the payroll tax year), a Congratulations screen appears with the new payroll years appearing in the Payroll Tax Year(s) field. Click **Finish** to close the wizard.

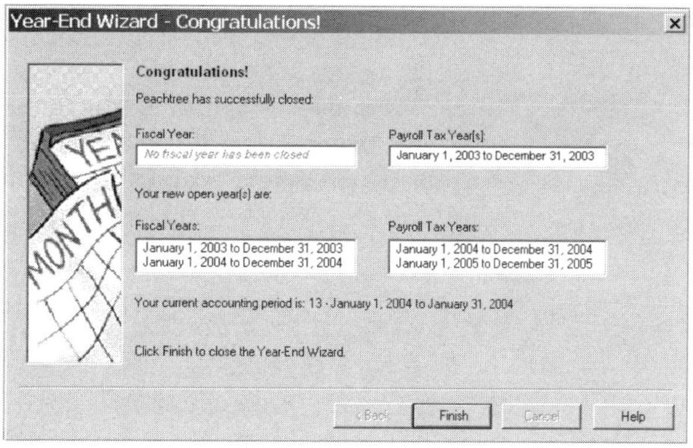

Once the payroll year is closed, you will need to install the tax tables before payroll can be entered for the new year. Also, verify that the state unemployment wage limit and percentage rate are changed to the new amounts.

Closing the Fiscal Year

As with closing the payroll year, closing the fiscal year does not have to be done immediately after the new year is started. Most of my clients do not close the previous year until they have reached Period 18 at least. Some wait until Period 24 to close and have me perform the final backups, closings, and tax updates all at the same time. (This means I'm always swamped about Christmastime and the first week of January.)

Warning!! Once the fiscal year is closed, you may not make any more changes to that year. One of the reasons for waiting until later in the year is to verify the accuracy of the data before closing. Any necessary changes will have to be done with beginning balances once the fiscal year is closed.

To close the fiscal year, follow the steps given below. This example is for Peachtree 2002 but is similar for earlier versions. The main difference is that the payroll and fiscal close procedures are accessed separately and the screens are slightly different.

1. Verify the accuracy of all data and account balances before proceeding further. Running the General Ledger report for all accounts and the entire year to be closed will assist you in locating and making changes.
2. Create your final backups for the year. You will be required to make a backup using the close wizard, but you can never have too many backups.

Tip: I have a special backup process for my clients that allows them to look at data in previous years without having to do a Restore. Because the Restore process can be so dangerous (I've had clients wipe out an entire year's worth of data accidentally), this process prevents tragedy. The process is not included in this book or in the companion files, but is available to interested parties who contact me.

3. Verify that all users are logged off the system.

Tip: Whenever possible, perform the close on the computer on which the company data resides. If the Peachtree program is loaded on a server, I suggest that the close process be performed on the server.

4. Open the Year-End Wizard by selecting **Tasks**, **System**, then **Year-End Wizard** from the menu bar. Those with older versions will use **Close Fiscal Year.**

5. The Welcome screen shows the Current Open Years. The Payroll Tax Years should show that the previous year has already been closed. Click **Next.**

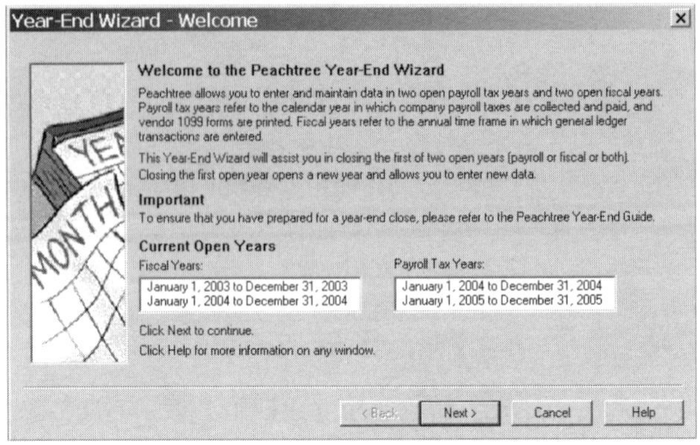

6. Because the payroll year was closed earlier, only the Fiscal Year option is available in the Close Options screen. Click **Next.**

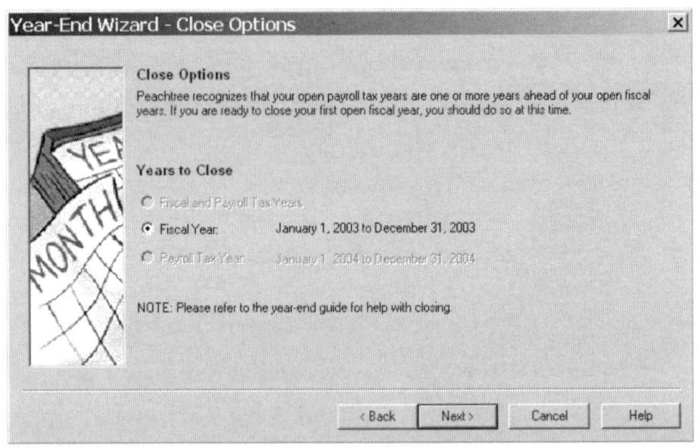

7. If there are any problems with the closing process, a Cannot Proceed screen will appear with information about the problem.

You will need to click the **Cancel** button to close the wizard. Correct the problems, restart the wizard, and return to this point.

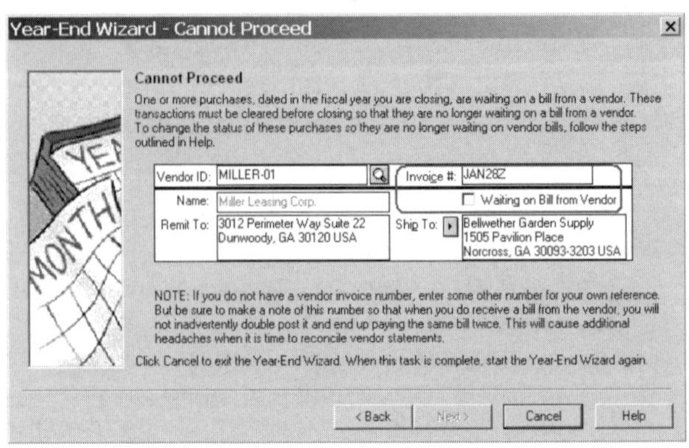

8. An Unprinted Items Warning may also appear.

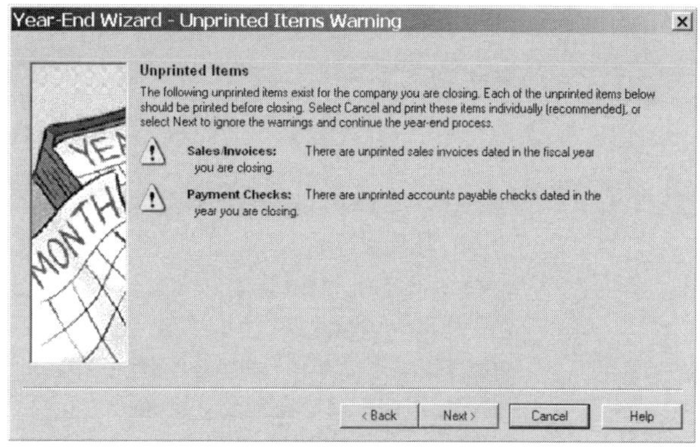

9. Once you are past all problems, the Reports screen appears.

   This screen allows you to print some or all of the journals before proceeding with the close process. Hopefully, those were done before you started the wizard. Click **Next** to print the reports or unselect the Print check boxes to ignore the reports and then click **Next**.

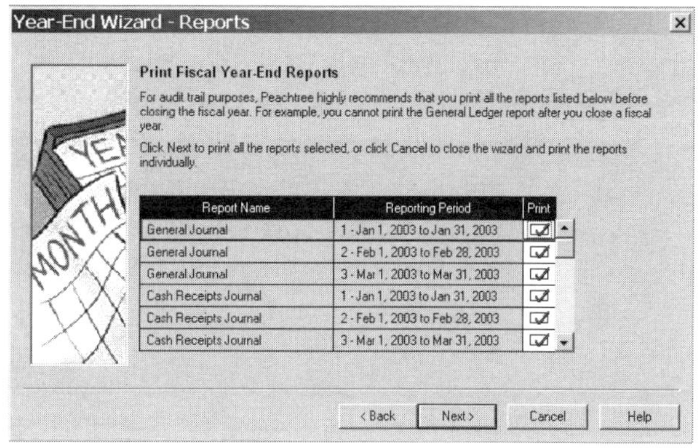

10. The Backup screen appears. Click the **Back Up** button to create the required backup and then click **Next**.

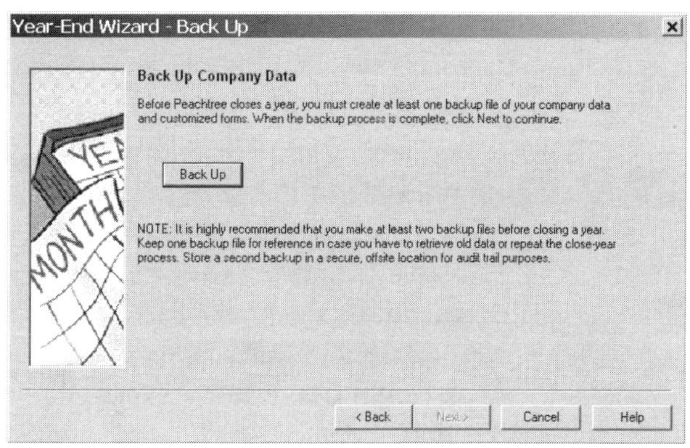

11. The New Open Fiscal Years screen appears.

    If you are closing 2003, the current fiscal year will be 2004 and the new fiscal year will be 2005. If the Next Fiscal Year option is selected here, the Period columns on the right will show the accounting periods for 2005. Occasionally, a company will want to alter its accounting periods for the next fiscal year. If the Current Fiscal Year option is selected, the current year will show. You cannot change the accounting periods for the current year; that is why they are read only. Click **Next**.

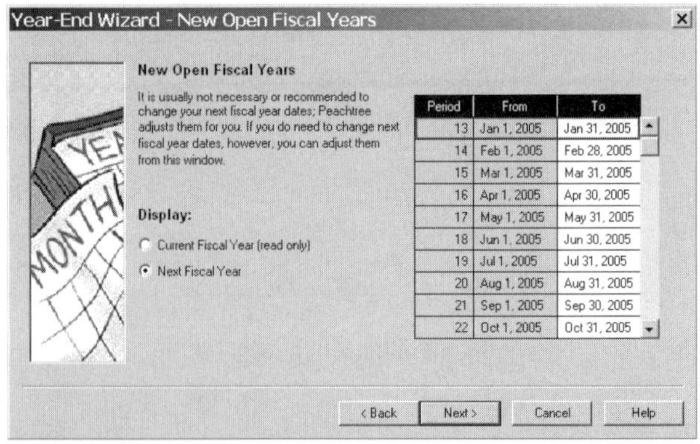

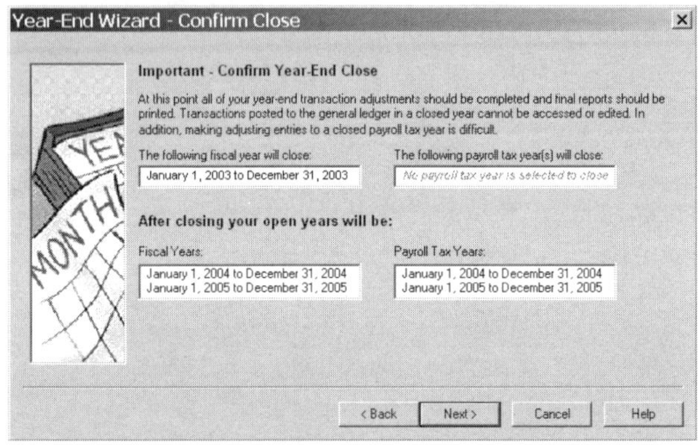

12. When the Confirm Close screen appears, verify the dates in the Fiscal Years and The following fiscal year will close fields. Click **Next**.
13. In the Begin Close screen, you are warned that the process may take some time and you may want to perform the close overnight. If this is a concern, you will need to wait to close. Click **Begin Close** to start the function.
14. The progress of the process will show in a status bar. (The Bellwether Garden file, with a 1.9 MB backup on a 1 GHz processor, took less than one minute to close the fiscal year.)

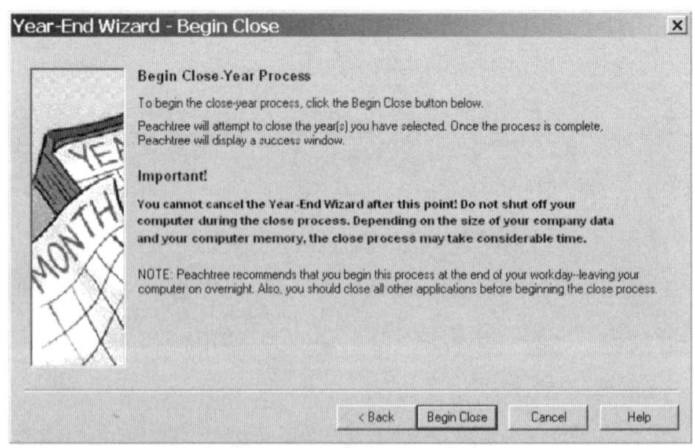

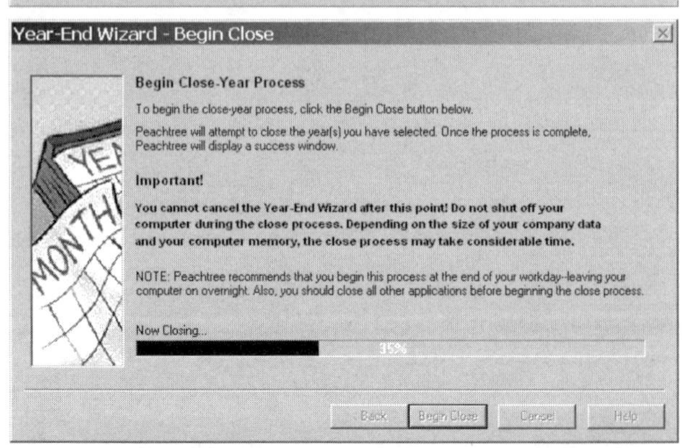

15. When completed, a Congratulations screen will appear showing the new fiscal year dates. Click **Finish** to complete the wizard.

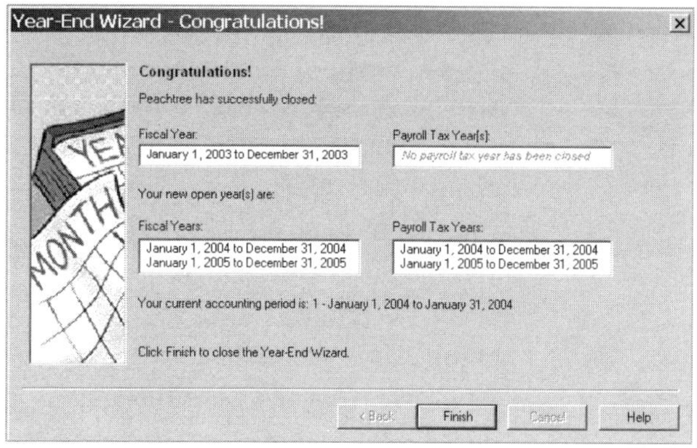

Purging Old Data from the System

Too many transactions in the system can slow it down. You may also have many customers, vendors, accounts, and inventory items that are inactive and have not been used in quite a while. Even though data in a closed fiscal year is not available, the information is still there. Purging data and removing old, inactive records can improve the performance of the system. Follow these steps to purge old information:

1. Make at least one backup before purging.
2. Select **Tasks**, **System**, **Purge Old Transactions/Inactives** from the menu bar. The Backup Before Purging screen appears.
3. After backups have been made, click **Continue**.

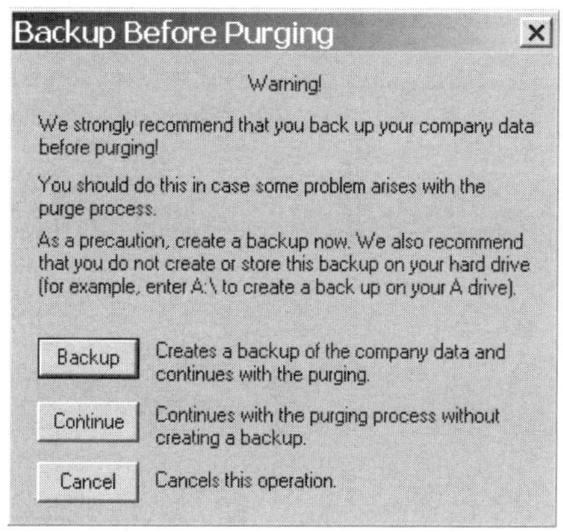

4. You will be asked if you want reports printed before purging. Generally, you will click **No**.

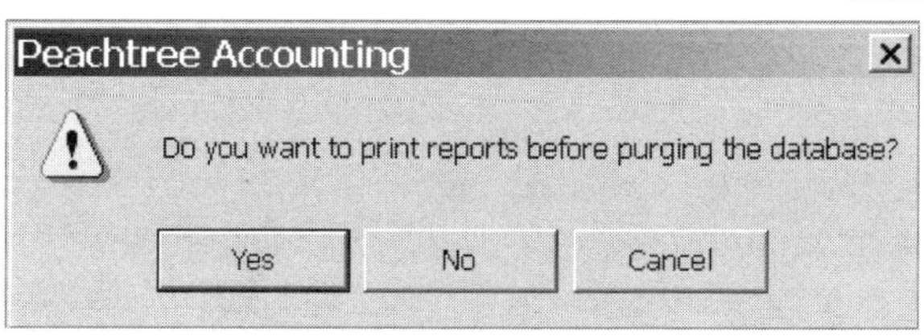

5. The database will be scanned and the Purge Guide screen will show.

Month 3

Tip: Although numerous screens appear after this, for most of my clients I select everything and make the Through date the last date of the previous fiscal year. I don't worry about whether the items selected to be purged are included in the company files, I purge them anyway to speed the selection process.

This screen allows you to select to purge quotes, closed purchase orders, and closed sales orders. Each selection has a Purge … through date associated with it. Generally you will select the last date of the previous fiscal year. If you just closed 2003, this date should be Dec 31, 2003. Some clients want to purge 2004 items in 2005 when 2004 is still open — bad idea. Click **Next**.

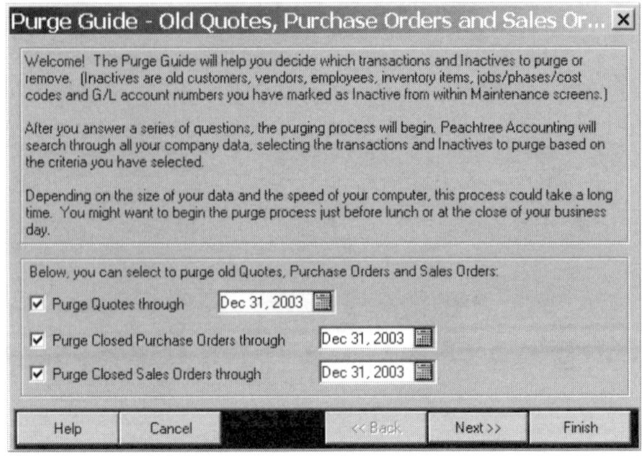

6. A Time and Expense Tickets screen appears. If you use time or expense tickets (which are not discussed in this book due to space constraints), you may select to purge those also. Click **Next**.

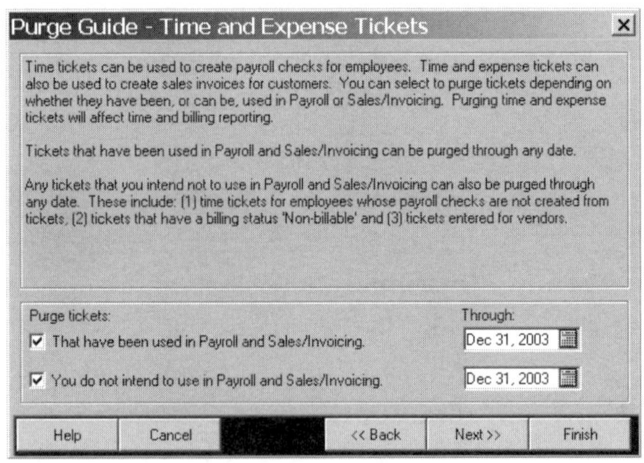

7. Another Time and Expense Tickets screen appears. It looks almost identical, but this screen is to purge tickets that are available. Click **Next**.

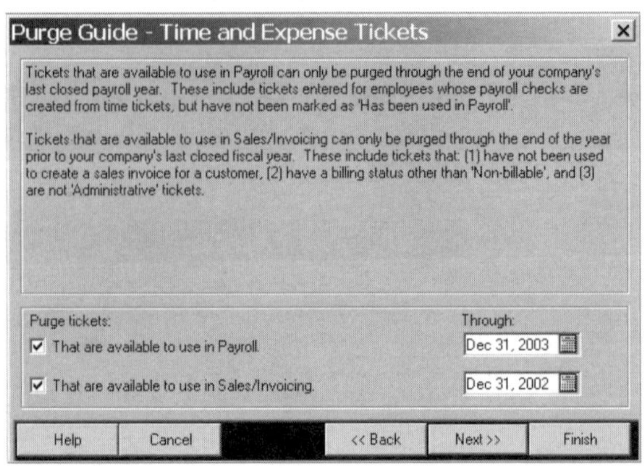

8. The Old Transactions screen appears.

   In addition to purging the items selected previous to the Old Transactions screen, it is important to purge the actual transactions themselves to improve Peachtree's performance. Click **Next**.

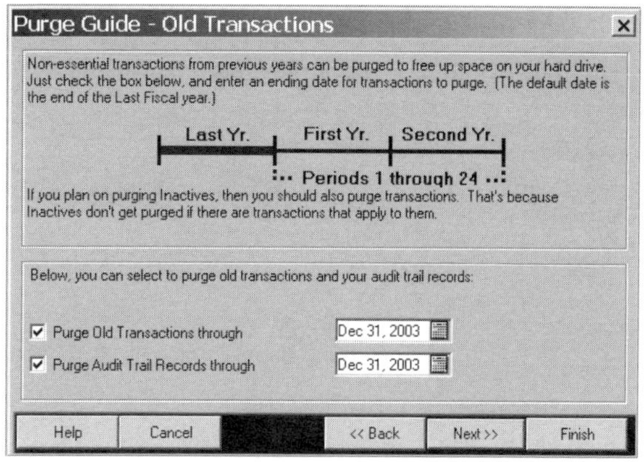

9. The Account Reconciliation screen appears.

   Choose **Yes** to retain any records or transactions that have not been cleared and are required by the reconciliation function, such as a check that has not been cashed by an employee. Click **Next**.

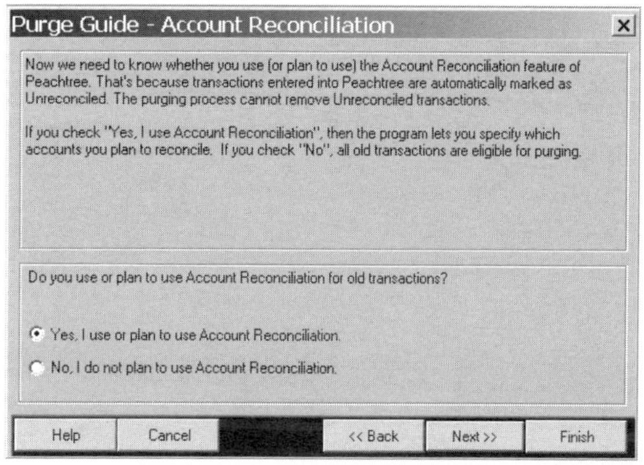

10. In the Account Reconciliation Select screen, select the accounts that may have transactions outstanding that need to be reconciled by clicking the **Use** check box. Click **Next** to select a date for purging checks.

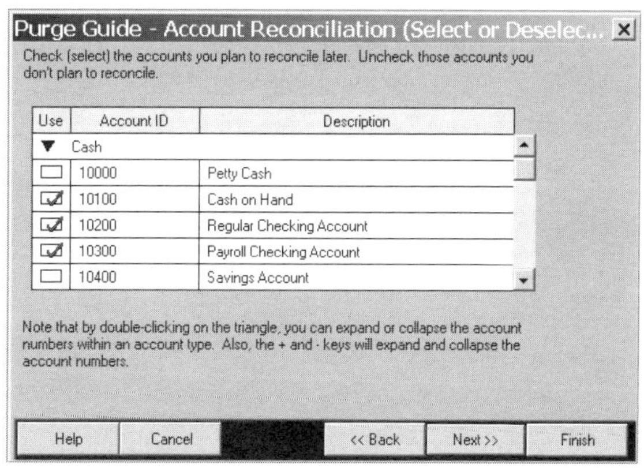

11. The date shown is the date of the oldest check or deposit that has not yet cleared. You will want to save this transaction, so leave the date as it is and click **Next** to continue.

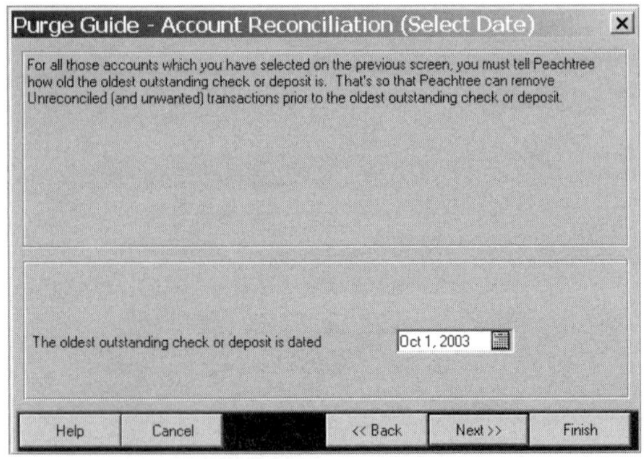

12. Select whether you are using reimbursable expenses and, again, click **Next**.

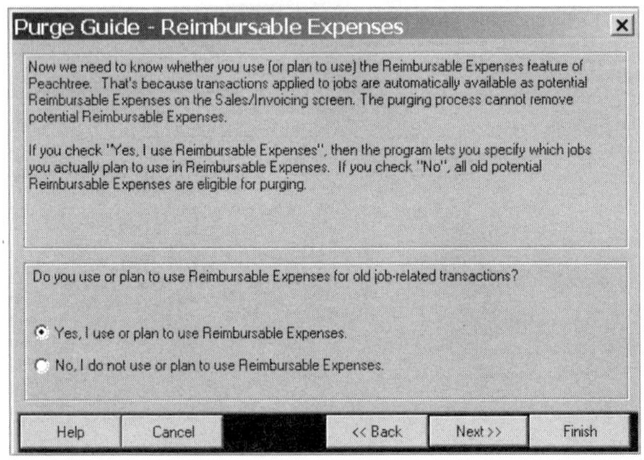

13. If you are using reimbursable expenses, select the **Use** check box of the Job ID lines for expenses that will be reimbursed. Click **Next**.

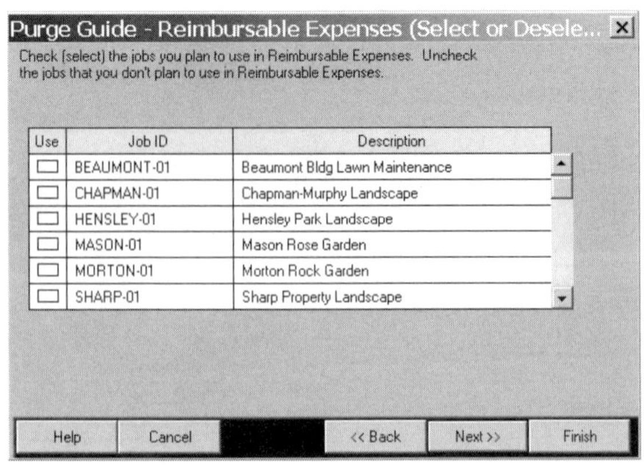

14. Here, enter the date of the oldest expense to be reimbursed that should be kept. Click **Next** again.

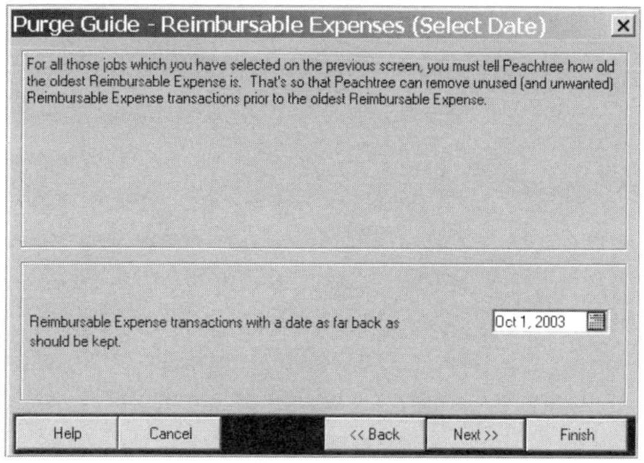

15. The Inactives screen lets you choose which records that have been made inactive can be purged. Only records without transactions, such as a customer without an invoice or receipt, can be purged. Sometimes, a customer, employee, or vendor will have an outstanding balance but no transactions. Peachtree will not purge the records until all balances are gone.

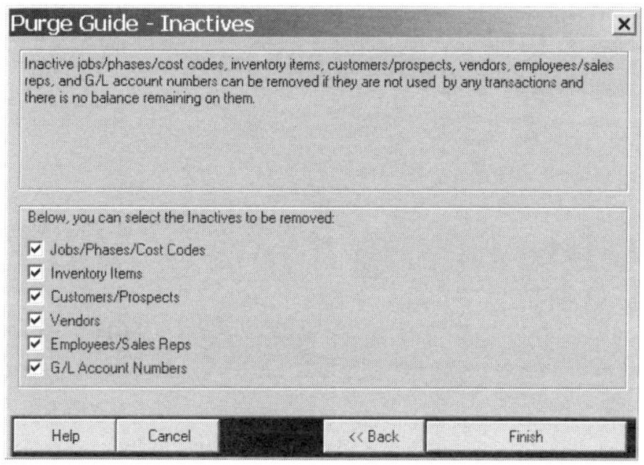

When all selections have been made, you can finally click **Finish**.

16. A last Summary screen will appear.

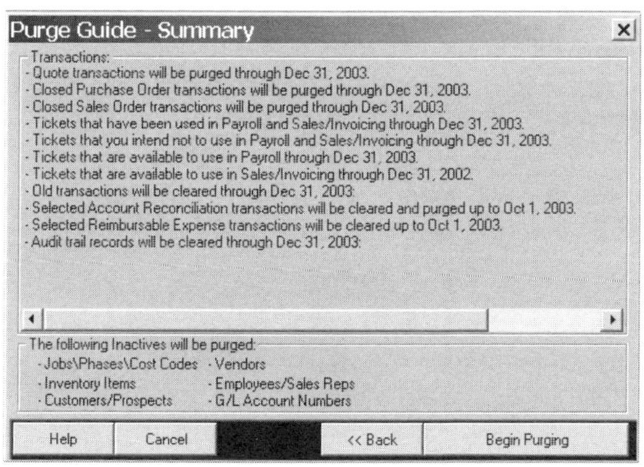

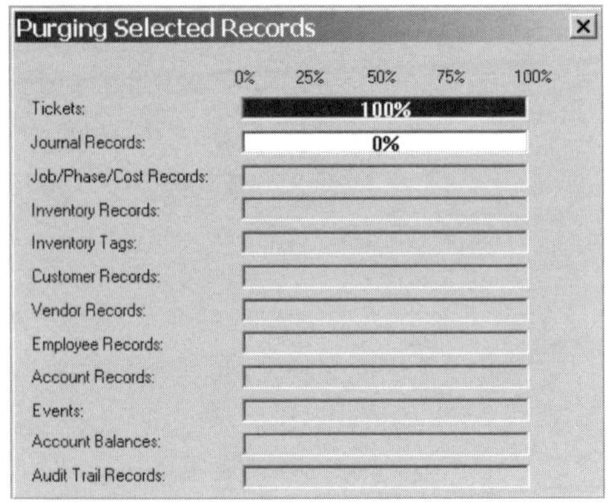

Verify the selections. If you need to make a change, click **Back**. If everything is correct, click **Begin Purging**. The system will show the status of the purge process.

17. I often find that the purge process takes longer than the closing processes, so be sure that you have plenty of time to purge. When the process is complete, a message will appear with that statement.

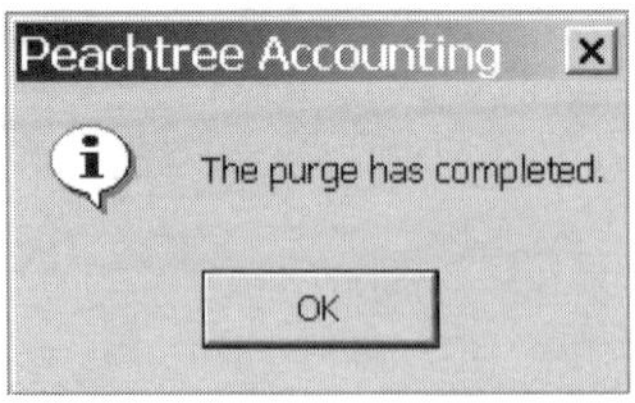

Click **OK**.

Customizing Reports and Forms

Many customers need forms and reports that have been customized. Changing the parameters or look of a report can be very easy, but for forms the process can be very time-consuming and it takes knowledge of many things to complete the task with accuracy. These skills include advanced desktop publishing experience, knowledge of Peachtree, and a talent for making a form or report look professional.

Reports

Several custom reports and forms are included with the companion files, which are discussed in the next chapter. In this section, I discuss some basics on customizing reports.

Note: Unfortunately, you cannot create reports from scratch but must start with an existing one, even when the result is nothing like the beginning report.

Once a report is the way that you like it, click the Save button on the toolbar to keep the changes. Always record the report with a new name, not the default name, because reinstalling or upgrading Peachtree will often overwrite the existing default reports.

The Fields Tab

Most reports can be made more informative and effective simply by adding or deleting a few fields. In Chapter 10, I showed how to use the Fields tab to add and move fields, thus improving a report's usefulness.

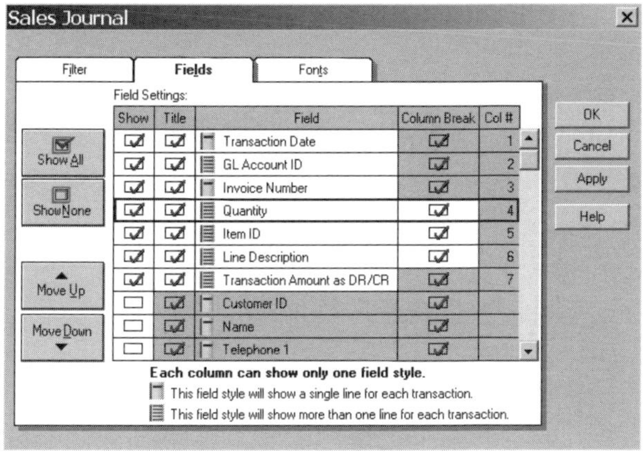

If a report almost meets your needs, look at the Fields tab to see if more information is available to you.

Report Filters

Another way to modify a report is to change the filters. For example, although there is a Quote Register to list all the quotes, that report does not show the journal transactions. The Sales Journal can include quotes, sales, or both. The default is both. If you wanted a journal all the time with just quotes, you could modify and save the Sales Journal by selecting Quote in the Sale/Quote filter range.

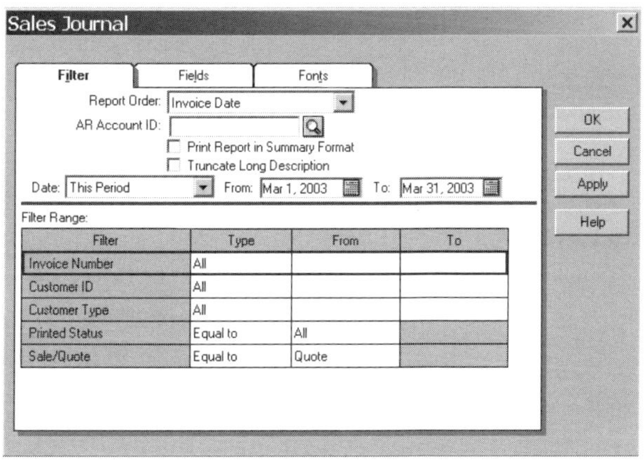

The Fonts Tab

We have totally ignored the Fonts tab up until this point. If you click on the Fonts tab in any report, it will look very similar on almost all of them.

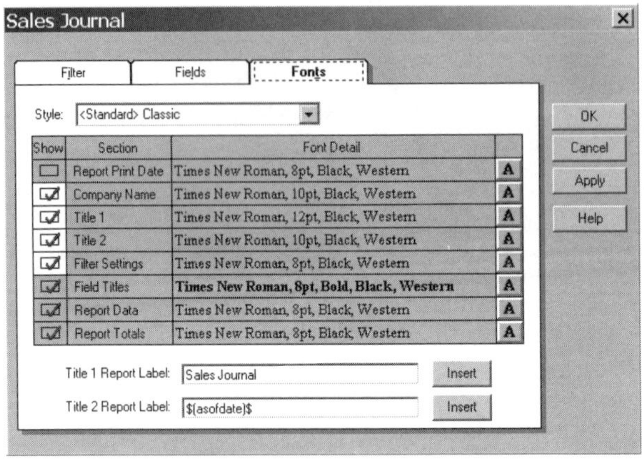

There are numerous formats that you can select from the Style drop-down list. These include Classic, Contemporary, Elegant, and Professional. You may also create your own custom style.

Some parts of the report may be viewed or hidden by checking or unchecking the Show column. The font may be changed or resized with the font button at the end of each line. The report must be saved under a new name to retain the changes made on this tab.

Forms

Many of my clients have tried customizing their own forms, without success, and have finally decided that they are better off having me create and modify their forms rather than wasting the time to do this themselves. The most popular forms to modify are the invoice and the disbursement check. If you decide to try it yourself, these instructions may help.

Because invoicing is one of the first functions a company starts with, a customized invoice with the company logo is very important. Most companies like to use laser printed invoices, but these instructions can be used with other types of invoices too. These instructions also may be used with other types of forms, like checks.

To create a custom invoice, I usually start with one of the plain invoices. Each of these is slightly different from the others. Decide which best meets your needs regarding the freight, partial payment, ship to, and quantity fields. A good way to look at the different invoices is to go to one of the sample companies and print an existing invoice using each of the different forms. Once you have decided which invoice to modify, select it in the Select a Report window and then click the Design button on the toolbar. The form will appear in Design mode.

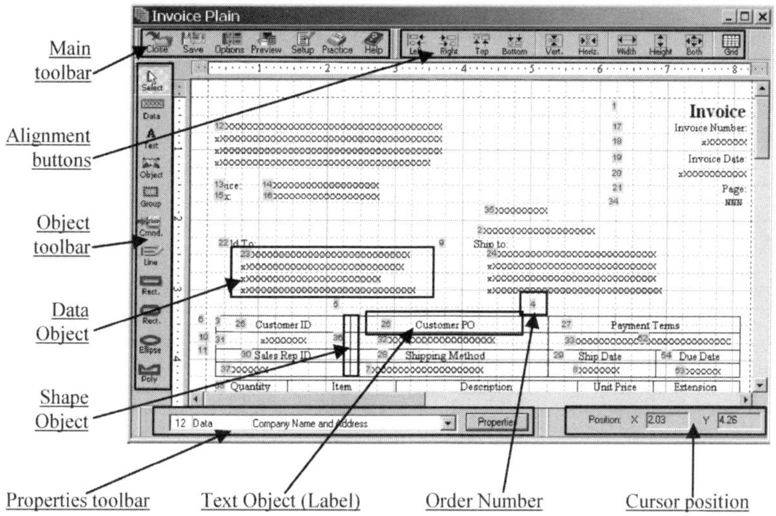

The design window has several toolbars around its edge. These may be dragged and dropped like other Windows toolbars. The inside of the design window contains the form. Different types of objects are placed on the form, and each object is printed in a specified order. The toolbars and many of the objects are labeled and shown in the above figure.

Design Options

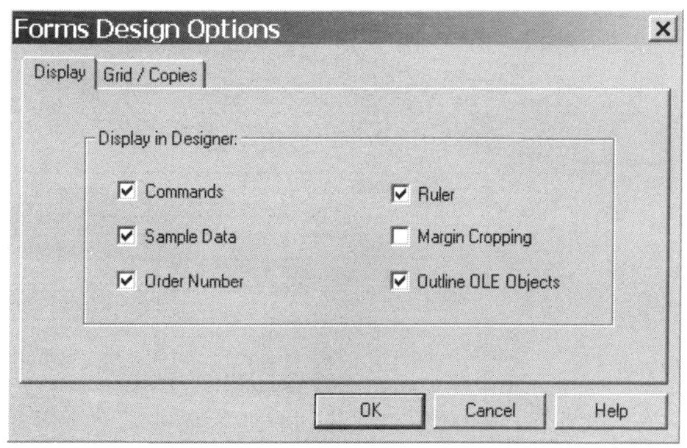

1. The main toolbar allows you to close, save, and view the form, plus it includes options for the design window. If you click the **Options** button, the Forms Design Options dialog box appears.
2. The Display tab controls the objects seen in the design window. The first check box allows you to see where commands are located on the screen.

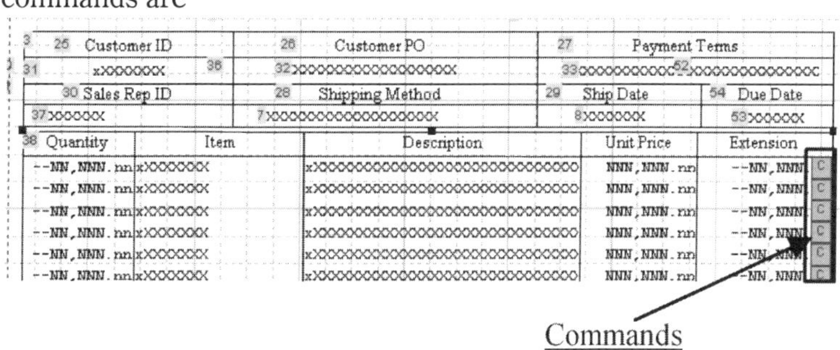

Month 3

In older versions, the commands are written out when they appear on the form and are included in the order. Removing the commands causes the placeholders to be removed from the design window.

3. Data objects can be shown with sample data consisting of X's (text data) and N's (numerical data).

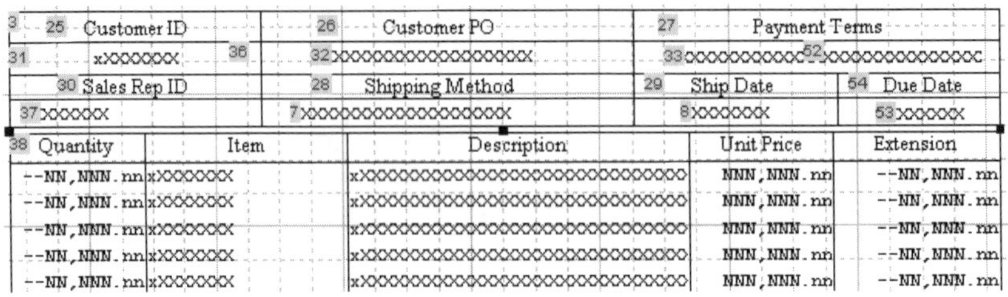

Unchecking the Sample Data check box replaces the sample data with the data field names.

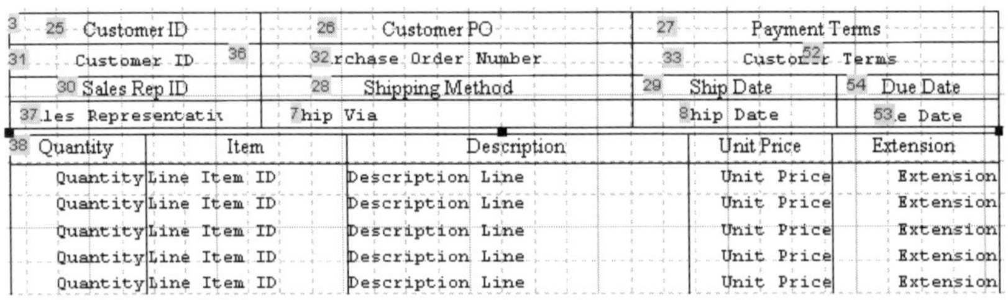

4. The third option controls the visibility of order numbers. Each object on the form is printed in a specific order. Changing the order is discussed later in this chapter. Uncheck the Order Number option to hide them.

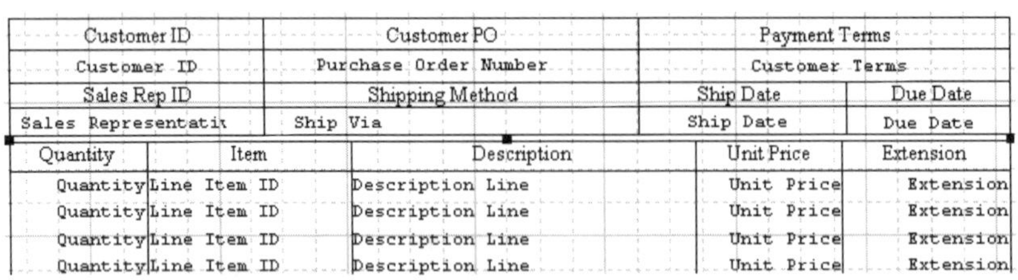

5. Notice that in the design window there is a ruler on both the top and left side of the form. Hide the ruler by unchecking the Ruler option.
6. The Margin Cropping option refers to the printing of a form. If this option is checked, any portion of a field that extends past the margin, denoted by red lines, will be cut off. If unchecked, the form will be printed with as much of the field as is allowed by the printer itself.
7. The last option concerns graphic objects. If a graphic is on the form, the Outline OLE Objects option will place a border around the object in Design mode. The border itself does not print.

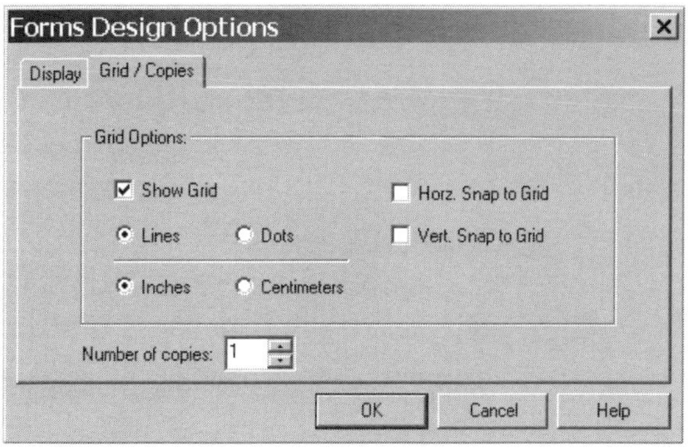

8. Click the **Grid/Copies** tab.

   The grid is the collection of blue lines that crisscross the form in Design mode. The grid can be useful in aligning objects on the form.
9. Hide the lines by unselecting the Show Grid check box.
10. You may choose to view the grid as Lines or Dots and in Inches or Centimeters by selecting the correct option.
11. The Horz. Snap to Grid and the Vert. Snap to Grid check boxes control how objects are dragged across the form. If checked, the object will "snap," or jump, to the closest gridline. Although these options make the alignment of objects easier, they are often more trouble than they are worth.
12. The last option is the Number of copies field. This controls how many forms print when the form is used. Some companies purchase laser paper or preprinted forms with sequential colors (like white, yellow, pink) to imitate NCR (no carbon required) paper. When a form, such as an invoice, is printed from the Sales/Invoicing screen, the printer automatically prints the number of copies shown here. This way with one click a copy is printed for the files and two copies are sent to the customer. Many companies also do the same but with plain white paper only.
13. Click **OK** to select the options from the dialog box.

Cursor Position

In moving objects around the form, the position of the cursor can become important. The Cursor Position toolbar contains two fields showing the location of the cursor on the form at all times. The fields are based on an X,Y coordinate system and are labeled accordingly. The form shown here has the cursor placed at a point that is four inches from the left margin and one inch below the top margin. The Position fields show the associated coordinates of X, Y as 4.00, 1.00.

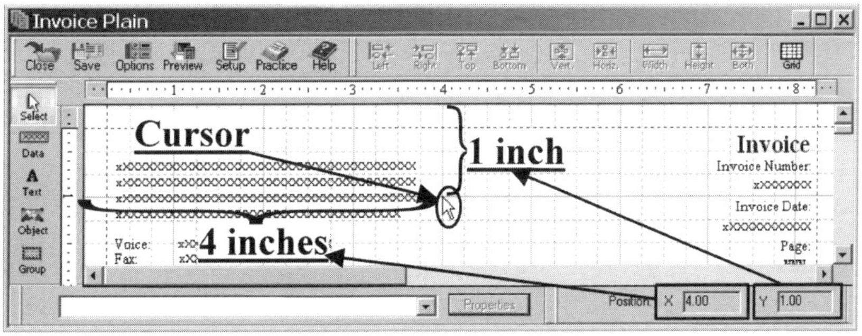

Month 3

Text Objects (Labels)

Text objects are the labels that guide the customer through the invoice. These include labels such as “Invoice” and “Sold To” or column headings such as “Unit Price.” You can change the look of the data on the form very easily.

1. To select a text object, such as the label Invoice, click on the object itself or select the object from the drop-down field in the Properties toolbar. When the object is selected, it will have object handles around it.

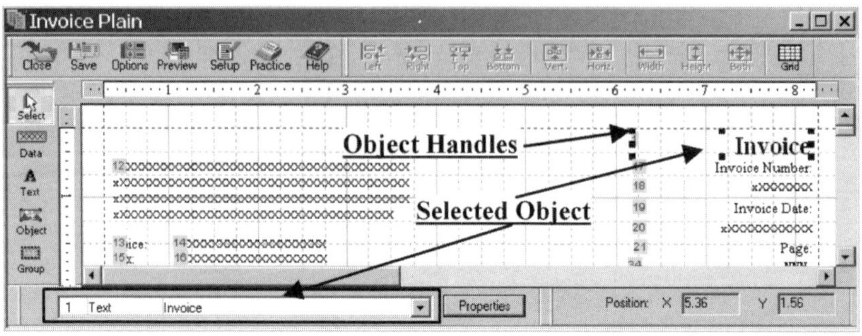

2. The coordinates of the object’s top left corner appear in the Position fields.
3. The object may be resized using the object handles.
4. In the Properties toolbar, the drop-down field displays the order number, the object type, and the name of the object.
5. To view additional properties or to change properties for the object, click the **Properties** button. The Text Object Properties dialog box appears.

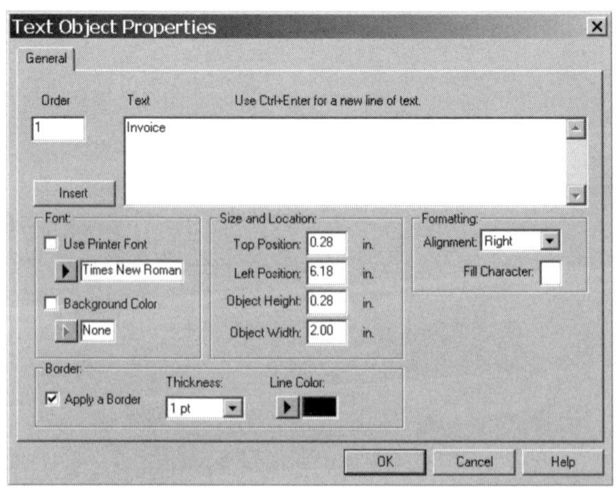

The Order field controls the print order. You can change the order number by entering a new number in the field. If fields on the form overlap, fields with a larger order number will appear on top of objects with smaller numbers. The text of the label appears in the Text field.

In the Font section, you may change the font by clicking the arrow next to the field name. If you check the Use Printer Font check box, a default font will be used. Printer fonts speed up the printing of the form and are desirable if you print a large number of forms at the same time and want to reduce print time. If you check the Background Color check box, you may select the field’s color behind the text using the color arrow. If a color is chosen, including white, the field will hide any information behind it.

The Size and Location section controls where the object is and how large it is. Changes may be entered in the various fields.

The Formatting section controls the object's alignment. Some fields may need a fill character, which can be entered here. These might include periods before a number (...49.95) or asterisks after a description (One hundred and no dollars******).

If you desire a border for the fields, check the Apply a Border option and select the thickness and color. Click **OK** to apply the new object properties.

Note: Some properties and the dialog box may be accessed by right-clicking on the object.

6. To add a new label, click the **Text** button on the Object toolbar. The cursor will change to a + shape. Draw the field in the desired location. The object handles and the order number will appear. Once the field is drawn, the Text Object Properties dialog box will appear so that you may type the text of the label and change its appearance.

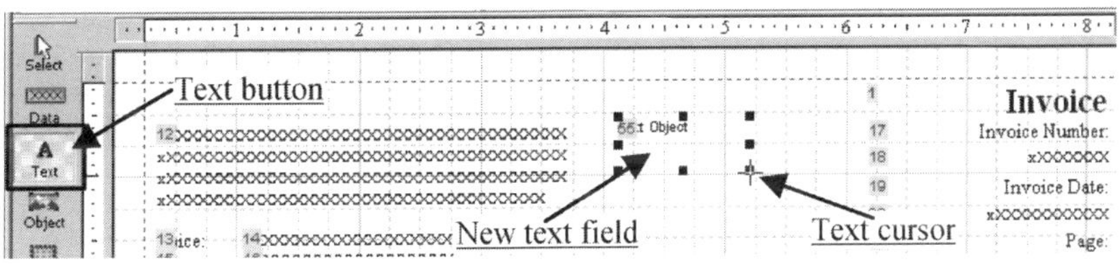

Data Objects

A *data object* is a field on the form that contains information from a Peachtree table or transaction. This information may be the quantity of an item sold to a customer, the customer's address, the invoice date, or your company's telephone number. Data objects appear as sample data or with the data field name appearing in the object, depending upon the options you have chosen. Having the sample data show assists you in separating text and data objects.

1. As with text objects, data objects may be selected by clicking on the object or selecting the object from the Properties toolbar drop-down list.
2. Access the object's properties either by right-clicking to bring up the shortcut menu and clicking the **Properties** menu item or by clicking the **Properties** button.

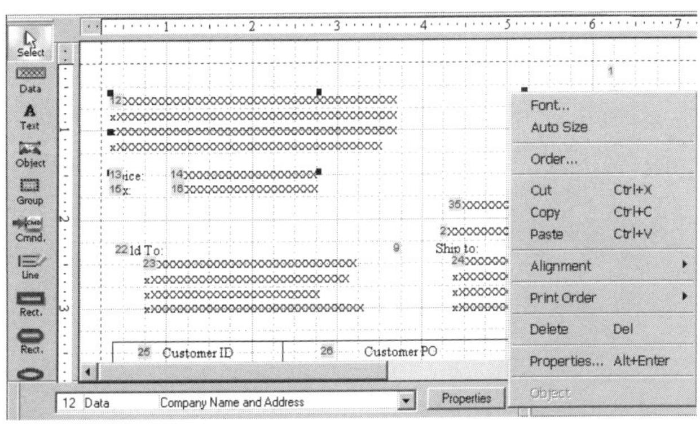

3. The Data Object Properties dialog is very similar to the Text Object Properties dialog. The Order field can be used to change the field's order number. The Sample Data field allows you to change the length of a field. By adding X's to the end of line, more of the data will appear on a line.

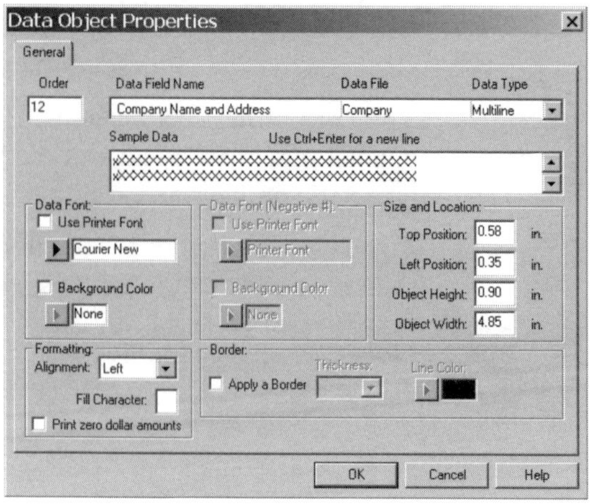

The drop-down list includes Data Field Name, Data File, and Data Type. Some data fields have a Multiline data type. This type of field includes several fields that have been combined, usually name and address fields or long fields such as item descriptions or comments.

The Data Font section is the same as for text objects.

Tip: For professional and classy looking forms, I generally choose proportional fonts, such as Times New Roman, for text objects and the printer font or a fixed-width font, such as Courier New, for data objects. This layout makes it easy to distinguish between the two types of fields on the form. I also apply different types of formatting to text objects so that some fields, such as Total, may be bolded, and some fields, such as a finance charge warning, may be italicized. I also find it helpful to accentuate the look of comments or memo fields to highlight them. Color can play a big part in designing fields too. Text fields may be in color, but data objects are almost always in black. If you use color, use it sparingly. Unless you have an expensive color laser printer, color printing is slow and eats up color cartridges.

The Formatting section has been moved below the Data Font section. This section includes a new option, Print zero dollar amounts, which determines whether a numerical field with a zero value is printed as 0.00 or is left blank.

A new section, Data Font (Negative #), is enabled for fields with a number or currency data type. These fields allow you to control the printing of negative numbers so they may be distinguished from positive amounts.

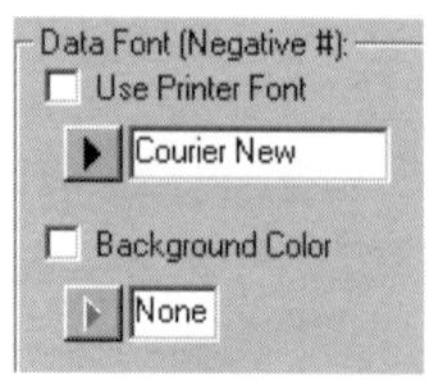

The Size and Location section and the Border section are used as shown earlier.

Click **OK** to apply the data object formatting.

The same data object may appear more than once on a form.

4. To add a new data object, click the **Data** button. The cursor becomes a + sign. Draw the new field in the desired location. When the Data Object Properties dialog box appears, select the field to be shown in the field. Change other properties as needed.

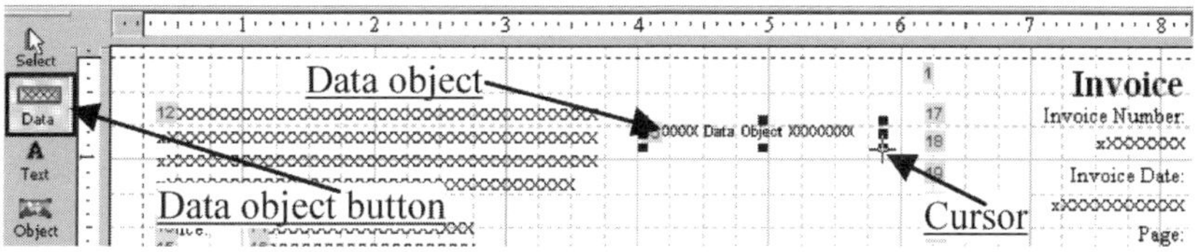

Group Objects

A *group object* is a collection of fields and usually contains line items in a check or invoice. All line items attached to the transaction appear and blank lines show as white space on the form. Group objects are generally shown in a table or grid format.

In earlier versions of Peachtree all the line items on an invoice or check were shown separately on the form. Moving, resizing, or aligning the objects was very difficult and time-consuming. Many times the objects and associated commands would become tangled and out of order so the entire process would have to be restarted. In later versions of Peachtree the group object has been perfected and is now easily modified.

1. Click on the line items of the invoice so that the group object is selected and the group name appears in the Properties drop-down.
2. Open the Group Object Properties dialog box.

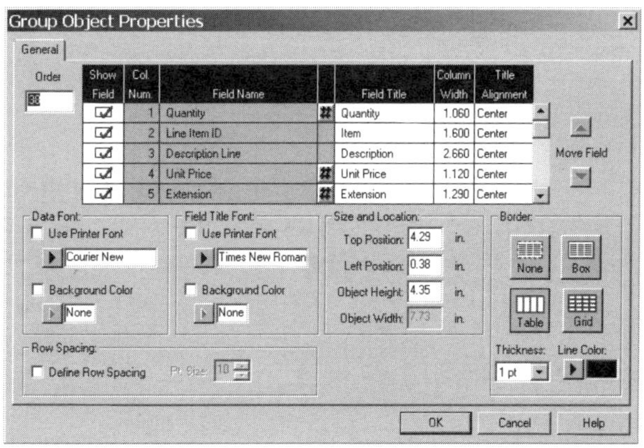

3. Many of the fields are the same as for the text and data objects. Notice that instead of one field name, a list of field names appears in the top section of the dialog box. If you want the data field to appear on the form, check the **Show Field** column.

Col. Num. holds the column number of the field from the left. The order of the columns may be changed using the Move Field arrows.

The column after Field Name allows you to modify the formatting of numbers where there is a number button.

Field Title is the column heading for the field and may be changed. Title Alignment is for the column heading also, not the line items themselves. The Field Title Font section controls the look of the headings.

If you choose Define Row Spacing in the Row Spacing section, you may increase or decrease the amount of space between the line items. Enter the amount of space in the Pt. Size field.

The Border section allows you to select from four options for the line items listing. The Line Color and Thickness may also be customized.

Click **OK** to save the changes to the group object.

Graphic Objects

The single most distinctive change that can be made to an invoice or form is to add your company logo. The process is extremely simple, although the size of the file will directly affect your print speed.

1. Your logo must be in electronic form and should be of excellent quality. I find that PCX, JPG, and BMP files work best. Compressed files are good because they print faster. Images that have been scanned rarely show up as well as electronically created files due to the lack of resolution and definition.
2. Click the **Object** button and the Insert Object dialog box appears.
3. If you choose Create New and then make a selection from the Object Type list, Peachtree will open a window within Peachtree to create the graphic after you click OK. It is better to create the file before opening Peachtree and then select Create from File.

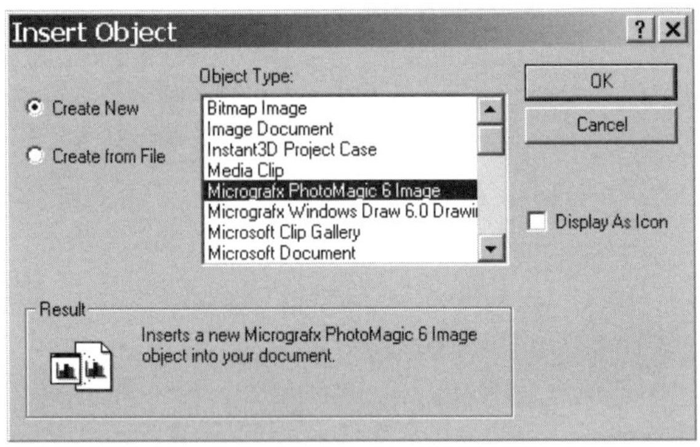

4. You may enter the location and filename in the File field or click the **Browse** button to locate the file.

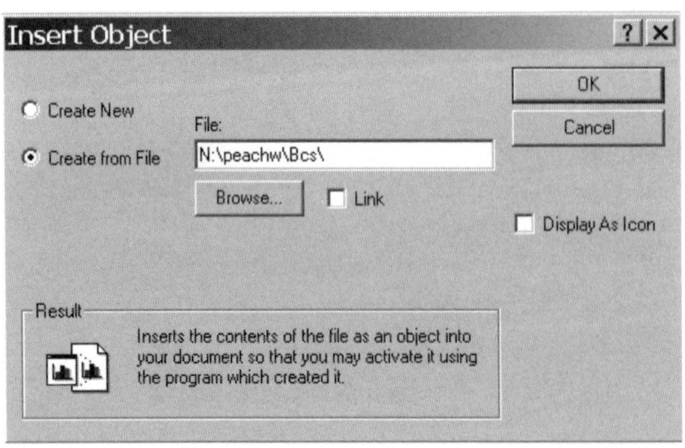

5. Check the **Link** check box if you do not want to embed the graphic in the form. Embedded graphics print quicker but greatly increase the file size. You may view the graphic on the form in Design mode or you can select the Display As Icon check box to insert a placeholder.

6. Click **OK** to place the graphic on the form. Resize and relocate as necessary.
7. Part of a redesigned invoice is shown here. Notice that the font of the logo, company address, web address, and the title "Invoice" have all been coordinated. Also notice that the address, phone, and web information are text objects, not data objects, for more flexibility. The other text objects all appear using a sans serif font and the data objects are shown using the Courier, fixed-width font.

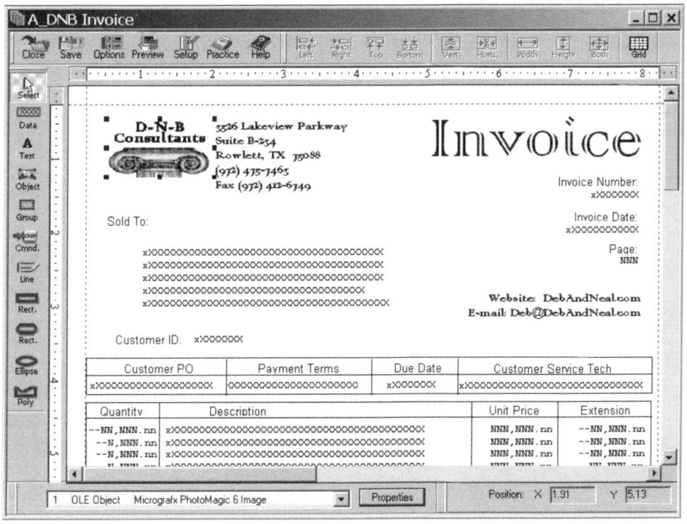

You can also use the Windows standard copy and paste functions to add a graphic to a form or report.

Saving Forms

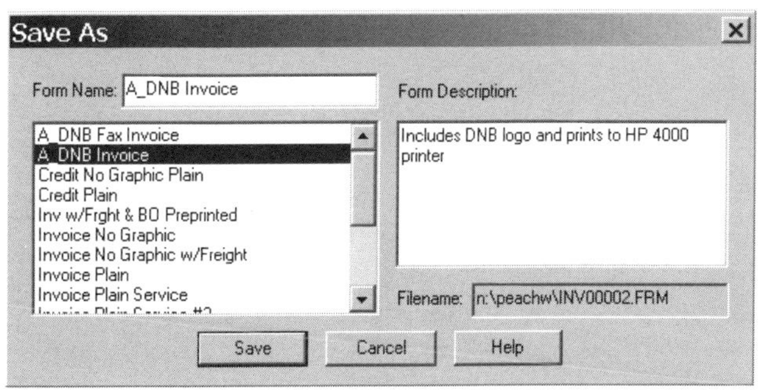

1. Once your form is complete, click **Save** in the toolbar. The Save As dialog box appears.
2. In the Form Name field, enter the new name of the form. It used to be important to watch the alphabetizing of form names in older versions of Peachtree. I still like to save customized forms at the beginning of the list by using A_ as the first two letters of the name.
3. In the Form Description field, enter any notes regarding this form.
4. The location and actual name of the Peachtree form will appear in the Filename field.
5. Click **Save**.

Tip: Because so many companies have computer-based faxing, I like to create a form that faxes directly from the computer. Select the printer, such as WinFax, in the design window by clicking the Setup button.

Financial Statements

Financial statements are a slightly different kind of report. Peachtree has added a wizard to simplify creating new statements.

1. In the Select a Report window, with **Financial Statements** selected in the Report Area, click the **Financial Statement Wizard** button.

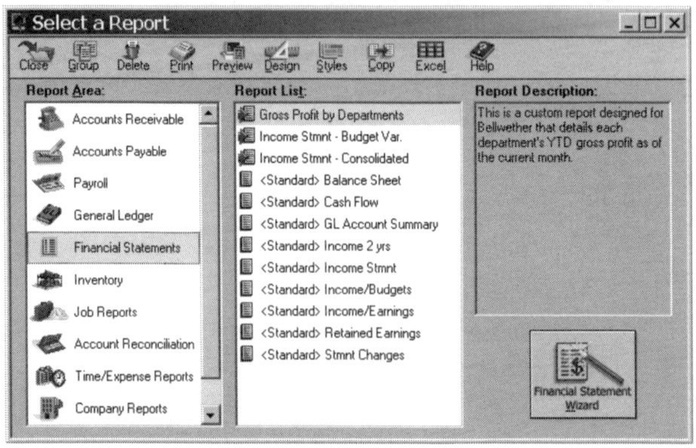

Follow the steps, clicking **Next** when necessary.

2. On the Financial Statement Name screen, select a template in the Financial Statement Template field and fill in the Name and Description fields.

   Keep clicking **Next** to continue.

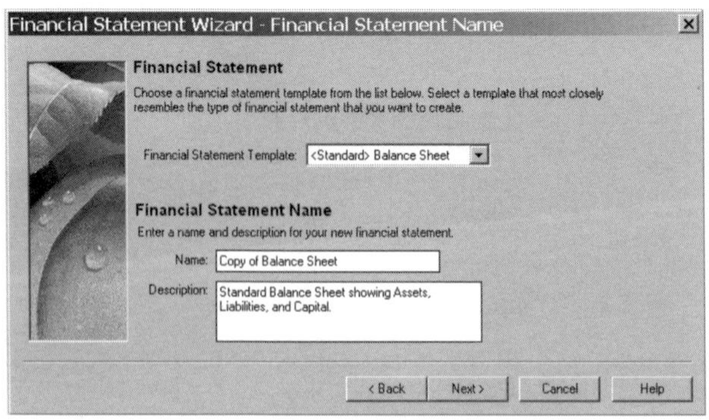

3. Each succeeding screen will walk you through selecting and formatting headers and footers, dates, department masks, and up to 30 columns. In addition, the page setup and default printer can also be modified.

   Although customizing many of the reports and forms is time-consuming, the results can give your company a more professional look when you send reports and forms to individuals and organizations outside your company. A number of customized forms are included with the companion files.

Summary

The problem with annual procedures, such as closing the fiscal and payroll years, is that they only occur once a year and, therefore, it is easy to misunderstand and make unrecoverable errors when working with these functions. Even clients that have watched me perform the functions for years have problems when they try to do it themselves. It is no wonder that many companies that are able to handle all the day-to-day tasks and month-end functions still call me year after year to have these procedures performed. Because I don't close one company file but dozens including my own, these steps have become second nature.

The same goes for customized reports and forms. The skills involved are so rarely used by the average accounting person that creating the forms can become a real nightmare. I include the information here because once in a while, a client has the skills, determination, and creative ability to really master this task. I have returned to a client and been pleasantly surprised to discover that they had created dozens of reports and forms to meet their company's needs.

Chapter 19

Finalization and Follow-Up

In This Chapter

- Setting up security
- Topics not discussed in this book
- Companion files

Setting Up Users and Security

Keeping your data secure is vital to the success of your business. The chances of your company information falling into the hands of a competitor or being made public are very real. The number of companies that have had trusted employees take customers, pricing data, and supplier costs and go to work for competitors or start their own businesses is higher than you would expect. I have even received calls from potential clients that had full backups of their boss's files.

If you are a one-person office and do not have to worry about anyone breaking into your computer, you do not need to worry about security or setting up as a user in Peachtree. If there is any chance that someone could get into your computer and therefore your company accounting information, you will want to set up security and a user account. You must set up security and users with a network installation.

An Important Message about Security and Passwords

The issue of security — how much and how restrictive — is an interesting dilemma. You want to keep your data secure, but at the same time you don't want to make it so difficult that you can't get to information easily. User accounts for your employees give you the capability to secure your work by allowing you to assign a password to your user account ID. Without the password, a person cannot sign on under your account name. Before going into details of how to set up a user ID and set a password, we need to present a few words of warning. First, a password-protected account is only as good as the password. We tell people not to use common ordinary words as their password because they are too easy to guess. Passwords such as PASSWORD, GOD, OPEN, and X are so common that when a person really wants to break into a system, these are the first words he tries. In a similar vein, your name, your kids' or other family members' names, pets, and social security numbers are almost as common and are easily guessed or located. If security is an issue, stay away from these common names.

So what makes a good password? The best password is a totally random combination of letters and numbers of at least six characters (but preferably more) — such as nH3iD97m. But most people cannot remember these, so choose a word, or better yet a phrase, that you will remember but others won't guess.

Passwords have pros and cons associated with them. By implementing security via a password you are attempting to keep others out of your work, but if you forget the password, security is equally as effective at keeping you out of your work.

The most effective password is one that only you know and which is not written down anywhere. Unfortunately, this is not a good idea for most companies. Some people try to safeguard their password by making a copy of it and placing it in a spot where they can refer to it if needed. I have heard reports of extremely sensitive systems being compromised because a person who could not remember a 10-digit password had it taped to the side of their monitor. On the other hand, I have seen cases of important data being lost when the only person who had the passwords died in a freeway accident or worse, changed all the passwords and left the company. Keeping a copy of the password is a good idea. Keeping it in an obvious spot isn't.

Sharing passwords between employees is also a no-no. I have been shocked to walk into offices and hear two employees yell across several cubicles asking and receiving passwords. It was no wonder that this company found that one of their employees was coming in and downloading important information on the night shift. He later opened up his own competing shop with all the information he needed to undercut prices to all the original company's customers.

Security Setup

Every company with more than one person entering data needs to sit down and think about their security procedures regarding company data. Ask yourself several questions while doing this:

- What would happen if one of my competitors got my vendor information and the discounts I had arranged?
- What would happen if one of my shop or customer service people could walk off with all my invoicing and client information?
- What would happen if one of my accounting people had full access to my invoicing and receipts functions and decided to cash checks for herself?
- What kind of nightmare would I have if payroll information was easily accessible?

All of these questions, plus the thousand and one that you can think of, can only cause you headaches. That's why you need to set up security from the beginning and then, more importantly, enforce it. Peachtree uses the Maintain Users form to implement security.

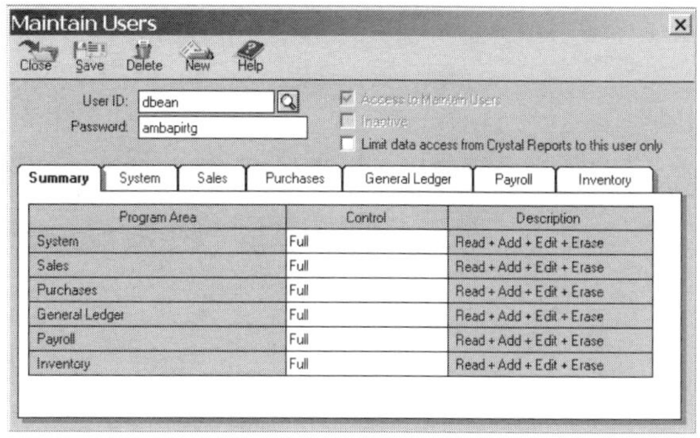

1. From the menu bar, select **Maintain** and then **Users**. The Maintain Users screen appears.
2. The first user entered is always the security administrator. In the User ID field, enter the user's name or logon. If you have network logons, it is often a good idea to keep the user name the same as that logon.
3. In the Password field, enter the user's new password. These may be assigned by the administrator or may be picked by the user. Remember the earlier notes about good passwords. I have recently come across a scheme using the first letter of a favorite quote or song as the password. This makes the password almost unguessable. The password shown in the above screen stands for "All my bags are packed, I'm ready to go," but translates to "ambapirtg." Unless someone guesses the scheme, the password is such a jumble of letters that no one will figure it out. Do not use the same scheme for every user!
4. Notice that the Access to Maintain Users check box is checked and disabled. The Inactive check box is disabled also. The security administrator is always active and always has permission to change or set up users, so these options may not be changed.
5. There is an additional option to limit data access from Crystal Reports. Crystal Reports is an add-on program and is not covered in this book.
6. Finally, on the Summary tab all the Program Area selections have Control set to Full. Full control means that the user has complete access to add, modify, and delete records and transactions. Read access is the ability to view information but not affect it in any way. Read access is great for upper-level managers who do not deal with the data on a day-to-day basis but need the information.
7. Record the user security record by clicking **Save**.
8. Other users who are added to the system should have access that is limited to just their duties. The Access to Maintain Users function should be given only to the security administrator and maybe one other person. In case of a tragedy, Peachtree security can be broken by Peachtree support and by one or two other hacking programs that have been created to break security.
9. Next, you want to add all other users to Peachtree. Each user should have their own user ID and password. If two users share a computer, each should have different user IDs. If one person leaves the desk and another takes over, the first person should log off and the new person should log on.

10. Each tab on the Maintain Users screen helps to define the users' limitations. You want to restrict their access to those parts of the program that concern their job responsibilities. With security enabled, users who attempt to enter a part of the program to which they do not have access will receive this message.

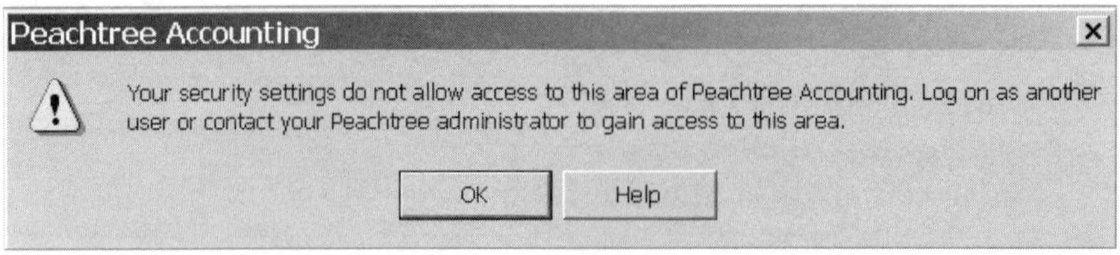

The Summary tab seen in the earlier figure controls access to the major portions of the program.

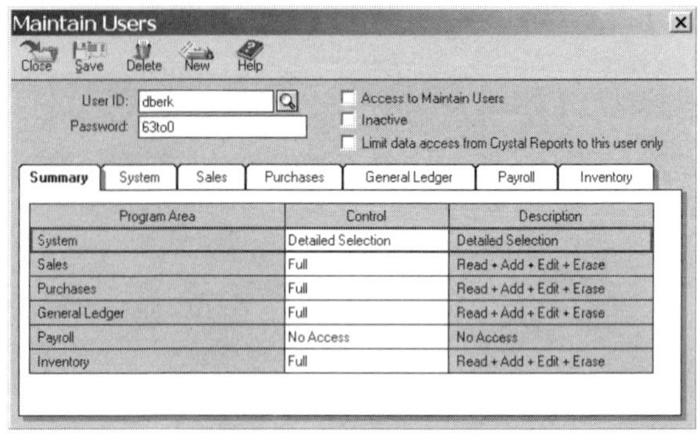

Summary Tab

Each Program Area on the Summary tab relates to the different Peachtree modules and system information. Each area also has its own tab. On the Summary tab, you can set the Control of the Program Area to Full or No Access. On the individual program area tabs, you can limit a user's access to specific areas of the associated module. When a user is only given partial access to an area, the Control on the Summary tab will then show as Detailed Selection.

The different control rights that can be assigned to a user vary according to the program area. Each area may have all or some of the available rights. The control rights are as follows:

No Access — The user cannot access this area of the system and will receive the warning message shown earlier in the chapter.

Read — The user may look at the data but cannot do anything with it.

Add — The user may add new records but cannot change or delete records.

Edit — The user may add new or change existing records but cannot delete records.

Full — The user may add new records, or change or delete existing records.

After the Summary tab are the tabs for the different modules.

System Tab

The System tab has Program Areas that relate to the Analysis module. Each Program Area has sub-areas that can be seen by double-clicking the triangle to the left of the program name.

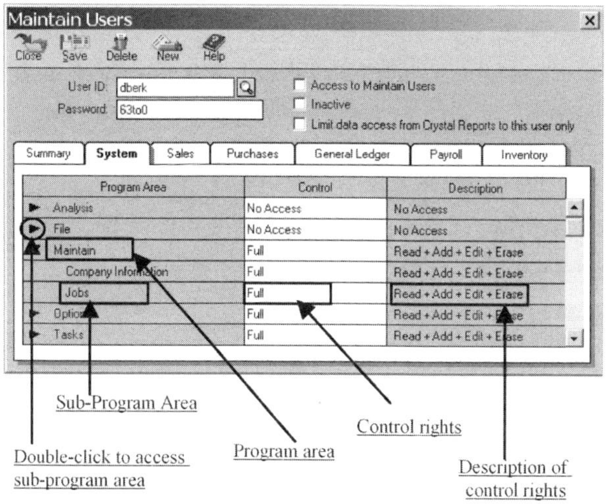

The program areas covered by the System tab are shown here. Think carefully about the rights given in this area. Most should only be accessible to managers.

Analysis — Includes the Cash Manager, Collection Manager, Payment Manager, and Financial Manager sub-areas located in the Analysis folder and menu. These functions should be made available to managers.

File — Includes the Backup, Import/Export All Files, Data Verification, and Restore functions under the File menu. These functions should be made available to managers.

Maintain — Includes access to Company Information and Jobs, which are found under the Maintain menu and under the Company folder. These functions should be made available to managers.

Options — Includes access to the Action Items/Event Log Options and the Change System Date function. The Action Items/Event Log Options may be made available to employees or managers. The Change System Date function should only be available to a manager.

Tasks — Access to the Action Items, Account Reconciliation, Change Accounting Period, Year-End Wizard, Find Transactions, Post, Un-Post, Purge, Time and Expense Tickets, and the Link to Other Apps (DDE) functions is included. If you use real-time processing, each user must have access to the Post sub-program area to add transactions and to Un-Post to edit or delete transactions. Each of the sub-program areas can be found throughout the program under menus and in folders. Access to these functions will depend upon each employee's duties.

Reports — Includes the Audit Trail Report, Jobs reports, Account Reconciliation reports, Time/Expense reports, and the Report Groups function. Access to these functions will depend upon each employee's duties, except for the Audit Trail Report which should only be available to higher-level managers.

Sales Tab

The Sales tab relates to the functions found in the Sales folder. Most of these functions should be available to the A/R people, salespeople, and managers. Some may only have partial access if job duties are split up. Only managers should have access to the forms or beginning balances.

Maintenance — This area allows you to add, edit, or delete Customers and Prospects, and to enter Customers/Prospects, Beginning Balances.

Tasks — All of the tasks to run accounts receivable, including Quotes, Sales Orders, Receipts, Sales/Invoicing, and the Credit Card Center, are available in this program area.

Reports — These include the Master Lists, Transaction Lists, Other Reports, and Forms.

Purchases Tab

This tab is for the A/P functions.

Maintenance — This area allows you to add, edit, or delete Vendors, and to enter Vendors, Beginning Balances.

Tasks — All of the tasks to pay bills, including Payments/Write Checks, Purchase Orders, Purchases/Receive Inventory, and Void A/P Checks, are available in this program area.

Reports — These include the Master Lists, Transaction Lists, Other Reports, and Forms.

General Ledger Tab

Tasks that cover those associated with the general ledger are here.

Maintenance — This area allows you to add, edit, or delete the Chart of Accounts, and to enter Chart of Accounts, Beginning Balances.

Tasks — The abilities to add, edit, and delete a General Journal Entry are in this area.

Reports — These include the Master Lists, Transaction Lists, and Financial Statements.

Payroll Tab

This is one area that most companies restrict first. They don't want anyone but the payroll people to access these areas.

Maintenance — This area allows you to add, edit, or delete Employees/Sales Reps, enter Employees/Sales Reps, Beginning Balances, and work with Payroll Tax Tables.

Tasks — The tasks to run payroll, Payroll Entry, and Void PR Checks are located here.

Reports — These include the Master Lists, Transaction Lists, Other Reports, and Forms.

Inventory Tab

Employees who manage inventory or the items used to speed data entry are given access here.

Maintenance — This area allows you to add, edit, or delete Inventory Items, enter Inventory Items, Beginning Balances, and enter Multiple Item Prices.

Tasks — The Inventory tasks are located here.

Reports — These include the Master Lists, Transaction Lists, and Other Reports.

Once all individuals have had security added, you should create a list of the users and their passwords. Keep this list in a safe location, such as in a file on the computer with a fake filename (not passwords.doc), as a written list in the company safe deposit box, or in a file at the owner's home. When I create users for client companies, I always take a copy of the list and put it in the client's file at my office. You would be amazed at the number of calls I receive from people who have forgotten their passwords.

Audit Trail

If you have security concerns, perhaps because your company has a lot of turnover or because there are a lot of individuals in the system when you are not around, you should implement the audit trail.

1. Select **Maintain**, **Company Information**.
2. Check the **Use Audit Trail** check box in the Maintain Company Information screen.
3. Click **OK**.

   You may now run the Audit Trail Report which is found under the Company Reports in the Report Area of the Select a Report window.

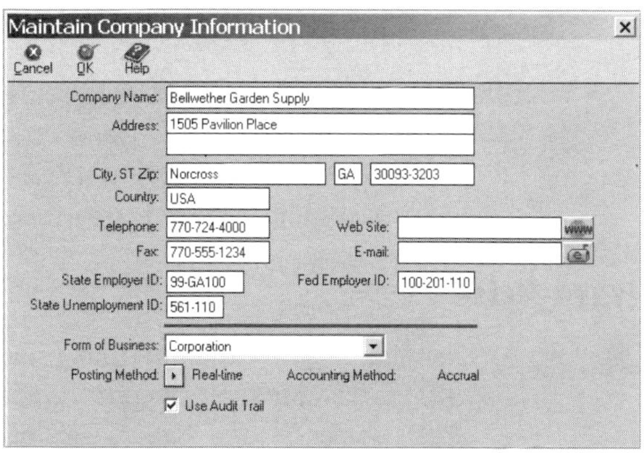

With security and the audit trail enabled, you can trace changes to records and transactions and make each user accountable for everything he or she does in the system.

What Was Not Covered in This Book

Unfortunately, due to the tremendous functionality of Peachtree and space constraints of this book, it is impossible to show every single function and capability of the program. Some of the parts that are missing include the following.

Time & Billing

The Time & Billing function can track time spent performing activities and record the use of company resources associated with work for a customer or on a specific job. Time and expenses that have been recorded can be billed to customers when they are invoiced. In the payroll function, activities can be timed and then applied to the employee's paycheck. Time & Billing can assist in managing other activities and expenses, like overhead, for your business. Activities are recorded using time tickets. Expenses are recorded on expense tickets.

Timeslips

Timeslips and Timeslips Express are used by professional companies such as legal firms, engineering companies, or software developers to charge billed time to their clients. Timeslips is an add-on to Peachtree. Information is recorded in the program and then transferred to Peachtree. The program may be purchased through Peachtree.

Jobs and Job Costing

Jobs are a way for Peachtree users to implement a type of job costing to the work performed by the company. It allows revenues and expenses to be estimated. Later, when bills are received and employees allocate their time to the project, the actual expenses of the job can be recorded. Invoice line items can also be assigned to a job. The manager can then go run job reports to discover how much money the company made or lost on a job.

The process can become quite time-consuming for smaller companies. It takes a lot of discipline to record all transactions to the job and only works well if project supervisors code their employees' time cards and expenses. Jobs may be broken down into phases and assigned cost codes.

Item Prices

For companies with numerous price levels for inventory items sold to different customers, the Maintain Item Prices function can help. It also assists when price increases occur. The item prices can be changed individually or as groups.

Crystal Reports

Crystal Reports is a reporting tool that can be used with programs and databases to create customized reports and graphs. It is a separate program that accesses the data to be reported on. Crystal Reports includes many wizards that walk you through the steps of acquiring and displaying data according to desired parameters. This outstanding program has been out for many years and I am glad to see the partnership between it and Peachtree. Crystal Reports will make important data available to managers, employees, and even customers and vendors without giving those individuals access to your actual data and the accounting program.

Although the program is not simple to use, the knowledgeable computer professional will find the program very easy to understand. Until Peachtree enables Microsoft Access on the database files, this will be the most important tool for those companies that want to take their data and make it go farther. You may want to send some of your employees to classes on Crystal Reports to enable them to understand and use the program.

The Companion Files

The companion files for this book contain a number of things that may be useful when setting up Peachtree and training employees. These files can be accessed at www.wordware.com/peachtree. See readme.doc in the downloadable file for more specific information.

Note: The information included in the companion files is for the benefit of small businesses and may be printed for the use of the purchaser of this book. The distribution of any of the information that has been developed by the author to other individuals or clients is strictly prohibited without the consent of the author.

Sample Companies

In addition to the sample companies provided by Peachtree, backups of numerous company files are included in the downloadable files. These can be restored over any existing sample company, even those with a different name, and viewed or used to follow the instructions in this book.

When restoring a backup using the Restore function, I suggest that you make a backup of the sample company file first. That way you may view the original sample company when you are finished with the file by restoring the original file.

Sample companies include files for sales taxes, reconciling the bank account, reconciling A/R and A/P, and annual procedures.

Spreadsheets

Also included in the downloadable files are a number of Excel spreadsheets that contain information for entering beginning balances, balancing payroll, and reconciling the checking account and a credit card statement. The spreadsheets require the use of Microsoft Excel, version 97 or better.

Lists

Throughout the book, I have referred to the procedures required to perform accounting functions in Peachtree. Some of these are quite long and others very short. The lists include procedures such as entering an invoice for a customer and the Three-Month Plan suggested to implement Peachtree. The lists are available in both spreadsheet and document form and require Office 97 or better.

Forms and Reports

Also included in the files are some customized forms and reports. These have been very useful to clients when they want forms that are more flexible than the standard forms included in Peachtree. Some modified reports are also in this section. The forms and reports may be accessed by copying them to the Peachtree directory. Verify that none of the form or report names already exist in the directory. If they do, either the old forms or the new ones will need to be renamed. The forms have all been created using Peachtree 2002 and may not be used with older versions.

Final Summary

I hope that this book has been helpful to you and your company. Peachtree is a great program and its use is of great benefit to those who are willing to maximize the functionality of the program. The time spent to set up your company will be rewarded tenfold by the information that is now available to use. I remain an advocate and a resource to any and all who want or need my assistance to build their business with the greatest of all small business tools.

Index

C

O

P

Q